Introduction to

GLOBAL HISTORY

Second Edition

RICHARD LEWIS

St. Cloud State University

Kendall Hunt
publishing company

Cover image credits:
Globe © Jupiter Images Corporation
Background © Digital Juice

Kendall Hunt
publishing company

www.kendallhunt.com
Send all inquiries to:
4050 Westmark Drive
Dubuque, IA 52004-1840

ISBN 978-0-7575-8181-6

Printed in the United States of America
10 9 8 7 6 5 4 3

Contents

Chapter Four: China 281

Chapter Five: South Africa 379

Chapter Six: Algeria 439

Introduction

Introduction to Global History presents a series of historical case studies of a variety of important civilizations. Russia, India, Japan, China, South Africa, and Algeria illustrate a number of historical differences. The book provides an opportunity for comparative study, for discovering similarities and differences, and explaining similarities and differences across time and across geography.

Each chapter and most sections focus on six broad themes: place in the world, political institutions, ideology and belief systems, social and economic developments, gender issues and the family, and diversity and community. It is possible, for instance, to trace the historical development of ideology and belief systems in South Africa from the sixteenth century to the present by reading all of the sub-sections dealing with that theme.

The theme of *place in the world* includes some attention to the geography of a country, territorial expansion, and relations with other nations.

The theme of *political institutions* includes attention to the structure of government as well as the actions and decisions of government.

The theme of *ideology and belief systems* includes some attention to the basic ideas that provide direction and justification for a country. Some belief systems are religious and others are secular. Christianity and Communism are examples of ideologies.

The theme of *social and economic developments* includes some attention to the structure of an economy and growth patterns, class structure, and social mobility.

The theme of *gender issues and the family* includes some attention to the nature of the family (the most basic social unit in almost every society) as well as to relations between men and women and the rights and roles of each.

Of special importance in this study is the theme of *diversity and community.* Various societies sought to build community in different ways and defined difference or diversity in various ways.

Important terms and names, as well as technical or advanced vocabulary are in italics. Some will be easy to identify through context; others may have to be looked up in a dictionary.

A list of the most important terms and vocabulary is found at the end of each chapter. You should be able to define or explain these terms.

Each chapter concludes with key questions, one for each chronological sub-division. You should be able to answer these questions.

Chapter One

RUSSIA

Introduction

Now a medium-sized power, Russia was once the largest state in the world, stretching from the middle of Europe to the eastern edges of continental Asia. Over the last five centuries Russia has changed profoundly. Starting as a small state composed of Russians, it expanded almost inexorably to become a vast multicultural empire that reached from Europe to the Pacific. The collapse of the Russian Empire during the First World War and Communist victory in revolutions and civil war created an opportunity for restructuring the new Soviet State. Initial decisions to establish internal borders on the basis of ethnic identity made it difficult to create a unified, single-nation state, based on socialist internationalism and attempts to create Soviet man. In the last decades of Soviet rule, efforts to create and reinforce cultural unity were abandoned and ethnic identity became so important as to threaten the survival of the Soviet Union. After the collapse of communism in 1991, the Soviet Union disintegrated and the rump state of Russia faced the challenge of restoring its domination over the now independent former Soviet republics and preventing ethnic unrest and separationism from breaking up the new Russian state.

From extreme poverty and a subsistence way of life, Russia, later the Soviet Union, advanced to become the second largest economy in the world, with tremendous wealth. This advance was quite gradual, as Russia found it difficult to move from a backward agrarian economy to an industrial society with great unrealized potential for economic development.

Throughout its history, however, certain factors have remained as constants. Russia has been dominated by authoritarian politics and political systems and has found it almost impossible to transform itself into a civil society in which broad political participation was the ideal and the norm. Sometimes rulers used their position to strengthen their power; sometimes they used their power to reform Russian society. Briefly in the early twentieth century, attempts were made to broaden political participation to include representatives of society as a whole. With Communist victory in 1917, authoritarian rule, this time by the Communist Party and its leadership, returned. The twentieth century created opportunities for much more thorough and all-encompassing autocratic rule. The collapse of Communism led to the introduction of open elections and an authoritarian-style democracy.

Ideology (belief systems) played a powerful role, even though the nature of the dominant ideology changed over time. Russians have seemed to be trapped by ideology, unable to escape its influence. Initially the Russian Orthodox Church provided a set of beliefs that provided direction for the Russians. That consensus broke down in the nineteenth century, when competing ideologies emerged. The victory of Communism brought ideological unity to Russia once again. Stalinism remained the dominant ideology until about 1990. After the fall of Communism the ideological consensus broke down and various ideologies now compete for attention and support.

For most of Russian history the family has been a powerful institution and an important arena for male domination. The state frequently provided justification and legal support for the role of the family and male domination.

Finally, Russia, like all of the other societies in this book, faced the problem of how to deal with diversity and how to build community. It could not be otherwise in a multicultural empire. In many ways the central thread of Russian history is the challenge of diversity and community in a multi-ethnic and multi-religious state.

A. RUDE AND BARBAROUS KINGDOM, 1500–1700

Russia (initially Muscovy) was a rude and barbarous kingdom, to use the title of a mid-seventeenth century book on Russia by German traveler George Herberstein. Muscovy made a major commitment to empire building. Russian expansion was accompanied and made possible by political changes. The increasingly authoritarian rule of the Muscovite princes culminated in the brutal rule of Ivan the Terrible. Upon his death several decades of political anarchy followed, embracing conflict over the throne, foreign invasion and lower class rebellions. When Michael Romanov was placed on the throne in 1613 the way was paved for the restoration of strong government and authoritarian rule. The rise of Muscovite and later Romanov power was enhanced by substantial support from the Russian Orthodox Church. Poverty and economic backwardness characterized the Russian economy. During these two centuries *serfdom* emerged to dominate social relationships and social structure. Squeezed between the estate-owning nobility and the serfs, a small intermediate class of educated people, clerks, artisans, and merchants stagnated, with no access to power. The family was the basic social institution, an institution subordinate to the power of church and state. Patriarchy and male domination characterized the family and violence and abuse were common. Leaders hardly recognized issues of diversity and community. The country became more diverse as Russia created a multi-cultural and multi-ethnic empire. Given primitive transportation and communication systems and the very limited ability of government to ensure that its will was carried out, religion provided most of the impetus toward community. Ironically however, the creation of empire undermined community building as well as the church's dominant ideological role. We define ideology as a set of values or ideals that influence or determine a society's basic behavior.

1. Imperialism and the Origins of Diversity

Russian geography placed limitations on human economic capacity and created parameters for political behavior. Muscovy made a major commitment to empire, conquering the area east of the *Volga River* and Western Siberia. Muscovy's victory over the Mongols, who had ruled most of central and eastern Russia from the mid-thirteenth century on, made this expansion possible. Renewed political strength and the revival of authoritarian government facilitated the conquest of Ukraine and the incorporation of the unruly and freedom-loving Cossack leaders of the Ukrainian lands into the Russian political system. The seventeenth century witnessed the exploration of Siberia and the extension of Russian military power and economic activity across Siberia until the Russians met Chinese resistance in southeastern Siberia toward the end of the seventeenth century. Imperialism made Russia more diverse—in religious, ethnic and cultural terms—and made political rule more difficult.

Geography Limited Russian Capacity. Several elements of Russian geography had a powerful influence on the country's history, especially early on. First, Russia's northerly location and climate meant that growing seasons were short and agriculture not very productive. Until the eighteenth century, the central and most important part of Russia had particularly low-quality soil. Given this northerly location, Russia lacked warm water ports and thus was relatively isolated, especially from Europe. Mineral resources were located on the western edge of Siberia and thus a great distance from the nation's population core. Most of Russia was a vast plain, with only the Ural Mountains (little more than hills) dividing the country. Other mountain ranges would eventually form Russia's southern borders. Thus, Russia was largely defenseless from the east and subject to frequent attacks from nomadic peoples, the most important of which were the Mongols. An extensive network of rivers enhanced transportation in the core of Russia, while in Siberia, most rivers flowed into the Arctic Ocean. The country was crossed by several east-west bands of vegetation, starting with the *tundra* in the north, a broad band of swamps, moss and shrubs. South of the tundra was the *taiga,* a huge area of coniferous forests. To the immediate south of the taiga was a forest zone of mixed forests. Further to the south was the agriculturally rich soil of the *steppe,* added to Russia in the seventeenth and eighteenth centuries. The semi-desert, arid lands of Central Asia were added in the mid-nineteenth century. But for this first period of Russian history, 1500–1700, Russia was limited to the core area, with Moscow at the center and its borders approximately 500 miles in each direction.

Across the Wide Volga. By 1500, Russia had effectively declared its independence from the Mongols but had not guaranteed its own safety. As long as the nomadic peoples of the Volga Basin could raid Russia with impunity, destroying Russian crops and cities and killing Russians, security could not be assured. The Volga River acted as a bit of a barrier but beyond, stretching eastward into Siberia were vast steppe lands that formed a broad, open road into Russia. The need for security offered one central motive for eastward expansion.

However, by this time the Russians, rude and barbarous as they might be, had already assumed a sense of superiority over the nomadic steppe peoples and had assumed the right to "civilize" them. Religious conversion, reflecting the powerful role of the Russian Orthodox Church, accompanied this civilizing mission. The concept of the *Third Rome,* well developed by 1500, gave ideological support to expansion. According to this theory, God's civilizing mission had first been the responsibility of Rome and then when it collapsed, the role was transferred to the eastern part of the Roman Empire, commonly known as Byzantium, centered in what is today Turkey. When the Ottoman Turks conquered Byzantium in 1453, Russia believed it was anointed as the center of Christianity; it was the Third Rome. Thus it was the responsibility of this Third Rome—Russia—to champion the faith among non-believers, best achieved through political-military conquests. Later, other myths were used to promote empire, but the thrust for empire never disappeared.

Russian victory over the Khanate of Kazan in 1552 marked the first major expansion of Russians into lands whose populations were non-Slavic and for the most part *Muslim.* Kazan, a Mongol successor state, controlled the area east of Muscovy where the Volga River halted its eastward course and turned southward, eventually to reach the Black Sea. Soon after this, Russian armies captured the Khanate of Astrakhan on the southern reaches of the Volga. Russia thus controlled that part of the Volga Basin west of the Volga River.

Russian treatment of Kazan and Astrakhan set a pattern for empire building. Assumptions of superiority and the practical limits of Russian administrative power guided policies that aimed to ensure captured lands would no longer threaten Russian security. The Russians drove out some of the population, killing others. They also used divide and conquer tactics, promoting conflict within the conquered elites and encouraging some elites, especially the Mongol (*Tatar*) elites, to enter Russian service. Russian officers were placed in power as military governors of newly conquered territories. The *tsar* (emperor) granted land to Russian military and political leaders and encouraged peasants to migrate to these *virgin lands.* This served both the needs of security and economic development. The Russians extended their power symbolically and practically by building a series of forts further and further out onto the steppes. In general the Russians had neither the inclination nor the ability to carry out a *cultural revolution* among conquered peoples and left the indigenous peoples free to follow local customs. The main exception to this was intermittent attempts to convert the local people to Russian Orthodoxy. Conquest of the Volga Basin left the lightly populated and geographically inhospitable Siberia open for exploration and easy *nominal* conquest.

Oh, Siberia! From the Kazan "beachhead," the Russians moved straight eastward, pushing across the Ural Mountains, which were little more than foothills in many places, or skirted the southern edge of these mountains. In spite of the climate and thick taiga, Russian entrepreneurs, Cossacks, and explorers avoided the steppe lands of Central Asia where relatively strong Muslim kingdoms were located. Instead they moved eastward at the expense of scattered, small tribes of indigenous Siberians unable to defend themselves against the primitive military power of the Russians. The *Stroganov* family of merchants and fur traders, which sought to dominate the Siberian fur trade, and *Ermak,* the Cossack adventurer, stood out. By the early 1580s Ermak had defeated the strongest force of resistance in western Siberia, the Khanate of Siberia. Adventurers, traders and small military forces continued to push eastward, reaching the Pacific Ocean by 1639 and founding a settlement at Okhotsk on the Pacific a decade later. Peasants followed in the wake of the military adventurers and traders, seeking freedom and economic opportunity. By the eighteenth century, the tsar began to grant estates in western Siberia to the nobles, who brought their serfs with them.

China saw itself as the arbiter of the fate of Northeast Asia. As a new and alien dynasty, the *Qing* from Manchuria began to consolidate their power in China (see Chapter Four). They halted Russian expansion. By the *Treaty of Nerchinsk* (1689) the Russians agreed to a *demarcation* of the border with China, which sharply limited the possibility of Russian expansion in Northeast Asia.

The Russian government slowly extended its power into Siberia, following the policies it had developed to deal with the Volga khanates: divide and conquer politics, settlement, military rule, lines of fortifications, and cultural autonomy for conquered peoples. In Siberia the native peoples were left alone in exchange for paying a heavy tax in furs. The small Siberian tribes offered resistance that was sometimes fierce but failed to push the Russians out. By extending their border into Siberia, the Russians gained much of the security they sought on the eastern frontier.

Cossack Liberties and Russian Power. Conquest of the Volga Basin still left the Russians vulnerable along their southern frontier, an area known as *Ukraine* (the frontier). As the Mongols withdrew from that area, disaffected people from Russia and the Polish-Lithuanian Republic to the west and northwest began to move into this no-man's land. These adventurers came to be known as *Cossacks,* from the Tatar word for free men. Initially they formed a small elite of farmer-warriors along the *Dnepr River.* They gave Russia and Poland-Lithuania some degree of protection from the last remaining Tatar stronghold in the Crimea. As the Ukraine became more secure and Russian and Polish serfdom more oppressive, more and more peasants fled into Cossack lands. Gradually, a two-tiered structure emerged, consisting of the "enrolled" Cossacks (the military leaders) and the peasants. In the mid-seventeenth century, the Cossacks rejected Polish *suzerainty* and transferred their loyalty to the Russians, assuming that the weakness of Russia would enable the Cossacks to maintain their independence. They were, of course, mistaken and in the eighteenth century the Russians incorporated Cossack lands into Russia, eliminating Cossack freedoms.

Until the early eighteenth century the Russians were unable to defeat the Tatars and thus ensure complete security on the southern frontier. The Crimean Tatars were a powerful military force in the south. They were supported by the Ottoman Turks, who saw Russian expansion as a threat to their own power and sought to block the Russians from access to the Black Sea and the Mediterranean Sea. Seeking slaves and demonstrating their superiority over the Russians, the Crimean Tatars were able to attack and destroy the Russian capital of Moscow as late as 1571. A series of forts in the Ukraine generally provided the Russians with some security, but their campaigns against the Tatars either succeeded only briefly or failed.

Creating Diversity Problems. In this period Russia was transformed from a small, rude, and barbarous kingdom of Russians into a multi-ethnic empire stretching across a portion of two continents. Empire building made it more difficult to build and sustain community. Two religions—Russian Orthodoxy and Islam—competed, both espousing *messianic* goals of conversion. In addition, the conquest of Siberia had brought into the Russian Empire people whose religious beliefs had little organized structure and little theology. Differences in levels of civilization increased, stretching the distance between sedentary Russian "civilization" and the nomadic cultures of the Tatars and Siberians. Distance became a severe barrier to community. The Russian government lacked the capacity to establish and maintain community, which was not always a central goal of its empire building. Religious leaders, whose influence over government policy gradually declined, articulated the vision of unity. By 1700, then, the Russian Empire lacked community and a vision of community for the various people who lived on the territory of the Russian Empire.

2. Creation, Disintegration, and Re-Creation of Authoritarian Government

During Mongol rule, most Russian principalities adopted *authoritarian* political systems, perhaps modeled after Mongol political structures. One of those principalities, Muscovy, combined aggressive expansion at the expense of its neighbors with the creation of authoritarian rule. Authoritarianism and Russian unity collapsed briefly around 1600. During the seventeenth century, a new dynasty, the Romanovs, gradually built up centralized power once again.

Creation of the Muscovite State. Moscow's relative isolation and its willingness to avoid antagonizing the Mongols enabled it to gradually increase its strength. Simultaneously, the Muscovite princes increased their power within the principality. By the reign of Ivan I (1328–40), Muscovy had halted tax payments to the Mongols, thus effectively demonstrating independence. The Muscovite princes gained stature through this victory over the Mongols. At the same time the princes began to use the title tsar (caesar or emperor), signifying their enhanced status. Though they sought to act as authoritarian rulers, the weakness of their bureaucracy and the counter force of the aristocrats (*boyars*) limited their power. Boyars still possessed the potential to destroy the ruling house.

Ivan the Terrible and the Time of Troubles. Ivan the Terrible (1533–84) introduced a new dimension to authority. Brilliant and lamentably unstable, Ivan sought to make himself an unchallenged ruler. He recognized that the boyar class and boyar political institutions represented the main threat to this goal. Ivan *Peresvetov,* a petty nobleman from Lithuania, provided Ivan the Terrible with an ideological vision of what a ruler should be like. Alluding to the concept of Russia as the Third Rome and its predecessor Byzantium the second Rome, Peresvetov blamed the collapse of Byzantium not on the power of the Ottoman Turks but on the treasonous behavior of the Byzantine aristocracy. He emphasized that the Turkish sultan, on the other hand, consciously selected his officials from society as a whole on the basis of merit. At the same time Peresvetov argued that the all-powerful ruler should act on the basis of law and not whim.

Influenced by Peresvetov, Ivan reached out to the lesser gentry by calling *assemblies of the land,* composed not only of aristocrats but of the rest of the upper class, too. When this strategy failed to weaken the aristocrats, in 1564 Ivan the Terrible turned to the *oprichnina (separate realm).* Ivan withdrew from Moscow, announcing that he would not return to the throne until the boyars surrendered their power to him. When the aristocrats gave in, Ivan further undermined them by confiscating estates and shifting aristocrats from their local power bases to other parts of the country where they were unknown. Ivan gave many of the aristocrats' lands to key allies, who carried out a campaign of revenge and violence against the population in general. Ivan's death ended the reign of terror but did not lead to peace and order.

Ivan's actions weakened the fragile political and social structures of Muscovy and led to *The Time of Troubles* (1601–13). By 1600 the ruling family had died off and a fierce power struggle ensued. Since no one had a legal right to the throne, contenders sought to legitimize their position by pretending to be members of the former royal family. Poland and Sweden invaded and the Polish king's claim to the throne almost succeeded. Finally, the issue of who was to be ruler was settled in 1613, when townspeople and Russian Orthodox Church leaders placed the young Michael *Romanov* on the throne. The Romanovs then ruled Russia for three centuries, sometimes brilliantly, more often ineptly.

Rebuilding Authoritarian Government—Early Romanovs. The first three Romanovs ruled for most of the seventeenth century. This was a period of major expansion at the expense of the Poles, a split within the Russian Orthodox church, the entrance of some western ideas, an increase in the power of the tsar and the gradually rationalization of his government.

3. Ideology of the Russian Orthodox Church

Russian Orthodoxy provided the basic ideals and beliefs by which the Russian people lived. In the second half of the seventeenth century, a split occurred within the Church, thus destroying ideological unity. For the most part Russia remained isolated from the rest of the world.

Basic Institutions and Theology. Russian Orthodoxy became and remained the primary source of ideas and beliefs in Russia throughout this period. Some Russians first converted to Christianity before 900 C.E. (Current Era), influenced by missionaries from Byzantium. Christianity spread gradually over the next several centuries, mixing with and influenced by pre-existing forms of religion. Eastern Orthodoxy was much more ritual-oriented than Roman Catholicism and by approximately 1000 C.E. had finalized a theology and ritual that no longer accepted change. Russians thus adopted this rigid form of Christianity and with it a language of religion, Old Slavonic, increasingly distinct from ordinary Russian. Byzantium's isolation from the West was replicated by Russian distance from Western ideas. In addition, Eastern Orthodoxy operated on a dual track, simultaneously promoting *asceticism* through the isolation of individual monks and minimizing the theological significance of personal behavior for the mass of believers. The Russians followed the structural model of Eastern Orthodoxy, with a single all-powerful leader, the *patriarch.* Russians also sought to emulate the wealth and political power of the Eastern Orthodox Church. The Russian church became a major landholder, eventually owning about one-third of the country's agricultural lands.

Church and State. Third Rome. Early in the Mongol period, the Russian Orthodox Church decided to support the princes of Muscovy, both against the Mongols and against other Russian princes. This religious support facilitated Muscovite domination of Russia. Into the second half of the seventeenth century, Russian patriarchs sought to influence policy and princes. For instance, Michael Romanov's father, Filaret, was head of the Russian Orthodox Church. Eventually the Church sought or needed a justification for its political role. The idea of Russia as the Third Rome provided such a rationale.

Isolation from the Western Renaissance and Reformation. Russia isolated itself from Western Europe by aligning with Eastern Christianity. At the time of the conversion of Russians to Christianity, Western Europe was little more advanced than Russia. However, in the next centuries Western Europe underwent a series of relatively radical changes and emerged from the Middle Ages quite different from Russia. Universities were created and nation-states established. Renaissance humanism, which emphasized the power of human beings, challenged the Catholic Church. Criticism of Roman Catholicism led to the collapse of religious unity and the formation of various Protestant religions. Finally, global exploration and the scientific revolution transformed the Western Europeans' vision of themselves and the world. At the same time, Russia changed little and weathered mild criticism of Orthodoxy, at least until the second half of the seventeenth century. Isolation thus increased the challenges Russia faced when it came into contact with Western Civilization.

Ukraine and New Ideological Initiatives. With the incorporation of Ukraine into Russia in the mid-seventeenth century, Western ideas began to slip into Russia. At that time Ukraine was part of the Polish cultural world. Renaissance ideas had penetrated Poland through its ties with the Italian aristocracy. The Counter-Reformation, the attempt to restore Catholic domination, recognized the importance of well-educated rational appeals and of "modernizing" Catholicism. Thus its emphasis on learning, which entered Ukraine largely through the Polish nobility, and the formation of institutions of religious education. With the incorporation of Ukraine into Russia, leading Ukrainian scholars moved to the Russian capital. Their more critical approach affected the way the Russians viewed Orthodoxy and acted as a catalyst for the internal church conflict known as the *Schism.*

Church Schism and Old Believers. Russia's first—and rather limited—encounter with the West contributed to a serious split within the Church. Perhaps influenced by ideas from the Ukraine and certainly dissatisfied with the condition of the Russian Orthodox Church, priests in central Russia, known as *Zealots of Piety,* criticized the poor quality of the clergy and the low standards of morality among the believers. They emphasized the importance of preaching and attacked the deadening boredom of the church service. The Zealots also sought a church cleansed of secular tendencies. *Avvakum* played an important role within this group. Other reformers, including the new patriarch, *Nikon,* aimed to purify the ritual of the church by eliminating mistakes that had crept into the church service over the centuries and been confirmed by the 1551 Church Council. In addition, Nikon championed a strong church able to dominate the state and provide the Russian nation with imperialistic leadership. Opposition to efforts to purify church ritual came from many of the Zealots of Piety and especially from Avvakum. Refusing to listen to these "traditionalists," Nikon pushed his reforms through the Church Council of 1655. He drove his opponents from the church and forced them into exile. The dissidents, who came to be known as *Old Believers,* retreated into remote areas of Russia, especially the far north and Siberia. There they formed religious/economic communities that operated illegally but were not destroyed by the state. Old Believers continued their opposition to the state, which they saw as the main force behind the reforms, into the nineteenth century. Old Believers were also major participants in rebellion in the 1670s, 1680s, and 1770s.

Nikon's efforts to achieve Church domination over the state met resistance from Tsar Alexei (1645–1676). When Nikon used the threat of quitting to enhance his power, Alexei accepted the resignation, thus ridding himself of a rival. With Nikon out of the way, Alexei called a new church council (1666–1667), which approved the reforms proposed by Nikon. The church schism weakened the Orthodox Church. Its vulnerability enabled subsequent tsars to transform it from Nikon's ideal of dominant partner into a bureaucratic sub-division of the state.

Non-Christians and the Issue of Conversion. Russian expansion created both opportunities and challenges for the Russian Orthodox Church. Generally the Russian government preferred not to disturb the culture and customs of newly conquered indigenous peoples. In practical terms, this meant that the Russian government did not encourage Church efforts to convert Muslim and shamanistic peoples to Orthodoxy. The situation was different in the West. With the incorporation of much of Lithuania and Ukraine into the Russian Empire, the Empire now had a large number of Catholics and *Uniates.* Polish efforts to expand into Ukraine and West Russia led to the creation of a religion that attempted to appeal to the Slavic peasants who lived in these areas. Lacking an ethnic identity, the peasants were converted to a religion that used the Russian Orthodox liturgy but remained part of the Roman Catholic Church organizational structure. This Uniate Church thus permitted rural folk to remain loyal to the religious experiences they knew well, while subordinating their priests to the Catholic Church hierarchy, and thus ensuring their loyalty to Poland-Lithuania. Once Uniate areas were captured, the Russians carried out programs of mass conversion to Russian Orthodoxy, using threats and force when necessary. Most Uniates "converted" to Orthodoxy, at least overtly, but continued to worship underground and illegally. The experience of the Orthodox Church showed religion to be an unlikely cement of unity in a multireligious state. Social differences also hindered the creation and maintenance of community.

4. Social Difference and Class Simplification

In this period, the nobility became increasingly powerful, while differences within the class diminished. At the same time, the peasants, mired in poverty and agrarian backwardness, were gradually enslaved. Outside the social structures of rural Russia, urban folk found it difficult to carve out a distinct social space. Substantial social unrest occurred, peaking in the frontier rebellion of Stenka Razin toward the end of the era. Economic growth characterized the period, except for a lengthy economic depression, from about 1560 to about 1620, provoked by the unrest of the Oprichnina and the Time of Troubles.

Nobility. Nobles dominated the Russian social landscape. At the beginning of the period the class was clearly divided into two strata, the boyars and the *servitors.* Boyars were the large landowners, who exercised power through the political structure, the *boyars' duma,* access to the Muscovite rulers, the heritage of being a traditional aristocracy, and the economic power of owning large estates. Anxious to weaken the power of the boyars, Ivan the Terrible introduced the Oprichnina, described earlier. During the ensuing Time of Troubles, the boyars sought to determine who would become tsar but failed to secure the throne for their candidates. Boyar power was weakened through their conflict with the tsars, who sought to build up the servitors as a counterweight. Expansion of the Muscovite state created great opportunities for the rulers to confiscate landed estates and then grant them to loyal servitors, especially military officers.

Over time, distinctions diminished between boyars, who owned their estates outright, and servitors, who held their property contingent upon continued service to the state. The noble class played a powerful economic role as large landowners in a largely agrarian society.

Peasants. Most peasants worked the lands of the nobility, the state, the royal family, or the Orthodox Church. During this era the peasantry was changed into a serf class, whose members became the property of their masters, primarily the nobility. Earlier, many types of cultivators had existed, many of whom had some degree of personal freedom and/or economic rights. Over time, distinctions diminished and by about 1600 two major types of peasants remained, those who owned land themselves, mainly on the frontiers, and those who were tenant farmers, working for a member of the nobility, the state, or the Church.

Geography, agricultural backwardness, and the introduction and strengthening of serfdom determined the peasant condition. Though some peasants relocated or were sent to southern Russia or the steppes east of the Volga Basin, most peasants lived in the central regions of the country, where soil was poorest and growing seasons relatively short. These geographical conditions combined with relatively primitive agricultural methods to perpetuate low levels of output and little economic growth. Peasants made the basic agricultural decisions and brought to their work their own tools and seed grain. Estate owners played little role in determining agricultural practices and did little to promote the kind of agrarian revolution that much of Western Europe went through in the eighteenth century. Superstitious and intent upon survival, peasants simply would not gamble that new methods and new tools would produce larger harvests. Besides, larger harvests would only find their way into the nobility's hands. Peasants used the three-field system of agriculture, in which only one-third of the land was used for growing grain each year, one-third was *fallow* and one-third left in pasture or gardens. Most villages used a system of periodic reallocation of land, which minimized a peasant's desire to introduce improvements. Peasant fields were laid out in narrow strips, based on the amount of land that could be plowed in a day. Quite a bit of land (perhaps 10%) was thus unavailable for farming because it was used to separate one farmer's strips from another's.

Peasants had some ability to move from estate to estate. However, by about 1600 labor shortages led the government to first limit movement, and then prohibit it. First peasants were limited to moving during a brief period after the completion of the harvest, around St. George's Day. As a consequence of the Time of Troubles and the need to restore order, the government was in a position to end peasant mobility.

The *Ulozhenie (Law Code) of 1649* prohibited peasants from moving from one estate to another and gave nobles unlimited rights to recover runaways. The peasants thus became serfs or slaves. The Ulozhenie was a momentous confirmation of noble power and peasant powerlessness. Serfs were little more than pieces of property, which could be bought and sold, beaten, raped, killed, or sent into the army at the whim of their owners. ***Serfdom* became a central**

defining characteristic of Russian history. Ironically, serfdom died out in Western Europe about the time it appeared in the East. Serfdom perpetuated agrarian backwardness and poverty. It thus limited the military potential of Russia. It eliminated the possibility of community, reducing elements of commonality to religious belief. Serfdom symbolized the inhumanity and injustice of the Russian upper class and the Russian state toward the rest of society.

Peasants responded to their enslavement in many ways. Passive resistance in the form of shirking work was the most common response. Peasants on the frontier participated actively in the rebellions of the seventeenth and eighteenth centuries. They also focused energy on religious experiences, ranging from sorcery and folk magic to support for the Old Believer movement.

Urban Folk. Russian cities played a minor role in this predominantly rural society. They were first of all administrative centers and only secondarily commercial and "industrial" sites. A typical city contained government officials, some members of the nobility, merchants, and artisans. The merchant and artisan classes were divided into strata. Wealthier merchants who engaged in regional and international trade were at the top of the merchant class, while storekeepers, who produced much of what they sold, were at the bottom. As in the West, artisan shops consisted of owners or masters, journeymen, and apprentices. Urban classes had no political power and little access to government authorities. They were to produce and sell goods and pay taxes.

Frontier Rebellion. As the autocracy sought to strengthen its grip on Muscovite society, unrest emerged. Urban riots in the middle of the seventeenth century were easily crushed. However, resistance to the centralizing efforts of the government were strongest on the frontier, where Cossacks had just been incorporated into Russia and where increasing numbers of peasants had relocated, fleeing serfdom. This unrest produced the rebellion of *Stenka Razin* (1670–1671), in which rebels marched up the Volga River, proclaiming independence from the authorities.

Economy. The Mongol invasion and the Black Death produced a lengthy economic depression that lasted into the 1400s. Economic growth thereafter resulted from the expansion of agricultural output due to a shift from slash and burn methods to the three-field system and an expansion of trade, especially trade in grain. Some international trade, primarily with England developed, as well. Government consumption, especially military spending, and church construction also promoted economic growth. This growth was interrupted by the economic depression of 1560–1620. With the return to political stability under the early Romanov and the acquisition of Ukraine, the economy recovered and grew more rapidly than earlier.

Conclusion. Russian society was rural in nature, dominated by a nobility that enslaved those who worked the land and refused to support the existence of a strong middle class. The broad outlines of this social structure lasted for several centuries. Economic growth and social unrest laid the basis for similar developments in the early empire.

5. Family and Gender Roles

Male domination (*patriarchy*) permeated all of Russian society. The Orthodox Church, as well as state law in the form of a family code, reinforced patriarchy.

Patriarchy. In this period Russians did not view sexuality from a puritanical perspective. Instead they attached little religious significance or limitations to it.

At the same time, the family was dominated by males (patriarchy) and encumbered by strict regulations outlined, for example, in the *Domostroi* (*Household System*) of 1550. Male domination was accompanied by familial violence and probably by limited affection. Russians viewed the family, the basic social institution, as a microcosm of society as a whole and as a model for the political structure. The family was an economic unit as well, with inheritance primarily in the male line, and property divided among all sons. Of course, for serfs, inheritable property was limited to farm animals, equipment, and the family hut. Family origins played an important role in determining social position, both within the nobility and for serfs as well. Although the actions of Ivan the Terrible and the period of anarchy weakened the power of the boyars and the importance of family origins in determining status, overall blood was the most important determinant of upper class rank. Only urban families functioned with fewer restrictions and greater freedom. Because of the nature of craft production and shop keeping, wives played a more important role in urban than in rural families. Patriarchy, thus, ruled the Russian family and gender roles in this period.

6. Diversity and Community

Between 1500 and 1700 Russia emerged as a multi-ethnic and multicultural empire, employing conquest and efforts at forced assimilation.

Empire building was justified by the idea that Russia, in contrast to the largely Muslim states it conquered, was civilized and had an ethical responsibility to bring civilization to the barbarians. Civilization was defined largely in religious terms, with Russian Orthodoxy, the true religion, viewed as civilized and other religions as pagan. The state expected newly annexed areas to be peaceful, productive, and capable of providing the necessary tax revenues. Sometimes quiescence was to be achieved by permitting conquered peoples to continue to use their native values and cultures. At other times, the state preferred forced assimilation. However, to ensure the productivity of the population, the Russian government sought to transform the newly acquired territory into farm land to be worked by the former nomadic peoples, Russian noblemen, and their labor forces or independent *(black) peasants*. Thus the Russian vision of civilization described an agrarian society rather than a pastoral one.

Though the Russians might permit some diversity, they sought to build a community based on Russian domination and a single state religion, Russian Orthodoxy. Two problems arose from this strategy. The government faced opposition to its centralizing efforts—in the Time of Troubles at the beginning of the seventeenth century and during the major rebellion led by the Cossack Stenka Razin, in the late 1660s and early 1670s. These and other *centripetal* tendencies demonstrated the reluctance or unwillingness of frontier areas to accept Russian centralization, thus threatening Russian unity. Thus the government's organized efforts at promoting conformity were always challenged but the state was able to prevent the break off of any frontier region until the First World War. The ability of the Orthodox Church to enforce religious conformity was destroyed by the Schism and the inability of the state to ensure religious conformity.

Still, the tsars made substantial progress toward political unity and control. Common political practices and bureaucratic behaviors gradually emerged, strengthened by efforts of the central government to create hierarchies that extended beyond the capital, through the regions, and down to the localities. Further efforts at the creation of a single society were reinforced by the *domostroi,* the single pattern of expected behavior within the family. At the same time, the introduction of serfdom divided Russia into classes whose differences would never be bridged, leaving it a badly divided country. No unifying principle, including Orthodoxy and Russian nationality, was strong enough to bridge the increasingly gigantic gap between serf and master.

So what diversity remained by 1700? A bit of urban freedom from the structures of rural Russia, some cultural and customary independence for conquered peoples, some freedom for frontier peoples such as the Cossacks, and the determined right to worship differently espoused and defended by the Old Believers (perhaps 20% of the Russian Orthodox population).

B. EARLY EMPIRE, 1700–1855

This was a period of great change. Russia expanded its empire to the south, extended its reach further into Siberia, and acquired Western outposts in Poland and Finland. A very modest Westernization began, intensifying in the first half of the nineteenth century. The state implemented political reforms that greatly strengthened the power of the rulers and the effectiveness of government. Ideological unity disappeared, while a variety of ideological systems were proposed and debated. None was able to attain the kind of dominance Orthodoxy had earlier. Economic growth, fostered by industrialization, helped produce efforts to restructure agricultural relationships. The government studied numerous proposals to weaken serfdom but did little. The family and gender roles changed little, though some upper class women gained prominence through education. The government tried to build community through ideology and the extension of the power of the central government more effectively throughout the country. However, the incorporation of European peoples, Poles, Jews, and Finns into the Empire increased ethnic and religious diversity. As the period ended Russia was poised for dramatic changes.

1. Imperial Expansion

This was the true age of Russian imperialism, as the Russians conquered the Caucasus and Western Siberia, made serious inroads into Central Asia, and extended their power into Europe, acquiring much of Poland and Finland. Land imperialism greatly increased Russian power but brought with it tense relationships with minorities and serious problems of governance.

Southern Conquests. Primarily, Russian military energies were directed toward expansion into the south.

Crimean Tatars. For much of the eighteenth century Russian attempts to extend power southward were halted by the Crimean Tatars, a residue of the earlier Mongol invasion, whose state was centered on the Crimean peninsula that jutted into the Black Sea. Finally, in the 1770s the defection of the Crimean Tatar allies, the Nogai, enabled the Russians to defeat the former and a decade later make the Crimea a province within the Russian Empire. The government introduced Russian political rule, incorporated the Tatar nobility into the Russian upper class, and permitted Islamic authorities to continue to exercise their religious authority locally. Conquest of the Crimea opened up the Black Sea to Russian influence and enabled the Russians to challenge Ottoman Turkish power.

The Caucasus. Next, Russia moved down into the mountainous *Caucasus* area. In the Caucasus, small Muslim tribes fought fiercely to defend their independence but were eventually defeated by the Russians. The Russians held ambiguous views toward the mountain peoples, extolling their bravery but brutally repressing their independence. Russian rule remained tenuous and rebellion *endemic.* In 1785, the *Chechens,* led by *Sufi* leader Sheikh Mansur, rebelled (see Chapter Two for a discussion of Sufism). In the 1820s Ghazhni Muhammad organized another rebellion that seriously threatened Russian rule in the Caucasus. Finally, a famous resistance movement led by *Imam Shamil',* lasted from 1834–1859. Shamil's execution and mass resettlement finally tamed the mountain rebels.

Trans-Caucasia. South of the Caucasus Mountains lived three larger states—*Georgia, Armenia,* and *Azerbaijan.* The Georgians were an Orthodox, agricultural people with a landed nobility and peasantry. The Armenians were Eastern Christians, whose religion had diverged from Orthodoxy centuries before the Russians were converted. They were a trading society of merchants, artisans, and professional peoples extending across the southern Caucasus into the Ottoman Empire. Both Georgians and Armenians saw the Russians, fellow Christians, as potential protectors but Russian guarantees of protection did not prevent a Persian invasion in 1795 that destroyed the Georgian capital. The Russians incorporated Georgia into the Empire at the beginning of the nineteenth century, yet the Georgians gradually constructed a strong sense of national identity and distinctiveness. Russian victory over the Persians in 1828 and the Turks the following year gave Armenia some degree of security and enabled Russia to peacefully bring it into the Empire. Many Armenians immigrated to Russia from Persia and the Ottoman Empire at this time. This inmigration of Armenians alarmed the Azeri, Shiite Muslims with cultural ties to Persia and language ties to the Turkish Empire. Conflict between Azeris and Armenians began, continuing down to today. Russia expended much energy, sacrificed many lives, and consumed huge amounts of resources to secure the Caucasus, in part to provide security on the southern flanks but also to exact revenge upon people who fought so fiercely and refused to surrender to the "invincible" Russians.

The *Trans-Volga* and Western Siberia. Though Russians had explored Siberia and reached the Pacific during the seventeenth century, they had initially avoided confrontation with the Muslim peoples of the Trans-Volga area and southern Siberia. Brutal warfare between Russians and the Bashkirs in the mid-eighteenth century opened up the southern flank of Siberia, where virgin soil could be turned into plow land. Russians defeated the tenacious Bashkirs in a series of wars that lasted from the late 1730s into the 1760s. Acting with tremendous brutality, the Russians *decimated* the Bashkirs, seized some of their lands, and forced the nomadic Bashkirs to turn to farming. The Russians then easily conquered the other Muslim peoples of southern Siberia. The way was open for the creation of new estates for the Russian nobility and small independent farms for peasants, many of them runaway serfs. These conquests of small "barbarian" Muslim tribes enabled Russia to do battle with the more sophisticated and better-organized Muslim kingdoms of Central Asia in the mid-nineteenth century.

Poland. Under Peter the Great (1682–1725), Russia turned westward, seeking ideas and conquest. The "rude and barbarous kingdom" sought to shed its archaic structures and become a modern, "western" society. Poland-Lithuania, Western and Catholic, stood in the way. At the same time, Poland-Lithuania still could be viewed as a legitimate heir to original Rus, through its long-term control over Kiev, the first Rus capital, and most of the western territories that had comprised the original Kievan state. Russians and Poles already hated each other. Weakened by a Swedish invasion, the defection of the Cossacks, the loss of Ukraine, and internal political conflict, Poland could not stand up to Russian power.

The Russians intervened in Polish domestic affairs, taking advantage of Poland's elective monarchy to support first one rival for the throne, then another. The Russians also supported *confederations,* armed groups that rebelled against the Polish government. Thus the Russians gradually gained a powerful position in Poland and prevented it from carrying out self-strengthening measures. The Russian armies were seldom needed, with the Poles almost intent upon committing national suicide.

Russia did not have the power to devour Poland by itself and feared the reaction of the Germanic states of Austria and Prussia. Working with one or both, the Russians engineered three *partitions* of Poland (1772, 1793, and 1795) that led to its complete disappearance. One multi-ethnic state, Poland, disappeared, making diversity an even greater challenge for the Russians.

Polish nationalism flourished, producing the November Uprising of 1830–1832. This rebellion tied down hundreds of thousands of Russian soldiers, preventing Russia from sending armies into Western Europe in support of monarchies threatened by revolution. Poland then lost most of its autonomy, while the Russians began the unsuccessful attempt to Russianize Polish life, language and its educational system. Poles continued to threaten insurrection, remaining the most rebellious and least patriotic of the peoples within the Russian Empire. Russia could not successfully incorporate the more civilized Poles into the rude and barbarous kingdom that Russia remained.

The Jews. As the Russians conquered the Poles, they also began to worry about the Jews, another alien group, reluctant to assimilate to Russian society. As early as the 1790s the Russian government prohibited Jews from living in the two main Russian cities, St. Petersburg and Moscow. However, in the early nineteenth century Russian policy changed and the *Jewish Statute of 1804* granted Jewish communities a large measure of local autonomy (*kabala*) in education and self-government. Jews were encouraged to engage in commerce and industry in the Ukraine, Western Russia, and the newly acquired Poland. Under Nicholas I (1825–1855), assimilation was again the main strategy, as exemption from military service was eliminated and conversion to Orthodoxy encouraged.

Conclusion. During the Early Empire, Russia expanded dramatically, incorporating an increasingly diverse variety of peoples into the Empire. It found it difficult to develop a single strategy that would create and ensure loyalty to the Russian state and its goals. Increasingly it seemed to conclude that native peoples could no longer be permitted to retain their traditional customs, way of life, or religion; that local political institutions could no longer be allowed; and that unity was essential if Russia was to become and remain a great power. Schemes for decentralization and federation emerged from time to time but centralization always won out.

2. Autocracy

The emperors transformed the Russian government into a *bureaucratized autocracy,* in which the powers of the ruler were quite substantial and the ability of the state to carry out the will of the ruler and his key advisors measurably greater than in the seventeenth century. Tsars attempted to enhance their power and improve the performance of the government.

Increased Power of the Tsar. During this period the tsar came to be viewed as and acted as the true leader of the country. The tsar dominated the national political agenda. Initiative for action and proposals for change came either from the tsar or could advance only with his support.

The nobility remained the only serious rival to tsarist autocracy. The actions of *Peter the Great,* Anna Ivanovna, *Catherine the Great,* and *Nicholas I* all weakened the power of the nobility but in very different ways. Peter forced the nobility to begin the process of Westernization that would alienate them from the mass of Russians—the peasants and serfs—preventing the nobility from providing leadership for the masses against the government. Westernization produced a split within the educated classes and this lack of unity made it difficult for the nobility to act jointly to push their agenda against the tsar. Too, Westernization was costly, ultimately impoverishing many noble families.

After the death of Peter the Great, autocratic power appeared to decline, giving aristocrats an opportunity to increase their political power. As Anna Ivanovna was poised to assume power in 1730, aristocrats tried to force her to make concessions that would have made her little more than their puppet in exchange for supporting her quest for the throne. With the assistance of the lesser nobility, Anna Ivanovna rejected the aristocratic plan and reestablished the idea of autocratic power.

Catherine the Great enhanced the power of the nobility, increased their control over the serfs, and established structures for noble community. In a sense, greater social power came at the expense of reduced political influence. Nobles did not seek the greater political power that seemed appropriate to their enhanced social status and economic rights. Catherine offered them only crumbs of political power.

Deeply anti-noble, in part in response to the unsuccessful army officer-led *Decembrist Uprising* (1825), Nicholas I attempted to increase his power and that of the central government at the expense of the nobility. In this he was aided by the economic decline of the nobility, caused by their efforts to "keep up with the Joneses." Discussions of peasant reforms and the introduction of modest reforms for the state peasants and private serfs on West Russian estates, owned primarily by Polish gentry, caught the nobility off guard. Nicholas undermined the independence of the nobility when he decreed that the government had the right to enforce laws on the property of the nobility. The nobles were sufficiently weakened that Nicholas' successor, Alexander II, had little difficulty imposing emancipation of the serfs on them.

Increasing Centralization. All of the tsars faced the problem of how to impose their will upon a gigantic landmass where transportation and communication systems were slow and primitive. They shifted between two grand strategies. Sometimes power was centralized in the hands of the tsar's bureaucracy. At other times it was centered in the hands of provincial governors, in theory subordinate to the central government.

Eventually a compromise was reached. Policy initiation was centralized and policy implementation was placed in the hands of provincial governors. Functional officials assisted each provincial governor and maintained ties to the appropriate functional department of the central government. The country was divided into approximately 50 provinces, each subdivided into regions and localities. Supervision of provincial government was conducted directly through inspections and indirectly through reporting mechanisms. The ruler thus had a rather clear idea of whether policy was being implemented effectively. Gradual improvements in the quality of the bureaucracy and substantial increases in their loyalty to the government enhanced its power at both the central and provincial levels.

Political Experimentation. Tsars sought to create the *rechstaat* (the well-run state), experimenting with various forms of government. Experimentation was most common during the reign of Alexander I (1801–1825). Coming to power upon the assassination of his father and feeling responsible, Alexander vacillated between mystical distance from action and reform planning. He sought reforms that would improve the efficiency of the government without diminishing his own power. Efforts at political change were interrupted by the lengthy Napoleonic Wars, the wars between the British and the French that lasted from the French Revolution until Napoleon's ultimate defeat more than two decades later.

Most proposals for reform were offered during the first half of the reign. Soon after coming to power Alexander permitted the *Senate* to propose a redefinition of its powers. Alexander ultimately rejected the Senate proposals, which included election of the Senate, which would have the power to levy taxes and nominate key government figures. Immediately after that, Alexander appointed a *Secret Committee* of trusted allies who were to discuss reforms. Nothing much came of their efforts.

In 1809, Michael Speranskii offered the most substantial set of reform plans. Speranskii called for a professional civil service chosen through an examination system. He also proposed the separation of powers. Though Alexander would head each branch of government, in other respects executive, judicial and legislative branches were to be separate. Speranskii suggested an elected *State Duma* (legislature) with budgetary power and the right both to ask questions of the ruler and offer suggestions. Bureaucratic in-fighting and jealousy of Speranskii, as well as the relatively radical nature of his ideas, doomed the plan. Late in the reign, other bureaucrats proposed a federal system, loosely based on the U.S. constitution. Reform planning produced increased bureaucratic efficiency under Alexander I but did not substantially change the nature of government.

Bureaucratic Class. During this century and a half, a bureaucratic class formed. Peter the Great recognized the inefficiency and ineptness of his government and sought to restructure the government and improve the qualifications of its servitors. He introduced a *Table of Ranks,* intended to promote social mobility and encourage and reward political or bureaucratic talent. Above the common clerical jobs, government officials started at the bottom of the Table of Ranks, which gave them the status of personal nobility. They then worked their way upward, eventually reaching a point where they became hereditary nobles, which conferred noble status on their families and heirs. Most of the bureaucrats came from the nobility but gradually foreigners, the sons of priests, and urban merchants entered the government. Over time, government officials transferred their loyalty from the nobility to the bureaucracy, thus forming a distinct class. Possessing a separate sense of identity, the bureaucrats began to see themselves as the spokesmen for the needs of the nation and not those of a single class—the nobility. This perspective helps to explain why the bureaucrats became social and political reformers, beginning under Alexander I and culminating in the Great Reforms of Alexander II.

Independence from the nobility predisposed bureaucrats toward reform. They also became interested in Western ideas of the Enlightenment and Utilitarianism. Discussing Western ideas in *salons* and other informal gatherings, bureaucrats acquired a rationale for and program of reform. These discussions produced a new law code, improvements in the condition of the state peasants, and the initial planning for the abolition of serfdom.

Conclusion. In the period from Peter the Great through the mid-nineteenth century the power of the tsar increased and the efficiency of Russian government improved. The power of the government was extended beyond the capitals to the fringes of the empire and to the estates of the formerly all-powerful "petty tsars"—the landed nobility. This more powerful and more efficient government was better able to carry out massive reforms, though its ability to successfully mobilize for military victory improved only somewhat after the seventeenth century.

3. Ideological Confusion

As the Orthodox Church declined, alternative sets of ideas surfaced, most focusing on the issue of Russian identity. Ideology was no longer a force for unification; it became a basis for conflict within the educated classes.

Decline of Russian Orthodoxy. From its dominant position in the first half of the seventeenth century, Russian Orthodoxy's influence continuously diminished. First weakened by the Schism, the church also suffered at the hands of Peter the Great. Though in many ways a deeply religious man, Peter eliminated the Church's independence. He made the Church a branch of the government, appointed its head, the Patriarch, and subordinated the church to a secular institution, the *Holy Synod.* The schism weakened the power of the church spiritually. Peter also weakened it politically. Catherine the Great (1762–1796) undermined the economic position of the Church by confiscating huge amounts of church lands and giving them to lovers, hangers-on, and military leaders. Alexander I supported western Protestant missionary societies' attempts to spread the gospel in modern Russian, while at the same time promoting mystical sects. Orthodoxy could no longer act as cement for Russian society, though Nicholas I tried to restore its ideological power and influence.

Condemnation of Russia. The decline in the power of Russian Orthodoxy left an ideological vacuum. Petr *Chaadaev* initiated discussion of alternatives in 1836, when he argued that Russia had neither identity, nor purpose. Russia was a barbaric land that had offered nothing to humanity. It was doomed to a wretched existence. Nicholas I responded by sending Chaadaev to an insane asylum, for one must be crazy to have such a negative view of glorious Russia.

Secularization of Orthodox Values—*Slavophiles.* A small group of nobles, many of them the owners of landed estates in the Moscow area, had a response for Chaadaev. These Slavophiles—lovers of Slavic life and culture—argued that Russia was indeed unique and possessed a richness and power greater than that of any other nation. They looked to rural Russia and, imagining a perfect world quite distant from reality, idealized the peasant community (the *obshchina*). Ivan *Kireevskii* and Aleksei *Khomiakov* focused on Orthodox faith and the concept of *sobornost,* which suggested a community that could preserve diversity. All benefited from and contributed to the community while retaining their own identity. As one Slavophile put it, "A commune thus represents a moral choir, and, just as in a choir one voice is not lost but is heard in the harmony of all voices, so in the community the individual is not lost, but renounces his exclusivity in favor of the common accord." Condemning autocracy, the Slavophiles offered a political alternative in which the upper classes would dominate politically. In a society increasingly fragmented ideologically and socially, the appeal to community, ironically, gained few supporters. As the Slavophiles posited a vision of an ideal society, they attacked the impact of the West on Russia. They condemned the West as individualistic, materialistic, and rational.

Westerners. "*Westerners*" reflected the increasing influence of Western ideas and culture upon Russia. Peter the Great opened the floodgates of Western influence, while Catherine and Alexander encouraged the influx of Western thought and customs. Increasingly the Russian educated classes were becoming westernized. For example, many used French as their language of daily interaction and reserved Russian for giving orders to serfs. The Westerners, especially historian Timofei *Granovskii,* emphasized that Russia's independent path had denied it access to a number of important Western ideas and institutions, including an independent judiciary, a parliament, and a tradition of dissent. More radical was Vissarion *Belinskii,* a literary critic who emphasized the need to introduce social reforms, especially emancipation of the serfs, and even hinted at socialism. Westerners easily defeated the small band of Slavophiles.

Official Nationality and Russian Nationalism. The government's efforts to create a set of ideals around which people could rally came to be known as *Official Nationality.* Initially defined by Minister of Education Sergei Uvarov, Official Nationality contained three main slogans—*autocracy, orthodoxy,* and *nationality.* Autocracy meant complete loyalty to an all-powerful tsar. Orthodoxy meant allegiance to Russian Orthodoxy as well as efforts to destroy other religions. The term nationality was rather unclear, combining a sense of Russianness with an elemental loyalty to the nation; that is, the people. If autocracy could be a rallying call for many—but not all—Russians, both Orthodoxy and nationality contributed to further disunity. Orthodoxy was a divisive slogan in a multi-religious empire. Orthodox believers were little more than half of the population of the Empire, if one excludes Old Believers and those who continued to follow Uniate beliefs. Nationality was also a divisive slogan for a multi-ethnic empire. Since the Russian Empire had become increasingly diverse in this period, this appeal to Russian identity could not be an effective force for unity.

Radical Critique. A few radicals began to criticize the Russian system. The radical tradition began with the Masons, Nikolai *Novikov's* quiet criticism and Aleksandr *Radishchev's* critique of autocracy and serfdom. The Decembrists, whose minor rebellion in 1825 transformed them into revolutionary martyrs, continued the radical tradition. They proposed political reform, especially transformation of Russia into a constitutional monarchy. Alexander *Herzen,* who emigrated during the reign of Nicholas I, was the most prominent radical critic. Eventually Herzen called for the creation of a utopia based on the peasant commune (*obshchina*). Thus radicals created an idealized portrait of a traditional society as the basis for a Russian future of justice and equality.

Ideological Disunity. Gradually, the ideological choir that had sung in harmony through the middle of the seventeenth century sang with discordant notes. With Orthodoxy no longer able to create and sustain community, a variety of voices could be heard. Slavophiles and radicals idealized the rural past, while Westerners championed republican ideals. Unsure of itself, the government too promoted an ideology, Official Nationality. Ideology could not produce community in the increasingly diverse Russian Empire.

4. Social Difference

Social difference continued to dominate Russian life. The nobility was still the most powerful class but it began to decline. No answers were found to the questions of serfdom, backwardness, and poverty. Urban life flourished through in-migration, cultural activity, and economic expansion. Russia's predominantly rural economy faced competition from the expansion of commerce and the beginnings of industrialization.

From Golden Age to Decline: the Russian Nobility. This was a golden age for most members of the nobility. The wealthiest aristocrats owned millions of acres of land and hundreds of thousands of serfs. With the expansion into the rich farmlands of Ukraine and diversification of agriculture, nobles' wealth increased. Access to Europe brought dramatic changes to the lifestyles of the nobility. French champagne, Wedgwood china from England, and travel abroad (especially to the German principalities) transformed many Russian nobles into European gentlemen and ladies. Catherine the Great's *Charter of the Nobility* (1785) enshrined noble privilege and rights. In addition, the Charter created a system of upper class self-governance, with elected class "officers," *marshals of the nobility,* providing leadership. Nobles had almost total power over their serfs. They could whip or kill their serfs, or send disobedient ones into the army (with a 25-year term of service, this was often a death sentence), and he (or she) could rape a serf without penalty. The state had no right to intervene on noble estates and thus was forced to accept all unspeakable noble actions toward serfs. Finally, most nobles continued to serve the government. Dragooned into service to the government by Peter the Great and forced to accept the principle of advancement by merit, most nobles recognized that service to the state gave them access to power and influence. Even when Catherine abolished compulsory service, most nobles continued to serve the government.

However, the façade of the golden age gradually tarnished. Economic decline set in, recognizable after the Napoleonic Wars. Many nobles went into debt to maintain their lifestyles and to meet daily expenses. They pledged their serfs as collateral for the government loans they received. By 1859 two-thirds of the serfs were loan collateral. Increasingly, indebtedness and near-bankruptcy became the fate of many noble families. As industrialization expanded, the agrarian sector of the economy, the mainstay of noble wealth, became less important.

Also, more and more nobles abandoned service to the state. This had two consequences. First, they lost access to the influence they had had earlier. Secondly, the state had to recruit persons from other classes to serve in the bureaucracy, promoting an independent bureaucratic perspective. The rise of a small group of individuals critical of traditional society put the nobility on the defensive. Finally, Nicholas I sought to reduce the independence of the nobility and the state began to intervene on nobles' estates. Thus in the first half of the nineteenth century the landed nobleman declined, his once new silk robe now tattered, as he slumped in his overstuffed easy chair.

Serfdom: "The Wretched Question." Peasant life worsened dramatically during this era. Increased noble expenditures led to greater pressure on the serfs to work harder and produce more. Peasants either made money payments, which the nobles frequently increased, or had labor responsibilities on the estates, with the number of days per week of labor for the nobleman increased, as well. Nobles treated the peasants with great brutality. The buying and selling of serfs, which disrupted their lives, became more and more common. The lives of serfs in Western Russia and state peasants improved as a result of state-sponsored reform movements during the reign of Nicholas I.

Urbanization and Urban Classes. Russia remained a largely rural society in which cities were relatively unimportant. Before the incorporation of Finland and much of Poland into the Russian Empire, Russia had only three major cities—Moscow, St. Petersburg, and Odessa. Cities were primarily administrative centers and secondarily commercial sites. Merchants, artisans, and unskilled laborers dominated, though the nobility and the educated classes increasingly built stately homes as part-year residences. City governments existed but primarily as structures for tax collection.

Catherine the Great issued the *Charter of the Cities* (1785), building upon earlier efforts by Peter the Great to establish city government. Authorities divided the urban classes into three strata—large merchants, small-scale merchants, and "city folk" (artisans and day laborers), with government dominated by the wealthier merchants. Urban residents had responsibilities but no rights. Cities did not become independent centers of political power, as they had in Western Europe. Crime, disease, and pollution made life unbelievably difficult but rural life was not much better. This helps to explain why urban population declined in relative terms from 11 percent of the population in 1740 to 7 percent in 1860.

Intelligentsia. Late in this period a new social group—the *intelligentsia*—emerged. The term described relatively well-educated persons who devoted some or much of their energy to thinking and talking about public issues, generally from a critical perspective. Their social origins were varied. Some came from the *raznochintsy* (people who had no clear social identity) and some from the increasingly important professional classes of professors, lawyers, and journalists. Many came from the nobility. Intelligentsia referred to a psychological and political orientation rather than to a class background or identity. The intelligentsia played an increasingly important role in Russia both within the government and in opposition.

Frontier Protest. Tsarist authority was seriously threatened by the *Pugachev Rebellion* (1773–1775), which began in the Western Ural Mountains and spread westward to the Volga Basin. With Russia at war with Turkey, authorities were slow to respond to this rapidly expanding uprising, which engulfed serfs, industrial and mine workers, Old Believers, and minorities, such as the Bashkirs and Tatars. Pugachev's appeal, in part, was based on his assumption of the role of Peter III, the assassinated husband of Catherine the Great. In part his call for social justice, an end to serfdom, and the end of government control over people's lives motivated frontier residents to support the rebellion. It is claimed that the Pugachev Rebellion and the unrest in France that soon became the French Revolution halted serious efforts at social and political reform in Russia.

Economic Growth. The economy expanded throughout much of the eighteenth century but probably declined in the first half of the nineteenth century, especially due to the government's focus on warfare. Economic expansion resulted from a broad set of factors. Government took the initiative in promoting industry, expanding its role as a consumer of industrial, especially military, products. The amount of cultivated land expanded, especially in the south after the incorporation of Crimea into the Empire (1783). Emigration to vacant lands in the Volga Basin and southern steppes and the incorporation of Poland into the Russian Empire added substantial amounts of farmland. Agricultural yields increased with the shift from the planting of rye to wheat (a grain with much larger yields per acre) and the introduction of new crops such as tobacco and grapes and new livestock, including Spanish and Polish sheep. However, there was little improvement in agricultural methods. Russia did not go through an agricultural revolution, as did the European countries. Finally, transportation improved, especially through a major program of canal building and the opening up of the Black Sea port of Odessa.

Commercial Expansion and the Origins of Industry. The Russian economy grew at a modest pace from the seventeenth through the mid-nineteenth centuries. When political chaos came to an end in the early decades of Romanov rule, the economy began to stabilize and grow. However, serf agriculture and an inadequate infrastructure were major drags on the economy. Population increases, territorial expansion, European demand for grain, and the opening up of the wealth of Siberia stimulated economic expansion. Peter the Great promoted the development of an industrial zone in the southern Ural Mountains, where iron and coal were found in abundance. Armaments were the main products of this industrial complex but warfare also increased demand for rope, textiles, leather goods, and ships. By the end of Peter's reign, Russian industry was producing more iron than any other part of the world. After his death, interest in promoting industrial growth and economic development waned. Industrial production expanded rapidly in the last quarter of the eighteenth century and in the first half of the nineteenth century, when textiles became a leading industry. Industrial expansion accelerated with the development of a textiles industry in Russian Poland, which quickly became one of the leading industrial centers in Russia.

5. Family and Gender Roles

Family life changed little in this period. Patriarchy dominated family relationships, while women from the nobility acquired some public role through Westernized education. Women from the royal family and the nobility organized salons where reform ideas were discussed.

Gentry Nest. Many families of the nobility moved to the frontier. Relatively isolated, they developed a closeness and affection lacking in families that lived in the heart of Russia. Such families were large and generally *extended* (three or more generations living together). Families remained institutions for social and economic advancement.

Serfdom, Family, and Gender. Most serfs were members of families; few were single for their entire lives. Serf families were patriarchal and extended. Owners had a great deal of control over the lives of their serfs, determining marriage partners and having sexual rights to the serfs. Alcoholism, violence, and abuse were common in serf families, as they replicated the kind of behavior they frequently received at the hands of the serf owner.

6. Community and Diversity

Diversity dominated, while community became more difficult to achieve in the early empire, 1700–1850. The expansion of empire, the introduction of serfdom, and the privileging of the nobility enhanced diversity.

The Russian Empire expanded to the Black Sea in the south, beyond the Urals in the east, and reached into Europe, with the absorption of Finland and much of Poland. Continued expansion to the east and south meant conquest of Muslim tribal peoples, including those such as the Crimean Tatars, who had had their own independent states. Thus, the government faced the tremendous challenge of incorporating all of these peoples into the Empire. Ethnic and religious diversity made community difficult. The Lutheran Finns and Catholic Poles created the greatest difficulties. During this period the Russians did little to develop strategies for building community, especially for *double minorities* (simultaneously ethnic and religious minorities).

Class intensified difference as well. The introduction of serfdom created an unbridgeable gap between the nobility and the peasants. The nobility was above the law; the peasants were beneath notice. The difference between the two social groups was intensified by the Westernization of the nobility, while peasants remained mired in a medieval world of poverty, filth, paganism, and superstition.

As Russia became more diverse, the state lagged behind in developing ways of dealing with difference. Other goals took priority. Territorial expansion was not accompanied by strategies for effectively incorporating the newcomers into the Empire. The government no longer followed the earlier method of not imposing Russian culture on newly acquired peoples.

Indirectly, attempts to improve the effectiveness of government promoted community. Efforts to ensure that the will of the government was effective, not just in the capital but in the country as a whole, helped to produce common standards and practices. People in different parts of the Empire were thus treated in a similar way before the law. The Law Codes of 1649 and 1833 created a common set of legal rules for the Empire as a whole, though law was applied differentially depending upon one's class.

Educated Russians saw ideology as a basis for unity. Ironically their inability to develop a consensus on belief systems made community building more difficult. In the seventeenth century conflict over theological issues and efforts to reestablish unity led to the break up of the Orthodox Church. Though the church and state used force, approximately 20 percent of the Church membership, the "Old Believers," rejected efforts to purify the church service and broke away. Neither the church nor the state successfully incorporated Western-influenced ideas from Ukraine into Russian culture and thought.

During the reign of Nicholas I, Official Nationality produced another flawed effort at unity of thought. Official Nationality responded to the recognition that Russia was a country lacking a strong sense of community. Autocracy supported the all-powerful role of the emperor but political dissent was beginning to challenge this perspective. Orthodoxy appealed only to the members of the Orthodox Church and alienated the Old Believers, Muslims, Catholics, Uniates, and Lutherans. Nationality had no resonance among the ethnic minority Poles, Turks, Finns, Tatars, Bashkirs, and others. Periodic and modest calls for federation did not enter the mainstream of Russian policy. Honoring diversity was rejected in the name of community building measures that backfired.

C. REFORM AND COLLAPSE: DEATH OF TSARIST RUSSIA, 1855–1914

The Russian star rose rapidly during the reign of Alexander II (1855–1881), and then crashed toward earth, burning up during its fall. Military losses acted as bookends for the period. Defeat in the Crimean War (1853–1856) forced the government to introduce substantial reforms; defeat in the First World War produced the collapse of the Russian imperial system. At the moment of its collapse Russia had reached its greatest extent, having conquered the Muslim kingdoms of Central Asia and tying Russia to the Pacific through the Trans-Siberian Railroad. Alexander II introduced dramatic changes in political and social institutions in an effort to revitalize a badly beaten Russia. However, these reforms alarmed conservatives who tried, with little success, to dismantle them. Political reforms introduced the idea of broadened participation in the political process, through *zemstvos* (local and provincial elected rural assemblies) and city councils. Facing revolution, in 1905 the government authorized the creation of a national legislature (*duma*). The government applied the strategy of *Russification* on the ideological front, as it tried to create a single culture and set of beliefs based on the superiority of Russian language, culture, history values, and religion. Frightened by the possibility of peasant revolution and building upon modest reforms under Nicholas I, the reform bureaucrats of Alexander II provided him with a plan for emancipating the serfs and transforming state peasants into freeholders. The emancipation of the serfs transformed rural Russia and provoked dramatic changes in almost every aspect of Russian life. Initial preoccupation with the rural economy soon turned into support for rapid industrialization. Rapid industrialization helped create two new social groups—an industrial middle class and an industrial working class. With industrialization came changes in the Russian family and in gender relations. A small women's movement, mainly concerned with political rights for women, appeared in the early twentieth century. Efforts at community collapsed and diversity exploded, producing the disintegration of the Russian Empire in the First World War.

1. Empire Completed

Early in the second half of the nineteenth century Russia completed its empire through the conquest of Central Asia. By these moves, minorities became half of the Empire's population, creating serious problems for the Russian government.

Central Asia. Russian armies moved into Central Asia, forcing the Muslim political leaders to surrender. Here were states with long traditions of independence stretching back to the days of the Mongols. Two states, *Khiva* and *Bukhara,* were permitted some degree of autonomy and were not formally incorporated into the Russian Empire. The Russians made no real attempt to assimilate these arid land kingdoms into the Russian administrative system. Local traditions and structures were left intact. Russians believed that completion of the Empire would guarantee Russian security against the possibility of British incursions, which were never a reality. More importantly, Central Asian lands were turned into cotton fields, whose harvests fueled the mills of Moscow and Russian Poland. Even this limited degree of Russian rule aroused resistance, a resistance centered in the lush *Fergana Valley,* the real center of Muslim political power in Central Asia.

The Balkans. Russia concentrated on expanding its influence in the Balkans. The Balkans, the area between the Black Sea and the Adriatic, had been part of the Ottoman Empire for centuries. The population consisted of Muslims, Eastern Orthodox, and Catholics. Russia's attempts to support the Slavic Orthodox populace had led to the Crimean War. Hoping that the European powers would not intervene and goaded by an increasingly nationalistic press and elite, Russia went to war with the Ottoman Turks (1877–1878). The Russians defeated the Turks, enabling the Serbs and Bulgarians to gain independence. The Russians could defeat the weak army of the moribund Ottoman Empire; other nations it could not.

The Far East. The conquest of Central Asia opened up southern routes to the Pacific. The *Trans Siberian Railway* (1898–1902) stretched across southern Siberia along the border with Central Asia. Cutting its losses by giving up its American empire, the Russians compromised with the Japanese by abandoning claims to the *Kurile Islands* and agreeing to the division of the island of *Sakhalin,* both off the eastern coast of Russia. Preoccupied with domestic reform, Russia had neither the energy nor ability to become an East Asian power during the reign of Alexander II. However, the emancipation of the serfs started a greater flow of peasant immigrants into Siberia. This migration peaked after the famine of 1891–1892, when the government encouraged peasants to move to Siberia.

2. From Reform to Reaction—the Government

During this period the government tried to expand political participation while reserving ultimate power to the tsar and his central bureaucracy. In the process, reform efforts were replaced by reactionary moves.

Alexander II (1855–1881). This was an era of dramatic political change, made necessary by the emancipation of the serfs. The government introduced two major political reforms—local self-government and a Westernized judicial system.

Zemstvos. In 1864 Alexander established assemblies of the land (zemstvos). In rural areas, landowners, separated according to class, elected delegates to local assemblies, and those assemblies elected representatives to provincial assemblies. The assemblies drew up broad policies that were to be implemented by administrative boards they appointed. Zemstvos were responsible for local taxation, education, health and welfare, and agricultural improvements. The central government frustrated most attempts at transforming the zemstvo system into a national network of elected bodies. Initially the zemstvos were not very effective but by the 1890s they had become organs for substantial local improvements (mockingly called "small deeds" by radicals). In the early 1890s the government introduced a new level of authority in the countryside, the land guards, who were to represent the will of the central authorities and ensure that the zemstvos were relatively powerless.

In the 1870s parallel municipal councils were established. These modest attempts to broaden participation in governance were limited to Russia and were not extended to minority areas. Thus an opportunity to bind the minorities to the Russian Empire was lost.

Judicial reforms. In the 1870s the government introduced major reforms in the judicial system, which had already been improved by the 1833 codification of law. Judges were appointed for life, the jury system was introduced for civil cases, and justices of the peace were appointed to provide judicial services to the peasantry. Modeled after the French legal system, the reforms did much to reduce the arbitrariness of Russian justice.

Nicholas II (1894–1917). Though Alexander II had received proposals for an elected national legislature, his 1881 assassination by disillusioned revolutionaries prevented adoption of the idea. The concept was reintroduced in 1906. Faced with massive opposition, Nicholas II (1894–1917) felt he had no choice but to permit Russians to have a voice in national affairs through an elected national legislature. This legislature, the *duma,* held four sessions between 1906 and 1914. Members of the legislature were generally chosen indirectly at provincial electoral assemblies. The nobility was well represented, the peasants less so, and urban residents badly underrepresented. Nicholas closed each of the first two Dumas because they were too radical. The government changed the electoral laws over and over again until Nicholas II was assured of a conservative majority. Political reform moved Russia toward constitutional monarchy but Nicholas II refused to acknowledge that his continued rule was really dependent upon broadened participation in the political process and greater political rights for citizens.

3. Ideology

Russian nationalism provided two main ideologies—*Pan-Slavism* and *Russification.* Opponents of the autocracy offered three alternatives—*liberalism, populism,* and *Marxism.*

Pan-Slavism. This ideological plan of action emerged in the 1860s, fostered by right-wing journalists and elements within the Russian military. Pan-Slavism argued that all of the Slavic peoples, with the exception of the Catholic Slavs (mainly Poles), had a common destiny to be united into a single alliance, and dominated by the Russians. Russians had a duty to free the other Orthodox Slavs from Muslim control and to bring them under Russian protection. Such ideas, especially as espoused by the fiery journalist Mikhail *Katkov,* pushed Russia into the Russo-Turkish War (1877–1878), while seeking to increase the Slavic element within a Russian Empire whose population was increasingly non-Russian and prone to rebellion. Support for Russification superceded Pan-Slavism, whose goals were mainly in the area of foreign policy.

Russification. *Russification* can be defined as a set of policies intended to create a uniform culture based on Russian values, beliefs, and traditions. Russification had a number of goals. A single culture and language throughout the Empire would produce bureaucratic efficiencies. Russification would end minority dissidence and rebellion. It would strengthen Russia by overcoming ethnic and religious differences. Russification was based on an assumption of Russian superiority, as well as a Russian civilizing mission, a *messianism* evident as early as the seventeenth century.

Policies included efforts to make Russian the language of all government activity throughout the Empire. For instance, the minutes of all peasant village meetings in minority areas were to be written in Russian and all court cases, including all testimony, were to be conducted in Russian. Education was the key to the potential success of Russification. Russian became the language of instruction in secondary and higher education and ultimately in primary education as well. In minority areas the native language was taught as a foreign language, with translation of passages into Russian the key pedagogical technique. Subject matter was Russianized as well. Throughout the Empire, students learned Russian history, geography, and literature. If they were not Russians they did not learn the history, geography, and literature of their native cultures. Authorities sought to eliminate minority identities. For example, Poland was renamed "The Vistula Lands."

Russification also meant a more active program of forced conversion to Russian Orthodoxy, a campaign directed mainly against Lutherans and Catholics. For example, the Russian government subordinated the Polish Catholic Church organization to the Russian Orthodox hierarchy, closed seminaries, and created barriers to entrance into the priesthood. Lutheran churches were transformed into Orthodox ones. Hundreds of priests and pastors were sent into Siberian exile.

Anti-Semitism was a particular *virulent* form of Russification. In a country long filled with anti-Jewish prejudice, the Russian government ultimately fostered anti-semitism. But in 1880 the future direction of Russian government policy was not yet clear. Anti-Jewish attitudes of the Romanov family, important officials, and the populace were transformed into a campaign against Jews in response to the report of a government study group, the *Pahlen Commission.* This Commission concluded that assimilation was the appropriate strategy for dealing with the Jewish question. Rejecting the report, the government of Alexander III turned to a more open program of exclusion of Jews from Russian society. In 1882 Jews were banned from acquiring property and moving to rural areas and prohibited from becoming lawyers. At the same time, quotas limited Jewish enrollment at universities and medical schools. At Passover in 1891, two-thirds of the Jews of Moscow was expelled, under the pretext that they were illegal residents. *Pogroms,* such as that in Kishinev in southwestern Russia in 1903, became increasingly common. Generally provoked or even organized by authorities, mobs of Russians burned and plundered Jewish districts.

Russification failed. The Russians simply lacked the ability to coerce all school children in the country to learn to become Russian. School strikes and the widespread emergence of underground educational institutions, including universities, preserved native cultures and offered an illegal alternative to public education. It is estimated that a majority of literate Poles studied in illegal schools, while thousands of students attended the underground "Flying University" of Warsaw.

Attempts at Russification met bitter resistance from minorities and from some educated Russians. Russification increased the alienation of minorities and helped explain why so many minorities played leadership roles in revolutionary movements. Russification actually promoted national consciousness among ordinary members of minority groups, especially peasants. Among educated members of minority groups, the question of their future relationship to Russia was a common topic from the 1880s on. Few thought independence was at all possible, a majority favored local autonomy, and a few sympathized with Russian rule, either out of despair or because loyalty to Russia gave them access to enhanced status and position.

Liberalism. Liberalism represented the most important alternative to loyalty to the tsar. It emerged out of three social groupings—landed nobles, rural professionals (the *third element*), and urban professionals. Landed nobles, gaining experience in the zemstvos, saw the need for a national legislative body. Rural professionals, such as doctors, veterinarians, and teachers, believed that political change at the national level was necessary to improve the lives of the rural masses. Urban professionals, deeply influenced by Western political thought, argued that a modern Europeanized Russia needed the same sort of parliamentary government as Western countries. Liberals wanted universal suffrage, an elected parliament, and either a constitutional monarchy or a republic. They offered vague support for improvements in the lives of ordinary people but weren't very clear about what social changes would produce such results. Recognizing that their movement was rather small, liberals unsuccessfully reached out to other political forces. They believed that only a unified opposition could defeat the autocracy of Nicholas II. Still, the liberals were the most powerful opposition force from the early twentieth century down through the first revolution of 1917, the February Revolution.

Populism. Populism had begun in response to the emancipation of the serfs. Populists concluded that the emancipation reforms were too modest and too pro-nobility. As they tried to figure out how to change government policy, they justified their role through the concept of the *critical thinking individual,* a term coined by a sociologist, Petr *Lavrov.* Critical thinking persons were to provide leadership in the struggle against the tsar. For the most part populists tried to "go to the people" in order to invoke revolutionary impulses among the peasants. Sometimes they settled in peasant villages, hoping to gain peasants' trust. Distrusting outsiders from educated (and Westernized) Russia, peasants turned many over to the police. Disillusioned, many populists concluded that the peasants could not be transformed into a revolutionary force (see a parallel disappointment with the peasants in China after the Communists came to power). Instead, populists would have to assume the burden of history by destroying the tsar. The assassination of Alexander II in 1881, however, was not the beginning of populist power but a major defeat. By the time populism recovered, it had decided to devote its energies to opposing the modernization of Russia. In the early twentieth century the populists returned to mass agitation and terrorism, achieving some degree of influence, especially among the educated peasants and village teachers.

Marxism. Russian Marxism emerged among former populist exiles in Western Europe. Rejecting terrorism, they turned to the ideas of Karl *Marx.*

Marx argued that material conditions—the means of production—determined all other facets of life. Essentially the economy determined a society's political system, its gender relations, and even its art and literature. Marx created a model of historical inevitability known as *dialectical materialism.* At a certain point in historical development a society (the thesis stage) would face internal contradictions (the antithesis). Out of these internal contradictions a new set of forces, based on a new means of production and reflected in a particular social class, would emerge (a new synthesis). Society thus would advance in a series of stages, culminating in the victory of socialism over capitalism. According to Marx, socialism could triumph only in the most advanced capitalist countries in the world. He passionately condemned the suffering of the proletariat, which he believed was caused by capitalist exploitation. Marx also identified a leadership that would make the revolution and bring socialism into being. This group would be the *vanguard of the proletariat.*

In the early twentieth century Vladimir *Lenin* (a pseudonym for Vladimir Ulianov) took this concept further, arguing that only a small group of dedicated, full-time revolutionaries could make a revolution. This narrow definition of a Marxist splintered the Russian Marxist movement, with Lenin calling his supporters *Bolsheviks* (the majority) and his opponents, the larger wing of the party, the *Mensheviks* (the minority). With its narrow base, the Bolsheviks had less influence than the Mensheviks, who emphasized mass agitation and worked to improve the living standards of the working class.

4. Social Difference and Conflict

Rapid social change characterized Russia in the second half of the nineteenth century. Emancipation of the serfs and relatively swift industrialization were the main engines of social change. These changes produced increased social conflict that culminated in the Revolution of 1905.

Emancipation of the Serfs. The emancipation of the serfs and parallel changes for state and other categories of peasants was the central event in modern Russian history. Emancipation acted as a catalyst for dramatic political, juridical, social, and economic changes. However, emancipation did not solve the "wretched question" of peasant backwardness and poverty.

The *Crimean War* (1853–1856) was the catalyst for emancipation. The war demonstrated Russia's military weakness, which many attributed to backwardness associated with a serf economy. The war also provided an opportunity for the expression of peasant unrest. Thus, two forms of insecurity, one associated with the inability of Russia to defend itself against Western powers, and another based on fears of social chaos, produced emancipation. Alexander II and his reform bureaucrats, many of whom had gained valuable experience in the earlier reform of the state peasantry and the reforms affecting serfs in Western Russia, provided the leadership.

Alexander and his key reformers based emancipation on several principles. First, emancipation would involve a transfer of land to the peasants. Second, nobles who lost land would be compensated for the loss of both land and labor. Third, allocation of land to peasants was intended to ensure relative equal economic conditions for each peasant family.

Promulgated into law in 1863 for serfs and in subsequent years for other types of peasants, emancipation occurred gradually. First, peasants were granted personal freedom. Next they were placed in the status of *temporary obligation.* While land was being surveyed and allocations determined, peasants continued to work on the lands of their former owners. By the late 1870s land was ready for allocation and peasants permitted to use their new property and move about freely. As landowners, peasants were required to make *redemption payments,* set at 6 percent of the value of the land (inflated to compensate nobles for the loss of free labor), to be paid each year for a 49-year period.

The village society (frequently known as the *commune*) replaced the nobleman as the determinant of peasants' fate. Except in western Russia and Poland, the village, not individuals, generally owned the land. Periodically villages redistributed land to take into consideration demographic changes, such as deaths, births, and the creation of new families. Village societies tried to keep peasant labor "down on the farm." But even a peasant who left the village to work in the cities had to continue to make allotment payments, as well as pay taxes and other dues. Peasants were transferred from the tyranny of the noble estate owner to that of the village society. In this way, peasants remained a separate social group, not integrated into the rest of society.

Emancipation did not lead to immediate economic improvements. The confusion, the lengthy process of determining allotments, and increased peasant fertility perpetuated rural poverty. Opportunities for grain exports, access to cheap capital, the emergence of a commercial dairy industry in northern Russia and Western Siberia, the opening up of new lands for cultivation in Siberia, and modest amounts of agricultural modernization contributed to improvements in the peasant condition in the late nineteenth century. Emancipation produced a chain reaction of reforms, including zemstvos, justices of the peace, and rural police and land guards.

Emergence of a Capitalist Class. Industrialization transformed urban Russia's physical and social landscapes in the second half of the nineteenth century. In spite of fears of accelerating urban unrest, the government promoted industrialization. It guided priorities; for example, emphasizing railroad construction. Officials devised incentives for industrialists. It encouraged foreign investment and developed other schemes for increasing the amount of capital available for investment. Industrialization grew quietly in the 1870s and surged from the 1890s to the First World War. The Ural Mountain industrial region ceased to be the center of industrial activity. Instead, the large cities in central Russia (including Moscow, St. Petersburg, and Ivanovo-Voznesensk), Ukraine, the Caucasus, the Baltic areas, and especially Poland became major industrial centers. At a time when Western Europe was going through a "second industrialization," which focused on heavy industry and chemicals, Russian industrialization was powered mainly by textiles and food processing, including vodka production.

Government policy and industrial expansion combined to produce significant changes in urban society. Alexander II eliminated internal distinctions within the merchant class. Municipal council legislation in 1870 expanded the role of local government to include security, welfare, and education, and not just taxation. Cultural life flourished and many urban residents joined a *civic movement* of professional, cultural and leisure activity associations. By the early twentieth century, large cities began to acquire amenities such as streetlights, sewers, and tram service.

An urbanized middle class began to flourish, dominated by industrialists. They replaced merchants as the leaders of urban society and began to displace the nobility as the country's elite. However, neither the right to serve local government nor civic participation prepared the capitalist class to play an active political role.

Emergence of a Working Class. A working class emerged, numbering over 10 million, including families (over 10% of the population), by the time of the First World War. These workers did not form a hereditary, urban proletariat. Many were first generation proletarians who retained their ties to the countryside, for reasons of psychological and economic security. Many factories were located in the countryside or in small towns. Gradually differences developed within the class, based largely on type of employment, education, and life goals. A "gray" workforce of skilled workers, many of them literate, distinguished itself from unskilled laborers from the countryside.

The government responded to the condition of the working class in a paternalistic manner, introducing labor legislation, beginning in 1882. This legislation attempted to reduce the ability of factory owners and their staffs to exploit workers. Legislation limited night work and work hours for children and women and in 1897 set the maximum workday at eleven and a half hours. Authorities introduced a factory inspection system. Initially factory inspectors focused on the mistreatment of workers and tried to convince factory owners and staff to treat workers better. Government paternalism improved workers' conditions only marginally. From time to time worker anger burst out in waves of strikes. These strikes were primarily economic, with better pay, shorter hours, more humane treatment, and fringe benefits the main objectives. Workers did not yet view the government as the main cause of their harsh lives. Overall, from the late nineteenth century on, except for periods of economic depression, working class conditions gradually improved. The cities clearly became the main centers for action and change in Russia from the mid-nineteenth century on.

Revolution of 1905. Though the nineteenth century had been a time of revolution in Western Europe, in Russia the populace was relatively calm, except in the minority areas, and never a threat to the power of the Romanovs. Globally, the twentieth century was an age of revolution, initiated by the Russian Revolution of 1905. *Revolution* may be described as an attempt to carry out a set of radical, comprehensive changes quickly and generally violently. In 1905 an attempted revolution focused on four major components—urban, rural, parliamentary, and minority.

Background. Unrest increased in both the cities and the countryside in the early years of the twentieth century, simultaneously with but distinct from the emergence of opposition political parties. Industrial strikes peaked in 1903. They threatened neither the economic position and power of the capitalist class nor political peace and autocratic power. However, the government made concessions, mainly in the area of social welfare, including the introduction of a pension system.

In rural areas in 1902 and 1903 peasants engaged in massive attacks on local authority figures, especially estate owners. Ironically, peasant actions were concentrated in southern Russia, where farming was undergoing substantial expansion and farm incomes increasing considerably. A sudden reduction in income after a decade of economic growth left peasants unhappy and fearful that the decline in income would be permanent. Peasants attacked estate granaries, the homes of the wealthy landowners, and sometimes the nobles themselves. Peasants argued that they had received the tsar's permission to attack the wealthy and powerful and showed golden books or red ones they claimed they had received from the tsar. The government sent in troops to crush peasant unrest.

Far Eastern Gamble. Aggressive foreign policy acted as a catalyst for revolution. Beginning with the Crimean War, Russia had focused its diplomatic efforts on the Balkans. Religious motives and preoccupation with access to the Mediterranean drove the Russians into the Balkans and kept them there. But Russia also had a Far Eastern policy made possible by the completion of the Trans-Siberian Railway in 1902. Russia sought to dominate Manchuria, that rich but vulnerable northeastern part of the decaying Chinese Empire (see Chapter Four). Though the Chinese Empire was no longer a major threat to Russian expansion, the island nation of Japan had used Western ideas and technology well enough to become a regional imperialist power and a player in the politics and diplomacy of Northeast Asia (see Chapter Two). The Japanese, too, coveted Manchuria.

Russian diplomatic aggression produced Japanese military aggression. Before the Russians were ready, in 1904 the Japanese launched an attack that turned into the *Russo-Japanese War* (1904–1905). The Japanese defeated the Russian armies in Manchuria and forced their surrender. The Japanese navy humiliated the Russians at sea, even destroying the Russian Baltic fleet just as it arrived from Europe. The war exhausted the Japanese economically, but the *Treaty of Portsmouth* (worked out by U.S. President Theodore Roosevelt) confirmed Japan as one of three Asian powers—Great Britain, Japan, and the United States. The war profoundly affected Russia as well.

War and Revolution. The Russo-Japanese War created opportunities for expressing dissatisfaction and open rebellion. It forced Russia to move much of its army to the Far East, leaving it unable to maintain order in the rest of the Empire. The government drafted large numbers of men, who saw no need to die without cause in a distant foreign country. The reduction of male labor created hardships in the villages and disrupted industrial production. Anti-war rallies and riots became increasingly common and focused on the conscription depots. Military defeat weakened public support for the government and gave hope to its opponents. If Russian autocracy could not defeat the Japanese, perhaps it was no longer strong enough to prevent the victory of the domestic opposition.

Urban Revolution in 1905. In this atmosphere of increasing tension and declining support for authority, in January 1905 authorities panicked and ordered soldiers to fire into a crowd of peaceful protesters led by the priest Gapon. *Bloody Sunday,* as the massacre was called, quickly turned into Russia's first nationwide general strike. Millions of industrial workers struck, initially protesting the massacre, then demanding economic concessions. The strikes generally lasted two weeks, after which the loss of wages and management's desire to make concessions led the workers back to their jobs. Economic concessions were substantial—generally 10–15 percent wage increases, shorter workdays, medical benefits, and even promises of more humane treatment of workers by factory staffs. During the strikes workers idled away their time in street gatherings and demonstrations. The government seldom had sufficient power to put down disturbances, unless they turned to violence and looting. Most local officials panicked, demonstrating their lack of competence to deal with urban unrest.

Urban Russia remained quiet until the autumn, but rebellion continued in the minority areas throughout the year. Beginning in late September better organized protests began, initially on the railway lines. Railway workers tended to be literate, more aware of political issues, and certainly possessed a great deal of power due to their control over transportation and communication lines. Strikes began among railroad workers in Moscow, then spread to other major railheads. The strike then expanded to the factories. These strikes clearly protested tsarist political authority. They were more threatening as well because of the emergence of fairly large political parties with some ability to mobilize and shape worker protest.

Constitutionalism. Gambling, the government made political concessions in October, agreeing to the creation of an elected *State Duma* (legislature). Issuing the so-called *October Manifesto,* Nicholas II hoped to divide the opposition and pull the more moderate revolutionaries to his side. He hoped that modest concessions would halt demands for his resignation. Guarantees of civil rights were intended to show that the autocracy was a modern, enlightened European government. Opportunities to act on the basis of civil rights led to massive street demonstrations, sometimes numbering as many as 500,000 participants, and the government soon reintroduced martial law. Quickly, civil rights disappeared.

Still, the electoral process moved forward. A complicated system gave workers (other than those in small factories), land owning peasants, educated urban residents, and the nobility the right to vote. The system was intended to ensure domination by the nobility. When the First Duma met in 1906 it had an anti-government majority, with the pro-peasant *Trudoviki,* the liberals and the national minority parties dominant. Expressing opposition to the tsar, the First Duma was soon closed down. Electoral laws were changed, decreasing opposition representation. The Second Duma met in early 1907 and it too opposed the autocracy and was *prorogued.* Finally, further changes in the electoral process gave the tsar a majority in the Third Duma, which first met in late

1907. The Duma was a platform for anti-government rhetoric, while government unwillingness to accept the will of the voters demonstrated that under no circumstances would it peacefully and voluntarily surrender any of its power.

Rural Revolution. Meanwhile, in the countryside, peasant unrest ebbed and flowed, based on the agricultural cycle and the availability of government troops. Agricultural laborers, mainly working on the estates of the nobility, struck before spring planting in 1905. They marched from estate to estate picking up supporters and releasing those who had been early participants. Sometimes they conducted *black strikes* (no one stayed behind to milk cows and feed farm animals); sometimes they forced nobles to "lead" them. At times the strikes turned violent but owners generally agreed to concessions that would not have to be implemented immediately. In the summer of 1906 peasant landowners and some agricultural laborers struck at mowing season, demanding a greater share of the harvest or access to large portions of the nobles' pastures and hayfields. Confrontations occurred again at the end of the harvest season, when nobles tried to turn out the strike leaders and refused to fulfill agreements reached in the spring. In the spring of 1906, farm workers conducted a series of strikes before the planting season, sometimes with leadership from political parties, after which peasant rebellion died out.

National Minority Revolution. The Revolution was most intense in the national minority areas. Russification had even driven conservative minorities into opposition. Strikes lasted longer in minority areas, both in the cities and the countryside. They were more violent and larger than those in Russia. Minorities even created a number of small-scale "independent republics." In the countryside, peasants not only took actions against the nobility but essentially drove away Russian power. By the autumn of 1905 minorities were calling for autonomy and in some cases independence from Russia. The Russian response was more violent as well, especially after the end of the Russo-Japanese War and the return of the army from the Far Eastern front.

In Russia the Revolution ended in December 1905 with barricade building in a working class district of Moscow. In the minority areas the Revolution continued into 1907, ending in Poland only in November 1907.

Conclusion. Revolution challenged autocracy in 1905–1907, yet it survived this serious threat to its power. While the government erred in concluding that the countryside was the real center of revolutionary threat and thus where reform efforts must be concentrated, opposition political parties either focused their energies on Duma politics or ceased to be a significant force in Russia—at least for a few years. The Revolution demonstrated that as long as the military remained loyal, no matter how grave the threat, autocracy would eventually triumph, largely unchanged. It would not have to give up its power or change its basic system. The Revolution demonstrated the power of spontaneous volatility and showed that opposition parties were not ready to lead an offensive against the autocracy. By 1908 Russia appeared to have returned to normal. But that was not true.

5. Family and Gender

Modest changes occurred in the nature of the family and gender relations. The changes were less radical than might have been expected in a society in which serfdom had been abolished and industrialization introduced.

Families. Families of the nobility changed least, remaining deeply patriarchal. However, in poorer noble families sons and daughters left to work in the cities and the nuclear family replaced the extended family. Middle class families turned to the *cult of domesticity,* in which women focused their energies on the home and family. Among peasants, the extended family largely disappeared, as younger sons and daughters moved to the cities and returned only intermittently. Many first generation workers remained single but gradually marriage became the lot of most members of the working class. Crowded apartments prohibited the extended family.

6. Diversity Without Community

During the second half of the nineteenth century strategies for building community failed.

Community-building? Recognizing that Russia was becoming increasingly diverse, the government sought to create community through the strategy of Russification. Obviously, if everyone in Russia saw himself or herself as Russian, diversity would have disappeared and community automatically created. Russification did not work, even superficially. The government understood that Russification could only succeed if the education system was nationalized and Russified. This required that all teachers believe in and totally support Russification. Not enough Russians were available to teach in the minority areas, even though wages and benefits were higher than in Russia. So Russian authorities tried to turn the teacher training institutes in minority areas into centers of Russification. These institutes prepared village school teachers. Authorities had partial success in Russifying its teachers. More importantly, it was almost impossible to make Russian the language of instruction in elementary schools in which almost no children knew Russian. Russification led to alternative, underground education, where minority values and patriotism were encouraged.

Russification also meant conversion to Russian Orthodoxy. Forced conversion and punishment of non-Orthodox church leaders and priests and pastors created resentment but few true conversions. Religious diversity could no more be eliminated than could linguistic diversity. Russification actually promoted opposition and clearly encouraged non-Russian patriotism among peasants who had been least committed to the non-Russian national cultures.

Ideologies became increasingly important to the educated class and the government. Ironically, the increased importance of ideologies helped to promote difference within Russia. Even though each of the ideologies had as one of its ultimate goals a unified community, its actions, as well as the proliferation of ideologies, contributed to difference and made community building more difficult.

Diversity. Russian authorities made almost no attempt to honor diversity. They did not believe that recognizing diversity could possibly be a strategy for building national unity.

D. REVOLUTIONARY RUSSIA, 1914–1922

The First World War created conditions that made revolution at least possible. Incompetent leadership, military defeat, a weakened security apparatus, and urban unrest combined to create a very volatile situation in Russia. However, the existence of these conditions did not guarantee that the tsarist socio-political system would be destroyed. Fate, accident, and leadership in support of alternatives produced revolution.

1. On the Eve: Russia, 1907–1914

Historians continue to debate whether the period after the Revolution of 1905 was one of "social instability" and inexorable movement toward chaos and revolution, or whether orderly, gradual change was leading Russia away from the abyss of revolution and anarchy. Evidence for both perspectives is available. The brief period saw economic growth fueled by both industry and agriculture. Petr *Stolypin,* the new Prime Minister, promoted universal education and attempted to transform the agrarian structure. In spite of improved work conditions and wages, labor unrest spread after 1910. Russia also embedded itself into Balkan politics, which led to the First World War.

Economic Growth. Recession, the Russo-Japanese War, and the Revolution of 1905 only briefly interrupted economic expansion. Continued industrial development produced much of the growth. Russia became an industrial leader, though not yet competitive with British, German, and French industry. Much of the growth was in heavy industry, especially iron and steel, but consumer goods production increased as well. Southern Russia was the scene of much of this expansion. In the countryside, farm production and productivity grew. Less successful farmers gave up, sold their land to others, and went off to the cities. Members of the lesser gentry did likewise. Thus more land was transferred into the hands of the most productive farmers and estate owners; those most interested in agricultural modernization. Continued migration to Siberia increased the amount of land under cultivation. Western European demand for Russian grain stimulated production. The elimination of redemption payments and arrears in 1906 also gave peasants more money for investment.

The Countryside. As economic improvements provided a calming effect, especially in the major grain-producing regions, the *Stolypin Reforms* may have created rural instability. Yet, improved living standards may have reduced the probability that the Reforms would produce rural rebellion.

From the Revolution of 1905 the government drew the lesson that the peasants were the main threat to the autocracy. Therefore the state must prevent a revival of peasant unrest. Stolypin sought to prevent a reoccurrence of rural instability through a massive program of rural restructuring, almost as substantial a social engineering project as emancipation of the serfs had been a half century earlier. Stolypin believed that if rural Russia could be turned into a land of individual landowners able to act independently of the conservative commune, revolution would be averted and peace and prosperity ensured. Between 1906 and 1911 Stolypin introduced the major components of his reforms. Peasants were given an opportunity to own the land they worked and if one villager wished to own land, then all villagers automatically became private landowners. The commune was abolished, at least officially, though it continued to function in many areas. Villages were authorized to eliminate the strip system of farming and to consolidate holdings into individual farms. Since emancipation had been carried out gradually, Stolypin expected his reforms to take decades. Private ownership was the most successful part of the reforms but only about 10 percent of the peasants acquired consolidated holdings.

Labor Unrest. Labor troubles proved a greater force for destabilization than did peasant unrest. Strikes began in the gold mines of central Siberia in 1911, then spread in the following year to the oil fields of the Caucasus and its oil capital, Baku. In 1913–1914 strikes spread to the large urban industrial centers, especially Moscow and Petersburg. At first the strikes had purely economic goals, as workers sought the restoration of income lost when industrialists cut wages. By 1914 workers had begun to direct their attacks against the government. In retrospect, it is clear that workers lost faith in the autocracy in 1905 and thereafter supported it only at the beginning of the First World War. With political parties either moribund or focusing on white-collar service workers, industrial workers and miners were left on their own. When parties in 1914 tried to assert preeminence by urging employees to return to their jobs, workers demonstrated their independence by remaining on strike. By the summer of 1914, Russia's large industrial cities were a tinderbox awaiting a match. Instead, the First World War poured water on the unrest, dousing the revolutionary fires—temporarily.

Balkan Crisis. Once again Russia turned its diplomatic attention toward the Balkans. This time, Russia's preoccupation with the Balkans took place in a very different power constellation than in the nineteenth century. Driven away by the other conservative multi-ethnic states, Germany and Austria, Russia had turned to France and England for support. Thus Russia's struggle with Austria over which nation should have a dominant role in the Balkans resulted in a conflict between two different alliances, rather than an internal conflict within one alliance. Russia was freer to act but also freer to blunder. Increasingly Austria asserted its influence in the Balkans, acquiring control over Bosnia and Herzegovina. Two Balkan Wars (1912–1913) made Serbia and Bulgaria the most powerful states within the peninsula. Since Bulgaria and Russia had fought earlier, Serbia was a logical Russian ally, the staging point for efforts to increase Russian influence in the Balkans.

When a Serbian nationalist murdered the heir to the Austrian throne, both camps mobilized, with the Germans, eager for a war that would enable them to dominate the continent, urging the Austrians to reject apologies and other concessions. War began officially in August 1914, when the Germans invaded France via Belgium. This war began as a glorious parade but turned into a brutal war of attrition and trench warfare.

2. War and Revolution, 1914–1917

The Great War brought greatness to neither the Russian military nor the Russian autocracy. Defeat promoted urban unrest and stimulated the emergence of an alternative leadership—the liberal opposition.

The Great War. Russia had the military capability to defeat all of its enemies except Germany, the leader of the Central Powers. After the Russo-Japanese War, Russia's military leaders had modernized weaponry and improved the training of troops. They had not, however, solved the problem of effective military leadership at the top. Incompetence in the general staff, power struggles among military leaders, and an inability to determine an appropriate strategy made it difficult for the Russians to defeat the Germans. Further, no country had any experience in total mobilization of resources for this new kind of war—total war.

At first the Russians drove into East Prussia (today northern Poland) but were crushed by German forces. A campaign against the Austrians across Galicia (today southern Poland) was successful. The Russians also pushed the Turks out of the Caucasus and back into Turkey. In 1915 the Germans drove the Russians out of Galicia and took the rest of Poland. The Russians were able to recover during the winter of 1915–1916 and in the summer of 1916 launched another successful campaign into Galicia before the Germans drove them back again. In 1917 the Germans pushed into Russia, perhaps threatening the autocracy.

The Home Front. The Great War tested the "home front" in profound ways. War-related industry expanded, in spite of the siphoning off of skilled labor for the army. However, neither the transportation nor the communication system could handle the increased traffic necessitated by the war. Patriotism died quickly in the cities but its absence did not immediately produce revolt. Reduced harvests, increased peasant consumption, inflation that reduced peasant willingness to sell food to the cities, and the terribly inadequate transportation system combined to produce reduced wages and hunger in the cities. Defeat at the front and suffering at home could not be sustained simultaneously. In the second half of 1916 the autocracy lost the support of the urban masses. Only a spark was needed to incite rebellion.

Political Vacuum. Meanwhile, the tsarist political leadership isolated itself from the realities of Russia. Nicholas II had appointed himself commander in chief at the front, while his wife Alexandra and their mystic priest *Rasputin* dominated the government in the capital. Incompetent minister replaced incompetent minister. The once vaunted bureaucracy was not up to the test handed it by the Great War. Rather quickly the Duma began to assume administrative powers associated with the war effort, playing a leading role in the War Industries Board, for example. A majority of the Duma, calling itself the Progressive Bloc, increasingly provided leadership for the country. Two elements necessary for revolution were thus present—massive urban unrest in the large cities, where power was concentrated, and an alternative group of leaders who could come to power upon a revolution. A catalyst and revolutionary leadership were still lacking.

3. The Era of the February Revolution, February–October, 1917

Bread riots and the unwillingness of the military—both ordinary soldiers and army leaders—to continue to support the autocracy brought an end to the Romanov dynasty after over 300 years of rule. The February Revolution delivered great opportunities to Russia and offered tremendous dangers as well. The future would be crimson in many different ways.

The Fall of the Romanovs. Bread riots, military mutiny, and disloyalty among military leaders combined to destroy the Romanovs. An especially brutal winter provoked and promoted a sense of despair. Disruption of transportation lines reduced the flow of raw materials and parts for industry and interrupted the supply of food to the large cities, especially the capital, Petersburg (called Petrograd during the First World War). Real wages declined sharply in the second half of 1916 and early 1917. News of defeat, or at least unconvincing victory, dampened patriotism. Few had confidence in the ability of the army to prevent a major German offensive from pushing deeply into Russia during the 1917 spring and summer campaign season.

Five Days in February. Conditions were thus ripe for revolution. In Petersburg the closing of a large munitions plant was followed by massive street demonstrations on February 23, International Women's Day. Women played an important role in the overthrow of the Romanovs. Police and soldiers were brought in but initial attacks on the crowds turned into fraternization. The size and volatility of street marches escalated.

February 26 became a turning point. Not only did massive demonstrations continue, but a regiment assigned to put down rebellion mutinied and urged other military units not to shoot at demonstrators. By March 1, the entire Petersburg military garrison had gone over to the side of the "revolutionaries." A *Petersburg Soviet* was established, to represent the masses. Leaders of the Duma founded a *Provisional Government.* On March 2, under pressure from the army general staff, Nicholas II abandoned the throne.

Quickly, with little opposition, revolutionaries had overthrown the tsar. This first of two 1917 revolutions had tremendous significance. First, the revolution was a spontaneous action by the working class and the soldiers stationed in the capital. For the first time, soldiers abandoned their disciplined obedience to authority and supported revolution instead. These soldiers were atypical in that they were mainly relatively fresh recruits that had not yet become accustomed to automatic obedience. Political parties, even radical ones, miscalculated, believing the demonstrations would lead to nothing. Thus they did not try to play a leadership role. The sudden demise of the Romanov government suggests that its power was already quite fragile and that almost unnoticed it had been on its last legs for some time. Finally, the overthrow of recognized political authority transformed the political situation in Russia. Revolution forced the Russian people to adapt to a situation in which recognized and predictable rule had suddenly disappeared.

Provisional Governance. Two political forces emerged out of this political chaos—a provisional government of the educated elite (many of a liberal or moderate socialist persuasion) and a Petersburg Soviet that represented the masses but was structured in such a way that the military dominated. Over time the differences between the Provisional Government and the Soviet diminished. By the summer of 1917, moderate socialists, whose views were almost identical to those of the Soviet, assumed leadership of the Provisional Government.

The Provisional Government came to power intent upon providing effective leadership in a period of crisis and effecting long-range political changes. It achieved neither. Ironically, it made more progress in dealing with the long-term restructuring of the political system. Upon assuming power, the Provisional Government announced the establishment of a *civil society,* with guarantees of civil rights and freedom of action for all political forces. The euphoria of revolution fed the masses for a brief period but eventually civil rights and democracy proved an inadequate diet.

Russia faced three serious problems—the war, mass urban discontent, and peasant demands for land. As the Provisional Government dealt with each issue, it aroused more and more opposition. It was obvious that the war created the possibility of continued domestic ferment, unless a quick and decisive victory could be achieved. As the German threat increased, the dilemma facing the government became clearer and clearer. It could make a separate peace with the Germans, or it could continue the war in futile hopes of victory. Deeply influenced by its pro-British ideals and its desire to respect the agreements the tsar had made with the Western allies, in late March 1917 the Provisional Government announced its intention to fulfill its obligations to its allies and thus to continue the war. On May 1, Foreign Minister Pavel Miliukov rejected the idea of a separate peace. Through these announcements, the Provisional Government lost much of the good will and support it had earlier received from the masses.

By June living conditions had worsened so much in Petersburg and other large cities that massive urban demonstrations threatened the existence of the government. Loyal troops came to the government's rescue. However, the government did not learn from the February Revolution and continued to underestimate the extent to which the masses were disaffected and the ease with which a new revolution could break out spontaneously.

Increasingly peasants demanded that all of the farmland be turned over to them. Peasants already owned 90 percent of it and possession of the rest would have had minimal impact on their lives. According to the Provisional Government, redistribution of land must wait until all the peasants were available to participate and thus such actions were to be postponed until war's end. Fearing civil war in the countryside, the Provisional Government announced that since it was only an interim government it did not have the right to make decisions concerning owners' property rights.

If overnight Russia was transformed from an autocratic regime into a democracy, its new government was unable to make effective decisions that would solve, or at least diminish, Russia's problems. The same had been true of the Romanovs.

4. The October Revolution

Urban unrest intensified while the Provisional Government was in power. The Bolshevik Party gradually became a potent force in Russian politics and Lenin worked hard to convince other party leaders that the time for revolution had arrived. The confluence of all three of these factors produced the October Revolution.

Urban Unrest. Recognizing their power, the urban masses became increasingly vocal and physical in their opposition to the Provisional Government. Between late March and the beginning of May it became clear that the city masses had ceased to support the government. Crowds manifested increasing opposition to the government through massive demonstrations. In June the Soviet led a huge demonstration in Petersburg, protesting the war and worsening living conditions in the city. In mid-July workers and soldiers clashed with military units loyal to the Provisional Government. The Bolsheviks assumed leadership of the rebellion but it collapsed due to the loyalty of some military units and the unwillingness of the Soviet leaders to attempt to assume power. Within a few days the masses had retreated from the streets, disillusioned with both the Bolsheviks and the Soviet but firmly opposed to provisional government rule.

Rise of the Bolsheviks. When the February Revolution began, the Bolshevik Party was a small, insignificant group whose key leaders were abroad. Support for the Bolsheviks increased gradually. Its membership grew from 80,000 in April to 200,000 in mid-August. Still it remained relatively unimportant.

In September, General Lavr Kornilov tried to take power. Bolsheviks assumed leadership of the effort to prevent Kornilov from capturing Petersburg. In this way they gained the support of armed workers, soldiers, and sailors, as well as access to huge stocks of weapons. By mid-September Soviets in large cities were approving Bolshevik proposals. Most importantly, the Executive Committee of the Petersburg Soviet elected Lev *Trotskii,* next to Lenin the most important Bolshevik leader, as chairman. The increase in support for the Bolsheviks took place largely at the expense of moderate socialists, especially the Social Revolutionaries. Support for the liberal Kadet party expanded modestly.

Lenin and the Revolution. With the assistance of the Germans, Lenin returned from Switzerland in April. However, he found it very difficult to reestablish supreme command over the Bolshevik Party. Most other party leaders rejected his April call for opposition to the war and the Provisional Government. After the defeat of the Bolsheviks in July they had little interest in conducting a revolutionary offensive.

From mid-September Lenin accelerated his offensive against the dominant Party view that a revolution was far away and efforts to make one were suicidal. Still, Lenin persevered. Finally, in mid-October the party agreed to consider the planning of a revolution. A Military Revolutionary Committee was set up to begin development of plans. Events moved faster than the Bolsheviks. Pro-Bolsheviks soldiers, sailors, and workers seized key points in Petersburg during the night of October 24–25. The night before the revolution triumphed, the Bolsheviks still hesitated, still fearful of failure. However, Lenin's views coincided with that of many of the city residents. So when the city was easily taken by the masses, Lenin alertly announced that the Bolsheviks had made the revolution and would immediately assume power and solve the country's problems.

Conclusion. This October Revolution brought the Bolsheviks to power for an eighty-year period. They transformed Russia in fundamental ways and presented an alternative model to capitalist liberal democracy—a model that had worldwide appeal especially after the Second World War. The October Revolution was one of the central events in Russian history and of momentous importance in twentieth century world history.

5. Civil Wars, 1917–1923

The October Revolution succeeded with little difficulty and little bloodshed. It was much more difficult for the Bolsheviks to remain in power, for within months they faced massive opposition. Brutality, suffering, and political chaos characterized this era of civil wars. Unlike the February Revolution that unleashed a brief burst of euphoria and unlimited optimism, the October Revolution quickly produced despair and hopelessness outside the ranks of the Bolsheviks, initially only a quarter of a million strong.

Causes. The civil wars resulted from three intersecting factors. First, those whom the Bolsheviks had driven from power soon saw opportunities for returning to office. Liberals, moderate socialists, and even monarchists recognized that parliamentary methods would not succeed. Military means seemed the only route. Second, massive discontent was generated by Bolshevik policies and by continuation of the First World War. Third, contrary to Bolshevik propaganda claims, the Revolution—and thus Bolshevik rule—never enjoyed broad popular support. Thus, an unpopular government carried out policies that antagonized the population, while terrible conditions and the reemergence of organized political-military opposition brought about the civil wars.

Course of the Civil Wars. Opposition began to form by the beginning of 1918. "*White*" armies formed in the periphery but especially in Siberia. There, Czech soldiers, who were to be sent through Russia to fight on the side of the Western allies, aided the anti-Bolsheviks. Though most of the military leaders of these forces were supporters of monarchy, either the return of the Romanovs or the creation of a new royal dynasty, much of the leadership came from moderate socialists and liberals—the groups the Bolsheviks had driven from power.

Incredibly complicated, the civil wars consisted of two phases, an initial period of dangerous threat to Bolshevik power (most of 1918) and a second period of more desperate and unsuccessful military campaigns by the Whites (1919–1921). Three separate military offensives from the spring through the autumn of 1918 threatened the very existence of Bolshevik power. Only the inability of the Whites to organize a coordinated campaign prevented the capture of Moscow and Bolshevik defeat. Thereafter White forces were weaker than the *"Reds"* (Bolsheviks) and in 1919 and again in 1920 Bolsheviks halted White offensives. In 1921 the Reds defeated White forces retreating into the Crimean Peninsula.

In the *Russo-Polish War* (1919–1920) the Poles first invaded Ukraine and then were driven back toward the Polish capital of Warsaw. There Red forces were defeated and forced to retreat back through Western Ukraine, which became part of Poland during the period between the First and Second World Wars. The Bolsheviks also failed to recover the Baltic states and Finland. Thus the Bolshevik state's borders were established substantially further to the east than tsarist borders had been.

At the same time that the Bolsheviks faced White armies, they encountered *Allied Intervention.* Russia's allies (or former allies) sent troops into Russia between 1918 and 1922. These troops were generally used to guard munitions depots and railheads. Initially they arrived at the invitation of the Bolsheviks. Once in place the Western soldiers were not neutral but pro-White. They did not participate in the civil wars, except indirectly by maintaining some degree of security behind the White front lines, thus freeing up White soldiers to fight against the Reds. By 1920 most foreign troops had withdrawn, as Western governments realized the futility of trying to influence internal politics in Russia. The Japanese, who had sent the largest interventionist force, stayed in the Russian Far East until 1922.

War Communism. The Bolsheviks tried to implement policies that would ensure survival of their regime. This goal outweighed any concern over the consequences of their decrees. *War Communism* included nationalization of all industry, a *crusade for bread,* and mobilization of labor, carried out violently and brutally. Factories were nationalized to ensure the production of goods needed for victory in the civil wars. The crusade for bread took grain from the countryside to feed urban residents, who, otherwise might have revolted and overthrown the Bolsheviks. The rural population felt the brunt of the Bolshevik campaigns. In many villages "committees of the poor peasants" informed on others that hid grain. Military units came in and seized all the grain they could, with a portion of the loot going to "poor peasants" who had identified the hoarding villagers. The crusade for bread and bad weather contributed to a horrible famine that killed several million peasants.

Rebellion of the Masses. Peasants rebelled in the main grain producing areas of southern Russia. Reports from the *Cheka,* the Bolshevik militarized secret police, suggested that by February 1921 over 100 peasant uprisings were occurring. The Bolsheviks lacked the military might to crush peasant rebellion and were fortunate the scythe of death—the famine—destroyed peasant rebellion.

In the cities, large numbers of factory workers began to strike. Reduced wages, unemployment, and the difficulties of daily life (especially the constant quest for food) produced high levels of urban unrest. The Bolsheviks were reluctant to use force against the restless urban masses, for this social group provided the Bolsheviks with much of their support. At the same time, the Bolsheviks were unable to improve urban conditions, even though they understood that two urban revolutions had occurred in 1917 for the very same reasons and with similar results—the overthrow of the existing government.

Threatened by military forces seeking their extinction and lacking the support of the masses, the Bolsheviks also faced a naval rebellion, the *Kronstadt Revolt* of 1921. Kronstadt, a naval base in the Petersburg harbor, had housed sailors who had actively participated in the October Revolution. Terrible conditions, some changes in the composition of the naval forces at the base, and most importantly, disillusionment with the Bolsheviks, triggered the rebellion. When negotiations failed to quell the riot, the Bolsheviks were forced to send an army of 50,000 loyal soldiers to destroy the uprising.

Causes of Opposition. The civil wars resulted from numerous factors. Most importantly, since the Bolsheviks had come to power through a narrow-based *coup d'etat,* they really could not claim to be a legitimate government, especially after they closed an elected Constituent Assembly, which was to draw up a democratic constitution. The Whites believed that they could easily topple the Bolshevik government and made an unsuccessful military attempt to do so. Under Bolshevik rule the people continued to suffer, and clearly suffered even more deeply during the civil war. In these conditions, it was easy to foster disillusionment with Bolshevik rule.

Reasons for Bolshevik Victory. In spite of massive domestic opposition, armed intervention, and armed rebellion, the Bolsheviks ultimately triumphed. Bolshevik military superiority eventually paid off. The Bolsheviks had a military force at least twice the size of the White armies. The Bolshevik armies possessed the inspired leadership of Lenin and Trotskii plus the military skills of many former officers in the Tsarist army. Defending a central core area against armies located in the periphery gave the Bolsheviks logistical advantages. The Cheka, a paramilitary secret police force with fanatical leadership and tremendous organizational abilities, strengthened Bolshevik might. Bolshevik propaganda was everywhere, emphasizing over and over again that the Whites wished to revive the Romanov monarchy and return serfdom to rural Russia. Though most Whites were neither monarchists nor proponents of serfdom, the emotional Bolshevik propaganda worked quite well. In addition, the Bolsheviks claimed they supported federalism and defense of the rights of the minorities, while the Whites clearly championed a centralized, **Russian**-dominated empire. Most of the areas initially controlled by the Whites were on the periphery of Russia, where a majority of the people was non-Russians. The White goals of reunification had little appeal to national minorities. Finally, the Bolsheviks were desperate to keep power, in part because they still believed it their historical destiny to create a Communist society.

Consequences. The Civil War left Russia devastated and hardly capable of economic development. Thus, strategies of gradual economic growth were necessary. Russia's population had little reason to support the Communists. Propaganda and force were alternative approaches to creation of a loyal populace. Clearly, neither a democratic Communist Party nor a democratic government was possible. Dictatorship seemed the only workable alternative.

6. Gender Roles and Family

The First World War, the Revolutions, and the civil wars had a profound impact on the family and gender relationships. These events weakened the power of men, strengthened the authority of women, and changed family dynamics.

Matriarchy. The most important reason for these changes was the absence of men, who fought, surrendered, or died in the war. In the absence of patriarchal power, women were forced to be independent, to make decisions, and assume authority within the family. Many families came to be *matriarchal.* During the civil wars women's power was enhanced further. Many women fought during the civil wars (perhaps as many as 100,000), either for the Reds or the Whites. In its quest for popularity, the Bolsheviks made a major effort to secure the support of women. In 1919, they established a Women's Department (*Zhenotdel*), reporting to the Party's Central Committee. Thus women were more and more important in the public sphere. Women's labor replaced that of men, especially in the countryside. There women became farm managers and not merely manual laborers. Women became involved in the market and offered opposition to war communism. Overall, the family weakened, as women became more powerful. Numerous families were led by a single parent, while many children were left orphans.

7. Diversity and Community

Community disappeared during this period of violence. Initial loyalty to the monarchy and to Russia as it defended itself against the Germans and Austrians soon collapsed. Political unity disappeared in conflict over how to win the war and over which revolutionary group to support.

Fewer Minorities. The First World War gave minorities an opportunity to seek independence from Russia. Those in the Western parts of the Empire, including the Poles, Latvians, Lithuanians, and Finns, generally gained their independence. Very briefly Ukrainians won their freedom but later Ukraine was divided between Poland and the Soviet Union. Independence movements in the Caucasus, northern Russia and the Far East were broken by Communist military force soon after the end of the civil wars. The Communists' Soviet Union recreated the Russian Empire, minus its western edges.

Bolshevik Community. The Bolsheviks sought to establish community on new bases. No longer was Russian nationality to be the basis for building community. A different ideology—Communism—was to cut across previous ethnic and religious alliances and loyalties and perhaps even ignore them. Loyalty to Communism was to be based on its ability to create the perfect society, as well as an essential element of defense against external enemies. Little progress could be made toward successfully establishing a new basis for community in this era of violence, suffering, and war.

E. CULTURAL REVOLUTION AND FREEDOM, 1920s

The 1920s were a period of relative freedom, continuity with the past, and efforts to transform Russian culture. These three elements, of course, conflicted with each other. The Communists created a political structure that bore close resemblance to the tsarist structure, with two major differences. First, a single political party, that is the Communist Party, was to play a central role in decision-making. In addition, the Communists created a party structure that paralleled the system of political institutions. The early death of Lenin led to intense conflict within the party leadership that was resolved only at the end of the twenties. Though the Party promoted its cause through relatively sophisticated forms of propaganda, freedom of expression and freedom of action characterized the Soviet Union. The failures of the war communism economic system led the party to encourage the continuation of private enterprise. Radical changes occurred in the family and in gender relations, as both the conditions of the war and revolution period promoted the weakening of patriarchy, the reduction in the importance of the family, and the emancipation of women. Ethnic difference remained a barrier to community. Overall this was a period of tremendous excitement and great change.

1. Creating the Soviet "Union"

Initial Communists decisions about national borders, political sub-divisions, and the ideal of "Soviet man" largely determined the future of diversity and community in the Soviet Union. The Soviet Union was isolated in the 1920s, with Weimar Germany its only friend. Soviet foreign policy pursued normal diplomatic relations with other countries and sought to subvert them through *covert* means.

New Borders. Soviet Russia's borders were defined during the civil wars and immediately thereafter. Unlike the Russian state, which had been characterized by constant imperial expansion, the Soviet Union did not expand its borders after 1923. All of the non-Russian areas sought independence during the First World War and the civil wars. In 1920 Ukraine was recaptured and in 1921 all of the Caucasus except Georgia was taken, as were Khiva and Bukhara in Central Asia. Georgia was recovered through military invasion in 1923. Eventually the Japanese withdrew from the Far East and that area was incorporated into the Soviet Union.

New Constitution. In 1922 the Communists adopted a new constitution. This constitution established a hierarchical system of governance, with a parallel Communist Party structure. The country was divided into republics, whose borders were determined largely by nationality. Minority enclaves within these republics were designated as autonomous republics or regions (*oblasts*). For example the Russian Federated Socialist Republic housed 17 autonomous republics and regions. In theory these republics and regions operated relatively independently of central government and party controls; in reality they had no independence. In this unintended way nationality was preserved and given an organizational framework. At the same time, the Communists began to espouse the idea of Soviet man. According to this view, the creation of a Communist society would gradually lead to the elimination of all ethnic differences, leaving people loyal only to Communism.

Foreign Policy in the 1920s. In this period the Soviet Union pursued two contradictory foreign policy methods. Initially it pursued "old diplomacy," signing treaties with those countries that defeated the Red Army. In the 1920s the Soviet Union sought recognition as a legitimate member of an international community of nations. Given its severe economic problems, Russia also sought to develop trade relations with European states. In 1922 at *Rapallo* in Italy, Russia and Germany signed a treaty of friendship. During the 1920s the Soviet Union was also recognized by France and temporarily by Great Britain.

Parallel to this effort to normalize relations with European countries, the Soviet Union sought to promote world revolution and subvert the governments of the Western powers. Russian subversive efforts in England, especially in 1920, 1924, and 1927, were defeated by British intelligence and led the British government to withdraw diplomatic recognition from Russia. Subversion, thus, prevented normalization and trade relations from being successful.

2. The Communist Party and Its Struggles

During the 1920s the Communist Party sought to establish its control over the Soviet people but was hindered by a lack of vision, an inept and inadequate bureaucracy, a lack of consensus on goals and methods, and fierce internal party conflict. Preoccupied by internal issues, the Party's propaganda campaigns had little success in convincing people to believe in Communism. The Communist Party had little choice but to leave the Soviet people alone.

Ready or Not. The Communist Party was not prepared to rule a country devastated by war and civil strife and filled with discontent and suffering. Many of the leaders of the Communist Party had spent lengthy periods in Siberian or European exile and barely understood their country. The Party had devoted most of its efforts to making a revolution and had hardly considered what it should do if it ever came to power. Lenin's main statement about the future state of Communism, *State and Revolution* (1917), suggested that after the victorious revolution, all political authority would disappear and people would naturally cooperate and work together, without the need for any forms of coercion.

Party leaders could not agree on what kinds of economic strategies should replace what some saw as the temporary *New Economic Policy (NEP)* (see the discussion that follows). Not only did the Communists lack a blueprint of what kind of society to create; they lacked the political apparatus to carry out substantial change. Though the Communist bureaucracy was quite large, most of its employees lacked skill and experience. One estimate is that only about 25,000 Communists (out of over two million officials) were dedicated and capable of providing administrative leadership at any level of government.

Added acronym

ital OK

Power Struggle. Most importantly, Lenin, the dominant Party leader, a man revered for having "led" the revolution and ensured victory in the civil wars, was dying. As soon as Lenin had a first disabling stroke in 1922, other party leaders began to jockey for position, seeking to succeed him. The power struggle lasted for most of the 1920s.

Factions. Four distinct factions emerged. The *Trotskii-left faction* called for the immediate introduction of state control over the economy in order to foster rapid economic growth. The *Stalin faction* (Joseph Stalin 1879–1953) promoted the power of Stalin and increasingly became pivotal in the party conflicts. The *Bukharin-moderate faction* (Nikolai Bukharin) favored continuation of the New Economic Policy and supported modernization of the countryside. The *Zinoviev-Kamenev-Petersburg faction* mainly aimed to preserve some degree of autonomy for themselves in Petersburg and ensure that no one else gained a dominant position.

First Struggles. After Lenin's death, the Zinoviev-Kamenev and Stalin factions joined to blunt Trotskii's drive for power. Closest to Lenin in perspective, Trotskii seemed incapable of asserting himself as the rightful successor.

He failed to take the lead in driving Stalin from important positions, even though Lenin's "Testament" indicated that Lenin saw Stalin as a dangerous threat to the Party and its Leninist legacy. After the serious weakening of Trotskii's group, Stalin and the Bukharin group joined to face the Zinoviev-Kamenev group that now attempted to align with the weakened Trotskii. By 1927 the Trotskii and Zinoviev-Kamenev factions had been defeated. Stalin then turned against Bukharin and easily defeated the Bukharinist-moderates. Stalin was thus left at the top, having skillfully manipulated the power struggles to his advantage.

Stalin's Triumph. Stalin acquired a dominant position in the Communist Party for several reasons. He clearly had superior political skills. He was willing to use ruthless tactics that included trying to isolate Lenin, spying on his enemies, falsely claiming to support certain views he did not believe in, and undermining others' regional power bases. Stalin had assumed a number of important roles within the Party—head of Workers' and Peasants' Inspection, the Organizational Bureau of the Central Committee, and the Commissariat of Nationalities. He used these roles to enhance his power and undermine that of his enemies. While others continued to emulate Lenin's methods of maintaining power—dogged, uncompromising rhetoric—Stalin undercut the power bases of his enemies.

Once he had consolidated his power, Stalin was able to carry out radical change. Stalin sought to be a new Lenin—a bolder figure in Soviet history than even Soviet Communism's founder.

3. Communist Ideology and Personal Freedom

Knowing how authoritarian and all-powerful the Communist Party became under Stalin, it is hard to realize how little influence the Party had over people's lives in the 1920s. Private lives and personal behavior generally remained outside the realm of Communist Party control. During the period of wars and revolutions, people had acted without worrying whether or not their private actions had any relevance or importance to government, which had less control over their lives than both earlier and later.

Creative Freedoms. Freedom extended to the world of culture as well. Russian artists had been in the avant-garde of European modernist painting. Vasilii Kandinsky, Marc Chagall, and Igor Malevich all supported Communism and painted in revolutionary styles. Kandinsky produced bold, modernist paintings. Chagall created colorful scenes of fantasy, while rejecting traditional notions of perspective. Malevich made painting into a minimalist science, with works such as "White on White" and "Red on Red"—geometric shapes painted on canvases of the same color.

Writers had the same kind of freedom. Though some engaged in proletarian prose—depicting the heroism of workers—most writers strove for fantasy, such as Iuri Olesha's *phantasmagoric* work, *Envy,* a series of vignettes that included soccer matches between capitalism and communism, inventions destroying their inventors, and the quest for the perfect sausage.

Freedom and imagination flourished in the 1920s in the public field of culture and in private life. The Party neither could nor would shape and limit cultural and personal freedom. The government had broader power over the economy.

4. Capitalism and the New Society

In economic terms, War Communism was an ad-hoc series of emergency measures intended to ensure victory in the civil wars and preserve Communist power. War Communism created economic distortions and hindered economic development. Lenin, the realist, recognized that the time was not ripe to introduce radical economic strategies and forms if the Communist Party wished to remain in power. Thus vague notions of Communist economics were abandoned, replaced by a mixed economy that used capitalist principles such as the market and the laws of supply and demand. Lenin called this mixed system the New Economic Policy (NEP), though it contained precious little that was really new.

The New Economic Policy. The New Economic Policy created a sort of market socialism with the market more important than socialism. Government ownership of industry continued, building on the tsarist system in which the state was also a major owner. Factories were free to decide what to produce, what prices to charge, what wages to pay, where to acquire raw materials and components, and where to market their goods. State-owned enterprises were thus encouraged to act the way capitalist enterprises did in the West.

A state planning agency, the Supreme Economic Council, was established. It employed many trained and untrained economists but had little practical impact on the economy and its ideas were not used to provide economic guidance. Many members of the tsarist economic bureaucracy held posts in the Communist government of the 1920s, as did non-Bolshevik political activists such as Mensheviks. Continuity rather than change marked the views of these bureaucrats. In addition, debate over what a Communist economy should be like and when the shift to Communist economics should occur occupied economic thinkers and politicians throughout the 1920s.

Agriculture remained in private hands, either owned by villages or by individual farmers. During the First World War, the revolutions and the civil wars, peasants had seized what little land was still held by the nobility and the state. Under the NEP, peasants were expected to meet a modest grain quota to be sent to the state (a kind of tax) but free to consume or market (at whatever prices the market would bear) any amounts above the quota. Private farming dominated. Most families owned or farmed no more than 20 acres, returned to the strip system and continued to use primitive farm equipment, such as the wooden plowshare. Modern farming was not introduced, though farmers produced nearly as much grain as before the war.

Private trade replaced state controls and forced levies. In a society in which the economy could not meet the demand for goods, prices rose rapidly, accentuated by black marketeering. Individuals bought up scarce goods as cheaply as possible, and then resold them for gigantic profits. For example, traders (commonly known as *NEP-men*), purchased vodka produced by peasants and resold it in the cities at profit margins of 400–1000 percent. Consumer goods purchased from factories were resold in the countryside at substantial profits, too. The market provided a much more responsive network of circulation of goods than would have been possible through government directives but the consequence was increasing inequality.

The New Economic Policy led to economic recovery. By 1927 the industrial sector of the economy was producing at the same level as before the First World War. Food output almost reached pre-war levels at the same time. With a smaller population than before the war and with grain exports reduced to almost nothing, the population as a whole was eating much better and had a higher standard of living than before the war.

Russia was still a poor, backward country in the late 1920s, with a relatively unproductive agricultural economy and a primitive industrial sector. The economy had produced recovery but it had not reached a take-off stage for accelerating economic growth. At the time, economists debated whether continued modest growth or a swift change to policies intended to promote rapid growth would be more beneficial.

New Society. Soviet society in the 1920s was very different from that of pre-war Russia. New classes emerged and old ones disappeared in this society of tremendous mobility. After the Civil War, the Soviet population was quiet until about 1927. At that point urban unrest, worker strikes, and peasant uprisings threatened the power of the government.

The New Elite. Obviously, a new elite determined by membership in the Communist Party and a position in either the Party or the state bureaucracy, emerged. This group came from various social origins. Many of the Party leaders came from the intelligentsia, the nobility or the middle classes. Those in the lower ranks of the government and the Party frequently came from the peasantry or the working classes. Thus a hierarchy was established within the Party, based in part on previous social position and in part on roles played during the Revolution and civil wars. The previous elite of landed aristocrats and wealthy businessmen were destroyed through emigration and the civil wars.

Commercial Class. A new commercial class emerged—traders, owners of small factories, artisans, and small shopkeepers. This group flourished, though generally disdained by others in society, until outlawed in the early 1930s.

The Working Class. The proletariat—supposedly the object of the revolution—was very different from the pre-war working class. That class had been militant, opposed to both government and managerial authority. Though many workers still had deep roots in the countryside, by the First World War a majority of factory workers came from families of workers or artisans. They were becoming a class of traditional proletarians. However, under Communism the working class was apolitical, nervous, almost frightened, and importantly, quiescent until the late 1920s. The vast majority of workers came from the countryside and had no prior experience in an industrial setting. Almost all of them were unskilled workers and the vast majority were illiterate. They felt ill at ease in the cities and joined the Communist Party as a way out of their isolation and loneliness, having little understanding of what the Communist Party stood for. When living conditions worsened in 1927 and unemployment rose dramatically, large numbers of workers began to strike. They were, perhaps, becoming a threat to Communist power.

The Peasantry. All of the urban classes—elite, commercial, and proletarian—were essentially new classes. Only the peasantry remained little changed by war, revolution, and civil wars. They remained mired in the mud of backwardness and rural isolation. Presided over by richer farmers, who had some understanding of the outside world and by semi-literate priests, the peasants inhabited a world of Christian-pagan beliefs and maintained a stubborn resistance to change. They ate better, in spite of the continued backwardness of their agricultural techniques, because their taxes were substantially lower. Further, the government left them alone. It had essentially retreated from the peasant sea onto the small island of urban life. When the Party tried to introduce Communist structures, the peasants either ignored them or transformed them into traditional peasant institutions. As long as the government left them alone, the peasants saw no need to care who was ruling the country. The Romanov tsar was gone, replaced by the Red Tsar.

5. The Revolutionary Family and Personal Freedom

The revolutionary era transformed the family and gender roles and relationships (see Chapter Four for parallel developments in China). The Communists provided ideological and political support for changes that had already occurred. Engels, one of the founders of Marxism, had followed the lead of German socialists in condemning the "bourgeois" family and male domination. Marxists viewed the capitalist family as a conservative institution, a barrier to social change.

Women's Rights. Forced to act independently and to lead the family, women sought equality. Before the First World War, a small Russian suffrage movement had promoted political rights for women. The Communists' Women's Department championed equal rights for women, including liberation of the "women of the East"—Muslim women. The Women's Department, led first by Inessa Armand and then by the radical feminist Alexandra *Kollontai* (author of *Red Love*), supported democratization of the Communist Party against Lenin's demands for centralization of power in his hands. Finding itself on the losing side of one of the most important internal struggles within the Communist Party while Lenin was still alive, the Women's Department faded into the background.

Women gained civil and political rights equal to those possessed by men. However, few women, except for Armand, Kollontai, and Lenin's wife, *Krupskaia,* had any real power within the Communist Party.

Women acquired numerous freedoms within the family. Equal property rights, civil marriage, paid maternity leaves, abortion, and divorce gave women much more control over their lives than under the old regime. Laws were passed to reduce the burdens of childcare. Communal dining halls, children's nurseries, and pre-schools all reduced the household responsibilities of urban women. Sexual freedom came too, as sexual behavior was "privatized," no longer controlled by law, the church, or peer pressure.

Women's economic roles changed, too. Many women entered the workforce and thereby gained some economic independence. Equal pay for equal work was championed by Lenin but not implemented. Many women remained in the consumer goods industries where pay was lower and few became skilled workers in the higher-paying fields of heavy industry. When unemployment increased from 1927 on, women were the first to be laid off. Peasant women continued to carry the burden of heavy farm work, from pulling the plow to carrying water from village wells or streams.

Changes in the Family. Changes reached the family, too. The government fostered the idea that it, and not the family, was the basic social institution. Male domination was reduced or eliminated and in many cases matriarchy replaced patriarchy. Many families were single-parent families, with the female as the single parent. Children's rights were fostered in order to reduce the power of patriarchy and to encourage the future revolutionary generation to be loyal to Communism. Still children had suffered the most during the revolutionary era and continued to suffer in the 1920s. Death sought out children. Millions died in famine; millions more remained homeless. Hundreds of thousands were sent eastward on orphan trains at the height of the famine of the civil war years. Millions were deported from cities and sent to child labor camps from 1927 on. Child abandonment and infanticide remained at high levels. An increase in youth crime, juvenile delinquency, and anti-social, and perhaps anti-government, behavior was predicted.

The ideals of gender equality and democratization of the family were promoted by the realities of the revolutionary era and the ideology of the Communists. Partially fulfilled, sometimes only temporarily, these ideals remained generally hidden for the rest of the Soviet period and through much of the post-Soviet era as well.

6. Community and Diversity

Diversity played a more powerful role than community building in this period. The people promoted diversity, while the government could do little to limit it and had little ability to successfully promote community.

Diversity. Diversity was fostered on a personal level. Personal freedom was not seen as incompatible with a sense of community. Thus, in many ways, the Soviet Union was a civil society, in which difference was viewed as a positive and not a negative. At the same time ethnic diversity was reinforced by the ways in which political boundaries resembled ethnic ones. The Communists created an ethnic mosaic within the framework of Communist rule. The Party used force to bring ethnic groups back into the empire but did not try to impose the kind of Russification employed by the last tsars.

Community. Propaganda in favor of a single culture, that of "Soviet Man," was ubiquitous in the cities but had little effect and hardly reached the rural masses. For a brief period of time, then, diversity was not viewed as a threat to community. Ideological community, though not really achieved, was more important than any other type of community.

F. STALINISM, 1929–1953

Stalin transformed a relatively free, largely capitalistic society into an authoritarian, socialist one, which came to be associated with his name—thus *Stalinism.* Stalinism had five major components. First, political power was concentrated in the hands of one person, Joseph Stalin, who encouraged the use of force and threats to assure obedience to his will. Second, in the countryside capitalism was replaced by collective farms and peasants were returned to a serf-like condition. Third, efforts were made to conduct an intensive industrialization drive, focusing on replacing the market with centralized determination of production, distribution, and even consumption, as well as heavy expenditures of capital, labor, and raw materials. Fourth, cultural freedom was eliminated, replaced by a single style of culture, *socialist realism.* Finally, the private freedoms of the Twenties were eliminated or driven underground. This all occurred in a country turned inward as Stalin sought to establish "*socialism in one country*" before expansion or response to external threats would be possible.

1. From Isolation to World Power

Soviet isolation was in part intentional. It also resulted from attempts to export revolution. The major powers, with the exception of Germany, also considered a pariah, ignored Russia. The smaller nations of Eastern Europe felt obligated, for security's sake, to align with the Soviets in non-aggression treaties directed, ironically, against the Germans. Alliance with Germany and then Japan at the beginning of the Second World War ended Russia's isolation. Quickly changing sides after the Germans invaded in 1941, Russia played an essential role in the Allied victory over the Germans. Russia was again in a position to build an empire.

War and Nation. Initially, Soviet ideology emphasized that ethnic and other differences would gradually disappear as Russia moved to higher and higher stages of socialism. Stalin abandoned this perspective during the Second World War. Propaganda emphasized the central role of the Russians, portraying the Russian Orthodox Church approvingly and hinting that non-Russians were traitors. Russian history was emphasized, especially that of Alexander Nevskii, a medieval prince, who had defended northern Russia against the Germans, and Ivan the Terrible, who had used violence against domestic enemies. When Russian armies rolled westward to take the lands, especially the Baltic states and eastern Poland, promised by the *Soviet-Nazi Non-Aggression Treaty* (1939), expansion again became a goal of the government. Stalin carried out a program of *ethnic cleansing,* removing minorities from border areas. When the Germans advanced into Russia, nations treated brutally by Stalin quickly joined the Nazi cause. Ukrainians initially believed that the Germans would be milder masters than Stalin. The Volga Germans and the Crimean Tatars also wavered in their loyalty to the Soviet Union. Promoting Russian patriotism, Stalin found it difficult to maintain the loyalty of the minority peoples in the borderlands.

Cold War Imperialism. Even before the war ended, Stalin began to plan for a modest empire, using principles of *indirect rule.* (In India the British also exercised indirect rule. See Chapter Two). As Russian armies swept westward, they placed in power Communist governments-in-exile, which were established in Moscow as early as 1943. Puppet governments were established all over Eastern Europe. Communists remained in power until 1987 in Poland and until 1989 in other Eastern European countries. In addition, some territory was taken from Japan, while North Korea became a Soviet satellite. Efforts to dominate Communist governments in Yugoslavia, China, and Vietnam were less successful. In addition, efforts to secure territory in Turkey and Iran, as well as control over Libya in North Africa, met opposition from the Americans and their British allies. Security was one Soviet goal. This expansion took place at a time of increasing domestic insecurity and campaigns against non-existent enemies and internal threats. The Cold War was in part a consequence of Soviet imperialism.

2. The Purges

What we know most about Stalinist Russia are the Purges; what the Soviets knew about least was the Purges. Coming from the Russian word *chistka,* which means to cleanse or purify, the Purges destroyed the lives of millions of people and deeply damaged almost every Soviet citizen. Yet, even to count the number of victims is to underestimate how profound was the impact of the Purges. How could you sleep, when the secret police in their blue uniforms rounded up people after midnight? How could you trust anyone since betrayal was so common? How could you find out what had happened to loved ones that had suddenly disappeared? How could you survive the forced labor camps located in the Arctic areas of the Soviet Union with inadequate food and brutal treatment? How could one remain a human being facing this nightmare of inhumanity? As we describe and explain the Purges, do not forget its brutal destruction of the human soul.

Origins. Though it appeared that Stalin had consolidated his power by 1929, opposition and criticism resurfaced in 1932. By that time the First Five-Year Plan (the first attempt at rapid industrialization) had come to a halt, declared a victory. Collectivization had destroyed the productivity of Soviet agriculture and famine stalked the land. Clearly Stalin's strategies for rapid economic development and modernization had failed. Other Party leaders began to criticize him. Trotskii called for his dismissal, others organized small petition campaigns, and his wife dared to criticize him publicly. Stalin offered his resignation, a political ploy he had used before, but no one dared accept it. Stalin then attacked the *Old Bolsheviks,* party leaders from the pre-Revolutionary era, such as Kamenev and Zinoviev, who were no longer a threat to his power.

When Sergei *Kirov,* head of the Leningrad (Petersburg was renamed Leningrad after Lenin's death) Communist Party organization, espoused a slightly more moderate and much more popular approach—concessions to the peasants and an end to attacks on the Old Bolsheviks—Stalin acted. Kirov was murdered in December 1934, probably through the efforts of Henrikh *Iagoda,* head of the secret police, who most certainly acted on Stalin's orders. Quickly, traces of conspiracy were covered up with the mass deportation and execution of thousands of secret police and Party officials from Leningrad. The Purges had begun.

Show Trials. The Purges operated on three levels simultaneously—public show trials, quiet attacks against Party organizations, and the random arrest, exile, and murder of ordinary citizens, especially urban residents. Party leaders and former Party leaders, most of them Old Bolsheviks, were tried and found guilty at three public trials. In the *Trial of the Sixteen* (August 1936), Zinovev, Kamenev, and their allies were found guilty of treason and executed. In the *Trial of the Seventeen* (January 1937), Old Bolsheviks were accused of betraying

Russia to the Germans and Japanese. Finally, in the *Trial of the Twenty-One* (March 1938), Bukharin and other leaders of the right wing of the party were condemned for trying to organize a plot to overthrow Communism and return the country to capitalism.

Almost all of those put on trial confessed in the courtroom. Fear for their own lives and those of their families, almost unbearably painful torture, and some twisted belief that their confessions would end the country's nightmare motivated those put on trial. Those strong enough to refuse to confess were tortured to death or executed.

Purge of the Communist Party. While the public half-believed the fiction of the show trials, Stalin's lieutenants went about purging the Communist Party and other important segments of Soviet society. In 1937 and 1938 the military was purged, in part because the Red Army and its commander Marshal Tukhachevskii had criticized the public trials. Most top military leaders were purged, as was half of the entire officer corps. In 1938 regional party organizations, including those of Moscow, Leningrad, and Ukraine, were decimated. Then the purge spread to the top of the party, the *Central Committee* and *Politburo* (the main decision-making organ of the Party), most of whose members had been put in power after The Purges began. Most of the country's entire political elite was purged.

Ordinary Citizens. Ordinary citizens had less chance of being purged through an overt decision by Stalin or the secret police. However, a campaign of denunciation, arrest, and exile spread throughout the country. An individual accused a friend, acquaintance, neighbor, or fellow employee of some outlandish crime. Many people acted in this way to save themselves. Ironically, most of the accusers were arrested too. The purge flowed through office buildings, apartment complexes, and cultural organizations. For ordinary citizens The Purges made no sense; they weren't supposed to.

The Purges End. Finally, in late 1938 Stalin purged the secret police, blaming excesses on them and their leader, N.I. *Ezhov.* In spring 1939, Stalin announced that The Purges, beneficial as they had been to the Soviet Union and the Communist Party—and to Stalin himself—were no longer needed and had been terminated. At least 5 percent of the country's population had been arrested and half of the urban population was on an arrest list. Hundreds of forced labor camps were hastily built to house the 18 million people arrested. Three-and-a-half million were executed or died in the forced labor camps. The transportation system strained to accommodate the flow of victims to North Russia, Central Asia, and northeastern Siberia.

Why? What took place was more important that why it happened. As historians, however, we need to ask why The Purges occurred. Clearly they took place because Stalin wanted them to. What were his motivations? To maintain himself in power Stalin needed to cover up his mistakes. This seemed possible only if all those who understood the consequences of his introduction of collectivization and rapid industrialization were no longer around to criticize him. How could he be the next Lenin if his policies were recognized as failures?

Some have argued that he was paranoid and that in order to eliminate his fears he had to destroy those who were a threat to him. Saying that he was mentally unstable gets him off the hook—and too easily. Stalin sought to create a Communist Party and a Soviet people totally loyal to him personally. This would preserve his power and ensure—he thought—the success of his programs. Eventually, he realized that millions of prisoners could work for almost nothing, thus reducing the costs of industrialization. They could also be forced to participate in labor-intensive projects in remote regions that could not possibly attract sufficient free labor.

Stalin was not alone. He had the enthusiastic support of the secret police. Millions of people acted out of self-interest by accusing others of treason and other crimes. They gained jobs, better apartments, new lovers, and a sense of power. In a society used to suffering, it was better to cause suffering than to be its victim.

Ordinary people viewed The Purges in an ambiguous fashion. Confused and uncertain as to the depth of The Purges, they almost cheered that the leaders who had made life so miserable for ordinary people were now being punished. This increased their support for Stalin. Frequently they concluded that if a person had been arrested, that person must be guilty. Yet, many ordinary citizens expressed sympathy for the victims through simple acts of kindness.

Consequences. The Purges were of great importance in Soviet history. They destroyed a generation of leaders and brought to the top or near the top a generation of less-talented people, who would rule the Soviet Union for over thirty years after Stalin's death. Military capability and thus national security were greatly weakened. Industrial and economic growth sputtered and ground to a halt, as factory managers, scientists, and engineers were purged. A new kind of society and a new kind of leadership emerged. Terror and fear characterized society and its leadership. The impact of the psychological trauma faced by individuals cannot be measured. The promise of socialism had drowned in a sea of bloodletting.

3. Stalinism

Stalin interpreted Marxist ideology rather differently than Marx did and focused on different issues than Lenin did. Stalin emphasized the power of the individual to mold environment and thus determine history. Seeing himself as an original thinker, Stalin tried to write theoretical works about nationality, science, and linguistics.

Stalin's Theories. As you recall, Marx had argued that socialism would inevitably triumph through fundamental changes in the economic system. Marx used the term dictatorship of the proletariat to suggest that after socialism was introduced, it would be structured to meet the needs of the working class. Lenin focused on the role dedicated elite played in actually making the revolution. For him, a revolution could be made only by a small group of professional revolutionaries, with the support of the workers and peasants, even though society had not reached an advanced state of capitalism.

Stalin faced new circumstances, for the revolution had succeeded and Communists were now in power. However, after a decade, the Soviet Union still retained substantial capitalist components and ways of doing things. For Stalin, the practical and ideological problem was what should Communism look like and how could this Communist society be actualized.

ital OK

Stalin made several contributions to socialist theorizing. First, he rejected the notion of world revolution, replacing it with the idea of *socialism in one country*. According to Stalin, the Soviet Union must first focus its energies on creating a socialist society at home. He abandoned the idea that security for the Soviet state could be guaranteed by world revolution. Instead, security was dependent upon the Soviet Union becoming a strong, modern nation—to be achieved through rapid industrialization.

term on p 55

Second, Stalin built upon Lenin's emphasis on the power of the individual to shape environment and history. He applied the idea not to destroying a capitalist society but to building a socialist one. Stalin simply could not wait for the nature of production to change naturally.

Third, Stalin argued that the world of ideas was totally determined by the system of production. There is of course a contradiction between the second and third points.

Finally, Stalin emphasized that under Communism, a single culture would emerge, one in which difference, including ethnic and linguistic difference, would disappear, replaced by uniformity. Ironically, the single culture was not to be an amalgam of all of the cultures in the Soviet Union but would be created through the total assimilation of non-Russians to Russian culture. Soviet Man was thus Russian Man.

Stalin's Reality. The reality Stalin created was quite different from his theory in many ways. Granted, the emphasis on the power of the individual to shape environment, contradictory to socialism, was implemented in practice, and world revolution was abandoned. However, the new synthesized culture of Soviet man was not created, nor did non-Russian culture and cultural identity disappear. Conformity was based on threat and fear, not on faith. Stalin thus created a system of beliefs that was internalized by some but accepted as true by others only because the alternatives were insecurity, punishment, and perhaps death.

4. Stalin's Social and Economic Revolution

Stalin introduced radical changes in the nature of the economy, destroying the old market socialism system. He brought about the changes with great brutality. Stalin wished to create a modern socialist industrial society. Instead his efforts produced an underdeveloped economy filled with contradiction and inefficiency. Changes in the economic system were accompanied by and produced dramatic changes in society.

Collectivization. Collectivization of agriculture produced the total transformation of rural life. State ownership of land, tools, and even seed grain replaced private ownership. State management of farming replaced private initiative. State control over disposition of farm production replaced the open market. The dictatorship of the collective farm manager replaced traditional village governance. Personal mobility was replaced by tying peasants to the soil once again. All of this was imposed upon peasants at gunpoint and in the face of massive resistance. Stalin conducted a war against the peasants and their way of life. In the long run this was a *pyrrhic victory*.

Why Collectivization? Marx had focused his energies on condemning capitalism, especially industrialization. Peasants, he wrote, were a "sack of potatoes," not worthy of any serious analysis. Lenin, on the other hand, thought about what agriculture might be like under socialism. However, he wrote mainly about the "Prussian" agricultural system of large estates worked by badly paid farm workers and the "American" system of large land holdings farmed by individual families. However, Russia had the traditional model of the commune, which involved collective ownership and decision-making by the peasants themselves, and the utopian communes of the 1920s, in which land and other property were owned jointly. None of these models appeared capable of producing substantial increases in productivity, let alone transforming the countryside through an agricultural revolution. In an unintended fashion the collective farm became Stalin's solution.

Collectivization became a solution to issues broader than agricultural modernization. By 1927, agricultural output appeared inadequate to meet the needs of the urban population. This occurred at a time when workers began to strike in large numbers, demanding higher wages. Stalin's solution to the problem of the inadequacy of the urban food supply was to force peasants to transfer a higher proportion of their harvests to the state. At the same time the Party concluded that industrial expansion could not continue unless substantially more investment took place. Again the countryside was seen as the source for additional income. First, the government decided to reduce the prices it paid for the grain peasants delivered to the state. The Party expected that the peasants would seek to maintain their income levels by selling more grain on the market and that, using the laws of supply and demand, increasing the supply would reduce prices. Therefore there would be more grain for the cities and more money for investment in industry.

Peasants soon realized that such a strategy did not maintain income levels and concluded that they might as well increase their own consumption of farm goods, reduce the amount of grain they produced, and shift to more profitable crops, such as vegetables and fruits. In 1928, Stalin ordered a return to the kind of forced requisitions employed by War Communism. Grain was simply taken from the peasants. Though harvests were lower, the amount of grain collected by the state actually increased.

Discontent in the countryside produced violence and even open rebellion in 1929. Over 1,000 rural Communist officials were murdered, state granaries were destroyed, and rebellions broke out, sometimes district-wide and in a few cases province-wide. The government was afraid to send in the army since most of its soldiers were of peasant background.

The Party faced a tremendous crisis, as both supplies of food for the cities and capital for investment were threatened. If the increasingly troubled cities exploded, the Communists might not be able to preserve their power. That was the dilemma Stalin faced; collectivization was the answer he gave.

Forced collectivization, 1930. By the late summer of 1929 Stalin had decided to embark upon a campaign of rapid, forced, compulsory collectivization. He announced his program in October, on the anniversary of the 1917 Revolution.

As a first step toward collectivization, Stalin conducted a campaign against the better-off farmers. The derogatory term *kulak* (fist) was used to identify farmers the Communists considered wealthy. In reality, the kulaks were not rich farmers but simply somewhat better off than others because they worked harder, had better land, more children, and/or a better understanding of the market and the outside world. But the kulaks were the village leaders and Stalin believed they might be potential leaders of opposition to collectivization. Besides, their land, farm animals, and tools could be used as a basis for collective farms. An anti-kulak campaign would strike fear in the hearts of other peasants, who would be more willing to accept collectivization without a fight. In December 1929, over one million kulak families were driven from their land, preparing the way for the collectivization drive.

Next, military units and groups of armed factory workers were sent into the countryside to collectivize the peasants. Force, surprise, and intimidation succeeded. Over half of the peasants were herded into collective farms in less than two months during the winter of 1930.

At first, peasants didn't know how to respond. Sometimes they wrote complaints to party officials or to rural newspapers. But as collectivization spread beyond the central Moscow region and into the richer farmlands of southern Russia, resistance emerged. Peasants destroyed their livestock. It is estimated that about half of all livestock was destroyed in February 1930. Rumors spread that peasants would refuse to do spring plowing.

The probability that massive urban starvation might occur and thus might threaten Communist—and Stalin's—power forced him to back down. In early March, the Communist Party newspaper, *Pravda,* published Stalin's statement, *Dizzy with success.* Blaming lower-level Party officials for the excesses that he had ordered, Stalin announced a return to voluntary collectivization. Within weeks most peasants left the collective farms, even though the best lands remained in the collective farms. Confident that forced collectivization was dead and that private farming would continue to flourish, peasants happily plowed their fields and planted their crops. Weather, hard work, and luck (Stalin's good luck) produced a bountiful harvest. As the harvest season ended, peasants were again forced into the collective farms. Collective farms retained their central role in Stalinism until the collapse of Communism in 1991.

Consequences. Collectivization produced unintended results. It restored order in the countryside, establishing Communist Party control in rural Soviet Russia for the first time. Millions of Party officials were sent into the countryside over the next few years. Peasant rebellion disappeared, replaced by suffering and sullen bitterness. The countryside never again threatened the power of the Communist Party. However, collectivization failed to achieve its economic goals. Agricultural productivity and modernization did not result. Overall farm production declined, though the destruction of livestock temporarily increased the amount of food available for humans. The Soviet Union lacked the infrastructure and the mechanized base to modernize agriculture. It lacked sufficient numbers of agronomists and veterinarians to provide peasants with the expertise they needed to modernize their farming. Resentment against collectivization meant that peasants did not work as hard as they had as private farmers. The disruptions of collectivization, along with drought conditions, produced a famine in the Soviet Union that lasted from 1932–1934 and destroyed the lives of up to 15 million people. Nor did agriculture provide additional amounts of capital for industrial development. In fact, the proportion of capital for investment generated by the agricultural sector declined substantially until the late 1930s. The urban population thus paid the costs of the rapid industrialization drive of the 1930s.

Rapid Industrialization. Rapid expansion of industry, in the guise of *Five-Year Plans,* sought to transform the Soviet Union into a mighty industrial power. This goal was to be achieved through massive investment of capital, labor and raw materials. Investment was to be concentrated in heavy industry rather than in consumer goods production. The Soviets thus reversed the order of industrialization pioneered by the British in the eighteenth century, and soon followed by the Americans—develop consumer goods industries first, then proceed to heavy industry (Japan also followed the British model. See Chapter Four.). Quantity was the goal, while quality and cost were irrelevant.

Planning. All of this was to be carried out through a system of centralized planning. The *State Planning Office* determined what would be produced, how much would be produced, and where it was to be produced. This meant that a particular factory was given a quota in tons of a particular item it was to produce—tons of sewing machines or dishes or steel, for instance. In Soviet terminology, this was known as the "gross."

Prices were set by the state as well, though little attention was given to pegging prices to costs of production. The planners simply had little idea what it cost to produce a sewing machine, a set of dishes, or a ton of steel. Prices were set in an arbitrary fashion, though two ideological criteria were used—culture was to be quite inexpensive, as were materials that supported Communism, such as the published works of Lenin. Efforts were also made to coordinate the distribution system, determining where a factory sent its finished goods and where a collective farm sent its products.

Inputs. Capital for investment could not come from the kinds of mechanisms used in capitalism—stock markets and investment banks. Nor were company profits available because most factories actually lost money. The population was heavily taxed, primarily through a very heavy turnover tax (a kind of sales tax). The government levied this tax on consumers, including urban residents and collective farmers.

Vast quantities of raw materials were poured into industry, creating new "complexes" where iron, steel, and coal deposits were located. Initial efforts to improve the transportation system were hampered by the inadequate railway and highway network as well as by poor management. Later, improved coordination of rail transportation facilitated the movement of raw materials and finished products.

Labor Mobilization. Labor mobilization, that is exploitation of the workforce, was an important input into the economy. Harsh discipline and prohibitions against changing jobs drove the workers hard. In addition, efforts were made to improve the organization of work. Under the *Stakhanovite system* the best practices of workers were used to raise production quotas and then applied to all workers. The best workers then worked even harder to get higher wages. Exhaustion led to the collapse of this approach. Workers were also encouraged to sacrifice for the future and for their children's future. They were also told that their hard work was essential to Soviet security.

Consequences. Economic growth was impressive, though uneven (over time and among sectors of the economy). It was bought at heavy cost in terms of declining living standards and brutal treatment of the workforce. Accurate data does not exist but real growth was as much as 5 percent per year on average during the 1930s. Substantial barriers existed to achieving the even higher annual growth rates (8–12%) typical of other countries undergoing rapid industrialization drives. The Soviet Union lacked the advanced equipment and machinery necessary to modernize. The country couldn't afford to import much machinery and only gradually developed the capacity to build its own machinery (*import substitution*). Increased defense spending diverted capital from industry as a whole. The workforce was initially quite inexperienced and inefficient. Pouring more and more labor into projects led to increased production but also dramatically increased costs. Later, greater emphasis on technical training led to improvements in the quality of work. Because many projects were quite large, they took many years to complete. These long-term investments did not produce short-term gains.

By the end of the 1930s the Soviets had completed much of the necessary infrastructure. However, the outbreak of the Second World War makes it impossible to guess what might have happened in the economy. Rapid industrialization became a core component of Stalinism—along with collectivization and The Purges. All brutalized the suffering Soviet people, while results were uncertain. The introduction of such rapid changes also affected the country's social structure.

Stalin's New Classes. Under Stalinism, the remnants of pre-Revolutionary Russian social structure disappeared, the proletariat expanded, and new classes emerged. Social and geographical mobility, which had characterized Russia from the emancipation on, intensified in the 1930s through rapid industrialization, collectivization and The Purges. Downward mobility marked many educated persons, as well as the families of those purged. Eventually social uprootedness was replaced by a frozen society.

Death of the Middle Class. In the early 1930s the Communist Party outlawed private trade, thus eliminating the class of small traders, artisans, and NEP-men that had flourished in the free market conditions of the 1920s. The true pre-revolutionary upper class and most of the middle class had already disappeared in the revolutionary era of 1914–1922. Only the lower strata of the middle class remained. At the same time, the intelligentsia was destroyed or transformed from an independent, critical thinking, creative social group into a lifeless group of supporters of the regime and its definition of intellectual and cultural life. The Purges destroyed most of those who had been outspoken advocates of intelligentsia ideals during the 1920s.

New Administrative Elite. Quite large, the bureaucracy became the most powerful social group in Stalinist Russia. Upon the foundation of the Soviet state, the government recruited large numbers of employees. These new civil servants were selected on the basis of some loyalty to Communism (frequently determined by having served in the Red Army), rather than on the basis of clerical or administrative skills. Inefficiency, petty authoritarianism, and low-level corruption characterized the new elite. This bloated bureaucracy grew even more in the 1930s. The government needed more and more personnel for central planning, republic, regional and local government agencies, the economic ministries, and the secret police. Industrialization demanded more factory managers, engineers, and technicians. Millions were recruited to work in the bureaucracies of the collective farms and the central agencies for agriculture. It is clear that the members of this social group saw themselves as occupying a special place in Soviet society. The upper ranks of this gigantic bureaucracy had special privileges, access to goods in a society of scarcity. Automobiles, apartments, and education for their children were available to bureaucrats. However, this new bureaucracy, which was clearly the new elite, was not a closed group. The Purges created a mechanism for mobility into and out of the bureaucracy. Once a person was purged, his/her family suffered as well, losing its special privileges, too. Loyalty to Communism—and thus loyalty to Stalin-determined whether one could enter or remain within this special group. Thus, this new elite supported and generally benefitted from Stalin's modernization agenda.

Proletariat. The Stalinist working class was very different from the proletariat of the revolutionary era in size, composition, and militancy. The working class grew tremendously in size. As in the early 1920s, the working class was overwhelmingly composed of persons escaping the countryside. The shift to industrial and urban life left them bewildered. Moving to Moscow was like going from one planet to another. Ill-adjusted, without a sense of class solidarity, the new working class accepted its situation. On the one hand, it was praised as the most important social group, especially for its role in industrialization. At the same time, its members suffered ill health, exhaustion, and a decline in living standards. The class was no longer militant the way it had been during the revolutionary era and the late 1920s. It caused the Communist Party no serious troubles. The class was also badly split between a small elite of skilled workers, the Stakhanovites, whose productivity and wages were higher than those of the mass of workers, and unskilled workers who were former peasants. The latter deeply resented the former. The class was hardly a proletariat in a Marxist sense.

"New" Serfs. Collectivization destroyed the peasantry, still two-thirds of the population by the late 1930s. In the 1920s it had been a class of landowning private farmers. Now it was enslaved, once again tied to the soil. Famine, Communist military force, and farm management ignorance circumscribed the lives of the peasants. Though large numbers of farmers left the collective farms, legally they needed the permission of the collective farm management in order to depart. Peasants lost freedom of mobility and the freedom to make decisions about farming. They became badly paid farm workers instead of property owners. In the mid-1930s the government introduced modest changes. Peasants were permitted to use a half-acre or so of collective farm land for growing food and raising livestock and could also market these farm goods. Only slowly did the light of literacy begin to shine in many peasant huts. Even in the 1930s a demographic imbalance developed in the countryside, as young people, especially males, fled the collective farms for opportunities in new industrial areas and in large cities such as Moscow. Thus began the transformation of the rural village into one of grandmothers. Stalinism dealt a terrible blow to the Russian peasants.

Prisoners. Prisoners occupied the bottom of society. They numbered approximately 5 percent of Russia's population. Brutal treatment and shortened lives were their fate.

5. Family, Gender, and Security

Eventually Stalinism changed the family and gender relations. However, into the mid-1930s, the Party continued to espouse the goals of the 1920s, attacking the traditional patriarchal family and promoting women's independence. Conditions changed very quickly in 1934–1935, due to the Stalinist modernization drive and recognition that policies of the 1920s were producing unruly youth and increased youth crime. In addition, changes in gender relations and in the family reflected the general tightening of discipline in society and a sharp reduction in personal freedom.

Return to Tradition. Stalin began to champion the nuclear family as a central institution of Communism. Divorce was made difficult and expensive. It became illegal for people to live together without being married. "Free love" was condemned. Stronger parental authority was encouraged.

At the same time, gender roles were modified. Men continued to dominate the political system and played an increasingly important role in economic development—in state planning, economic ministries, and factories. At the same time women moved into the workforce in even larger numbers. By the mid-1930s a higher proportion of Soviet women worked than in any other industrialized country.

The Communist Party emphasized two contradictory roles for women—participation in the workforce and motherhood. Women were encouraged to have large families and to enter the workforce. Thus a "double burden" was imposed upon women. The situation was made worse because the state did not make social welfare a priority, nor did it have the money to build and staff all of the day care facilities that would have been needed because of the large numbers of mothers in the workforce. Stalinism profoundly affected the family and gender relations and shifted the direction of government policy away from permitting a great deal of personal freedom to limiting freedom through the return of patriarchal institutions from the past.

6. Community, Diversity, and Security

Soviet citizens underwent a number of common experiences that did not produce community. Diversity had greater influence than community, though Stalin tried to emphasize community based on Russian patriotism from the Second World War on.

Community. Official propaganda bombarded people with the Stalin cult, portraying him as the greatest hero in all of human history. Soviet citizens were all encouraged to accept and participate in the common national agenda—modernization and national security. They were all exposed to the idea of the Soviet Man—that modernization would eliminate all ethnic and religious differences, leaving a single Soviet culture (speaking Russian, of course). In some way or another, rapid industrialization, collectivization, and The Purges influenced everyone's lives. In reality, these common experiences made community building more difficult.

Diversity. Differences actually increased in the Stalinist period. Little progress was made toward reducing ethnic identity. In fact, Stalin saw ethnic identity as dangerous. Stalin's revolutionary changes affected minority areas more deeply than they did Russia. For instance, collectivization damaged the peasantry in Ukraine more than it did Russian peasants in the Moscow area. The famine of 1932–1934 was centered in Ukraine, the most important grain producing area. During the Second World War, national minorities initially viewed the Germans as saviors, especially in Ukraine and the Baltic areas. When the war ended, Stalin punished the unreliable minorities, resettling millions of people of minority background—Crimean Tatars, Estonians, Latvians, Lithuanians, and others—to Central Asia. Volga Germans who had settled in Russia in the eighteenth century were also exiled to Central Asia. The Purges hit the minority populations disproportionately. Russians were less likely to be purged, shot, or sent to a forced labor camp than were minorities. After the Second World War, Stalin launched an anti-Semitic campaign, as part of his effort to find scapegoats for his failures and as a means of reestablishing tight control over the population.

Class differences grew. The distance between the collective farmer and the urban resident widened. A special elite emerged within the working classes. Most importantly, the large, privileged bureaucratic elite expanded. Finally, the nation was divided between those who remained loyal to Stalinism—or professed to be loyal—and those charged with and punished for treason. The Soviet Union became a nation of the guilty and the not yet guilty.

G. REFORMING COMMUNISM, 1953–1985

For the Soviet people, the death of Stalin was almost as painful personally as living under Stalin had been. The basic issue facing the nation and more importantly the Communist leadership was whether to preserve the Stalinist system or modify it. The power struggle that became public after Stalin's death masked this question for several years. Leaders who favored continuation of the system unchanged had little thinking to do. Those who concluded that reforms were needed had to engage in critical analysis. Critical analysis was beyond their previous experience, something they were unprepared to do. Under Stalin, critical thinking was dangerous and automatically treasonous. Those who came to the conclusion that changes were needed had to identify what was bad about the old system, what had to be changed, what the post-Stalinist Soviet Union should look like, and how proposed changes were to be carried out. The period of reforming Communism easily divides into two sub-periods, that of Nikita *Khrushchev* (1953–1964) and that of Leonid *Brezhnev* (1967–1982). Each period will be dealt with separately because the Khrushchev forces and the Brezhnev clique had very different answers to the above questions. Khrushchev believed that Stalinism could be reformed to produce a better kind of Communism and improve the lives of the Soviet people. The Brezhnev people recognized that reforms were needed but feared that change would lead to upheaval, unrest, or perhaps the collapse of Communism.

1. Khrushchev, 1953–1964

Nikita Khrushchev gradually worked his way up in the party, first playing a major role as one of Stalin's henchmen in the 1930s. Upon Stalin's death, Khrushchev became head of the Communist Party and soon defeated rivals to become the single most powerful figure in the Soviet Union. Khrushchev shifted from being a Stalin loyalist to being a Stalin critic. He recognized some of the weaknesses of the Stalinist system, especially its impact on people's lives and the nation's psyche. Determined to carry out reforms that would improve socialism, he continued to believe that it was a workable system—for the Soviet Union and the rest of the world. Substantial opposition from anti-reformers hampered Khrushchev. In addition, many of his reforms were crackpot ideas. However, neither he nor others were able to apply any critical analysis to reform plans. Still, life improved greatly under Khrushchev, as he undertook major efforts to change the Soviet Union. Though unable to carry out his threat of burying capitalism, he left the Soviet Union a more modern, better-educated, and better-fed society than it had been under Stalin.

Empire Threatened. Soviet Man. Even before the end of the Second World War, Stalin began to dream of empire and to plan for an enlarged zone of post-war Soviet influence. As Soviet armies advanced, the Eastern European peoples fell into the Soviet camp. Taking advantage of the unwillingness of the Western powers to intervene in Eastern European politics, the Soviets provided military and internal security support for Communist Parties. Building on popular support for programs of recovery from the war, Communist Parties gradually consolidated their power. After internal Party struggles brought victory to the Muscovites (pro-Moscow rather than native Communists), the Communists, by 1948–1949, were in a position to introduce Stalinism. This included collectivization, rapid industrialization, Soviet-style planning, propaganda campaigns, and authoritarian party dictatorship. In Asia, the collapse of Japanese power created a power vacuum in China. As Nationalists and Communists struggled militarily to come to power in China, the Soviets vacillated, unsure whether Communist or Nationalist rule would be more beneficial to the Soviet Union. When the Communists won in 1949, the Soviets decided to provide them economic assistance (see Chapter Four). Korea and Vietnam were divided into north and south partitions, with Communists dominant in the northern parts of both countries.

The Soviet Empire was quickly weakened. Unrest broke out in Eastern Europe, especially in East Germany, Czechoslovakia, and Bulgaria, soon after Stalin's death, reaching an early peak with the East German Uprising of 1953 and turning into multiple rebellions in 1956. In both Poland and Hungary, anti-Muscovite factions came to power, carried by urban revolt, in Poland through the actions of workers and in Hungary by student rebellion. Collectivization was abolished in both countries and small-scale private trade legalized. Some freedom of expression was permitted and levels of public anxiety diminished greatly. Incomplete reform efforts faltered, and then sometimes disappeared. For example, in Poland, ideas such as working class power on the shop floor were initially accepted and then gradually withdrawn. The Polish October and the Hungarian Uprising and the reforms that followed became models for

Communist reform later—in Czechoslovakia in 1968 and in the Soviet Union under Gorbachev.

China escaped from Soviet control at the end of the 1950s. The Chinese decision to test an atomic bomb led Khrushchev to denounce the People's Republic and withdraw financial and technical support for Chinese industrialization. The Chinese condemned Khrushchev's efforts to reach accommodation with the much more powerful West, while the Soviets criticized China's unsuccessful attempts at radical reform, such as the Great Leap Forward (see Chapter Four). The real issue was not differences over domestic or diplomatic policy but over which Communist Party would dominate the world Communist movement.

Khrushchev identified American power as the central Soviet foreign policy issue. Twice in the early 1960s the United States and the Soviet Union came close to war. Soviet efforts to force the West to abandon Berlin led to the mobilization of Western support for Berlin (symbolized by the visit of American President John F. Kennedy at the height of tension) and soon thereafter the building of the Berlin Wall, which prevented East Germans from fleeing to the West. Simultaneously the Soviets tried to put nuclear missiles into Cuba, which had moved into the Soviet camp after Fidel Castro's rebellion of 1959. Faced with the possibility that Americans would use their nuclear might, Khrushchev agreed to remove missiles from Cuba. Unable to gain an advantage at the expense of the Americans over these two flash points, Khrushchev turned to a strategy of *peaceful coexistence.* He agreed to limitations on nuclear testing and on the spread of nuclear weapons. Neither aggressiveness nor accommodation reduced the disparity in power between the United States and the Soviet Union.

Khrushchev also faced renewed conflict with Yugoslavia. Though Stalin tried to isolate Yugoslavia when the latter refused to submit to his will, Khrushchev initially tried to improve relations with the Yugoslavs. However, Chinese support for the Yugoslavs led to a revival of tension between the Soviet Union and Yugoslavia in the late 1950s and early 1960s, generally known as the *Second Yugoslav Crisis* (1958–1961).

Khrushchev had difficulty in preserving the informal Soviet Empire Stalin had created at the end of the Second World War. Yugoslavia maintained its independence, Eastern Europe reluctantly remained within the Soviet orbit, and China and the Soviet Union angrily broke with each other. Khrushchev lacked the skill and experience to control the Soviet bloc, especially given the economic failings of Stalinism and the absence of the kind of ruthless power available to Stalin.

Political Change. Despite Stalin's death, the political system changed only modestly. Initially, one-man rule was replaced by collective leadership. Since the early 1930s Stalin had faced no significant internal opposition; the Party accepted his dominant role. In contrast, constant conflict among party leaders continued throughout the Khrushchev era. This prevented Khrushchev from emerging as an all-powerful ruler. In general the conflict was between those who sought to reform Stalinism and those who wished it to continue unchanged.

Eventually Khrushchev emerged as the single most powerful leader, though his power was never secure. By 1957 he was clearly the nation's most important leader, as he survived an effort by the so-called *anti-party group* to oust him. His power was challenged again at the beginning of the 1960s. At that time he lost control over the Central Committee, which earlier had provided the margin for his victory over the anti-party group. Badly weakened by the Cuban and Berlin Crises and by his increasing authoritarianism, he finally fell from power in October 1964, accused of abuse of power and incompetence.

In addition, the Party reduced the power of the secret police, symbolically by executing secret police chief Lavrenti Beria. Arbitrary arrests diminished and some of the victims of The Purges were "rehabilitated," that is released from forced labor camps or prisons or posthumously restored to Party membership.

De-Stalinization and the Thaw. Khrushchev also challenged the dominant ideology of Stalinism and in so doing encouraged challenges to socialist realist artistic conceptions through a movement known as the *thaw.* Criticism of Stalinism was known as *de-Stalinization.*

De-Stalinization. Khrushchev had several reasons for attacking Stalinism. First, he sought to separate himself from his own Stalinist past, which included a major role in purging regional party organizations. Second, Khrushchev believed that Stalinism could not produce a higher form of socialism and had serious faults that needed to be corrected. Third, if Khrushchev was to change the Soviet Union, he had to prove that the past was flawed. Khrushchev also understood that the challenges of modernization required that the educated classes, including scientists, engineers, and technicians support the system; this required a critical approach to the past.

The course of de-Stalinization was uneven. Decisions to reduce the power of the secret police and introduce collective leadership were implicit criticisms of Stalinism. In 1956, Khrushchev denounced Stalin at a meeting of party leaders. He emphasized that from 1934 on Stalin's leadership had been destructive for the Soviet Union and for the cause of socialism. Khrushchev's speech eventually leaked to the public, causing consternation as well as incentives for a more critical perspective among the educated classes. By the end of 1957, Khrushchev had become alarmed at the levels of open criticism and placed limits on de-Stalinization. De-Stalinization disappeared until Khrushchev revived it again in 1961. At that time he faced serious threats to his political power. Criticizing Stalin, he charged that his own main political enemies were "closet" Stalinists who wanted to bring back Stalinism. These attacks backfired, as other party leaders, including his allies, began to worry that Khrushchev would become another Stalinist dictator.

The Thaw. De-Stalinization appeared most prominently in the sphere of culture, especially in literature, art, music, and theater. The *Thaw,* named after the title of a novel by *Ilya Ehrenburg,* manifested itself as a criticism of socialist realist style, the Stalinist past, and the Soviet present. Critics of poetry and theater especially condemned the principles of *socrealism,* as it was called. Real human beings had disappeared, replaced by cardboard figures, they charged. The complexities of behavior and motivation had been replaced by single-minded structures in which perfect champions of socialism—especially of meeting industrial goals—defeated personifications of evil, usually secret supporters of capitalism and monarchy. Critics argued that the purpose of art was not to promote socialism but to explore life.

The thaw passed through two stages, a humanistic period followed by social criticism. Poets and dramatists portrayed human beings facing real dilemmas. Writers tried to praise humanity without criticizing Soviet reality. This was difficult to do. Soon they began to criticize the Soviet system, generally directing their remarks against the bureaucracy. The bureaucracy was portrayed as a barrier to the creation of a modern socialist society. In time, criticism of individual failings came close to expressions of disillusionment with Communism in general. The most famous novel of the period, *Not by Bread Alone* by Vladimir Dudinstsev, described the struggle between an idealistic engineer and a party bureaucrat. Eventually the bureaucrat used the engineer's invention to increase factory productivity. The bureaucrat was rewarded and the engineer forgotten. The novel crossed the line separating humanist and political criticism.

In 1958, Boris *Pasternak,* was awarded the Nobel Prize for his novel, *Doctor Zhivago,* which praised the apolitical individual trying to preserve his own way of life during the whirlwind of the civil wars. At this point, Khrushchev and other Party leaders acted quickly to prevent continued criticism of the system. Pasternak was denied permission to leave the country to accept the prize. Khrushchev bluntly announced that criticism of socialism was unacceptable, though he forced the Stalinists who controlled the arts organizations to accept a multitude of styles as long as the works did not criticize socialism.

The thaw demonstrated that artists had not accepted the idea that there was only one legitimate style and only one approach to subject matter. The Party rejected the idea that freedom of expression was compatible with Communism.

Economic Problems and Incompetent Reforms. By Stalin's death, the Soviet Union faced a fairly severe economic crisis. The new Soviet leaders had little choice but to try to overcome economic stagnation.

The economic crisis resulted from specific factors, as well as the overall nature of the Stalinist system. Agriculture remained backward and relatively unproductive, with half of the population still engaged in farming. Drought and bad harvests were typical of most years from 1945–1953.

Dislocations brought about by the return of millions to civilian life and distortions produced by heavy spending for the Korean War hindered economic growth. Propaganda and threat could not overcome the physical and psychological exhaustion of the Soviet people.

In addition, planning could not respond to the complexities of the economy, nor could the nation's leaders eliminate bureaucratic incompetence and confusion. The costs of increasing production were great, for economic growth depended on extremely heavy outlays of increasingly expensive labor, capital, and materials.

Farming. Agriculture was the most pressing problem, for the collective and state farms, which were expected to provide sufficient food for the population and raw materials for industry, were quite unproductive. Initially Khrushchev introduced a series of modest and fairly technical reforms that increased output.

Not content with modest, technical changes, Khrushchev turned to radical gambles, based on the goal of surpassing U.S. levels of agricultural output. His ideas were wild, ill-conceived, and subject to sabotage by agricultural officials and his political enemies. In 1957, Khrushchev transferred agricultural decision-making power from the central ministries to 107 *Regional Economic Councils.* Decentralization of decision-making, based on the idea that those at an intermediate level understood the economy better than those isolated at the center, failed and was gradually abandoned. Later, Khrushchev divided the country into approximately forty agricultural zones, with bureaucrats deciding which three or four crops could be planted in a particular zone.

Khrushchev also introduced the idea of the virgin lands. Beginning in 1954, young people and others were encouraged to move to northern *Kazakhstan* to establish and work on newly created collective farms. Initially harvests were quite good, then leveled off as enthusiasm and soil quality diminished. Ultimately some 90 million acres were turned into agricultural lands, producing 15–20 percent of the Soviet Union's grain, giving the country a reserve for times of agricultural crisis. Still the results were less spectacular than Khrushchev's propaganda claimed.

Two wild schemes failed miserably. First there was the *Riazan fiasco.* Khrushchev pledged that the country would double its meat production. Officials in Riazan Province in southern Russia stepped forward, promising to double their meat production in a single year. To achieve this goal Riazan had to slaughter dairy cattle and breeding stock. The quota was met but in the following year meat production fell to 50 percent of normal years.

Corn production was another disaster. Having seen the bountiful harvests of Iowa corn farmers during a visit to the United States, Khrushchev determined to increase corn production in order to expand meat production. Climate and the relatively short Russian growing season meant that the corn harvest could not reach expected goals. Collective farm officials developed a complicated scheme to make Khrushchev believe that the harvest was enormous. He was not very happy when he found out that he had been tricked.

Industry. Industrial reform was much more successful. Here, too, Khrushchev introduced structural reforms that were later abandoned. The Regional Economic Councils were to coordinate industry as well as agriculture. Later, Khrushchev proposed dividing the Communist Party into two functional parts—one to be responsible for agriculture, the other for industry. Leaving no room for the largest party organization—propaganda—this idea was dead on arrival. Khrushchev emphasized consumer goods industries, which expanded output and improved quality somewhat. To fund this emphasis on consumer goods, Khrushchev had to cut military spending, not a popular option. However, this expansion failed to meet the needs of consumers. Less radically, Khrushchev placed more emphasis on technical education and expanded the number and status of scientists and engineers. New industrial complexes were built—in Western Siberia/Northern Kazakhstan and in the Soviet Far East. This more balanced investment, along with an emphasis on improving the quality of human inputs, produced an economy that grew at a rate of about 5 percent until the early 1960s. Thus Soviet citizens breathed more easily and lived better than under Stalin.

Strengthening the Family and Women's Rights. Much more attention was paid to family conditions and the position of women. Abortion and divorce were made possible once again. Women continued to enter the workforce, encouraged to do so by the Party. At the same time women gained greater opportunities for advanced education. Khrushchev also suggested that women should be active in Party affairs and even appointed a woman to a central ministry, the first time a woman had held important formal office since the mid-1920s. As part of a major anti-religion campaign, Khrushchev promoted secular wedding ceremonies, creating special "wedding palaces," which turned out to be very popular with young couples.

Community and Diversity. Khrushchev took some steps to improve the position of national minorities, especially trying to remove the label of "treasonous" applied to them by Stalin. He also returned peoples such as the Crimean Tatars to their homelands from exile imposed upon them during the Second World War. Greater opportunities for higher education were made available in minority areas. At the same time, emphasis on the Soviet Man concept reached new heights. Khrushchev argued that the Soviet Union was in the final stages of eliminating all difference and thus creating a new Soviet citizen whose only identity was Soviet.

At the same time, Khrushchev emphasized national unity through attempts to universalize use of the Russian language. No longer were Russians expected to learn the language of the non-Russian republics in which they lived. The Virgin Lands program devastated the traditional way of life of the Kazakhs in Kazakhstan, transforming the Kazakhs into a minority within their republic.

Thus, under Khrushchev, diversity broadened and community weakened.

2. Brezhnev and His Successors

Brezhnev, who had also risen to a high position under Stalin, did not abandon the cautious approach he had developed then. In the Brezhnev era discussions of reform took place but the Party leadership refused to attempt radical change. Party leaders recognized that Communism was floundering but feared taking action. Internal problems and international successes balanced uneasily.

Détente and Challenges to Empire. The Soviet Union reached its most extensive global power during the Brezhnev period, while unrest simmered in Eastern Europe. Soviet foreign policy followed the idea of *détente*—a relaxation of tensions. The Soviet Union used the relaxation of tensions, as well as American preoccupation with Vietnam, to dramatically expand Soviet influence in Africa, Latin America, Asia, and even Western Europe.

After the "adventurism" of Khrushchev's foreign policy, his successors moved more cautiously. Recognizing U.S. military superiority, Brezhnev faced the dilemma of how to match and supersede American power without provoking a sharp increase in American military spending. Détente was a strategy for reducing short-term insecurity and military inferiority. The Soviets reduced tensions in Europe, especially by making peaceful overtures to West Germany. Brezhnev and American President Lyndon Johnson met to affirm their dedication to world peace and negotiations were conducted to limit the arms race. This produced SALT I, which placed modest limits on nuclear weapons.

At the same time Brezhnev consolidated his support within the military by embarking upon a crash program of military spending. The Soviets did not believe that their support for the North Vietnamese and Viet Cong, as well as revolutionary forces in southern Africa and Latin America, violated the spirit of détente.

Détente broke down in 1979 when the Soviets invaded Afghanistan to keep their puppet Communist forces in power. What began as a power struggle among Afghan elites soon turned into a civil war between modernizing Communists and traditionalist Muslim tribesmen. Though the Soviets could control the cities, they found it difficult to conduct a guerilla war in unfriendly mountainous rural terrain. The war lasted a decade, absorbing huge amounts of Soviet resources, alienating the Soviet people, and undermining the Soviet image of peace builder. At war's end the military gap between the Soviet Union and the United States was wider than ever and the Soviet Union lay economically exhausted. The Afghanistan gamble was the last major battle in the half-century-long Cold War, lost by the Soviet Union.

Unrest continued within the Soviet internal empire. After the turbulence of the mid-1960s, all of the Communist regimes of Eastern Europe had adopted policies to ensure relative domestic tranquility. The Poles called this *petty stabilization.* In exchange for domestic peace, Communist governments promised to improve living conditions. Poland, however, was restless throughout the Brezhnev era, while the Czechs rebelled in 1968. They tried to introduce *socialism with a human face;* that is socialism with less insecurity, some freedom of expression, and more consumer goods. The Soviets invaded, compelling acceptance of the newly established *Brezhnev Doctrine,* which essentially stated that the Soviet Union had the right to use military force to ensure the loyalty of every country within the Soviet bloc.

In Poland, unrest began with student demonstrations in 1966–1968 and continued with major labor strikes in 1970 and 1976. All of this prepared the way for the *Solidarity* movement, which surfaced in 1979 after Pope John Paul II returned to his native country. Strikes and demonstrations mobilized the support of millions of Poles and led to a serious weakening of the Communist Party. The Polish military intervened in late 1980, ending a year and a half of freedom. It instituted martial law, arrested most of the Solidarity leaders, and tried to destroy the main Solidarity mass organizations. Brutal, Stalinist-style rule fell upon Poland. For example, the secret police arbitrarily beat up people standing in line waiting for busses. Eventually secret police agents murdered priests, destroying the last bit of public support for Communism. The Communists ruled through force alone. Thus in spite of détente and a massive military build-up, Brezhnev could not increase Soviet military power and security in relative terms and his attempts exacerbated economic difficulties. Détente, thus, failed.

Tensions increased with the other major Communist power, the People's Republic of China. Though the Brezhnev group had blamed Khrushchev for increased ideological conflict with China, the Soviet-Chinese relationship improved only temporarily in the Brezhnev era. Ideological warfare turned into border skirmishes in 1969. The possibility of nuclear war between the Soviet Union and China was greater than the possibility of nuclear war between the United States and the Soviet Union. In 1971 relationships between the two countries worsened when U.S. Secretary of State Henry Kissinger "played the China card" and Chinese leader Mao Zedong "played the American card." It appeared that the Americans had successfully pulled China away from the possibility of another alliance with the Soviet Union, thus weakening the Soviet global power position.

Bureaucratic Rule. Brezhnev abandoned the idea of implementing dramatic changes in the decision-making structure. Continuity of leadership characterized the upper ranks of the Party. As long as you did not challenge Brezhnev, you need not worry about losing your position. He sought to build up a coalition of interest groups within the party, including the economic ministries (the *metal eaters*), the military, and the secret police. Seeking to maintain itself in power, the Brezhnev clique consciously avoided risk-taking. Bureaucratic rule, with fairly independent regional Party chieftains, was common. A hereditary Communist elite with special privileges, known as the *nomenklatura,* emerged. In addition, the Communist Party became more and more powerful at the expense of government ministries.

Dissent Crushed and Conformity Installed. By the time Brezhnev came to power, Communism had ruled the Soviet Union for a half-century. A half-century of Communist power and propaganda extolling the virtues of Communism had produced a population generally willing to accept Communist rule. The people were unenthusiastic in their support of the Communist Party, yet reluctant to express discontent. *Socialization* programs no longer worked on Soviet youth. Brezhnev also tried to ignore the sensitive issue of Stalin's legacy. Finally, open critical opposition emerged, primarily from three groups within the educated elite—national minorities (discussed later), writers, and scientists.

Socialization. The *Communist Youth League* (*Komsomol*) and the *Pioneers* (for children) and the million or more Party members employed full time in propaganda activity promoted loyalty to the cause of Communism. Increasingly, however, their efforts produced passive acceptance or fell on deaf ears.

Re-Stalinization. Very quickly the Brezhnev group concluded that the issue of Stalinism should be buried as deeply as possible. After an initial burst of positive assessment of Stalin, the Brezhnev regime grew silent. It permitted no public discussion of the Purges and other aspects of Stalinism. The term *re-Stalinization* is sometimes used to describe this approach.

Dissent. At the same time, discontent appeared among the educated classes once again. Though short-lived, this unrest among the intellectuals came to be known as *dissent.* The dissent movement included writers, as well as part of the scientific community. The emergence of dissent threatened neither the power of the Brezhnev group nor that of the Communist Party. Dissent illustrated the ultimate power of the Communist Party to repress civil liberties and criticism, using imprisonment, exile, and even forced admission to psychiatric hospitals. It also showed that a small number of well-educated Soviets had begun to think critically and to express their concerns openly.

The dissent movement emerged before Brezhnev had consolidated his power and determined the "correct" line toward criticism. The 1966 trial of two writers, Andrei *Siniavskii* and Iuli *Daniel,* acted as a catalyst for dissent. The two authors had published their work in *samizdat* (underground, illegal publications). Siniavskii criticized the principles of socialist realist literature, while Daniel attacked Stalinism more directly. Both were found guilty of treasonous acts and sentenced to lengthy terms of hard labor in Siberia. Angrily, the intellectual community organized a *legalist* campaign, intended to convince the Communist leaders that they should act within Soviet law, rather than in the arbitrary manner of Stalinism. By 1970, the dissent movement had expanded, numbering leading scientists, such as the nuclear physicist Andrei *Sakharov,* in its ranks. Sakharov emerged as a powerful leader, especially through his underground journal, *The Chronicle of Current Events.* The *Chronicle* presented accounts of government repression of dissenters. The scientists, as well as people like the historian Zhores *Medvedev,* still believed in socialism and thought that a government of law would receive the respect of the rational thinking educated classes and that their ideas would lead to a workable socialist system.

Writers tended to be much more critical of the Stalinist past and the Soviet present and much more pessimistic about the possibilities of creating a successful system of Communism. Alexander *Solzhenitsyn* was the most vocal critic of socialism. An early novel, *One Day in the Life of Ivan Denisovich,* published in the Khrushchev period, depicted the horrors of daily life in a forced labor camp in Siberia. *Cancer Ward* (published abroad in 1968) used the metaphor of cancer to describe the Soviet system. Ironically, only terminal patients were released from the cancer ward. *The First Circle* presented a brutally frank condemnation of Stalin and Stalinism and explored their terrible consequences for Russia.

At the beginning of the 1970s the Communist leaders decided to destroy the dissent movement. Leading dissidents were sent into exile in the West and deprived of their Soviet citizenship. Lesser figures were quietly sent to labor camps. The Party successfully destroyed domestic opposition. It was less successful in promoting economic development.

Economic and Social Stagnation. After the wild reform impulses of the Khrushchev period, Soviet leaders were reluctant to introduce major changes into the economic system. Consideration of relatively radical changes in the command economy continued and a few experiments were implemented, then gradually abandoned, until they disappeared about 1970. The sharp rise in oil prices in the early 1970s, beneficial to the Soviet Union, masked underlying economic weaknesses.

Economic Strategies. The economist Evsei *Liberman* offered three major, radical proposals. First, decision-making should be centered neither in Moscow (as under Stalin) nor in the regions (as under Khrushchev); instead each local enterprise (factory) was to make basic economic decisions beyond what to produce and how much. Second, Liberman emphasized quality control. Finally, and most controversially, he proposed socialist profitability. Enterprises should be judged not by how much they produced but by productivity and efficiency. Enterprise-level decision-making was introduced gradually and rather extensively in some consumer goods industries but the reforms did not last. The other proposals were ignored or judged too dangerous.

Party leaders understood that economic growth was slowing, moving toward stagnation. They did not fully understand why this was happening. They complained of a labor shortage, especially in European parts of the Soviet Union, where most factories were located. Authorities poured more and more capital into industry, not recognizing how wasteful and inefficient this use was. They did little to improve the ability of human capital to work productively. Raw materials were wasted as well. Costs of production rose steeply, especially in the mineral extraction industries. The Stalinist model was predicated on using huge amounts of labor, capital, and raw materials to generate economic growth. The Party leaders failed to understand that this strategy no longer worked, especially as all of the other industrialized countries of the world were focusing on increased use of technology, improved quality, and greater efficiency. The Soviets were left in the dust, with the lowest living standard among all of the industrialized countries.

Farming. Agriculture was a drag on the economy as well. Bad harvests occurred every year from 1979 through 1985, requiring the importation of huge amounts of foreign grain. It was cheaper to buy grain abroad than to produce it at home. Peasants turned more and more to their private plots, which became efficient sources of large amounts of food, except grain. Economic stagnation was accompanied by social stagnation.

Social Stagnation. Social mobility declined for almost every group in society except the scientific elite, which continued to grow in importance. The *nomenklatura* occupied the top of society. Privileged status was transferred from one generation to the next, creating a hereditary aristocracy quite at odds with Communist rhetoric of equality. Below the party elite was a growing middle class of white-collar employees, many of them university graduates. This group had prospered under Khrushchev and had contributed a new energy to the Communist Party. The working class, which included many with low-paid, unskilled jobs, was further down. Party propaganda gave special honor to the proletariat but in reality workers were not the real rulers of the country. At the bottom of society were the peasants. Aging, burdened with harsh working conditions in under-mechanized operations, they clung to their small private plots; the land that had not been left an "orphan." Regional party leaders had proposed joint ownership of the land by small groups of peasant families (the *link* concept), but the idea of "group capitalism" was unacceptable to the Brezhnev leadership. Thus social stagnation and relatively low living standards characterized the lower classes.

Crisis in the Family. In the Brezhnev era party leaders became aware of and concerned about a "family crisis." The Party believed the family had failed to fulfill its obligations to socialism. From the perspective of the Party two problems had arisen. First, the birth rate had fallen sharply in European Soviet Russia and was expected to decline even further, which would lead to a smaller workforce in the future. Second, discipline among youth had declined, as had youthful enthusiasm for Communism. According to Soviet leaders, these interconnected problems resulted from the "family crisis." This crisis had several dimensions. The proportion of single-parent families had grown significantly; females headed most of the single-parent families. According to family sociologists, the absence of fathers had produced both the lowered birthrate and the decline in discipline, with its consequent reduction in worker productivity.

The Party offered a number of solutions, some rather silly, to the family crisis. For example, there was a propaganda campaign against the "militant bachelor." Men were also encouraged not to abandon wives who had become pregnant. Women were also expected to have larger families. Men were urged to avoid heavy drinking and alcoholism and to help with the housework.

Authorities also recognized that Soviet women were overburdened, responsible for the family and expected to participate in the workforce. By the Brezhnev era the idea of equal pay for equal work had been realized. There was relatively equal access to the professions, some of which (such as medicine) were dominated by women. However, many women were stuck in low paying, menial jobs. A disproportionate number of women performed unskilled jobs on the collective and state farms.

Women played little political role. Though women were 25 percent of Party membership, only 5 percent of the Central Committee was female. No women served in the main decision-making body, the Politburo. To rise in the political world required a substantial time commitment, thus creating a "triple burden"—family, work, and politics—for which few women had the time and energy.

Merely recognizing the existence of a family crisis and the unequal treatment of women produced no significant improvements for women.

Community and Diversity. Diversity increased in the Brezhnev era, largely as a consequence of the increasing sense of national identity among minorities. Two contradictory policies were employed. On the one hand, the Brezhnev crowd emphasized the *fusion of nations*—a campaign to Russify the population through Russian language and Russianized education. On the other hand, many policies promoted the decentralization of the Soviet Union and thus the enhancement of minority rights. Brezhnev moved leaders of Communist Parties from the minority republics into the center of the Party, including the Politburo. He ended the system by which a Russian served as First Secretary of the Communist Party in a minority republic and a representative of that nationality held the position of Second Secretary. Brezhnev bought the loyalty of republic level party leaders by permitting them a great deal of freedom to engage in corruption. He poured huge amounts of capital investment into the minority areas, especially Kazakhstan and the rest of Central Asia. The Party also encouraged a renaissance of minority cultures. Ukrainian film, Lithuanian pop art, and Uzbek novels flourished, frequently honored at the national level. Gradually a sense of national cultural identity formed among minorities. In a few areas, where people perceived themselves as *double minorities,* cultural identity was transformed into political dissent. This was true among Lithuanian Catholics and Ukrainian Baptists, for instance. Political dissidence was as strong in the Ukraine as in Leningrad. Brezhnev worried about the political power of the Ukrainian Communist Party, removing its leader, Peter Shelest, in 1972 and replacing him with a more subservient party leader.

Large numbers of Russians moved into the minority republics, while the Turko-Muslim population grew by almost 50 percent in the Brezhnev decades.

Minority discontent did not reach dangerous levels during the Brezhnev era. At the same time, efforts to promote Soviet community, especially through propaganda, failed utterly. Increasingly fractured, without the kind of powerful authoritarian rule of a Stalin, the Soviet Union was gradually moving toward a state of "disunion." These and other weaknesses became more and more apparent to Brezhnev's successors, who presided over the collapse of Communism and the Soviet Union.

H. COLLAPSE OF COMMUNISM, 1985–1991

Mikhail *Gorbachev* came to power understanding that Communism was in shambles. The economy was on the verge of a lengthy depression and badly in need of basic reform. Security had been weakened by the inability of the Soviets to compete with the United States in the arms race. Brezhnev's aggressive foreign policy had mired the Soviet Union in Afghanistan in the same kind of war the United States had faced in Vietnam, also with little possibility of victory. Russians were a bare majority of the country's population, as minorities became more and more restive. The whole social fabric was fraying, reflected in increasing crime and alcoholism rates, declining life expectancy, serious environmental dangers, and continuation of the family crisis.

Gorbachev, however, confidently marched into the midst of these challenges, sure that he could successfully implement reforms that would solve these problems and simultaneously strengthen Communism. The depth of the crises, his career as a specialist in propaganda, as well as very brief exposure to the West, gave initial direction to his reforms. He believed in the power of propaganda to secure appropriate behavior. He also recognized that the Soviet Union was very backward in comparison with the West. The West and reform ideas from both the 1920s and the Khrushchev period provided the initial plans. However, each reform forced Gorbachev to introduce greater changes and to move further from Stalinism and socialist principles. He was being forced toward a decentralized union, a market economy, and democracy—all alien to the history of the Soviet Union. The quick sands of change captured and swallowed Gorbachev. All of this happened very quickly—it took only six years for the Soviet Union and Soviet Communism to collapse.

1. Break Up of the Empire, the Crisis of Russian Nationalism and "*New Thinking*"

The Soviet Union broke up unexpectedly. Economic decentralization, environmental crises, and freedom of expression led to the emergence of national movements in various parts of the Soviet Union, especially in the Baltic states. Gorbachev's inability or unwillingness to accommodate the minorities' requests for autonomy radicalized the minorities, which established full-fledged national liberation movements. Unwilling to compromise, the strongly nationalistic Gorbachev used force against rebellious minorities, then gave up. The rise of nationalist feeling among minorities triggered the emergence of potent feelings of Russian nationalism and anguished soul-searching by the Russians after the collapse of the Russian-dominated Soviet Union. Gorbachev introduced major changes in foreign policy, which he called "new thinking."

Gorbachev's Position. Gorbachev inadvertently promoted minority unrest in a number of ways. First, he had very little understanding of and appreciation for the non-Russians. As a Russian, he had spent his entire Party career in the Russian Federation, unlike predecessors who had spent time in minority republics. Second, his effort to reduce the power of Party chiefs in the national minority areas, which he saw as essential to successful reform, backfired. For example, when he fired the head of the Communist Party in Uzbekistan, massive anti-Gorbachev demonstrations broke out.

National Liberation. After initial efforts to improve economic performance through propaganda failed, Gorbachev permitted some degree of economic decentralization in the republics and promoted some freedom of criticism. The minorities increasingly used freedom of expression to criticize Russian domination and to promote their own national identities. At the same time environmental degradation and catastrophes in the minority republics were a flash point for mobilizing anti-Russian feelings. The 1986 explosion at the *Chernobyl* nuclear power plant (on the border between Ukraine and Belorussia) produced high levels of radioactive fallout across the Baltic states. Chernobyl symbolized not only environmental disaster but the entire Soviet system, too. In the minority areas, "*green*" movements emerged, mobilizing mass demonstrations against environmental crimes attributed to the Russian-led Soviet government.

Gorbachev and the Party addressed the issue of minority unrest and the future destiny of the minority republics at a *Party Conference* in July 1988. Party leaders rejected proposals for autonomy and could not come to a consensus on any policy toward the nationality question. In the Baltic states in 1989 demonstrators had stretched from Riga, the capital of Latvia, through Tallinn, the capital of Estonia, to Vilnius, the capital of Lithuania. It was clear that only independence would satisfy the Baltic peoples. Gorbachev first used economic sanctions, cutting off supplies of energy and other raw materials. When unrest increased in January 1990, he sent in elite secret police military units to crush demonstrations in Estonia and Lithuania. Efforts to create a mechanism through which the republics would have greater power within a centralized state, the *Commonwealth of Independent States,* provoked a right-wing *coup d'etat* against Gorbachev. These efforts were rejected by a majority of the republics anyway. When the Russian Republic withdrew from the Soviet Union, it collapsed in 1991. In reality it hardly existed at that point anyway.

Ethnic Conflict. National liberation was associated with increased nationalist feelings. Open conflict between ethnic groups was another. Such conflicts were most intense in the Caucasus. The most serious conflict erupted between the Azeri of Azerbaijan and the Armenians. The Azeri were of Turkic-Muslim stock, while the Armenians were Christians. The Azeri looked back to the glorious days of medieval Turkic kingdoms in Central Asia and further back to *Chinghis Khan.* The Armenians saw themselves as martyrs, especially recalling the massacre of Armenians in Turkey in 1915. Two increasingly militant nationalistic neighbors were ready to fight. An Armenian enclave within Azerbaijan, *Nagorno-Karabakh,* provided the catalyst. Violence broke out when the Nagorno-Karabakh Armenians held massive demonstrations, demanding that Armenia annex their area. Street fighting and guerilla warfare followed. Gorbachev sought to mediate the dispute but found neither side willing to talk. Eventually Gorbachev sent in troops to maintain order. He rejected the Nagorno-Karabakh request mainly because he was afraid the example would spread to other ethnic enclaves.

Russian Nationalisms. As the Soviet Union disintegrated and its global power collapsed, Russians became angrier and angrier. The Communist Party had provided cement that kept the Soviet Union together, while Russian unity existed in the context of being the dominant ethnic group in the Soviet Union. In the Gorbachev period several types of Russian nationalism were apparent. *Nationalistic imperialism* was one response. Supporters of this position argued that Russia needed to recover its rightful place as the central force in a unified Soviet Union. They rejected the idea that minority groups could have either independence or autonomy. They called for aggressive use of force whenever necessary. The Communist *bureaucrats* formed a second group of Russian nationalists. They believed that effective government required a large degree of centralization with a single national language-Russian. This group also wanted to preserve its own power. Finally, a small group of *democratic nationalists* appeared. They argued that Russians should focus on strengthening Russia and that the multi-ethnic nature of the Soviet Union was a barrier to the creation of a democratic political system. They suggested that the original Russian political systems had been democratic and that foreigners, the Mongols, had imposed authoritarian rule on the Russians. Gorbachev ignored both the national minorities and the Russian nationalists, intent upon reforming Communism within a united Soviet state. His efforts failed.

"New Thinking." New thinking offered a different approach to Cold War strategy. Most importantly, new thinking explored ways of reducing the possibility of nuclear war with the United States. Gorbachev was fortunate that American president Ronald Reagan had, by late 1983, come to the conclusion that the only way to prevent nuclear disaster was through the elimination of all nuclear weapons. Their joint efforts in 1987 led to the *INF (Intermediate Nuclear Forces)* treaty, which eliminated intermediate range nuclear weapons.

Gorbachev also sought better relations with Western Europe, arguing that Eastern and Western Europe formed a "common European home." In this way Gorbachev tried to drive a wedge between the United States and its NATO allies. Gorbachev's "Asian offensive" was less successful. Attempts to improve relations with Communist China disintegrated when the Chinese government cracked down on dissidents in 1989 during a Gorbachev visit (see Chapter Four). In part they blamed Chinese dissidence on the example of Gorbachev's political reforms. Japan was willing to offer economic assistance only if the Soviet Union returned the *Northern Territories,* seized by the Soviets at the end of the Second World War. Gorbachev, however, refused, fearing that surrender of these territories would act as a catalyst for national liberation movements back home.

2. Democratization

Gorbachev had not intended to establish democracy after over seven centuries of authoritarian rule in Russia. He promoted political reform in order to consolidate his power and build up support for economic change. Initially he attempted to restructure the Party. When this did not yield desired results, he turned to broader political reform—democratization. Democratization of the national political system was followed by democratization at the local level.

The Usual Methods. Initially Gorbachev sought to consolidate his power in the usual ways, packing important Party bodies with his supporters and removing those who did not support him. He added his supporters to the Politburo and removed enemies. He filled the Secretariat with his allies, increased the authority of a restructured Secretariat and moved key Secretariat members into the Politburo. He replaced one-third of the Central Committee and 40 percent of central government ministers. By August 1987, he had replaced three-fourths of the First Secretaries of the Communist Party at the republic and region levels.

Communist Party Elections. Still, much of the old guard remained entrenched in power. Gorbachev then turned to "party democracy"; election of Party officials at the local level. Again Gorbachev could not gain a majority. At the same time a number of interest groups, known as "*informals,*" emerged, lobbying locally.

The Parliament. Next, democratization spilled over to the "legislative" branch of government. In 1989 elections were held for the Congress of People's Deputies and for President of the Supreme Soviet. Only about a third of those elected strongly supported Gorbachev. The Congress elected an executive Parliament of approximately 500, which acted as the real legislative body. The Parliament passed only a few pieces of key legislation, primarily in the area of economic reform. However, it served two more important functions, *constituent services* and *parliamentary investigation.* Legislators were swamped by constituents who saw them primarily as powerful *ombudsmen* who could intercede with the bureaucracy or solve individual problems in other ways. This demonstrated the extent to which citizens believed in the power of their representatives to overcome bureaucratic authoritarianism. Legislative committees were formed to deal with various policy areas. They spent considerable time investigating problems, a necessary prelude to effective legislation. For example, the legislative commission on military reform compiled one of the most active investigative records. Legislators studied military readiness, hazing, and mistreatment of recruits in basic training and "draft dodging." The Parliament was a semi-democratic institution with the power to legislate, but it was not a puppet in the hands of Gorbachev.

Reform Victory. Gorbachev also pushed for local and regional elections, first held in 1990. Reformers triumphed in many large cities. In part, the scale of campaigning meant that a vigorous, hard-working candidate had a chance of victory. In addition, reformers had gained experience in campaign strategy and were better able to carry their message of reform. Also, at the local level, the appeal of reform had greater resonance. People could see the potential of reform and expect positive results. Finally, by 1990 there was greater general support for reform than earlier, making it easier for reformers to come to power.

Conclusion. Democratization did not bring Gorbachev the hefty pro-reform majorities he expected and needed. This lack of support certainly undermined his power. However, Gorbachev planted the idea that the Soviet Union should have democratically elected local and regional officials, as well as a democratically elected national legislature and presidency.

3. Glasnost

Glasnost had a profound impact on the Gorbachev era and was a major solvent loosening the grip of Stalinist institutions on Soviet life and contributing to the collapse of Communism and the Soviet Union. The term means non-secret and is generally translated as openness. More accurately, glasnost meant the right to criticize openly (within limits) without fear of punishment. The press was not truly free, for the Party retained control over the media. Glasnost arose after Gorbachev and other party leaders recognized the fallacy and dangers of keeping things secret.

The Past. Initially glasnost focused on the past. Criticism of the immediate past, the Brezhnev period, predominated at first. The period was depicted as an *era of stagnation* (the inability to respond to the country's problems), tremendous corruption, and flawed policies, especially those related to national security (Afghanistan and the arms race). All of the problems facing the country were blamed on the Brezhnev crowd, giving Gorbachev some breathing room before he, too, became a target of criticism.

Glasnost also directed attention to earlier periods, as historians tried to "fill in the blank spots." Boldly, Stalinism was addressed, especially after Gorbachev in 1987 openly criticized Stalinization and especially forced collectivization. Party leaders were not the only critics of Stalinism. The public, led by historians, sought to understand Stalinism. Archives were opened up and soon studies of collectivization and The Purges were published. Interest groups, such as *Memorial,* sought to understand the purges using another source, the memories of victims and their families. Memorial sought to establish a database on victims of The Purges and even interviewed guards and labor camp commandants. It was difficult for people to accept the brutal reality of Stalinism, for it brought into question all that they had believed, their faith in the system, and the authority of the Communist Party.

Gorbachev used this *new de-Stalinization* for some of the same purposes as Khrushchev. Condemnation of Stalinism was a strategy for building up support for Gorbachev and for change. Gorbachev faced the problem of where to set limits, finally concluding that it was unwise to set any limits to the investigation and condemnation of Stalinism.

Criticism of Stalinism led to reconsideration of the more "moderate" Soviet leaders, Khrushchev and Lenin. The economic ideas of the New Economic Policy, as well as those of the Khrushchev period (including Libermanism), were used by the Gorbachev reformers. Eventually both Khrushchev and Lenin were subjected to a more critical evaluation and this facilitated the rejection of Communism.

Contemporary Faults. The press also investigated the shortcomings of contemporary Soviet society. Poverty, alcoholism, and health problems were the subject of much investigative reporting. It became obvious that 70 years of Communism had neither brought the good life to the Soviet people nor made "life more joyous," as Stalin had claimed in the mid-1930s. These investigations also undermined support for the Communist Party.

Glasnost and Nationalism. Glasnost also encouraged nationalistic feelings among the minorities. Openness led minorities to a greater understanding of how much they had suffered under Stalinism. Glasnost created opportunities for looking critically at the past relationship between the Soviet leaders and the minorities. For example, the publication of the secret clauses of the Nazi-Soviet Non-Aggression Pact that gave the Soviet Union the "right" to conquer the Baltic states fired the patriotic fervor of the Latvians, Lithuanians, and Estonians. Glasnost fueled the alienation of the Ukrainians and Crimean

Tatars, also treated brutally by Stalin. It created opportunities for mass demonstrations in the minority areas and led to the organization of national liberation fronts, most prominently in Lithuania and Ukraine.

4. *Perestroika* (Restructuring)

Over time Soviet construction workers piled cement block upon cement block for a new government building in Moscow. From every angle the building seemed to lean more and more the higher the pile of cement blocks rose. Soviet citizens knew that the Leaning Tower of Pisa had leaned for many centuries and had not yet collapsed. Ultimately the Soviet citizens were wrong; this building—Soviet Communism—collapsed. So did the Soviet economy. The collapse resulted from the inherent fallacies of Stalinist economic theory and practice; the requirement of diverting large amounts of labor, capital, and raw materials into the arms race; and the reforms implemented under Gorbachev.

Gorbachev's Dilemma. Gorbachev focused his energies on what he saw as the cardinal problem facing the Soviet Union—its inability to develop a productive, quality-oriented, efficient socialist economy and its failure to provide for the basic needs of the Soviet people. Gorbachev knew that a productive economy was essential if the Soviet Union was to maintain a high degree of national security. Instead, the socialist economy was weakened by Gorbachev's reform efforts and eventually collapsed, replaced by a mixed market economy that was also problem-laden.

Stalinist modernization theory was based on using maximum amounts of labor, capital, and materials to build a gigantic heavy industry-military base. Efficiency, cost, and quality were ignored. Economic growth was paid for by under consumption of consumer goods, heavy taxation of the people, and forced labor. A harsh life today was to pay for a joyous life for children and grandchildren in the future. That future never arrived.

As long as almost unlimited amounts of labor and materials were available and large amounts of capital were squeezed out of the people, some economic growth occurred. Real growth under Khrushchev was followed by artificial rates of growth under Brezhnev until the mid- to late-1970s when growth rates leveled off and began to decline.

By the time Gorbachev came to power there was little likelihood that continued use of the Stalinist model would ever again generate substantial growth. Yet, this was a time when national security "threats" required a much higher growth rate. The supply of excess labor had disappeared through declining birth rates, the maximization of female participation in the workforce, and expansion of industrial plant. No huge influx of workers could be expected to promote rapid economic growth. Heavy military spending, huge government budget deficits, the decline in capital-generating oil prices, and the unavailability of foreign capital due to the global economic recession of the 1980s left the Soviet Union short of the capital it needed to modernize its aging industrial plant. Waste had been promoted by lack of labor discipline, corruption, and the emphasis on quantity of production. Costs of production rose, especially in less accessible northern Siberia, from which raw materials of the extraction industries were now being drawn.

For Gorbachev the question was what was the real nature of the economic crisis, how severe was it, and how could it be overcome. He and his economic advisers had real difficulty with all three questions. Peeling off one layer of the question revealed new problems. For example, no one had realized that the government ran a substantial budget deficit each year. This meant that the government had little money to put into economic reform. Soviet economists were not used to "thinking outside the box" and had very little experience in looking critically at the economy. Thus it was hard for them to discover exactly what was wrong. As the economy continued to worsen, Gorbachev had to face the ultimate question of whether a socialist economy was at all workable in the Soviet Union or whether it would need to be replaced by market mechanisms.

Industry. Gorbachev first tried the strategy with which he was most familiar—mobilization of labor through propaganda. Then he turned to the kinds of modest structural reforms Khrushchev had introduced. Ultimately Gorbachev agreed to a mixed economy that included market elements.

Sloganeering. Since Gorbachev had spent much of his early career in the Komsomol, where the primary focus was on changing people's behavior through exhortation, he tried the same approach to the economy. He assumed that if people worked harder and better there would be no need for structural reform. In 1986, he introduced a work hard campaign, and red banners with the slogan "Intensity '86" flew from the gates of every factory.

In the same year he began a campaign against alcoholism. Gorbachev assumed that a reduction in alcoholism would translate into a surge of productivity. Since the government had a monopoly on the legal production of alcohol, it was easy for it to manipulate supply, variety, and price. However, the alcohol monopoly was a major source of income for the government, estimated at up to one-third of the value of the entire consumer goods trade. By cutting the supply of alcohol, Gorbachev reduced government income at a time when more money was needed for capital investment. When prices were raised to compensate for the reduced production, drinkers turned to *samogon* (home brew). Approximately one-third of all alcohol consumed in the Soviet Union was home brew. Limits on the hours vodka stores could be open and efforts to close them on payday had little effect. Campaigns against public drunkenness sent thousands to work and rehabilitation camps but had no long-term impact. Gorbachev urged abstinence, though he did not call for prohibition. Gorbachev's campaign against alcoholism had no impact on hard-core drinking and alienated Soviet citizens for whom drinking was both a social and psychological necessity. Labor productivity did not increase.

Structural Reform. When propaganda did not lead to improved productivity, Gorbachev turned to structural reform, especially since the economy had moved into recession by 1988. Three major decrees were issued: the *Law on State Enterprise;* the *Law on Private Enterprise,* and the *Law on Quality Assurance.* The Law on State Enterprise sought to impose upon individual firms some degree of accountability. Individual enterprises were responsible for securing a small portion of their own raw materials and for marketing a small percentage of finished goods. The reformers assumed that factories would produce higher-quality goods if they were no longer assured of a market for everything they produced. However, in an economy of shortage, even badly produced products would sell. Scrounging that involved bribing producers was already an integral part of the Soviet supply system so the Law on State Enterprise merely legalized informal procedures that already existed. Finally, factory managers continued to obey ministerial bureaucracies, which ignored the law. In the short run this structural change had little impact.

The Law on Private Enterprise authorized small-scale private production and service activities. Private restaurants, taxi service, repair shops, and fruit and vegetable stands could operate but only if permitted to do so by local governments. Local authorities made it very difficult for private enterprises to operate legally. As a result *mafia* activity emerged.

The Law on Quality Assurance had propaganda value, promoting the importance of quality. In practice it did little to foster improved quality of industrial production. The law focused on inspection as the key to quality control. Factories could be punished for producing too many shoddy products, but they were able to sabotage the law. Inspection was, of course, the most primitive form of quality control. Little was done to organize production so as to minimize human error.

Though Gorbachev emphasized the importance of high tech and introduced a few pilot projects tying pure research to technological application, he rejected the idea of importing high tech equipment from abroad.

Market Economy. Gorbachev's efforts to improve the Stalinist economic system failed, forcing him to accept the idea of a market economy in 1990. Before the changes could be implemented, Gorbachev and the Communist Party fell from power, leaving it to his successors to try to figure out how to introduce a market economy where bureaucratic centralized decision-making was so deeply entrenched.

Agriculture. Agriculture was in even graver difficulty than the industrial economy. Geography continued to limit agricultural productivity. Some 50,000 state and collective farms covered the rural landscape. Mostly unproductive, these farms suffered from an aging workforce and decades of inadequate investment. Increased investment in the Khrushchev and Brezhnev eras had come too late to create modern farming. Labor productivity was low, while storage facilities and transportation were hopelessly inadequate.

As party chief in a major grain producing area and for a short time responsible for agriculture for the country as a whole, Gorbachev had developed great confidence in his ability to solve the farm crisis. He achieved little, however. Initially he decreed a program of mega-centralization, putting all agricultural decision-making in the hands of a Minister of State Agricultural Industry. Along with this, Gorbachev provided substantial increases in subsidies for meat and dairy production. Farm output did not increase, but public demand for improved diet forced the government to import food from abroad.

In 1988, Gorbachev turned to ideas implemented during NEP and others suggested in the early Brezhnev era. He proposed a system similar to the *link* idea first suggested in the early Brezhnev period. Land would be leased to small groups of farmers for a 50-year period. The state would retain ownership but peasants would treat the land as their private property and would thus work more productively. Gorbachev also reintroduced ideas from the NEP, including compulsory delivery of specific amounts of grain, with farmers permitted to sell the surplus on the open market. In addition, inefficient collective farms would be denied a state bail out and permitted to go bankrupt. Once this happened, the farm's land would be leased to farmers. The Ministry of State Agricultural Industry was abolished, too. These ideas were stillborn. Both the agricultural bureaucracies and the peasant farmers were deeply conservative, incapable of change.

Conclusion. Gorbachev failed to transform the socialist economy into a globally competitive one. Reform attempts created confusion in the economy and contributed to economic depression that began in 1988 and continued to the twenty-first century.

5. Family Crisis Continues

The crisis in the family worsened under Gorbachev and the position of women declined.

The energy that the Gorbachev leadership put into political, ideological, and economic reform movements left little energy for dealing with social issues, including the family crisis and the position of women. Single-parent families and overburdened mothers remained a problem. The economic position of older women worsened, both on the collective farms and in the cities. Women focused their energies on economic survival and played no significant role in the reform activities.

6. Community, Diversity, and the Collapse of Communism

Though Gorbachev came to understand that the Soviet Union was disintegrating, he failed to recognize that his power and that of the Communist Party was collapsing as well. Ironically, his efforts to create an alternative structure intended to keep the Soviet Union together produced the failed attempt to drive him from power in August 1989. The ineptness of the secret police-military *coup d'etat* illustrated how weak the system had become, while it deeply wounded Gorbachev. Immediately and publicly criticized by Boris *Yeltsin,* President of the Russian Republic and disgruntled former ally, Gorbachev hung on to power for another year and a half, then quietly slipped into the winter darkness. The collapse of the Soviet Union, the Communist party, and Gorbachev's power were interrelated.

Diversity. The Soviet Union became increasingly diverse during the Gorbachev era. The reemergence of non-Russian nationalism had a profound effect. Glasnost, the new de-Stalinization, and decentralized economic decision-making all promoted nationalism. The idea of Soviet Man collapsed. No longer did people believe in a common culture, in which the advance of socialism would eliminate all cultural and ethnic differences, leaving a single Russian culture in place. The rise of nationalism produced national liberation movements in the Baltic states and the Caucasus and to a lesser extent in Ukraine, Belorussia, and Muslim Central Asia. Ethnic conflict also arose from increased nationalism and reduced the ability of the central government to maintain control. The conflict between Azerbaijan and Armenia was merely the most violent example of inter-ethnic conflict, which the government was generally powerless to contain.

The collapse of support for a single national agenda also reduced unity. From the time of Stalin this national agenda had emphasized modernization, security, and empire. Economic policy produced neither modernization nor national security and the Soviet Union began to lose control over its empire. Revolt in Poland and defeat in Afghanistan weakened the Soviet Union's ability to project its power globally. The economy was neither modern enough nor productive enough to generate sufficient wealth to enable the Soviet Union to remain a great power. Many doubted the value of empire, and others worried how the Soviet Union could maintain its national security when it could no longer compete with the United States in the arms race. Others were concerned about the consequences of modernization in terms of impoverishment of the population and environmental degradation. Still others concluded that the Stalinist strategy of modernization was no longer workable. The retreat into the family and individual interests that had begun with the decline of enthusiasm for Communism in the 1960s left many unwilling to support any national agenda.

Community. Diversity had cracked the Soviet Union so deeply that no effective basis for community remained. Threat and fear no longer could be employed and when they were, as in Lithuania and Latvia, they were quickly withdrawn. A single bureaucratic set of rules began to disintegrate with economic reform and efforts to restructure the legal system. As the Communist Party weakened and its power dissipated through democratization, its efforts to ensure unity had less success. Propaganda that still outlined the Stalinist vision of Communism fell harmlessly to the ground. Gorbachev found no replacement for the elements of community associated with Communism.

Increasingly, the republics of the Soviet Union established their own policies, ignored the laws of the Soviet Union, and refused to send tax revenues to the center. Having failed to approve autonomy in 1988, Gorbachev now worked for the creation of an alternative structure—the Commonwealth of Independent States—intended to prevent the disintegration of the Soviet Union, while leaving him and the Russians in power. Delayed by the unsuccessful attempt to remove Gorbachev from power, it was established too late to keep the Soviet Union together. When the Russian Federation withdrew from the Soviet Union in 1991 (it was one of the last republics to withdraw), the Soviet Union disappeared. The momentous events of 1991 created opportunities for a new Russia, a Russia very different from the dominant player in the Soviet Union.

I. QUEST FOR A NEW RUSSIA, 1991–PRESENT

Over seventy years of Communist rule and Soviet power disappeared very quickly, attesting to their weakened condition. What would a new Russia be like? No one knew and everyone feared the future. The post-Communist period can be divided into a chaotic-democratic era (to 2000) and a return to authoritarian rule since then. Nostalgia for empire continued to motivate Russian policy toward the West and toward the former Soviet states, commonly called the *Near Abroad.* Authoritarian democracy, introduced in the Gorbachev period, continued. In the 1990s, however, the basic political conflict was between a reforming executive branch and a legislature opposed to it. By 1993, the administrative branch had triumphed over the legislature, making reform more likely. As Russia sought identity and purpose, many of its citizens felt lost. Until the year 2000 economic decline continued, as Russia sought to transform bureaucratized communism into a market economy. Thereafter the economy grew, fueled by sharp increases in global prices for oil, gas, and metals. The family crisis worsened and women bore the brunt of economic and political transformation. No strong sense of community emerged to overcome diversity. Russia continued to undergo a slow, very painful transition away from Stalinism and toward democracy and a market economy. Will Russia return to a Stalinist system? The answer is unclear.

1. What Is Russia? What Is a Russian?

The collapse of Communism and the disintegration of the Soviet Union created a political and psychological dilemma for the Russian people. On the one hand, they faced the issue of whether to accept the existence of small Russia or seek to restore Russian control over the former Soviet states. At the same time, the Russians had to figure out how to move from feelings of worthlessness to a sense of pride in being Russian. Both dilemmas were interrelated and answers to one might resolve the other. Russia focused its foreign policy goals on the main powers—the United States, China and the European Community—seeking to prevent American global domination. In addition, Russia attempted to increase its influence in the Near Abroad.

The Search for a New Sense of Nation. It is hard to imagine the depth of the morale problem Russians faced in the early 1990s. Economic reform produced a lower living standard. Russians could no longer lord it over other people of the Soviet Union. Russia lost its stature as one of the two world powers and became a secondary player internationally. Many Russians felt betrayed. They had worked hard and suffered greatly for Communism, based on the hope that they were building a better future. Now that better future seemed so distant as to be unattainable. Various strategies were developed to deal with the resultant psychological malaise and sense of powerlessness.

Some argued that the nation should accept the new reality and focus its energies on domestic problems. Others displayed nostalgia for empire. This nostalgia for empire arose from a need to demonstrate worth through power over others, especially Russia's neighbors.

Russia and the Big Powers: New Thinking Transformed. Russian foreign policy toward the most important power blocs was characterized first by the "Primakov Doctrine," applied by Yeltsin in the 1990s, and the "Ivanov Doctrine," introduced by Vladimir Putin and still in force. In the 1990s Russia sought economic ties with the Western nations, primarily seeking economic assistance. Russia supported the First Gulf War, directed against its ally, Iraq, and did little to exert Russian influence in the Balkans as Yugoslavia broke up into independent nations. The Russian government received much criticism for its "powerlessness."

Believing that cooperation with the West had weakened Russian national security, Putin turned to confrontation, beginning in 2003. Putin and his allies sought to project Russian power abroad, or at least pretend it had much international influence. Putin focused energies on confronting and combating the "*hegemon*"—American global power. This approach led Putin to two more specific strategies. One strategy was to try to build up an anti-American coalition with China and to create an anti-American grouping at the United Nations. China and Russia moved closer together. Common concerns, including proliferation of international drug traffic, immigration, and the American presence in Central Asia associated with the American conflict with al-Qaeda and the Taliban in Afghanistan. The two countries joined Central Asian states in the *Shanghai Coalition.* Secondly, following the Ivanov Doctrine, Putin engaged in saber-rattling, threatening the Americans, condemning American influence in the Near Abroad and American plans to put missile systems into Eastern Europe. The war of words reached a peak in the summer of 2006, when American Vice President Cheney condemned Russian authoritarianism and Putin *caustically* commented on Cheney's "shooting prowess." Elected President in 2008 Dmitry Medvedev has cautiously moved away from the confrontation strategy. This has been reflected in the recent US–Russian agreement on further modest restrictions in nuclear weapons stockpiles.

Russia and the Near Abroad. Little able to influence global events, even in the Middle East and the Balkans, where Soviet influence had been extensive, Russia tried to project its power over the former republics of the Soviet Union—the Near Abroad. Recognizing that the Baltic states were adamantly opposed to a Russian takeover and of limited value as well, the Russians focused their energies on the other Slavic states, the Caucasus and Central Asia. In the Near Abroad Russia has opposed "color revolutions," democratization and human rights. Ukraine and Kazakhstan were the most important former republics. Both were relatively wealthy and contained sizeable Russian minorities. The Russians applied a long-term strategy of economic reintegration toward these two states and Belorussia. Belorussia moved close to Russia but the other two states maintained their independence. The Russians even accepted the idea that the Crimean Peninsula, whose population was mainly Russian, remain part of Ukraine and the two nations amicably settled their dispute over who should own the rusting Black Sea Fleet. Russian efforts to influence the formation of a pro-Russian government in Ukraine failed, leading to the "Orange Revolution" (2004–2005) and a pro-western independent Ukraine.

Russia used force to increase its influence in the Caucasus and the eastern parts of Central Asia. The situation in Georgia is illustrative of Russian strategies. The Russians also intervened in Georgian politics and tried to prevent *Edvard Shevarnadze,* formerly a close ally of Gorbachev, from becoming head of the Georgian state. In 2008 Russia supported the *Abkhazians,* a minority that rebelled against the Georgians. Russia provided military equipment and even air support for the Abkhazians. In more remote areas such as *Tadzikistan,* the Russians sent in troops, in theory to put down rebellion against the Tadzik government. The presence of Russian troops enabled Russia to influence domestic policies in various states and to prevent the Muslim nations of Central Asia from aligning with Muslim states elsewhere. The Russians also intervened militarily in the dispute between Azerbaijan and Armenia, largely to ensure access to oil deposits. Russia's efforts in the Near Abroad gave her some leverage but did not lead to the reincorporation of lost territories into a New Russian Empire.

Regionalism and the Quest for Autonomy. Political decentralization appeared in Russia. Russia contained 83 political sub-units, many of them dominated by non-Russians. Some political sub-units, such as *Sakha* in Siberia and *Nizhnii Novgorod* along the Volga, sought a large measure of autonomy in order to maximize their own economic opportunities. Others sought ethnic autonomy. Such was the case for *Chechnya* and *Bashkortostan* (home of the Bashkirs). War broke out in Chechnya, when Yeltsin sent in troops to crush an uprising. Brutal guerilla warfare continued for two years (1994–1996) before the Russians withdrew. To permit Chechnya to be independent might have produced a domino effect and the breakup of Russia, with only the Muscovite core remaining intact. A bloody second Chechen-Russian War, initiated by Putin, lasted until about 2005, though unrest continued after that. When rebellion broke out in nearby Dagestan in 1999, the Russians bombarded Chechnya, accusing it of providing a safe haven for the rebels.

Most of the political sub-units that had inched toward independence by passing their own laws, failing to remit tax moneys to Moscow, and operating their own foreign trade withdrew from the brink in the fall of 1993 after Yeltsin used military force in his attempt to crush Parliament. Russia was weakened by the political sub-units' drive for autonomy. Yeltsin lacked the power, and the good health, to reestablish firm centralized control over the provinces and other sub-units. In the Putin era, the regions abandoned their drives for autonomy after Putin dismissed all elected governors and replaced them with men loyal to him.

2. Authoritarian Democracy

Russia had an authoritarian form of democracy. Many preferred a return to strong leadership, ala Stalin, seeing no contradiction between democracy and authoritarianism. Yeltsin continued to use the democratic system to maintain himself in power. Two key political developments characterized Yeltsin's Russia—the conflict between the presidency and the parliament and the weakening of the presidency because of Yeltsin's ill health. Under Putin (1999–2008) authoritarian, one-man rule returned, continuing after he formally completed his second term, after which he continued to exercise great authority.

President vs. Parliament, 1991–1999. Yeltsin and the Russian Parliament remained bitter foes throughout. Both Yeltsin and the Parliament were holdovers from the Gorbachev system. Both tried to become all-powerful and to destroy the other's influence. Though the struggle was partly over power, it was also a conflict over policy. A majority of Parliament members were former Stalinists, opposed to capitalism, democracy, and Russian weakness. The president represented the reformers, though his policies and support were inconsistent. Conflict intensified in 1993. Both sides issued conflicting decrees, especially over economic policy. For example, Yeltsin abolished the collective farms, while the Parliament reestablished them. In late summer 1993, the Parliament attempted to deprive Yeltsin of his office and he tried to close the Parliament. As the conflict escalated in the autumn, Yeltsin decided to use force, ordering the army to surround the "White House," the parliamentary building, and fire artillery shells into it until the members of Parliament surrendered. Yeltsin pushed a weakened Parliament to permit his own people to draw up a new constitution. Though the new constitution, approved in

December 1993, was intended to consolidate Yeltsin's power, anti-reformers retained control of the Parliament and were frequently able to block Yeltsin's reform moves. The gridlock in the Russian political system was again demonstrated in the 1996 elections. Yeltsin was elected president, using a pro-Yeltsin political party, United Russia, while anti-reformers won a large majority in the Parliament. The main opposition parties were the Communists (one-third of the presidential vote), the semi-fascist Liberal Democratic Party, and the very small democratic parties, which retained some influence over Yeltsin.

Putin Presidency (1999–2008) and Beyond. Putin gradually consolidated his power during his first term and easily won re-election in 2004. Putin created a one-man authoritarian rule, with the trappings of democracy through elections and the existence of other branches of government, the legislature, and the judiciary. The *siloviki* (strong ones) formed his power base, centered in the secret police and the military. Most of his key officials came from the secret police, as he had, too. Putin ensured that the loyalist political party, United Russia, had a solid Parliamentary majority. Increasingly, Putin ruled by decree, ignoring the legislature. Until his second term, Putin faced intermittent opposition from the Constitutional Court (the supreme court), which found over 200 of his laws and decrees unconstitutional. During the second term the constitutional court ceased to oppose him. Putin also moved to halt the efforts of the regions to go their own way. In an arbitrary fashion, Putin dismissed all 80 plus governors, replacing them with his appointed loyalists. Federalism thus disappeared. Finally, limited to two terms as president by the Russian constitution, Putin stepped aside but did not relinquish power, instead running things as Prime Minister. His successor, Medvedev, has generally followed the Putin line, though he has promised to introduce measures to improve living conditions for the Russian people.

3. Loss of Identity and Lack of Unity

No single set of ideas prevailed in Russia after the collapse of Communism. Some still retained their faith in the ideology of Stalinism. A small minority championed democratic ideals. Most espoused authoritarianism and cautiously supported capitalism. Nearly everyone saw nationalism as a potentially unifying ideological force.

Nationalism. The break-up of the Soviet Union shattered Russian unity as well. A number of different varieties of Russian nationalism emerged. In common was their search for a new kind of Russian nationalism appropriate to changed conditions and their desire to provide the basis for a powerful Russia and a strong sense of national identity and optimism about Russia and the Russians.

However, it was not clear what this nationalism should be like. Most people seemed to have lost their ideological bearings and supported one of many variants of nationalism. *Imperialist nationalism* garnered a great deal of support, especially because of their opposition to American power. The imperialist nationalists argued that Russians would gain respect and a sense of self-worth by recovering lost territories and by exerting as much influence abroad as possible. Their ultimate goal was reestablishment of a Russian

Empire that would include all of the former Soviet republics, except the Baltic states. The imperialist nationalists espoused anti-Semitism and a general hatred of minorities.

A second group can be called the *identity* or *cultural nationalists.* Mainly from the educated elite, these individuals focused primarily on the nature of Russian identity in a post-Soviet Russia. Some attention was given to the relationship between the Russians and the non-Russians in Russia. The quest for identity seemed an end in itself, rather than a first step toward action. Some, however, have argued that it is time to halt the endless discussion of identity and, instead, act.

Democratic nationalists represent a third and less important group of Russian nationalists. This group clearly overlapped with the identity nationalists. The democratic nationalists had little interest in Russian power and its projection beyond the country's borders. They also displayed little interest in the multi-cultural nature of Russia. Their focus was on redefining Russia as a capitalist democracy. By accepting the reality of "small" Russia, the Russians would be able to successfully complete the transition to democracy and capitalism, they argued unsuccessfully. "Democracy in one country" paralleled Stalin's "socialism in one country" idea. The lack of ideological unity and the difficulty of creating common values and beliefs had an impact on efforts to create a market economy.

Eurasianism. *Eurasianism* has been increasingly influential in the Putin era. Reminiscent of the debate between the Slavophiles and the Westernizers in the first half of the nineteenth century, Eurasianists have asked whether Russia is part of Europe or part of Asia. Some argue that Russia is part of Asia and that Russian power depends on Russia's ability to dominate the Eurasian land mass. Others see Asia as a threat. That threat comes from Islamic terrorism, an expansion of the drug trade, and the challenge of Chinese illegal immigration into the Russian Far East. In general, Eurasianists champion the increased projection of Russian power globally, but especially in Asia.

Glasnost. Building on the practices of the Gorbachev period, Yeltsin continued to support glasnost, though he sought to manipulate the media to support his electoral campaigns and his policy positions. Putin, on the other hand, achieved almost total control over the media and saw little value in the critical approach central to glasnost. The Putin administration eliminated freedom of the press. The government acquired ownership of all television networks, taking them from oligarchs. Especially during political campaigns the media has provided Putin with a constant barrage of positive press. Under Putin, nostalgia for the past replaced criticism. Those elements of the past that are strongly praised are strong government, order, and stability.

4. Russian Capitalism

Russia moved toward a market economy with great difficulty. Major changes have been introduced, though initially the creation of a market economy failed to halt Russia's economic decline. The Russian economy remained in transition—moving away from the Stalinist command economy toward capitalism. Some segments of the economy made the transition; others still operated under Stalinist rules. In spite of (some would say because of) the transition to capitalism, the Russian economy functioned poorly and produced little economic expansion until the twenty-first century. Under Yeltsin the GDP (total value of goods and services produced) declined by 40 percent. Significant economic growth in this century has resulted from increases in global prices for the raw materials Russia exports.

Mixed System or Mixed-up System? The Russian economy retains parts of the old Stalinist structure as well as capitalist elements. Centralized planning still exists for the state sector. Much privatization took place but further action stalled more recently. Much of the service sector has been privatized, in part through the start up of new firms, stores, and shops. Most industry has been privatized, but the most inefficient sectors still remain in state hands. Initially Russian citizens received vouchers with which to purchase stock in various enterprises. However, management, with the collusion of the workforce, privatized many enterprises. Workers were offered job security in exchange for the formal transference of factory ownership to management. Consolidation of privatized industry soon followed, with a few firms dominating entire industries. A kind of monopoly capitalism, earlier attacked vehemently by Lenin, emerged. Money-losing factories remained in government hands, soaking up subsidies in order to survive. In the early Yeltsin years, when opponents of economic reform controlled the State Bank, it printed money so the state could pay the bills of unproductive companies.

Under Putin the economy has been renationalized, with allies of Putin responsible for supervising nationalized firms. In theory, "profits" are to be used by the government to address social welfare needs.

The service sector has been largely privatized, a process begun under Gorbachev in the 1980s. The state distribution system continued in shambles, yet attempts to plan distribution of raw materials, components, and finished products for the state sector continued.

Centralized price setting disappeared, with the market now determining prices. In the 1990s high inflation resulted from the shift to market setting of prices. The absence of increased productivity contributed to the rise in inflation. In the early Yeltsin period inflation was as high as 100 percent per year, dropping to 20–50 percent. Under Putin inflation remained over 10 percent.

Capital is now generated from a variety of sources. Previously capital was accumulated through low wages, low prices for agricultural goods, and a national turnover (sales) tax. The Russian stock market produces small amounts of money. In the 1990s much more money came in through foreign loans, including money from the World Bank, the International Monetary Fund, and foreign investment. Russia's huge budget deficit directed money into interest payments, reducing the amount of funds that might be available for investment. By August 1998, the state's inability to pay off its loans created a severe financial crisis that further weakened the Russian economy. Recovery began by the end of the century. Under Putin most investment money poured into the energy and metals sector.

In the twenty-first century, oil and natural gas profits in renationalized firms flowed into the central coffers. Little of this money became available for investment; instead it has been used to create millionaires among Putin loyalists. Two-thirds of Russia's economic growth comes from oil and gas profits.

Motivation of the labor force had been central to the Stalinist system. No new system of motivation has been successfully implemented. Appeals to working for the future would be unsuccessful. A patriotic appeal has not been tried. Unsure of receiving wages on time or at all, until recently workers had no incentive to increase production or productivity.

Agriculture. Yeltsin found it very difficult to secure support for the elimination of collectivization. Finally in 1996 Yeltsin issued a decree abolishing collectivization. Nothing changed quickly. Eventually a few collective farms passed into private hands, generally when collective farm managements assumed ownership. Seldom were collective farms divided up into small farms owned by individual families. De-collectivization, however, produced neither increased yields nor increased productivity. Ninety percent of Russia's grain is still produced by state or collective farms, 10 percent by private farms.

Continuing Economic Crisis. Some saw capitalism as a panacea that would magically transform Russia into a modern, wealthy society. Efforts to introduce a market economy, attempts to sabotage this, as well as the continued presence of a substantial segment of the Stalinist economy, all contributed to economic decline. The more the economy declined, the less capital was available for investment that might produce economic growth. Quality, efficiency, and productivity were still neglected, except in the service sector. Rust-belt industrial plants continued to build up heavy losses. Money used to bail them out could not be used for investment in modernizing sectors of the economy. The economy could not produce sufficient amounts of necessary consumer goods. It was impossible to quickly restructure an economy that had overemphasized heavy industry. The national GDP continued to decline until 2000.

Economic Recovery. The 1990s were characterized by substantial economic decline (a serious recession). From 1999, economic recovery has been taking place, reaching a 7 percent growth rate in 2005 and continuing at a rate of 7–8 percent until the 2007–2009 global economic crisis. Now the growth rate has slowed to 4–5 percent. Inflation has declined, though it remains relatively high.

Social Conditions and Social Problems. Overall living standards continued to decline. High inflation was especially damaging to those on fixed incomes. Unemployment and underemployment, as well as unproductive employment, continued. Capitalism moved forward at a glacial rate, while the economy declined more quickly. In spite of increasing inequality and the widening gap between the "millionaires" and ordinary people, Russians grumbled but did not rebel.

Russians face very serious social welfare and health problems. Russian population continues to decline, due in part to a very low birth rate but primarily a response to health problems. The country's population declined by 3 percent between 1992 and 2003 and continues to go down. Life expectancy in Russia is the lowest of all industrialized countries. For men, life expectancy is less than 60, for women only 65. Russia has extremely high rates of alcoholism, *cardiovascular disease,* HIV-AIDS, and fatalities due to road accidents.

Inequality. Increasing inequality has characterized Russian society, widening sharply under Putin. The 100 richest persons in Russia, known as *oligarchs,* possess 25 percent of the national wealth. At the other end, 20 percent of the population remains in poverty, with the elderly and children most at risk to live in poverty.

5. Family and Gender in Crisis

"New Russia" has witnessed the deepening of the family crisis, the return of patriarchy, and a worsening of the position of women.

The birth rate continued to decline, while the number of single parent families grew. Family violence increased, especially during the period of decline in living standards, despair over the collapse of certainties, and increasing lawlessness in society. The family may have also acted as a haven and life-support system in those difficult times. It is clear, however, that overall the position of women declined. The unemployment rate was much higher among women than men, as women were the first to lose their jobs during the economic decline. In addition, women were the main component of the pensioner class. Pensions fell far behind the inflation rate, so real income of the elderly declined. Recent increases in pension levels have produced little improvement in living standards. Much of the rural work force was composed of women, especially elderly women. These women worked extremely hard for meager wages and survived through work on private plots, raising chickens, and berry and mushroom picking. Democracy and capitalism brought few benefits to women and did little to strengthen the family.

6. Community and Diversity

What held Russia together in these very trying times? Inertia and the lack of external enemies, along with a vague, continued belief in the recovery of Russia and Russian cultural loyalty appear to be the main forces keeping Russia united.

Absence of Unity. Certainly centralization found few supporters outside the Moscow region and Putin's recentralization actions have not brought the regions together. Russian nationalism provided insufficient common ground. No cause or future agenda brought people together. The economy was mixed, and society suffered more and more fissures. The rural population has become more and more distinct from the Westernized urban residents. (See Chapter Four for the parallel experience in China's modernization program.) True, all Russians had experienced a common fate—the collapse of their knowns and their replacement with unknowns. How long could the similarity of experience bind the Russians together?

Russians Abroad and Ethnic Minorities. When the Soviet Union collapsed, many Russians found themselves outside of Russia, citizens of other countries, such as Latvia or Kazakhstan. Once part of the elite—as Russians—they became minorities overnight. The Russians lost their privileged status and frequently faced discrimination, both social and legal. In general Russians were expected to learn the majority language to attain citizenship. Under these circumstances, initially many Russians returned to Russia. However, others were stuck in their new countries, where they had homes, jobs, and social ties. Most of the Russians living abroad no longer are returning to Russia and have now come to see themselves as citizens of the countries in which they live. Russians, thus, have become Latvians and Kazakhs.

At the same time, Russia remains a multi-ethnic state. Some 20 percent of the population of Russia is non-Russia, with Muslims the predominant minority. Russians display much animosity toward the Muslims. September 11th and the wars with Chechnya have provoked and justified Russian prejudice against Muslims.

CONCLUSION

Modern Russian history is filled with brilliant achievements and tragic failings.

From Muscovy to the present, Russian rulers have tried to build and maintain an empire. Expansion has been a central characteristic of the country's history. From the small core of the Muscovite state, Russia expanded eastward to the Pacific Ocean and westward to Europe. Eastward expansion and settlement met only limited resistance from societies generally less well-developed than Russia. Throughout, Russian efforts to acquire European territory met strong opposition. During the nineteenth century Russia gained control over important parts of Eastern Europe and exercised informal rule over all of Eastern Europe from the late part of the Second World War to the fall of Communism around 1990. Empire building was costly, straining Russia's financial and administrative resources. Imperialism created serious diversity problems and made community building extremely difficult.

Russian governments have been authoritarian, even since the fall of Communism. Princes, later emperors, and now presidents have sought to gather all political power into their own hands. The vast size of Russia and the seriousness of the problems it generally faced made it impossible for rulers to be all-powerful. They were thus forced to create structures of administration intended to guarantee that their will would be implemented. Efforts at centralization generally failed before the twentieth century. Instead, rulers were forced to accept some degree of administrative de-centralization to have hopes of effective rule. Once the Communists came to power, they created a gigantic bureaucracy, which in the 1930s gave them effective control over the country and made centralization of all authority a practical reality. Though possession of power was an end in itself for many rulers, authorities also believed that the initiative for change should come from the center. Emperors thus were reformers, sometimes promoting administrative changes that would enhance their power but also carrying out revolutionary social and economic reform programs. Emancipation of the serfs and associated reforms, the Stolypin reforms of the twentieth century that sought to establish private farming, and the radical Stalinist changes of the 1930s attest to the self-confidence of rulers and their belief that they could radically change the country without difficulty and with great support. Stalin's Communist successors also had faith in their ability to change the country, to establish a better form of Communism. With the collapse of the Soviet Union, Russia continued on the path of radical reform—toward capitalism and democracy. The pace of change has now slowed.

Parallel to this emphasis on the monopoly of political power by the supreme ruler, Russians tried to establish ideological unity. For much of the country's history, Russian Orthodoxy gave Russians a universal belief system. Not only did Orthodoxy provide a required set of beliefs, it also emphasized that those beliefs should not be changed. The Russian Orthodox Church could not prevent the appearance of alternative ideas. Other kinds of ideas came from the West, in the seventeenth century through Ukraine and Poland and later more directly. Though Peter the Great emphasized the value of Western ideas and downgraded the role of Russian Orthodoxy, Orthodoxy remained dominant into the nineteenth century. In the nineteenth century, Western ideas battled with domestic revisions of Orthodoxy, including Slavophilism and Pan-Slavism. Western ideas, in the form of Marxism, triumphed through the Revolutions of 1917 and from that point on until the fall of Communism, a new ideological unity emerged—that of Communism. From the mid-nineteenth century Russian nationalism became more and more important ideologically. With the collapse of Communism, nationalism seemed the only possible basis for ideological unity.

Economic backwardness and social inequality have been present throughout Russian history. Geography and peasant conservatism placed severe limits on agricultural productivity. Industrialization came relatively late to the Russian Empire and was not powerful enough to compensate for low levels of agricultural output. Both tsarist economic experts and the Communists sought to develop comprehensive plans for economic development. Stalin based economic development on centralized planning and administration, giving priority to heavy industry and investing huge amounts of capital labor and material. The Russian economy remained relatively unproductive, in spite of planned commitment to economic growth. Post-Communist capitalism brought only modest improvements in economic performance.

Social inequality resulted from economic factors, government policy and the desire of the elite to maintain a dominant political, social, and economic position. Even under the Communists inequality was not eliminated but fostered by the power of the Communist Party and its desire to provide privileges for its leaders and members. The elite had its special position confirmed by government decrees under the tsars and informally under the Communists. Governments also took actions that created a badly treated lower class. Both the legalization of serfdom and the collectivization of agriculture had a devastating impact on the lives of the peasants. In spite of government definitions of social structure that would appear to establish a frozen social structure, considerable social mobility took place.

Patriarchy dominated family structure and dynamics. In the pre-Communist era patriarchy was reinforced by Russian Orthodoxy and by state law. Briefly under Communist rule women acquire some degree of independence and power, at least in their private lives. Both war and revolution gave women opportunities for independence and personal power, which were confirmed by government policy. Recognition of the burdens facing women did not eliminate them. Women were economically active, primarily as peasants and workers under the tsars and as white-collar workers, collective farmers and low-level administrators and professionals under the Communists. Women never played a significant political role. Brief improvements for women under Khrushchev, especially through educational and employment opportunities, faltered under the double burdens of work and family in the 1970s and 1980s and under the pressures of radical economic change associated with the introduction of capitalism.

Community-building attempted to overcome the diversity created by imperialism. However, the strategies used generally backfired, promoting difference instead of the desired community. Before the revolutions of 1917, the government sought to create community based on conformity to Russian beliefs and culture. This alienated the non-Russians whose numbers reached over half of the population by 1900. Authorities made no real efforts to recognize diversity, except for intermittent actions that permitted native cultures to exist unchallenged by the Russians. The government tried explicit and comprehensive strategies of Russification in the late nineteenth century but they met little success. The Communists saw loyalty to socialism as the main basis for unity and championed the idea of "Soviet man." Gradually all sense of ethnic identity would disappear, replaced by loyalty to socialism. However, Soviet man came to be viewed as "Russian man" and Russian language and culture became the pattern all Soviet citizens were to emulate. Minority nationalism remained of little importance until the last years of Communism. Since then ethnic nationalism has surfaced as a threat, first to Soviet unity and temporarily to the unity of the Russian Federation.

Name: ______________________________ **Date:** ____________________

Chapter One: Russia

IDENTIFICATION: IMPORTANT TERMS AND VOCABULARY

Allied intervention (45)

anti-Semitism (29)

asceticism (8)

authoritarian (7)

Avvakum (9)

black peasants (13)

Bloody Sunday (35)

boyars (7)

bureaucratized autocracy (17)

caustically (89)

centripetal (13)

Chaadaev (20)

Charter of the Nobility (22)

Chechens/Chechnya (15)

Cheka (45)

chistka (56)

civil society (42)

commune (32)

Communist Youth League (Komsosmol) (74)

constituent services (81)

coup d'etat (46)

Crimean War (31)

Name: ______________________________ Date: ________________

Chapter One: Russia

KEY QUESTIONS

Rude and Barbarous Kingdom, Muscovy, 1500–1700: What basic elements of Russian history emerged in the "rude and barbarous kingdom" period, 1500–1700?

Early Empire, 1700–1855: What major changes occurred in Russia in this Early Empire period?

Reform and Collapse, 1855–1914: What were the main causes of the decline and eventual collapse of the Russian Empire, 1855–1917?

Revolutionary Russia, 1900–1922: What were the main causes of revolutions in 1905 and 1917?

Cultural Revolution and Freedom, 1920s: Why was Communism not introduced into the Soviet Union immediately after the Communists came to power?

Stalinist Russia, 1929–1953: What were the main characteristics of Stalinism?

Reforming Communism, 1953–1985: Why were the post-Stalin leaders unable to successfully reform Communism?

Collapse of Communism, 1985–1991: What was '*glasnost*' and what role did it play in the collapse of Communism?

New Russia, 1991–Present: How did the Yeltsin Presidency, 1991–1999, and the Putin Presidency, 1999–2008, differ?

Chapter Two

India, Pakistan, Bangladesh

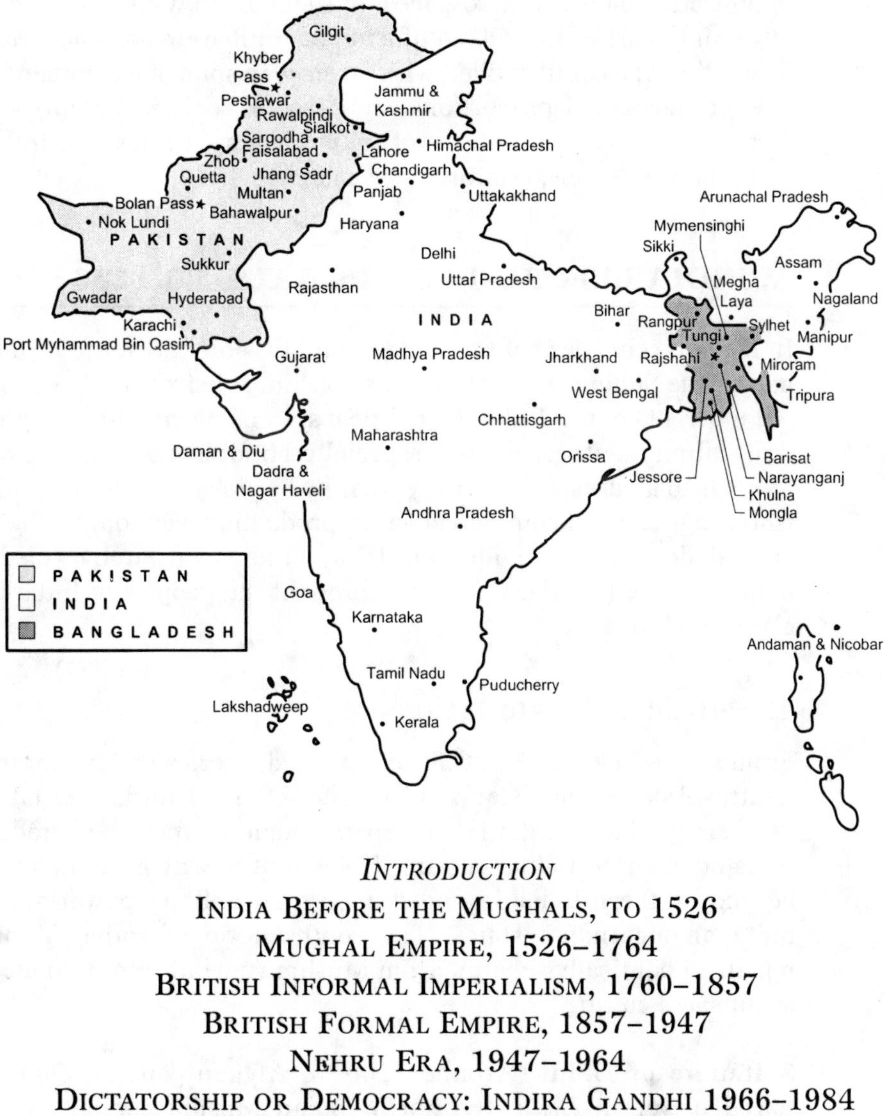

Introduction

Diversity and continuity have characterized the history of India. Geography reflects this diversity. The mountainous Himalayans slope down to northern plains traversed by broad rivers such as the *Ganges.* Further south, low mountain ranges near the coastline act as borders for a central highland, the *Deccan.* The southern triangle of *Tamilnad* has a tropical climate. Two major world religions—Hinduism and Buddhism—were created in India, one of the great civilizations of world history. Almost always lacking political unity, India was the scene of a struggle between Hindus and Muslims that lasted over 1,000 years. The history of India is also one of invasion and the assimilation of invading peoples. Only the Muslim Mughals and the British, both external forces, came close to projecting their rule across most of India. Even with Indian independence in 1947, only part of the sub-continent was united under single rule. Indian history is that of a country filled with poverty, in spite of a commercial-crafts economy of substantial proportions. In addition, social inequality—especially the *caste system*—was at the heart of Indian history. Castes also influenced family and gender relations, reinforcing patriarchy.

A. INDIA BEFORE THE MUGHALS, TO 1526

In the two centuries before the Mughal invasion, much of Northern India was part of the Sultanate of Delhi. This Muslim rule frequently extended throughout much of central India. Its political system is generally known as a centralized military state. Religions, especially Hinduism and Islam, dominated the ideological landscape. Relatively wealthy by global standards, India had a flourishing agricultural-commercial-craft production economy. The caste system created deep social divides for Hindu India. Patriarchy ruled over India's family-centered world. Geography brought the peoples of India together; little else united them.

1. Political Constellations

From about 1000 to 1500 C.E., India faced a series of Muslim invasions from Central Asia, Afghanistan, and Persia. After an initial period in which the invaders tried to maintain their separate identity, they were gradually absorbed into and changed Indian culture. The extent to which the invaders penetrated beyond northern India depended upon their military power and the degree of unity among Indian states. The southern tip of India, Tamilnad, always remained politically separate from Muslim rule but was influenced by Muslim actions and culture.

Sultanate of Delhi. Around 1200 an Afghan general, *Outb-ud-din Aybak* seized power in *Delhi,* the north Indian Muslim capital, and founded the Sultanate of Delhi. *Sultan* was the title of the supreme ruler of the Umayyad Muslim dynasty (661–750 C.E.) in the Middle East and the term was later brought into India. The Delhi sultanate gradually expanded into central and southern India. The Mongol invasion by Timur the Lame (c. 1400 C.E.) broke the power of the sultanate, which was replaced by a series of Turkish and Afghan rulers. Eventually *Babur* (1483–1530), a Turkish general brought in to provide military leadership for one of the warring Muslim principalities, conquered the other Muslim states and founded the *Mughal* dynasty (1526). The power of the Delhi Sultanate had been reduced earlier when a number of Hindu feudal monarchies in central India had slipped out of the Sultan's grasp. The most important of these Hindu monarchies were Vijayanagra, Gujarat, and Bengal.

2. Central Monarchy and Military Feudalism

The centralized monarchy of the Sultanate of Delhi and the Hindu feudal states had one common characteristic. Their rulers tried to enhance their power through military force. To achieve maximum military power, they needed to assure themselves of almost unlimited tax revenues, thus treating their populations harshly.

Centralized Monarchy. The Sultanate of Delhi was a centralized state, whose ruler claimed to be all-powerful. Obviously the monarch's control over outlying and newly conquered provinces was frequently quite weak. A military elite, initially Turkish, and later Afghan, aided the monarch. Eventually India-born Muslims comprised the civilian and military bureaucracies.

The main purpose of government was military and territorial expansion. Rulers devoted a great deal of attention to the tax system, which applied differential burdens to Muslims and non-Muslims. In the early fourteenth century *Ala-ud-din Khalji* and *Muhammad Tughluq,* the sultans most interested in economic policy, introduced basic changes in the tax system. Ala-ud-din raised the tax to 50 percent of the harvest and added taxes on milk cows and dwellings. Muhammad abolished the poll tax (a tax on individuals) on non-Muslims, though he required them to pay the *zakat* (alms gift). At the same time, he taxed upper class Hindus, the *Brahmans,* who had been previously exempt. Organized for military expansion, the Sultans paid less attention to other issues facing India.

Military Feudalism. The Hindu states were decentralized, feudal structures. *Feudalism* is a term generally applied to medieval Western Europe and describes a system of political decentralization and local economic self-sufficiency. It is organized around the *manor* (landed estate) that a *vassal* (subordinate) held as long as he performed military duty for and remained loyal to the *lord.* In India, the rulers (*maharajas*) granted tax-free land to their warriors (*samanta*). In turn the warriors agreed to maintain an armed force ready to participate in the ruler's military actions, to send the ruler a portion of the taxes they collected, and to offer their daughters in marriage to the maharaja. Frequently the rulers made grants of land to Brahmans, recognizing their role as the elite caste. Warfare was common among the Hindu states and acted as a divisive force, though not nearly as much as the animosity between Hindus and Muslims.

3. Hinduism and Islam

India was dominated by two great religions—Hinduism developed within India and Islam was brought in by merchants and invading armies. Islam dominated in northern India and Hinduism in the south, with central India a battleground between the two religions. Discrimination against Hindus was common in areas under Muslim control. The most common form of discrimination was economic—the differential tax system. Both religions had deeply felt support. They were both changing, as well.

Hinduism. Hinduism evolved into a religion of personal devotion to regional or local deities. *Vishnu* became the most powerful god, the savior of mankind, who protected believers against demons intent upon destroying Hindu belief. Vishnu manifested himself in a variety of forms but most importantly as *Krishna. Shiva* was the other central Hindu deity.

Otherworldly in direction, Hinduism emphasized the concept of *dharma*—the responsibility to act properly. By fulfilling your obligations to caste, gender, and political ruler, you reached a higher status in your next life (or *reincarnation*). By continuing to fulfill your destiny, you eventually reached *nirvana* (salvation), escape from the endless cycle of birth, death, and rebirth and dharma obligation. Proper behavior thus was the key to salvation.

These common beliefs encouraged political obedience and acceptance of inequality and poverty. Hinduism thus helped promote and maintain a strong conservative quality to Indian life. Art and architecture, science, and mathematics also flourished under the influence of Hindu religious ideas. Hindus believed that theirs was the only true religion and justified the use of force to convert others. Islam had a similar perspective.

Islam. Founded in seventh century Arabia, Islam expanded along the shores of the Mediterranean Sea then spread eastward through Persia to Afghanistan and Central Asia. Shortly after 700 C.E., the Muslim Persians sent a military expedition into India. Beginning about 900 C.E., Muslim tribes from Afghanistan invaded and conquered northern India.

Islam was a *monotheistic* religion, much simpler than Hinduism. Islam was action-oriented. A Muslim surrendered to Allah's (God's) will. All Muslims were members of the community, or brotherhood (*umma*), of believers. Muslims had to affirm their monotheism and *Muhammad*'s role as prophet, give alms to the poor, pray five times a day facing the holy city *Mecca,* fast during the lunar month of *Ramadan,* and make at least one pilgrimage to Mecca. In addition, Muslims believed they had a responsibility to conduct a holy war of conversion (*jihad*) against non-believers. The *Qu'ran* (the Holy Scriptures of Islam) and subsequent Islamic law (*shar'ia*), tradition (*hadith*), and commentary outlined detailed behavior for all Muslims. Islam emphasized the distinction between itself and other religious communities, applying different laws to Muslims and to non-Muslims.

4. Caste in an Agrarian-Commercial Society

Centered in North India, Islam emphasized the equality of all believers, while the caste system applied primarily to the rest of the country. Caste, based on and reinforcing inequality, operated in an agrarian-commercial realm.

Caste. Caste had emerged before 1000 B.C.E., perhaps as a means by which the invading *Aryans* maintained a distinct culture as they expanded throughout India. Originally the system had racial implications, for the term first used for caste was *varna* (color) and seemed to distinguish the light-skinned Aryans from the dark-skinned Tamils of southern India. Eventually caste became an integral part of Hinduism. Society was divided into four castes, which were further divided into sub-castes. Beneath the caste system were the *untouchables* or *outcastes*. The castes, arranged hierarchically and initially vaguely representing occupation, were the *Brahmans* (religious elite), the *Kshatriya* (warrior/political elite), the *vaisyas* (farmers), and the *shudras* (laborers). The shudras were much lower than the other castes and could not reach salvation through fulfilling dharma. Hinduism justified this social inequality and stressed that social mobility took place very gradually, with its ultimate purpose the otherworldly one of salvation. Caste reinforced economic inequality.

Agrarian-Commercial World. Agriculture was the primary source of wealth in India, with different types of farming in numerous parts of the country. Both grain and specialty crops were grown. Trade, both domestic and international, was also important. Domestic trade involved the circulation of food products and artisan production. International trade was conducted primarily with Southeast Asia, though Europeans had arrived by the end of this period. Trade was in spices, tea, and hand-made luxury items. Commerce and agriculture produced relatively high levels of wealth, though economic growth was very modest. In this period, India was one of the wealthier parts of the world. However, economic inequality mirrored the social inequality of caste. Economic inequality clearly was a barrier to higher rates of economic growth and produced extremely high levels of poverty.

5. Family and Gender

Inequality characterized the family, which was patriarchal. Caste created divisions that could not be bridged and prevented intermarriage between caste members.

Both Hindu and Islamic law and traditions defined women as subservient. They were left with almost no human rights. Child marriage was common. Women were the property, first of their fathers and then of their husbands. Divorce was impossible. According to Hinduism, upon the death of husbands, widows were to be cremated *(sati)*. Otherwise, they barely had a legal existence, since they could not inherit property.

Families were extended, with several generations living together in a common household. The family was enlarged by the presence of daughters-in-law. The eldest male, the patriarch provided leadership for the entire group. The wife of the senior male ran the household and supervised women's work. Since conflict was quite common, the patriarch and his wife were responsible for maintaining harmony within the family.

Considerable conflict took place among the women, especially between the senior female and the daughters-in-law and between unmarried daughters and daughters-in-law. In addition, women were treated as inferiors.

6. Community and Diversity

Geography meant diversity of economic activity and separation of the country into distinct regions. Religion also provided a powerful basis for diversity.

Religious Diversity. Religious diversity was represented not only by the fault line separating Hinduism and Islam but also by the existence of a number of other religions such as *Sikhism* and *Jainism.* In addition, Islam was divided into two major sub-groups, *Shi'a* and *Sunni.* Late in this period more emotional forms of worship emerged in both Hinduism and Islam, centered on the experience of individuals working with a religious master. In Hinduism this was the *bakhti* movement and in Islam it was *Sufism.*

Other Types of Diversity. Even though not universal, caste was deeply divisive as well. Ethnic and linguistic diversity also existed. No common language united the population. No single culture could form the basis for community. Political unity could not be achieved. The need for security that in many societies created a common national interest did not operate in India because not every part of the country felt threatened by invaders.

All believed in the central role of religion and religious worship. However, differences in religious faiths minimized the overall role of religion as a source of community. No real bases for community existed. The Mughals, however consciously sought to create community in India, with different rulers applying various strategies.

B. MUGHAL EMPIRE, 1526–1764

The *Mughals* (the term *mughal* is the Persian word for Mongol) swept out of Afghanistan and into India in the 1520s. Within thirty years they had captured all of northern and central India, while southern India fell under their influence. The early Mughal rulers showed great ability and by 1600 their empire reached its maximum power. The empire was sustained at this level for most of the seventeenth century. However, Mughal power gradually declined in the eighteenth century. The Mughals introduced a new administrative structure intended to foster centralization and ensure a steady flow of talent into the government. Westerners provided a third ideology, a secular one that would increasingly compete with Hinduism and Islam. Islam exerted a powerful influence on Indian life, in spite of Hindus' efforts to preserve their culture. The caste system, for example, remained unchanged. At the same time, the Indian economy was further internationalized, in part through a determined Western attempt to dominate foreign trade. Few changes occurred in the family and in gender roles. India became a much more diverse society. Mughal rulers understood that diversity and lack of community were serious challenges facing the country. Some recognized the validity of Hindu culture and espoused toleration and the reduction of anti-Hindu discrimination. Others sought to create community by destroying Hindu religion and culture and replacing them with Islam.

1. Building, Preserving, and Losing Empire

The Mughals devoted much of their energy to building and sustaining their empire and preventing its collapse. The initial conquest of north India was quick but expansion into central India took many decades.

Empire-building. Invited in to defend a Muslim principality, Babur the "Tiger"—the first Mughal emperor—recognized the wealth of India and in 1526 sent his army to sack the twin capitals of the Deccan Sultanate—Delhi and Agra. The sultanate's treasury provided the wealth for the conquest of north India, which was completed within three years. Intrigue and conflict within the Mughal elite halted further expansion until the reign of *Akbar* (1556–1605). In the early 1570s Akbar conquered large Hindu states including Gujarat, Surat, and Bengal. In the 1590s he pacified central India. By the time of his death, the Mughal Empire encompassed all of northern and central India. The Mughals presided over the largest Indian Empire that had existed to that point. The Mughal Empire may have been the most powerful empire in the world in the seventeenth century, stronger than China, France, the Netherlands, and Russia.

Sustaining the Empire. The glorious Mughal Empire of the seventeenth century is best known for the actions of two emperors, *Shah Jahan* (1592–1666) and *Aurangzeb* (1658–1707). Both were dynamic leaders, who ruled for long periods of time. Both were activist rulers, though they had different goals. Shah Jahan, who built the *Taj Mahal* in honor of his beloved wife Mahal, created a brilliant court culture. He used the country's wealth to carry out a tremendous program of monumental building and conspicuous spending. In the process he nearly bankrupted the country. Aurangzeb was a militant Muslim, intent upon transforming all of India into a Muslim nation. He used violence and promoted fear among the populace in order to ensure his dictatorial rule. He employed military force to expand Mughal power and put down unrest among the Sikhs and *Rajputs* of western India and the *Marathas* of central India.

The Mughal bureaucracy acted with great efficiency, though the innovation and creativity present earlier in the government later disappeared. Inertia pushed the bureaucracy to fulfill its responsibilities. Government officials aped the behavior of the emperor, under Shah Jahan carrying out monumental building projects in their localities and under Aurangzeb acting as petty dictators. The Mughals seemed unaware that threats to their rule were beginning to surface.

Collapse of the Mughal Empire. For centuries historians have been fascinated with why once all-powerful empires collapsed. They have less often asked the question, "What enabled an empire to last so long?" The long slide of Mughal power ended with its final collapse in 1764. The empire had been weakened by a number of forces, all occurring more or less simultaneously. In addition, certain common conditions had existed throughout. In isolation they were not a threat to Mughal power but together they added to the cumulative forces for disintegration.

Internal divisions weakened Mughal leadership. The power and glory associated with being a Mughal emperor was so appealing that upon the death of an emperor, his sons often fought for the throne. Eventually one emerged victorious. Emperors did not develop a system of regular succession that would have eliminated these fierce struggles. At the same time, the conflict within the royal family spilled over into the rest of the elite and factional coalitions supporting one candidate or another emerged.

In the eighteenth century the long line of talented emperors disappeared. The last Mughal emperors and their courts were filled with greed and incompetence. *Opulence* and warfare drained the Mughal treasury, making it difficult for eighteenth century rulers to respond to external and internal threats.

South India drifted out of Mughal hands almost without protest. In the first half of the eighteenth century *Maratha federations* routinely defeated Mughal armies. Religious discrimination and increased taxes made it easier for the Maratha princes to mobilize opposition to the Mughals.

Outside threats of two sorts emerged. A much more expansionist Persia appeared on the northwest border. In 1732 the Persians invaded India, sacked the capital Delhi, and seized huge amounts of gold and jewels. Westerners were a greater long-term threat to Mughal power and Indian independence. Though Westerners arrived about 1500 and gradually increased their role in India's international trade, it was only in the eighteenth century that they sought territorial possession of parts of India.

It is easy to see how this combination of conflict within the Mughal elite, the rise of Hindu independence movements, Persian invasion, and the increasing involvement of Westerners in India would combine to topple the Mughal Empire. But we should also ask what enabled the Mughals to create and sustain the richest and most powerful nation in the world for over two centuries. Certainly dynamic leadership characterized the Mughal emperors, at least before the eighteenth century. The ability to generate large amounts of money through an efficient tax collection system in a relatively wealthy country was important. The Mughals generally possessed large amounts of money for support of military power and used it to expand and consolidate their control. The Mughal northwestern frontier was an open one and the opportunity for power and riches acted as a magnate for Muslim warriors from Central Asia, Afghanistan, and Persia. Thus there was a constant influx of talent, at least until the eighteenth century, by which time the Afghans and Persians had blocked the flow of new blood. Mughal rule over India was harsh but not haphazard or arbitrary. People generally had little interest in resistance to Mughal rule. This was especially true of the privileged group—the Muslims—whose loyalty was based on religion and on the recognition that as members of a minority in India, they must stick together. Finally, Mughal rule was certainly enhanced by the relatively high quality of their governance.

2. Imperial Rule

The major goals of Mughal administration were to extend centralized authority over all of India and to develop a tax system that would assure adequate resources for the consolidation of their power. Mughal rule was supported by Islamic law and by the emperors' attempts to portray themselves as almost god-like rulers.

The Mughals introduced a system of hierarchical administration known as *mansabdari.* (The Russian Table of Ranks operated on the basis of similar principles. See Chapter One.) The Muslim elite were divided into 33 ranks based on the number of cavalry to be provided to the emperor. Initially, most of the elite (about 70% of those in the higher ranks) were foreign-born Muslims. Identification as a member of the elite required service to the emperor, either in the military or the civilian bureaucracy. Within the elite, upward mobility was based on service to the ruler.

In addition, the country was divided into twelve provinces, then into districts and sub-districts. City governors, relatively independent of the provincial governors, ruled large cities. City police and rural military police maintained domestic order.

Governance was informed by Islamic law (*shar'ia*) and tradition (*hadith*), as interpreted by legal scholars (*ulama*) and enforced by Muslim judges (*qazis*). In general Hindu law applied to relations among Hindus.

Mughal rulers projected a greater than life image. Akbar portrayed himself as a god, based on the Persian model of the ruler as divine. Shah Jahan created an image of himself as a superior mortal through monumental building, especially the *Taj Mahal.* Aurangzeb demonstrated his inhumane brutality. Mughal emperors thus viewed themselves as god-like and not as mere mortals. This image certainly strengthened their power.

Tax policy engaged the energies of the Mughal rulers. Akbar eliminated the differential tax system by which non-Muslims paid higher taxes. The idea of private property ownership did not exist; instead a right to use land was in place. Peasants worked for overlords (*zamindari*). Under the Mughals in the sixteenth century peasants normally paid a tax of one-third of the harvest. In years of bad harvests the tax might be cancelled. Once every ten years the tax was recalculated to take into consideration changes in land usage and rates of inflation. Under Shah Jahan the tax was raised to one-half of the harvest. Aurangzeb reintroduced the poll tax (*jizya*), a tax on adult males, in 1679 and taxed goods sold by Hindu merchants at a rate twice that paid by Muslim merchants. In addition to stabilizing tax incomes, the Mughals improved the efficiency of tax collection, with the assistance of the city and rural military police.

3. Religion and Culture

Religious and cultural life became much more complicated in this period. Four major developments can be noted.

First, Persian culture had a profound impact on the Mughals. Persian became the language of Mughal administration and law. By the end of the reign of Akbar (1605), Mughal culture had become a national one, fusing Persian, Afghan, and Hindu elements to form what became known as *Mughlai* culture. Akbar also promoted Hindu culture, even appointing a Hindu poet laureate, Raja Birbal. Birbal translated the classic Indian text, the *Ramayana,* into the Hindi language.

Religion. Secondly, in 1581 Akbar created his own personal religion, known as the *Divine Faith.* Akbar believed that he was divine and should be worshipped by all of the people of India. Akbar sought to create community through a new religion intended to supercede both Islam and Hinduism. His efforts to establish a personal religion, based on Persian models, aroused the opposition of orthodox Muslims. In addition, the Shiite Muslim sultan of the Deccan led an unsuccessful rebellion against Akbar.

A new religion appeared in northwest India, the *Sikh* religion. Founded by *Nanak,* Sikhism flourished in the seventeenth century, especially appealing to the peasants. Sikhism sought to fuse Hinduism and Buddhism, while focusing on actions in this world, rather than on the spiritual life. Aurangzeb tried to destroy the Sikh religion. However, his efforts failed, fostering a Sikh sense of alienation from and opposition to whatever government ruled the country.

Finally, Hindu-Muslim conflict continued, less so in the sixteenth century when there was some Mughal toleration of Hinduism, and more so in the seventeenth century under Aurangzeb, who tried to destroy Hinduism (see section 6).

4. Society and Economy

India's economy expanded during the Mughal period, while social unrest increased, in spite of the caste system and the Hindu concept of dharma.

Economic Growth. In the Mughal period India's population grew to 100 million, making it only slightly smaller than China and about the size of Europe. Craft production, including common goods such as textiles and luxury items, increased dramatically. Exports expanded substantially, in part because Europeans increased their participation in India's international trade. Spices, indigo, and opium were major exports. Heavy government spending on weapons and monumental building projects acted as an engine of economic growth, too. The Mughal elite also spent heavily on personal luxury goods.

The caste system remained unchanged in non-Muslim areas. Income disparity increased. Peasant discontent multiplied, especially in the last third of the seventeenth century. Rural unrest resulted from central government tax hikes and illegal increases in taxes by provincial and local officials trying to line their own pockets, as well as from famines and plague. The typical peasants' response was flight from the lands they worked. Some *millenarian* movements emerged, such as the *Truth Names* (*Satnamis*) Hindu sect of peasants. On rare occasions peasants rebelled.

5. Family and Gender Roles

The family changed very little. However, some changes occurred for elite women.

Nur Jahan was the real ruler of India for almost two decades. Her husband, Shah Jahan, idolized her. Elite women were placed on a pedestal but also expected to bear large numbers of children. Patriarchy still characterized the extended family, as did the primacy of sons and tension among the female members of the household. The family remained an economic institution. Among the Hindu population, caste continued to be a barrier to marriage across social boundaries.

6. Community and Diversity

Mughal rulers recognized that they ruled a diverse society and developed two different strategies for building community. Akbar and Aurangzeb represented these two very different approaches to this dilemma.

Toleration. Akbar, an early Mughal emperor, understood the need to reach out to the Hindu community. He promoted religious toleration and equal treatment (non-discrimination). Akbar first acted symbolically, marrying the daughter of a Hindu prince. He also recruited non-Mughals into government service. Akbar abandoned the earlier Mughal policy of promoting forced conversion to Islam. He eliminated the tax on Hindu pilgrims traveling to holy places. He ended the poll tax on non-Muslims. Further, Akbar promoted the reduction of cultural differences within India, especially through the fusion of Persian, Afghan, and Hindu elements to create *Mughlai* culture. Akbar's emphasis on reducing conflict among the religious communities, eliminating discriminatory polices, especially taxes, and promoting cultural fusion continued until Aurangzeb ascended the *Peacock Throne.*

Muslim Supremacy. Aurangzeb (the World Conqueror) sought to establish total Muslim domination of India. He used *censors of public morals* (*muhtasibs*) in each province and region to ensure that Islamic law was obeyed. Militantly anti-Hindu, he prohibited the building of new Hindu temples and forbade the repair of existing ones.

Aurangzeb's actions alienated large segments of the Indian population and promoted political unrest, especially among the Sikhs in the Punjab and the Hindus of the Maratha. Sikhs, especially peasants, rebelled several times. Motivated by hatred of the Muslims, *Shivaji Bhonsle* (1627–1680) pushed for independence for the Maratha and for religious freedom. Shivaji called himself Lord of the Universe and led several Maratha rebellions against the Mughals. Thus Aurangzeb's efforts to promote Muslim domination backfired, producing instead political and religious opposition that weakened Mughal rule. In general the Mughals ignored the Western threat, which became serious in the mid-eighteenth century.

C. BRITISH INFORMAL IMPERIALISM, 1760–1857

Though Westerners had begun to trade in India by 1500, it was only in the eighteenth century that they moved beyond trade to political domination. Defeating the French in the second half of the eighteenth century, the British became the strongest foreign power in India. The *British East India Company* provided leadership in British India. Ironically, this private corporation had both a political and an economic role. The British gradually extended their power over India, using political pressure, economic strategies, and military force. By the time the British had "conquered" all of India in the mid-nineteenth century, the Indians had begun to rebel against foreign rule. Throughout, tension existed between the British East India Company, primarily interested in profits, and the British government, concerned about domestic peace in India and global security for its national interests. Increasingly the British government exerted a more and more direct influence over Indian governance. India's British rulers found it difficult to decide whether the British had a *civilizing mission* to perform or whether they should respect India's classical heritage. Those who emphasized Western superiority won this ideological debate. As one might expect, the British East India Company developed strategies for profit-making that involved promoting the economic development of

India. Few changes occurred in the area of family and gender roles, though the British encouraged improvements in the position of women. Recognizing the religious, linguistic, ethnic, and social differences within India, the British strategy for building community was to convert the Indian elite to British culture. Thus, a unique Anglo-Indian upper class and culture emerged. However, by the mid-nineteenth century, differences between the British and the peoples of India widened irrevocably.

1. Creating the Jewel in the Crown

India became the central jewel in the crown of the British Empire. British imperialism gradually emerged as the dominant force in India from the mid-eighteenth century until independence in 1947. The British came late to the business of imperialism, in large part because they were not as strong initially as a number of other European states better located to build an empire based on sea power and naval ability.

The Portuguese and Dutch. In 1498, the Portuguese sea captain Vasco *da Gama* reached the coastal port of Calicut in Western India after a lengthy voyage around the southern tip of Africa. This inaugurated European activity in India. Quickly the Portuguese moved beyond merely sending a few trading ships each year by establishing small enclaves known as *factories* or foreign port facilities. *Dom Alfonso d' Albuquerque,* Portuguese viceroy for Asia, developed this strategy and established Portuguese headquarters along the west coast of India at Goa, which remained in Portuguese hands until the 1960s. The spice trade (especially pepper and cloves) brought great wealth to Portugal.

By 1600, the Dutch had created the *Dutch East India Company,* whose purpose was to control and promote Dutch trade interests in Southeast Asia and India. (See Chapter Five for its role in South Africa). In part the Dutch saw themselves as leaders of a Protestant crusade against the Catholic powers of Portugal and Spain. The British arrived a few decades later and set up a factory at the main Mughal port of Surat. By 1623, the British and Dutch had become deadly enemies, after the Dutch executed British, Japanese, and Portuguese merchants for supposedly plotting against the Dutch East India Company. Gradually and quietly the British built up commercial ties with India, trading for cotton, silk, pepper, and indigo. Still, the Dutch remained the most important European commercial presence in India until the end of the seventeenth century.

The French. French interest in India produced the *French East India Company* in 1664. Moving aggressively, by the 1730s the French were generating 25 percent profits from their commercial activities in India. Soon after that Joseph Francois *Dupleix* (1698–1764) assumed direction of French operations in India. Recognizing the profits to be made and the importance of India in the eighteenth century global struggle between the European continental power of France and the European sea power of England, Dupleix developed a strategy for French domination of India. In the 1740s the French captured Madras, the largest city in southern India. Next the French defeated the major Indian ruler in southern India, *Nizam-ul-Mulk.* Thus France gained a dominant role in southern Indian international trade.

Conflict with the British, who were led by Robert *Clive,* reached a peak during the *Seven Years' War* (1756–1763), known in the United States as the *French and Indian War.* The Seven Years' War was a global struggle, fought in North America, the Caribbean, and India, as well as in Europe. The British defeated the French in several major battles in south India. Though not driven from India, the French ceased to be a serious rival to the British. During the Napoleonic Wars (1790s–1815) the British destroyed the remnants of French power in India.

British Victory over the Indians. Having destroyed the ability of its European rivals to play an important role in India's trade, the British turned to expanding their power in India. By the 1790s, the British East India Company controlled the southeast and southwest coasts of India. Still in its way were the inland kingdoms of southern India, the Maratha in central India, and the principalities of the Deccan and northwest India, including the Punjab. In 1818, the British crushed the greatest threat to their domination of India, the Maratha. In the 1840s, they captured northwest India, including *Sind* and Punjab after fierce warfare. Finally, in the 1850s, the British conquered the Deccan kingdoms such as Orissa and Oudh.

The British used a variety of approaches, and not just military action, to create British India. However, they also gained a dominant influence over native states by permitting their rulers to remain in power, while at the same time securing most of the states' income. Initially, the British lowered taxes and avoided social reforms that might disrupt Indian customs.

British India was a patchwork. The British directly ruled some parts of India and permitted native princes to remain nominally independent, though subservient to British will. The British devoted much energy to developing a system of governance for India.

2. The Political System of the British East India Company

The British East India Company, primarily seeking to enrich itself through trade and tax collection, formed the government of India. The company created a political structure for achieving these goals. Over time the British government came to the conclusion that the interests of the British Empire were different from those of the British East India Company. The British government in London then took steps to increase its role in the governance of India.

Formal Governing Structure. After the defeat of the French, the British turned their attention to creating a viable governing structure for India. This involved establishing British government controls over the administrative functions of the British East India Company. Initially the *Court of Directors* for the British East India Company governed the Company's three scattered territories. In 1784, Parliament passed the *India Act,* which created a *Crown Board of Control* that included several members of the Cabinet and had ultimate decision-making power for British India. It could overrule decisions made by the BEIC Court of Directors. The Board of Control focused on taxation, war, and peace and relationships with the independent native princes. The Court of Directors made all appointments, including that of governor-general, though the British government could remove high officials.

Lord Cornwallis, the British general defeated in the American Revolutionary War, became the real architect of British governance in India, primarily by creating a professional British civil service. He eliminated corruption within the BEIC and removed Indians from leadership roles in the *Indian Civil Service.* Cornwallis developed a series of rules known as the *Code of 48 Regulations* (1793). He abolished the Indian judicial system and replaced it with British judges operating in four provincial circuits. He merged judicial and police functions. Cornwallis also established the *Office of Revenue Collector,* to be staffed by the British. He ended all Indian taxes in areas under British control and gave the British government in India power to levy any taxes it wanted to. Cornwallis regularized the *zamindar* system of permanent taxes levied on harvests. Cornwallis also gave the BEIC a monopoly over the production and sale of salt and opium. He also Europeanized the officer corps, though the vast majority of soldiers were Indians. Finally, Cornwallis encouraged a British sense of supremacy that evolved into an aristocratic arrogance and power hunger that led the British ruling class in India to be called the *New Mughals.*

Finally in the mid-1830s, Thomas Babington *Macauley* joined the Council as law representative and initiated an emphasis on social legislation and the transformation of Indian custom through legislation. Sometimes this policy approach is derogatorily called *legislating happiness.*

Thus by the mid-nineteenth century almost all of India was ruled directly or indirectly by the British, operating through an administrative structure that included a small group of executives and a larger group of administrators (still only a thousand or so), the Indian Civil Service. The British government had come to see India not only as a source of wealth but as a place for implementing radical social change. But until the British began to legislate changes in basic Hindu beliefs and customs, a tension existed between those who espoused British supremacy and those who recognized the significance of Indian civilization.

3. Ideological Differences

Huge differences remained between Hindus and Muslims. Most Indians espoused Hinduism or Islam, or one of the other major religions, Sikhism or Jainism. Western ideas, however, increasingly gained support, especially among those educated in British culture. Initially the British in India lacked a consensus on what role Western ideas should play. The two key questions were whether Western or Indian civilization was superior and whether Indians should receive a British-style education or one that emphasized Indian culture. By the mid-1830s the conflict was resolved by the victory of the *Anglicists* over the *Orientalists.*

Orientalism. A number of the British developed great respect for Indian civilization, recognizing it as a vibrant, glorious culture. By espousing the positive qualities of the Indian past and present, ironically, the British promoted a revival of Indian interest in their own past. Sir William *Jones* founded the Asiatic Society of Bengal in 1784 and emphasized the need for the Indian elite to study Indian civilization through its classics written in Sanskrit or Persian (Urdu). Horace Hyman *Wilson* prepared a Sanskrit-English dictionary and attacked the "cultural imperialism" of the Anglicists. Out of these efforts came the *Bengal Renaissance* (1813–1825), whose key figure was *Ram Mohuym Roy.* Roy studied ancient Hindu texts, especially the *Upanishads,* a series of philosophical writings that became central to Hindu belief. The *Friendly Association,* led by *Roy* and *Dwarkanath Tagore,* discussed Hindu theology and philosophy. This group sought to present a Hindu alternative to Christianity at a time when missionary activity was spreading rapidly. Roy also founded the *Society of Brahma,* a key organization for those involved in the Bengal Renaissance. In 1816, David Hare and other British Orientalists founded a *Hindu College* that provided university education for Indian youth.

British ideals of toleration and respect for other cultures were presented in the *Liberal Charter* of 1833. The charter called for equality of opportunity within the BEIC and prohibited discrimination based on race, color, ethnicity, religion, and/or language. The charter also established the principle that Indian customs and laws should take precedence over British civilization and law. Preferring the Anglicist position, the British in India soon abandoned this ideal.

Anglicism. Eventually the Anglicists triumphed. Missionary reformers espoused the initial Anglicist position. They translated the Bible into Indian languages and called for British education for upper class Indians. Initially the BEIC had opposed missionary activity as bad for business and British missionaries were forced to settle in the Danish enclave. However, in 1813, the ban on missionary activity was lifted.

Macauley provided the intellectual framework for the Anglicist position, though others later espoused a more extremist perspective. A historian and legal scholar, Macauley codified Anglo-Indian law and emphasized the importance of English education for the Indian elite. He believed Indian youth should receive an English education instead of an "Oriental" education in native subjects. Macauley sought to create a new social group in India, an Anglo-Indian upper class; Indian by birth and British by education and culture.

Macauley and others emphasized that the British had a responsibility to civilize the Indians. When he became governor-general, *Lord* William *Bentinck* aggressively espoused the superiority of British civilization and condemned the barbarity of Indian culture. He banned *sati* (widow burning) and the *thugi/thugs* (a cult of highway robbers). Eventually the Anglo-Indian class used its English education to achieve Indian goals—independence from the British.

4. Economic Development and Social Reforms

As one might expect, the BEIC and the British government developed clear strategies for increasing British revenues, stimulating the economic development of India, and promoting social change. During the 1830s British leaders in India concluded that Indian "barbarism" must be destroyed, replaced by "civilized institutions." The British government in India issued decrees to force the elimination of traditional Indian customs.

Economic Development. In the eighteenth century, the British strategy for economic development focused on improving agricultural output and thus British income. With the late eighteenth century industrial revolution in

England, the British dramatically changed their view of India's economic role. India came to be viewed not only as a source of food supplies but also of raw materials, such as cotton, for British industry. To improve India's ability to fulfill this role, the British promoted improvement of India's communication and transportation infrastructure.

Government Revenues and Rural Change. New tax policies dramatically increased British revenues and produced significant social change in rural India. Since revenues came largely from taxes on farming and farmers, the British tried to ensure a stable income from rural taxes.

In North India this was achieved through the *zamindar settlement* (1793). To ensure a stable income from rural taxes the British introduced the idea of private ownership, replacing the traditional Indian concept of *rights to use land.* Zamindars were intermediaries between the government and those who worked the land. Under the British, zamindars were assigned ownership of the land they had supervised. Peasants thus became farm workers or tenant farmers. Zamindars had the right to buy and sell land and remove peasants from the plots they had worked for generations. The relationship between zamindars and peasants, as oppressive as it frequently was, was paralleled by a mutual relationship between zamindars and the British. The former became a class loyal to the British. When bad harvests made it difficult for zamindars to collect and pay taxes, they sold their land to bankers and moneylenders, who represented a new layer of absentee landowners. The zamindars and absentee owners became a new upper class, replacing the Mughal aristocracy. At the same time, the British changed the nature of taxation from a percentage of the harvest to a flat tax, or poll tax, on each peasant family. The tax was constant and did not increase over time. This change promoted greater agricultural productivity, since increased output left a larger amount of wealth in the hands of the peasants and promoted economic growth.

In southern India, Thomas *Munro* introduced the *ryotwari* (peasant) *settlement.* In this case a fixed tax was levied on the peasant family and this tax could be readjusted after a 10–30 year period. Peasants benefited by knowing what their taxes would be each year, while the British could change the tax rate only at specified times. When peasant landowners could not pay their taxes because of bad harvests, they turned to moneylenders and subsequently lost their property if they could not repay their loans. This produced a group of absentee landowners from the banking class. The British collected taxes directly and not through intermediaries and this required British district officers to increase their direct contacts with the peasants. BEIC income was also affected by the *Charter Act of 1833* that eliminated its monopoly over trade, except in opium and salt. Thus increased productivity and overall improvements in peasant living standards accompanied increasing social inequality and differentiation in the countryside.

Economic Development Strategies. The British also sought to increase profits by direct involvement in economic activity. The British began to see India as a source of raw materials, such as cotton and indigo, and as a market for British finished goods. This is especially true in cotton textiles. Until the nineteenth century India exported its homespun cotton textiles throughout Asia and Europe. After 1810, they faced increasing competition from machine-made goods from England. The 1830s destroyed the homespun textiles industry, which was incapable of competing with British imports. Massive unemployment and suffering hit the hand-made cotton textiles workforce.

At the same time some Indians began to participate in the British sector of the Indian economy, primarily as middlemen. Among them was Dwarkanath Tagore, who joined the first *Anglo-Indian Managing Agency* (1834).

The British also promoted improvements in infrastructure, including port facilities, railways, and the telegraph. The latter became especially important in India from the 1840s on.

All of these actions produced healthy profits for the BEIC, other British businessmen, and the British government. Only a small percentage of the Indian population profited from the overall expansion of the economy in the first half of the nineteenth century.

Caste and Social Reforms. Initially the British avoided entanglement in Indian domestic social issues. The Hindus, especially, resented and opposed efforts to destroy traditional customs—no matter how barbarous the customs might seem to the British. In England attempts to "civilize" the British were known as *humanitarian reform.* We might also see these as efforts at *Cultural Revolution*—transformation of the basic values, customs, and institutions of a society (see Chapter Four).

The British, especially through the efforts of Macauley, transformed the Hindu law code to make punishment less cruel and less inhumane. Widespread use of the death penalty was eliminated and treason remained the only crime for which the death penalty was appropriate.

Attempting to minimize violent and cruel behavior, the British outlawed infanticide and human sacrifice. The British military successfully wiped out the *thugi* (thugs), whose religious ceremonies included the murder of travelers. This halted the murder of 20,000–30,000 travelers annually. *Sati* (widow burning) was also outlawed.

Most boldly, the British outlawed the caste system, but the law was ignored. Elimination of caste, if it had been successful, would have created the impetus for bold social change and social mobility. The British passed the *Caste Disabilities Act,* which permitted Indians who converted to Christianity to inherit property. In practical terms, conversion to Christianity enabled a person to escape from the *untouchables.* The British believed that elimination of restraints on mobility would produce a large middle class (loyal to the British, they hoped). Caste and sati were so much a part of Hindu religion and customs and British rule so superficial that radical social change was impossible. Still, the ideals of social equality, social mobility, and equal treatment gradually became key components of the Indian freedom movement, especially after the First World War.

5. Family and Gender Roles

Under British rule, few changes occurred in family and gender roles. Indians who received a British education retained traditional attitudes toward the family, for the British family at this time was also patriarchal.

Family. The family was still patriarchal, dominated by the father, to whom all other family members were to be totally obedient. The family remained an economic unit. Tension characterized the relationship among female members of the household. Laws abolishing sati did not improve the relative position of women.

Gender Roles. Women remained embedded in the patriarchal family, with no opportunity for alternative or additional roles. Only one group of women escaped the Indian patriarchal family—Indian women who married British men and their Anglo-Indian daughters who were raised as British.

6. Community and Diversity

India now possessed a more complex kind of diversity than previously. Religious differences were intensified because of the activity of Christian missionaries. Along with the Hindu-Muslim conflict, the Sikhs became much more militant in their opposition to the British, resulting from and producing British incorporation of the Sikh lands, the Punjab, into British India. The British vacillated between a policy of promoting religious tolerance and playing the religious card—setting the Hindus and Muslims against each other.

The British and the Peoples of India. A central issue of diversity and community was the relationship between the British and the Indian peoples. The British were, of course, not India's first foreign conquerors. Previously, outside forces, mainly Islamic, had tried to extend their domination over all of India, but seldom controlled the south. They made accommodations to Indian cultures and failed to maintain separation from the Indians. Some fusion of Indian and conquerors' cultures took place.

For over half a century the British, and especially the BEIC, tried to disturb Indian culture as little as possible. The BEIC assumed that since their main goal was the maximization of profit, any interference in deeply held Indian beliefs would undermine British economic efforts. Leaving the Indians alone permitted freedom of activity for the Orientalists, who recognized and promoted respect for traditional Hindu civilization.

The triumph of the Anglicists brought to power those who had two goals for community and diversity. The Anglicists sought to create a single middle- and upper-class culture, based on British education. This, of course, separated the upper-class Indians from the peasants even more than before. The Anglicists also championed the superiority of Western Civilization, which in effect reinforced difference. Toward the end of this period both the British and the peoples of India began to view each other with more and more suspicion, while racism replaced tolerance. This ambiguous legacy bore bitter fruit in the Great Rebellion of 1857–1858 and ultimately led to direct British rule in India.

D. BRITISH FORMAL EMPIRE, 1857–1947

A series of bloody rebellions broke out in the late 1850s, forcing the British government to abolish the British East India Company and assume direct control over India. British and India actions focused on the future political relationship between the two. The British favored modest political reform and a gradual increase in Indian political responsibilities. By the late nineteenth century some Indians became impatient with the slow expansion of their political rights. Out of this situation came a *freedom movement.* The movement was relatively moderate in aims and methods until after the First World War. From the end of that war until independence (1947) the British and Indians fell into broader and more violent conflict with each other. Compromise and gradualism no longer worked. At the same time that the British gradually surrendered some of their political power, they continued to pursue the economic development strategies of the informal empire period. Social conditions changed little. Caste and poverty still dominated the lives of most Indians. As India moved toward independence, religious difference increasingly produced greater violence, which came to be known as *communalism* (local religious violence). By 1947, the key issue was neither whether India would be independent nor really when it would be free. The main question was the distribution of power between Hindus and Muslims in an independent India. Inability to resolve this issue led to intensified religious conflict and to political partition.

1. Geography of British Rule

In the aftermath of the Great Mutiny, the British government controlled India in two different ways. Much of the country—especially much of northern and central India—was ruled directly by the British government and civil service. The frontier areas and much of inland southern India were ruled indirectly though native princes. The British put tremendous pressure on these princes to follow British directives.

2. Challenges to British Rule

During the century of direct empire, the British faced serious challenges. The first was the Great Rebellion of 1857–1858, actually a series of uprisings across northern India that almost drove the British out of the country. The freedom movement, which began in the 1870s, represented the second major challenge.

Great Rebellion, 1857–1858. The Great Rebellion illustrated the cultural gap between the British and the Indians and the economic and social consequences of a century of economic exploitation of lower-class Indians. Increasing "racial conflict," acceleration of technological modernization, and British use of force to complete the annexation of India lands produced widespread opposition to the British. For the first time in a century Indians began to reject British rule.

Cultural differences acted as a catalyst for the beginnings of the revolt, a rebellion in which both sides acted with great brutality. In 1857, the British introduced a new rifle, the Enfield, into India. Cartridges needed to be lubricated with animal fat, requiring the Indian soldiers to touch the fat. For religious reasons Hindus were banned from handling beef fat and Muslims were prohibited from touching pork fat. Both Hindu and Muslim soldiers feared that the Christian English were plotting to force them to disobey their religions. Showing no sympathy for the religious beliefs of the native soldiers, the British abolished military units that refused to use animal fat in loading their weapons, and dismissed "rebellious" soldiers from the military. At one point eighty-five soldiers were imprisoned for disobeying orders to lubricate their cartridges with animal fat. The next day all military units at the camp mutinied and marched to the capital, *Delhi,* some thirty miles away. Delhi soldiers joined the mutiny, which then spread across north India.

The rebellions centered in Delhi, Lucknow, and Cawnpore. In general the rebellious soldiers called for the restoration of traditional monarchies—either the Mughal Emperor or Indian princedoms. Wealthy landowners from areas such as Oudh, who had recently lost their political power and much of their revenue, provided leadership for the rebellion. At the same time, military revolt triggered peasant rebellion, largely directed against the British tax system.

Gradually the British military recovered, motivated in part by the murder of British civilians. The British attacked innocent peasants and burned down entire villages. The British "flayed" some rebels, since hanging was "too good for them." Other rebels were shot out of cannons. By the autumn of 1857 the British had recovered the capital Delhi and most of North India. Rebellion continued in the highlands of central India for another year.

The Great Rebellion of 1857–1858 had great consequences. It was the bloodiest struggle in Indian history. On the one hand, it represented the last gasp of traditional India's opposition to British rule and especially British efforts at modernization. At the same time, it presaged the Indian freedom movement and its opposition to British power. The Great Rebellion demonstrated that British efforts at Cultural Revolution and technological modernization had fostered bitter hatred, which could easily lead to inhumane brutality by all parties. A few Indians concluded that the British were not all powerful and that it would be possible to acquire independence from them at some point in the future. The rebellion also showed that the people of India were not yet ready to subordinate personal, class, and religious interests in the name of a greater good—Indian nationalism or opposition to British rule.

The British also learned from the rebellion. They concluded that the strategy of assigning political and military responsibilities to a commercial organization did not work. The British East India Company was abolished and direct British rule replaced company governance. The new government recognized that efforts to change the basic beliefs of the Indian people had backfired and had intensified opposition. The British living in India increasingly isolated themselves from the native population, fearing contact would lead to Indian violence against the British. A great divide had been created and could not be crossed.

Gradual British Retreat. The British now faced a series of difficult challenges. Soon after reestablishing firm rule over India, the British began to plan a gradual political withdrawal. They sought to transfer some power to the Indians, so that the issue of independence would not have to be addressed. Over time the British implemented three changes that added up to a substantial increase in Indian political rights and power and laid the basis for Indian autonomy. The British reduced the power of the British executive branch of government in India, increased the power of provincial legislatures and permitted Indians to play a greater role within the British government and bureaucracy in India.

Direct Government. Though the ultimate British objective was to withdraw from India, the British first had to reestablish order and create a political structure that would ensure effective administration. First, the British East India Company was abolished, for the British government needed a scapegoat. The *Secretary of State for India* assumed complete responsibility for the Indian government and its revenues. The Secretary of State was to be advised by a *Council of India,* almost half of whose membership were former British East India Company officers. Previously, competitive exams for the Indian Civil Service had eliminated the BEIC's patronage powers. In 1861, the cabinet of the Calcutta's Viceroy was transformed into a twelve-person *Legislative Council,* only half of whom could be British. The Indians appointed to this legislature were conservative loyalists. Also, the Viceroy's cabinet was reorganized so that each member had a functional responsibility to oversee one department, such as revenue or law.

The British also attempted to build up a loyal majority among the elite of India. The government ended its policy of confiscating the lands of Indian princes. Instead it guaranteed the preservation of the remaining 560 principalities. The princes, then, became strong supporters of the British.

Toward Indian Political Rights. This system remained unchanged until the late nineteenth century. The British strengthened the role of the bureaucracy, especially at the district level, where the tax collector and magistrate-judge acquired great power. The cabinet system by which members were responsible for a single portfolio was extended into the provinces. Under Viceroy George *Curzon* the central government tried to reestablish tight control over provincial and district bureaucracies. In 1892, the *India Councils Act* gave the governors of Calcutta, Madras, and Bombay the right to appoint Indian representatives to the legislative councils from among those nominated by Indian constituencies such as universities and chambers of commerce.

The so-called *Morley-Minto Reforms* (*Indian Councils Act of 1909*) greatly enhanced the power of provincial legislatures and Indian representation in the central and provincial legislative councils. The councils were tripled in size and Indians given a majority on the provincial councils. Indian membership was to be determined by democratic elections, though the number of voters was relatively small. In the first elections (1910), Indians gained over 60 percent of the provincial and national legislative seats. The legislative councils could debate government proposals, especially in the budget area, and introduce legislation.

Within a decade, additional reforms were introduced, especially through the efforts of Secretary of State Edwin *Montagu* and Viceroy *Lord Chelmsford.* Before the end of the First World War Montagu announced that the British were determined to increase Indian participation in the government and gradually move India toward self-government. In 1919, the *Montagu-Chelmsford* reforms were passed. Indians were to have a "large measure of responsibility" at the provincial level, with complete self-government as soon as possible. A bureaucratic division of responsibility was to be introduced, with the British responsible for finances and law and order and the Indian-dominated legislative councils in charge of other matters. The central legislature, now to be known as the *Imperial Legislative Council,* was expanded and made more representative. In the 1923–1924 elections, Indians won a majority of seats in the central legislature and large majorities in the legislatures of most provinces and large cities.

The bureaucracy was opened up to greater Indian participation. Examinations for the India Civil Service were held in India, as well as England, making it easier for Indians to participate.

From the early 1920s a more radical Indian freedom movement emerged, making compromise and gradual progress toward self-government unacceptable. The British rejected Indian independence and struggled to find a structure for autonomy that would satisfy the Indians. In the *Government of India Act of 1935,* the British made a final attempt to balance the conflicting British and Indian political goals. India was transformed into a complex political system, with a federation of 11 provinces, each with full self-government; the 560 Princely States; and a small number of Chief Commissioners' Provinces run directly by the Indian Civil Service and reporting directly to the British central government. This compromise was unacceptable to the princes and to the leaders of the India freedom movement. In spite of this opposition, in 1937 the British declared provincial autonomy. Efforts to balance the political goals of the Muslims and Hindus led to the creation of single religion constituencies. Half of the provinces had bicameral legislatures; the others had unicameral ones. All legislators were elected in voting which attracted 35,000,000 including 6,000,000 women and 3,000,000–4,000,000 untouchables. Moreover, *Congress,* the Hindu-dominated freedom movement, polled 716 seats, while its chief rival, the Muslim League, won only 109.

After the 1937 elections, the people of India seemed satisfied with the new system and expected the British to continue to provide over-all leadership. However, the Second World War led to a further radicalization of Indian aims, which made continued British rule unacceptable and impossible. The main British objective, especially after the Nazis gained control over most of continental Europe west of the Ural Mountains, was to defeat Hitler. Policy toward India was to serve that goal.

The British position was most clearly reflected in the *Cripps Mission* of 1942. Sir Stafford Cripps came to India to assess the situation but also to tell the Indian leaders that the British contemplated no changes in India's status until after the war. He promised full dominion status after the war and suggested that any province or state that wished to opt out of a future India would be permitted to do so.

The Congress movement found unacceptable an autonomy accompanied by continued legal ties to Great Britain and the possibility that India might be split up into a number of separate states. Mohandas Gandhi gave the Congress response when he initiated a *Quit India Campaign.* British efforts to create a temporary compromise failed, setting the stage for unsuccessful post-war negotiations.

Indian Freedom Movement. After the failure of the Great Rebellion, Indians began to try to redefine their relationship to the British political system. An Indian freedom movement emerged, passing through three stages:

- Political moderation and cultural nationalism, to 1905
- Transition to radicalism, 1905–1920
- Radicalism, with independence as the main goal, 1920–1947

The freedom movement rested on an ambiguous interpretation of the British presence and legacy. The increasing racist and isolationist behavior of the British widened the distance between them and the Indians. Symbolic of British discrimination was the inability of the Liberal viceroy, *Lord Ripon,* to gain the support of British in India for his reform program. For instance, in 1883, the Anglo-Indians protested changes in the criminal code that would have allowed Europeans to be tried before native judges, as long as half of the jurors were Europeans.

At the same time, some British actions facilitated the emergence of an Indian opposition movement. Improvements in transportation and communication, as well as the creation of a mass press, made it easier for Indians to communicate with each other. In addition, the British provided the Indians with a set of political ideals, including the *rule of law, representative government,* and *national sovereignty.* The British school system in India enabled Indians to drink deeply from the cup of British culture. The British ability to set goals and work together to achieve them also appealed to the Indians. Indian responses to the British assumed three different orientations—political reform, cultural nationalism, and radicalism. Most participants in these movements were middle- or upper-class Indians with British education. They came mainly from the largest cities that had long been under British control, including Calcutta, Bombay, Madras, and Poona.

Political Moderates. Initially, the freedom movement was moderate. Mahadev Govinda Ranade founded the All People's Association (PSS) in 1870. PSS called for the use of British political institutions and ideas to establish Indian self-government. Surendranath Banarjea formed another political reform group, the Indian Association, in 1876. Most political reform movements were regionally based. Among such groups were The Madras Native Association, which supported political reform and renewed interest in Tamil culture and the Mahajana Sabha (Great People's Society), composed of Madras Brahmans.

In 1883, a group of British and Indians, including Allan *Hume* and Womesh *Bonnerjee,* founded the *Indian National Congress* (generally called Congress). Congress became the single most important nationalist organization in India. Most of its members were high-caste Hindus and Parsis (those of Persian origin). Few Muslims felt comfortable in the organization. In the moderate period Congress called for greater Indian participation in the governance of India, both in the civil service and in the higher levels of administration. Congress believed government should drastically reduce military spending and promote economic development more effectively.

Cultural Nationalism. Cultural nationalism, a renewal of interest in past cultural traditions also emerged. By emphasizing the glory and values of earlier cultural traditions that had flourished when India was free of foreign control, without identifying specific political goals, cultural nationalism indirectly provided a basis for opposition to the British. Cultural nationalism built on the earlier revivals of Indian tradition, such as the Bengal Renaissance.

Balwantrao Gangadhan *Tilak* (1856–1920) was the most important cultural nationalist of the first two phases of the freedom movement. Using the Marathi language, Tilak spread his message of the superiority of Hindu tradition over British civilization among the urban masses. Gopal Krishna *Gokhale* also promoted cultural nationalism. A proponent of modernizing Indian life, including women's rights, Gokhale created a number of Hindu festivals in Maharashtra that became a model for other areas. First, he established a festival honoring

Ganesh, son of the main deity Shiva. Then he founded a festival honoring Shivaji, the military leader of Maharashtra opposition to British incorporation of Maharashtra into British India. For Gokhale, enthusiasm for the Hindu revival turned into anti-Muslim feelings.

In Bengal, Banarjea, Motilal *Ghosh* and his brother, Arabinda *Ghosh,* played a leading role in a second Bengal literary revival. The Ghosh brothers were very close to Tilak. A deep dedication to Indian nationalism and Hinduism was reflected in the literary work of Bankim Chandra *Chatterji,* whose poem, "Hail to Thee Mother," became the Indian national anthem.

Cultural nationalism emerged in the Muslim community, too. *Sir* Sayyid Ahmad *Khan,* a member of the Mughal aristocracy and a British civil servant, tried to synthesize Islamic ideas and Western thought. At the same time he called for Islam to once again militantly seek converts. His was a nostalgia for the good old days of Mughal glory. In 1870, he founded the *Muhamadan Anglo-Oriental College at Aligarh,* modeled after Cambridge University. Aligarh became the center of the Muslim revival and the main training site for future Muslim leaders.

At this time, most Indian activists either called for political reform, thus espousing a secular approach, or promoted the revival of interest in Hindu traditions. Few called for Indian independence.

Transition to Radicalism. During the years 1905–1920, the Indian freedom movement began to undergo profound changes. This period of transition began with the Bengal protests of 1906. Hindus organized fierce protests in response to the British decision to divide the huge Bengal province into two parts. The *svadeshi* movement to boycott British goods followed the riots. Bipin Chandra *Pal* and Arabinda Ghosh led the protest movement. This group called for the boycott of British manufactures and British institutions, including schools, colleges, law courts, and the civil service. Their goal was to prevent the British government from operating effectively. From Bengal the protest movement spread to Poona and to the Punjab, where Lala Lajpat Rai led the Arya Samaj.

The split within the Congress Party was as important as mass protest. A radical faction, the *New Party* emerged under the leadership of Tilak, Pal, and Rai. This New Party encouraged the boycott and called for anti-British violence as a way of achieving independence. Gokhale, moderate president of Congress, mobilized overwhelming support against the views of the New Party, preventing its candidate, Rai, from becoming president of Congress.

Essentially driven out of Congress, the New Party felt free to pursue its agenda of extending the boycott and conducting anti-British terrorism. Rai and the other leaders of Arya Samaj were arrested, while radical youth, influenced by Russian anarchism, began a campaign of public terrorism. Tilak declared that the bomb would be a magical weapon that would drive the British out of India. During the First World War Sikhs in the Punjab launched a terrorist campaign against British rule. Terrorism was met by harsh British repression.

The division of Bengal also mobilized Muslims. They concluded that it was essential to gain British support for Muslim political rights. In 1906, a group of Muslim leaders, led by the Aga Khan, met with Viceroy Minto, who agreed that Muslims would have fair representation in the legislative councils, based not on their proportion of the total population but upon their political significance. By the end of 1906 Muslims had formed the *All-India Muslim League,* first led by Mohsin-ul-Mulk and Nawab Viqurul-Mulk and supported by the Aga Khan. The Muslim League announced its loyalty to the British government and its intention to defend Muslim political rights. In 1913, Mohammed *Ali Jinnah* joined the Muslim League and soon became leader of its almost desperate campaign to ensure political power for Muslims within India. The creation of the Muslim League prefigured greater Hindu-Muslim conflict over political rights and roles.

The existence of two distinct political organizations, each with a different religious base, threatened to destroy the possibility of India acquiring greater political rights. Two efforts at reunification achieved but temporary success in 1916, when Congress was reunified. Also, Congress and the Muslim League signed the *Lucknow Pact,* designed to reunify the broader freedom movement. Tilak and Jinnah played central roles in devising the agreement. They agreed that Muslims would be overrepresented in the legislative councils in proportion to the overall population. Ideally their membership in provincial legislative councils would range from 15–50 percent. More generally, both sides agreed to push for broader overall Indian participation in governance, including a guarantee that half of the members of the Executive Council be Indian. They urged that the right to vote be extended to a much broader group of the population. They also decided to demand that the costs of the British administration in India be paid by British and not Indian taxpayers. This platform still represented the moderates' point of view, ideas that would be destroyed by events after the First World War.

Radicalism. Radicalism emerged out of the sudden rise to leadership by Mohandas *Gandhi,* who introduced a new strategy, *satyagraha* (*truth-force*); Indian reassessment of British goals and power arising out of the First World War; and bloody repression by the British.

Gandhi became the most powerful leader of the radical freedom movement, whose principal goal was Indian independence. After studying law in England, Gandhi dramatically abandoned his infatuation with Western Civilization and came to praise traditional Indian civilization. Gandhi turned to *swaraj*—freedom from human desires, independence from the modern economic world created by the British, and political independence. Gandhi next went to South Africa and became a defense lawyer for Indians discriminated against by the Whites (see Chapter Five). In South Africa, Gandhi developed the strategy of *satyagraha*—peaceful civil disobedience. Back in India once again, Gandhi quickly became convinced that India must be freed of British control. Gandhi established a persona that appealed to the Indians' sense of traditionalism.

His assessment paralleled that of many educated Indians, including those active in Congress and the Muslim League. Educated Indians recognized that British global power had diminished substantially and that the British lacked the will to send large numbers of soldiers back to India. With reduced financial resources, the British could no longer afford their empire. The Indians understood that the British were leaving India—politically, economically, and psychologically. However, the future relationship of India and Great Britain and the timing of Indian independence remained unresolved during the period from 1920–1947.

The British massacre of Indians at *Amritsar* (1919) drove the moderates underground and pushed radicals to the head of the Indian freedom movement. Freedom no longer meant autonomy, it meant independence. Social unrest toward the end of the war and the influenza epidemic after the war (which left 12,000,000 dead) set the stage for the massacre. Amritsar was a Sikh center in the Punjab. The British arrested Sikh leaders who protested the continuation of martial law-like regulations. Sikhs then marched to the home of the British official who had ordered the arrests. When the British army killed several in the crowd, it went berserk, burning British banks and attacking British citizens. A new British military commander first ordered his troops to surround a public meeting and then to fire on the crowd. Four hundred Indians died and 1,200 were wounded. The British governor of Punjab expressed his full support for the massacre and declared martial law. Eventually *General Dyer,* the officer who had ordered British soldiers to fire into the crowd, was sent home to a hero's welcome. In Punjab, the British and the local population carried out acts of terrorism against each other. There was no turning back. Independence now seemed the only alternative.

The freedom movement, now dominated by radicals, followed a rhythm of radical outbursts and intermittent lulls that repeated itself until independence. The Amritsar massacre; the Calcutta Congress of 1919, which was stacked with large numbers of ordinary people, rather than the elite; and the death of Tilak left Gandhi as undisputed leader of Congress. Congress then embarked upon a brief campaign of *satyagraha.* At the same time it constructed a hierarchical organization, a 15-person Working Committee at the center, reaching down to the villages.

Pushed by radicals such as Subhas Chandra *Bose,* Gandhi conducted a campaign for immediate independence. Temporarily he redefined *swaraj* as "abandonment of the fear of death." British repression and religious violence accompanied this radicalization of the freedom movement. The Hindu Mahasabha party and Arya Samaj carried out a campaign of violence against Muslims in the Punjab. Muslims in the Malabar area of southern India conducted a holy war against Europeans and wealthy Hindus. In Bombay, Hindus and Muslims attacked Parsis, Christians, and Jews. Violence got out of hand, leading Gandhi to abandon *satyagraha* in favor of a *constructive program*—hand spinning and weaving, education, and sanitation efforts in the villages. Many became disillusioned with Gandhi's failure to fulfill the promise of independence and believed the shift to a constructive program a mere rationalization.

In 1922, Gandhi was arrested and after his release he abandoned political action until 1929. For the rest of the 1920s, communal violence, efforts at rebuilding the Hindu-Muslim alliance, and the issue of untouchability dominated politics. This gave the British a breathing space, since independence no longer seemed the main goal of the Indian peoples.

While Ali Jinnah and Gandhi condemned communalism and emphasized the need for Hindu-Muslim unity, violence continued, especially in the mid-1920s. Muslims were disappointed by the collapse of a Muslim reform movement, while the Mahasabha and Arya Samaj organizations attacked Muslims. The British did little to stop the local terrorism.

Gandhi sought to build up support rather than engage in direct confrontation with the British. In addition, he turned more and more to the issue of untouchability. Touring the country, he identified the untouchables as *harijans* ("children of God") and criticized Brahman treatment of these outcastes. Gandhi argued that swaraj was possible only when untouchability was eliminated. His efforts placed the issue of untouchability on the national agenda and built up support for him among the masses but failed to convince upper caste Hindus to reject untouchability.

By the late 1920s the possibility of Muslim-Hindu cooperation had largely disappeared. Gandhi was forced to turn once again to *satyagraha,* pushed in that direction by the newly created Socialist Independence for India League founded by Jawaharlal *Nehru* and Subhas Bose. This group called for immediate, total independence, while Gandhi still favored an independent India within the British Empire. When Nehru was elected president of Congress in 1929, Gandhi was forced to embark upon a new *satyagraha* campaign.

The Nehru-Gandhi alliance bore fruit in the *Salt Tax Campaign* of 1930. Salt was a government monopoly heavily taxed at the retail level. It was illegal for private citizens to manufacture or sell salt. Gandhi used the salt tax to mobilize mass support for the freedom movement. Gandhi and almost 100 followers marched from the interior to the coast, a trip of 240 miles. Each day crowds gathered, registering their support. Newspapers and wire services carried news of the march across the nation and worldwide. Gandhi challenged the British to arrest him and thus provoke massive opposition to British rule or to leave him alone, demonstrating British powerlessness. At the Indian Ocean Gandhi picked up some natural salt and called on all Indians to do the same. The Salt March dramatically expanded the power of the freedom movement, demonstrating that the Indian masses, and not just British-educated intellectuals, wanted freedom.

Gandhi was arrested after the salt tax campaign. Massive strikes and an anti-British terrorism campaign ensued. The British arrested over 50,000 Indian activists. Confrontation continued making peaceful resolution less likely.

During the 1930s, efforts at negotiations alternated with satyagraha campaigns. In 1930, British and Indian leaders met fruitlessly in London in the *First Round Table Conference on Reform.* Gandhi was soon arrested and after his release accepted what became known as the *Gandhi-Irwin* (Viceroy Lord Irwin) *Pact* of 1931. Gandhi agreed to end the civil disobedience campaign and the boycott of British goods and participate in the next Round Table. The British agreed to accept the idea of svadeshi (native production).

Nothing was achieved at the Second Round Table Conference (1931), whose participants included Gandhi and representatives of the Muslim League, the Sikhs, and the untouchables. The non-Congress groups demanded that separate electoral communities be established for each of them. In response to Gandhi's unwillingness to accept this arrangement, the British quickly jailed him, outlawed Congress, and arrested some 80,000 Congress activists. Tax boycotts, especially among the peasants, accompanied terrorism. In 1932, British Prime Minister Ramsey *MacDonald* announced the *Communal Award,* in which he agreed to separate electorates. Gandhi saw this as a strategy for destroying Hinduism and embarked on a fast. B. R. Ambedkar, leader of the untouchables, criticized Gandhi and Hindus for their treatment of untouchables. This led to the *Yeravada Jail Agreement,* by which Gandhi and Ambedkar, both in jail, agreed that untouchables would receive increased legislative representation and that untouchability would be abolished. The Congress left wing then criticized Gandhi for fasting in support of the untouchables. In 1932, Congress activism dissipated and a Third Round Table achieved no consensus.

Congress then turned its attention to the 1937 elections. It easily triumphed over the Muslim League and other contenders. The distance between Congress and the Muslim League widened, as the latter concluded that Muslims would not receive self-government in an independent India. Ali Jinnah suggested that Hindu political movements threatened Indian Islam. At the same time Congress was weakened by a power struggle between Bose and Gandhi. Bose was briefly victorious but Gandhi engineered the resignation of most of the Working Committee, undermining Bose's authority.

At the outbreak of the Second World War, Congress seemed no longer a militant threat to British power, while the Muslim League seemed hardly a player in Indian politics. The war made independence the only alternative, though the British were reluctant to accept this conclusion. In addition, the war drove a deeper wedge between Congress and the Muslim League, as the Congress and Hindus in general attacked the British, while the Muslim League sought to work with them.

Instead of pledging loyalty to the British, Congress embarked upon a satyagraha campaign early in the war. In August 1940, Viceroy *Linlithgow* offered to invite a number of Indians to join his Executive Council and proposed a War Advisory Council that would include representatives of various constituencies, including the princes. He promised that no changes in the political system would take place without consulting the Indian people. Instead of viewing this *August Offer* as a step toward independence, Congress viewed it as an attempt to bribe the Indians to be quiescent. After Gandhi initiated a satyagraha campaign in October 1940, the British responded with massive arrests and Bose organized a widespread terrorist action. Gandhi insisted that Indian independence must precede Indian support for the British war effort. The British believed that the Indians should support the war effort and after the war receive independence. The Cripps Mission (March 1942) symbolized the conflict between the two approaches. Cripps promised full dominion status after the war was over. Gandhi rejected this proposal and immediately initiated a new *Quit India Campaign.* Massive arrests and riots followed.

In 1943, Bose created a pro-Japanese Indian army and with Japanese assistance established a Provisional Government of Free India. Using Indian troops captured by the Japanese, Bose attacked India, reaching as far as the frontier capital of Imphal in northeastern India in March 1944. After that the Bose army was pushed back, finally surrendering in May 1945.

In contrast, the Muslim League supported the war effort. It was content to await the end of war, after which it expected to see an independent Muslim state. The British favored the Muslims because the latter supported the war effort. Discussion at Lahore in 1940 produced a general agreement that after the war there would be two Muslim states—Pakistan in the West and Bangladesh in the East. The Muslims expected that their support for the war effort and Hindu opposition would lead to an independence settlement favorable to the Muslims.

After his release from prison in 1944 Gandhi met with Ali Jinnah but both had hardened their positions. Gandhi argued adamantly for a unified India, while Jinnah insisted on independent Muslim states. The inflexibility of the Congress position was reflected in the collapse of the *Simla Conference* of June 1945. The British offered to turn over the government of India, with the exception of the viceroy and the military commander-in-chief, to the Indians. Recognizing that total independence was imminent, Congress rejected the idea. In the years before independence the British and Indians tried unsuccessfully to decide whether there should be one state in India or more than one.

In August 1946, Ali Jinnah initiated *Direct Action Day,* which turned into a bloodbath that continued even past the formal declaration of independence. Starting in Calcutta, Muslims attacked Hindus and Sikhs, who reciprocated. Ali Jinnah thus showed that the Muslims refused to be part of a unified India but great bloodshed resulted. Communal conflict would have been extensive even without the Direct Action.

In February 1947, the British Prime Minister Clement *Attlee* announced that India would be granted its independence by June 1948. He sent *Lord Mountbatten* to India to conclude an independence settlement. Finally a compromise was worked out. The British transferred power to a Dominion of India, in which each part of India would have the right of self-determination based on a *plebiscite.* Boundary committees were to be formed to determine exact borders.

Communal violence occurred on an unbelievable and inhumane level. Punjab, with its Muslim, Sikh, and Hindu populations was the scene of the greatest violence. Sikhs, using the slogan "Death to Pakistan," initiated violence against the Muslims when the latter established a government. The violence became a three-way struggle. Gandhi tried to stem the carnage with a *pilgrimage of love* but brutality only intensified. After independence, violence intensified even more. One million died as they tried to move from one country to the other in order to live in the religious motherland. Fear and death stalked India, not an auspicious way to begin independence in August 1947.

3. Ideological Differences

Ideological positions hardened in the era of formal empire. The British gradually lost faith in the idea of Western superiority. Unity among the Indians disappeared. Except for their support for liberal political ideals, the Hindus and Muslims had little in common. The Hindus emphasized the superiority of a Hindu civilization, looking back to an ancient golden age. The Muslims rejected the idea of cooperation with the Hindus and called for Muslim separation.

Decline of British Civilization in India. The idea that the British had a mission to perform in India, based on the superiority of Western Civilization, gradually lost its hold on the British in India. The Great Rebellion of 1857–1858 had weakened support for the ideal. At the same time, the granting of political rights to Indians automatically weakened support for the concept of British superiority. Political withdrawal and a diminishing economic role reinforced the weakening of British interest in a civilizing mission. Abandonment of the idea of a civilizing mission left a void in British ideology in India. A more defensive ideological approach emerged, an anti-ideology. The British begrudgingly granted more and more political rights and power to the Indians, yet rejected the idea of Indian independence. Pragmatism, more than ideology, motivated the British.

Common Indian Ideological Components. As the possibility of independence became more a reasonable prospect than a distant hope, Indians found it harder to maintain ideological unity. Certain common ideological elements derived from the British and British ideas. Independence became a goal for most Indians in the 1920s or 1930s. Justification for independence came from British learning and British ideology, including ideas such as self-determination, liberty, and civil rights. The Indians concluded that Indian civilizations were superior to British civilization. This is most clearly presented in Mohandas Gandhi's *Hind Swaraj* (*Free India*), written in 1909. However, religion divided the Indians irreconcilably.

Hindu Supremacy. From the last third of the nineteenth century on, Hindu political activists came to believe that traditional Hindu civilization was superior to British and Islamic ones. Ancient Hindu civilization was seen as the model for future India. Idealizing the pre-British and pre-modern period, some Hindus turned to traditional garb, hand spun and hand woven. The campaign for the restoration of traditional Hindu civilization drew large numbers of people into the freedom movement. This was especially true of the Brahmans, who longed to dominate India once again. The campaign for traditional Hindu civilization separated the Hindus and Muslims and made a case for Hindu superiority. For the first time in almost one thousand years, Hindus had an opportunity to control all of India and to banish foreign domination and influence. To ensure that Muslims would not be able to dominate India, the Hindus called for a religious-based, centralized state, rather than a federation. History and religion were thus the basis for this anti-British and anti-Muslim ideology.

Muslim Ideology. Rather than look back to past glories, such as the Mughal period, the Muslims looked to the future. They recognized that they had a better chance of maintaining some degree of power and influence in India by cooperating with the British. They began to espouse self-government within India and eventually independence from India for the Muslim areas. The Muslims thus abandoned the idea of a unified India, preferring a separate Muslim state. They recognized that a unified India would be Hindu-dominated. Muslims would have limited political power and be subject to attacks by Hindu supremacists. Ideologically, then, the Muslims equated religion with state-building, ultimately rejecting federalism and political decentralization and a secular state. As British ideology lost its influence, these competing religious-based ideologies came to the forefront.

4. Economic Development Strategies and Disengagement

The British government pursued some of the same economic development strategies as did the British East India Company. However, especially after the First World War, British business began to leave India. At the same time Indians began to engage in *import substitution,* moving from commercial activity into industry and international trade. Thus the British gradually withdrew from their dominant economic position in India. This shift did not reduce Indian poverty, suggesting that imperialism was not the sole cause of poverty, as Indian radicals claimed.

Economic Development Strategies. The British government continued to promote the technological modernization of India's infrastructure. They built metal-surfaced highways and extended the major east-west highway, the Grand Trunk Road, from Delhi to Peshawar in northwest India. Railroad construction boomed. By 1900 25,000 miles of track criss-crossed India. Until that time everything was imported, from track to locomotives to rolling stock. New irrigation canals led to dramatic increases in agricultural harvests in northern India.

The British government continued the BEIC strategy of treating India as a source of raw materials for the British domestic market and as a market for British finished goods. Building on indigo, opium, and cotton as commercial crops, the British promoted tea and coffee plantations in the second half of the nineteenth century.

The British acquired large amounts of land for tea plantations after passage of the *Assam Clearance Act of 1854.* Assam, located in northeast India, had an ideal climate for tea. Under the Act of 1854 British citizens could receive up to 3,000 acres of land if they promised to grow tea for export. The number of tea plantations increased from one in 1850 to almost 300 in 1871 and the harvest rose from 200,000 pounds of tea to over 6,000,000 pounds in the same twenty-year period. Coffee plantations grew rapidly between 1860 and 1885 eventually, producing 30,000,000 pounds of coffee per year. After that disease destroyed the industry.

India remained a market for British goods, not only iron and steel, but especially cotton textiles. In spite of the growth of a mechanized textile industry in India, British imports still supplied 90 percent of the cotton cloth consumed in India and over half of all imports. This continued British domination of India's textiles market was due to substantially lower British costs of production and to a policy of charging no import taxes on British goods but levying heavy export taxes on Indian-produced goods.

Jute represented the first major effort at import substitution. Industrial hemp was grown in India and made into jute bags, especially for the international grain trade—and later for sandbags used in warfare. Scottish mill owners began to shift their operations to India. By the 1880s, Bombay on the west coast had become a major jute mill center. Eventually Indian merchants gained control of futures trading in jute and used this leverage to shift supplies of raw materials to the jute mills they, rather than the Scots, owned.

Responding to a British decision to arbitrarily subdivide the large province of Bengal, in the early twentieth century Indian radicals initiated a "boycott British and buy India" campaign (the *svadeshi movement*). Indians purchased large amounts of handmade Indian cloth. Ironically, the campaign to buy traditional hand-woven cloth hampered the development of India's mechanized textile mills. The Indians also boycotted other products such as sugar, matches, glasses, shoes, and metal products.

In the decade before the First World War Indian capitalists moved into heavy industry. The leader in heavy industry was Jamshed N. *Tata,* who had gained his wealth from the largest mechanized cotton mill in India, the Empress Mill. He plowed his profits into the *Tata Steel Works,* which became the largest industrial enterprise in the country.

The trend toward increased Indian participation in industrial production and in the economy as a whole accelerated after the First World War. The war produced a shift of British capital away from India and that capital did not return. This lack of capital slowed economic development.

British businessmen began to withdraw from India, selling their holdings to local entrepreneurs. Since India faced serious economic difficulties in the 1920s, compounded by the Great Depression of the 1930s, it was a less profitable venue for British economic activity than it had been earlier. The radicalization of the Indian freedom movement and the svadeshi movement convinced many British businessmen that they could not maintain the profitability of their operations in India and thus it was better to leave. At the same time, Indian industrialists and bankers increasingly used their capital to promote Indian economic activity.

The Second World War brought renewed economic vitality to India. Native industrialists and landowners were the main beneficiaries of a British demand for Indian goods. Indian industrialists diversified as well, expanding into paper, cement, bicycles, locomotives, rolling stock, automobiles, chemicals, pharmaceuticals, and electric motors.

Thus, just as Indians gained a greater role in governance of the country, they also gradually increased their economic activity, so that by the end of the Second World War, Indians dominated the Indian economy. Much less change took place in Indian society.

Social Status Quo. Recognizing that efforts to promote radical social change in the first half of the nineteenth century had contributed directly to the Great Rebellion, the British government abandoned efforts to implement social change. Rarely did they try to deal with the vast social inequalities embedded in Indian society. However, British decisions indirectly promoted gradual social changes.

After the Great Rebellion the British made no attempt to promote social reform. Missionaries were ordered to minimize overt efforts to convert Indians to Christianity. Instead, Christian churches focused their energies on education and translating the Bible into various Indian languages.

By avoiding efforts at social reform, the British hoped to gain the support of the Indian elite. In addition, the British consciously sought to create a new loyalist land-owning elite. In 1859, the British restructured land holdings in newly acquired parts of northwestern India, returning to former owners previously confiscated land. These land owners, *taluqdars,* were to hold their land forever and could transfer the land to a single heir, the eldest son. The *taluqdars* fulfilled local government duties and professed their loyalty to the British. Zamindars and *sirdars,* (aristocrats from the Punjab) also became local magistrates. In 1862, the local elite in central India, the *malquzars,* also assumed positions in local government. In this way the British created and sustained a new elite of generally loyal landowners and local office holders. These actions extended the difference between landowners and peasants.

Indian industrialization also increased differences among the industrial classes. Industrialization expanded the size of the Indian proletariat, while making it possible for factory owners to acquire great wealth. Industrialization and increased urbanization placed great stress on the working class. Harsh treatment led to increased strike activity, especially after the First World War.

From the 1890s on, the position of peasants worsened dramatically. Bad harvests and subsequent famines led to massive suffering. The commercialization of agriculture reduced grain production, except in the wheat-rich area of the Punjab. The agricultural crisis of the 1920s turned into the suffering of the depression. The gap between the rural rich and the rural poor widened substantially in the first half of the twentieth century.

In this period of direct British rule, India became a more and more unequal society due to the continuation of caste, British efforts to create a loyal elite, industrialization, and a general crisis in agriculture. Differences based on gender and difference in roles within the family continued as well.

5. Gender Roles and the Family

Modest changes occurred in the family and in gender roles in the second period of British rule. The British government passed a few laws that formally affected the position of women and the nature of the family. Industrialization and urbanization had a deeper impact.

Women. British laws that redefined the position of women had little impact. In 1856, the British government passed a law permitting Hindu widows to remarry. In practical terms, this was a way to eliminate sati. In 1891, the British addressed the problem of child brides by raising the legal minimum age of marriage to twelve. These laws touched the edges of gender inequality but did not reach to the heart of the problem—a Hindu religion that promoted gender inequality and male domination.

The Family. Increased industrialization and the accompanying urbanization produced changes in gender roles and the nature of the family. Those who moved from the countryside to the cities partially separated themselves from the paternalistic, extended family. In urban families women frequently worked outside the home. With broader horizons and a separate income, working women had greater independence from males and greater power within the family. Access to education became a reality for a few urban women. Conflict within the family was a microcosm of conflict in society as a whole.

6. Communalism

No major changes occurred in the mosaic of difference that was India in the century from the Great Rebellion to independence. However, forces shifted from debate over differences to violent conflict. The Great Rebellion was a foreshadowing of this turn to violence. Some, mainly Muslims, looked to self-government or independence, while Hindus sought a Hindu state in which non-Hindus would have few rights. A few British officials, and sometimes Gandhi, espoused a multicultural society based on toleration and respect. Increasingly India was divided into a British world and an Indian world and the Indians further separated on the basis of religion. Caste and economic distinctions increased the degree of disunity.

The British against India. After the Great Rebellion, the British withdrew behind a high wall of isolation and then gradually abandoned India. Suspicious and fearful, the British retreated into British settlements, known as *civil lines* (British suburbs and urban districts). Servants were not to be trusted and the

British even felt ill at ease among Indian aristocrats and princes. Intermarriage disappeared almost completely and single British males sent home for British brides. British life centered in the local British Club. Efforts to create a loyal class of landowners and Muslim leaders worked in the nineteenth century but fell apart after the First World War. The British controlled India through the army, while dreams of a common destiny lay shattered.

Religious Communities. The conflict between Hindus and Muslims had been muted in the second half of the nineteenth century. Economic prosperity, the British policy of not antagonizing the Indians with proposals for radical social change, and hopes for gradual increases in Indian political rights helped to minimize Hindu-Muslim conflict.

However, communal violence increased in the period between the First and Second World Wars. Violence peaked in the 1920s, and then revived again on the eve of independence. Conflict occurred on two fronts—in the local communities and on the national political arena. Religious hatred motivated local mob actions. Hindu crowds attacked Muslims and their property; Muslims reciprocated. Thousands died in this undeclared religious civil war.

Political conflict intensified. The British and the Indians faced the obvious question of whether India should have self-government or independence and how quick the transformation should be. Of great consequence was the issue of how to structure a political system that would meet the conflicting demands of Hindus and the other religious and social groups who saw themselves as distinct from but equal to the Hindus. The Hindus and Congress wanted a unified, centralized state (which of course would be controlled by the Hindus). The Muslims, Sikhs, and other minorities wanted a political system that would guarantee them self-rule. With some hesitation, the British tended to support the decentralized model, in which each group would have a large measure of control over its affairs. British policy was reflected, for instance, in the *Communal Award* of 1932. Muslims, Sikhs, Indian Christians, Anglo-Indians, Europeans, and outcaste groups would each have separate electorates that would choose representatives to legislative councils. No compromise bridged the differences between the various groups. Terrorism gained the upper hand and Indian independence was accompanied by *religious cleansing.*

E. NEHRU ERA, 1947–1964

After the Second World War the British had little stomach for remaining in India but felt an obligation to promote an independence agreement that would keep India together and minimize violence. However, the British quickly gave up and an independent India, with a Hindu majority, and a Muslim-dominated Pakistan emerged out of communal violence. Soon after independence, a Hindu extremist who opposed Gandhi's vision of a diverse and tolerant India murdered him. Under his logical successor, Jawaharlal Nehru, India faced tremendous challenges. It needed to create a viable political system and establish a position in the post-colonial world. Rejecting British liberalism, the Indians sought to establish a set of alternative principles for Indian society and used religion as a basis for structuring ideology. In a country of great poverty, authorities tried to establish a successful economic development strategy.

Responding to the native impetus for radical social change coming from Gandhi, the Indian government addressed social inequality and the caste system. Economic development that promoted greater industrialization and urbanization further loosened the shackles of patriarchy. Though an independent Muslim state had been created, India was still not a homogeneous society. English was the most commonly spoken language, while no native language commanded a majority of the population. In addition, some 20 percent of the population was Muslim. India struggled unsuccessfully to deal with this new diversity. It built a new society, but not a true community.

The rest of the chapter deals with the histories of the three countries into which former British India was split. Sections E, F, and G trace the history of independent India, 1947–present. Sections H and I present the history of Pakistan, 1947–present. Section J describes the history of Bangladesh from its formation in 1971 to the present.

1. Independence and World Politics

Two tasks faced India immediately—defining itself geographically and determining its global role. Three princes had difficulty deciding whether to join India. Eventually only *Kashmir's* fate remained undetermined. The Kashmir issue has still not been settled. As one of the largest nations in the world, but a relatively powerless nation, India decided to seek a leadership role among countries trying to avoid alliance with the superpowers.

Borders and Allegiances. Though Pakistan had been created out of two largely Muslim areas in the west and in the east, native princes still had to decide whether to join India or Pakistan or remain independent. Very quickly all but three of the 550 native princes joined India. Hyderabad and Junagath had Muslim leaders and Hindu populations, while Kashmir, the largest of the princely states, had a Hindu ruler and a largely Muslim population. Surrounded by India, Hyderabad and Junagath meekly surrendered to Indian military forces in early 1948.

Kashmir. Kashmir's position was different. With a 75 percent Muslim population and bordering on Pakistan, Kashmir occupied a very strategic position. The Hindu ruler, Hari Singh, preferred independence but Nehru found that unacceptable. After Muslim peasants rebelled, Hari Singh agreed to transfer Kashmir to India. The British argued that the fate of Kashmir should be determined by a plebiscite after order was restored. Nehru agreed to this but after the British withdrew, he refused to hold a plebiscite. At the beginning of 1949 a cease-fire was concluded, dividing Kashmir into separate Muslim and Hindu parts, with the latter incorporated into India.

Leader of the Non-aligned Nations. As Prime Minster, Nehru personally directed foreign policy. Given his socialist background and India's desire to totally sever ties with Great Britain, it is easy to see why India would seek to be a leader among non-aligned nations. India's position was reflected in its participation in the 1955 Afro-Asian Conference in *Bandung,* Indonesia, the real beginning point of the third world non-aligned movement. Still, India could not ignore the major world powers. Relatively weak, India had to balance its relationships with the three major Asian powers, the Soviet Union, the People's Republic of China, and the United States. India saw the Soviet Union as a model for economic development strategies and a buffer against Western power. Initially India and China signed a Treaty of Friendship that meant that India would not oppose *Sinification* of Tibet. However rebellion among Tibetan peoples in China promoted unrest in Tibet. China decided to punish India when it accepted Tibetan refugees and appeared to be a staging point for the rallying of Tibetan nationalism. Border skirmishes broke out in 1959 and turned into a major war by late 1962. Though the Chinese easily defeated Indian troops, the Chinese suddenly withdrew. India's tilt toward Communist countries ended when the Indians turned to the United States for military assistance. Constitution building and politics in a newly independent state accompanied this creation of new boundaries and the development of foreign policy strategies.

2. "New Politics"

Independent India built upon the British constitutional tradition to form new political institutions. At the same time Congress had to transform itself from an opposition group into a ruling party, while challenges to its rule gradually surfaced. Jawaharlal Nehru was the architect of the new Indian political system. A handsome, regal-looking Brahman from the left wing of Congress, Nehru dominated constitution-making, foreign policy, and the creation of an economic development strategy.

Constitution. The Indian constitution combined British and American principles. The new constitution went into force in January 1950. Several broad concepts informed it. The constitution was to create an institutional structure that would preserve broad ideals, including justice, liberty, equality, and fraternity—the bases of Western liberalism. The constitution abolished untouchability, too. Sovereignty was to reside with the people (the concept of *popular sovereignty*). All Indians were to have the right to vote (173 million voted in the first elections in 1951). India was to be a *parliamentary democracy,* with real power centered in the *House of the People* (*Lok Sobha*), or lower house of the Parliament. The Prime Minister came from the largest party in the Lower House and simultaneously led both the legislature and the executive branch of government. The constitution provided for a complicated federal structure that included three types of states. State legislatures elected representatives to the upper house, the Council of State, with equal representation from each state. The central government was to have authority over defense, atomic energy, foreign affairs, transportation, energy, shipping, postal and telegraph service, and the monetary system. States were responsible for police, justice, public health, education, agriculture, forestry and fishing, and local government. Some powers were to be held jointly. These *concurrent powers* included economic and social planning, commerce, regulation of monopolies and trusts, and trade union issues.

In addition the constitution provided for *emergency powers.* The President, whose powers were largely ceremonial, could declare a state of emergency if he/she felt national security was threatened. A state of emergency could last up to six months. During a state of emergency all civil rights and constitutional procedures could be suspended, though decisions made during the state of emergency could be made permanent only through legislative action after emergency rule had ended. Finally, the constitution was easily amended. This meant that changes in political structure were easy to introduce when changes in political power occurred.

Congress Politics. Overnight India became the largest democracy in the world. On the basis of its leading role in the drive for independence and its nation-wide political network, Congress dominated Indian politics in the Nehru era. In 1951, Congress won 362 of 484 seats in the Lower House. The 1962 results were almost identical. Thus, ironically, Indian democracy produced one-party rule that lasted, with two short breaks, for some 40 years. Few changes took place in the new ideology of independent India.

3. Ideology

Independent India operated on the basis of a few broad principles, including democracy, non-alignment, socialist economic planning, Hinduism and the preservation of inequality.

Democracy. For India, the idea of democracy was a complex one. Of course it meant that everyone had the right to vote. But in practice it meant that the democratic duty of citizens was to confirm the Congress Party in power, unless its actions were so egregious that it should be removed from office.

Non-alignment. Non-alignment was a strategy to ensure that India did not fall under British sway. India sought to play one Asian power against others to its own benefit. Because it was the second largest country in the world in terms of population, India had an advantage in terms of access to support from all of the major global players. The Cold War enhanced India's opportunities. The danger, of course, was that India might be perceived as not really neutral but tilting toward one power or the other. In such circumstances, it might lose access to resources. Since India could not control the behavior of the powers it sought to balance, there was always the danger that a particular country might decide to use force against India, thus destroying the fragile balance of power that India wished to preserve in South Asia. Except for brief periods of conflict with China, India was fairly successful in remaining in the good graces of the Asian powers.

Socialist Economics. Having rejected the British model of economic development as well as the Gandhi ideal of returning to a pre-industrial economy, Nehru enthusiastically turned to socialist-style long-range planning, though with some modifications (see section 4 below).

Hinduism. Most leaders of Congress came from the Brahman caste and thus sought to ensure that the government supported Hinduism, though they declared India a secular state. The Party generally avoided overt introduction of laws that discriminated against non-Hindus and placed a token Muslim or Sikh here and there in the government. But it is clear that Congress saw India as a Hindu nation.

Inequality. Though laws were passed that legally ended discrimination and even established a kind of *affirmative action* program for the untouchables, Nehru and other national leaders espoused elitism in which former caste membership and wealth were the main determinants of power. Opportunities for social and political mobility were limited. Informal inequality reigned supreme.

Conclusions. Tensions between values—democracy vs. inequality and Hindu supremacy in a multi-religious state, for example—produced significant levels of unrest and violence. At the same time, leaders used economic planning to address the issue of poverty.

4. Social and Economic Change

Impoverished and lacking a modern industrial and agricultural base, India sought to develop strategies that would promote modernization and eliminate poverty without creating dependency on outside nations. At the same time it sought to honor Gandhi's social reform agenda.

Planned Economics and Unplanned Poverty. At independence India was a land of great poverty. It had lost part of its most important grain producing area, the Punjab, to Pakistan. Famine stalked the land in 1952–1953 because of bad weather. Population increased quite rapidly. Most of the population lived in deep poverty, while a few were "filthy rich." Peasants were extremely conservative, making agricultural modernization difficult to carry out. Most of the population was illiterate (in 1961, 24% of males and 13% of females were literate). Life expectancy was only 32. After the First World War the British had essentially halted their efforts to improve infrastructure, so existing irrigation systems, canals, and power grids were decaying and inadequate. However, since the British had been gradually withdrawing from a dominant role in the Indian economy and Indians had gradually assumed leadership roles in the economy, India did have talented and experienced industrial managers and technicians. Thus it was necessary for the government to develop economic strategies that would promote rapid economic growth.

Central planning. Nehru and Congress attempted to reduce poverty through a centralized system of planned economic development and through grass roots rural development projects. As a socialist, Nehru was an advocate of Soviet style centralized economic planning, thought to be the best way to transform a backward country into a modern industrial giant quickly. He had come to espouse socialist planning before anyone realized that long-range planning did not work well in the Soviet Union. Nehru's planning was tempered by three conditions. First, the economic plans were not merely bureaucratic documents decreed by the *National Planning Commission,* which Nehru headed. They also had to go through the parliamentary process. This produced rather modest plans that had some possibility of success.

Second, Nehru recognized that the plans should not merely promote the development of heavy industry. Different plans had different emphases, with agricultural frequently the main objective. The First Five-Year Plan (1951–1956) emphasized agriculture and consumer goods. In 1954, Congress declared that its main goal was the creation of a *socialistic pattern of society,* including the nationalization of all industry. The Second Five-Year Plan

(1956–1961) more ambitiously stressed heavy industry and family planning. The Third Plan sought to make India the seventh largest industrial power in the world through investment in power and heavy industry, but it also devoted substantial resources to battling illiteracy.

Third, many of the most important supporters of Congress were wealthy industrialists who ignored directives that would have interfered with their production of wealth. This was especially true of the proposed nationalization of industry. Since government, the private sector, and foreign aid (including the International Aid-to-India Club) paid the costs of the five-year plans, the government could not directly confront the capitalist economy.

Socialist planning promoted greater industrialization and an increase in the overall wealth of the country, but population growth left the country little better off per capita than before independence.

Grass Roots. Local community development sought to include citizen participation in the process of improving infrastructure and living conditions in the villages. Vinoba *Bhave,* Gandhi's closest disciple, carried out the first grass roots effort to deal with rural poverty. He traveled around the countryside asking wealthy landowners to give him land, which he then transferred to landless agricultural workers. Through this campaign, landless laborers received about one million acres of land.

With the assistance of the Ford Foundation, the government introduced the *Community Development and Rural Extension Program* in 1952. Ford's role was to fund the training of agricultural specialists and community organizers, who would then train villagers. Local projects included land reclamation, well digging, school construction, attempts to eliminate mosquitoes and other pests, greater emphasis on better seed, and the use of chemical fertilizers.

Though the focus was on local action at the village level, a complex, hierarchical structure was created to coordinate efforts and allocate resources. At the village level was the *panchayat,* said to be the ancient form of Indian democracy. Groups of five villages were gathered into project areas of 100 villages each and project areas combined into *community development blocks,* which encompassed about 200,000 peasants and approximately 150,000 acres of farmland. By the end of 1952, 55 community development blocks had been created.

Democratic elections always gave power to the largest landowners. Councils elected an executive officer to supervise individual projects and representatives to project areas and then blocks. Community development produced major improvements in living conditions in rural India and gave peasants a sense of ownership over the changes taking place. In this way, the cycle of peasant conservatism was undermined, though not destroyed.

Persistence of Caste and Emergence of Class. The legal abolition of caste had few practical consequences. Caste was so deeply embedded in Hinduism that its elimination would have been viewed as a betrayal of deeply held religious belief. Caste stigmas continued and social contacts between persons from different castes remained minimal and condemned.

Untouchability. Attitudes toward the untouchables changed—at least modestly. Gandhi's campaigns against untouchability gradually sank into the Hindu psyche. At independence some 60 million people were identified as untouchables (almost 20% of the population). In 1955, the parliament passed the *Untouchability Offences Act,* which established penalties for mistreatment of untouchables. A kind of *affirmative action* system was introduced for untouchables. The government established a quota system for central government positions, seats in state legislatures and the lower house of the national legislature. Universities were also required to set aside a certain number of places for untouchables (see Chapter Five for the use of affirmative action in South Africa).

Class. Though caste remained a vital symbol of inequality and opposition to change, a class system began to appear. This class structure overlapped with but was not simply imposed on top of the caste system. The elite remained virtually unchanged, consisting of university graduates and wealthy industrialists and bankers. Almost all came from the Brahman caste. An intermediate commercial class with ties to lower castes remained important. Greater industrialization reduced the distance between the city and the countryside. Workers began to identify themselves as proletarians rather than to identify with their caste position. Peasants remained the largest social group. The loss of part of the Punjab initially acted as a leveling force, for a large number of wealthier farmers found themselves in Pakistan. However, over time economic differentiation increased among the peasants. Still, caste remained a more powerful way of defining social position than did class. Gradual changes in gender roles and the family paralleled gradual changes in the social system.

5. Women and Family: Independence and Economic Development

Industrialization, urbanization, and literacy combined to produce significant changes in gender and family.

Women's Rights. Conditions changed after independence. All women were granted political rights, especially the right to vote. By the mid-1950s, 40 percent of women voted. Five percent of the members of the Lower House were female and over 100 women were elected to state legislatures. Modest opportunities for political leadership appeared as well.

Family. Efforts to eliminate caste differences were reflected in the *Hindu Marriage Validating Act* (1949), which permitted upper caste Hindus to marry people from other castes. In 1955, the *Hindu Marriage Act* granted women the right to divorce and raised the minimum age of marriage to eighteen for males and fifteen for females. Wives were permitted to seek divorce if their husbands had "co-wives" (concubines/mistresses). The *Hindu Succession Act* (1956) granted female children inheritance rights equal to males. None of this legislation applied to Muslim women, whose position remained defined by the *Qu'ran,* Islamic law, and tradition (*hadith*).

Laws only slowly changed gender roles and the structure of the family. Urbanization and industrialization pulled many young people from the villages into the cities. Many of the labor émigrés were female. An independent income and greater freedom to meet potential spouses modified the roles of urban women. The ability of the patriarchal extended family to control its urban members was weakened. In the cities the nuclear family became more common, in part because of the separation of rural and urban, and in part because economic circumstances neither required nor allowed for the extended family.

Improved literacy rates among women and the 1959 decision to introduce family planning also permitted greater independence for women. Declines in family size made it possible for some women to escape from a life-long cycle of childbearing and child rearing.

Independence led to improvements in the position of women and to the weakening of the role of the patriarchal family. Independence did not create a homogeneous, violence-free India.

6. Communalism and Attempts at Hindu Domination

Independence produced a more homogeneous India, but minorities remained. Twenty percent of the population was Muslim, while Sikhs rejected acculturation. Tribal groups on the frontiers opposed incorporation into the Indian governance structure. Kashmir remained a serious issue. The government, in spite of pledges to be a secular government, frequently promoted the interests of the Hindus over other Indians. For almost everyone, the tolerant multicultural society envisioned by Gandhi was a mirage, not a dream. Violence remained the major weapon for dealing with difference.

Difference. Many varieties of difference and conflicts over difference existed, including religious, linguistic, regional, ethnic, and social. Intense conflict existed for many reasons. In general, the government sought community by supporting one party to a conflict rather than by trying to bring both sides together. In this sense, authorities promoted violent resolution of conflict rather than peaceful methods. History played an important role, too. Millennia of conflict could not be quickly erased just because India was now independent. Building community was not a central priority for the government, which devoted its energies to the creation of a new constitutional structure, the development of economic policies intended to reduce poverty, and the establishment of a global position for India. The reduction of violence was seen as essential for the survival of India but not part of a conscious decision to build the kind of multicultural society envisioned by Gandhi.

Religious conflict continued, worsening after the death of Jawaharlal Nehru. In the year immediately following the declaration of independence, communal conflict continued with great ferocity. Gradually, conflict declined but animosity remained intense.

Conflict based on linguistic differences was intensified by government policy. India was a land of many languages, none spoken by a majority of the population. The most commonly used language was English, obviously not a candidate for national language. The Indian Constitution designated *Hindi* in the Devanagari script as the official state language. However, it was used by only 20 percent of the population.

Of equal importance was the issue of how to define political boundaries. Using a model similar to that introduced by Lenin in the Soviet Union, Congress had in 1920 reorganized the party into twenty-one provincial committees, with provincial boundaries determined by language. After independence, various language groups began to demand that political subdivisions be created for them. For example, in 1953, after their leader fasted, the Telugu speakers in southern India successfully lobbied for a separate state of *Andhra.* Nehru then created a study group, the *States Reorganization Commission,* in 1956. The Commission proposed and the government approved a reorganization plan that divided the country into twenty states and administrative territories, each based on a single language population. Apparently the central government was worried about the potential of a *Dravidian* separatist movement, the Dravidian Progressive Federation, which called for an independent Dravidistan in southern India. The Commission proposal blunted much of the support for a separate Dravidistan.

Sometimes language and regional issues overlapped, as in Bombay State. The northern part of the state had a Gujarati population, while the southern part was Marathi. Conflict between two nationalistic parties, the United Maharashtra Party and the Great Gujarat Party, turned violent. In response, the central government divided Bombay into two states—Gujarat and Maharashtra.

Disillusioned with these regional and linguistic struggles, Nehru concluded that India could not be kept together. Having a common enemy had held the Indians together, until the Muslim-Hindu conflict became too intense to permit a united India. Within the India that remained after the creation of Pakistan, conflict continued, threatening to tear India apart. This was apparent in the push for autonomy by tribal groups such as the Assamese, in northeastern India.

Caste was also a basis for conflict, in spite of laws prohibiting discrimination against untouchables. In many parts of India anti-Brahman riots broke out, focused primarily on destruction of their property. Anti-Brahman riots were strongest in areas where the Mahasabha organization had been strongest. Economic inequality thus became a basis for violence.

Symbolic of India's inability to conquer communal violence was the 1948 assassination of Mohandas Gandhi, murdered by a Hindu extremist, as he fasted in protest against the continuation of communal violence. This tragic inability to resolve internal conflict and build community continued to haunt India in the subsequent period, dominated by Nehru's daughter, Indira Gandhi.

F. DICTATORSHIP OR DEMOCRACY: INDIRA GANDHI, 1966–1984

Complex and controversial, Indira Gandhi came to power soon after the death of her father, Jawaharlal Nehru. She differed from her father in almost every way. Though she espoused the third world neutralism he championed, she also took advantage of tension between East and West Pakistan to invade East Pakistan and promote its independence as the new state of *Bangladesh.* This ensured Indian domination of South Asia. As leader of her own Congress Party faction, Indira Gandhi presided over almost constant political crisis, provoked mainly by her authoritarian style and corruption within her party. Ultimately she backed away from replacing democracy with personal dictatorship. Indira continued the Stalinist style economic planning introduced by her father, yet promoted modernization of the more advanced sector of agriculture through Western ideas, the *Green Revolution.* Family planning could not keep pace with the population increase, leaving the country little better off economically. Further changes occurred in the family and gender roles, including reduced male power within the family, the decline of the extended family and greater freedom for women. Communalism increased and spread beyond the Muslim-Hindu conflict as Indira sought to force centralization upon autonomy-oriented areas and promoted Hindu religious interests at the expense of Sikhs, as well as Muslims.

1. India and the World

Indira Gandhi continued her father's efforts to make India a world power, while devoting much energy and military might to become the dominant force on the sub-continent of South Asia.

India and the Third World. India continued to play an active role in the coalition of Third World nations, though the influence of these countries declined, as the United States turned away from global involvement and Soviet power gradually declined when the Soviet Union's Brezhnev leadership lost its grip on international activism. Ironically, the decline in the importance of the non-aligned movement enabled Indira to direct her energies to ensuring India's position as the most powerful state in South Asia.

South Asia. Twice in less than a decade India and Pakistan went to war. In 1965–1966 the two fought over Kashmir and Jammu in the Northwest. India was victorious but the truce that ended the war left the fate of Kashmir and Jammu unchanged and the issue unresolved (see section 6). In 1971, terrible economic conditions led millions from East Pakistan to immigrate to India, causing turmoil among the Indian frontier populations. India took advantage of the situation to declare war on Pakistan. Defeating the Pakistani army in the east and declaring India victorious, Indira paved the way for an independent East Pakistan, Bangladesh. In this way the Muslim populations of South Asia were divided into two separate states, weakening Pakistan and making it much less dangerous to India. At the same time Indira came across as a champion of Hindu superiority and demonstrated her ability to weaken Muslim power on the sub-continent. Her push to dominate South Asia was paralleled by her drive for total power within the Indian political system.

2. Politics and Political Conflict

Intense power conflicts marked the Indira Gandhi decades. Gradually the idealism and drive that had motivated the ruling party turned into corruption and lust for power. The weakening of Congress gave hope to its opponents, who briefly held power twice during the two decades between the death of Nehru (1964) and the assassination of Indira Gandhi (1984).

Conquest of Power. After Nehru's death, a collective Congress Party leadership assumed power. Though Lal Bahader Shastri became Prime Minister, a close Nehru associate, Kumaraswami Kamaraj Nader, held real power. Kamaraj believed that Indira Gandhi, a minor cabinet member in charge of the Ministry of Information and Broadcasting, was weaker and could be manipulated more easily than veteran Congress leaders. When Shastri died in 1966 Kamaraj threw his weight behind Indira, rather than the senior party leader Morarji Desai.

Initially Indira had great difficulty consolidating her power and gaining broad popular support. In 1967, the elected Congress won a bare majority in the Lower House and only 48 percent of the seats in the state legislatures. Conflict within Congress intensified and in 1969, Indira broke away, forming a *New Congress Party* extremely loyal to her personally. She and her followers represented the left wing of Congress. By 1971, she had consolidated her hold over the central government and strengthened the power of New Congress. The 1971 elections gave New Congress a landslide victory, as it won 68 percent of the seats in the Lower House. New elections the following year confirmed the broad popularity of Indira Gandhi and support for her program of socioeconomic reform.

However, her dream of total power was soon shattered. In 1974, economic difficulties produced huge riots, a fast by Desai, and the formation of a coalition of parties that aimed to drive Indira Gandhi from power. This coalition, known as Janata Morcha, seemed poised to achieve electoral victory.

Emergency Rule. In 1975, Indira Gandhi faced a constitutional crisis that threatened Indian democracy. A High Court judge found her guilty of committing campaign violations during the 1971 elections. The judge banned her from holding or running for office for a six-year period. In effect, she was expelled from office. Instead of meekly accepting the judicial ruling, Indira declared a state of national emergency. Her forces broke up anti-government rallies and arrested most leading opposition politicians. Eventually at least 10,000 were jailed for political opposition. Civil rights, including freedom of expression, were suspended. All political parties, except her Congress Party, were outlawed. She called the Parliament into session and forced it to approve the emergency measures. She pushed through constitutional amendments (according to the Indian Constitution, the Parliament approved all constitutional amendments) that prohibited the courts from challenging emergency rule. The frightened Parliament gave her immunity from judicial action and rescinded the high court's ban on her holding office. In 1976, she destroyed the power of her political opponents at the state level.

Indira Gandhi called her new regime *Disciplined Democracy*. Her foes mounted little resistance to this authoritarian regime. Some have argued that Hindu culture, with its emphasize on *dharma* or duty to fulfill one's responsibilities, made it easy for the Indian people to accept the overthrow of democracy. Certainly the repressive power of her government made opposition unlikely.

Janata Morcha. Suddenly in 1977, Gandhi announced an end to emergency rule, released political prisoners, rescinded the ban on political parties and called for new elections. She clearly believed that she had consolidated her position so solidly that she could afford to have elections confirm her power. She miscalculated.

Janata Morcha reappeared, now aligned with a party of ex-untouchables, the Congress for Democracy, which represented the 100 million ex-untouchables. Campaigning under the slogan, "Freedom and Bread," the coalition won

43 percent of the vote, while only 34 percent supported Indira's Congress Party. The defeat was made more humiliating by the fact that both Indira and her son Sanjay, projected as heir apparent, lost their seats in the Lower House.

Desai became Prime Minister of the Janata Morcha minority government. Janata failed to address the major issues facing India; instead it conducted a public puritanical campaign. Corruption and factional struggle monopolized the energies of Janata. In 1979, the left wing of the coalition abandoned Janata and Desai turned more and more to the support of orthodox Hindus within the government. Janata lost a vote of confidence and resigned.

Indira's Return. After parties made two additional attempts to form a government, new elections were held in 1980. Indira swept to victory, with her Congress-Indira Party winning two thirds of the seats in the Lower House. In office again, Indira became more and more authoritarian, while permitting more and more corruption in her government. Finally at the end of October 1984, two of her Sikh bodyguards assassinated Indira Gandhi. Her younger son, Rajiv, became Prime Minister, since Sanjay had earlier died in an accident.

Conclusion. The authoritarian government of Indira Gandhi increased support for pro-Hindu policies, introduced an agricultural revolution and continued support for state planning. Poverty still stalked the land, largely because of the continued population explosion. Though accepted by the Indian people, authoritarian democracy brought them few benefits.

3. Mixed Ideologies

Indira espoused two seemingly contradictory sets of ideas—cultural traditionalism and socialism. Each appealed to a different segment of Indian society.

Hinduism. She championed Hinduism and especially Brahman elitism, while using force against other religious groups, especially Muslims and Sikhs (see section 6). Support for traditionalism cushioned the blows of socioeconomic change. It also provided a broad political base, especially among the still very powerful Brahmans. Encouragement of traditional Hinduism lent credence to her anti-Western foreign policy, too.

Socialism. At the same time, Indira Gandhi continued to promote socialism and state planning (see section 4). She still believed that the Stalinist economic model provided the most effective basis for modernization and thus national strength. World socialism reached its greatest influence during the period that Indira Gandhi was in power in India and rejection of socialism would have left India relatively isolated in Asia and among non-aligned countries as a whole. Socialism also differentiated India from Pakistan.

This tension between cultural traditionalism and socialist modernization added to the trouble Indira Gandhi faced during the two decades of her rule.

4. Socialism, "Green Revolution," Poverty, and Caste

During almost fifteen years in power, Nehru had addressed the issue of poverty, concluding that rapid modernization through socialist-style planning was the best way to overcome it. His efforts brought only small improvements to the lives of ordinary Indians. His daughter, Indira, too faced the problem of deep poverty. She continued his strategy of rapid modernization through socialist planning, even placing greater emphasis on a socialist economy through further nationalization. She faced the same barriers to rapid modernization, including a poorly educated population, a lack of technical training and skills and continued rapid increases in population (by 1969, the population of India was 530 million, only half of whom were literate). Gandhi added two weapons to the arsenal of strategies to pull India up from poverty—agricultural revolution and family planning.

Socialist Economics. Indira concluded that socialist economics had failed because it had not gone far enough. The economy still retained too many capitalist elements, she believed. Therefore, she was determined to make India a more socialist country. In 1969, she called for nationalization of banks and limits on corporate earnings and individual income. By this time the government owned almost all of heavy industry. In 1973, further nationalization took place. Coal mines were nationalized and the government assumed control over all wholesale food markets. In 1975, when the population reached 600 million, planners emphasized heavy industry and energy sectors, especially in response to the energy crisis of 1973–1974. At the beginning of the State of Emergency, Gandhi announced a *Twenty Point Program* of economic reforms. This hodgepodge of programs sought to limit inflation through state price controls, reduce corruption, including tax evasion, and promote hand production.

The economy responded to expanded government decision-making. By 1969, India had the seventh largest industrial economy in the world. The industrial growth rate reached 6 percent in 1975 and 10 percent in 1977. Increased capital investment (some of it from abroad), as well as a peaceful labor scene, contributed to this growth.

Green Revolution. Even greater success reached agriculture, largely through the *Green Revolution.* The Green Revolution produced a major increase in the size of harvests in the primary grain producing areas of India. The Green Revolution introduced high-yield Mexican wheat and Taiwanese and Philippine rice, all developed through U.S. research. These much more productive strains of grain had shorter growing cycles but required relatively fertile soil and more fertilizers, pesticides, and water. Farmers needed to manage the soil more effectively and had to work more diligently than average peasants.

Thus the Green Revolution was applied primarily in areas where farmers were already better off and better educated. It was not extended nation-wide and may have contributed to greater differentiation among peasants. It reduced the threat of starvation and contributed to the overall increase in grain production that enabled the country to feed its growing population but did not generate a surplus.

At the same time, Gandhi promoted plans for the redistribution of farmland—away from the wealthier farmers, who were producing additional grain, to the landless peasants, who were less productive farmers. Three years of near-famine in the 1970s halted efforts at land redistribution. However, a bountiful harvest in 1975 made it possible for the Twenty Point Program to include a radical call for redistribution of the land. Proposals to provide owners with compensation for land surrendered could not counter the reduced productivity that the plans incurred. In reality, Gandhi could not afford to accept reduced agricultural production and the loss of political support from wealthier farmers that radical land distribution would have produced. Thus the redistribution plans were dropped.

Family Planning. Family planning was another major approach to reducing poverty. The population was growing at alarming rates, over 10 million per year. In the late 1960s Gandhi began to invest heavily in family planning, focused primarily on educating women. In 1975, Gandhi turned her attention to the male population, introducing a program of vasectomies for men who had fathered too many children. She met the resistance of a male-dominated society and traditional concerns that the high infant death rate required almost constant pregnancy of rural women. Family planning was most successful in the cities, especially among educated middle-class women.

Filled with contradiction, the economic policies of Gandhi brought greater wealth to India and a more productive economy, though Indian economic growth was not at all unique among Asian nations at this time. Poverty was not erased; Gandhi's policies barely reduced it.

Persistence of Caste and Rise of the Middle Class. Caste, too, persisted; though increasing evidence of class differences appeared. Village vigilante actions against inter-caste marriages represented the most brutal of informal prohibitions against contact between persons of different castes. The former untouchables remained social outcastes, in spite of legislation outlawing untouchability and a strong interest group movement supporting the former untouchables.

At the same time, industrialization and urbanization began to produce clearer class divisions in the cities. An upper class of the intelligentsia and industrialists began to distinguish itself from the urban proletariat.

5. Women and the Family

Change came slowly to gender relationships and the family. That the most powerful person in India was a woman was a model for some but Indira's power came from her family ties, her Brahman caste status, and her authoritarian personality, not from her gender.

Gender Traditionalism. The government did not pass laws to improve the position of women, as it had under Nehru. Instead, change was gradual, resulting from economic forces, educational improvements, and the declining birth rate resulting from family planning. India thus followed the pattern of other countries in the early stages of industrialization and rapid urbanization.

Little changed in the countryside, even though the younger generation of women began to receive some education. Rural families were still patriarchal. Conflict within the families generally took place among the women, especially between unmarried daughters and daughters-in-law who had been added to the extended family.

Modest Changes. In the cities, more and more families had nuclear structures, with two breadwinners. This produced smaller family sizes and less inequality between husbands and wives. Still the rural extended family acted as a magnet attracting sons and daughters who had moved to the cities.

Thus socioeconomic change rather than government policy weakened the patriarchal family and produced greater independence for women. Government policy, heightened by Indira's authoritarianism and tendency to see violence and force as the best way to resolve issues, was at the heart of the deepening crisis of diversity.

6. Communalism Transformed and Continued

Poverty and diversity were the greatest problems facing Gandhi. Her actions exacerbated rather than reduced diversity issues. Almost every part of India was racked with conflict based on diversity. Ironically, for the first time, Muslim-Hindu discord became less important than other types of conflict.

Regional Conflict. Some of the conflict was regional in nature. Tamils and Hindus fought in southern India. Bihari and *Bengalis* came into conflict in east central India. Gujarati and Marathi clashed in west central India. Communal conflict broke out periodically in Gujarat, Uttar Pradesh, Punjab, Bihar, and Maharashta (central and western India).

On the northeastern frontier, barely connected to the rest of India by a small strip of land, rebellion smoldered throughout the entire period. The peoples of the area were organized into seven tribal states, including Assam, Nagaland, and Manipur. Northeast India had contained a mixed religious population of Hindus, Christians, and Muslims. The original inhabitants of northeast India were known as *tribals,* people organized on the basis of tribe and hardly incorporated into the Indian political system. Ethnically the tribals were quite different from the other people of India. They were Burmese-Mongoloid and spoke Sino-Tibetan and Tibeto-Burman languages. Though primarily Buddhists, some were Christians and others were *animists.* In northeast India, religious differences were thus less important than local rights.

On the one hand, Indira Gandhi sought to increase Indian control over these remote areas. Assamese, Mizo, and Naga tribals, along with Hindu and Christian urban residents attacked the Muslims, including those who had lived in the region for centuries.

In 1965, Gandhi sent troops into Nagaland to put down an uprising. The civil war that produced an independent Bangladesh led to the migration of millions of Muslims into the northeast. They cleared the jungles and turned to rice cultivation. Both their numbers and their sedentary life style seemed a threat to the tribals. Unrest was heightened by the Indo-Pakistani war of 1971, when as many as 5–10 million Muslims fled to the Northeast. They added to the millions of Muslims who had gradually migrated into the northeast since independence. The tribals feared that Islamic customs would inundate their societies and outsiders take over their political systems.

Unrest gradually grew until open rebellion broke out in 1979–1980. Assamese were the most militant, forming an *Assam Liberation Army* that used the satyagraha against the Indians. In addition, they threatened to close down the Assam economy, which was based on oil, tea, and jute. The Assamese demanded that Muslim immigrants be sent back to Bangladesh. The Indian government responded by introducing martial law. Finally a united front was created, the *Seven United Liberation Army,* composed primarily of Naga, Mizo, and Assamese tribals. Unrest continued in the Northeast in the last years of Indira Gandhi's reign. In northeast India, religious differences were less important than local rights.

The Sikh Situation. Sikhs in the Punjab posed the greatest diversity problem for Indira Gandhi and other Hindus. Though most Indian states had a largely homogeneous population, this was not true of the state of Punjab. About one-third of the state's population was Sikh, concentrated in the northwest half (which also contained a sizeable Muslim minority, too). Hindi-speaking Hindus were concentrated in the southeast half, known as Haryana. In addition, Sikhs were prominent in the Indian officer corps. Finally in 1966 the government divided Punjab into three states—Punjab, Haryana, and Himachal Pradesh. This, however, did not reduce Hindu-Sikh conflict. Extremists increasingly dominated both sides. The Sikh radical party was *Akali Dal* (The Eternal Party). Arya Samaj and Jan Sangh, which organized "Save Hindi" demonstrations, led the Hindus. Akali Dal increasingly called for an independent Sikhistan or Khalistan (land of the pure). The Sikhs strongly opposed the state of emergency and came to power in Punjab from 1977–1980. Gandhi tried to undermine the power of Akali Dal by promoting a rival Sikh "saint," Jarnail Singh Bhindranwale. Bhindranwale, instead, turned radical, espousing Sikh independence more firmly than Akali Dal did.

Violent conflict became inevitable after Bhindranwale and his followers occupied the *Golden Temple* in the Punjab capital of Amritsar in 1984. They announced that they would not leave until Punjab was independent. Sikh and Hindus fought with great ferocity. Under pressure from Hindu extremists, Gandhi initiated *Operation Bluestar,* a siege of the temple by Indian soldiers. The temple was taken in June and thousands of Sikhs killed. Within six months, Sikh bodyguards assassinated Indira Gandhi. Violence produced more violence. In retaliation Hindus attacked Sikhs in New Delhi. A reign of terror resulted, with the police ignoring Hindu violence against Sikhs. Hindu gangs were encouraged to attack Sikhs and Sikh property. Sikh-Hindu hatred temporarily replaced Hindu-Muslim animosity as the main diversity problem in India.

Kashmir. Kashmir faded into the background during this period. India had defeated Pakistan in the 1965 war but the 1966 truce left the boundary between the Indian province of Jammu and the rest of Kashmir where it had been under Nehru. Conflict was muted, as well.

Conclusion. Communalism took precedence over community building in Indira's India. The murder of Indira Gandhi, who had championed government sponsored and/or approved violence against minorities, symbolized the failure of violence as a means of dealing with diversity.

G. CONTEMPORARY INDIA, 1984–PRESENT

The death of Indira Gandhi launched a new era in Indian history. The Indian oxen began to change course. Though the Nehru-Gandhi family continued to play an extremely important role in Indian politics, new forces appeared, threatening the family's power. Hindu fundamentalism emerged as a powerful and disruptive force, while Congress found it difficult to maintain control over Indian politics. India's non-aligned tradition was weakened as India tilted more and more to the west, the consequence of the Soviet invasion of Afghanistan and the collapse of Communism almost everywhere. Increasingly, capitalist enterprise, Western investment, global trade and the information technology revolution drove the Indian economy. On other fronts, future direction was unclear. Gradual changes occurred in the family and in gender roles, still propelled slowly by modernization and urbanization. The government oscillated between toleration and community building on the one hand and Hindu supremacy on the other, generally preferring the latter.

1. India and the World

Indira Gandhi's death brought about debate and disagreement over India's role in the world. Eventually India resolved this issue by moving closer to the West, especially the United States.

Four trends emerged. First India turned toward the West, especially opening its economy to Western financial assistance and trade. This enabled India to begin to move away from Soviet-style economic planning, especially after the collapse of Communism. This transformation began in 1984 with American president Reagan. After India-Pakistan border clashes in 1999, the United States offered to mediate. This shift toward ties with the West culminated in U.S. support for India's nuclear technology program, in a sense violating provisions of the 1968 Nuclear Non-Proliferation Treaty. This decision came in 2005–2006.

Secondly, India increasingly saw China as a threat because of tense Indian-Chinese relations on the northeast border. The two countries clashed over possession of some 100,000 square miles of mountainous land. India also saw China as an economic rival, especially as India sought to expand its exports to the West and to Southeast Asia. This possibility of conflict with China also pushed India more and more toward the West. Basically India sought to prevent China from becoming too powerful globally.

Tension with Pakistan intensified, as India continued to dominate the South Asian sub-continent. In 1998, India had tested nuclear weapons; Pakistan soon followed suit, launching its own nuclear weapons' tests. Now each country has approximately seventy nuclear weapons and is thus capable of destroying the other. Conflict intensified, especially from 1998–2004, when the Hindu fundamentalist *Bharatiya Janata Party (BJP)* was in power in India. The two countries also battle over Kashmir. Pakistan supports militant, pro-Pakistan forces in Kashmir. Pakistan sent military units across the line of control at Kargil three times between 1999 and 2005, with the Indian army defeating the Pakistanis each time. The two countries remain close to war.

The fourth development—a turning inward—has been heightened by Hindu traditionalism and domestic unrest in Pakistan. Chaos in Afghanistan, resulting from the American victory over the Taliban and the destruction of part of al Qaeda after September 11th, has further exacerbated Pakistani-Indian conflict.

2. Politics

The long period of Nehru-Gandhi rule drew to a close, with no clear future political direction evident. The power of the Nehru-Gandhi tradition died slowly. Since the mid-1980s no consensus has emerged over which political forces should run the government. In this sense, Indian politics has come to resemble politics in much of the rest of the democratic world (See Chapter Three for Japanese parallels). Instead of an authoritarian, one-party democracy, India has become a democracy in which shifts in power and direction are frequent and voters fickle in their attachment to particular parties. This has produced a series of coalition governments and thus a shift from one party (Congress) domination to fragmentation. Regional, caste, and class-based parties have replaced national political parties. Congress and BJP remained the two strongest parties. Policy now focuses on economic liberalization and, as always, the reduction of poverty and inequality.

Historically disadvantaged groups, such as lower caste and untouchable groups, have considerable electoral power. Lower caste groups vote at much higher rates than do the elite and the middle class.

Rajiv Gandhi. A mammoth outpouring of emotional support gave Rajiv Gandhi a landslide victory in the 1984 elections. The public expected much of Rajiv and saw him as a representative of "modern" India. Though he tried to move India away from state domination of the economy and to "westernize" the country, Rajiv could not overcome high levels of corruption within the Congress Party. Increasingly he faced an emerging Hindu fundamentalism that opposed modernization.

Political Instability. After Rajiv fell from power in 1989, a series of short-lived governments ruled India. First Vishwanatu Pratap Singh, from the Janata Dal Party, came to power with the support of the Bharatiya Janata Party (BJP). BJP soon moved into opposition, forcing Singh to resign. Then Rajiv tried unsuccessfully to manipulate Indian politics from behind the scenes. With the approach of new elections in 1991 three competing forces emerged: Singh's Janata, Rajiv's Congress Party, and the Bharatiya Janata Party, led by L. K. *Advani.* Just before the elections Rajiv met the same fate as his mother—assassination—this time at the hinds of a Tamil (southern Indian) extremist. Once again communalism produced death. Once again, Congress came back into power, though BJP strength was growing.

Led by Narasimha *Rao,* Congress remained in power for five years. Rao emphasized secularism and social justice. Secularism and efforts to promote the interests of the lower classes alienated the upper class Hindu activists. In 1995, the increasingly powerful *Hindutva* (Hindu-ness) movement produced Bharatiya victories in much of northern and central India.

In the 1996 elections, Rao focuses his energies on attacking Advani, accusing him of bribery. A number of Congress cabinet members were also indicted for corruption. Charges and counter-charges of corruption reduced public interest in the election. Bharatiya emerged with the largest number of seats but its minority government stayed in power for less than two weeks. The new government, a coalition known as the *National Front,* came into office, led by H. D. Deve *Gowda.* In 1999, another coalition government came to power. Lack of consensus and lack of political direction continued, with Hindu fundamentalists remaining a powerful force and the Gandhi family continuing to be a force to be reckoned with on the political stage. Sonia Gandhi, Rajiv's widow was elected president of the Congress Party, while her son, Rahul, flexed his political muscles.

Politics Today. After a six year period of a BJP-led coalition government, Congress returned to power in 2004, first as part of a coalition with left-wing parties and then by itself. Monmohan Singh became Prime Minister. Congress power was reconfirmed by 2008 elections. Whether this represents the beginnings of another long period of Congress, and thus one-party, rule, is uncertain.

3. Ideology

Two broad sets of ideas competed in the post-Indira period—*liberal secularism* and Hindu fundamentalism.

Liberal Secularism. Secularism espoused Western ideas, viewed India as part of the Western world, and focused on issues of social justice, especially eradication of poverty. Secularism opposed a state religion and supported socialism and democracy. The secularists argued that India had much in common with Western societies, especially in terms of democracy. This was a rejection of the anti-Westernism that had dominated Indian politics since Mohandas Gandhi arrived on the scene at the end of the First World War. Politically, these ideas are found in the Congress Party.

Hindu Fundamentalism. Hindu fundamentalists rejected secularism and Westernization. Seeing Hinduism as the vital core of Indian life, they believed in the value and morality of violent confrontation with Muslims (see section 6).

Authoritarianiam is a central tenet of Hindu fundamentalism. As a political movement, represented by Bharatiya Janata Party (BJP), Hindu fundamentalism has championed the market economy. Its "India shining" campaign in the 2004 elections shows a contradiction between modernism and fundamentalism. This contradiction is, perhaps, resolved, by the argument that market capitalism will create an India on the same high level (economic rather than cultural) as traditional Hindu India of the classical period.

Neither the secularists nor the fundamentalism could dominate the ideological front.

4. Capitalism and Prosperity

During the last two decades India has introduced major changes in its economy. It has moved away from state planning and toward a more capitalist economy. Abandoning the idea that they should have an *autarkic* economy (one totally independent of outside economic forces), Indian authorities have encouraged foreign investment and international trade. After a serious recession in the late 1980s, the economy has grown rapidly, reaching 6 percent from 1990–2000 and 6–8 percent per year more recently. The growth rate under socialism was about 4 percent.

Rejecting Planning. Upon coming to power, Rajiv Gandhi began to reduce bureaucratic rules, lower taxes on the wealthy, and eliminate socialist elements in the economy. It was easier to carry out planning when the government owned substantial portions of the economy, the "commanding heights" of some heavy industry, transportation, energy, and banking. Rajiv dismantled much of the planning system. However, the process of selling off government economic properties has gone slowly, though it has accelerated in the last few years. Deregulation has been a government privatizing strategy. Agriculture remains backward in part because of continued regulation. Instead of accumulating investment capital primarily through the tax structure, capital is increasingly generated by two stock exchanges, which rank third and fifth in the world in terms of numbers of transaction.

Service Sector. India has emphasized the service sector, especially information technology, telemarketing, and pharmaceuticals. Half of the economy's growth has been generated by this sector. The service sector represents 51 percent of GDP (Gross Domestic Product/total value of goods and services), while manufacturing totals 17 percent. In China, manufacturing represents 30 percent of GDP.

Globalization. Rajiv Gandhi and Foreign Minister Manmohan Singh led a globalization campaign that opened up the Indian economy to the world and to capitalism. Initially the Indian government sought loans from the *International Monetary Fund* and the *World Bank.* Later the government encouraged foreign investment. A breakthrough came when IBM and Ford signed *joint-venture* agreements with Indian firms. Between 1991 and 1996 $10 billion in foreign investment flowed into India. Pepsico, Xerox, and Kentucky Fried Chicken, among others, entered the Indian market. Though initially Americans were the principal foreign investors, Japan and Singapore later made major investment in Indian industry. India emphasized high-tech industries and a *Silicon Valley* emerged in the *Bangalore* area of southern India. Here software engineering, call centers, and telemarketing firms came to dominate.

From 1991–1996, growth was so rapid that many talked of an *Indian economic miracle.* In this short time frame the Indian economy grew as much as it had in the entire period 1947–1991. In this five-year period exports increased 20 percent per year; industrial production grew by 10 percent annually, while inflation was brought under control. Still, exports totaled only 2 percent of world trade. Asian economic problems of the late 1990s did not slow the Indian economy. In the early years of the twenty-first century Indian economic growth ranked second to that of China among major countries.

From time to time Indian leaders have regretted the economic changes, especially globalization, which meant Westernization. They have called for a return to traditional Indian economic principles, especially hand production. Such efforts had little impact on the changed direction of the Indian economy.

Barriers to Economic Growth. Still, India faces serious barriers to further economic growth. Illiteracy remains high, especially among women. Only half of all Indian women cannot read and write. Agriculture remains backward, trying to sustain the glory days of increased agricultural output that came about through the Green Revolution. Plots are small, equipment primitive, and the countryside overcrowded. Infrastructure remains backward, with only modest modernization of the British-built infrastructure of the imperial period. For example, 40% of the Indian fruit crop spoils before it can be transported to urban markets. Poverty limits the domestic consumer market and is thus a drag on economic development. Though much has been done to reduce government's decision-making role in the economy, business law discourages entrepreneurialism and the creation of new companies.

Population. Substantial population growth accompanied this rapid economic expansion. By the end of the twentieth century India's population had reached one billion. Population projections suggested that by the year 2030 India would surpass China in population, reaching 1.5 billion. Life expectancy has increased from 34 years at independence to 65 today.

The movement toward free enterprise and globalization has had and will continue to have profound effects upon India, reducing the differences between it and other Asian countries.

Social Classes. India is divided into classes, and in practice differentiated by caste. At the top of society are the Brahmins (10% of the population). The middle class, increasing in size, numbers 25 percent. Peasants number 25–30 percent of the population. The lower class numbers 20–25 percent and is comprised mainly of landless agricultural laborers. The untouchables are approximately 20 percent of the population.

Toward Social Equality? Great inequality has continued to characterize Indian society. Caste, long prohibited legally, remained a common social practice. However, wealth increasingly became very important in differentiating people, especially in the first years of the twenty-first century. Economic growth also produced increasing economic and social differences as upper and middle classes benefited most from the economic miracle. Over 300 million landless peasants, urban slum dwellers, and homeless people gained little from economic growth.

Responding to increasing inequality, Prime Minister Rao proposed a major program of social welfare, including free school meals for poor children, maternity pay for poor mothers, pensions for poor senior citizens, and assistance for OBC (other backward classes). The government found it difficult to fund these social welfare programs. Inequality has been regional with half of the poor located in four states.

Poverty has declined only modestly, from 36 percent in 1990 to 25 percent in 2004. The poverty rate is set at a daily income of $1 per person. Average daily income is about $3 per person.

5. Family and Gender

Economic change also promoted social changes as well. A dramatic tension existed between traditional and modernizing forces.

In spite of improvements in the position of women, India has remained a land of much gender inequality. Patriarchy flourishes. The death rate for baby and young girls is much higher than that of boys.

The revival of Hindu fundamentalism led to an increase in violence toward women. This was reflected in *kitchen fire deaths* of women, especially young brides. If the parents of the bride failed to pay the bride price, the husband and his parents might murder the bride. Dowry burnings still number 11,000–15,000 per year. Sometimes such a murder is just an easy way for a husband to rid himself of a wife for whom he didn't care. Also, especially in the predominantly Hindu area of Rajastan, *sati* (widow burning) returned.

Approximately 50 percent of families are nuclear and 50 percent extended. In the cities the nuclear family has predominated, while in the countryside extended families were still common. Close familial relations between urban and rural relatives were common as well, as urban residents frequently returned to ancestral homes for important celebrations, such as weddings.

At the same time women's position has improved through continued gains in education and modernization of the economy, which have created greater job prospects for women. Campaigns for family planning reduced family size (2.2 children per family in India; 2.1 in the U.S.), providing women with greater opportunities and some alternatives to traditional roles.

Women have been increasingly active in politics since the early 1990s. A kind of affirmative action has been introduced, with one-third of seats on regional and local councils reserved for women. Untouchable and lower caste women tend to be more active politically than upper caste women. Hindu women are extremely active in anti-Muslim efforts. Hindus criticize Muslim men for "oppressing" Muslim women and suggest that Muslim women could be "saved" by subordination to Hindu men.

6. Diversity and Violence

Community is of declining importance in India. Belief in democracy remains the most important unifying force. In spite of an official policy of secularism, religious difference has played a powerful and violent role. Difference remained a serious issue. Perhaps in reaction to the murder of Indira Gandhi, who had promoted violence against non-Hindus, a brief period of toleration ensued. However, by the end of the 1980s, Hindu fundamentalism and the government's centralizing tendencies had produced bitter conflict once again. The situation was complicated by a dispute over affirmative action. In spite of the high levels of conflict, India remained a single state, with the issue of Kashmir a potential disintegrative force.

Diversity. India is characterized by religious diversity. 82 percent of the population is Hindu, 12 percent Muslim, and 2 percent Sikhs. Smaller numbers are Christian, Jewish, or Buddhist. Over 22 languages are spoken by over 1 million people. The government recognizes over 600 "Scheduled Tribes," which demand special rights. Caste and class differences are huge.

Hindu Fundamentalism, Terrorism, and the Punjab. Hindus, a privileged elite, dominate the government and use its powers to promote Hindu values.

Anti-Muslim riots occurred in Bihar in 1989 and in Gujarat in 1992 and 2002. One of the most controversial developments was the Shah Bano decision of 1995. The national legislature overruled a government decree authorizing Muslim custom to hold sway among Muslims. In 1999, Hindus began to attack Christians. Great violence has taken place in the Punjab. Rajiv also sought to resolve issues involving the Punjab but with little success. Through the *Punjabi Accords,* the Punjab had been redistricted, with some primarily Hindu areas detached and added to Harayana state, while Chandigarh was selected as the capital of Punjab. The pro-independence for Punjab party, Akali Dal, won the 1985 elections, after which the Indian government suspended the Punjab Accords for a six-year period. The decision backfired, leading to a sharp increase in violence. Large numbers of Indian police and soldiers, brought in to restore order, killed many Sikh youths. The governor of Punjab tried unsuccessfully to bridge differences between the Indians and the secessionists Sikhs, leading Rajiv to impose *President's Rule* (a form of martial law) on Punjab. Director General of Police, Julio *Ribeiroas,* promoted intensified violence and arrested large numbers of Sikh youths. Between 1989 and 1991 Prime Ministers Singh and Shekhan tried to resolve the conflict but could not. This led to the *Ayodhya* crisis.

Ayodhya. Ayodhya was the location of a sixteenth century mosque, Babri-Masjid, built by the Mughal emperor Babur. Hindus demanded that the mosque be torn down and replaced by a new Hindu temple in honor of Ram (hero of a famous Hindu epic poem). Hindus claimed that the site was the actual location of the birthplace of Ram, who had been honored with a Hindu temple, later torn down by Babur. Millions of Hindus made pilgrimages to Ayodhya.

A crisis broke out when Advani, head of Bharatiya Janata, had loyal followers pull him in a golden chariot toward Ayodhya. The Brahman *Universal Hindu Society* mobilized many villagers to join the pilgrimage. In a sense, both the Brahmans and Advani used the deep faith of ordinary Hindu villagers to seek their own aims—for the Brahmans continued domination of Hindu society and for Advani the quest to become Prime Minister. Fearing violence and rejecting the idea that India should become a Hindu state rather than a secular one, Prime Minister Singh ordered Advani's arrest. Bharatiya then withdrew from the governing coalition and Singh's government fell, leading to several years of political instability. In late 1992 Hindus finally stormed the mosque, destroying it and killing all of its inhabitants.

Anti-Muslim Attacks. This act of violence triggered attacks against Muslims, including the murder of thousands of Muslims in Mumbai (Bombay). In Mumbai the *Shiv Sena Party* (*Shiva's Army*) led the pro-Hindu initiative. Muslims in Pakistan and Bangladesh responded by destroying a number of Hindu temples in their countries. Hindu fundamentalists, organized in Shiv Sena, called on all Muslims to become Hindu or leave "Hindustan." By 1995, support for these ideas enabled the Bharatiya Janata Party to gain control over state governments in much of central and north India. Bharatiya had manipulated the religious fervor of Hindu masses for its own political purposes.

Northeast India. Conflict centered in northeast India, the Punjab, central India, and Kashmir. In northeast India, religious differences were less important than local rights. Rajiv reduced tension by turning political power over to appropriate tribal political movements, including the Assam People's Party and the Mizo National Front. In 1987, the Mizo area became the state of Mizoram. These agreements permitted the Indian army to withdraw from the Northeast. However, the agreements began to fall apart very quickly. Tribal political movements then began to demand that all outsiders leave the Northeast. As violence intensified, the Indian army was sent back into Assam.

Gurkhas. Unrest also broke out in Gurkhaland, the Darjeeling area of north India. The *Gurkhas* were best known for their skills as mountain climbing guides. Many of them had served in the British army in India, spoke Nepalese, and were much closer to the Gurkhas in Nepal than to the neighboring Bengali. Indian police and soldiers tried to crush the Gurkha National Liberation Front, which sought either independence from India or union with Nepal.

Central India. Central India was also the scene of substantial conflict over diversity. Separatist movements emerged in Maharashta, Uttar Pradesh, Orissa, and Meghalaya states. Groups demanded independent Uttarkhand, Jharkand, and Garoland nations.

At the same time, Hindu fundamentalism flourished, centered on the *Lord Ganesha miracle.* Ganesha was the younger son of the Hindu god, Shiva, and appeared in an elephant's head. In 1995, reports of Lord Ganesha drinking milk spread in large cities, leading tens of thousands of Hindus to bring milk to temples. Millions believed that Shiva and his entire family had returned to earth in need of milk and that the rule of Rama had returned.

Kashmir. Kashmir, where India still kept 600,000 soldiers to "occupy"/ "defend" it, remained a flash point. In the 1980s violence was on a relative low level, as some thirty people were killed. Two groups of insurgents espoused different ideals. The Jammu and Kashmir Liberation Front is secularist and calls for an independent Kashmir. The Islamic Hizbul Muhadeen seeks unification with Pakistan. In 1989, the India government and the Indian Intelligence Bureau put down mass Kashmiri protests. Provoked by the Indian Intelligence Bureau, most Hindus (some 100,000) have fled Kashmir. Conflict intensified in the years 1989–1996. Violence intensified in 1995 when Kashmir separatists kidnapped the daughter of the Home Minister. In 1996, several Western tourists were kidnapped. Violence escalated. The vast majority of Kashmiris sought independence. Only a minority wanted Kashmir incorporated into either India or Pakistan. The situation became tenser with the migration of a number of Muslim tribals from the independent portion of Kashmir into the Indian state of Jammu and Kashmir. The pro-Indian party lost the 1999 elections. At the end of the twentieth century pro-independence Muslim guerillas captured mountain ridges in Kashmir but a large Indian army finally drove them into Pakistan. After September 11th, India claimed that Muslim Pakistanis in Kashmir were agents of international terrorism. No solution to the violence in Kashmir seemed in sight, despite intermittent negotiations and a decline in violence in the early twenty-first century.

Conclusion. A nation of great diversity, India has been unable to successfully employ non-violent means to address such issues. Violence has produced further violence rather than solutions. Governments have encouraged violence, as have religious fanatics. The notion that India is a secular state in which all religions are tolerated and none control the government has remained an unrealized ideal.

H. PAKISTAN, 1947–1971

The newly independent Pakistan was left with fewer natural resources than India and the disadvantages of being divided into two parts quite distant from each other. Attempts to create a civilian, democratic government came up against a military whose main goal was national security. To justify its illegitimate rule, the military encouraged an increase in the public role of Islam. Pakistan's economy was based on two sets of outside ideas—socialism, from the Soviet Union, and the Green Revolution/agricultural modernization, from the United States—neither of which was able to overcome the nation's poverty. Government played a key role in defining and supervising the basic social institution—the family. Though women secured political rights, they could not escape from patriarchy. The separation of Pakistan into two very different subparts ultimately proved more important than ethnic diversity in the West and religious conflict in the East.

1. Independence and Weakness

For Ali Jinnah and the Muslim League, independence and the creation of a Muslim state had been a dream. In reality, it was much more of a nightmare. Independence produced a divided Pakistan, dominated by the west Pakistanis and threatened by the absence of internal cohesion and difficulties of communication. Pakistan, the size of California, lost key agricultural lands to India and faced a national security threat from a much larger and much stronger independent India. With the fate of Muslim Kashmir not settled, Pakistan could expect fierce resistance from India if Pakistan tried to add Kashmir to Pakistan.

Consequences of Division. Because the Muslim population of India had been concentrated in two geographical areas a thousand miles apart, the possibility of creating a unified, cohesive state was remote. A concentration of Muslims in central India that might have connected both parts would have created an India unacceptably divided into North and South, so India invaded and captured the Muslim areas of central India. India also prevented Kashmir, a Muslim state in the north, from either becoming independent or being attached to Pakistan.

The two parts of Pakistan were Muslim but had little else in common. West Pakistan was a bit larger (170 million), ethnically diverse, and lacking in natural resources. However, it was able to dominate the country, even though east Pakistan had a slightly smaller population (130 million), greater natural resources, and ethnic cohesion (mainly Bengals).

Geopolitical Insecurity. Thus, at independence Pakistan found itself in a weak position geopolitically. To compensate for weakness, especially against India, Pakistan turned to outside alliances. Pakistan looked westward and joined both the Baghdad Pact that included its western neighbor, Iran, and aligned with SEATO (South East Asian Treaty Organization) to the east. Neither treaty gave Pakistan much security and actually helped to pull Pakistan apart because western Pakistan was closest to members of the Baghdad Pact and eastern Pakistan to the nations of SEATO. Toward the end of this period relations with the United States turned sour, leaving Pakistan relatively isolated. Pakistan's only friend was China, which also saw India as a threat.

Pakistan and India. India became and remained the main national security threat for Pakistan, a threat that could not be overcome by participation in weak and fragile alliances, whose main aims were to blunt the expansion of Communism.

Kashmir symbolized the conflict between India and Pakistan. The first of three wars was fought in 1948, as the Indian army invaded Kashmir. Though India defeated the Pakistanis, it was not able to secure control of all of Kashmir. Under international pressure, Kashmir was divided into two zones, one Indian-occupied and the other closely tied to Pakistan. Though Nehru promised to support a plebiscite through which the people of Kashmir could decide their fate, that plebiscite was never held. In the 1965 war, India badly bruised the Pakistanis, demonstrating its military superiority. The third war between India and Pakistan broke out in 1971 and led to the independence of East Pakistan, which would call itself Bangladesh.

2. Military Rule vs. Democracy

Though it had the same kind of political background as India, a legacy of British ideas, Pakistan travelled a very different route. For the period 1947–1971, Pakistan was primarily under military rule. In 1953, the *theory of necessity* was announced. According to this idea, the military had the authority to dismiss a civilian government and rule in its place if national security was threatened. National security demanded that Pakistan have a strong military. The military saw domestic order as an essential component of security—and thus continued independence—and feared the civilian government was not strong enough to meet the challenge from India. From independence until 1958 Pakistan struggled to develop a constitutional system. Military rule, especially through the dictatorship of Ayub *Khan*, lasted until the disintegration of unity in 1970–1971. The 1970 elections brought the East Pakistanis to power, produced a civil war between East and West Pakistan, and divided the country into two independent nations, Pakistan in the west and Bangladesh in the east.

Foundations, 1947–1958. Initially Pakistan retained British-era political institutions and only developed its own constitution in 1956. The constitution created a unicameral legislature and declared Pakistan an Islamic Republic. Power was in the hands of the westerners, especially the Punjabi, the largest ethnic group in western Pakistan. At first Pakistan had a civilian government led by the Pakistan People's Party (PPP). However, civilian rule was corrupt and when attempts were made to replace democracy with authoritarianism, the army stepped in, placing Ayub Khan in power.

Ayub Khan's Military Dictatorship, 1958–1971. Khan created the illusion of democracy through *Basic Democracies*. Basic democracy established a type of *oligarchy*—rule by the few. Khan reduced the number of citizens—those with the right to vote or hold office—to an elite of 80,000. He thus rewarded the elite in a country of great social inequality and limited political rights to those who could understand the importance of national security and political stability. Ordinary people, he claimed, were incapable of making the right decisions.

Bangladeshi Independence. Yahya Khan, who ousted Ayub Khan in 1969, decided to hold democratic elections in 1970, the first since 1956. The *Awami League*, led by Sheikh Mujibur *Rahman*, won the elections. The Awami League was headquartered in East Pakistan and mainly represented the Bengali Muslims of the east. The League won a few seats in the west and thus held a majority of places in the national legislature. However, Yahya Khan rejected the results of the election and refused to call the national assembly into session. Infuriated, the east Pakistanis rebelled. Pakistan then sent in an army to quell the uprising. However, a Bangladeshi (Bengali) National Liberation Movement, aided by the Indian army, badly defeated the Pakistani army. Rahman then declared independence, thus splitting Pakistan into two separate states. The unwillingness of the westerners to share power with the east and their failure to recognize Bengal as a national language had produced intense resentment in the east. This history of Pakistan, from 1971 to the present, is thus a history just of the western half of the Pakistan that was created in 1947.

3. Secularism vs. Islamism

Secular ideas initially gave direction to Pakistan. Ali Jinnah, the founder of Pakistan, represented this perspective. However, from the beginning, in practice Pakistan was a religious state in which most people were Muslim. The 1956 constitution declared Pakistan an Islamic Republic, though what that meant was not clear at the time. Presumably the citizens were Muslim and their government would be guided by Islamic ideals. Military leaders justified their illegal seizure of power by increasing the Islamic content of their governance. Eventually, an Islamist Party—*Jamaat-i-Islam (Islamic Society)*—emerged and later even joined the government. Islamism is a conservative strain of Islam that calls for a theocracy and the application of Islamic provisions to all aspects of public and private life. (See Chapter Six for the emergence of Islamism in Algeria.)

Two Nations Theory. In 1940, Ali Jinnah, leader of the Muslim League, developed the concept of *two nations*. He argued that Hindus and Muslims should have their own, separate states. In addition, he made a distinction between Pakistan as a secular country in which a Muslim majority lived (his goal) and Pakistan as a Muslim state where Muslim law determined public policy. Pakistan began independence loyal to the ideas of toleration and secularism, as espoused by Ali Jinnah. His early death (1948) made it easier to abandon these ideals.

Jamaat-i-Islam (Islamic Society). Jamaat-i-Islam was a *cadre* organization and not a mass movement. It consisted of a small cadre of dedicated leaders. The group saw Islam as a political ideology and not just a set of religious imperatives. Jamaat-i-Islam argued that Pakistan should become an Islamic theocracy dominated by the Qu'ran, shar'ia, and hadith. The group was anti-Western, condemning the Western impact on daily life and Western influence over the political system. Western Civilization, they argued, had provided the rationale for secularism. Later Jamaat-i-Islam assisted the Pakistani army in its unsuccessful attempt to break the Bangladeshi independence movement and later entered Pakistani coalition governments.

4. Poverty and Slow Economic Growth

In the years 1947–1971 Pakistan remained a poor country with substantial amounts of inequality. Strategies to reduce poverty and inequality—socialism and the Green Revolution—did little to modernize the economy and improve living conditions.

Disadvantages of Independence. Independence brought few economic advantages to Pakistan. Partition caused economic dislocation, especially the elimination of complementary trade relations. India acquired most of the natural resources and much of the industry. At first Pakistan's sole economic advantage was rich, productive soil in East Pakistan. Given the location of two of the three great South Asian rivers in Pakistan, substantial hydro-electric power was available, and the huge irrigation system was well-watered. Eventually large deposits of natural gas were found along the shoreline of both West and East Pakistan. To overcome these economic disadvantages, Pakistan turned to the creation of a socialist industrial economy. Later, Pakistan would employ the Green Revolution to feed its population. Pakistan, however, remained a very poor country with huge social differences, especially in the western parts of the country.

Socialist Industrial Sector. In the 1970s Pakistan turned to the introduction of a socialist industrial sector, nationalizing key factories and instituting a loose system of central planning. The strategy did not work well, given the limited role of industry in the agriculturally-based Pakistani economy. The economy grew at a rate of about 4 percent, not enough to improve per capita GDP and the living standards of the Pakistani people.

Green Revolution. The Green Revolution was introduced in 1963, at a time of terrible famine and soon after the program was launched in India. The Green Revolution involved high-yield varieties of grain; sufficient watering through irrigation, chemical fertilizers and pesticides; and much more careful and scientific work by the farmers. The 1965 war with India slowed down the expansion of the Green Revolution. However, by 1968, Pakistan was self-sufficient in wheat. The wheat harvest doubled from 1965–1970. Money no longer needed to buy food abroad gave Pakistan more funds for industrial investment. Pakistan seemed to have begun to turn the corner economically. However, the 1971 break-up of Pakistan reduced the successes of economic development.

Social Differences. Poverty and inequality were deeply imbedded in Pakistan's complex social structure. The caste system did not apply in Pakistan, even among the many Hindus who initially lived in East Pakistan. West and East Pakistan had very different social structures. This had broader implications for differences in political systems, ideology, and ideals of community. In West Pakistan there was great inequality, as society was divided into two social classes—an elite class of very large landowners and a large lower class of peasants, many of whom were agricultural laborers.

There was less social and economic inequality in the east. Here the dominant group was a middle class of business men and the intelligentsia—doctors, lawyers, professors, teachers, and journalists—and a lower class of smallholders—peasants who owned their own small farms.

5. Gender and Family

Patriarchy, deeply influenced by state sponsorship of Muslim family law, created parameters within which women and the family functioned. Women's relative freedom at independence was continuously reduced. (See Chapter Six for parallels in Algeria.) The subordination of women was greatest in the countryside.

Women and Patriarchy. At first women were active in public life. In 1947, women received the right to vote in local elections. The 1956 constitution extended rights of citizenship for women to national elections. In addition, a small number of seats in the national assembly were set aside for women. Political activism was soon replaced by social exclusion. At independence, female literacy was relatively high. However, the small number of girls in schools reduced the rate over time.

Muslim Family Law Ordinances of 1961. Initially Pakistan retained British law related to the family. The military government was determined that government play a major role in determining marriage law. In 1961, it thus issued the *Muslim Family Law Ordinance*. The law demonstrated a rather liberal interpretation of Islam and gave the government an important role in determining rules of marriage. Marriages were viewed as secular acts and were registered with the government, rather than approved by religious institutions. Polygamy was strictly controlled. The local government council ruled on a husband's petition to have more than one wife. Local government had to be informed of divorces. Finally, responding to the question of child marriage, the law set the minimum age of marriage at eighteen for boys and fourteen for girls. Thus the government gave itself the power to be deeply involved in the most basic social institution—the family.

6. Community + Diversity

Difference was of great importance in both West and East Pakistan. However, the nature of the diversity was quite distinct. Diversity brought much greater conflict and violence to the west than to the east. Difference was maintained in the west and reduced in the east.

Ethnic Difference. Ethnic differences played an important role throughout Pakistan, though the ethnic composition of the two parts of the country was quite different and yielded different consequences. Numerous ethnic groups lived in West Pakistan, while almost all of the east Pakistanis came from the same ethnic group.

East Pakistan. In East Pakistan almost everyone came from the same ethnic group—the Bengalis. Bengalis were found in both East Pakistan and in the eastern parts of India. This ethnic unity shaped the Bengali's political goals. At first a *language movement* acted as a substitute for nationalism, as the east Pakistanis rejected the idea of Urdu as the sole national language and demanded equal privilege for the Bengal language. The west Pakistanis refused.

West Pakistan. Tremendous ethnic diversity characterized West Pakistan, where the largest—and politically dominant—ethnic group was the Punjabi (some 60 percent of the population of West Pakistan and thus about one-third of all Pakistanis). The next largest group was the Pashtuns, located in northern Pakistan (some 15 percent of the population of West Pakistan). The Sinds from southern and central Pakistan were only slightly less numerous (14 percent of the population of the west). Seven percent were *muhajirs*, Muslims who had moved from India to Pakistan after independence. Four percent were Balochs, a Persian-Syrian people in western and coastal Pakistan. In West Pakistan, the Balochs were the strongest opponents of Punjab domination. Finally, in the northwest were a number of *tribals*, members of small, unruly tribes, never pacified by the British and relatively independent under Pakistan.

Baloch Resistance. The Balochs have continued to protest inclusion in Pakistan. In 1947 the Balochs declared their independence, only to be overridden by the Pakistani government and military. In this period, the Balochs rebelled three times—in 1948, 1958, and 1961. The discovery of natural gas in Balochistan in 1952 intensified Baloch desire for independence and Pakistani insistence on retaining the territory. The main strategy of the Pakistani government was to try to undermine Baloch tribal structures and institute centralized control over Balochistan. Rebellion became fiercer after Bangladesh gained its independence from Pakistan, raising similar hopes among the Balochs.

Religious Minorities. Most Pakistanis were Muslim but there were significant numbers of religious minorities, especially in East Pakistan.

West Pakistan. In West Pakistan 98 percent of the population was Muslim, split between Shi'ia (25–40 percent but gradually dwindling in proportion) and the majority Sunni. There were small numbers of Hindus, Christians, Sikhs, Jains, and Buddhists, many of whom had been untouchables before independence. The most important—or most dangerous from the perspective of the Muslims—were the Ahmadi (Ahmedi in the Bengal language). The Ahmadis claimed to be Muslims who emphasized tolerance and rejected jihad. They were condemned as non-Muslims, outlawed, and persecuted. Their mosques were destroyed and they were prohibited from public worship and from seeking new members publically.

East Pakistan. The vast majority of east Pakistanis were Muslim but at independence Hindus numbered as much as 20 percent of the population. That number quickly dwindled, remaining rather constant at about 10 percent. The Muslim government enacted expulsion policies and confiscated the property of Hindus. Religious difference trumped ethnic commonality—the east Pakistani Hindus and Muslims were both Bengals. The initial emphasis on Bengal nationalism soon took a back seat to religious identity.

Economic and Social Differences. Economic and social differences characterized the Pakistanis, especially in the west. This vast gap between the small landholding elite and the mass of impoverished landless peasants also divided the Pakistanis.

Muslim Community. Though Ali Jinnah had dreamed of a Pakistan in which all of its citizens were deeply nationalistic, possessed a common Muslim faith, and were tolerant of difference, Pakistan emerged in independence as a deeply divided society. True, most Pakistanis were Muslim and this gave Pakistan the semblance of community. Religious commonality was not enough to overcome other differences, especially in a country in which the largest ethnic group—the Bengals—was discriminated against and powerless.

Ethnic and religious differences and intolerance promoted by the government created serious problems for Pakistan, both as a united country and after division into Pakistan and Bangladesh in 1971.

I. PAKISTAN, 1971–PRESENT

This smaller Pakistan faced a number of challenges. Most important was the question of how to guarantee national security to this more vulnerable Pakistan. Again, the key factor was the value and reliability of allies. The Pakistani military wondered whether its rule would become permanent, largely giving a positive answer to the question. The military believed that it could best justify its power through an appeal to conservative Islamic ideas. Still committed to socialism, authorities only belatedly expressed a preference for capitalism as an approach to reducing poverty. There seemed little need to change the family, while women's rights were largely ignored. Tolerance and peaceful resolution of difference seemed luxuries Pakistan could ill-afford.

1. Small Pakistan and National Insecurity

Defeat in the 1971 war with Bangladesh and India damaged the Pakistani economy and undermined Pakistan's national security. It left India, the mortal enemy, a dominant power in South Asia. Indian-Pakistani relations and the Kashmir issue dominated Pakistan's foreign relations.

Consequences of Bangladeshi Independence. The economic weakening of Pakistan reduced its ability to adequately fund its military. India was emboldened, now certain it would easily dominate Pakistan. This made it more difficult to secure a resolution of the Kashmir issue.

Kashmir, India, and Pakistan. Conflict with India continued, with Kashmir the central scene of battle. In 1972, Pakistan was forced to agree to a *line of control*, dividing Kashmir between India and Pakistan. The Indian army occupied its part of Kashmir and set about consolidating its control. Pakistan's power over the rest of Kashmir was much weaker.

During the War in Afghanistan, Pakistan concentrated on supporting the mujahidin against the Soviets. The coalition of Pakistan, the United States, China, and Saudi Arabia enhanced Pakistan's security. Once that war was over, relations between India and Pakistan became tenser. In part this was due to the rise of Hindu fundamentalism and in part to Pakistan's renewed isolation, resulting from the weakening of the war-time coalition. In 1998, first India and then Pakistan acquired nuclear weapons, producing grave danger to the South Asian sub-continent. In this tense situation, a brief war broke out in Kashmir. In the twenty-first century relations have improved as both sides have sought to reduce conflict.

Geopolitics. Pakistan was part of the geopolitics of Asia, as the Soviet Union, the United States, and China sought to involve Pakistan in broader geopolitical issues. From 1965 until 1980 U.S.-Pakistani relations were quite strained, largely because of Pakistani military rule. In 1979, America cut off all economic and military assistance to Pakistan. However, the War in Afghanistan produced an abrupt turnaround and a return of significant U.S. military and economic assistance. After the War in Afghanistan, U.S.-Pakistani relations again soured. The War against Terror again brought improved relations, huge amounts of American military assistance, and intense pressure on Pakistan to end the terrorist safe havens along the Pakistani side of the Pakistan-Afghanistan border.

China and Pakistan retained close relations throughout. At first, China saw Pakistan as a counter to Soviet power in South Asia. After the collapse of the Soviet Union and the increase in India's global economic power, China saw Pakistan as a thorn in the side of the Indians, a means of forcing India to divert resources from economic development to military preparedness against Pakistan.

2. Militarism and Democracy

The military dominated politics in "Small Pakistan." It found it even easier than earlier to make the argument that only the military could ensure domestic stability that was such an essential part of national security. Democratic elections were held but the military dominated the government.

Civilian Government of Zulfiqar Ali Bhutto. Two major political parties generally alternated in office, though they had limited power. They were the Pakistan People's Party (PPP) and the Pakistan Muslim League (PML). The key figure in the 1970s was Zulfiqar Ali Bhutto, who primarily served as foreign minister. In 1973, the constitution was amended to substitute a bicameral legislature for a unicameral one.

Military Dictatorship of Zia ul-Haq. Mohammed Zia ul-Haq seized power in 1977 and ruled Pakistan until his death in a plane crash in 1988. The American ambassador and key Pakistani military figures also died in the crash.

During his reign, the military made Islam a powerful political force in Pakistan (see Section Three).

Alternating Parties. In the 1990s the military remained powerful but retreated into the background. Led by Benazir Ali Bhutto, Zulfiqar Ali Bhutto's daughter, PPP held government reins from 1988–1990. Nawaz Sharif of PML then came to power from 1990–1993. Ali Bhutto came back into power for the years 1993–1996. Nawaz Sharif replaced her from 1997–1999. These civilian governments placed greater emphasis on economic development, family planning, and anti-poverty programs.

Military Dictatorship of Musharraf. Condemning the weakness of civilian rule and arguing that India's possession of nuclear weapons necessitated a stronger Pakistani government, Pervez Musharraf instituted a military dictatorship in 1999. He remained in power into 2008. Musharraf ruled through a National Security Council. Though in 2007 he appointed himself to a five-year term as President, public protests forced him to resign the next year. Under pressure from the United States, Musharraf took military action against the Pakistani Taliban and began to reduce the power of Islamists and overturn pro-Islamist legislation such as the Hudud Ordinance.

Return to Democracy? Both Ali Bhutto and Sharif were permitted to return from exile imposed upon them by Musharraf to compete for political power. However, Ali Bhutto was assassinated in late 2007 as she campaigned for office. Her husband Asif Ali Zardari was elected head of the government. However, he had little sympathy for democracy and tried to become a dictator. Public unrest forced him to abandon those goals. Pakistan remained a country in which civilian rule was weak and the military constantly ready to take power.

3. "Ideology of Pakistan"

Under Zia ul-Haq Islam came to occupy a central place in Pakistani public life. This was personified by an anti-blasphemy law and the Islamization of the educational system. Jamaat-i-Islam came to play an important national political role, in spite of its limited electoral appeal.

Triumph of Islamism. In 1974, Khursid *Ahmad* outlined the key ideas of Islamism. Pakistan needed to become an ideal society, known for its Islamic purity. He condemned the "axis of evil"—the United States, India, and Israel. According to Ahmad, only the Islamists stood in the way of American domination of the world and the total destruction of Islam.

Blasphemy. In 1979, Zia ul-Haq issued a *blasphemy law*. To say anything that could be interpreted as defaming Islam, the Qu'ran, Allah, or any religious personage became a capital crime, punishable by death. The law was a little-used symbol of intolerance (five cases from 1984–2004) but a powerful threat to dissent. At the same time the Islamic penal code replaced the secular law code. In 1981, Zia ul-Haq announced the abandonment of secularism, replacing it with the "ideology of Pakistan"—the idea that to be Pakistani was to be Muslim.

Islam became the state religion. Zia ul-Haq drastically expanded the role of Islam in the educational system. Religious instruction was introduced during school hours and the reading of the Qu'ran became a secondary school graduation requirement. Madrassahs (religious schools) were declared the equivalent of public schools and graduates of madrassahs were eligible to attend state universities. An Islamic University was created and "Islamic Studies" introduced at universities. Arabic became Pakistan's second language.

Rise of Jamaat-i-Islam. The government's support for Islamism strengthened the political power of Jamaat-i-Islam, especially within the military. The party continued to call for a theocracy and a dominant role for shar'ia (Islamic law). However Jamaat-i-Islam had little broader influence among the citizens of Pakistan. For instance, in the 2008 elections, Jamaat-i-Islam secured only 2 percent of the vote.

4. Socialism and Poverty

With the fall of the Soviet Union and the failure of socialism to generate a strong, productive economy, in the 1990s Pakistan turned to economic liberalization, as Bangladesh had a few years earlier. Under Zia-ul Haq and subsequent democratic leaders, the focus was on improving the basic lives of the Pakistani people. Population growth and low levels of economic productivity kept Pakistan a very poor country. Improvements emerged in the twenty-first century. Society changed little, though the elite came to include a Westernized commercial class.

Socialist Economy. Pakistan retained its socialist economic structures into the early 1990s. Civilian authorities attempted to liberalize the economy, promote privatization of state-owned companies, and reduce the role of central planning. However, liberalization didn't work well until the twenty-first century. At the same time, the governments of Zia ul-Haq and later civilian leaders focused more on programs to improve the lives of Pakistanis. Zia ul-Haq introduced programs of rural aid, land reform, and improved local infrastructure. In 1992, the government initiated a Social Action Program that increased funding for elementary education, health and welfare, and agricultural improvements. Musharraf made greater efforts to strengthen capitalist elements in the economy. He reduced subsidies to government firms, privatized a number of corporations, liberalized international trade, and in general deregulated the economy. Under socialism the economy grew at a rate of 4 percent; in the transition to capitalism in the 1990s the growth rate slowed to 2-4 percent; and in the twenty-first century, as international trade expanded, growth soared to 7 percent a year.

Poverty. For the period from 1971 to 2000 basic survival was a challenge for 80 percent of the population. In the twenty-first century the poverty rate declined sharply to 35 percent. The most vulnerable were women, ethnic minorities, the disabled, landless peasants, beggars, and servants. According to the Human Development Index, Pakistan was in the bottom one-fifth of all countries in the world. Thus much more needed to be done to raise Pakistan from the depths of poverty.

Social Inequality. The social structure changed very little. Pakistan still had a small elite of large land owners, government bureaucrats, and military leaders. To this was added an emerging middle class of business men, whose families lived a very Westernized lifestyle, even including residents in gated communities. At the bottom were the many poor peasants, industrial workers, and the servant class.

5. Gender and Family

Though the 1973 constitution guaranteed gender equality and women's full participation in all aspects of life, in reality women faced discrimination and violence. The family, as defined by the Muslim Family Law Ordinance of 1961, changed little.

Status of Women. Equality and civil and political rights were guaranteed to women. Initially, 5 percent of seats in the national legislature were reserved for women. Today a quarter of representatives are female. Ten percent of all government jobs are set aside for women. Zia, however, strongly emphasized *purdah*, the isolation of women.

Women have a limited role in the workforce. Approximately 8 percent of all employees are female. Women are primarily found in the professions, especially nursing and teaching. Laws passed to guarantee equal pay for equal work have not been enforced. In 2010, a law was passed prohibiting harassment of women in the workplace.

Women have been the victims of "honor killings." Women have been killed because they rejected the marriage partner chosen for them by their parents, thus for seeking a "love marriage." Women seeking divorces have also been the subject of honor killings.

***Hudud* and Vengeance against Women.** Under Zia ul-Haq's military dictatorship, the Hudud Ordinance was issued in 1979. Parallel to the blasphemy law, it operated on the basis of fear and intimidation. It was also part of the strategy to legitimize the authority of military rule. The Hudud Ordinance called for punishment for a number of offences against Islam, but especially *zina* (extramarital sex) and consumption of alcohol. The maximum punishment was death by stoning but more commonly imprisonment or 100 lashes were meted out. Hudud infractions were tried in anti-terrorist courts. Those most commonly accused of zina were women who had been raped, those who had sought divorce, or daughters who had rejected arranged marriages. Local clerics and local elites most commonly accused women of zina. The Hudud Ordinance was thus a part of the arsenal of power of local officials and clerics. Several thousand, mainly women, were accused of hudud offences each year, though most were eventually released from prison.

The Hudud Ordinance was revoked in 2006, while the repeal was confirmed by the Supreme Court in 2010.

A Few Improvements. The military dictatorship of Zia ul-Haq marked a low point in the lives of Pakistani women. Under Musharraf and since, modest improvements have occurred.

6. Conflict

Conflict has characterized the recent history of Pakistan. Conflict was primarily based on religious differences but also included ethnic conflict. Since 2005, the government has tried to ban hate speech and hate publications. Under Musharraf discrimination against religious minorities was reduced.

Religious Conflict. Pakistan is a predominantly Muslim country (96 percent Muslim, 4 percent other religions). The 1973 constitution set aside six seats in parliament for religious minorities. That number has been increased to 10.

Much religious discrimination has been directed against the Ahmadi, declared non-Muslim by the government in 1974. Ahmadi were prohibited from possessing mosques, worshipping publically, *proselytizing* openly, and serving in the government or bureaucracy. Vigilante attacks were launched against Ahmadi property.

Shi'a-Sunni conflict continued, peaking in the 1980s. Shi'a still sought local autonomy, while they joined terrorist groups much more often than the Sunni.

The small Christian community (2 million) has been the subject of attacks, especially after 2000. Christian churches were burned and Christians accused of blasphemy. Attacks against the Hindu community (also 2 million strong) intensified from the mid-1990s. When Hindu fundamentalist attacks against Muslims increased in India, the Pakistani Hindus found themselves the victims of attacks.

Ethnic Conflict. The Sindhi still resent Punjab domination of Pakistan, while ethnic and sectarian violence is common in Karachi, the largest city in India.

The Balochs represent the main challenge to Punjab domination. The Balochs are among the most impoverished of all Pakistanis and have the highest level of illiteracy in the country. One Baloch uprising lasted from 1973–1977, before it was finally crushed by the government. More recently, rebellion lasted from 2001–2006. Violence was greatest in 2005 and 2006.

The Disabled. Large numbers of the disabled live in Pakistan. Estimates are that 14 percent of the population is disabled. In 2003, the authorities passed a law calling for "mainstreaming" of persons with disabilities. In workplaces with 50 or more employees, 2 percent of jobs were set aside for the disabled. Thus, the disabled have been less subject to discrimination and violence than have religious and ethnic minorities.

Over the last three decades Pakistan has changed, though much has remained the same. Geopolitically Pakistan still faces a serious threat from India, while its allies, especially the United States, remain fickle. Social structure has been quite similar throughout, while poverty remains a major challenge. The military still dominates the political system, sometimes behind the scenes but more commonly directly. The fundamental social institution, guided by Muslim law, has changed little. In several areas, there has been a return to original directions. This is true in the revival of secularist ideology and in improvements in the position of women. Probably the most important change has been the shift from socialism to a market economy.

J. BANGLADESH, 1971–PRESENT

1. "Bengal Country"

Independence benefitted the Bangladeshi, who retained the best farm land and now could determine their own fate. Foreign policy was characterized by participation in international initiatives, first non-alignment, then UN peacekeeping operations. Initially a two-party system was introduced but, just as in Pakistan, civilian leaders quickly turned authoritarian, leading the military to intervene and assume power. The military remained in power until 1990. From that point, two parties, the Bangladeshi National Party and the Awami League, alternated in power. Mistrust and corruption characterized the political system. At first Bangladesh declared itself a secular state, but by the early 1980s Islamist ideas had captured the government, which saw support for Islamism as a strategy for justifying military rule. In the twenty-first century an act of anti-government violence led to a return to secular ideals. Making little economic progress under socialism, Bangladesh turned to economic liberalization and to significant economic growth that almost pulled Bangladesh, once one of the poorest countries in the world, into a middle-rank economic status. With independence, the government decided that marriage and family law were political responsibilities of the government. However authorities perpetuated the marriage law of each religion in the country. In contrast to most Muslim countries, women increasingly secured some power in Bangladesh. Two women alternated as prime minister from 1990 to the present. In addition, rural women worked with NGOs (non-governmental organizations) to create some independent economic space for women. Ethnic unity contrasted with religious diversity, and Muslim discrimination was directed against the Hindu minority. Bangladesh remains a poor country but has made great progress toward democracy, economic viability, and equality for women.

Independence. In the early twentieth-century the British had divided the Bengals into two provinces, primarily along religious lines. At independence, that boundary became the border between India and East Pakistan. However, many Hindus remained in Pakistan, while fewer Muslims remained in Indian Bengal.

The two parts of Pakistan had little in common. The Easterners resented their powerlessness and the lack of Punjab sensitivity to Bengal nationalism. The 1970 elections seemed to create an opportunity for the east Pakistanis, through the victorious Awami League, to right past wrongs and to rule Pakistan. Rebellion in the east brought the Pakistani army to East Pakistan, where it was defeated by combined Bangladeshi and Indian military forces. Pakistan had no option but to accept Bangladeshi independence. The alternative was a full-scale war with India and possibly the destruction of Pakistan.

Geographical Forces. Bangladesh is a small country about the size of Wisconsin, with a population of 130 million at independence and approximately 160 million now. Western Pakistan lay 1000 miles to the west. Bangladesh is a densely populated country. Much of the country forms the delta of the *Brahmaputra River* that outlets into the Bay of Bengal of the Indian Ocean. The coastal area consists of marshes and jungles. Two small portions of the country are hilly and the home of the last wild Bengal tigers. Bangladesh has a monsoonal, tropical climate and is the frequent victim of natural disasters, including floods and cyclones (Asian hurricanes). The soil is quite fertile, permitting *triple cropping* (three crops per year on the same piece of land).

Non-alignment and Global Citizenship. Bangladesh has been an international voice for moderation—in the non-aligned movement, in UN peace keeping, in support of issues facing developing nations, and in the Organization of Islam Conference.

Non-alignment. By the time of Bangladesh's independence the non-aligned movement had existed for two decades and increasingly leaned to the Soviet side. Bangladesh emphasized the need for non-aligned nations to be truly neutral. From 2009, Bangladesh became increasingly pro-American, in part because of substantial American economic assistance and the opening up of American markets to Bangladeshi textiles and clothing exports.

Global Citizenship. Bangladesh has been a strong supporter of the United Nations and especially of U.N. peace-keeping missions. It has sent troops to various war zones in Africa, Kosovo, Bosnia, and Haiti, where Bangladesh had the second largest number of troops. Bangladesh has also played a leading role in emphasizing to the international community the importance of addressing the terrible problems facing developing nations. Finally, Bangladesh has been a moderate voice among Muslim nations loosely gathered together in the Organization of Islam Conference.

Friends and Neighbors. Unlike most nations, Bangladesh has no real enemies. Bangladesh and Pakistan have warm relations, with both accepting the rationality of being two separate nations. China is a close friend, investing substantially in Bangladesh and seeing it as a counterweight to the power of India. Relations with India are sometimes strained. India has angered Bangladesh by constructing a border fence to prevent illegal immigration from Bangladesh, especially by Burmese refugees. Sometimes Bangladesh resents the willingness of India to use its power to impose measures on its eastern neighbor. Still, the two have come to a peaceful agreement on the central issue of sharing water from up-stream rivers, which have their sources in the Himalayan Mountains.

Since independence, Bangladesh has been a peaceful citizen of the globe, with neither enemies nor an aggressive foreign policy.

2. Political Stability, Military Rule, and Democracy

When Bangladesh gained its independence, its political leaders had decades of experience (the Awami League had been formed in 1954), as well as the popular support that accrues to victorious national liberation movements. A constitution was quickly written and Mujibur *Rahman*, head of the Awami League, won the first elections. However he was assassinated by mid-level military figures. Military rule began in 1975 and lasted until 1990. Military leaders tried various strategies to rationalize their rule and gain the support of the people. Finally, in 1990, civilian government returned, with *Sheikh Hasina* (Awami League/AL) and *Khaleda Zia* (Bangladesh National Party/BNP) alternating in power. In office, each party sought to consolidate its power and destroy the political capacity of the other. Out of power, each party tried to wreck the parliament dominated by the other. In spite of corruption, intense party conflict, and weak governance, Bangladeshi democracy survived.

New Constitution, 1972. In 1972, Bangladesh produced a constitution. The country was to be a parliamentary democracy, with a strong executive centered in the office of prime minister. The national legislature was unicameral. Universal suffrage for men and women was declared. The constitution espoused four basic principles—Bangladeshi nationalism, secularism, democracy, and socialism.

Origins of Party Politics, 1971–1981. Mujibur Rahman and the Awami League ruled Bangladesh until Rahman's assassination in 1975. He was replaced by a military dictatorship led by Ziaur (Zia) Rahman, whose civilian power base was the Bangladesh National Party. In 1981, Zia, too, was murdered. In that period the institution of Martial Law Administrator was created to provide leadership in the power vacuum between two periods of rule.

Mujibur Rahman, 1971–1975. Winning a landslide victory in the first national elections in 1973, Mujibur initially focused on economic and social reconstruction, including the introduction of socialism and anti-poverty measures. Soon he turned away from democracy, declaring a state of emergency. He forced through parliament an amendment that limited its own power. He created a new one-party system, known as BAKSAL. Junior military officers then murdered Mujibur and most of his family, except for two daughters studying abroad. One of them was Sheikh Hasina, a future prime minister.

Military Dictatorship of Ziaur (Zia) Rahman, 1975–1981. Zia, Chief of Staff of the Army, declared himself military dictator. He assumed the role of Martial Law Administrator and banned all political parties. He argued that political party conflict and civilian authoritarianism had led to the assassinations. Only the military, and not a new civilian government, could restore order, he argued. Initially, Zia focused on further socialist reforms and on family planning to slow the rapid population increase. In 1978, he declared himself president for a five-year term. Changing his mind, he called for open democratic elections, reinstating both AL and BNP. BNP won the elections, but Zia was assassinated in 1981, thus ending the attempt to return to civilian rule.

Politically Bangladesh was not off to a good start. The government was more successful on the policy front than in the political arena.

Ershad Era, 1982–1990. In 1982, another military leader, Hussain Mohammed *Ershad*, declared himself Chief Martial Law Administrator and President. He feared a return of instability if civilian government was restored immediately. Therefore, Ershad decided on a gradual process beginning with democratization of local government that was to be followed by national elections. Ershad believed that decentralization of political power would leave the military as the sole national political force and also diminish political strife. Local government council elections were held in 1985 and won by pro-government forces.

In 1986, Ershad began the process of reviving democracy at the national level. First, citizens were again guaranteed civil rights. Next he created his own political party, *Jatiyo* (*the National Party*). Parliamentary elections were held in 1986, easily won by Jatiyo. BNP, now led by Zia's wife, Begum Khaleda Zia, boycotted the election, while the Awami League, under Sheikh Hasina, participated. In the same year a presidential election was held. With BNP and AL both refusing to participate, Ershad won easily. Parliament lifted martial law. However both BNP and AL protested, organizing demonstrations and strikes when Ershad tried to add military representatives, appointed by him, to local government councils.

Both BNP and AL boycotted the 1988 parliamentary elections, which were thus won by Jatiyo, which gained 70 percent of the seats. Local council election ran peacefully in 1989.

However, the opposition turned increasingly to protests and strikes, forcing Ershad to resign in 1990. His resignation paved the way for a return to free elections and democracy.

Democratic "Alternance," 1990–Present. Democracy returned in 1991, after which BNP and AL alternated in power. Hardly accepting the results of elections, the losing parties tried to sabotage the legislative efforts of the victors. It seemed never clear whether democracy would survive or the military reassume power, even after twenty years of the two parties alternating in office. Between elections the Chief Martial Law Advisor assumed power and prepared for new elections. Eventually the Chief Martial Law Advisor's office was held by civilians. Thus was formalized a process for maintaining government and political stability in periods between elections.

BNP in Power, 1991–1996. Parliamentary government, under the leadership of Prime Minister Begum Khaleda Zia, returned in 1991. AL and other opposition parties claimed in 1994 that the 1991 elections had been rigged and thus boycotted parliament. AL representatives then resigned from Parliament, making it easier for BNP to rule. Early in 1996, BNP won new parliamentary elections. However, boycotts by the opposition led to increased political turmoil. Parliament dismissed Zia and appointed a *Chief Advisor* to prepare new elections.

AL in Office, 1996–2001. AL won the second set of parliamentary elections in 1996 and Sheikh Hasina formed a *Government of National Consensus* with Jatiyo. Initially announcing it would not participate in the parliament, BNP decided to take its parliamentary seats but walked out a second time in 1996 and again in 1997. In 1997, BNP organized a series of nation-wide general strikes. In 1999, four minority parties boycotted parliament and refused to participate in local elections. These actions failed to force AL to dissolve its government. Finally, in 2001, AL resigned and a new caretaker government was established to halt political violence, seen as a prerequisite to fair, peaceful parliamentary elections.

BNP Government, 2001–2005. In 2001, Khaleda Zia returned to office, with her BNP sharing power with three other parties. AL rejected the results of the election and boycotted parliament in 2002, 2003, and 2005. In 2004, the constitution was changed, setting aside forty-five parliamentary seats for women. Then in August 2005 the terrorist organization *Jama-atul Mujahideen Bangladesh (Islamic Jihadists of Bangladesh/JMB)* organized attacks on sixty-three of Bangladesh's sixty-four political units, demanding the replacement of secular law with shar'ia courts. Their main targets were government courts. The government moved quickly and arrested seven JMB leaders for murdering two judges. At this point AL decided that the stakes were too high to continue to oppose the legally elected government and returned to parliament. Mutual verbal assaults continued but on a relatively low level.

When the parliamentary session ended in 2006, the president was appointed as the new Chief Advisor and tasked to prepare for new elections.

"Interregnum," 2006–2009. New elections were not held immediately. AL refused to participate in scheduled parliamentary elections, which were then cancelled. The Chief Advisor abolished civil rights and ordered the arrest of a number of prominent politicians, accusing them of corruption. Both Khaleda Zia and Sheikh Hasina were arrested for corruption, then released in 2008, and permitted to contest the election, now scheduled for 2008.

AL in Power, 2009–Present. AL and Hasina won a landslide victory in the fall 2008 elections, with BNP refusing to participate. Neither Zia nor Hasina seemed to have learned very much; neither placed the need for national unity above partisan interests. They continued to attack each other. In spite of its huge majority, AL failed to pass anti-terrorist legislation. It failed to restore civil rights, reintroduce decentralization that would have left a great deal of power in the hands of local officials, and establish neutrality of judges. When border guards mutinied in 2009, the Hasina government was slow to respond.

Bangladesh has found it difficult to effectively operate its political system. It suffers from the tendency of the military to step in to restore stability, from intense political conflict between the two major parties, and from the government's inability to define and achieve major goals that would benefit the people of Bangladesh. Fair elections and the creation of a mechanism for maintaining order during the preparation of new elections seem to have been the main achievements of the central political system. At the local level government has been willing to cooperate with NGOs in improving the daily lives of Bangladeshi.

3. Quest for Bangladeshi Identity

From the beginning of the twentieth-century Bengali Muslims have sought a unique identity, one that would distinguish them from both the Hindu Bengalis and from Muslims in the western part of South Asia. Language united them with other Bengali, and religions divided them from Hindu Bengalis. Religion united the Bengali Muslims with Muslims in the West but language and ethnicity kept them apart. At first ethnicity and language were the main Bangladeshi identifiers. By the mid-1980s religion had replaced ethnicity as the key to their identity. In recent years the government has begun to see religious identity as a threat to the stability of the Bangladeshi nation. Especially in the early decades of Pakistan, Muslims in the east practiced discrimination against the minority Hindus, driving many of them into India. When the proportion of Hindus settled at about 10 percent, discrimination declined in independent Bangladesh, in spite of the rise of Islamism.

Secularism, Nationalism, Socialism, and Democracy, 1971–1983. At first, religion played a secondary role to nationalism and secularism in independent Bangladesh. Secularism, democracy, nationalism, and socialism were viewed as the primary goals. The 1972 constitution prohibited the use of religion in the political sphere and Bangladesh's leaders espoused religious toleration. Mujibur Rahman emphasized Bengali nationalism to distinguish Muslim

Bengalis from Hindu Bengalis. There was an early concern that an inter-faith Bengali nationalism would bring Bangladesh into the Indian state or subordinate it to India. AL tended to be a secularist party, while BNP was closer to the Islamists.

Rise of Islamism, 1983–2005. Once Zia came to power, supported by BNP, Islamist tendencies increased within the government. Zia clearly sought to justify his rule by arguing that his support for Islamism demonstrated that he identified with the religious ideals of the people of Bangladesh. In 1977, an amendment deleted secularism from the constitution. Bangladesh became a Muslim state, not a Bengal one. Zia re-legalized the Islamist parties, especially Jamaat-i-Islam. In 1983, a constitutional amendment proclaimed Islam as the state religion. In the Ershad period, government became increasingly involved in providing support for Islamic schools, the madrassahs.

Islamist terrorist groups began to form in the 1990s after the close of the War in Afghanistan. However, Islamists never gained much electoral support. Jamaat-i-Islam won only 6 percent of the vote in the first free election after the end of military rule. Though it was part of the BNP coalition, its electoral support remained small, demonstrating that though the people of Bangladesh had deep faith in their religion, they did not accept the idea that Islam should be a political movement.

Return of Secularism, 2005–Present. When Islamist terrorists launched the violent attacks of 2005, they destroyed both government and popular support for terrorism. Instead of seeing Islamism as beneficial to providing popular support for not very legitimate governments, the government now saw Islamism as a threat to the survival of the political system. Between 2005 and 2010, the government introduced a number of reforms that reduced the ability of Islamists to play an active role in politics. All religion-based parties were required to drop the word *Islam* from their names. Secularism was restored to the constitution. The Fifth Amendment, which had made Islam the state religion of Bangladesh, was repealed.

Bangladesh returned to a position similar to its starting point. Bangladesh was a country in which most people were Muslim, but whose government was secular, tolerant of all religions. Government was not to be used to strengthen the power of Islam in Bangladesh.

4. Progress in a Least-Developed Country

Throughout its history Bangladesh has been a very poor country, hampered by a lack of natural resources, initial dependence on a socialist economy, illiteracy, and rapid population growth. Less unequal than West Pakistan when the two areas were united, inequality increased in Bangladesh, only declining in the twenty-first century.

Agriculture. Rich soil and abundant moisture, through rainfall and irrigation, have enabled Bangladesh to be nearly self-sufficient in food, in spite of rapid population increases. Rice, jute, wheat, corn, vegetables, and tea are the main crops. Triple-cropping is common in Bangladesh. Bangladesh experienced the introduction of the Green Revolution in the 1960s, just as West

Pakistan and India did. More recently rural Bangladesh has benefitted from micro-credit, the provision of small amounts of money, primarily to women, to fund agricultural improvements. NGOs have worked with local women's groups to strengthen the rural economy.

Socialism, 1971–Mid-1980s. Introduced when Bangladesh was part of Pakistan, socialism was continued into the mid-1980s. Nationalization of industry and long-range planning were the key components of Bangladeshi socialism. The first five-year plan, 1973-1978, emphasizing industry, produced a growth rate of 4 percent per year. Under a subsequent five-year plan, the economy stagnated, growing at a rate of only 1 percent in the 1980s.

Economic Liberalization, Mid-1980s–Present. Economic liberalization, begun in the mid-1980s, responded to the economic stagnation. In the twenty-first century, some privatization was introduced—in banking and jute mills, for example. Some inefficient government-owned firms were closed. The government promoted private entrepreneurship and investment, as well as participation in international trade. Major exports included clothing, textiles, and pharmaceuticals. International loans have become increasingly important, especially through the International Monetary Fund's Poverty Reduction and Growth Facility program. Natural gas deposits have provided funds the government uses to improve social welfare.

Results. Bangladesh has made considerable economic progress. After significant growth in the early years of socialism (4 percent per year) the growth rate declined to 1 percent, rebounding in the 1990s to 3 percent. Until the recession of 2008–2009 Bangladesh was growing at about 8 percent per year in the twenty-first century.

Poverty. Today, 40 percent of the people live below the poverty line (down from 60 percent in 1992). Life expectancy has increased from 50 at independence to 64 in 2007. Literacy has doubled and child mortality has dropped. Improvements have almost lifted Bangladesh out of the category of least-developed countries and up into that of lesser-developed nations.

5. Religion, Women, and the Family

Bangladesh retained British-era family law, with different laws applying to people with different religious beliefs. This created considerable differences in the nature of families. Women are treated much better in Bangladesh than in Pakistan. Bangladeshi women, especially at the local level, have acquired substantial amounts of economic power and independence, threatening the local male power structures.

Religious Laws and Families. Separate marriage laws apply to different religious groups, most importantly Muslims, Hindus, and Christians.

Muslim Law. The nature of the Muslim family is determined by the Muslim Personal Law (Shariat) Application Act of 1937, as confirmed by the Muslim Family Law Ordinance of 1961. The law applies to important aspects of the Muslim family including marriage, property rights, inheritance, dissolution of marriage, *dower*, and guardianship.

Marriage is a civil contract, and the local government council registers all marriages. According to Qu'ranic law, those who are closest to the deceased receive the largest shares of inheritance. Limits are placed on the rights of husbands to have more than one wife. The husband needs the first wife's permission to take on additional wives.

Divorce can take place whenever the husband wishes; the wife can seek a divorce if her husband permits her to do so, if he has taken an additional wife without the first wife's permission (Dissolution of Muslim Marriages Act of 1939), or if the woman waives rights of financial compensation and rights to the children. Dower is an amount of money the wife is entitled to receive from the husband in return for marrying him.

According to the Guardian and Wards Act of 1890 a divorced mother has custody of male children until they are seven and over female children until puberty. These provisions were codified by the Muslim Marriage and Divorces (Registration) Act of 1974. A 1986 court ruling makes the child's welfare the main determinant of whether the mother or father has custody of children after the divorce.

A law of 1984 set the legal age of marriage at 21 for men and 18 for women. However, in about 40 percent of marriages, the couple is under aged.

Thus the Muslim family is closely guided by secular law, which generally follows Muslim family law.

Hindu Law. Hindu marriage law applies to Hindus and Buddhists. Marriage is viewed as a religious sacrament and the husband as a god. Marriage is indissoluble and divorce illegal. Hindu women acquire "use" of the deceased husband's property and can dispose of their own property in any way they wish.

Christian Law. Guidelines for the Christian family are provided by the Divorce Act of 1869 and the Christian Marriage Act of 1872. With so few Christians in Bangladesh, the government has seen no reason to update these British-era laws.

Organizing Women's Power. The Bangladesh constitution provides women with certain rights, including the right to vote and hold office, freedom of expression, and the right to work. Government has the legal responsibility to defend the rights of women. Women have held the office of prime minister from 1990 to the present. At a local level, women have worked with NGOs to challenge the power of local authority figures, including Muslim clerics, and rural patriarchy. These challenges led to increased violence against women, especially in the early 1990s. The clergy and rural elites have organized attacks on poor women who have worked with NGOs. In the late 1990s women demonstrated in the capital, Dhaka, against Islamic extremists who issues *fatwas* (religious injunctions) against women and NGOs they worked with. Violence against women has declined in the twenty-first century.

6. Ethnic Unity and Religious Difference

Most Bangladeshi are ethnic Bengali. At the same time the existence of a sizeable Hindu minority has fostered discrimination against Hindus.

Ethnic Bengalis. Ninety-eight percent of the residents of Bangladesh are Bengali. There are small numbers of tribals, or hill people, who gained a measure of autonomy in 1997. There are approximately 270,000 Rohingya, Muslim refugees from Myanmar, and 200,000 Bihari Muslims, who had fled from West Pakistan to Bangladesh at the time of independence.

Muslims vs. Religious Minorities. Though there are small numbers of Christians, Buddhists, and Ahmedi in Bangladesh, the two major religious groups are Muslims and Hindus. The Hindus may have numbered over 20 percent of the population when Bangladesh gained its independence in 1971. Those numbers have dropped to about 10.5 percent today. Eighty-eight percent of the population is Muslim.

Anti-Hinduism in the Pakistan Period, 1947–1968. Hindus are subject to discrimination, even having to pay the *jizja* (tax on non-Muslims). While Bangladesh was still part of Pakistan, the government carried out a number of actions against the Hindus. The East Bengal Evacuees Act of 1951 and the *Enemy Property Act* (1966) gave the government authority to seize the property of those who fled the country. The second law responded to the 1965 India-Pakistan War of 1965. India followed with a similar law in 1968. Even if they later returned, they could not recover their property. Large amounts of Hindu-owned property were thus seized from 1947–1968. In addition, in 1964, a series of Hindu-Muslim riots broke out.

Anti-Hinduism in Independent Bangladesh, 1971–Present. From the 1990s on, Muslims have carried out a lot of violence against Hindus, reflecting the greater activism of Islamists. In 1990 and 1992, crowds attacked Hindu temples and destroyed temple property. There is evidence that the government either instigated such actions or did nothing to halt them. This was a period during which the BNP and its ally, the Jamaat-i-Islam, were in power. At the time of the 2001 election there was much violence against Hindus, mainly conducted by BNP. Yet five Hindus were elected to the national assembly in that year.

Community. Ethnic unity has not overridden religious difference. Though almost all residents of Bangladesh are Bengali, religious conflict between Muslims and Hindus weakens a strong sense of community.

Having been part of an independent country for almost twenty-five years, Bangladesh had certain advantages that newly independent countries lacked. It had a large measure of unity, built up in opposition to west Pakistani domination of the country. It had a greater share of natural resources than the new, smaller Pakistan. Bangladesh had seen the consequences of military rule and tried to create limits to military political power. Economic reforms—socialism and the Green Revolution—were already in place. The principle of government control over the nature of the family was in place. Bangladesh followed the less-than-successful Pakistan strategy of ignoring minority rights. Overall, Bangladesh in 1971 had advantages not available to Pakistan in 1947.

CONCLUSION

Throughout its history, India has faced the challenges of diversity and poverty.

Boundaries based on the Indian Ocean and the Himalayan Mountains have defined the borders of India with precision. At the same time this separateness has been relative, for India has frequently been subject to invasion. Invasions generally produced new ruling dynasties. These dynasties secured control over northern India but had some difficulty extending their power into the south. This tension between centralizing governments, mainly of foreign origin, and local kingdoms, seeking relative autonomy or independence, has continued throughout India history.

Until the second half of the nineteenth century India had authoritarian governments led by kings or emperors. The rulers sought to create effective administrations that focused on tax policy and defense. Some rulers were activist authorities, seeking to improve India but in general they avoided efforts to promote social change. After the British assumed direct rule over India in the middle of the nineteenth century, they began to broaden political participation. Provincial governments assumed more responsibility, while the proportion of the male population authorized to vote and hold office expanded. With independence, universal suffrage was introduced. In spite of corruption and authoritarian tendencies by political leaders, India remains the largest democracy in the world.

Religions provided the principal ideologies. However, no religion gained a dominant role. Hinduism drove Buddhism out. The arrival of Muslim invaders created another religious conflict—between Hinduism and Islam. The conflict between these two relatively militant religions was sometimes violent, especially in the transition to independence. Western liberalism—the primary secular ideology—challenged these religious beliefs. Liberalism condemned traditional Indian, especially Hindu, cultural practices and offered an alternative—rationalism and democracy. Because liberalism was a Western set of ideas it had only modest influence during the colonial period. Ironically, after independence liberalism became a more powerful ideology.

Poverty and economic backwardness, as well as rigid class structure, continued throughout the country's history. Rapid population growth both accompanied and produced poverty. Low levels of industrialization did little to reduce poverty. India participated in the global economy throughout its modern history, though during the colonial period, the international economy primarily benefited Western nations. India's social structure provided little opportunity for social mobility, for the caste system froze people in specific social categories. Though officially abolished after independence, caste still dominates social relations.

Traditionally, Indian families were patriarchal and extended. Women's power was confined to the senior female, whose main responsibility was to promote harmony within the family. Religion emphasized the importance of female obedience. After independence women acquired some independence though the patriarchal family retained its strength, especially in the countryside. Women gained the right to vote and increasingly entered the urban work force. Economic independence provided the basis for some personal freedom.

Diversity remained a constant in Indian life. Religious, ethnic, social, and geographic diversity were abundant in India. From time to time rulers sought to build community by accepting and fostering diversity. At other times, leaders sought to build community by requiring conformity to a particular religion. The colonial period, which brought the British to power, complicated community-building. In general, British actions promoted community through improving communications and by articulating a vision of a single culture that recognized some diversity. Since independence, religious difference and communalism have remained a powerful force in Indian history in India, Pakistan, and Bangladesh.

Name: ________________________________ Date: ____________________

Chapter Two: India, Pakistan, Bangladesh

IDENTIFICATION: IMPORTANT TERMS AND VOCABULARY

Ahmadi (170)

Ali Jinnah (129)

All-India Muslim League (128)

Amritsar massacre (129)

Aurangzeb (111)

autarkic (156)

Awami League (164)

Ayodhya (160)

Balochs (167)

Bangalore/Silicon Valley (157)

Basic Democracies (164)

Bengal Renaissance (119)

Bengali (152)

Bharatiya Janata Party (BJP) (154)

Brahman (107)

British East India Company (115)

caste (109)

Caste Disabilities Act (121)

Charter Art of 1833 (120)

chief advisor (177)

civil lines (137)

Kshatriya (109)

legislating happiness (118)

Lucknow Pact (129)

Macauley (118)

millenarian (114)

monotheistic (108)

Montagu-Chelmsford reforms (125)

Morley-Minto Reforms (125)

Musharraf (170)

nirvana (108)

non-aligned nation (139)

parliamentary democracy (140)

Peacock Throne (115)

plebiscite (133)

President's Rule (160)

Punjabi (160)

Qu'ran (108)

Quit India Campaign (126)

Ramadan (108)

reincarnation (108)

religious cleansing (138)

rule of law (127)

Salt Tax Campaign (131)

sati (109)

satyagraha/truth force (129)

Name: ______________________________ **Date:** __________________

Chapter Two: India, Pakistan, Bangladesh

KEY QUESTIONS

India before the Mughals, to 1526: How did the caste system affect Indian life and history?

Mughal Empire, 1526–1764: List the main strategies the Mughals used to deal with diversity. Which strategies worked best and why?

British Informal Imperialism, 1760–1857: Analyze British efforts to change India in this period. What changes did the British try to implement? To what extent were they successful?

British Formal Empire, 1857–1947: What main strategies did the Indian independence Movement employ?

Nehru Era, 1947–1964: What were the main characteristics of the Indian economy under Nehru?

Dictatorship or Democracy: Indira Gandhi, 1966–1984: Why did conflict based on diversity dominate the Indira Gandhi era?

Name: ______________________________ **Date:** ____________________

Contemporary India, 1984–Present: What role has India played in the world from the mid-1980s to the present?

Pakistan, 1947–1971: Why couldn't Pakistan maintain the democratic tradition of British India?

Pakistan, 1971–Present: Why did the ideas of fundamentalist Islamism triumph in Pakistan, which began as a secular state?

Bangladesh, 1971–Present: How was democracy able to survive in Bangladesh?

Chapter Three

Japan

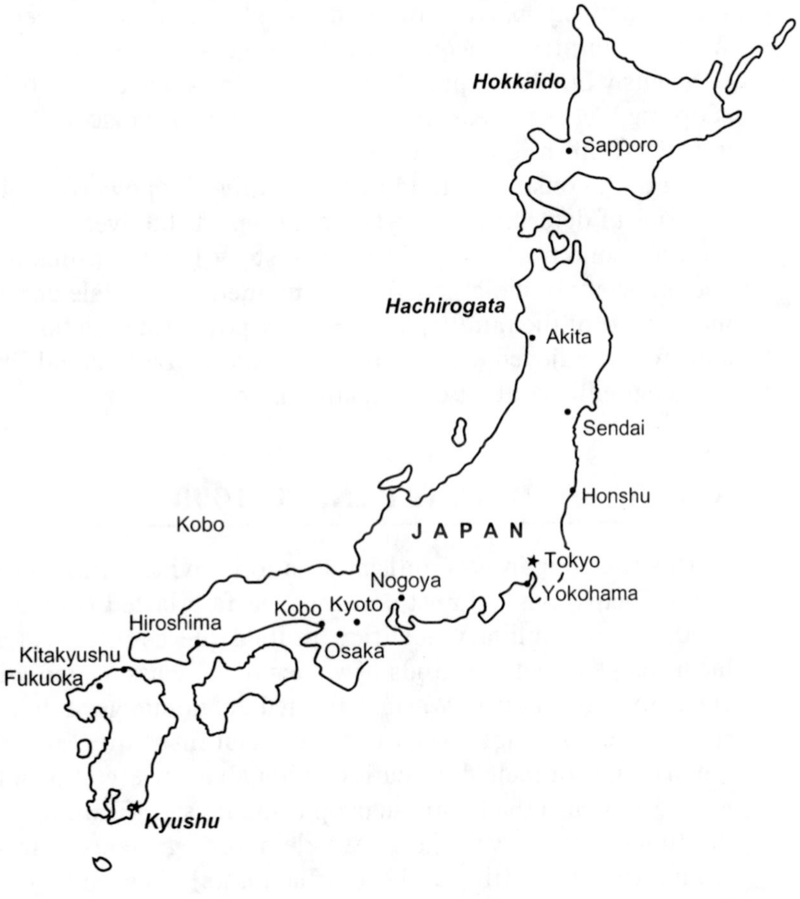

Introduction

In Japan cherry blossom viewing (*ohanami*) is very brief, lasting about a week before the blossoms fall from the trees. Beauty and its swift disappearance seem appropriate symbols for Japan. At the same time the sword represents strength of purpose and permanence. Japan has balanced support for tradition with a willingness to change in response to challenges. We first look at Japanese history when it was a feudal, militaristic society generally isolated from the rest of the world. Today it is a major global power, a generally pacifist and democratic society actively participating in globalization. Japan became the first non-Western country to acquire a modern great power status. It achieved this by judiciously building upon its past, rejecting some elements of its traditions and adopting Western ideas. In this chapter you will discover how Japan made this journey from insignificance to power.

Certain constants stand out, including the powerful role of the state, both in terms of determining the key qualities of the lives of citizens and in directing the economy. Very early in its history Japan became a relatively homogeneous society in which outsiders remained alien. Male domination occurred in the context of the family playing a very powerful societal role. Finally, in Japan culture has enjoyed a very important status. Late feudal Japan existed within the geographic context of an island nation.

A. LATE FEUDAL JAPAN, TO 1600 C.E.

At this time, Japan was an island nation, divided into a large number of military principalities. Almost constant warfare lasted from about 1400 to about 1600, when a military coalition unified the country. As a militarist society Japan emphasized the kinds of values usually associated with warfare—valor, endurance, obedience. Warfare limited economic growth and kept population stable. The household was the basic social institution and embedded in it was the principle of male domination. Though a variety of peoples had immigrated to Japan to form the Japanese people and no significant migration had occurred for almost 1,000 years, Japan was less homogeneous than it proclaimed. One group, the *Ainu* (the earliest inhabitants), had not been assimilated into Japanese culture and had been gradually pushed into the more remote parts of northern Japan.

1. Japan and the World

Geography provided a context for Japanese history and placed limitations upon the country's people. Relative isolation off the coast of a superior Chinese civilization affected Japan, too.

Geography. Lying close to the coast of East Asia, Japan was relatively isolated. This isolation enabled Japan to change gradually and to have a great deal of control over the pace of change. For much of its history and certainly for this period, the primary outside influence was China, the most powerful nation in the world and certainly the dominant power in Asia at this time.

Japan comprised four larger islands, *Kyushu, Shikoku, Honshu,* and *Hokkaido,* as well as over 1,000 smaller ones. Japan did not yet include the *Ryukyu Islands* (*Okinawa*) to the south. A long coastline and an *Inland Sea* gave Japan a sea orientation that belied its geographical isolation. Japan is a small country, with an area somewhat less than 150,000 square miles (slightly smaller than California). Three major mountain chains divide the country into fairly small regions. This has left little arable land and only a few large plains, the most important of which are the *Kanto Plain* and the *Kansai Plain.* At this time, Japan was largely self-sufficient economically, as the available natural resources met the needs of the population. Marked seasonal changes and frequent natural disasters (earthquakes, volcanic eruptions, and typhoons) made the Japanese very sensitive to the power of nature, which they romanticized.

Neighbors. Japan's primary neighbors were China and Korea, the latter deeply influenced by Chinese culture. Only 75 miles of rough seas separated Korea and Japan. Small-scale migration gradually disappeared during this period. Japanese pirates raided the coast of China and attacked Korea periodically. In the 1590s the Japanese sent two naval expeditions against Korea but failed to conquer any of the Korean kingdoms. Japan also set its sights on expansion southward, conquering the *Kingdom of Okinawa* on the Ryukyu island chain in 1609.

Christianity and Western Influence. Late in this period Jesuit missionaries from Portugal began to enter Japan. It is easy to understand the appeal of Christianity at a time of warfare and uncertainty. By 1600 over 300,000 (2–3% of the population) Japanese had converted to Catholicism. Thus, for the first time, Western ideas began to have an impact upon Japan, a Japan that was still feudal.

2. Feudalism

Feudalism (see Chapter Two for a definition of feudalism) created structures of governance for Japan and promoted constant warfare. In Japanese feudalism, lords (*daimyo*) had suzerainty over vassals (*samurai*).

Feudal Institutions. Japan was divided into some 300 militarized kingdoms, or *daimyo.* The leader, also known as a daimyo, of each kingdom maintained a feudal relationship with his samurai, warriors. The daimyo, or lord, provided the samurai with income in exchange for their service as warriors and administrators. Each side felt an obligation to fulfill their responsibilities to the other. At the base of the political system were villages, each operating on the basis of peer pressure and elected leadership.

3. Feudal Values and Religious Beliefs

Japanese ideologies included religious elements, as well as those derived from military feudalism. *Buddhism* and *Shinto* were the main religious belief systems. Christianity, which entered Japan late in the period, had localized influence, primarily in southern Japan. Values, known as *bushido,* derived from militarism and affected the upper class, the samurai, and to a lesser extent other social groups. The Japanese had little sense of national identity at this time. Except for Christianity, all of these sets of beliefs fit together to form a broader whole of complementary values.

Shintoism. *Shinto* was a traditional religion that became more structured as time went on, as it had to compete with imported Buddhism. Initially Shintoism was a form of *animism,* a belief that spirits, foxes, ghosts, and other creatures determined what happened to people. Shintoism involved belief in deities *(kami)* that had little shape or form but could ensure beneficial results, such as good harvests, or harm people. Each village had its Shinto shrine, for Shinto celebration took place primarily through village festivals. Shintoism emphasized the power of nature and the need for humans to cooperate with nature. It also emphasized the magical power of purity.

Buddhism. Originating in India (see Chapter Two), as you recall, Buddhism entered Japan from China via Korea. Buddhism used its well-organized structures to exert great political power. According to Buddha, the purpose of life was to overcome suffering. This was achieved by ridding oneself of personality or being. Suffering resulted from efforts to satisfy the desires of the self. Through an eight-stage process the individual could rid himself/herself of ego/personality and achieve the state of pure joy, *Nirvana.* Buddhist ceremony and art impressed the Japanese, as did its ability to organize religious institutions. A number of specialized sects emerged within Buddhism. The most important for Japan were the Pure Land Sect and Zen. The latter emphasized self-reliance and the achievement of enlightenment through meditation and self-reflection. Zen Buddhism gave support to the martial values of the bushido, especially discipline, courage, and *stoicism.*

The Bushido. *Bushido,* the way of the warrior, provided the military elite with a set of stable values in a period of chaos. Warriors were to fulfill their responsibilities completely, including total obedience to the lord, willingness to die bravely, and acceptance of one's fate. If the warrior failed to fulfill his responsibilities, it was his duty to commit suicide through *hara-kiri* or *seppuku.* Death thus provided the disobedient or defeated warrior with an honor not available in life.

Christianity. Christianity fit in less well in Japan than other sets of beliefs and appealed to a small proportion of the Japanese population during its brief period of legal existence there. The form of Christianity imported into Japan was counter-reformation Catholicism. Though Counter-Reformation Catholicism is usually viewed as rigid and authoritarian, in Japan the Jesuits adapted Catholicism to Japanese conditions. They had developed the ability to appeal to people during periods of turmoil. Ironically, conversion became more important than ideological purity. Catholicism offered an ideology that challenged Japanese feudalism, as well as Shintoism and Buddhism, and thus was seen as a threat. The first attacks on Christianity came in 1587 when Christian missionaries were ordered to leave Japan.

4. War-Time Economy and Rigid Class System

Constant warfare affected both the economy and the social system. The core economic area of Japan stretched from northern Kyushu, near the Inland Sea, through the Kansai Plain to the Kanto Plain (near Tokyo). This area contained much of the country's population, as well as the best farmland. The west coast was less densely populated, with only a narrow shoulder of good farmland near the Japan Sea. Northeastern Honshu was lightly populated and its residents the poorest Japanese. The Ainu were the main inhabitants of part of Honshu and all of Hokkaido.

Economy. Warfare and class difference played an important role in determining the broad outlines of the economy. Much of the economy was agriculture-based. *Wet-rice farming* provided much of the grain, which acted as a form of currency and economic calculation. Farmers diversified, engaging in silk worm cultivation and the spinning and weaving associated with it. Peasants near the sea also engaged in fishing. Military activity acted as a drag on the advance of agriculture. Armies destroyed crops, confiscated grain reserves, and drafted peasant labor.

Commerce was a secondary component of the economy. Warfare and the needs of the upper class provided the main motives for commercial activity. The governments were also a major consumer, for warfare required the production and sale of weapons. In addition, the upper classes sought a lifestyle that required luxury goods. Peasants had very limited consumption expectations and sought to be self-sufficient. So commerce essentially met the needs of the upper classes and governments.

Society. In spite of warfare, which usually creates high levels of mobility, Japan had a fairly rigid class system. Obviously, battle produced heroes who moved up the social ladder and it destroyed the lives of others. Yet most of the movement was incrementally within social classes.

At the top of society was the *samurai* class—the warrior caste. This hereditary class had its origins in a much earlier period of Japanese history. The samurai class was divided into a number of sub-groups, arranged hierarchically. It was almost impossible to enter the samurai class from below, so upward mobility was within the upper class but not between classes.

The class in the middle of society was the peasant class, even though economically it was the poorest. The ordering of classes was based on the *Confucian* model, imported from China (see Chapter Four). According to this perspective, the governing class (in this case the samurai) was at the top of society and the other productive class (the peasants) came next. At the bottom of society were the merchants, who, according to Confucian ideas, merely moved goods from one place to another and thus served no useful purpose.

Even though some merchants were quite well off, literate, and well traveled, their status and prestige were very low. Most merchants had originally been peasant traders who had expanded their activities. Two kinds of merchants existed—local traders and those engaged in long-distance commerce.

At the bottom of society were the outcastes, people below the social structure. The group may have had its origins in occupations considered unclean by

Shinto, such as butchers, leather workers, and funeral workers. Others engaged in occupations such as sandal making. About 1 percent of the population was in the outcaste category. Japan thus had a stagnant economy and a closed, stagnant social system.

5. Household and Gender

The household (*ie*) was the basic social institution in this period. Within the household, men were dominant and women subordinate.

Household. The household had existed in previous periods and individual families had been less important. People were recognized as members of a household, rather than members of a specific family. Most households were extended families that operated on the basis of Confucian ideals. Marriages were arranged, primarily for economic reasons. Upon marriage, wives joined their husbands' families and their names were added to the husband's family's registry.

Gender. Women were subordinate, though not necessarily ill-treated. The distance between men and women was greatest in upper-class families and less so in merchant and peasant families. In the non-samurai classes, men and women worked together—in the fields or the shops. Children were seen as unimportant and were expected to be submissive to the eldest male in the family.

6. Diversity and Community

Japan gradually became a homogeneous society ethnically by the sixth century. However, distinct differences remained.

The Ainu. The most important difference was between the "*indigenous people*"—the Ainu—and the Japanese. Ethnic and lifestyle differences marked the two groups. The Ainu were seen as non-Japanese barbarians and were not considered citizens.

Other Differences. The main religions, Buddhism and Shintoism, were viewed as complementary rather than exclusive. In addition, there were differences in Chinese and Japanese cultural elements. Regional and local cultural differences existed as well. For example, there were significant cultural differences between the Kansai area (encompassing the cultural capital *Kyoto*) and the Kanto Plain (the Tokyo area).

Class differences divided the Japanese but were minimized by ethnic similarity.

Community. Geographical isolation, many centuries of racial mixing, minimal religious conflict, and cultural unity and common values united Japan and gave it a large measure of community. Community existed in spite of constant military conflict among the daimyo.

B. TOKUGAWA JAPAN, 1603–1867

Japan changed greatly in the Tokugawa period. It entered the world as a result of Western pressure. Unification of the country, while permitting some degree of decentralization, became the basis for the political system. Though Confucianism dominated, Western ideas (first Christianity, then Western scientific and rational thought) became increasingly important. Significantly, some Japanese thinkers began to question Confucianism and to develop an alternative ideology, native learning. This was a period of substantial economic growth, especially through the diversification of agriculture and the introduction of *proto-industrialization*—hand production in a factory setting. In this rigid class system, peasant rebellion became more and more common. Few changes occurred in the family, though the household became less important. Finally, Christian proselytizing threatened to destroy the homogeneity of Japan. In response, Japanese intellectuals put more emphasis on *Japaneseness* or *nativism.*

1. Japan's New World

Japan's isolation was broken during this time period. Westerners had increasing influence, in spite of the destruction of Christianity.

Western Intellectual Influence. Though Shogun Tokugawa Iemitsu persecuted Christians and in 1639 sought to isolate Japan from all outside influence, his efforts were unsuccessful. The Dutch, Chinese, and Koreans were permitted to trade with Japan in a very limited way. After 1720, non-religious books freely entered Japan. Western ideas came to be known as *Dutch learning.* The Japanese were deeply influenced by Western scientific ideas.

2. Politics—Emperor Shogun and Daimyo

In 1600, *Tokugawa Ieyasu* organized a large military coalition that defeated a rival military grouping and thus "unified" the country. In 1603, he established himself as *shogun* or military dictator. His next task was to create effective rule. The system he established combined a thrust toward centralized government, along with some degree of decentralization through the continued existence of daimyo. Tension between center and periphery continued to affect Tokugawa politics.

Tokugawa Political Structure. Social divisions were at the center of the political system. The daimyo were divided into three categories: the members of the Tokugawa clan, those who had joined the Tokugawa before they united Japan, and those daimyo who retained some degree of independence.

The central administration, or *bakufu,* consisted of two levels of administrators, senior councilors and junior councilors. Senior councilors dealt with national affairs such as taxation and military questions. Junior councilors supervised the shogun's military and the samurai class in general. Over time, the shogun receded into the background and key advisors made policy, acting informally. Throughout, the goal of the shogunate was centralization and uniformity—of loyalty, of ethical practices, and economic behavior. Daimyo governed the military principalities and headmen provided leadership at the village level.

The shoguns sought to dominate the daimyo through promoting feudal relationship, uniform administrative practices, economic superiority, and an impressive military. In addition the shogun required that the wives and children of the daimyo live in the capital, Edo (Tokyo), as virtual hostages. The daimyo were also required to assemble periodically in Edo.

3. Confucianism vs. Nativism

Confucian ideas, or more accurately, neo-Confucian ones, dominated educated Japan in the seventeenth century but battled with nativism and foreign ideas in the next century. The eighteenth century was characterized by a great deal of intellectual unrest. This unrest centered on a critique of neo-Confucianism but also represented disillusionment with the quality of Tokugawa rule and the "softness" of the samurai.

Confucianism. Confucianism was a system of *public ethics* developed about 500 B.C.E. Though it entered Japan simultaneously with Buddhism it did not become a dominant ideology until the Tokugawa period. By this time, a *metaphysics* (an explanation of the universe) had been added to it. Japanese Confucianism emphasized loyalty to political authority, ignoring the quest for proper personal behavior that had been at the heart of original Confucianism. Confucianism, thus, offered a rationale for obeying the Tokugawa.

Dutch Learning. A number of Japanese thinkers adopted Western scientific ideas and emphasized experimentation and observation. *Hiraga* Gennei tied scientific experimentation to economic development. A number of thinkers, known as rationalists, argued that Japan must have a strong government whose main responsibilities were to promote economic development and national security, using Western scientific principles. Among the leading rationalists were Honda Toshiaki and Sato Nobuhiro.

Native Learning. Very gradually, an alternative to Confucianism—an ideology of foreign origins—appeared. *Native Learning* emphasized that Chinese civilization was an alien one and unthinking acceptance of Chinese thought had driven Japan away from its original spiritual and intellectual sources. Confucianism was the reason for Japan's backwardness and weakness. Japan must abandon Chinese ideas and return to the true roots of Japanese culture if it wished to be a strong, secure nation. *Motoori* Norinaga argued that purified Japan was unique and superior to all other civilizations. Similar views were expressed by Hirata Atsutane, who emphasized the superiority of Japan and Shinto religion, as well as reverence for the emperor. Ironically, the proponents of Native Learning had come to recognize the power of Western ideas and the inability of Confucianism to respond to Western pressure.

Mito School of Nationalism. Thinkers associated with the daimyo of Mito emphasized the superiority of Japan over Western ideas. They saw the emperor as the symbol of Japanese superiority, even though the emperor had been a figurehead for many centuries. Intellectually Japan was preparing for a future contest that would challenge Japan's internal resilience.

4. Economic and Social Change

Social and economic change accelerated in the Tokugawa period. Agriculture went through some modernization, resulting in much greater agricultural productivity and rural wealth. Proto-industrialization, which was organized production by dozens of workers using division of labor but hand tools, prepared the way for an industrial revolution. Population more than doubled, though much of the growth was in the seventeenth century (1600–12 million, 1700–28 million, and 1800—31 million). Social changes occurred too, as the samurai class lost some of its privileged status, the prestige and wealth of merchants grew substantially, and many peasants grew wealthier. Class boundaries were blurred as well. In the mid-nineteenth century Japan was quite different than it had been at the beginning of Tokugawa rule in the early seventeenth century. Urbanization, sophisticated business practices, increased literacy and numeracy rates, and greater per capita wealth similar to that of England when it embarked upon the industrial revolution, prepared Japan for parallel radical changes.

Economic Growth. The economy grew relatively rapidly during the Tokugawa age. The end to domestic civil war had a major impact. Population grew, resources could be devoted to reconstruction rather than to destruction, relative security promoted an interest in regional and interregional trade, and governments turned to specific economic development strategies.

Daimyo and the shogun promoted economic activities. Daimyo engaged in land reclamation and irrigation projects. The shoguns encouraged highway construction that made the transport of goods quicker and cheaper. Domestic demand increased, in part due to greater urbanization, in part due to population increase. By 1800, 10 percent of the Japanese population lived in large cities, with Edo at one million and Osaka at 400,000. Edo was one of the largest cities in the world. Japan became a consumer society rather than a frugal one, with the samurai leading the way in the area of conspicuous consumption of luxury goods. Merchants and peasants also consumed more, with peasants for the first time abandoning their spare way of life. These changes are clearly evident in agriculture.

Agriculture. Agriculture remained the most important source of wealth. The country underwent substantial agricultural modernization that produced significant increases in agricultural output and productivity. Rice production expanded from 100 million bushels in 1600 to 155 million in 1700 and 190 million in 1800. The introduction of new strains of rice permitted *double-cropping* (the growing of two crops per year on the same piece of land). This increase was accompanied by the diversification of agriculture, including new crops such as the sweet potato, imported from the Americas. Peasants also turned to commercial crops, such as hemp, fruits, vegetables, tobacco (also from the New World), safflower, rapeseed, and indigo. Better tools, aided by the introduction of commercial fertilizers, produced larger harvests. In many areas the peasants grew silk worms on a broader scale than earlier. Peasants became involved in commercial agriculture, leading to improved literacy and mathematical skills among peasants and merchants. They became a part of Japanese society, not merely sources of tax revenues. Most of the land was divided into small plots worked by single households. Proto-industrialization was also small scale and largely non-mechanized.

Proto-industrialization. Proto-industrialization is the production of goods for markets by small groups of workers using traditional technology but organized by concepts of division of labor. Proto-industrial firms were located in the countryside and organized by small-scale capitalists. The abundance of labor meant that there was little interest in mechanized power and labor saving machinery. However, small improvements in technology occurred in a very gradual way throughout the Tokugawa period. These small shops, each with 10–40 employees, produced bean paste, sake, vegetable oil, or iron. In addition, a different type of division of labor—*the putting out system*—was introduced in the textile industries. Merchants purchased raw materials and then distributed them to spinners. Then the merchants sent the thread to weavers and sold the finished cloth to wholesale merchants.

Commerce. Commercial expansion occurred as well. The shoguns promoted commerce by eliminating tariff barriers between daimyo and promoting highway construction and new shipping routes. Osaka and Edo became the main commercial centers, with Osaka markets setting national prices for rice and other products.

Three groups actively participated in commercial activities—merchants, retailers, and the daimyo. Wholesale merchants engaged in interregional trade, based on urbanization and regional specialization. They conducted business through paper credit transactions. Merchants loaned money to the shogun, to the daimyo and to the samurai, charging annual interest rates of 15–20 percent.

The bakufu tried to create order in the commercial world, as well as raise funds for itself, by granting monopolies to local merchants. The shogun issued charters to associations of wholesale merchants specializing in a single product, such as cotton textiles, tea, or silver goods. Each association paid a fee to the shogun in exchange for enjoying monopoly rights in a single commodity. Associations also determined prices and quality standards.

Retail merchants or shopkeepers sold locally produced goods or items purchased from long-distance wholesale merchants. Daimyo also engaged in commercial activity as a means of supplementing their income. They acquired monopolies of locally produced goods and sold them at both the retail and wholesale levels. Samurai officials and castle town merchants provided business expertise. Commercial expansion generated increased wealth and helped create a national economy.

Social Changes. Considerable social change accompanied economic transformation. Changes occurred within and among classes. Class lines blurred slightly, social mobility expanded and accelerated, and social unrest increased.

The samurai class faced increasingly serious economic challenges. Samurai income remained stable, so inflation produced a *real* decline in samurai income. Most samurai had few formal responsibilities and masked this by increased *conspicuous consumption.* Unable to afford the luxurious lifestyle they assigned themselves, samurai borrowed money from merchants. Some samurai secured supplemental income in the private sphere, even working as artisans and store clerks. Others married their daughters into merchant families in order to maintain their wealth. Still, the samurai remained the most powerful class in Japan, though one can see some indications of potential weaknesses.

The merchant class rose in significance, even though the Confucian model still applied in theory. Its wealth, and especially its role in financing shogunal, daimyo, and samurai activities, provided increased access to the upper classes and greater prestige. Its commercial activities gave it increased power to influence the direction of the economy. Just as the lines between the samurai and the merchants blurred somewhat, so did the boundary between the merchantry and the peasantry.

Peasants came to be recognized as productive members of society. Changes in the position of peasants resulted from a system of fixed taxes that over time, because of inflation and higher agricultural productivity, left the peasants with a greater portion of the harvests. Agricultural modernization also increased peasant income substantially. Changes took place in land usage and ownership rights. Peasants were no longer prohibited from buying and selling land. This enabled better-off peasants to purchase more land and thus increase their distance from poorer peasants. Wealthier peasants engaged in lending money, pawn broking, silk textile production, and proto-industrial activities such as sake brewing and cotton textiles.

The increasing gap between richer peasants and ordinary peasants, especially those that no longer owned land, led to increasing tension in the villages and, at times of famine (1780s and 1830s), to attacks on wealthier peasants by poorer ones.

Social Unrest. Social unrest increased during the Tokugawa period. The causes of unrest were several, including greater inequality, a reduced social welfare safety net, greater vulnerability due to natural disasters, and increased poverty for some.

Until the 1780s most protests were directed against the government's tax policies. In northern Japan in 1739 almost 100,000 peasants protested high taxes and attacked the daimyo's castle. In the early 1750s, almost twice as many protested high taxes. Taxes were lowered but the rebellion's leaders were executed. In the 1760s 200,000 peasants protested excessive labor obligations imposed upon them by the Tokugawa, who ordered a major program of road-building.

From the 1780s on, famine formed the primary cause of rebellion. In addition, participation shifted from the peasants alone to peasants and urban residents. In the Temmei Famine Riots of 1783–1787 starving peasants rose up, as did urban residents. They protested the failure of the Tokugawa to move food surpluses to areas of starvation. The Tempo Famine Riots of 1832–1836 centered on Osaka, the main commercial city. In Osaka urban residents burned rice granaries and pawn shops.

Unrest reflected the failings of the Tokugawa distribution system but were generally localized and quickly crushed by government military forces. However the government failed to solve the problems that produced rebellion.

5. Gender and Family

The family was the central institution in Japanese life. Japan had a patriarchal system, with the position of women in decline during the Tokugawa period.

Family. The patriarch had complete control over the lives of all family members. Parents arranged marriages. Husbands could divorce wives but wives could not initiate divorce. Women were to endure a marriage, not protest against it. Ideally, when a husband committed ritual suicide, his wife was to join him in death. All property passed to the eldest son upon the death of the patriarch. Samurai and peasant women could not inherit property. In urban families the husband-wife relationship was frequently seen as an equal one and patriarchy much weaker.

Women. The position of women was determined by samurai values, which extended to the rest of society and by Buddhism and neo-Confucianism. Buddhism claimed that women could not reach nirvana. Confucianism emphasized that the relationship between husband and wife was a vertical one, with men all-powerful and women powerless, or inferior. Men were free to engage in promiscuous sexual relations. Women could not. An unmarried samurai woman who was not a virgin was expected to commit suicide.

6. Emergence of Japanese Nationalism and the Challenges of Community

Centuries of isolation enabled Japan to become an increasingly homogeneous society. However, differences remained. The Japanese policy toward the indigenous people, the Ainu, shifted back and forth from assimilation to separation. Denigrated occupational groups, the *burakumin* or outcastes, remained socially and physically isolated and subject to discrimination. Expansion placed the Ryukyu Kingdom under Japanese control, challenging the push for homogeneity. Western Christianity threatened cohesion and stability, or so the Tokugawa thought. More broadly, even after the expulsion of Western Christians and repression of Japanese ones, Western ideas, broadly known as *Dutch learning,* continued to reach and influence Japan. In the eighteenth century, Japanese nationalism emerged in response to so-called threats to unanimity.

Ainu. The Ainu were the earliest known inhabitants of Japan. The Ainu organized themselves into small self-sufficient communities, which were grouped into regional associations, the *kur,* or *clan* (a group of blood-related persons). Gradually pushed northward by the Japanese, from the thirteenth to fifteenth centuries they were located in northern Honshu and southern Hokkaido, an area under the control of the *Ando* samurai family. Trade flourished between the Ainu and the Japanese in the century before the Tokugawa.

In the Tokugawa period the Ainu were partially incorporated into the decentralized political system (see Chapter One on Russian treatment of indigenous people at a similar point in time). Some Ainu were placed under the control of the *Matsumae* samurai family. Other Ainu remained independent, beyond the borders of the Matsumae daimyo. The Matsumae clamped down on the open trade between the Japanese and Ainu, making trade a Matsumae monopoly. This led to an uneven trade relationship in which the Japanese charged much higher prices than previously. By the late seventeenth century the Matsumae had set up fisheries that exploited Ainu labor. Feeling betrayed, the Ainu rebelled in 1699. This *Shakushain War* led the Japanese to view the Ainu as uncivilized and incapable of being assimilated. Government policy prohibited Ainu from learning Japanese or from wearing Japanese-style clothing. Ainu were discouraged from engaging in farming.

The Japanese began to change their policies toward the Ainu in the middle of the eighteenth century, in response to the expansion of Russians into the northern *Kurile Islands.* The Ainu became the target of Russification. To defend its northern borders the Japanese decided to claim the Ainu as Japanese and to embark upon a program of assimilation. Assimilation, which had already begun in northern Honshu, was extended to Hokkaido and to the Kuriles. The importance of protecting the northern border was reflected in the shogun's decision to assume control over Ainu territories in eastern Hokkaido and the southern Kuriles in 1799 and in western Hokkaido and southern *Sakhalin Island* in 1807. The Japanese focused on external assimilation, dress, life-style, etc., assuming that others could be transformed into Japanese. (See similar attitudes in the discussion of Russification in Chapter One). Though the Russian threat had not disappeared, in 1821 the Shogun returned the Ainu frontier areas to the Matsumae daimyo, which abandoned assimilation.

Ryukyu Kingdom. Known in the West as Okinawa, the Ryukyu Kingdom lay southwest of Japan, occupying a strategic space between Japan, China, and Korea. Early in the beginning of the Tokugawa period, *Satsuma* daimyo invaded and conquered Ryukyu, though the latter kept its tributary relationship with China. Satsuma demonstrated its control over the Ryukyu Islands by taxing the population. Later the Ryukyu leaders sent a tributary mission to the shogun's capital. The Japanese then claimed that the king of Ryukyu was a descendant of a famous Japanese warrior, Minamoto no Tametomo.

Burakumin. For many centuries *marginal groups* had existed, the object of discrimination. These marginal groups had occupational origins and included criminals, prostitutes, tattoo artists, dyers, bamboo workers, river boatmen, stone masons, and leather workers. They wore distinctive clothing and tied their hair up with straw cords. In modern times they came to be identified as *hisabatsu buraku* (*discriminated villages*).

Challenge of Christianity. The Tokugawa saw Christianity as a threat, as one more rival with whom to contend. Christianity was viewed as one more obstacle to unity and Tokugawa domination of Japan. The Tokugawa viewed the Christians as subversive outsiders. Anti-Christian actions continued long after Christianity had disappeared from Japan. A common ceremony was that of treading on *fumie* (Christian pictures).

Beginnings of Japaneseness. Until the mid-eighteenth century the Japanese did not define themselves as Japanese. Increased contact with outsiders and the emergence of nativist ideas produced a desire to define differences between the Japanese and others. Still, the Japanese were deeply influenced by Chinese culture and Chinese conceptions of the world. Very broadly the Japanese began to see Japan as the center of the world surrounded by concentric circles of greater and greater *otherness.* In the first circle were the Chinese and those nations under the Chinese sphere of influence, such as Korea. A second circle consisted of the *outer barbarians,* including the peoples of Southeast Asia, India, Spain, and the Netherlands.

Always a porous society, with outside influences seeping in at varying rates, Japan was not a completely homogeneous society in the Tokugawa age.

C. MEIJI ERA, 1868–1912

The *Meiji* (great change) era brought great change to Japan. Increased pressure from the West, beginning in the 1850s, led to a civil war in which reformers defeated Tokugawa conservatives. This *Meiji Restoration* led Japan to break out of its relative isolation and absorb Western ideas and practices. The country also became a major East Asian power, copying its imperialism from the West. Abandoning military dictatorship, the Meiji government gradually introduced a constitutional regime in which party politics assumed increasing importance. The Japanese became citizens, loyal to their nation. Initially Japanese nationalism provided some degree of unity against foreign power but later nationalism emphasized more traditional Japanese virtues. All of this was accompanied and influenced by radical social and economic change. Building upon the economic strengths of the Tokugawa period, Japan created a modern industrial economy with global aspirations. At first the government authored social changes, including the destruction of the former elite class, the samurai. Economic and political changes brought about other social transformation, including the rise of the business class and the emergence of an industrial working class. The stagnant Tokugawa social structure disintegrated, replaced by open, rapid social mobility and social instability. Gender and family roles were transformed by law (influenced by Western ideas) and socioeconomic change. Ironically, Western ideas played an important role in the growing homogeneity of Japanese society, its willingness to distinguish itself from other Asian powers, and its desire to align itself with other "modern" Western societies.

1. Meiji Revolution, 1854–1868

Foreign challenges weakened the Tokugawa and created opportunities for its enemies to challenge the ruling regime. Conflict turned from *bakufu* and court maneuverings to violence and finally to civil war. The destruction of Tokugawa power brought to office young reformers determined to introduce policies that would guarantee Japanese security. They recognized that the West was both a threat and a source of ideas and technology needed to ensure Japan's independence. Their victory over the Tokugawa created the opportunity for radical changes in almost every sphere of Japanese life.

The Western Military Challenge. The Russians first applied Western pressure against Japan by moving down the archipelago that included Sakhalin and the Kurile Islands. Later the British and ultimately the Americans attempted to open up Japan to trade and diplomatic relations.

Initial Threats and Responses. Russians provided the initial threat to Japan's isolation and security. By the 1790s, Russian trappers and missionaries had moved down through Sakhalin to the Kurile Islands and appeared poised to move onto Hokkaido. In 1792, the Russians sent a peace mission but the shogun refused to acknowledge them. They also tried in 1807 but were turned away again. Simultaneously, the Russians began to attack Japanese settlements on Sakhalin and in the Kurile Islands.

The following year the British showed up, acting more decisively than the Russians did. The British sailed into Nagasaki harbor in southwest Japan and intimidated the Japanese into providing their warship with provisions. After this encounter the shogun became more determined to maintain Japan's isolation and prevent foreign contacts. When a British whaling ship landed in Japan in 1825, the bakufu ordered daimyo to destroy all foreign ships and arrest and execute their crews.

The shogunal government and the daimyo debated two different options. Some, especially at the center, argued that Japan must strengthen itself in order to preserve its isolation and independence. *Tokugawa* Nariaki, lord of *Mito,* championed isolation, too. Samurai intellectuals in Mito such as *Fujita* Toko and *Aizawa* Seiheisei argued that trade with the West would drain precious metals from Japan, produce moral decline, and encourage the return of Christianity. Instead, they proposed that Japan engage in a program of *moral strengthening* that would enable it to defend itself. They emphasized that Japan needed to return to traditional samurai values such as frugality, loyalty, and obedience. They saw Japan as the moral center of the universe, with the emperor at the top of Japanese society. However, the connection between moral strengthening and military power was tenuous.

Others recommended increased use of Western scientific and technological thought, in order to strengthen the military. Advocates of Dutch learning espoused this view, recognizing that Japanese military backwardness left it vulnerable to the Western threat. Shimazu Nariakira, daimyo of *Satsuma,* championed this view as well. Satsuma and other southern and southwestern daimyo had had greater contact with the West and were most vulnerable to Western actions.

Those who believed it necessary to learn Western skills to defend Japanese principles were strengthened by awareness of the Opium War of 1839–1842, in which the British easily defeated the Chinese (see Chapter Four). They became further convinced that Japan could not ignore Western military power. A new chief minister, *Abe* Masahiro, encouraged the daimyo to avoid confrontations with the West and instead provide them with fuel, water, and provisions, if requested. At the same time he established a new *Office of Coastal Defenses* that built up coastal defenses, especially near the capital. Abe encouraged the daimyo to devote more resources to coastal defenses and the acquisition of Western military equipment. He hoped that this common defense policy would bring the various political units closer together, for he recognized that unity was essential if Japan was to successfully defend itself against the Westerners.

Arrival of the Americans. Ironically, American actions led to the opening up of Japan. Americans were primarily interested in China but saw Japan as a stopping off point. The 1848 acquisition of California and the Gold Rush of 1849 increased American interest in the Pacific. In 1853, Commodore Matthew Perry arrived with a small flotilla but was rebuffed. Promising to return with a more powerful fleet, Perry came back the next year, with a fleet of seven black ships, a crew of "red-nosed barbarians" and examples of American culture (including a toy train and barrels of Kentucky bourbon). Cultural sharing included Japanese sumo wrestling and banjo playing by sailors in blackface.

Briefly seeking the advice of the daimyo, the shogun accepted a *wood and water treaty* in 1854. The Japanese agreed to diplomatic relations and the opening up of two minor ports to American ships. Applying the concept of *most favored nation,* other Western powers received the same concessions.

The Americans smelled the blood of greater concessions and in 1856 the American consul at Shimoda, one of the two open ports, began negotiations with the Japanese that led to a new treaty in 1858. Additional treaty ports were opened up and Americans gained the right to charge customs dues on goods they sold to Japan. The concept of *extraterritoriality* was invoked, permitting Americans to be tried in U.S., rather than Japanese, courts if they committed crimes in Japan. Americans were permitted to have diplomatic representation in the Japanese capital. In spite of American pressure, the Japanese refused to permit the importation of opium.

Internal Power Struggle. Though most daimyo had supported the new agreement with the Americans, Japanese leaders soon began to seriously doubt the wisdom of having signed the treaty. At the same time conflict arose over who should become shogun to replace the ill Tokugawa Iesuda. This power struggle became increasingly complicated and violent, with policy toward the West a key issue.

Reformist daimyo, including Satsuma, Echizen, Mito, and Date supported *Tokugawa Yoshinobu,* the son of Nariaki of Mito, for shogun. These daimyo tended to be fairly independent of the shogun. The daimyo closest to the bakufu supported a boy, who was daimyo of Kii.

This conflict broadened beyond the controversy over the 1858 treaty to encompass the role and power of the emperor and his court. The 1858 treaty was submitted to *Emperor Komei,* nominally a mere formality. However, the deeply anti-foreign Komei rejected the treaty and called on the shogun to canvas the daimyo, who had already given their support to the treaty. The emperor claimed to be the ultimate political authority and not merely an impoverished figurehead living an isolated existence in Kyoto. The shogun sought to reassert his authority. He appointed *Ii* Naosuke as *Great Elder,* second in command. The shogun decided to sign the treaty in spite of the emperor's opposition. At the same time the shogun declared that selection of his successor was an internal matter not to be influenced by campaigning by the daimyo. The shogun appointed the daimyo of Kii as heir apparent. These actions alienated both the treaty opponents and the daimyo reformers and unleashed a decade of civil war that eventually led to the destruction of the shogunate.

Tensions and Civil War. Western trade produced high inflation, which further undermined the economic position of the samurai class. Urban riots and peasant uprisings accompanied unrest in the upper class. Out of this milieu of social stress emerged the *sonno-joi* (*men of determination*) movement.

Centered in Kyoto, these men sought a way out of their sense of humiliation at the hands of the West and their resentment that the rulers of the country could not prevent foreign inroads. Ironically, this group had support both from the anti-foreign clique around the emperor and the reformists in daimyo such as Satsuma, Mito, and Choshu. In 1860, the men of determination began a terrorist campaign against those who had supported the treaty. Ii and a number of other high bakufu officials were assassinated. The bakufu responded by arresting and executing a number of the men of determination.

Civil war replaced individual terrorism in 1863. Samurai from *Choshu* persuaded Emperor Komei to order the daimyo to expel foreigners. However, only Choshu acted, firing on an American ship. In 1863 and 1864, Western ships bombarded Satsuma and Choshu for attacking Western vessels. The bakufu ordered Satsuma troops to drive Choshu rebels out of Kyoto. By itself, Choshu was not strong enough to stand up to the power of the central government. In 1864, Choshu tried to depose the shogun and transfer supreme power to the emperor. Satsuma and Aizu daimyo defended the shogun and once again Choshu was defeated.

Though it appeared that the shogunate had defeated its foes, it continued to decline. The effort to patch up the relationship with the emperor through a marriage between the boy shogun Tokugawa Iemochi and Princess Kazunomiya, the emperor's sister, actually demonstrated the weakness of the bakufu. The central government hired a number of reformists from the relatively independent daimyo of Satsuma, Mito, Echizen, and Tosa and listened to their suggestions.

Anti-foreigners gained power in Choshu, Satsuma, and Tosa daimyo. Increasingly they recognize the need for national unity against the West and began to put together an alliance of large daimyo. Both the daimyo and the central government embarked upon crash programs of coastal defense and military modernization. The daimyo became more and more worried about the center's increasing military power. This led to an alliance between formerly bitter rivals, Satsuma and Choshu. When the shogun attacked Choshu in 1866, Satsuma joined with the latter to defeat the bakufu army.

Rebellion. In 1867, a new shogun came to power, the reformer Tokugawa Yoshinobu. Recognizing the Western threat, Yoshinobu proposed a centralized, unified Japan, an idea unacceptable to the daimyo. Satsuma, Tosa, Choshu, and Echizen decided to establish a new imperial government in place of the bakufu. Tosa and Echizen proposed to the shogun that he transfer authority to the emperor but Yoshinobu wished to retain much power in his own hands. Fearing that this compromise would break down, Satsuma and Choshu captured the imperial palace, where the new Meiji emperor had just assumed power. Satsuma and Choshu reformers convinced him to issue decrees that abolished both the bakufu and court offices and created a new government.

Yoshinobu responded to these events of late 1867 and early 1868 by declaring war on the rebellious daimyo and the emperor. By April 1868, rebels had surrounded Edo castle, forcing the surrender of the Tokugawa. Resistance continued in the northeast until June 1869, when supporters of the shogun surrendered in Hokkaido.

Conclusion. The civil war was brief, though bloody, and ended two and a half centuries of Tokugawa rule. The Meiji Restoration overthrew a weak and incompetent government and used traditionalist rhetoric, the restoration of imperial rule, to justify a program of strengthening Japan through Western ideas and practices. Ultimately Japan developed a strong sense of loyalty to nation and became a regional imperialist power, as well.

2. Nation, Citizenship, and Empire

Under the impact of Western ideas and example, Japan developed new ideas about citizenship, civilization, and empire.

Civilization. Intellectuals and politicians devoted much energy to the issue of whether Japan was part of Asian or Western Civilization. The debate over Japan's place in the world was a central concern for *Fukuzawa* Yukichii. Fukuzawa was the leading Japanese "Westernizer" of the period. He believed that the West was an advanced civilization and Japan an intermediate one. By using Western ideas Japan could advance to the highest level of civilization—that occupied by the West.

Nationalism. Closely related to the discussion of civilization was the emergence of a stronger sense of nationalism. The proponents of native learning had emphasized the superiority of core Japaneseness over the veneer of Chinese Confucianism. Destruction of the Tokugawa and implementation of the Meiji Revolution intensified and modified the Japanese sense of nationalism. National unity was necessary for Japan to preserve its national security and maintain its strength, the reformers argued. Ironically, a strong sense of nationalism, centered on the Meiji Emperor, accompanied the need to emulate the West. Some argued that the Japanese race was closer to the Aryan or Central Asian races than to other East Asians. This made the Japanese "almost Europeans." The Japanese believed that they, too, had a civilizing mission. (See British attitudes in Chapter Two and French views in Chapter Six). They believed that it was their responsibility to bring modern civilization to the rest of Asia. They saw themselves as a bridge between East and West. The Japanese also portrayed themselves as representatives of the "spiritual East" in contrast to the "materialist West." Though the Japanese depicted their role in the world variously, they clearly emphasized that their country was unique, representing the best of both East and West.

Creating a Colonial Empire. Japan became a regional imperialist power, one of the strongest countries in Asia. The nation sought to create an empire for several reasons. It desperately wished to emulate the Western imperialist powers and saw imperialism as a mark of civilization and Westernization. Japan wanted to build up a buffer zone around the Japanese core to ensure its national security. Since the first generation of Meiji leaders came from military backgrounds, they sought to demonstrate their military prowess abroad. They recognized that imperialism could be an effective strategy for promoting and strengthening national unity in a period of government-led rapid change. Parallel attitudes could be found among leading European powers at the end of the nineteenth century.

The desire to become a global power could be actualized in part because Japan acquired the necessary industrial base and military technology and expertise. In addition, Japan's drive for empire occurred during a power vacuum in East Asia. China was disintegrating, facing massive domestic rebellion and foreign threat with inept, weak political leadership. Russia had pretensions of being a regional power but faced huge logistical problems in moving troops and military equipment, even with the completion of the Trans-Siberian Railway. In addition, Russia was increasingly troubled with internal difficulties. The other Asian nations, such as the "Indo-Chinese" and the Koreans, were already colonies and thus had no independence. The European powers were neither able nor willing to oppose Japanese expansion. The French were preoccupied with Indo-China and even more so with North Africa and had begun to compete with the British in sub-Saharan Africa. The British sense of superiority led them to underestimate the potential of Japanese power. More importantly the British had reduced their imperial goals after the Great Rebellion in India (see Chapter Two) and focused primarily on India, their most important colony. The British had little desire to expand their power in East Asia. They sought to preserve their strategic position in Southeast Asia and southern China and prevent anyone else from gaining a dominant economic influence in East Asia. Finally, in spite of its role in opening up Japan, the United States was not yet a major player in East Asia.

Japan's strategy for empire building was to use military power to gain territorial and economic concessions and to back away from confrontation if initial efforts were unsuccessful. At first, the Japanese did not articulate a clear, long-range strategy of becoming a major East Asian power. Only gradually did Japan recognize that it had the ability to become a major regional imperialist power.

Expanding National Borders. The country's first step was to "round out its national borders." In 1874, China and Japan agreed that the Ryukyu Islands were part of Japan and not a Chinese tributary. In return, Taiwan was considered a Chinese client state. In 1879, the islands were incorporated into Japan as the prefecture of *Okinawa.*

In 1875, the Japanese and Russians agreed on a geographical demarcation to the north of Japan. The Japanese abandoned their claims to the island of Sakhalin and the Russians gave up their claims to the Kurile Islands. Thus each nation retained the disputed territory closest to its homeland.

Gradual Conquest of Korea. The Japanese first proposed "opening up" Korea to Japanese trade and diplomatic ties in 1873 but the idea fell helplessly to earth because of internal struggles within the Japanese leadership. Later, a display of Japanese naval power produced the 1876 *Treaty of Kangwha.* Korea opened up three ports to Japanese trade and accepted the idea that it was no longer a Chinese tributary. The Japanese were also granted rights of extraterritoriality. The Japanese approach and demands were very similar to those of the Americans two decades before.

However, the situation in Korea turned out to be much more complicated. In the 1880s, Japan asserted itself more aggressively into Korean affairs. The Japanese also attempted to dominate the Korean economy, especially its international trade. The Japanese rationale was the need to civilize both Korea and its former master, China. Japanese aggressiveness was met by renewed Chinese influence within Korea. The two countries backed different Korean factions. The Chinese supported the conservatives, including the Korean ruling family, the Min. The Japanese aided Korean modernizers.

In 1882, the Japanese assisted rebels who overthrew the House of Min. However, the Chinese intervened, crushed the rebellion, and placed Korea once again in a tributary status. This Japanese effort to dominate Korea by controlling its rulers was followed in 1884 by Japanese support for another rebellion—this time by the pro-Japanese modernizers, known as the enlightened faction. The Chinese general *Yuan Shikai* defeated this rebellion (see Chapter Four for the further role of Yuan Shikai). Military confrontation between China and Japan was avoided when both sides agreed to withdraw their troops, through the *Li-Ito* (or *Tianjin*) *Convention.* Both countries continued to desire to dominate Korea.

Sino-Japanese War. By the 1890s, Japan had begun to focus on the need for colonies, naval bases, and a *line of interest* that would delineate its sphere of influence. Arguing that only Japanese military power could preserve peace in East Asia, the Japanese began a major military build-up. This build-up played an essential role in ensuring Japanese victory in the Sino-Japanese War of 1894–1895.

Another rebellion in Korea in 1894, the Tonghak uprising, led to the Sino-Japanese War. The Tonghak was a religious-based, peasant-oriented sect. It was anti-foreign, especially anti-Japanese. It believed that its religious beliefs would protect Koreans against "foreigners" (see the Chinese parallel, the Boxer movement, in Chapter Four). When the Korean government invited Chinese general Yuan Shikai to put down the rebellion, the Japanese sent troops into Korea. The Japanese feared that an unstable Korea would undermine Japanese economic activity there. When the Chinese proved unwilling to negotiate a settlement, the Japanese declared war.

The Japanese easily defeated the Chinese. They drove the Chinese armies out of Korea and destroyed the Chinese navy. Japanese armies then marched into Manchuria. With naval superiority, the Japanese took the Liaodong Peninsula of Manchuria and part of the Shandong Peninsula in north China. Japanese troops threatened the Chinese capital of Peking (Beijing) but feared that the consequence might be Western intervention.

The two nations negotiated a peace settlement, the *Treaty of Shimonoseki* (1895). China surrendered Taiwan, the Pescadores Islands, and part of the Liaodong Peninsula to Japan. China also agreed to pay a huge indemnity, substantially greater than Japan's war costs. Further, China recognized the "independence" of Korea. Japan secured "most favored" status in China, including extraterritoriality and the right to trade and manufacture products in China. Japan thus gained a foothold on the East Asian mainland.

However, its gains were short-lived. Russia, France, and Germany imposed the *Triple Intervention* upon Japan, forcing it to return the Liaodong Peninsula to China. Ironically, Russia soon annexed the Liaodong Peninsula and the British acquired part of the Shandong Peninsula.

Overall, the Sino-Japanese War marked a turning point for Japanese imperialism in East Asia. The war demonstrated that China could no longer halt Japanese expansion. A much smaller and less Asian country, Japan, had defeated the greatest civilization in East Asia. Having defeated China, the Japanese turned to the other threat to its expansion, Russia. At the same time, the Japanese recognized the importance of naval power for a would-be Pacific power and embarked upon a major naval build-up.

Western Recognition. Simultaneously, the Japanese pursued equality with the Western powers. In 1894, the British agreed to a phase out of the unequal treaties applied to Japan. Then in 1902 Japan and Great Britain, still the most powerful imperialist nation in the world, signed the *Anglo-Japanese Alliance of 1902.* Great Britain declared its neutrality—and guaranteed that all other Western European powers would remain neutral as well—should Russia and Japan go to war. The British also recognized the special position of the Japanese in Korea. For the first time a Western power and a non-Western nation signed a treaty that recognized their equality. Japan had clearly joined the league of Western imperialists.

Russo-Japanese War. Korea and Manchuria soon became bones that the wild dogs, Russia and Japan, fought over. Initially the Japanese were willing to exchange Russian recognition of Japanese domination over Korea for Japanese acceptance of Russian control over Manchuria. The Japanese offer fell through for Russia saw no need to withdraw completely from Korea. Japanese support for the modernization of Korea produced rapid social change and intensified conflict between the enlighteners and the conservatives. With Japanese support, opponents assassinated Queen Min (1896). The plan backfired as pro-Russian conservatives came to power.

In 1898, at the time of the Boxer Rebellion (see Chapter Four), Russia took advantage of Chinese weakness to ensure Russian control over Manchuria. At the same time, Russia agreed to defend China in case of another Japanese attack. The weakened Chinese leadership agreed to transfer the Chinese Eastern Railway and the Southern Manchurian Railway to the Russians. They began a military and naval build up at Port Arthur on the Liadong Peninsula.

Negotiations to define spheres of influence (lines of interest) continued into early 1904. At that point Japan broke off negotiations, attacked Port Arthur, and then declared war on Russia. Once again, Japan easily defeated a mainland Asian power, though here they had gambled more than in the war with China. Russia had superior military power while Japan had surprise and a temporary geographic advantage on its side. The Japanese navy destroyed the Russian Far Eastern fleet and then launched major landings in Manchuria. In addition, Japanese armies advanced from Korea into Manchuria, finally capturing Port Arthur in early 1905. After capturing the other major Manchurian city, Mukden, the Japanese offense sputtered to a halt. The ground war became one of attrition. The final Japanese victory came through the destruction of the Russian Baltic Fleet, soon after it arrived off Japanese waters.

Exhausted, they both accepted President Theodore Roosevelt's offer to mediate. By the *Treaty of Portsmouth* (1905), Russia recognized a Japanese predominance in Korea. Japan also received the Liaodong Peninsula, the Southern Manchurian Railway and the southern half of Sakhalin. The western nations, especially Great Britain and the United States, recognized Japan as a major Asian power.

Concerned about the possibility of a revival of Russian power in Asia, Japan agreed with Russia on the division of Manchuria into lines of interest—with Russia to have a dominant role in north Manchuria and Japan in the south. In 1910, Japan annexed Korea and embarked upon a major program of economic development there. The Japanese improved infrastructure, built industry, modernized education, and improved agriculture.

Thus, at the end of the Meiji period, Japan was recognized, reluctantly in East Asia, and more positively in the West, as a major regional imperialist power. The Meiji reforms and an aggressive foreign policy provided Japan with the security it had lost with the American opening up of the country. Japan became the strongest Asian power in Asia and the first non-Western country in many centuries to become an equal partner to the West.

International Business. A close relationship existed between Japan's emergence as an imperialist power and its economic expansion into Asian markets. Initially, Japan was a net importer of Western goods. Most of the early imports were ordered and paid for by the Meiji government. Gradually private firms imported machinery and equipment as well. Japan paid for these imports with *specie.* Over time the Japanese began to export teas, silk, and craft products.

By 1900, Japan increasingly exported cotton and silk yarn, thus not raw materials but finished goods produced by mechanized industry. Japan continued to import machinery and raw materials for industry, though the proportion of imported machinery declined, leading to *import substitution* (see Chapter One where the term is first introduced).

Trading companies carried much of Japan's international commerce. The most prominent of these companies was the *House of Mitsui,* one of a handful of Tokugawa-era commercial enterprises that flourished in the Meiji period. Second, the Japanese government recognized that competitiveness required high quality goods. The government set up stations at ports that inspected export goods such as silk yarn to ensure high quality. The government further supported international trade through the creation of the *Yokohama Species Bank* (1880), which gave credit and foreign currency to Japanese businesses involved in international trade. The government promoted the sale of Japanese goods through commercial officers at embassies and consulates, international trade exhibitions and fairs. Trade with the West provided a major lift for Japanese business, introduced foreign goods and lifestyles and produced higher living standards for the Japanese people. At the same time Japan was exposed to global economic cycles, which meant that world depression spread to it, too.

The Japanese recognized that it would be easier to sell goods to China than to the West. In 1895, Japan became a participant in the unequal treaties Western powers signed with China a half century before. These treaties gave Japan a distinct trade advantage with China. With Britain's colony India sending its cotton goods to Britain, the Chinese market was left open to Japan. Japan exported large amounts of cotton yarn to China, receiving in exchange raw materials, especially coal and iron ore.

3. Meiji Constitutionalism

Japan created a constitutional government based on a written document. Ideas for a Meiji constitution came from an eclectic mix of Western ideas. The Tokugawa system was discarded, as were its Confucian underpinnings. Through the Emperor, the oligarchs outlined the ideals of the Meiji era in the *Imperial (Charter) Oath* (1868). A national assembly would be created to permit public discussion of important issues. Social differences would be eliminated, with a common position for all citizens. Remnants from the past would be destroyed as a new and glorious future was being created. Finally, the oath reiterated the strategy of using outside ideas to strengthen Japan.

Beginnings of Central Government. In the early Meiji era, new rulers, the *oligarchs,* applied their pragmatic approach, searching for workable political institutions. In 1868, they created a national assembly and a Council of State. In 1871, the Council of State was divided into functional boards. The Central Board was the main decision-making body, while the Board of the Left conducted policy studies and the Board of the Right administered the various departments of the bureaucracy.

Destruction of Daimyo Power. At the same time, the oligarchs consolidated their position by eliminating the power of the daimyo. First the daimyo surrendered their authority, beginning with those daimyo that had led the Meiji Restoration. These daimyo "gave" their lands to the Emperor in 1869. Other daimyo were shamed or forced to do likewise. The economic loss was softened by compensation equal to one-tenth of their previous income as well as by the new government's assumption of daimyo debt. In 1871, the governments of the daimyo were abolished, replaced by *prefectures.* New boundaries were drawn up, cutting across former daimyo borders. The oligarchs appointed governors, mainly from the lower samurai from Satsuma, Choshu, and other daimyo that had led the rebellion. Daimyo castles were demolished, both symbolic and practical actions. A hierarchical structure was established, with power flowing from the central government to the prefectures, then to districts, then on to towns and villages. Complementing the administrative structures were consultative assemblies at the village/town, district, and prefecture levels. These assemblies were appointed by members of the next higher level and could only discuss issues. This structure was in place by the mid-1870s, though still just in skeletal form. The Home Ministry (1873) played the primary role in supervising government beyond the capital.

Central Bureaucracy. Having created government outside the capital to ensure that daimyo opposition would not surface, the oligarchs then turned their attention to strengthening and improving the central government. Key to this was the reorganization of the central bureaucracy. The government established academies to train government officials. In 1886, it established the Imperial University of Tokyo, primarily as a training center for high-level bureaucrats. Its Faculty of Law became a major source of government officials.

Popular Rights. Though the oligarchs expected to rule Japan without any real participation by the Japanese people, by the mid-1870s they were forced to deal with a *popular rights movement.* Several factors produced this effort to democratize the political system. The Charter Oath had promised that the Japanese people would have the right to participate in the political process through popularly elected assemblies. Second, there was general opposition to authoritarian rule by the oligarchs. Educated Japanese had promoted democratic ideals, especially Western democratic thought. In addition, some oligarchs disagreed with official policy and used popular rights to oppose the government.

Initial leadership of the popular rights movement came from *Itagaki* Taisuke, *Goto* Shojiro, and others who had opposed the government intention to invade Korea. Most supporters of popular rights came from the samurai class and the professions such as journalism, law, and the professoriate. In 1874,

Itagaki and others called for the creation of an elected national assembly. Opposed to popular participation in governance, the oligarchs banned public meetings, introduced censorship of the press, and arrested the movement's leaders. However, the oligarchs failed to crush the popular rights movement. By the late 1870s over 600 pro-democracy groups existed, many emphasizing local rights.

Political parties emerged out of the popular rights movement. Neither the oligarchs nor the leaders of the popular rights movements had expected or planned for political parties. In 1877, Itagaki founded the first political party, the Patriotic Society. By 1881, he had formed the *Liberal Party,* which stood for representative government. In 1882, *Okuma* Shigenobu and Fukuzawa formed the *Constitutional Reform* (later *Progressive*) *Party.* Okuma called for the introduction of a British-style parliamentary government. Thus a two-party system emerged, later expanding into a three-party system when the government created its own party, the *Imperial Party.* These political parties were quite fragile and disintegrated easily, especially after the government co-opted the political reform program of the popular rights movement.

The popular rights movement played an important role in defining the nature and direction of the Meiji constitutional program. It pushed the government to introduce constitutionalism. It legitimized peaceful opposition as an alternative to oligarchic rule. It developed methods of mass mobilization.

The Meiji Constitution. By the late 1870s the issue was not whether to have a constitution but what kind to adopt. The Japanese gradually created the institutions that formed the basis for constitutional government. The written constitution neither created new institutions nor established a particular ideal form of government. Instead it described what Japanese governance was actually like. In 1881, the Emperor announced that a constitution would be written and implemented by 1890. It was to be a "gift" from the emperor, representing His (the oligarchs) will rather than popular will.

Most of the key government institutions were created in the second half of the 1880s. In 1884, a new upper class was established, the *peers,* from whose membership an upper house of the legislature would be created. In 1885, the oligarchs established a *cabinet system.* The Cabinet took major policy decisions. Ten functional ministries, including a Prime Minister, were to be appointed by the Emperor and to report to him through the Prime Minister. The Army and Navy Ministries remained separate, reporting directly to the Emperor rather than to the Cabinet. The Home Ministry was extremely powerful, responsible for all governance at the prefecture, district, and local levels. In 1887, a civil service system was established for all except a few top officials in each ministry, who would be political appointments. All other government officials were selected on the basis of a civil service examination. In 1888, the oligarchs established a Privy Council, responsible for giving advice to the Emperor. Essentially the Privy Council, comprised of oligarchs, rather than the Cabinet, became the primary decision-making body. In 1888, a system of local self-rule was established, with government in the hands of mayors and assemblies. Oligarchs did not have the time to micromanage down to the local level.

The constitution was drafted between 1887 and 1889, with most of the work completed in the few months before the Emperor "gave" the constitution to the Japanese people. The government, and not a constitutional convention, drafted the document. The Privy Council reviewed it before promulgation. The constitution described the operation of the institutions created in the 1880s, defined the role of the emperor, and established a bi-cameral legislature, the *Imperial Diet.* The Emperor was declared sovereign (though having his responsibilities defined in a constitution limited his power). He had ultimate administrative power, with the Cabinet responsible to him and not to the legislature. He could issue decrees, though they had to be countersigned by the Privy Council and the Cabinet. The Emperor also had the power to veto bills passed by the Lower House, the House of Representatives. The Legislature had the power to issue tax legislation and debate and approve the budget. It could also petition the Emperor. The members of the House of Representatives were elected through open (not secret) balloting. Only a small percentage of the male population could vote, as the *franchise* was based on levels of taxes paid. In the first elections in 1888, 1 percent of adult males were eligible to vote.

Politics of Governance. Constitutional government lived uneasily with oligarchic power for the rest of the Meiji period, 1889–1912. It was difficult to fit political parties into the authoritarian system. The constitution provided no role for political parties, while the idea of elected representatives with real power was a revolutionary idea hard to implement.

The political system was hampered by the weakness of the parties. The parties were pro-imperialist and thus always gave in to the government on the domestic agenda in order to ensure that external goals were met. Political parties were faction-ridden, each lacking a unified sense of purpose.

On the other hand, the oligarchs tended to stick together against the parties. In addition, all actions were taken in the name of the emperor but he was not personally held responsible. This made it difficult to locate responsibility. The oligarchs had powers not available to the parties. They could use the emperor system, the bureaucracy, and the police and could count on public support, as well. The oligarchs used divide and conquer tactics, taking advantage of the disruptive nature of the political parties. At the same time, oligarchs possessed a sense of dedication and determination to serve the state and public good.

Initially both the oligarchs and the parties tried to assert their total domination of the political process. In the first Diet session in 1890, the largest political party, the Liberals, tried to assert legislative control over the Cabinet. This would have produced a parliamentary form of government. However, neither side was able to achieve total domination; both were forced to compromise.

Oligarchy-Party Cooperation. Abandoning confrontation, politics entered a new stage in which the oligarchs ruled with the support of one party or the other. Oligarchic efforts to use force and bribery to prevent the victory of opposition parties backfired in the 1892 elections. Twenty-five were killed and 400 injured because of military and police brutality. The Progressives and Liberals won most seats in the House of Representatives, as well. From 1893–1895 and again from 1896–1898 the oligarchs ruled with the support of the Progressive Party. In 1895, the Liberals briefly aligned with the government. At the same time, Choshu and Satsuma oligarchs alternated as Prime Minister, reducing conflict within the oligarchy.

The era of oligarchy-party cooperation ended in 1898 when the Liberals and Progressives formed a coalition as the Constitutional Party headed by

Itagaki and Okuma. The coalition soon disintegrated, splitting into the Constitutional Party (the Liberals) and the Real Constitutional Party (the Progressives). Conflict between the two major parties enabled the government to successfully reintroduce the idea of a pro-government party.

Pro-government Party. From 1900 to the end of the Meiji period the oligarchs ruled with the cooperation of the pro-government party, the *Constitutional Government Party* (or *Seiyukai*). Liberals and government officials were the main components of this party. *Hara* Takeshi played a central role in ensuring that most governors supported Seiyukai, thus giving it some grass roots ties. Seiyukai was an openly pro-business party and thus had the support of the business community.

This was a period of relatively stable government, interrupted only by widespread dissatisfaction with the Treaty of Portsmouth settlement at the end of the Russo-Japanese War. *Katsura* Taro and *Prince Saionji* Kimmochi alternated as prime minister. This was also an era of transition for the oligarchs, who had ruled Japan for over thirty years. As oligarchs left the political scene, second-generation government leaders, who were much more willing to work with the political parties, replaced them. Relations improved between the government and the opposition parties, even though the government no longer needed their support in order to rule.

Thus during the Meiji period Japan underwent a revolutionary transformation of its political system. For the previous thousand years the Japanese political system had been a military dictatorship. In the Meiji period constitutional government triumphed, with power shared between the self-appointed oligarchs and the political parties, representing the Japanese people. The primary political institutions and their powers were formally defined by the constitution, though informal decision-making was still important. A cabinet system was established, the prelude to parliamentary democracy. A professional civil service was formed, partially replacing favoritism and cronyism.

4. Citizenship and Loyalty

Western ideas formed the basis of the new Meiji ideology. Progress and enlightenment were the watchwords of this new set of ideals. The ideology of the Japanese was almost identical to that of the Western liberal tradition. The Japanese people demonstrated strong support for the new ideology.

Westernism. At the center of the ideology was the principle that Japan must be a strong, secure nation, to be achieved through Western ideas and technology. Japan was to be a "democratic," capitalist, imperialist, and Western society.

Fukuzawa played a central role in popularizing Western ideas. His 1866 account of the West, *Conditions in the West,* sold 150,000 copies that year. Fukuzawa emphasized the inevitability of human progress and certainly the Meiji reforms seemed to confirm this perspective. He sought to define Japan's place in the world, suggesting that there were three types of societies, the civilized countries of the West; the semi-civilized, including pre-Meiji Japan, China, and India; and the savage barbarians, the rest of the world. Japan's goal was to move as quickly as possible from the state of semi-civilization to that of civilization. This emphasis on the inevitability of reaching a specific stage of human development gave the reformers great confidence in their ability to achieve this *cultural revolution*. However, agreement on what civilization actually looked like was lacking. Most, like Fukuzawa, saw civilization in terms of the secular, rational, individualistic West. A few, such as Nakamura Masanao, depicted civilization in Christian terms, especially idealizing the Protestant work ethic.

The first cracks in Japanese ideological unity came in the 1890s with the fostering of the imperial cult and the restructuring of education to achieve socialization of children into loyal, patriotic citizens.

5. Economic Modernization and Social Revolution

Japan transformed itself from an agrarian-commercial, autarkic economy into a modern industrial, global one in the second half of the nineteenth century. Changes occurred in the nature of economic activity, business, agriculture, and industrial production. At the same time, the social system was transformed. The class system was turned upside down and new classes emerged. High levels of upward and downward mobility replaced the rigid Tokugawa social structure. Protest and unrest accompanied these changes.

Economic Modernization. Rapid economic development produced a basic change in the nature of the economy. The Japanese industrial revolution was based on the British model of economic development. Wealth generated from expanded commercial activity and agricultural production made possible modest investment in light industry, especially textiles. After production skills and capital had been generated and work skills improved in light industry, Japan could begin to develop heavy industry, which was much more capital-intensive. Industrial development seemed essential if Japan was to become a modern society capable of maintaining its national security. Western capital, technology, and technical expertise made industrialization possible. Changing business attitudes were important, too. The Japanese emphasized material progress, the legitimacy of making private profits, and a commitment to a work ethic. Increased population (from 33 million in 1872 to 41 million in 1882 and 51 million in 1892) provided increased demand for goods as well as additional labor for industry. Building upon the Tokugawa base of relative prosperity, the Meiji transformed Japan into a modern, industrial society—one of the great stories of economic achievement in the modern world. Economic change is most evident in the industrial revolution.

Industrial Revolution. Japan underwent an industrial revolution rather swiftly, taking about three decades to become a modern industrial power. Industrialization went through three overlapping stages. During the 1870s and 1880s the government sponsored industrialization. In the second stage, private entrepreneurs promoted light industry, especially in the 1880s and 1890s. Heavy industry was emphasized in the third stage from the 1890s to the end of the Meiji period.

Government played the initial, central role in the development of industry. The oligarchs established the national goal of security through modernization, which required industrialization. It provided political stability that made it easier for private individuals to invest in economic development. Government reduced the restrictions on business activity that had been common in the Tokugawa period. It provided support to specific individuals and groups of samurai, including the upper samurai, the *seisho.* The government acted as the main customer, especially for products new to Japan. It imported foreign technology, including entire model factories.

In the 1870s the government tried to modernize the economy through foreign technology. The Ministry of Industry, created in 1870, built railways, telegraph lines, and lighthouses. It operated mines and textile mills. It imported entire factories that produced glass, cement, woolen cloth, and silk yarn. The government also invested in *strategic industries,* especially iron and steel. The government developed the gigantic Yawata Iron and Steel Works that produced three-fourths of Japan's steel in the first decade of the twentieth century.

Banking specialization played an important role, too. In 1902, the government established the Industrial Bank to fund heavy industry. In contrast to Britain and the United States, government played a dynamic role in the industrial revolution.

Private enterprise played the primary role in light industry, especially in cotton and silk textiles. Central to the development of light industry were entrepreneurial initiative, improvements in the organization of production, the mechanization of power, capital generation, and the shift from domestic to international marketing.

The shift from water to steam power in light industry began at *Shibusawa* Eichii's *Osaka Spinning Company.* By 1900, steam powered mechanization dominated industry, both light and heavy. Capital was abundantly available from domestic sources. First, individual industrialists plowed profits back into their firms. In addition *joint stock companies* were created as a means of generating capital. By 1898, 1 percent of the population had invested in stocks or company shares. Finally private banks, known as *organ banks,* appeared. Each bank provided capital to a few firms with which it had close ties. Large companies set up their own banks to provide capital for investment in the firm.

Light industry developed in the textile industries, first in silk, then in cotton. Initially the Japanese exported raw silk but soon turned to mechanized *silk reeling* (the making of thread). Initially large reeling mills were not very successful because the Japanese lacked experience in managing large-scale operations. However, by 1890, half of all silk output came from mechanized reeling production; by 1913, three-fourths of silk thread came from mechanized reeling mills. Expansion of silk production resulted from improvements in technology, increases in the size of reeling mills, and *vertical integration* of the silk industry from the production of cocoons to the weaving of cloth. A dual system of production developed. Mechanized mills met the foreign demand for standardized products, while hand reeling met the needs of domestic weavers. Commission houses purchased the cocoons at harvest time and later sold the thread to exporters, who had provided the capital. The government played an important role by introducing government inspection facilities at ports in Yokohama and Kobe.

Machine weaving of silk cloth developed more slowly than silk reeling. Silk weaving remained a cottage industry, with peasant households receiving silk thread to weave into cloth. After the cloth was woven wholesalers sent it out for dyeing and finishing and then supplied it to distributors and retailers. Limited amounts of silk weaving took place in small shops with power looms.

Gradually cotton textiles replaced silk textiles as the most mechanized and most important light industry. At the beginning of the 1870s government and private cotton mills were established, using imported Western machinery. The government purchased the necessary equipment for ten spinning mills and sold them at a discount to private entrepreneurs. Officials tried unsuccessfully to promote samurai cotton textile entrepreneurship. These mills were small and produced low-quality yarns. They were not competitive with yarn imported from India.

The founding of the Osaka Spinning Mill (1883) marked a turning point for the cotton textiles industry. From the mid-1880s to the mid-1890s private individuals founded a large number of large mechanized mills. Access to the Korean market and China's ban on Indian cotton goods due to an epidemic in Bombay stimulated Japanese cotton textile production. Japan thus entered two major East Asian markets—China and Korea. Initially raw cotton came from China, later from British India, and toward the end of the Meiji period primarily from the United States. By 1890, mechanization spread to weaving mills. Just as in silk, specialization of weaving occurred in cotton cloth. Large cotton weaving mills, owned by cotton spinning firms produced wide, standardized cloth for export. Thus the mechanized cotton industry was characterized by vertical integration. Small power loom mills or hand loom shops produced narrow cloth, mainly for kimonos for the domestic market.

By the end of the Meiji period textiles were the most important Japanese industry, employing some 60 percent of the industrial work force. Cheap labor, low costs of mechanized production, and entrepreneurial initiative drove the industrial revolution. Building upon this base, heavy industry became an important component of the Japanese industrial revolution.

From the mid-1890s, Japan emerged as a major participant in heavy industry. The most important heavy industries were iron and steel, shipbuilding, armaments, and machinery.

Agricultural Improvements. Substantial changes occurred in agriculture. First, agricultural output grew sizably. Second, continued improvements occurred in agricultural techniques. Third, ownership shifted from the daimyo to individual peasant households. Finally, rural equality declined, replaced by substantial economic inequality, especially the disparity between the positions of landlords and tenant farmers.

Agricultural output grew much faster than the population. Estimates of the annual increase in agricultural production range from 1.0 percent to 2.4 percent. Improvements in technology were modest but overall had a significant impact. Higher-yielding strains of rice were planted, irrigation systems were introduced, and fertilizers were used more extensively. Peasants, especially those with larger holdings, committed themselves to being better farmers. Expansion of farming on Hokkaido included cattle ranching.

In the 1870s the government transferred ownership of the land to peasant households, primarily to ensure a steady state income from rural taxes. Some of the increase in agricultural production was a consequence of farmers' rational decision to produce as much as possible, since the tax was based on landholding and not total harvest.

Temporarily the amount of land worked directly by owners increased but by the end of the Meiji period tenant farming was again a major part of rural Japan. Since the landlord was a rural resident, rather than an absentee owner, as in India (see Chapter Two), little exploitation took place. Landlords had a responsibility for their tenants, especially in hard times. In general the tenant and the landlord agreed upon payment of a certain percentage of the harvest and thus did not have to convert the crop into cash. Though over time economic differences increased, growth in harvests produced improvements in living conditions for most peasants.

Social Revolution. Japan also underwent a social revolution. New bases for definitions of class identity were created. The social structure became much more open, with opportunities for upward and downward social mobility. Social differences declined and the social distance between the top of society and the bottom diminished. The samurai class was destroyed, losing its elite status to the business class and the new governing elite. Many of those from the Tokugawa merchant class also failed to adjust to the Meiji revolution and fell to near the bottom of the social ladder. Peasants made major gains in economic position but the ideology of capitalism and mobility left them a lower class, not a middling social group as earlier defined by Confucianism. The proletariat formed a new class of increasing dynamism and volatility. At the bottom of society were the urban déclassé—unskilled day laborers, impoverished samurai, thieves, prostitutes, and the burakumin. These dramatic social changes and vastly increased social mobility were accompanied by social protest. However, given the degree of change that occurred in people's lives, the extent of unrest was actually rather modest.

Destruction of the Old Society. The Meiji Revolution destroyed Japan's old structure, a system that had been moving toward frailty in the first half of the nineteenth century. The Meiji Restoration brought about dramatic changes in the social structure, as almost all classes were destroyed or redefined. To some extent the oligarchs followed a conscious policy of social change. This is especially evident in the destruction of the samurai class.

In spite of some disagreement, the oligarchs decided to redefine the structure of the samurai class and later to destroy it. This redefinition took place from 1869–1872. The daimyo and court aristocrats (500 families) were designated as peers (*kazoku*). Some 320,000 samurai were assigned as upper class samurai (*shizoku*). Most samurai became lower-class samurai (*sotsu*), who were then made commoners in 1872.

The government reduced the special privileges of the samurai, including eliminating the symbolic demonstration of its power, the right to wear swords. No longer could samurai kill commoners with impunity. However, some legal differences remained in the Law Code of 1873. Peers and upper-class samurai who committed minor crimes paid a fine rather than serve a prison term. If they committed a major crime they were sentenced to prison but not to hard labor, as commoners were.

Economic decline was an even more important cause of the collapse of the samurai. In part the oligarchs acted against the economic privileges of the samurai in order to reduce government expenditures. At first samurai lost their state salaries, receiving instead annual pensions. These pensions were substantially lower than previous income. In 1876, the government caused financial ruin for many samurai when it commuted the pensions to government bonds, with variable interest rates dependent upon the strata they came from. Inflation further reduced the value of the bonds. Kazoku retained almost all of their previous income, shizoku income declined by half to three-fourths, and lower-class samurai income was reduced to 10 percent of previous levels. The average salary of a lower-class samurai was equivalent to that of an ordinary soldier.

Samurai also faced changes in occupation. Most lost their political offices upon the elimination of Tokugawa and daimyo governments. Yet, former samurai held most of the positions in the new government. Most kazoku became bureaucrats, especially in the central ministries. Approximately 10 percent of the samurai became government officials. A few became merchants, industrialists, or bankers. Most samurai, having lived a life of security, found it difficult to deal with risk and insecurity and were not very successful as businessmen. This is especially true of those samurai who were encouraged to pool the value of their bonds and go into banking. Samurai who formed tea cultivation companies in Western Japan were an exception to the samurai failures in business.

Literacy enabled some samurai to enter the teaching profession. Two-fifths of teachers came from the samurai. Many others went into careers that paralleled samurai background—the police and the military. The introduction of conscription in 1873 meant, however, that samurai entered the military not as officers but as ordinary soldiers or seamen. The government encouraged those who had lost their samurai status to purchase or lease government land on Hokkaido and thus become farmers.

Many samurai could not adjust to the new environment of the Meiji. They became part of the *lumpen proletariat* or urban underworld. Some had to become manual laborers. Others squandered their wealth and fell into poverty. Some became criminals or male prostitutes. Others sold their daughters to houses of prostitution. Some became unemployed and homeless.

Though there was some protest from the samurai, in general the class accepted its fall from the top of society. Economic necessity forced most samurai to accept their new fate. The restructuring of the class based on degree of loyalty to the new regime made class solidarity and cohesion impossible to maintain. Many samurai believed it was their patriotic duty to obey the new government, even if it meant the decline of their own positions.

The Tokugawa merchant class found it very difficult to adjust to capitalism and industrialization. Many merchants had made large loans to the Tokugawa government, the daimyo, and the samurai. The fall of the Tokugawa undermined their financial position. Having supported the old regime, merchants were viewed as suspect by the new government and lost access to guaranteed government contracts and monopolies. In addition, merchants found it difficult to adjust to the new economy. No longer did they operate under a system that minimized risk and ensured them a steady income.

A New Society. New classes emerged and some pre-existent social groups were redefined or their relative positions changed. This transformation left Japanese society very different than it had been at the end of the Tokugawa, thus the term social revolution.

With the demise of the samurai, the government created a new aristocracy, the peers. The peers included the oligarchs, the daimyo chiefs, leading court officials, the kazoku, high government officials, and prominent scholars. Entrepreneurs were of great importance in the Meiji period. Since the business class had been denigrated in the Tokugawa period, the entrepreneurs faced the practical problem of how to ensure that they would be highly valued in the new era. Led by Shibusawa Eiichi, the new business community embarked upon a public relations campaign to convince the government and the educated public that entrepreneurs played an important role in Japanese life. They saw themselves as distinct from and superior to the old business class, and thus not to be viewed in the same negative light. Businessmen emphasized that they were serving the interests of the nation and not merely making money. They argued that they were playing a central role in the building of a modern Japan capable of defending its national security and building an empire.

The entrepreneurs became increasingly politicized. Initially they lobbied the government for economic assistance, especially subsidies and protection against foreign competition. From the late 1890s the business class directed its attention to increasing its political rights. The right to vote depended on the amount of taxes a person paid. Since most tax revenues came from the land tax, only a few wealthy businessmen paid high enough taxes to vote and hold office. The businessmen campaigned to lower the tax threshold for voting rights. After the Russo-Japanese War, the business community lobbied through a national organization, the *National League of Chambers of Commerce.* They also sought to influence policy through bribery. For example, when the Japan Sugar Refining Company faced severe financial difficulties, it bribed dozens of legislators and government officials to support nationalization of the sugar industry. The strategies of the business community were quite successful. Their activities generated much wealth. At the same time, the public came to view them positively.

Two lower-middle class groups grew in size. *Indoor craftsmen,* skilled artisans who sold the goods they produced and thus were also merchants, increased in importance. *Outdoor laborers* were skilled construction workers who usually did contract labor for specific projects. As contract workers they had an autonomy and freedom that industrial workers lacked.

Peasants formed one of the lower classes. Overall the economic and social position of peasants was much better than in the Tokugawa period. When the government restructured the tax system in 1873, bureaucratic efficiency led it to assign ownership rights to peasants who worked particular pieces of land. Since the new tax was based on the amount of land they held rather than a percentage of the harvest, peasants had an incentive to produce as much as possible and they could see the visible difference between the Meiji harvest levels and those of the Tokugawa. The land tax totaled about 3 percent of the value of the land and represented a much lower burden than that of peasants in Russia (see Chapter One) or India (see Chapter Two). Still, the tax burden rested primarily on the peasants, who provided 80 percent of government revenues for much of the Meiji period. Peasants also gained the right to buy and sell land and to determine what crops they grew.

Though peasants were generally better off, they still faced heavy burdens. Universal military conscription was a temporary hardship for peasant families. Fluctuations in the price of basic farm products, especially rice and silk, left peasants without economic security.

Social and economic differentiation increased in the countryside. Many villages had one or more "gentlemen farmers," generally merchants. Their literacy, contacts with the outside world, and wealth gave them an opportunity to dominate village society and politics.

Tenant farming also continued. The amount of land worked by tenant farmers varied from 30–40 percent in the Meiji period. A tenant farmer paid over half of the harvest to the landowner. Tenant farmers especially suffered during periods of bad harvests or low prices for crops.

In part because expectations had risen and no system was in place to deal with intermittent declines in income, peasants expressed dissatisfaction with their situation. However, peasant discontent was substantially less than in other modernizing societies. Peasants developed several strategies to deal with their plight. Some "escaped" to the cities, where they became day laborers, rickshaw coolies, or rag pickers. These jobs were used as a springboard for work in factories or shops. Peasants also engaged in social protest (see below).

Industrialization created a new class—the industrial working class. Increasing numbers of workers took jobs in factories. Until the twentieth century most factory workers were young women employed in the textiles industries. Farm girls were recruited because of their submissiveness and finger dexterity. They worked and lived in little better than slave-like conditions. They worked long hours and lived in barracks provided by the company. Long hours produced a high accident rate, while the dampness needed to prevent breakage of thread led to upper respiratory diseases. Wages were lower than in Indian mills. Harsh conditions also existed in the mines, where prison labor gradually disappeared.

Skilled workers had much better lives, at least until the twentieth century. The demand for skilled workers was huge and this gave the small minority of workers who were skilled job mobility and the freedom to avoid discipline for tardiness and absenteeism. Factory owners thus insulated the contract workers from harsh treatment. By the early twentieth century conditions began to change, as factories sought to impose greater discipline and direct control over their workforces. Sub-contracting disappeared, replaced by the organization of work to maximize productivity. Skilled workers were transformed from craft workers into industrial workers. In addition, firms began to emphasize company loyalty and a long-term mutual commitment by the company and its workforce.

At the bottom of society was the lumpen-proletariat. In the Meiji era its composition and sources of recruitment changed. The burakumin, or outcastes, continued to face discrimination, even though Meiji legislation had abolished the category. Some 400,000 persons (1%) of the population were in this group. There were a similar number of urban poor who couldn't adjust to modernization and were "homeless." Though the Meiji outlawed slavery, thousands of prostitutes were treated as slaves, unable to escape from such a life.

Modernization and overt social policies brought dramatic changes to Japanese society. Though a majority of people were much better off, some were worse off, at least intermittently. Social protest was one response, especially for those who had difficulty adjusting to the new world of the Meiji.

Social Protest. Social protest has captured the interest of large numbers of historians in recent years. Though clearly the Meiji revolution did not go as smoothly as earlier generations of historians had thought, it is obvious that the level of protest was lower in Japan than in other countries going through the same kinds of modernization. Some protests were a last ditch effort by Tokugawa society, a nostalgic, conservative protest. Other expressions of discontent resulted from the harshness of modernization and industrialization. Four types of protest occurred: samurai rebellion, popular rights riots, peasant uprisings, and labor strikes.

Samurai Rebellion. Tokugawa defeat in the civil war blended with samurai protest, much of it bloody. The *Satsuma Rebellion* of 1868–1869 formed the last phase of the civil war. Easily crushed, the rebellion showed that even among the samurai few wanted to return to the past and that the government was already much too strong to be overthrown by these warriors of the past.

In 1870, samurai from Choshu tried to organize an anti-Western uprising that cut across class lines to include samurai, peasants, and urban folk. Dissatisfied with Japan's Korean policy, in 1874, Eto Shimpei led some 2,500 samurai in Saga Prefecture to attack the government. The group wanted to restore the daimyo system and samurai rights. Central government forces easily subdued the rebels. Samurai from Choshu, Kumamoto, and Fukuoka organized a series of small uprisings in 1876 to protest the *commutation* of bonds.

The largest samurai protest, the *Saigo Rebellion* of 1877, represented a delayed effort to organize the overthrow of the Meiji. *Saigo* Takamori dominated political affairs in Kagoshima Prefecture (formerly Satsuma daimyo). Kagoshima remained fairly independent, refusing both to introduce the reforms that destroyed samurai power and to forward taxes to the central government. Saigo attempted to reinforce traditional values through the creation of Confucianist academies. These academies not only emphasized traditional Japanese Confucianism; they acted as sites for the training of paramilitary forces. Saigo led his army of over 40,000 against the prefecture capital of Kumamoto. However, the conscript army defending the city drove off the Saigo rebels. In humiliation, Saigo committed suicide. Both sides suffered heavy losses; the government 16,000 casualties and the rebels 20,000. The government dealt harshly with the insurrection, executing 3,000 rebels. The suicide of Saigo mirrored the suicidal effort of the samurai to preserve the past.

Popular Rights Protests. Popular rights protests represented an effort to create a new future. These rebellions were directed against an oppressive and undemocratic government that had not yet introduced a constitution. The Liberals' impatience produced several rebellions in 1883 and 1884. In general Liberals led uprisings against authoritarian government at the prefectural level. In 1883, they protested against the despotic governor of Fukushima Prefecture. The next year they led rebellions against authorities in Gumma and Tochigi Prefectures. Liberals recognized that they dare not contest the power of the central government, thus they focused on protest at the prefectural level. This meant, of course, that their actions did not produce basic changes in central government policy. The response of the central government was repression that caused the collapse of the Liberal Party. Indirectly, though, such efforts pushed the government to draw up a constitution.

Peasant Unrest. Peasant unrest was relatively widespread from the beginning of the Meiji Revolution to the mid-1880s. After that peasant protest diminished. At first peasant disturbances were directed against the shogun, protests called *uprisings to reform society.* The disturbances were directed against the Tokugawa government and reflected a deep sense of injustice based on the harshness of peasant life and the socioeconomic transformations associated with commercialization and proto-industrialization. Pro-imperial groups actively incited peasants to rebel against the shogun. These protests also reflected rising expectations related to the overthrow of the shogun and introduction of a new government.

From the late 1860s through the mid-1870s peasants rebelled in response to economic problems, especially crop failures and inflation. These rebellions were generally localized and directed against local officials and wealthy peasants. For example 70,000 peasants in Nagano Prefecture rioted, demanding reduced rents. In 1876, a major rebellion took place, protesting high taxes, including new tax burdens such as school taxes. In response the government cut the tax rate from 3 percent to 2.5 percent of the value of the land. Increasingly, in the second half of the 1870s the government sought to placate the peasants.

Peasants also protested the policies of the Meiji. In 1873, for example, 37 peasant disturbances took place, mainly directed against conscription, compulsory education, and high taxes. The Meiji reforms infringed upon the lives of the peasants, who protested government "interference."

In the mid-1880s peasant poverty peaked, a consequence of world recession, which reduced prices for raw silk and other farm products, and the *Matsukata Deflation.* Better organized, a result of over a decade of experience in rural protest, peasants established protest groups such as the *Debtors' Party* and the *Hardship Party* that campaigned for the reduction of peasant debt.

In 1884, *Tashiro* Eisuke led the Hardship Party in the *Chichibu Uprising* on the Kanto Plain southwest of Tokyo. The Hardship Party called for a ten-year moratorium on debt repayment and the extension of debt payments over a forty-year period. It also demanded a reduction in local government taxes. For example, it called for the closing of all schools for a three-year period to hold down government expenses. Crowds attacked moneylenders and local government offices and destroyed debt certificates, as though this would eliminate the debts themselves. Government troops moved in, crushed the rebellion, and executed rebel leaders.

After the mid-1880s peasants became quiescent, quietly suffering their fate. Emigration to the cities and abroad increasingly became a safety valve against rural protest. The government first tried to put down disturbances immediately and then addressed some of the causes of unrest. Authorities also cut taxes and encouraged migration as a way to reduce rural overpopulation.

Labor Strikes. Harsh factory conditions did not immediately produce protests. Most factory workers were primarily female from rural areas where the patriarchal family and authoritarian father dominated. The young women were conditioned to automatic obedience. In addition, skilled workers were in such short supply that they had opportunities to seek the best work conditions and the highest pay. Thus, they had no need to engage in labor protest. Their situation was so different from ordinary workers that class solidarity was impossible. The sub-contracting system meant that it was easy to fire dissatisfied, unruly workers. Working class protest emerged parallel to the expansion of heavy industry.

In the first strike, 100 women protested at a textile mill in Yamanashi Prefecture. After the Sino-Japanese War inflation reduced real wages and led to efforts to organize workers. In 1897, *The Society for the Protection of Trade Unions* was formed. This initial effort led to the creation of skilled crafts unions, such as the Association of Ironworkers, the Society to Reform the Railroads, and the Printers' Association. These were mutual aid societies whose goals were to protect members' economic position against unexpected events, such as on the job injury or illness.

The emergence of *Christian Socialism* served similar goals. These groups emphasized mutual aid, education, and self-improvement. They also argued that owners and employees had common interests, thus making strikes unwelcome. With the support from the powerful businessman, Shibusawa, *Suzuki* Bunji created the first Christian Socialist organization.

The government sponsored factory legislation intended to ameliorate conditions and prevent working class protests. Legislation in 1905 sought to improve work and safety conditions in mines. The Factory Act of 1911 established a maximum workday of eleven hours for women and children under fifteen. Ten was set as the minimum work age. Factory legislation did little to ameliorate the harsh conditions of factory life.

Conclusions. Dramatic changes occurred in the nature of the class system. The old elite, the samurai, disintegrated and were replaced by a new elite of government loyalists (peers) and wealthy capitalists. The old merchant class disappeared, while a new crafts trade lower-middle class clearly emerged. Peasants saw their status enhanced through land ownership but they fell increasingly under the influence of external economic forces. Industrialization produced a new lower class, the working class. Industrialization brought large numbers of women from the countryside to the cities, part of a general rural to urban migration pattern. In addition to this geographical mobility, upward and downward social mobility became quite common. Japan became a society whose classes were fluid and their borders open to entrance and exit. Overall, Japan experienced a relatively peaceful social revolution in the Meiji period.

6. Transformation of Family and Gender Roles

The Meiji was also an age of dramatic change for gender relationships and the family. Responding to a desire to have institutional arrangements similar to those of the West, many educated Japanese called for dramatic changes in the position of women and in the nature of the family.

Proposals for Equality. Many leading intellectuals offered ideas on how to transform the position of women and the nature of the family. Fukuzawa presented his views in *Greater Learning for Women.* First he argued that women should not be treated as inferiors or sub-humans. He condemned *concubinage* (men having secondary wives or mistresses), calling instead for monogamy. Because husbands and wives signed marriage contracts, such action implied equality within marriage, he insisted. Women should have equal rights, including property rights and access to Westernized education.

Nakamura Masanao suggested that women should play an important role in the creation of proper attitudes of good citizenship among new future generations. Women were the moral foundation of society, teaching children proper behavior and preventing husbands from straying from the path of morality, he stated. Portraying women as having an important national function broke with previous definitions that women's main roles were reproduction and work (for non-samurai women). Home rather than family lineage was now most important.

Women were affected by the new civil code of 1898, which was based on samurai family patterns. This pattern emphasized the tremendous power of the patriarch and the special significance of family lineage. The patriarchal head of household could overrule the decisions of all other household members, determining marriage partners, place of residence and property rights. Men under twenty-five and women under thirty had to get their father's permission to marry. The civil code reinforced the idea of the good wife and wise mother model. Monogamy was sanctioned and concubinage delegalized. Marriages continued to be arranged and daughters joined the families of their husbands. Women gained the right to divorce. However, in practice, men sometimes divorced wives and wives almost never divorced husbands. Women could receive a divorce because of cruel treatment, desertion, and imprisonment but not on the basis of adultery. The divorced wife received no alimony and lost custody rights to the children. Peer pressure made it difficult for a wife to exercise divorce rights. Men obtained divorces more easily. Changes in gender relationships and the family spread slowly from the capital to other cities and only rarely to the countryside. Changes extended downward in society from the wealthy to the commoners.

Women were to be prepared for this new role of serving the nation through education. Compulsory elementary education applied to girls as well as boys. By the end of the Meiji period almost all girls and boys acquired a basic education. The girls' elementary education curriculum gave attention to literacy, numeracy, and household management. Few girls went to school beyond the elementary grades. Those who did so generally went to private, missionary-sponsored schools. Women could not enroll at Tokyo Imperial University. Instead they attended private post-secondary institutions such as the *Women's English College.* The expansion of elementary education increased the demand for teachers. The government responded by establishing teacher-training programs for women.

Women played no significant role in politics. A few women participated in the popular rights movement, most importantly *Kishida* Toshiko, who was eventually arrested for her public condemnation of traditional marriages and for promoting women's rights. In 1890 and again in 1900 the Diet passed laws prohibiting women from participating in political parties or political meetings.

Women, thus, saw major improvements in their position in the Meiji period, though equality was still some distance away.

7. Community and Diversity

In the Meiji period community was emphasized and diversity ignored. The nation's leaders made conscious efforts to promote unity and cohesion.

Diversity. Japan was a nation of very little diversity. No more than 2–3 percent of the population was defined as minority (primarily the burakumin), the Ainu, and the Okinawans. The burakumin had a caste-like existence, with no possibility of escaping to a new identity. Policy toward the Ainu vacillated between assimilation and isolation. The Japanese made little attempt to define a relationship with the Okinawans. Some diversity existed as a consequence of the huge influx of Western influence. Only after the Meiji period was there a delayed anti-Western reaction.

Community. Building community was extremely important to the oligarchs, the Westernized intellectuals and ordinary citizens. Meiji reforms reduced the extent of social differences and social distance. Boundaries between social groups were blurred and mobility much more fluid than previously. In social terms the Japanese formed a single nation.

National unity was seen as a prerequisite for national security. Thus the oligarchs sought to make the central government an all-Japanese government that would overcome tendencies toward decentralization. Legal uniformity and uniformity of administration contributed to overall unity. A common national agenda and success in achieving it brought the Japanese people together. Still regional and class differences remained.

Importantly the government and Westernized intellectuals created a new image of Japan—an imagined community. They portrayed Japan as an enlightened society on the way toward the level of civilization characterizing the West. Japan was a society in which progress was assured and problem-solving ability taken for granted, they announced. Japan recognized the Emperor as the central image and reality of the nation's life. The Japanese people were citizens, members of the Japanese nation, though only a small minority of males had the right to participate in the political system. These ideas were promulgated in the press and inculcated in the compulsory educational system, especially after the 1890 restructuring of education.

Thus community became an essential characteristic of Meiji Japan—a country in which patriotism and contribution to a common cause were the responsibility and the destiny of its citizens.

D. FROM PEACE TO WAR, 1914–1945

Japan appeared to be following the straight ascent line of progress, fulfilling its destiny of modernization, Westernization, and power. However, that straight line of progress was broken in the 1920s and 1930s. Japan moved away from the ideals of the Meiji period into the murky waters of authoritarian government and militaristic aggression. This section will describe these changes and explain why Japan abandoned Meiji ideals and turned to alternative beliefs and behavior.

1. Imperialism

Japan both engaged itself deeply on the continent of Asia and applied a policy of peaceful coexistence and arms limitations toward the Western powers that had a deep interest in Asia. Japanese leaders did not always agree on which strategy should be followed. In general both aims were pursued simultaneously. Ultimately these two strategic goals came into conflict with each other, leading to the War in the Pacific.

Trade and Migration. Japanese involvement on the continent included peaceful penetration through migration and trade as well as the use of sterner, military measures. As population increased and economic problems heightened in Japan, more and more Japanese emigrated. Their preferred place of immigration was the United States but limits on Japanese migration to California in 1906 and then an almost complete ban issued by Congress in the mid-1920s forced the Japanese to go elsewhere or stay at home. By 1910, almost a half million Japanese had migrated, primarily to the colonies of Taiwan and Korea and to Manchuria. Immigrants came largely from the lower-middle classes, especially traders, shopkeepers, and artisans. In the colonies they engaged in similar occupations and had higher incomes and standards of living than the local population. Parallel to the British in India in the period of formal empire (see Chapter Two), the Japanese created their own isolated communities, ran their own Japanese schools, and made little contact with the native peoples.

Taiwan and Korea provided markets for Japanese goods and supplied Japan with food staples—rice from Korea and sugar from Taiwan. China became Japan's leading trading partner. China provided Japan with coal, iron, and cotton. The shift to heavy industry meant that Japan could not produce sufficient amounts of iron and coal from domestic sources. Though initially Japan imported cotton for use in its textile mills, eventually the Japanese purchased or built cotton textile mills on the continent, especially in the Shanghai area. Investment in China increased from 1 million dollars in 1900 to 220 million on the eve of the First World War. Much of that investment was in Manchuria, which Japan considered extremely important for economic and strategic reasons. In 1906, Japan acquired the Southern Manchurian Railway Company, which became the main engine for economic development in Manchuria. Diplomatic threats and military pressure gradually replaced peaceful penetration of the Asian mainland.

Peaceful Coexistence. Japan pursued a policy of peaceful coexistence and arms limitation with the Western powers, especially Great Britain and the United States. The 1902 Treaty of Friendship with Great Britain marked the beginning of this approach. The Japanese also supported the unequal treaties China had signed a half century earlier and the Open Door Policy, which guaranteed all Western powers commercial access to China. After the Russo-Japanese War, Japan quickly applied the strategy of peaceful coexistence toward northeast Asia. In 1907, Japan and Russia signed a Treaty of Friendship, which delineated Russian and Japanese lines of interest in Manchuria. Joining the Western side in the early stages of the First World War, Japan easily defeated the weak German forces in the South Pacific and on the Shandong Peninsula of China. However, Japanese pressure on China threatened to undermine the policy of peaceful coexistence.

During the 1920s and early 1930s the civilian government actively pursued arms limitations agreements both to ensure national security and to maintain trade opportunities with the West. This strategy was carried out at the *Washington Conference* (1921–1922). Japan reaffirmed the open door policy, gave up its holdings on the Shandong Peninsula and signed a naval limitation agreement. The major powers agreed on maximum ratios for naval vessels, with United States and Great Britain to have equal size fleets, Japan 60 percent that of the British and Americans, and the Italians and French fleets half the size of the Japanese navy. The United States and Great Britain agreed not to improve coastal fortifications in the Pacific between Hawaii and Singapore.

However, the British refused to renew the British-Japanese Treaty of 1902 that had created an alliance between the two countries.

Under *Shidehara* Kijuro (foreign minister for most of the period from 1924–1931), Japan pursued a policy of "peaceful coexistence and co-prosperity" with China. Japan tried to avoid political involvement in China, which faced brutal civil wars (see Chapter Four). Changes in policy surfaced in 1927 as the Nationalists began the "Northern Expedition" that threatened to end civil war and unify China. Japan sent in troops to protect Japanese citizens and property and supported Zhang Zuolin, the dictator of Manchuria. Japan also claimed that Manchuria was a separate country, not part of China.

In 1929, Japan signed the *Kellogg-Briand Treaty.* Participants agreed to renounce war and to submit disputes to peaceful solution. An idealistic statement of hope for world peace, the Kellogg-Briand Treaty soon collapsed. In 1930, Japan participated in the London Naval Conference, which extended Japan's 60 percent quota to light cruisers and submarines.

Peaceful coexistence, combined with expanded trade with the West, dominated Japanese foreign policy for three decades. However, it met increasing resistance from military leaders and the public. Increasingly the Japanese applied military intervention to the continent of East Asia, which undermined the policy of peaceful coexistence and profitable international trade.

Military Intervention. Japan increasingly involved itself in continental Asian affairs, responding in part to its economic and national security strategies and to opportunities created by the political and social chaos affecting China.

Japan's cabinet reacted cautiously to the overthrow of the Chinese ruling house. Initially it supported the idea of a unified China rather than its breakup into numerous small military kingdoms.

However, when the First World War began, the Japanese government saw an opportunity to gain a significant foothold in northern China. Not only did the Japanese seize the former German holdings that included part of the Shandong Peninsula that jutted out into the sea toward Japan but they attempted to gain political control over China. Japan felt confident enough to issue a set of *Twenty-One Demands* (1915). The Chinese ultimately accepted the economic demands that confirmed Japanese control over the economy of Shandong Peninsula, extended Japanese economic influence in Manchuria and placed important iron mining facilities under joint Chinese-Japanese control. However, China rejected the political demands that would have transformed it into a protectorate, with Japanese advisors to key government posts; gave special privileges to Japanese nationals; and required China to purchase its weapons from Japan. The Chinese responded with popular protests and threats to Japanese property and citizens.

Japan intervened on the continent in another unstable situation—Russia. The Bolshevik Revolution and subsequent Civil War left a power vacuum in the Far East. Japan sent in a force of 70,000 to provide security in the Russian Far East and along the eastern portions of the Trans-Siberian Railway. Though Japanese forces moved as far west as Central Siberia and supported anti-Bolshevik governments, the Japanese impact was slight. After almost four years, Japanese troops withdrew in 1922. Thus twice within a decade the

Japanese tried to take advantage of political and social instability on the East Asian continent but had little long-term impact.

For most of the 1920s Japanese military leaders reluctantly accepted the peaceful coexistence strategy of the civilian cabinet. However, from the late 1920s on, the Japanese military became much more aggressive on the mainland. Military expansion was achieved through the initiative of intelligence officers and local commanders on the continent and not through the direct actions and decisions of supreme military leaders in Tokyo. However, government officials felt compelled to acquiesce to the actions of the troops in the field. In 1928, Japanese soldiers blocked the advance of Nationalist soldiers (see Chapter Four) onto the Shandong Peninsula. Though at first the Japanese supported the warlord of Manchuria, Zhang Zuolin, against the Nationalists, later the Japanese military, known as the *Kwantung Army,* bombed Zhang's train, killing him. The government in Tokyo refused to take advantage of Zhang's death.

In 1931, Japanese officers in Manchuria exploded dynamite near the Southern Manchurian Railway, blaming the Chinese for acts of sabotage. The Kwantung Army then seized all of Manchuria. The next year the Japanese military established the puppet state of Manchukuo. Both the military and civilians supported the conquest of Manchuria, enabling Japan to ignore the League of Nations resolution labeling it an aggressor.

The Japanese military gradually expanded beyond Manchuria into northern China. The 1933 *Tangku Truce* authorized Japan to occupy all of northeast China north of the Great Wall and called for the area between the Great Wall and the Chinese capital Peking (Beijing) to be a demilitarized zone. This left China's capital vulnerable to attack. The Japanese military advanced further into China from 1932–1936.

Gradual military expansion in north China led to full-scale warfare after the 1937 *Marco Polo Bridge Incident.* The Japanese army faked an attack on its own units near Peking. They then used this as an excuse to drive toward Peking. Japan quickly conquered much of populated China leaving the Chinese in control of only the remote areas of northwest and southwest China. Thus peaceful co-existence had been abandoned and the *China Incident* had begun.

China Incident. Broadly the Second World War in Asia consisted of two campaigns, the China Incident—the war in China and Southeast Asia—and the *Pacific Incident*—Japan's efforts to defeat the Americans and British in the Pacific.

Decision to Go to War. Looking back on the events of the summer of 1937, we can clearly see that the Incident at Marco Polo Bridge marked the beginning of the Sino-Japanese War, 1937–1945. The situation was not nearly as clear at the time. Japanese leaders hesitated, not sure their country should initiate war with China.

Initially, efforts were made to localize the incident and a cease-fire was worked out. The Japanese military was divided on what further steps should be taken. Ishihara Kanji, Chief of Operations of the General Staff, led the group that urged caution. Naval leaders, too, opposed military operations in North China. At this time many Japanese leaders viewed the Soviet Union as a greater threat and a weakened China preferable to a combatant one. However, Minister of War Sugiyama Gen convinced the cabinet to send a large force to north

China and Prime Minister Konoe demanded that China apologize and come to the bargaining table. As tensions increased in north China, on August 14, 1937, the Chinese airforce bombed Japanese naval vessels in Shanghai harbor. The Chinese followed this with a general mobilization. The Japanese cabinet decided to launch an all-out attack on the Chinese in north China and in the Yangzi (Yangtze) River Valley in central China.

Initial Japanese Conquest. War thus began, without a declaration of war and without adequate Japanese preparation. Japan had developed no detailed plans, stockpiled no weapons, and had not prepared the Japanese people for war. However, the Japanese offensive quickly captured much of heavily populated China. By the end of 1937 all of north China was in Japanese hands. The Japanese took the lower Yangzi Valley in late 1937. In December, Japanese officers permitted their soldiers to rampage through the Nationalists' capital, *Nanjing.* Two hundred thousand Chinese were killed and as many as 20,000 women were raped. The *Rape of Nanjing* initiated the brutality that characterized Japanese treatment of civilians and prisoners of war for the rest of the conflict.

Toward the end of 1937 the Japanese government sought a diplomatic settlement but its demands were unacceptable to the Chinese. The Japanese demanded that Inner Mongolia be granted autonomy and that the Chinese recognize Japanese control over most of North China and the Shanghai area. The Japanese also sought trade concessions. When the Chinese rejected the Japanese demands, Japan declared war on China in January 1938.

During 1938, Japan conducted major military offensives in central and south China and by October had captured the industrial cities of Wuhan and the major port of Canton. Japan occupied most of China including almost all of its largest cities, all of its major ports, most railroad lines, most heavily populated and industrialized areas, and the major river valleys. Japan also set up a puppet government under the former Nationalist leader *Wang* Jingwei. Still the Chinese refused to surrender. Not strong enough militarily to engage in open warfare with the Japanese, various Chinese groups conducted guerilla operations that tied down large numbers of Japanese soldiers. The stalemate continued. Finally, in July 1940, Japan dramatically changed its military strategy and goals, as it struggled to escape victoriously from the Chinese quagmire.

Into Southeast Asia. By the summer of 1940, Japan faced a dilemma. It controlled much of China but the Chinese refused to surrender. Military conquest of China had destroyed the policy of peaceful coexistence and alienated the Western powers. Japanese leaders only slowly came to a consensus on what to do next.

Two options existed. First, Japan could end the war in China by making generous concessions, withdrawing troops from China, except Manchuria and perhaps the Shanghai area, and profiting from the war in Europe. Japan thus would have acquired some of the most valuable parts of China and strengthened its Asian Empire. However, withdrawal from China meant a loss of honor for the military. The civilian government would have faced an angry population and the probability of an assassination campaign. The Americans made it difficult for the Japanese to exercise this option, not understanding the importance of a face-saving opportunity. The United States made it quite clear that it would not participate in any discussions about the future of China until Japan had withdrawn from all of the territory it had taken from 1931–on.

A second option was to "go for broke." Japan could attempt to seize Southeast Asia, including Indo-China and the Dutch East Indies (later Indonesia). This would have meant war with Great Britain, the Netherlands, and probably the United States; although the Japanese leaders hoped the Americans would stay out of the Asian war. Japan took the second option through a series of decisions they made in July 1940.

Pacific Incident. The decision to attack Southeast Asia led to Pearl Harbor and war with the United States. Though the Japanese hoped that diplomatic negotiations would bring the Americans to accept the Japanese perspective, they planned for the consequences of unsuccessful diplomacy.

The abrupt change in Japanese policy, the shift from a continental to a Pacific strategy, took place at a late July 1940 meeting of the Cabinet. By this time the Nazi-Soviet Non-Aggression Treaty had been signed, eliminating the threat of a two front war, and the pro-British Prime Minister, Admiral Yonai, had been dismissed. The Cabinet approved the *Main Principles of Basic National Polity,* a plan to prepare for and engage in a broad war against the Western powers in Asia. The plan envisioned military expansion as well as preparation for it through the transformation of the educational system into little more than a gigantic nationalistic propaganda machine, a more authoritarian government and a planned economy. The Cabinet and military leaders agreed to strengthen ties with Germany and Italy, sign a non-aggression treaty with the Soviet Union, and conquer the Asian territories of the European powers. Japan wished to avoid conflict with the Americans and prevent them from interfering with plans to create a Japanese-dominated *Greater East Asian Co-Prosperity Sphere.*

Japan, Italy, and Germany merged the wars in Europe and Asia through the September 1940 *Tri-Partite Treaty.* Each recognized that the others had the right to use force to expand territorial holdings. Most importantly, they would consider an American attack on any of the three as an act of war against the others, which were to come to the aid of the "victim" of American aggression. This agreement was soon followed by the *Japanese-Soviet Non-Aggression Pact,* which had similar provisions. Having been badly beaten by the Soviets in border skirmishes in 1938 and 1939, Japan sought to neutralize Soviet power.

At an "imperial conference" in July 1941, the Japanese decided to create the Greater East Asian Co-Prosperity Sphere as a way to achieve economic domination of East Asia and expand into South Vietnam. Japanese leaders spent much of the rest of 1941 trying to preserve Japanese gains while avoiding war with the United States. At the same time the Japanese prepared for the possibility of war.

Talking to the Americans. The American position was essentially non-negotiable. Only Japanese acceptance of every American demand would prevent war. In March 1941, Secretary of State Cordell *Hull* presented the United States position to Japanese ambassador Nomura Kichisaburo. The American demands were very broad and included respect for the territorial integrity and sovereignty of all nations, non-interference in the internal affairs of other countries; equality of economic opportunity; and a return to the pre-1931 situation in Asia. In June the Americans were much more specific. The United States wanted Japan to negate the Tri-Partite Treaty and withdraw from China. At the same time the Americans refused to guarantee an end to economic sanctions against Japan.

When Japan invaded South Vietnam in July 1941 (having conquered the northern part of the country in the autumn of 1940), the United States froze Japanese assets in the U.S. and banned American exports to Japan, except for food and cotton. Great Britain and the Netherlands followed the American lead. Since the American-led embargo included oil supplies (Japan had only a two-year supply), it provoked a change in Japanese thinking. The navy began to champion a more aggressive position centered on the conquest of the Dutch East Indies.

Prime Minister Konoe offered to hold a summit conference with President Franklin D. Roosevelt but the Americans refused to meet with him. Both sides set pre-conditions that made a successful summit impossible. The Japanese pre-conditions included an end to U.S. aid for China, U.S. acceptance of the Tripartite Pact, and the return of normal economic relations between the two countries. The United States reconfirmed that Japan would have to accept the American March 1941 proposal before negotiations could begin.

Negotiations continued throughout the fall. In early September an imperial conference concluded that if diplomatic agreement could not reached by October, Japan would prepare for war with the United States. When the Americans restated their basic position in early October, Japan moved closer to war. The army wanted an immediate decision to go to war, while naval leaders and Prime Minister Konoe were reluctant to support this view. The army forced Konoe from power and replaced him with *Tojo* Hideki. By early November Japanese leaders had agreed that if diplomatic agreement could not be reached by December 1, Japan would go to war against the United States a few days later.

The Japanese negotiating strategy was to offer a more moderate proposal first and if that was rejected to present a stronger ultimatum. By the moderate plan the Japanese agreed to a gradual withdrawal from China, except for parts of north China, Manchuria, Mongolia and Hainan Island, and from Southeast Asia. When the Americans rejected the idea of a gradual Japanese withdrawal from most of the areas they had conquered, Japan issued its second proposal, which called for a U.S.-Japanese division of spoils in Southeast Asia, an end to U.S. support for China, and Japanese withdrawal from South Vietnam. In response, the Americans demanded that Japan withdraw from all conquered territories. On December 1, the Japanese decided to go to war with the United States and to start the war with an attack on Pearl Harbor.

Japanese Offensive. After Pearl Harbor, Japanese forces expanded across the southern Pacific and even landed in the Aleutian Islands of Alaska. Singapore fell in mid-February 1942, followed by the Dutch East Indies, the Philippines, and Burma in the ensuing few months. In May the Japanese defeated the American and Australian navies in the Coral Sea, northeast of Australia. Japan seemed poised for an attack on Australia and had already reached the Aleutian Islands.

Japanese Retreat. The turning point came in June 1942, only half a year after the war in the Pacific had begun. Americans surprised and destroyed the Japanese fleet off Midway Island, ending Japan's naval advantage. In the autumn of 1942 the Japanese offensive across New Guinea collapsed. The Americans then employed an *island hopping* strategy, with one force driving across the central Pacific and another moving northward from New Guinea to the Philippines. By June 1944, the Americans had reached the island of Saipan.

From there American planes could reach Japan. To the island hopping strategy now was added the bombing of Japanese cities, focusing first on military targets and then switching to the firebombing of major cities. In March 1945, two major air attacks on Tokyo destroyed most of the city, killing almost 80,000 and leaving 1.5 million homeless. After almost five months of battle, the American military retook the Philippines in February 1945. Between April and June American armies captured their first Japanese territory, Okinawa.

Unconditional Surrender and the Atomic Bomb. By this time the war in Europe was over. As the Americans prepared for the invasion of Japan, Japanese leaders could not agree on whether to accept American terms, try to negotiate with them, or fight to the last live Japanese citizen. During the summer of 1945 the emperor began a quiet campaign to convince military leaders to search for a way to end the war. New Prime Minister Admiral Suzuki Kantao also favored a negotiated peace. That effort was made more difficult by the July 26 ultimatum, the *Potsdam Proclamation,* in which the allies reiterated the need for Japan to surrender unconditionally.

The Americans were convinced that the Japanese would not accept unconditional surrender. Faced with a bloody and lengthy invasion of Japan or the deployment of atomic weapons, American leaders decided to use nuclear weapons. On August 6, an A-bomb was dropped on Hiroshima. Though Japanese deaths were over 100,000 and the city literally destroyed, the Japanese refused to surrender. Three days later, a second atomic bomb was launched, this time on Nagasaki. By this time the Soviets had already invaded Manchuria and were poised to attack northern Japan.

The emperor called on military leaders to accept defeat but they ignored him at first. Emperor Hirohito then turned to the public. On August 14, he publicly called for Japan to surrender. The next day he announced over radio that the war was over. Though the war was fought abroad rather than on Japanese soil, it also deeply affected the home front.

On the Home Front. During the war, Japanese leaders built upon initiatives and directions proposed or started earlier. Military rule was introduced, efforts were made to ensure total government control of the economy, and the government sought to ensure that the public completely supported the war cause.

Governance. Civilian government had disappeared and political parties and the Diet had no real power. The government determined much of the membership of the Diet. When the two major parties tried to unite in order to offer an alternative to military rule, the military banned political parties and closed the Diet. Military rule was in the hands of the Supreme Command, with Tojo, Minister of War and Home Affairs, the spokesperson. Military government was extended from Japan to all conquered territories.

Coordination of the Economy. The military demanded that the economy be coordinated and perhaps controlled by the government in order to maximize military production. Several initiatives were attempted; some of them successfully opposed by big business. Ideas for centralized economic coordination came from the Stalinist model, the examples of Nazi Germany and Fascist Italy, and the military's experiences in promoting economic coordination in the colonies, especially Manchuria.

The *National General Mobilization Law* of 1938 gave the government the right to issue economic decrees without consulting the Diet. The government could set prices, implement rationing, and allocate materials and labor. In 1940, military leaders proposed a *New Political Order* that would transform Japan into an *advanced national defense state* in which the government would make all key economic decisions. Big business again opposed this plan. Some military leaders proposed the nationalization of all industry but this idea failed, too. Finally, in 1943, the government created a new Munitions Ministry, responsible for coordinating the war economy.

The Japanese economy was one of scarcity. With inadequate capital, labor, and raw materials, Japan could not match the U.S. economic machine. Japan found it difficult to acquire the necessary raw materials, especially because of allied bombing of shipping lanes. The inadequate labor supply affected both industrial and agricultural production. From 1940–1944 the Japanese economy grew by only 25 percent, the U.S. economy by 65 percent. From 1941–1944 the Japanese produced 59,000 aircraft, Germany 93,000, England 96,000, and the United States over a quarter of a million. The Japanese economy was structurally incapable of achieving military victory over the Western powers.

Many Japanese leaders supported *totalitarian* or *corporatist principles.* Forced national unity imposed from the top was their goal. Political parties were replaced by the *Imperial Rule Assistance Association,* which acted as an umbrella organization coordinating efforts at grass roots nationalism. Military leaders and government bureaucrats fought for control of the organization, limiting its effectiveness. Beneath the IRAA were small neighborhood associations, which formed a nationwide network by mid-1941. These neighborhood associations applied peer pressure to potential opponents of the war, distributed government propaganda, collected "gifts" for the war cause, and performed civil defense duties.

Military leaders also sought to fuse all organizations in Japan into supra-organizations. All universities were united, all newspapers combined, and all unions fused into a single union. These corporate bodies created the illusion that each group had some influence but in reality they were used to carry out government policies.

Thought Control. The government also engaged in "spiritual mobilization." Massive propaganda emphasized the imperial mission, applauded Japanese superiority, condemned the West, and gave glowing reports about Japanese military victories. Most Japanese accepted the propaganda as true, having been previously socialized to believe in the superiority of the Japanese way, symbolized by the god-like Emperor.

Initially the Japanese people were wildly enthusiastic about the war. This high morale diminished only slightly, even as the war turned against the Japanese. The government used the *Peace Preservation Law* to punish dissidents and potential dissidents. This law made it a crime to advocate the overthrow of the Japanese way of life and values (*national polity*). The concept of Japanese way of life was sufficiently vague that almost any behavior could be considered treasonous. The military police, as well as the *Special Higher Police,* brutally enforced the law.

Strict censorship of the press existed. All war news had to be approved by the supreme command. The press provided general statements about Japanese military victories and remained silent about defeats.

Indoctrination continued and accelerated. Textbooks were revised to reinforce nationalism and militarism. Movies emphasized patriotism, as well as the unity of all Asian peoples against the West. Much of the propaganda focused on vague concepts that were to be believed emotionally rather than evaluated rationally. Thus the many references to the Japanese mission, the Japanese essence, and the Japanese spirit. Praise and emulation of the West was replaced by harsh condemnation of almost all Westernized elements of Japan, except baseball. Golf, for instance, was condemned and English-derived words were removed from the Japanese language. Overall, authorities achieved great success in controlling the people's thoughts.

The People Suffer. Civilians suffered hideously, especially during the last year of the war. Food shortages resulted from crop failures, the diversion of foodstuffs to the military, and the interruption of food imports by Allied bombing. Malnutrition was common. Almost a million civilians died in American bombing. Entire cities were destroyed and at least 10 million people were sent from the cities to rural areas. In spite of the suffering of the civilian population, there were no anti-war demonstrations, no riots, and no social disorders. Isolated individuals openly opposed the war but were silenced by imprisonment.

2. From Taisho Democracy to Military Rule

From before the First World War and throughout the 1920s, Japan moved toward a Western-style parliamentary democracy. However in the 1930s military dictatorship replaced civilian government. Such dramatic changes deserve explanation.

Taisho Democracy. Political leaders of the *Taisho* period (the Taisho emperor held the throne 1912–1926) built upon the Meiji legacy. They moved Japan toward parliamentary democracy and improved the functioning of political parties. They promoted economic growth in spite of global economic difficulties. They implemented an international strategy based on peaceful coexistence and the expansion of international trade, while trying to prevent military domination of policy-making.

Political unity disappeared as a number of interest groups within the government and outside began to focus on the narrow goals of particular blocs. Among the interest groups were high imperial court officials, civilian bureaucrats, the military, the Diet, and big business.

At the beginning of the Taisho period a political crisis produced the *Taisho political change* (1913), the introduction of a two party, cabinet form of government. Basically, conflict broke out between the army and the leading political party, the *Seiyukai* (Association of Political Friends). Concerned that Seiyukai was becoming too influential and wishing to counter that power, Prime Minister Katsura organized a new party, *Minseito* (the Popular Government Party). At the same time a *movement to preserve constitutional government,* with broad public support, emerged, pushing for acceptance of the idea that the Cabinet should be responsible to a parliamentary majority. *Yoshino* Sakuzo led this pro-democracy movement, which appeared in response to the Rice Riots (see section four) of 1918. Tokyo University students also pushed for parliamentary democracy and universal male suffrage. After the Taisho political change, Seiyukai and Minseito alternated in power, with cabinets responsible to the largest party in the Diet. Thus Japan became a parliamentary democracy, though the military, reporting directly to the emperor, remained independent of and outside the parliamentary structure.

Japan experimented with various electoral formats and expanded the right to vote among the adult male population. In 1919, single-seat districts replaced multiple seat districts. Instead of each electoral unit selecting several Diet members, smaller units elected single representatives. This shift reduced the probability of a multi-party system. In addition, the legislation lowered the property qualification, enabling one-fourth of the adult male population to vote. Universal male suffrage was introduced in 1925, as was a form of *proportional representation.* Under proportional representation more than one person was elected from each electoral district, with a party's representation proportionate to its percentage of the vote. For example, if five representatives were to be elected and one party received 60 percent of the vote it would gain three seats, while a party that won 20 percent of the vote would win one seat.

As Japan searched for an ideal electoral system, the political system became more and more corrupt. The party in power sought to "buy votes" by increasing government spending, especially for local infrastructure, defense plants, and higher education. Voters in districts in which public works projects were built tended to vote for the party that had authorized the expenditure. Bribery, especially in connection with contracts for local construction projects, became fairly common. Corruption soured some voters on the democratic process. Other sources of dissatisfaction with parliamentary democracy also became more and more common in the 1920s.

Dissatisfaction with Parliamentary Democracy. Ironically, opposition to parliamentary democracy surfaced just as political leaders finally accepted it. Japanese democracy, like most democracies in the 1920s and 1930s, was quite fragile, easily attacked, and sometimes destroyed. Of the six nations discussed in this book, only Japan had a democracy in the 1920s and into the 1930s. Many powerful persons were opponents of democracy or only lukewarm supporters. Among those who offered little support for democracy were the conservatives who dominated the upper house, members of the Privy Council and high court officials. The press was especially critical of political corruption and the role of big business in policy making. Eventually the middle classes abandoned democracy, too. Most Japanese were motivated much more by nationalism than by democratic ideals.

Intellectuals generally rejected democracy. Liberalism's emphasis on the positive value of political conflict and debate were at odds with perceptions that Japan was a harmonious, cohesive society. Liberalism had little support. *Minobe* Tatsukichi, proposed the *organ theory,* arguing that the emperor was the highest organ of the state. This emphasis on the role of the emperor reinforced a sense of Japanese nationalism. Marxists condemned democracy, too. They saw it as derived from the socioeconomic base of capitalism and inherently class oriented, a system to ensure domination by the business class.

Taisho democracy collapsed in the 1930s. Though historians focus primarily on the inability of democracy to survive attacks from right-wing militarists, Taisho democracy had a number of achievements. First, the memory of Taisho democracy played an important role in Japan's acceptance of the democracy imposed by the Americans during the post-Second World War Occupation. Taisho democracy successfully promoted economic development in conditions of global economic difficulties. It established parliamentary democracy and the peaceful transition from one party to another. Finally, it created a successful foreign policy that placed Japan among the leading powers of the world, while emphasizing resolution of differences through peaceful negotiations and the common interests that resulted from increasing international trade. These are ideals of great importance today.

Terrorism and the Military Take-over. Though they had many reasons for being dissatisfied with civilian government, military leaders eventually assumed power to restore order, not to destroy civilian government. The military blamed the civilian government for rural poverty, while officers developed a paternalistic attitude toward their soldiers, who came mainly from the more impoverished areas in northern Japan. The military saw civilian government and urban society as "decadent and Western," and thus promoting an *effete* weakness. The military also attacked the government for corruption. More specifically they rejected the strategy of peaceful coexistence and resented the substantial cuts to the military budget. In spite of their conflict with the civilian government and the political parties, military commanders did not lead attempts to overthrow the civilian government.

Right Wing Terrorism. Right wing terrorists, within the military and outside of it, made numerous attempts to destroy the civilian government. Right wing terrorist ideology developed in the 1920s. *Kita* Ikki was the most important proponent of right wing terrorism. Ikki and others believed that democracy was the cause of all of Japan's problems. Since Western ideas were the source of Japanese democracy, it was necessary to eliminate all Western influence in Japan. Terrorist acts against government and business leaders would demonstrate democracy's impotence and lead to the collapse of the civilian government. The military could thus easily take over in this power vacuum.

Gondo Seikyo represented another group of right wing radicals, those who were *agrarian romantics.* Gondo idealized the countryside and saw the village community as representative of traditional Japanese values and as an anchor of stability in a rapidly changing nation. He argued that Western modernization models had destroyed traditional values and harmed the country's peasants. Japan should return to a pre-Western, pre-modern state, he argued. He failed to explain how a pre-industrial nation could be a twentieth century global military power.

Military Terrorism. A number of patriotic organizations appeared, many of them associated with the military. The Imperial Reservist Association, the Amur River Society, the Golden Pheasant Society, the Blood Pledge Regiment, and the Cherry Society were among the most important. In the early 1930s membership in these organizations rose to 600,000.

Junior officers attempted to apply the ideas of the civilian terrorists. Terrorist attacks began in 1930 when members of the Blood Pledge Regiment assassinated the Prime Minister to protest the London Naval Agreement. In 1932, military terrorists assassinated the Minister of Finance, attacked Seiyukai party headquarters and the Mitsubishi Bank and killed a Mitsui executive. That same year, Prime Minister Inukai *Tsuyoshi* was killed in the "May 15 Incident." Terrorist attempts were repeated in 1933, 1934, and 1935, and culminated in the *February 26 Incident* (1936). Led by a Lieutenant Hashimoto, the Cherry Society plotted to murder all government leaders and restore the emperor to true power. Though the terrorists mobilized the support of the First Division stationed in Tokyo, the plotters were ineffective terrorists. They killed two former Prime ministers and the Finance Minister but Prime Minister Okada escaped because the terrorists failed to recognize him.

At this point some military leaders stepped in to crush the rebellion. The navy, as well as a number of leading army officers, known as the *Control Faction,* championed modern warfare based on industrial superiority. They feared that a collapse of discipline and the independence of junior officers would undermine the authority needed by a strong Japanese military. Minister of War *Araki* led the supporters of terrorism, known as the *Imperial Way Faction.* This group believed the terrorists were fulfilling the samurai tradition, carrying out spiritual acts, not murder. The Control Faction defeated the Imperial Way group. It then dissolved the First Division and sent its soldiers home, then executed the ideologist Kita Ikki. Rebel officers who had participated in the failed plot sought to preserve their honor by committing suicide. Throughout the military, radical officers were purged—dismissed from the military.

Having restored order and this threat to civilian power and military effectiveness, the army assumed indirect control. It demanded, and the civilian government accepted, the military's veto over cabinet appointments and the budget and a major increase in military spending. Thus the military came to power, not through initiating the overthrow of civilian government but under the guise of maintaining order. The military remained in power until the end of the Second World War.

3. Rejection of the Meiji Ideology

During this period the main elements of Meiji ideology were questioned, challenged, and overthrown. In place of the pro-Western, pro-private enterprise, pro-democracy, pro-social equality, pro-economic growth through free trade approach, the world of Japanese ideas was dominated by nationalism, ideas of forced community and war as the common cause.

Ideology of Military Nationalism. Japanese ideology during the war was quite blunt. It emphasized Japanese superiority, represented by purity. Much attention was given to the emperor as spiritual leader of the country. Old samurai values were carried out, especially courage, endurance, and honor. Sometimes Japan emphasized its role as leader of the Asians against Western civilization and power. Most Japanese accepted the idea of Japanese superiority, seen both in terms of essential character and military might.

4. Rapid Industralization, Class Differences, and Social Discontent

Japan experienced substantial levels of economic growth in spite of global economic difficulties. Economic growth and economic problems contributed to growing class differentiation and social discontent.

Economic Growth. Economic growth was impressive, especially in heavy industry. Per capita income doubled in the three decades between 1912 and 1932. Living standards improved, though primarily in the urban, industrialized areas.

First World War and 1920s. Along with this positive economic performance, Japan faced a number of economic difficulties, primarily of a structural nature. The First World War was a period of industrial growth and economic expansion since Western powers needed goods Japan could provide. It took over markets the Europeans abandoned as they focused their attention on the battlefields of Europe. The Japanese invested heavily in China, especially in textiles. Japan also doubled the size of its merchant fleet to meet the demand for carrying trade in Asia and across the Pacific.

After the war, the country was beset by economic problems. The decline of London as the world's financial center created problems for international trade. Prices for industrial goods and especially raw silk and rice collapsed in 1920. This produced reduced business profits and economic hardship for farmers. A banking crisis took place as well. Banks had made risky loans and as firms could not repay their loans and went bankrupt, banks had less money to loan to stimulate economic activity.

Just as economic stability was achieved (1923), the Kanto Plain suffered a huge earthquake that was accompanied by destructive fires. The earthquake left over 70 percent of the Tokyo population and 85 percent of the population of Yokohama homeless. The economic loss was estimated at 70 billion yen. Money that might have been used to promote industrial development or agricultural modernization was diverted to the reconstruction of Tokyo. Though rebuilding from this earthquake provided some economic stimulus, overall it caused economic devastation.

Great Depression. The Great Depression was preceded by another banking crisis, which forced the closing of a number of banks and the consolidation of others into fewer banks. Only government loans kept a number of other banks in business.

As one of the more industrialized nations and one deeply engaged in the international economy, Japan was deeply affected by the depression. Silk and rice prices collapsed again, while export markets disappeared. At first the government followed the traditional policy used to deal with economic crises, *deflation,* that is reduced government spending. It was believed that reduced government spending would leave more money available for the private sector to stimulate its own recovery. This strategy failed.

Finance Minister *Takahashi* Korekiyo followed a *Keynesian model* (named after the British economists John Maynard Keynes), arguing that the most effective strategy for dealing with a serious economic recession or depression was for the government to increase its spending, and thus stimulate the rest of the economy. The government expanded spending, especially for military projects, and rural public works. Authorities froze taxes and reduced the interest rate. The yen was devalued, making Japanese exports cheaper and thus more competitive and foreign imports more expensive and thus less competitive with Japan-produced goods. By the mid-1930s Japan was recovering from the depression.

Structural Changes. Structural changes also took place during this period. *Zaibatsu* (gigantic conglomerates) became powerful economic forces. The largest zaibatsu with roots in the Meiji period tended to be *vertically integrated,* specializing in a single industry and anchored by a conglomerate bank and a trading company. The family leaders had great financial and decision-making power. Mitsubishi, Mitsui, and Sumitomo were among the largest zaibatsu. Mitsui controlled 15 percent of the assets of all Japanese business. Newer and smaller zaibatsu tended to be *horizontally integrated,* engaging in a number of different businesses. The new zaibatsu tended to focus on new technology and advanced engineering. Among the most important of these was the Japan Industrial Company or *Nissan. Aikawa* Yoshitsuke, an engineer who had studied in the United States, branched out from his Nissan Motor Company to military contracts. Nissan's Manchurian Heavy Industry Company was a dominant force in the Manchurian economy.

The Japanese economy is frequently described as having a *dual structure,* in which zaibatsu coexisted with large numbers of small mechanized firms. These small firms met consumer needs, sold some products abroad, and supplied parts and components for conglomerates. They offered lower wages to workers and no job security. These companies did not have deep pockets and frequently went bankrupt.

Parallel to the rise of big business were efforts to increase the role of "big government" in the economy. The military as well as bureaucrats who moved back and forth between the bureaucracy and private firms, played a central role in promoting the so-called *national defense state.* Sometimes the term *industrial policy* is used to describe situations in which government plays an important role in giving direction to the economy. Through industrial policy, government provided support for key industries important for international trade and the military, including automobiles, machine tools, synthetic oils, aluminum, and chemicals. Companies received tax breaks, subsidies, and guarantees against economic losses. In general, big business, other than the new zaibatsu, strongly opposed the national defense state.

In 1937, a *Central Planning Agency* was established. However its proposal to give government the power to control the economy was rejected. Instead a *National Mobilization Law* placed key economic decision-making power in the hands of a council that included the military, political parties, bureaucrats, and business leaders. In this way the military's push for centralized planning was muted and diluted.

Class Differences. Economic change promoted increased class differences. Four groups dominated the top of society: big business, the military, the bureaucracy, and political parties. At the same time, Japan was becoming a middle class society. The most visible part of this class was the urban youth culture of leisure and pleasure. If the upper classes and middle classes represented the success stories of post-Meiji Japan, the lower classes rode the waves of rapid change less well.

The working class increased in size and split more and more into a *labor aristocracy* of skilled workers and a mass of semi-skilled and unskilled workers. Wages increased, living conditions improved, and government protection eased life for workers. Still they had few civil rights.

Near the bottom of society were the peasants, also increasingly divided into sub-groups. In contrast to wealthier peasants and absentee landowners, a majority of peasants fell into tenancy in this period. Increasing rural inequality combined with a general decline in income for a majority of farmers to create a large impoverished peasantry located mainly in northern Japan. The masses tried to organize themselves and to express their discontent.

Social Discontent. Expressions of discontent were concentrated among factory workers and tenant farmers. Unrest was associated with suffering caused by economic crises.

Rural Unrest. Rural unrest began with the *Rice Riots* of 1918. Sharp increases in rice prices and rumors that farmers were hoarding grain led to rallies, demonstrations, and attacks on rice warehouses. Seven hundred thousand participated in disturbances in some 300 towns and cities.

The countryside was relatively poor, in spite of increases in productivity due to chemical fertilizers and greater use of mechanized equipment. Competition from cheap rice from the colonies kept prices for Japanese rice quite low.

Tenant farmers lived very harsh lives, yet their numbers were increasing. Approximately half of the peasants owned no land, paid very high rents for its use, and had very low incomes. Intellectuals discovered the countryside and its problems in the 1920s and reminiscent of the Russian movement to the people (see Chapter One) began to organize tenant farmers. Their first organizations were deeply influenced by *Christian Socialists* such as *Kagawa* Toyohiko. Tenants' unions increased in number from under 200 in 1917 to 4,500 in 1927. At the same time, an All Japan Farmers' Union was created to coordinate the tenants' union movement. The movement was strongest in central Japan, the area where agricultural conditions were best. Tenant demands for improved conditions led to modest reductions in rent.

Labor Unrest. Labor organizations also had minimal impact. Here, too, Christian Socialism played a major role. *Suzuki* Bunji organized a *Fraternal Association* that emphasized labor management cooperation and harmonious labor-management relations. The movement gradually became more radical, eventually becoming the All Japan Federation of Labor. Workers became increasingly militant during the First World War when real wages declined. The labor movement was influenced by the reorganization of the work place that occurred in the large zaibatsu, where sub-contracting was replaced by direct management control over work. Increased literacy also promoted worker "consciousness." The labor movement developed a broad program that included the right of workers to organize and strike, a minimum wage, an eight-hour day, and an end to child labor.

The strike movement was strongest from 1919–1925. In heavy industry a campaign for the eight-hour day was successful, first at the Kawasaki Shipyards and then elsewhere. In light industry, especially textiles, where most employees were still female, the 11–12 hour workday remained common. Strikes expanded after the 1923 earthquake and became increasingly violent. Management responded with lockouts and the government brought in soldiers to halt strikes.

In the mid-1920s the government broke up the labor movement. Labor unity was destroyed when Communist unions broke away from the All Japan Federation of Labor. The Peace Preservation Law gave authorities the necessary legal justification to use force against workers. At the same time the government introduced compulsory arbitration in key industries, as well as some social welfare legislation, including a national health insurance system and a minimum wage for workers. Company paternalism, especially the guarantee of lifetime employment for the labor aristocracy, also muted unrest.

Left wing parties also emerged. In 1920, the Socialist League was established but the government easily destroyed it. An underground Communist Party formed in 1922 but the police crushed it within a year. The most important left wing organization was the *Social Mass Party,* a moderate socialist group.

Social reform movements organized, articulated ideologies and sets of goals, and recruited members. However their actions brought little improvement to the lives of the Japanese lower classes. Reformist Christian Socialism, with its emphasis on social harmony, had greater appeal than radical confrontation. At the same time the government overreacted, using very repressive measures against a weak opposition. The women's movement had somewhat greater impact than the political parties.

5. Gender and Family

Modest changes occurred in gender relationships, in part a response to various women's movements. These changes affected the familial, political, economic, and cultural roles of women.

Within the family, patriarchy continued to prevail. Male domination was reinforced in the 1930s by the emphasis on nationalism and militarism. In the 1920s a *cult of domesticity* emerged, similar to that which developed in Great Britain and the United States in the second half of the nineteenth century. The magazine, *The Housewife's Friend,* played an important role by focusing on child rearing, marital relations, cooking, and sewing. The *Women's Review* encouraged discussion of whether women should work or remain in the home. Especially in the 1930s women were expected to bear children and raise them to be responsible, loyal, patriotic citizens.

The women's movement pushed for political rights. *Ichikawa Fusae* convinced the government to drop the ban on women attending public meetings and joining political organizations. The *Women's Suffrage League* pushed for the right to vote. In 1928, women were permitted to campaign—for male candidates—while in 1930 a bill to grant women the right to vote failed in the Diet. When the suffrage bill failed, the Women's Suffrage League encouraged women to turn their attention to local community issues. The suffrage campaign represented the political awakening of middle class women.

Increasing numbers of women worked outside the home. The dual structure economy fostered this trend. Opportunities for young women to hold unskilled jobs in light industry continued. White-collar jobs increased considerably, especially with the expansion of clerical work and elementary education, which provided many jobs for women. During the war, many women were drawn into factory and clerical jobs to replace men who entered the military. In many cases, the opportunity to have an income gave women greater independence and power.

Women also played an important role in literature. Founded during the First World War, the first feminist organization, *The Blue Stocking Association,* published a journal that addressed feminist issues and also provided a forum for women's writing.

Though patriarchy remained entrenched in family-oriented Japan, women acquired greater political, economic, and cultural opportunities.

6. Community and Diversity

In the 1920s differences became greater, while from the 1930s through the end of the Second World War community was emphasized. At the same time, discrimination continued against the burakumin, the Ainu, and non-Japanese Asians who lived in Japan, especially Koreans. Attitudes toward foreigners were reflected in the *comfort woman* issue, forced prostitution by young women from other parts of Asia brought in to work in military brothels.

Increasing Difference. In the 1920s difference became more pronounced. Class differences increased and the confrontation between labor and management threatened to undermine factory and government paternalism. Economic inequality increased, too. The urban-rural split widened, in economic and cultural terms. The countryside remained relatively important only in terms of political influence. Parallel to this split was the clash between Western pop culture, espoused primarily by youth and the intelligentsia in the cities, and traditionalism, championed by the right wing radicals, the military, and rural residents. In this era many questioned the Meiji legacy, focusing primarily on whether the impact of Western ideas was beneficial or destructive. Over time the critics of Westernism triumphed over its advocates.

The burakumin, Ainu, and foreigners continued to be subject to discrimination. Koreans, who had moved into Japan to work in factories, were especially subject to discrimination.

Community. Increasingly, but especially in the 1930s, government emphasized the need for unity and solidarity more and more. Community was to center around traditional values, patriotic devotion to the nation (national polity), and the Emperor. Community was not to be voluntary but enforced by peer pressure and government law and law enforcement.

Multicultural Empire. The building of empire and the military expansion of the Second World War created a multicultural empire (see Chapter One for Russian parallels), raising the question of how to treat non-Japanese Asians. On the one hand the Japanese emphasized the idea of a *Greater East Asian Co-prosperity Sphere,* hinting at the unity of all Asian peoples. This meant that other Asians should be assimilated to Japanese culture. The idea of Japan as leader of the Asians against the white Westerners was little more than propaganda, but many Asians outside of China initially accepted the Japanese perspective (see Chapter Two for Indian responses). At the same time the Japanese clearly saw themselves as a superior race, whose responsibility was to conquer and civilize other Asians. This period, thus, saw a shift from increasing diversity to demands for conformity and forced assimilation.

E. AMERICANIZATION OF JAPAN—THE OCCUPATION, 1945–1950

The American Occupation brought major changes to almost every aspect of Japanese life. The Americans believed that they had a responsibility to bring about the radical transformation of Japan into a peace-loving, democratic, egalitarian, capitalist society in order to preserve security in the Pacific. At the same time, the Japanese, devastated physically and psychologically, eagerly accepted and cooperated with this Americanization.

1. Background

It is important to understand the attitudes of the Japanese and Americans toward the Occupation reforms. Japan was in ruins at the end of the war. It had suffered almost 2 million casualties. Thirty percent of its industrial capacity and 25 percent of its national wealth had been destroyed. Almost half of the property in its sixty-six largest cities had been destroyed, while one-third of the population had lost their homes. Japan had to absorb 6 millions soldiers and repatriates from the colonies and provide them with food, housing, and employment. At war's end, Japan suffered from a tremendous food shortage and much of the population, especially in the cities, was close to starvation. Orphans and homeless people abounded. Public order broke down as robbery, violent crime, prostitution, and black market activity skyrocketed.

Japanese Motives. The Japanese people were exhausted, angry with their leaders, and concerned primarily with survival. Thus they were ready for change. Defeat had undermined confidence in the value and validity of the Japanese way of life. American victory convinced most Japanese of the superiority of American institutions, which thus should be copied.

The Japanese were now powerless militarily and had to accept American decisions. Parallel to the Tokugawa period, military defeat discredited the militarist-authoritarian system. Once again the Japanese were open to foreign ideas, many of which had been proposed or discussed in interwar Japan. Japanese leaders also recognized that cooperation with the Americans would end the Occupation more quickly. *Yoshida* Shigeru, the most important Japanese leader of the Occupation era, emphasized this idea of the *Friendly Japanese.* Japanese bureaucrats offered the Americans some understanding of Japan and worked out the details for American reform plans. Finally, American rule turned out to be quite mild and the Americans quite friendly toward the Japanese.

American Motives. At the center of American thinking was the determination that Japan becomes a peace-loving country, unable and unwilling to go to war in the future. The American decision to transform Japan into a mirror image of what American leaders thought the United States was like was based on certain assumptions. Americans believed that democratic societies were automatically peace loving and not capable of military aggression. They believed that democracy and capitalism were so intertwined that each required the other. They also thought that democracy and equality were closely interrelated. Underlying this democratic idealism was the desire to ensure that Japan did not become an Asian rival to the United States. The Americans had the power and self-confidence to impose their will on the Japanese.

Structure of Reform. Two American groups made plans for post-war Japan, largely agreeing on reforms but disagreeing over methods and timetable. A Washington-based group of Japan experts, a *Coordinating Committee,* argued that the reforms must not confront Japanese culture and values. They believed reform would be difficult to achieve and thus should be introduced very gradually. The views of the Coordinating Committee were largely ignored.

Another group of planners emerged from the staff of General Douglas *MacArthur* at *SCAP* (the *Supreme Command of the Allies in the Pacific*). These individuals knew very little about Japan. Instead they focused on pragmatic issues, recognizing that Japan had no real power to resist American ideas. They improvised, acting primarily on the basis of their American experience and heritage. Central to the success of the Occupation was the overpowering figure of General MacArthur. First the Americans destroyed "old Japan," then set out to create a new Japan.

2. Loss of Empire

The Americans destroyed Japan's military capacity and weakened the psychological and cultural supports for militarism. Their actions included demilitarization; the purge of Japan's elite, considered responsible for the war; a reduction of the status of the Emperor and of Shinto religion; and the renunciation of war.

Demilitarization. The Americans took immediate steps to eliminate the remnants of a Japanese military threat. They abolished the Ministry of War, disbanded the military and demobilized all military personnel. They destroyed remaining aircraft, naval vessels, and weapons, as well as all factories producing munitions and military equipment.

The Purge. The Americans decided to prevent Japan's wartime leaders from returning to power and to punish leaders who had committed war crimes. The *Tokyo War Crime Trials* focused on three types of crimes. Class A crimes were *Crimes against Peace.* In this group were twenty-eight Japanese leaders accused of planning, initiating, and waging an aggressive war. Seven from this group were hanged. Class B crimes were for *Violating the Rules of War.* Twenty officers were accused of commanding troops that committed atrocities. All were acquitted. Class C crimes were identified as *Crimes against Humanity,* including the mistreatment of prisoners of war and committing minor atrocities—6,000 were accused and most were found guilty; 920 were executed and most of the rest were imprisoned.

In addition, certain categories of people were "purged without trial"—they lost jobs and civil rights including the right to vote and hold office. Approximately 210,000, most of them (180,000) military officers, were included in these classifications. Business leaders, journalists, teachers, professors, and police were also deemed guilty because of membership in specific groups. The civilian bureaucracy was not touched by The Purges, in part because it was needed to carry out the Occupation reforms. Further, repressive police units, such as the Special Higher Police, were abolished, the Peace Protection law was rescinded, and censorship abolished.

Weakening Traditional Japanese Values. SCAP assumed that traditional religion and worship of the emperor could still be a rallying point for nationalism and opposition to the Americans and acted to reduce the status of Shinto religion and the emperor. Shinto lost both its privileged position as a state religion and its financial subsidy. What to do about the emperor was a more sensitive issue. The unconditional surrender clearly stated that the emperor would no longer be viewed as divine. The Americans treated the emperor as a constitutional monarch, a symbol of loyalty, and a bulwark of obedience and discipline. He was left with no real political power, only ceremonial responsibilities.

Pacifism. Japan renounced war, while the Constitution of 1946 prohibited the nation from having a military. This anti-war clause reflected not only the power of the Americans to impose pacifism on the Japanese but also drew upon a basic change in Japanese attitudes. The unexpected defeat in the Second World War produced among the Japanese a dramatic rejection of war.

Loss of Empire. Japan lost its pre-1931 empire, which had included Korea and Taiwan, as well as territory on the mainland of Asia, especially Manchuria. The southern Kurile Islands (the *Northern Territories*) remained in dispute between Japan and the Soviet Union. Soviet armies had conquered Sakhalin and the Kurile Islands and refused to return any territory to Japan. Only the Ryukyu Islands remained from what had been a gigantic empire. Political changes were just as dramatic.

3. Democratic Constitutionalism

The Americans imposed dramatic political changes upon the Japanese. Popular sovereignty, parliamentary democracy, universal suffrage, federalism, judicial review, and civil rights were key components of constitutional change.

New Constitution. MacArthur directed the Japanese cabinet to write a democratic constitution. Concluding that the draft constitution was not sufficiently democratic, he assigned a small group of American officers to write a constitution for the Japanese. Using their recollections of the American Constitution and a copy of the German Constitution of 1870 found in a Tokyo library, the Americans wrote the Japanese constitution in six days in 1947. The Japanese government made a few modest changes and the Diet approved it. This constitution has remained almost unchallenged and certainly unamended in the over sixty years of its existence. It represents a remarkable effort to create an ideal political system and contrasts with the 1889 Constitution, which merely described existing political institutions.

Central to the Constitution was the idea of *popular sovereignty,* that ultimate power rested with the people. Thus the document rejected *imperial sovereignty,* that final authority lay with the emperor. Japan became a parliamentary democracy, with the Cabinet responsible to the Lower House, the *House of Representatives.* The House of Representatives thus controlled both the legislative and executive branches of government. The elected Upper

House, now to be known as the House of Councilors, was elected but had little power.

The Americans also tried to reduce the power of the political center, providing for greater local autonomy. The Home Ministry, which had exercised great power throughout the country, was abolished. Prefectural governors and assemblies and local mayors were to be elected. These assemblies were to have taxation powers. Local police powers replaced the centralized police force. Local school boards were placed in charge of education.

The judiciary was to be independent of the administrative branch of government. The Supreme Court was to have the power of *judicial review,* the right to determine whether laws were constitutional.

The Constitution guaranteed civil rights. These rights were broader than those included in the American Bill of Rights, for they included equality for women and the right of collective bargaining. Universal adult suffrage was introduced, giving women the right to vote.

The Japanese Constitution provided the legal basis for democracy. The functioning of the political system ensured that the Constitution was neither ignored nor circumvented.

Politics. At first, politics produced no clear mandate. Initially, Japan was divided into two broad political camps, the *progressives* and the *conservatives.* The progressives deeply distrusted the surviving elements of pre-war political parties and favored socialist or communist ideas. Intellectuals, labor, and the urban population tended to support the progressives. The conservatives' support came from pre-war political figures, the business community, the small towns, and the countryside. The conservatives espoused Japanese nationalism, honored the emperor and favored big business. In 1946, progressives won the election, though the Liberals, the largest party, won only one-third of the Diet seats. Shortly before the elections the Liberal leader *Hatoyama* Ichiro was purged and Yoshida replaced him. Yoshida held the office of Prime Minister for most of the next seven to eight years. Socialists led a left-wing centrist coalition from 1947–1949, supported by the Progressives and the Cooperative Party.

In 1949, the Liberals, led by Yoshida, won almost 60 percent of the seats in the Lower House. Because he sought to change some of the policies of the occupation, his efforts are identified as a *reverse course.* The government recentralized the police, reduced restrictions on big business, and launched a campaign against labor and radical political parties. Authorities also placed restrictions on civil rights, especially the right of assembly. Increased confrontation and conflict replaced the harmony of the early post-war years.

The Socialist Party broke apart in 1951 as a result of pressure from conservatives and the signing of a peace treaty with the United States. A split within labor further weakened the socialist movement. Blue-collar workers, concentrated in *Domei,* supported moderate economic goals and the right wing of the Socialist movement. The *Sohyo,* the federation of white collar and public employees unions, focused on international issues and direct political action. It supported the left wing of the Socialist Party. The Communist Party, whose strength had been increasing, was weakened by its use of violence and torn apart by a Stalinist purge of leaders thought to be pro-Chinese Communist or insufficiently loyal to the Soviet Union.

Yoshida's expanding power and increasing authoritarianism produced a backlash, which was fueled by internal conflicts within the Liberal Party. When The Purge ended, former politicians returned to action and directed their anger against the conciliationist, pro-Occupation Liberals, especially Yoshida. Hatoyama tried to take over the Liberal Party. When these efforts failed, he took his faction out of the Liberal Party and joined with Progressives to form the Democratic Party. In 1954, Hatoyama became Prime Minister.

In the following year the *1955 System* was established. First, the factions within the Socialist Party reunited. Fearing that the Socialists would thus come to power, the two conservative parties, the Liberals and Democrats, joined to form a *Liberal Democratic Party (LDP)*. Until almost 1990 this political configuration continued little changed. The Liberal Democrats stayed in power, challenged by the Socialists and less so by the Communists.

Thus in the immediate post-war period a new democratic constitution was approved and a workable political party system was gradually created. This represented a substantial achievement, as militarist authoritarianism was replaced by pacifist democracy.

4. Westernism and Pacifism

The Occupation era was one in which Western ideas dominated and the traditional emphasis on Japanese nationalism receded into the background. It was to be expected that Western ideas would dominate Japanese ideology. What was less obvious was the powerful influence of Marxism, which successfully challenged liberal democracy among some from the educated classes.

Liberalism. Liberalism championed individual freedom and autonomy and democracy. The Occupation sought to instill such values through the educational system, emphasizing that social studies could teach responsible citizenship. Liberalism was pro-American.

Marxism. Marxism, on the other hand, emphasized class consciousness and collective solidarity. Japanese Marxists applied traditional Marxist concepts, including the primacy of the material, the inevitability of the triumph of socialism, and historical progress through conflict between existing structures and emerging ones (see Chapter One). Japanese Marxists eagerly sought confrontation with existing political and economic structures, the overthrow of capitalism, and the elimination of American influence.

Quite different in their basic approaches, liberalism and Marxism had in common claims of universality, belief in the superiority of Western Civilization, and a rejection of nationalism.

5. Economic and Social Restructuring

The Americans mainly emphasized political reform but they also saw a connection between the nature of pre-war Japanese economic structure and society and the rise of militarism. Therefore, according to SCAP it was necessary to destroy big business and promote social and economic equality. MacArthur sought to break up concentrations of economic power and promote the influence of alternative groups, including labor and the peasantry.

Break up of Zaibatsu. The Americans quickly moved to break up the zaibatsu and prevent their reemergence. In 1945, eighty-three large zaibatsu holding companies were dissolved. A commission was established to sell off their assets. Eventually 5,000 large firms were dissolved. In 1947, the Americans forced the Japanese to pass an *Anti-Monopoly Law.* This law banned holding companies and all other forms of monopolies. In addition, it limited the extent to which financial institutions could hold stock in companies. These measures reintroduced a large measure of competition into Japanese business and thus promoted economic growth. In 1953, the Liberal government weakened the anti-monopoly law by permitting cartels and interlocking directorates during times of economic difficulty and when it was necessary to develop new technology.

Economic Development Strategies. While the Americans sought to create an economic leveling in business, the Japanese emphasized economic recovery and economic development. Even before the war ended a study group led by *Okita* Saburo, had begun to formulate an economic recovery plan. The group proposed that Japan focus on the development of technologically advanced large private industries, aided by government guidance (*indicative planning*). Industrialists quickly shifted to the production of consumer goods.

With the Americans showing little interest in economic redevelopment, the Japanese emphasized targeted investment (see Chapter Four for Indian parallels). Finance Minister *Ishibashi* Tazan, deeply influenced by the Keynesian emphasis on government's role in stimulating economic development that would produce full employment, emphasized the need to invest in key industries, especially coal, steel, fertilizers, and housing construction. In 1946, the government established a Reconstruction Finance Bank that provided credit to key industries, especially coal. Its strategy was called the *priority production system.* The government also formed an Economic Stabilization Board that established price controls, rationing, and subsidies for the production of basic consumer items.

The Americans became interested in promoting economic development beginning in 1947. They slowed down the program of breaking up large companies, eliminated restrictions on foreign trade, and encouraged the importation of raw cotton from America. In 1949, the Dodge Mission investigated the Japanese financial system and recommended a series of economic stabilization measures, including a balanced budget, more efficient tax collection, controls over inflation, and a foreign exchange rate that would promote Japanese exports. At the same time, the Yoshida government moved away from government subsidies and direction to a private market system.

Rural Reform. The Occupation sought to end rural poverty largely through measures to ensure economic equality. Land redistribution was the basic strategy. In 1946, the Americans forced the Diet to pass a liberal land redistribution bill (see Chapter Four for a discussion of Chinese efforts at land redistribution). Each absentee landlord was forced to sell all except 2.5 acres of land. Ten acres was set as the maximum amount of land anyone could have. Seventy percent of the farmers purchased land at low prices with low interest rates. Tenant farming almost disappeared. In 1950, tenant farmers worked only 10 percent of the land. Now owners of land, farmers worked harder and produced more. This generated much higher standards of living for the farmers and left them conservative supporters of the status quo.

Rise of Labor Militancy. The Americans encouraged strong, independent trade unions as a counter to the power of business. A 1945 labor law gave workers the right to organize, bargain collectively, and strike. Americans even provided training for union organizers. By the end of 1946, 40 percent of workers belonged to unions. Initially unions were organized on the basis of the enterprise, with white- and blue-collar workers in the same union. A moderate federation was formed, as was a Communist union federation. Unions were sophisticated, creative, and militant in their tactics. In 1945 and 1946, workers emphasized *production control,* locking out management and white-collar personnel but continuing production. When SCAP expressed concern about this strategy, the communists turned to strikes in essential industries, hoping to set up standard contracts and settlements that could be extended to all industry. A *living wage* was the goal. That is, wages should be based on age, seniority, and family size and not on factors such as company profits and increases in the cost of living. Next, labor emphasized *workers' control*—efforts to determine wages, assign promotions, and eliminate the status differential between white- and blue-collar workers.

In 1947, conservatives became alarmed over the militancy of unions and the extent of strikes. Yoshida rejected a proposed wage settlement. When unions threatened a general strike, MacArthur stepped in and prohibited it. However, strikes intensified again in the early 1950s, especially in heavy industry. Companies turned increasingly to corporate paternalism, promises of lifetime employment, company discounts, company-sponsored vacations and recreation facilities, and wage increases based on seniority.

The Americans successfully promoted unions as a counter to the power of business. However, the unions acquired much more militancy than Americans expected, leading the Americans and the Japanese government to try to weaken the labor movement.

6. Revolution in Gender and Family

Legislation, the Constitution, and the gender imbalance that resulted from the war brought dramatic changes in gender roles and the family. Authorities issued a number of policies that were generally accepted by the people, suggesting that some changes had already occurred.

Gender and Family. The Constitution granted women equality within the family. Marriage was declared an act between two equal individuals. The 1948 Eugenics Protection Law extended legalized abortion beyond medical reasons to include all conditions. Women were permitted to initiate divorce. The patriarchal model was rejected, though not destroyed. Authorities promoted the nuclear family and the rights of individuals within the family. *Primogeniture* was abolished, replaced by equal inheritance regardless of gender.

Women remained in the labor force to some extent. A Women's and Minor's Bureau in the Ministry of Labor was assigned to protect women and youths in the labor force.

By the Constitution, women were granted the right to vote. In the first postwar elections in 1946, thirty-nine women were elected to the Diet.

Women continued to be prominent in the cultural sphere. Co-education was introduced as well.

7. Diversity and Community

During the war, authorities placed great emphasis on unity and conformity. After the war, the near unanimous support of militarism quickly disappeared. Japan became a relatively unimportant country, occupied militarily by the most powerful nation in the world. Once again, an influx of Western ideas contributed to community.

Diversity. Minorities remained, primarily the Ainu, burakumin, and Koreans. Large numbers of Americans arrived, looking and behaving quite differently from the Japanese. The Americans mixed little with the Japanese people, thus reducing the need to deal with this type of difference.

Community. Community was provided by the need to survive, the psychological trauma of defeat, and by the need to respond to Occupation policies. Nationalism faded into the background, replaced by remarkable unity in support of radical change.

F. MATURE JAPAN, 1950–1988

In general these four decades were quiet ones. Radical changes had already been introduced and digested. Japan's international position was largely determined by U.S. foreign policy aims. The LDP dominated politics, supporting conservative, pro-business, and pro-economic development goals. Japanese nationalism became the center of debate, as pro-Western feelings diminished and Communist ideals were pushed to the periphery. This was the age of an *economic miracle.* On the surface Japan appeared to be satisfied with improved living standards and relative social and economic equality. Beneath the surface, modest levels of discontent festered and some people began to worry about the consequences of rapid economic growth, especially materialism and pollution. Little change occurred in family and gender, though there were indications of growing conflict within the family and the increased importance of wives and mothers. The minorities were silent, as the majority Japanese triumphantly championed homogeneity as superior to diversity. This was an era of great achievement, though the Americans treated Japan like a satellite nation.

1. Independent Course?

Japanese-U.S. relations became almost a necessary obsession for the Japanese. Japan remained under the thumb of the United States, though it gradually began to assert a small measure of autonomy in foreign policy. As the Cold War intensified, the possibilities of an independent foreign policy disappeared. The government was united on two main components of foreign policy, though opposition parties and the Japanese public frequently disagreed, at least into the 1960s. Japan needed access to American markets and, given the ban on domestic military strength, this tied the hands of the Japanese.

Japan and the United States. The 1951 *San Francisco Peace Treaty* and the accompanying *Mutual Security Treaty* determined the broad outlines of Japanese-U.S. relations. The security treaty gave the United States indirect control over Japanese foreign policy and the right to use Japanese soil as a launching point for American military action in Asia. At the same time, Japanese dependence was reinforced by U.S. sponsorship of Japanese participation in world trade organizations, including the World Bank, GATT (*General Agreement on Trade and Tariffs* now the World Trade Organization), and the OECD (Organization of Economic Cooperation and Development). Though the Japanese and Soviets reestablished diplomatic relations in 1956, the two sides did not sign a peace treaty, largely because the Soviet Union refused to return the *Northern Territories* (the southern Kuriles) it had occupied at the end of the War in the Pacific.

Events leading up to the 1960 revision of the mutual security treaty confirmed Japanese subordination to the Americans. Many Japanese preferred neutrality in the Cold War, in part fearing that continued alignment with the United States, coupled with increasing Soviet power in Asia, threatened Japanese security. Many wanted a non-alignment strategy similar to India's. Socialists, Communists, and the university students' organization, *Zengakuren,* initiated a massive and violent campaign against treaty renewal. Unrest was so great that the Japanese called off a planned visit by U.S. President Dwight D. Eisenhower. However, the violence failed to prevent renewal of the treaty and ironically encouraged the public to support the government. The campaign against the mutual security treaty was the last gasp of Japanese radicalism and its failure marked the end to hopes that the left wing would be able to come to power. By the 1960 Mutual Security Treaty the United States confirmed its willingness to defend Japan. The United States agreed to consult the Japanese government before it deployed additional U.S. troops in Japan or launched military actions from Japan. The Americans also promised not to interfere in Japanese foreign policy. The treaty was extended for ten years.

No major changes occurred in Japan's foreign policy and its relationship with the United States until the late 1970s. Japan's insignificance was demonstrated in the early 1970s when the United States initiated talks with the Chinese Communists that led to U.S. recognition and President Richard Nixon abandoned the gold standard, thus devaluing American currency, without even notifying Japan. This *Nixon shock,* along with the OPEC oil crisis of 1973–1974, was a serious, if only temporary, blow to the Japanese economy.

In 1978, Japan and the People's Republic of China signed a non-aggression treaty. This "declaration of independence" from the United States marked the beginnings of a quest for an independent foreign policy. However, Japan remained closely tied to the United States.

Diplomacy centered around three issues. First, as détente collapsed with the Soviet invasion of Afghanistan (see Chapter One) and military build up in East Asia, Japan felt threatened and clung more tightly to the United States. At the same time the Japanese agreed to pay part of the costs of American bases in Japan. Prime Minister Nakasone Yasuhiro developed even closer ties with the United States and agreed that Japan would increase its military spending and defend the Pacific up to 1,000 miles from Japan. The Japanese military build up concentrated on shore defenses, the airforce and the navy. By 1987, Japan was spending a bit over 1 percent of its GDP on military, but this was enough to vault the Japanese into third place in the world in overall military spending.

International Trade. Second, Japan tried to expand its economic ties with China, Pakistan, Turkey, and countries in Southeast Asia. Economic assistance tripled in the 1980s. Japan concluded that it needed to expand its economic activities especially into Southeast Asia, since it could no longer depend on huge profits from its U.S. and European operations. However, the countries of Southeast Asia found it difficult to forget Japanese aggression and brutality during the Second World War.

The conscious decision to expand trade with Southeast Asia resulted in part from increasing trade friction with the United States and Europe. As Japan competed more and more successfully with U.S. products, beginning with steel and cotton textiles in the 1960s, the United States responded by pressuring the Japanese to institute *voluntary export restraints.* The trade friction reached a peak in the late 1980s. In 1988, the United States passed the *Omnibus Trade Act,* which included the so-called *Super 301 Clause.* This provision permitted the American government to retaliate against countries that engaged in unfair trade practices, as determined by the United States. The Americans also sought to expand exports to Japan in specific sectors, especially semi-conductors and food products, including beef and oranges. Finally, the Americans argued that the trade imbalance was in part due to the way Japan structured its economy, especially the effort to minimize domestic consumption, and the existence of non-tariff restrictions that made it almost impossible for foreign companies to compete in Japan.

Internationalism. Especially under Nakasone the Japanese began to argue that their country was not an insular, isolated satellite of the United States but a nation very interested in and capable of having an "international" focus. Much debate took place within Japan over what it meant to be a member of the international community and many Japanese argued that they were quite global in perspective. Japan believed that its new international power, economic rather than political, should allow it to become a permanent member of the United Nations Security Council.

Still the primary characteristic of Japanese foreign policy in this period was its emphasis on international trade. Though it increasingly emphasized its ability to protect its own national security, it recognized that it could not really defend itself against the Soviet Union and thus was dependent upon and subordinate to the United States. Relative stability in foreign policy was paralleled by a similar stability in domestic politics.

2. LDP Domination

In politics, the Liberal Democratic Party dominated, never seriously threatened by other political forces until the late 1980s. Continuity of LDP domination, policies, and bureaucratic influence balanced shifts of power among LDP's larger *factions.*

Liberal Democrats. The Liberal Democrats won a majority of seats in almost every election from 1957 through 1986. In the few closer contests, a large LDP plurality joined with splinter parties and independents to form a majority. The LDP vote declined in response to scandals and the oil shocks of the early and late 1970s. Liberal Democratic domination resulted primarily from its strengths, though the weakness and disunity of its foes was important, too.

The Liberal Democrats' platform of economic growth and improved living standards appealed to most Japanese. Successful and continued fulfillment of these goals meant that voters rewarded the LDP by continually returning it to power. In addition, the core supporters of the LDP, rural residents, were over-represented. Electoral laws were not changed to reflect the decline in rural population and the huge increase in urban population. Elections were expensive. By 1969, it is estimated, winning legislative candidates each spent about a million dollars. Big business, especially the national business associations such as the Japanese Economic Federation, provided huge subsidies to LDP factions. These contributions guaranteed that government policy promoted business interests. Japanese legislators used *pork barrel* tactics, ensuring that much money was spent on local infrastructure and construction projects, including local railways, roads, schools, and public office buildings. Thus each legislator could demonstrate to his or her voters that he/she had made sure that the district received its fair share of tax dollars.

Opposition. The Liberal Democrats benefited from the weakness of other political forces. The opposition was never able to create a coalition that might have seriously challenged the Liberal Democrats. Internal splits within the Communists and Socialists weakened each of the parties, while mutual animosity kept them apart. The faction-ridden socialists generally won about 20 percent of the seats. The Communist Party was much smaller and divided into pro-Soviet and pro-Communist Chinese factions. Their strength peaked at 11 percent in 1972, after the party abandoned its militant anti-Americanism. In 1964 a new party, the *Clean Government Party* (*Komeito*), appeared. An offshoot of a Buddhist organization, Soka Gakkai, it drew most of its support from immigrants from the countryside who drifted into unskilled work and jobs in the secondary industrial sector. Its rise cut into the Socialists' vote. Its support peaked in 1969 at 11 percent of the seats in the Lower House. Generally it won about 10 percent of the vote and frequently supported the LDP in Parliament. Very broadly, the Socialists and Communists focused on foreign policy issues, especially anti-Americanism, while ordinary Japanese voters were little concerned with international relations, instead concentrating on work and improved living standards.

Factionalism. Two other characteristics of Japanese politics stand out. First, each political party was composed of a number of competing factions. Within the Liberal Democratic Party, for example, five or six factions competed to win the party presidency. The party president's faction determined who would hold leadership positions in the Diet and in the government. Negotiations among factions determined government policy. Most factions emerged out of the original conservative parties, the Liberals, Democrats, and the Cooperativists. For example, the Hatoyama faction produced the strong mid-1980s Prime Minister Nakasone. Each faction had independent access to campaign funds. The relative success of a faction led "independents" to join it and sometimes produced defections from one faction to another.

The bureaucracy formed one leg of the *iron triangle* that ruled Japan (parties and big business were the other two legs). The central ministries, especially the Ministry of International Trade and Industry and the Ministry of Finance, had a great deal of power. These ministries determined policy rather than merely implemented legislation.

Corruption was another important component of LDP rule. The Lockheed bribery scandal of 1973 was typical. Gift giving, kickbacks, fraud, tax evasion, bribery, and blackmail all played a significant role in decision-making.

For almost thirty-five years, the "system of 1955" dominated Japanese politics. LDP rule, supported by or controlled by the bureaucracy and big business, pursued two broad policies—promotion of the economic miracle and subordination to the United States. These successful policies and the disunity of its opponents enabled LDP rule to continue for decades. LDP policies also promoted increased emphasis on nationalism, which became the dominant ideology during this period.

3. Westernism and Nationalism

Japan remained committed to Western ideology, including an emphasis on progress, democracy, equality, and internationalism. At the same time nationalism, a protest against Western ideology, became increasingly important. Two forms of nationalism emerged—*nostalgic patriotism* and *cultural nationalism.* Both were a response to American domination and Japanese subordination.

Nostalgic Patriotism. Nostalgic patriotism was reflected primarily in reassessments of the Second World War that portrayed Japan in a most favorable light. In 1963, Hayashi Fusao published *Affirmation of the Great East Asia War* which depicted the Second World War as a further stage in the lengthy conflict between the United States and Japan that had begun with Commodore Perry's opening up of Japan. By implication, the struggle continued as Japan rebuilt its economy and embarked upon the economic miracle. By the late 1970s, the Japanese had begun to glorify their role in the Second World War, reflected in ceremonies at the *Yasukini Shrine.* The Second World War came to be viewed as a just cause for Japan, while the brutal behavior of the Japanese was ignored.

Cultural Nationalism. In the 1960s the Japanese began a renewed quest to define a distinctive Japaneseness. This search became the *Nihonjinron* movement. Japan was defined as unique and distinctive. Japanese unique qualities included industriousness, tenacity, politeness, and kindness. Intellectuals argued that traditional Japanese values had made possible the economic miracle. From this came a mystical nationalism that emphasized uniqueness, purity, and nostalgia for military values.

Internationalism. At the same time the Japanese also claimed that they had become part of the international world. Foreign language study, international travel, and greater global diplomatic activism were viewed as indications of Japan's internationalism (see section 1).

4. Economic Miracle, Social Change, and Discontent

During this era, Japan experienced two lengthy periods of substantial economic growth, punctuated by economic crises. Rapid economic growth produced modest social changes and small amounts of social discontent.

First Economic Miracle, 1950–1973. Prime Minister Ikeda Seihin announced a goal of income-doubling. Japan successfully doubled its economy, experiencing an average 10 percent growth per year from 1955–1973. The *economic miracle,* common among industrialized countries that had suffered extensive damage during the Second World War, occurred for many reasons. The government was committed to economic growth, while the public expressed strong support for this goal. The Japanese had a clear strategy—to promote economic growth through exports. Initially they focused on core industries, especially textiles, shipbuilding, coal, and power.

International conditions were favorable into the early 1970s. Free trade was the order of the day, promoted especially by the Americans and codified by GATT. Cheap raw materials and cheap energy meant that costs of production were quite low. Consumer demand, after the lean years of the war, was extremely strong, thus permitting relatively high prices.

Japanese business operated in a period of political certainty. Business could depend upon LDP political domination and thus pro-business legislation and administration. The bureaucracy played an important leadership role. Bureaucrats, such as those in MITI and the Economic Planning Agency, had enormous power. The government allocated foreign currency, limited foreign investment, provided tax breaks to protect industries that could not compete with foreign firms, and promoted economic growth through spending on infrastructure. Both business and government focused on the future, engaging in long-range planning. The government's policy, and that of big business, too, was to invest in industrial potential and not in declining industries. The government engaged in *indicative planning*—suggesting areas of potential growth (*sunrise firms*) and discouraging continued support for *sunset industries.* For example, Japan reduced investment in textiles and shipbuilding when those industries became less competitive globally and instead increased investment in consumer electronics and automobiles.

Human resources were very important. Japanese employees were well educated, hard working, and deeply loyal. Lifetime employment in large firms reinforced the importance of employee attitudes. Company unions reduced the probability of conflict between management and labor and championed the idea of the company as a community of common labor and management interests. The six-day work week enhanced production as well. Japanese management, experienced but also trained by the American military during the Occupation, was extremely capable.

Capital was readily available and huge amounts of capital were invested in the economy. Consumer credit was not very accessible, while the absence of an extensive social security system meant that people saved large proportions of their income. The savings rate rose from 7 percent in the 1950s to over 20 percent in the 1970s. In addition, profits flowed to banks, which then invested large amounts of money. Low interest rates on savings meant that lower rates of interest could be charged borrowers. Japan was thus rich in human resources and capital but resource poor in terms of raw materials. Japanese firms emphasized building up market share rather than profits. Growth was more important than dividends.

Japanese business was reorganized, largely as a result of the Occupation. Horizontal combinations, much looser in form than zaibatsu, emerged. These *keiretsu* (enterprise groups) consisted of coalitions of companies that engaged in a variety of types of productions. Each keiretsu had its bank and trading company. A keiretsu might include up to 100 individual companies. These firms were tied together by monthly "presidents' luncheons" (where investment strategies were worked out), a common bank and a common trading company, and interlocking directorates and overlapping shareholding. Unlike the zaibatsu that sought to establish and maintain monopolies, the keiretsu competed against each other and shared trade secrets. These actions promoted productivity.

First Economic Crisis. This system that produced the first economic miracle worked well until the early 1970s. The first miracle was undermined by the Nixon shock, which made Japanese products more expensive and thus less competitive, and by the oil shock of 1973–1974, which caused energy prices, and thus costs of production, to soar. This threatened the international trade-based Japanese economy. However, the economy quickly recovered, developing strategies for dealing with sudden, unexpected sharp increases in costs.

Second Economic Miracle. The second economic miracle resulted from restructuring required by the oil crises of the early and late 1970s. Prosperity was thus sustained up to the end of the 1980s. Japan responded to unfavorable international economic conditions centered on sharp increases in energy costs with a clear sense of strategy. The government and the private sector focused investment in knowledge-based, high tech, and low-energy consumption industries, especially micro-electronics. Companies also emphasized *offshore manufacturing,* shifting production to other countries where costs, especially labor, were much lower. Japan championed economic growth through exports, especially to Southeast Asia and Europe. Business placed increased emphasis on quality in order to give Japanese exports a competitive advantage. This was a period of extraordinary labor peace as workers recognized the need for total loyalty to the company so that it could remain competitive. Involuntary retirements and an increase in part-time workers also reduced excess labor and labor costs. Lean management, reduced inventories, robotics, and cost cutting were also employed. The savings rate increased and Japanese businesses invested quite heavily. The focus on market share rather than profits remained, as did the emphasis on long-range planning. The bureaucracy continued to play an important role, though the Ministry of Finance was now relatively more important than MITI. Though Japan twice restructured its economy in the 1970s to respond to cost pressures, it was less successful a third time, at the end of the 1980s.

Social Changes. Modest changes occurred in Japanese society, most resulting from the Occupation and the economic miracle. The Occupation had produced a real leveling. In a sense almost all Japanese were equal. Though they began the post-Occupation period in poverty and thus may be considered lower class, the economic miracle pulled almost the entire society up into the middle class. Japan was also a society of great opportunity, especially due to the broad expansion of higher education. However, by the 1980s social differences were increasing, in part because of property speculation. Still, Japan remained the least unequal of all industrial societies.

Though class differences were small, political and economic power tended to be concentrated. One analysis suggested that by the 1980s Japan had become a three-class society. At the top of society was a power elite of about 2,000 families. LDP leaders, top bureaucrats, and the executives of leading keiretsu formed this group. Below this power elite was the *mass middle class.* At the bottom of society was a small lower class consisting of the old, the less well-educated employed in unskilled jobs in the secondary sector, the self-employed, and the burakumin.

Social mobility remained at high levels through the 1970s. For example, one-third of the students at Tokyo University, the best university in the country, came from working class backgrounds. Education, immigration to urban areas, and economic opportunities fostered mobility. During the 1980s mobility slowed because of the entrenchment of the elite, which became self-perpetuating (half of the members of the parliament were the sons or daughters of former Diet members) and the economic crises of the 1970s.

Social Conflict. Social conflict was greatest in the 1950s and again in the late 1960s. Throughout the 1950s, workers, especially white-collar employees, engaged in *wage offensives*—brief militant strikes in support of higher wages. Wage offensives were briefer and less militant thereafter. Labor and youth mobilized against the renewal of the U.S.-Japanese Mutual Security Treaty in the 1960s. Radical students in the Zengakuren engaged in violent protests again in the late 1960s.

From the 1970s on protest remained on a low level. Most common were *citizens' movements,* local protests, primarily directed against environmental catastrophes, such as the chemical spills at Minamoto Bay. By the 1980s, local issues groups, known as *resident movements,* directed their efforts at forcing local governments to change policies. Local governments were fairly weak and not prepared to stand up to organized pressure. Overall, the level of protest in Japan was quite low. Protest was directed against "injustice" but not against the Japanese system or way of life.

5. Gender, Family, and the Economic Miracle

Rapid economic growth also affected gender relations and the family. The nature of the family changed, while women became relatively more important. However, Japan remained very conservative in gender relationships and family roles. The ideal of the *good wife, good mother* still ruled.

The Family and the Economic Miracle. Changes occurred in family structure, power relationships, and emotional relationships. The nuclear family triumphed, while the extended family and corporate household (*ie*) lost much of their significance. Family size declined from 5 in the mid-1950s to 3.5 in the mid-1970s. The birthrate declined to 1.3:1000, with replacement of current population requiring a rate of 2.1. The new ideal was husband, wife, one son, and one daughter. Several factors produced the decline in family size. Immigration to the cities involved large numbers of single persons and created delayed marriage. Small, crowded apartments discouraged large families. In addition, SCAP had encouraged abortion and contraception as a remedy for "overpopulation."

Fathers ceased to dominate the family and mothers moved to the center of family life. Long work hours meant that fathers were not home many waking hours, leaving mothers in charge. Mothers were expected to follow the maxim "good wives, good mothers." Especially important was the role of mothers as "education moms," responsible for ensuring that their children passed the difficult entrance exams to various levels of education. Women assumed responsibility for controlling the family's finances. *Primogeniture* was abolished, replaced by the requirement that all children share in the family inheritance.

As family size declined and the nuclear family replaced more extended family relationships, parents gave more attention to their one or two children. Affection, especially between mothers and sons, strengthened. Still, family life was not perfect. Child abuse, child neglect, mother-child suicides, and single-parent families undermined the picture of harmonious family life. In addition, family members acquired loyalties and important friendships beyond the home. Men spent much of their free time with their work buddies and women associated more and more with neighbors and fellow members of organizations such as the Parent-Teachers Association.

Women's Roles. In addition to dominating the family, women played a specific economic role. As the economy improved in the 1960s, some women withdrew from the workforce. However, women's participation grew again in the 1970s and 1980s. Most women worked in clerical jobs, where opportunities expanded as knowledge-based economic activities became more and more important.

For most women, employment was a two-phase process. Women worked until childbirth and returned to the work force after their children began school. Most women were employed in the secondary sector of the economy where wages were lower. At the end of the 1980s women's wages were only half those of men.

Some indications of changes in the work environment for women appeared in the 1980s. For the first time a higher percentage of women than men participated in higher education, though generally at two-year community colleges. The purpose of higher education for women was still to prepare them to be good wives, not career women. In 1980, Japan signed an international treaty that banned sexual discrimination. In 1985, the Diet passed an equal employment law. Under the law mediation was used to resolve possible instances of unfair treatment of women with respect to employment. At the same time the law eliminated the special protections women had traditionally received at work in terms of limits on the length of the work day, night work, etc. Leave from jobs was granted for parents of newborns.

Ironically, then, women gained much more power within the traditional space—the family—but achieved only modest gains in the public sphere of politics, the work place, and higher education. In a parallel fashion, only limited support for diversity emerged during the economic miracle era.

6. Community and Diversity

Community still dominated Japanese thinking, while minorities were generally ignored. Japan's preoccupation with community and solidarity left little place for difference.

Community. In this era community and consensus became more and more important. Two broad sources of community were at work. First Japanese nationalism (see section three above) became increasingly powerful. The emphasis on uniqueness separated the Japanese from others and enhanced the importance of the Japanese community. Second, Japanese global economic successes produced a sense of superiority. Homogeneity was used as an argument for Japanese economic achievement. Homogeneous societies were automatically superior to diverse ones, many Japanese argued. If this was true, of course, Japanese minorities had to be viewed as invisible.

Diversity. Two groups remained outside the definition of Japanese—the burakumin and the Koreans. Increasing numbers of foreigners, *gaijin,* some in the business community and others in the low-paid service sector, were alternatively invisible or exotic "clowns."

Burakumin. Discrimination continued against the burakumin. Little was done to end overt discrimination in housing, employment, and higher education. Burakumin organized politically and aligned themselves with Communists and Socialists. At the national level this alliance had no impact. At the local level, where from time to time left wing city governments came to power, changes occurred. For example, the left came to power in Kyoto, where a large number of burakumin lived. The city government built burakumin neighborhoods, with separate schools, social welfare services, and entertainment. Thus, ironically, segregation was a path to improvements in the lives of the burakumin.

Koreans. Koreans continued to face discrimination. Numbering over 600,000 by the mid-1970s, most of the Koreans in Japan were second or third generation residents of Japan. Most no longer knew the Korean language and had never been to Korea. Still they were discriminated against.

It was almost impossible for a Korean to become a citizen of Japan. The *naturalization law* based citizenship on parentage, not place of birth. To become Japanese one needed to change one's name to a Japanese one. Noncitizens were excluded from social security, health insurance, and public housing. Discriminated against in employment, most Koreans were forced to take low-status jobs.

Within the Korean community two strategies emerged. The *separationists* tended to identify with North Korea, sent savings to relatives there, and created self-contained communities. These communities had their own schools, universities, banks, and other businesses. This self-segregation left Koreans outside Japanese society.

Assimilationists tended to identify with South Korea and sought to become Japanese, with little success. They tended to turn to the courts to support their charges of being discriminated against.

Burakumin and Koreans remained outsiders, excluded and ignored by the Japanese.

G. JAPAN CHALLENGED, 1988–PRESENT

Political instability, economic difficulties, and uncertainties left by the end of the Cold War produced a serious crisis in Japan that ranged across most areas of public life for some two decades. Solutions seemed to avoid the Japanese leaders. The bubble economy collapsed, LDP domination fell apart, and Japan's relationship with the United States became strained.

1. Japan and the World

Japan sought to assert itself in world affairs, but political instability, economic problems, dispute over the use of its military abroad, and the nuclear threat from North Korea weakened its efforts. The American eagle still loomed large over the Japanese global landscape.

Japan's Global Image. Japan sought recognition as a major player in world politics. For the Japanese, the main mechanism for achieving high global status was its quest for a permanent seat on the United Nations Security Council, a goal blocked by China. Japan also sought to promote global economic growth and cultural and scientific exchanges.

The Gulf War, the West's decision to attack Iraq for invading Kuwait, demonstrated Japan's limited ability to act as a world leader. Japan had tried to avoid alienating countries with whom it had important trade relations or upon whom it was dependent for oil. Yet, it participated in the economic boycott of Iran and provided 13 billion dollars of support for Iraq's neighbors and the war effort. However, when Japan was criticized for spending its money but being unwilling to shed its blood, Prime Minister *Kaifu* Toshiki tried unsuccessfully to persuade the Diet to authorize the Japanese military to participate in the first Gulf War. However, Article 9 of the Constitution, which prohibited Japan from engaging in military action, constrained Japanese global action, especially in a world in which non-governmental entities were the main threat. Even this modest shift in policy provoked a great deal of domestic discussion and some opposition.

Japan and the United States. The end of the Cold War created opportunities for Japan to assert greater independence from U.S. foreign policy goals. Its need for U.S. protection declined. With Russia no longer as serious a threat to Japanese security as before, Japan need not always acquiesce to the United States. At the same time, however, the United States could afford to be more assertive toward Japan, since it had less need of Japan as a bulwark against Soviet expansionist impulses in East Asia. The end of the Cold War brought a shift from military to economic issues. Here the United States became increasingly irritated with Japan over the trade imbalance. Conflict peaked in 1995, when President Clinton threatened high tariffs against Japanese luxury automobiles and took the issue to the World Trade Organization. A compromise was worked out over this specific issue but did not remove the main basis for conflict—the trade imbalance and the American perception that Japan had little interest in making changes to reduce the U.S. trade deficit. In the same year three American soldiers raped a young Okinawan girl, setting off a major protest in Okinawa and in Japan. Relations remained tense, even though the two countries had much in common in terms of trade and East Asian security issues, especially China's economic power and military expansion.

Japan and Asia. Japan also struggled to carve out for itself a more important role in Asia, especially Southeast Asia. The policy shift had come in 1987 but it was only slowly implemented. By 1993, Japan's trade with Asia was greater than its trade with the United States. Japan provided large amounts of aid to Southeast Asia, especially in terms of infrastructure construction and investment. However, memories of the Second World War remained a powerful force for other Asian peoples. Japanese colonialism was not easily erased. In addition, the comfort women issue surfaced. During the Second World War women from all over Asia were forced into prostitution to serve the needs of the Japanese military. In the mid-1990s, survivors began to sue the Japanese government. The government made sizeable payments to the survivors but that could not erase the image of sexual exploitation.

Further, the Japanese still ignored the brutality of their actions during the war. Conservatives saw the war as an act of Asian liberation from Western colonialism. In 1995, the Japanese faced the question of how to "celebrate" the end of the Second World War. The Diet barely passed a resolution expressing "deep remorse for acts of aggression." Socialist Prime Minister *Murayama* Tomichii offered an official apology but many doubted the sincerity of Japanese "remorse."

Commemorating the atomic bombings was also controversial. On the one hand, the Japanese could portray themselves as the victims of the most hideous weapons in human history. Yet at the same time, the Japanese had shunned the surviving victims of nuclear radiation and were reluctant to draw too much attention to "Hiroshima."

North Korea. The fall of the Berlin Wall and the subsequent union of Germany produced hopes for the reunification of the Korean peninsula. North Korea's poverty led the United States to pressure Japan to provide economic assistance to the North, in spite of its Communist dictatorship. However, North Korean abduction of Japanese civilians and its launching of a Tripodong missile in 1998 led Japan to halt humanitarian aid to North Korea. Japan's expectation that North Korea would be starved into returning abductees and ending its military build-up proved false. The crisis intensified in October 2006, when the North Koreans detonated a nuclear device. Japanese insecurity reached higher levels than during the Cold War.

Deployment of Japan's Self Defense Force Abroad. Possible revision of Article 9 of the Japanese Constitution, which banned the use of the Japanese military, the Self Defense Force, abroad, resulted from increased Japanese nationalism and international demands, especially from the United States, that Japan employ its Self Defense Force in international peacekeeping operations and in anti-terrorist actions. In 1992, the Diet passed a law permitting Japan's National Defense Force to join U.N. peacekeeping operations in a noncombatant role. Subsequently, Japan conducted peacekeeping activities in Cambodia, Timor, Mozambique, and the Golan Heights (Israeli-occupied Syria).

After the September 11th attacks on the United States in 2001, the Diet passed laws that permitted the sending of a naval force to patrol the Indian Ocean. Japan also deployed military units to Iraq for reconstruction and medical (but not combat) efforts and for airlift operations from Kuwait into Iraq. Discussion of revision of Article 9 intensified with the appointment of Abe Shinzo as prime minister in October, 2006.

A Permanent Seat on the U.N. Security Council. In recent years, Japan has sought recognition as an important global power through its campaign for permanent membership on the U.N. Security Council. By 2008, Japan had not yet achieved this goal, in spite of an alliance with Germany, India, and Brazil, three other important nations, which also sought permanent seats on the Security Council. Chinese opposition and support for China's stance by many countries in Africa have blocked these efforts. Chinese insecurity seems to be its motivating factor.

Japan has not been very successful in becoming recognized as a world leader and it asserted independence from the United States primarily by rejecting American demands for changes in Japanese economic policy that would have reduced the U.S. trade deficit. Having a positive trade balance with the United States and Europe seemed one way in which Japan could demonstrate its superiority.

2. Political Instability

Some two decades of relative political instability began in 1988 when it first appeared that LDP domination was finally seriously threatened. Eventually the LDP lost its political majority but efforts at basic political reform and attempts to establish an alternative political power constellation have proven elusive. The political crisis began with a scandal based on corruption, sex, and taxes.

LDP Challenged, 1988–1993. Corruption had erupted publicly from time to time in Japanese politics but had never brought down an LDP government. However, beginning in 1988 scandals took place in an atmosphere of general and massive dissatisfaction with LDP rule. In the summer of 1988 *Recruit Cosmos,* a real estate firm, sold shares cheaply to government officials, including the secretary of Prime Minister Takeshita Noboru. When the company went public, the shares were worth millions. Though there was no proof that Takeshita was involved, he was forced to resign. He was replaced by Uno Chiyo. Then, Uno's mistress went public, criticizing him for not treating her in the fashion due the mistress of a Prime Minister. Beyond that, the government had levied a 3 percent sales tax that was extremely unpopular among one of LDP's key constituencies, small business. The conjuncture of sex, corruption, and taxes seemed to make LDP especially vulnerable.

When Socialists won control of the Upper House, the House of Councilors, in the summer elections of 1989, LDP seemed doomed. Led by a woman, Doi Takeo, the Socialists expected to win in the autumn, 1989 Lower House elections. However, Japan did not turn to the left. LDP won easily. Deeply fearing a fall from power, the LDP worked very hard to ensure victory. Pork barrel legislation "bought" many votes. LDP also campaigned on a platform of economic patriotism. It claimed it had presided over Japan's rise to become the most influential economy in the world. To defeat LDP was to endanger this status. LDP also spent a great deal of money on the campaign, up to 3 billion dollars, much of it from the business community. Though a woman led the Socialists and the sex scandal seemed to create the opportunity for a female protest vote, there was no women's vote. Only a minority of women voted for opposition candidates. LDP victory was also made possible by failure of the Socialists to run an effective campaign.

Recognizing that popular support for reform was strong, LDP appointed Kaifu Toshiki, a supporter of political change, Prime Minister. Kaifu's government introduced a bill that would have given greater voice to urban residents and smaller parties but the bill was defeated in the Diet. The inability of LDP to carry out significant political reform; the lingering recession, for which LDP was blamed; and another scandal led to the fall of the Kaifu government and to the collapse of LDP domination. In 1992, the president of a fast-delivery trucking firm, Sagawa Kyubin, gave money to about 100 politicians, laundering the money through companies with ties to the Japanese Mafia. The scandal reached Vice Prime Minister Kanemaru Shin, who had tucked away 6 billion yen (approximately 500 million dollars) from gifts and bribes. Shin was convicted of tax evasion. LDP had clung to power for over four years after the first serious challenge that had begun in the summer of 1988. From 1993 on, no clear majority emerged and no party or coalition remained in power for long.

Short-lived Governments, 1993–2001. From the summer of 1993 to the present, Japanese politics has been dominated by a confusing, rapidly shifting balance of power. In the summer of 1993 *Hosokawa* Masahiro, who had earlier formed a LDP break-away group, Japan Renewal Party, joined with several small parties that had split from LDP, the Japanese Socialist Party, and the Clean Politics Party to form a new government. The Hosokawa government passed a reform bill that created 300 single seat constituencies, with 200 other Diet members elected through proportional representation. However, the coalition fell apart over tax proposals and was replaced by another minority government.

In 1994, the Socialists and LDP joined in a coalition government with the Socialist Murayama as Prime Minister. Though the two parties had opposed each other for half a century, they actually had much in common. In a sense both were part of the old political establishment. The coalition was short-lived and was replaced in 1996 by an LDP minority government, led by Hashimoto Ryutaro. The pro-political reform groups formed the *New Frontier Party,* headed by Ozawa Jizaburo. Elections in 1998 gave LDP another plurality and the prime minister's position.

These short-lived governments meant political fragmention, a lack of stability and continuity in decision-making, and a general weakening of the power of government. It was thus difficult to respond effectively to crises that broke out. The collapse of the Socialists and Communists meant that the political spectrum was confined to the center (the Liberal Party, the New Clean Politics Party, and the Democratic Party of Japan) and the right (the LDP, the New Conservative Party, and later Your Party).

Return of LDP, 2001–2009. LDP's position was strengthened with victories in 2001, 2003, 2005, and 2007 elections. A wildly popular LDP maverick, *Koizumi* became Prime Minister promising major reforms. Opposition to reform centered in *zoku giin* (special interest politicians), who represented powerful groups whose political power and economic positions were threatened by reforms. Among these were the post office and construction industry *zoku.* Consolidating his power within the party and acting cautiously, Koizumi Junichiro initiated a number of reforms intended to reduce the power of the central government and to reduce the extent of Japan's public welfare safety net (pensions and nursing care for the elderly). The goal was to create greater private and personal risk (or insecurity) and reduce government responsibility. Privatization of the postal system was at the heart of these reforms. Thus the largest savings bank in Japan, the postal savings bank, was privatized, creating greater economic risk for most Japanese citizens. After Koizumi, the reform momentum ran out of steam.

Politics Today. Formed in 1993 in the chaotic days of the collapse of LDP domination, the Democratic Party of Japan (DPJ) briefly held power. Unpopular foreign policy decisions by LDP from 2005–2009 gave DPJ another opportunity to rule Japan. Its electoral support rose from 24% in 2005 (LDP 62%) to 40% in 2007 (LDP 28%) and 47% (LDP 39%) in 2009. Led by its general secretary *Ozawa* Ichiro, DPJ has suffered from charges of corruption and popular dissatisfaction with its inability to remove an American military base from Okinawa. Declining support for it and for LDP, as well, suggests continued political unease and instability. This will weaken Japan's ability to solve its many problems.

3. Nation

Changes occurred in the Japanese belief system in the period of crisis. At first some of the chauvinistic forms of nationalism were softened because of domestic problems. Westernism then revived, as the Japanese began to emphasize the need, once again, to learn from the West. More recently, more aggressive forms of nationalism have gained increased support, especially among political leaders. This has been symbolized by the annual visits of Koizumi to the Yasukini shrine, a war memorial that houses the remains of Japan's Second World War leaders executed for crimes against peace.

4. Economic Bubble Bursts

In the early phases of the political crisis, the Japanese economy entered a severe decline that has lasted to the present. This crisis was powered by long-term structural problems, as well as by ineffective decision-making by the government and business. In the past, economic challenges had been met with successful restructuring of the economy and changes in its rules of behavior. Earlier, economic difficulties had been dealt with quickly. In the last two decades, the Japanese government and business community failed to meet the challenge.

Crisis of the 1990s. The crisis of the nineties was long lasting and yielded no clear solutions. In the late 1980s growth slowed and from 1992 on the economy was either in recession or grew less than 1 percent per year. The Asian economic crisis of 1998–1999 deepened Japan's economic difficulties. As the new century began, a modest recovery set in but the growth rate has generally been only about 1 percent.

The crisis had many origins. Interest in minimizing costs of doing business diminished. Companies maintained bloated work forces, especially white collar ones, caused partially by the guarantee of lifetime employment. Firms had overbuilt in the 1980s and now had excess plant and capacity. Companies had borrowed large amounts of money to pay for expansion in the 1980s and now found it difficult to repay loans because profits had declined. Also, many large banks had issued very risky loans that now threatened their viability. For example the eighteen largest banks had 350 billion dollars out in bad loans.

One financial crisis hit in 1990 and another in 1998. In 1990 the Bank of Japan, following the advice of the Ministry of Finance, raised interest rates. Confidence in the stock market disappeared and it collapsed. The *Nikkei Index* of the Tokyo Stock Market fell from 39,000 yen to 12,000. The real estate market, built on speculation, also collapsed. At the same time the value of the yen appreciated by 20 percent, making Japanese exports more costly and Japanese products less competitive. In turn the economy slowed down dramatically.

It was clear that the Japanese had now become less effective at strategy and innovation. The emphasis on conformity and reduced spending on research and development had hindered the planning of new products. The bureaucracies, government, and private, applied their heavy hand, also stifling creativity. The Japanese were falling behind in key areas of the information revolution, including software, satellites, cable TV, telecommunications, and microprocessors. Unlike the past, Japan has not been able to move into new core areas of industry. A recent study suggested that Japan had increased its market share in only 10 percent of some 1,600 industrial products.

Less than dynamic sectors, including retailing, banking, housing, construction, and agriculture, dragged down the economy. These are highly regulated, protected, and subsidized parts of the economy. For example, the government has continued to encourage small-scale farming and to oppose consolidation into larger, more efficient holdings. This has benefited farmers and produced extremely high food prices for consumers.

The economic crisis occurred in the midst of the political power vacuum and this prolonged the crisis. However, some efforts were made to overcome the crisis. Companies sought to reduce costs. They did this by reducing the number of parts in a product and by expanding their multiple uses. Some workers were pushed out. The Obuchi government made 200 billion dollars available to enable banks to survive losses resulting from bad loans. The money was thus not used to promote productivity or economic growth. The crisis grew worse again in the late 1990s.

The Economy Today. In the twenty-first century the Japanese economy has been relatively stagnant, generally with growth rates of about 1 percent per year, rising to 2% from 2003–2007. The global financial crisis of 2007–2009 affected Japan but for different reasons than in the rest of the industrialized world. Default on sub-prime mortgages and collapse of major financial institutions did not occur in Japan. However, reduced Japanese domestic investment and the increasing costs of an aging and declining population led Japan into recession (–1 percent in 2008 and –5 percent in 2009). Modest growth returned in the second decade of the twenty-first century. However, Japan has remained a major player in the world economy and still has the second largest economy in the world, with a GDP of over five trillion dollars

Society. Japan remained a society in which people were members of the "mass middle class." At the same time, a social group known as the "new" middle class has emerged from this social group. This new middle class is considerably wealthier than the rest of the middle class. It has also been suggested that Japan is now a four class society: capitalists (9%), new middle class/upper middle class (22%), the old middle class (22%) and the working class (45%). Beneath this class system is a lower class of about 2 percent, comprised of burakumin, resident foreigners, new immigrants, the day laborers, and the unemployed. Once the most equal society in the world, in the twenty-first century, greater inequality has crept in. Today Japan's level of inequality is similar to that of European industrialized countries, such as Germany and France.

5. Family and Gender

Changes in family and gender relationships continued earlier trends.

Family. The declining birth rate meant that many families now had only one child and these children grew up much more self-centered and less family-oriented than children earlier. Recently, the family has been affected by so-called "parasite singles"—employed singles living with their parents. Almost half of all persons age 20–34 are in this category. Thus the trend toward later marriage has continued.

By 1999, the birthrate had declined to 1.3 per thousand, while the birth rate needed to maintain Japan's current population was 2.1. This meant that Japanese population had begun a gradual decline, as its aging accelerated. To promote a higher birth rate the government has increased child subsidies and offered tax incentives.

Within the family power conflicts have been muted and husband-wife relations have become more intimate and less formalized. However, relations are not perfect. That a "Law for the Prevention of Spousal Violence and the Protection of Victims" was passed in 2001 suggests that spousal and child abuse remain a problem. At the same time, divorce has become more common, doubling in the last fifteen years. The increase was especially pronounced in marriages that had lasted over 20 years, increasingly divorce is initiated by women whose husbands have recently retired. Child support laws remain largely unenforced.

Women's Roles. Women still dominate the household and have not responded to government encouragement to have more children. There are some indications that women are dissatisfied with participation in the workforce and are returning to the traditional role of mother. Women's economic power has weakened as businesses have sought to reduce costs by shifting to more non-regular, part-time workers, many of whom are females, especially young mothers. Wages for non-regular and part-time employees are substantially lower than for permanent employees. Equal opportunity employment legislation has been strengthened with the addition of a prohibition against discrimination in hiring and promotion and continuation of the provision for equal pay for equal work. Among permanent employees men's and women's wages are almost equal. In the business world, few women have moved into management. In Japan, 9 percent of managers are female, in the United States that number is 45 percent.

6. Community and Diversity

The community of the Japanese nation has remained the ideal, while minorities have appeared largely invisible.

Community. As in previous periods, Japan remained a very homogeneous society, with strong support for community. As Japanese nationalism has become increasingly powerful, pressure to ignore diversity has increased.

Diversity. As the number of Ainu has diminished and the burakumin have sought isolation from the Japanese, the problem of immigrants and long-term residents has attracted increasing public attention.

Ainu. While throughout the 1980s emphasis on Japan as a homogeneous nation seemed to suggest that there were no non-Japanese in Japan, the 1990s witnessed an effort to legislate a cultural revival for the Ainu. In 1997, the government enacted the Ainu Cultural Promotion Act, a first step toward encouraging a multicultural perspective. The official population of the Ainu is 24,000, with the Ainu located almost entirely on the island of Hokkaido. Support for Ainu cultural rights came largely from the Socialist Party, which temporarily formed a coalition with the LDP. One Ainu member of the Socialist Party was elected to the Japanese Upper House. The Act provided funding to preserve Ainu identity and to promote its culture. In addition, the Act abolished the 1899 law that had confined Ainu to reservations. Further, a plan to improve living conditions for Ainu on Hokkaido was introduced in 2002 and completed in 2008.

Non-citizens. The other key issue of diversity relates to long-term resident foreigners and newer immigrants, who together number about 2 million. These immigrants are less than 2 percent of the Japanese population, compared to 5 percent in Great Britain, 10 percent in Germany, and 12 percent in the United States. Though most of the "special permanent residents" are third- or fourth-generation Koreans, a new wave of immigration began in the 1990s. The largest group of these new immigrants is Japanese-Brazilians (250,000). Each year a very small number of permanent non-citizens (12–14,000) become citizens. Most of these new citizens are spouses of Japanese.

Japan thus seeks simultaneously to deal with diversity and pretend it does not exist.

CONCLUSION

The Japanese mastered reform while creating the illusion of stability. Relative isolation and a capacity to selectively adapt ideas from other civilizations characterized Japanese history.

Over many centuries immigration gradually formed the Japanese nation. Then in splendid isolation, the Japanese pushed the first inhabitants, the Ainu, northward, expanding north of the large northern island of Hokkaido, and conquering the Ryukyu Islands to the south. Trying to prevent outside influences from weakening Japanese attempts at internal unification led to the ejection of Christian missionaries and to conscious isolation. Western ideas seeped in and in the middle of the nineteenth century Western powers opened up Japan to Western trade and, more importantly, to Western ideas. Abandoning its isolationist policies, Japan emulated Western imperialism and began to build an Asian empire of its own. Korea and Manchuria became colonies, while Manchuria (northeast China) fell under Japanese influence. Japanese expansionism reached a peak during the Second World War when China and Southeast Asia were conquered. As a consequence of military defeat, Japanese power retreated to the traditional borders of Japan, dominated by the United States. Having abandoned military power, the Japanese had little ability to play a role in world politics. International trade created self-confidence and from the late 1970s Japan began to take small steps toward an independent foreign policy. The nation found it difficult to participate on the international stage.

The Japanese political structures represented a tension between centralized control and decentralization. In the Tokugawa period the shogun only gradually expanded the power of the central government. The ability of the daimyo to maintain some degree of independence made possible the Meiji Restoration, which destroyed the centralized political system. Very quickly, though, the new rulers established centralized government. They created a constitution that included provisions for elections that eventually had broad participation from the male population. Political parties emerged and by the 1920s principles of parliamentary rule had been established. However, during the 1930s Japan returned briefly to military dictatorship. Military defeat led to an American-imposed political system of representative parliamentary democracy, with some measure of decentralization. Until the late 1980s this democracy produced one-party rule by the Liberal Democrats and political instability thereafter.

For much of Japanese history a number of ideologies co-existed, largely complementary to each other. Buddhism, Shintoism, and Confucianism provided guidelines for behavior. When the Tokugawa came to power they espoused the military values of bushido and the acceptance of authoritarianism implicit in neo-Confucianism. Criticism of neo-Confucianism became louder and louder in the eighteenth century and fused with Western ideas to create a new ideology. This ideology emphasized the potential superiority of Japan based on traditional Japanese strengths and Western methods. Gradually the Japanese components became more and more important, culminating in the Japanese patriotism of the 1930s and the Second World War. De-nationalization and a return to Westernism responded to the terrible defeat in the war. Concern over the nature of Japaneseness emerged, though the ideas of Western capitalistic democracy dominated.

Japan possessed a relatively productive economy and fairly advanced business methods for much of its history. Gradual economic growth accelerated into rapid growth in the Meiji period and again in the first four decades after the Second World War. Japan moved from an autarkic agricultural-commercial economy in the Tokugawa period to an industrial-international trade-based economy from the Meiji period on. Until the Meiji era Japan had a rigid social structure that limited social mobility. Beginning with that period, rapid social mobility and fluid class lines dominated. Japan achieved relative economic equality, with increasing but very modest levels of inequality emerging from the 1980s on.

Japan remained a patriarchal society throughout its history. The Japanese saw the family as the country's most essential institution. The family had great power over its members. Women acquired some degree of cultural power in the twentieth century and the right to vote after the Second World War. Women exercised political power primarily at the local level through various citizens' action groups. Both a new constitution and laws guaranteed equal rights to women and provided some protection against discrimination.

Japan remained one of the most homogeneous large countries in the world. The minority population was quite small and generally discriminated against. Community was based on ethnic identity and loyalty to the Japanese nation. The Japanese made conscious efforts to maintain community. This sense of Japaneseness sometimes turned into a strong feeling of superiority over other nations.

Name: ______________________________ **Date:** ____________________

Chapter Three: Japan

IDENTIFICATION: IMPORTANT TERMS AND VOCABULARY

agrarian romantics (241)

Ainu (194)

Anglo-Japanese Alliance of 1902 (231)

bakufu (199)

Buddhism (195)

burakumin (204)

bushido (195)

Christian Socialism (228)

comfort women (247)

Confucian (197)

Constitutional Government Party (Seiyukai) (218)

Control Faction (242)

daimyo (195)

double-cropping (201)

Dutch learning (199)

economic miracle (255)

extraterritoriality (208)

Fukuzawa (210)

Greater East Asian Co-Prosperity Sphere (235)

horizontally integrated (244)

ie (198)

Name: ______________________________ **Date:** ____________________

oligarchs (215)

peers (216)

popular rights movement (215)

pork barrel (258)

primogeniture (254)

priority production system (253)

proportional representation (240)

proto-industrialization (199)

putting out system (202)

reverse course (251)

Rice Riots (245)

samurai (195)

SCAP (Supreme Command of the Allies in the Pacific) (249)

seisho (220)

Shibusawa (220)

Shinto (195)

shogun (199)

silk reeling (220)

sunrise firms (260)

sunset industries (260)

thought control (238)

Tojo (236)

Tokugawa Ieyasu (199)

Tokyo War Crime Trials (249)

Twenty-One Demands (232)

Name: ______________________________ Date: ____________________

Chapter Three: Japan

KEY QUESTIONS

Late Feudal Japan, to 1600 C.E.: How did warfare affect Japan before unification (before 1600)?

Tokugawa Japan, 1603–1867: Why did "native learning" emerge as an alternative to Confucianism?

Meiji Era, 1868–1912: What enabled Japan to maintain its independence from Western power?

From Peace to War, 1914–1945: What brought the military to power in Japan in the 1930s?

"Americanization" of Japan—the Occupation, 1945–1950: Why were the Americans able to dramatically change Japan right after the Second World War?

Mature Japan, 1950–1988: What factors produced the Japanese "economic miracle" in the 1950s and 1960s?

Japan Challenged, 1988–Present: What foreign policy aims did Japan seek to achieve in this period?

Chapter Four

CHINA

INTRODUCTION

A GREAT CIVILIZATION (MID-MING TO MID-CHING), 1400–1800

NINETEENTH CENTURY CHALLENGES

REVOLUTION AND ANARCHY, 1911–1949

CHINESE STALINISM, 1949–1957

AGE OF MAOIST RADICALISM, 1956–1976

FOUR MODERNIZATIONS, 1980–1989

CONTEMPORARY CHINA, 1990–PRESENT

CONCLUSION

INTRODUCTION

China's "long march" to the future has passed beyond the Great Wall of isolation from the rest of the world, through remote and backward peasant regions to port cities open to the West and Western ideas. For centuries China saw itself as the center of the universe, self-sufficient and superior. This idea gained greater significance in the rule of the *Ming* (Brilliant) dynasty, which replaced foreign Mongol rule. Yet in the first half of the seventeenth century, a new group of invaders, the *Manchu* (*Qing Dynasty*), seized the Chinese throne, which they held until the Revolution of 1911. During the two and a half centuries of Qing rule, China moved from being the most powerful and wealthiest country in the world, ruled by a very effective government, to a nation devastated by domestic rebellion and foreign pressure. Generations passed before a measure of stability and independence returned to China, in the garb of Chinese Communism. The Chinese Communists sought to create a radically different and brilliant future but ultimately had to accept a state capitalist economy in order to remain in power. Today China has become a relatively successful economic and regional power.

Throughout an authoritarian government, China's rulers administered a vast geographical expanse. Rich soil and abundant natural resources fostered a large population and created a relatively wealthy and very powerful country. For many centuries, China had been an agrarian nation in which interregional and local trade was extremely important. China has remained a peasant country, though the shift away from Communist economics has encouraged industrial activity, especially light industry, consumer spending, and international trade. Until the Communists came to power, China had a rigid social system, with a well-educated *gentry* (upper) class, a middle group (the peasants), and a relatively well-off lower class (the merchants). When the Communists came to power, social leveling occurred and the gentry and merchant classes were destroyed, leaving everyone in the lower class. Over time a small number of Communist Party officials assumed an elite status (see Chapter One for parallel developments in the Soviet Union).

The family remained patriarchal until the Communists came to power. Males dominated and females were subordinate, justified by Confucian ideas that certain groups were superior to others. The Communists tried to destroy the patriarchal family, viewing it as a conservative bastion of opposition to Communists. They also supported women's rights as a strategy for enhancing their power.

The Chinese saw themselves as having a single culture, with ethnic and dialect differences relatively unimportant. They were very successful in assimilating outsiders to the dominant Chinese culture. Yet in the nineteenth century, ethnic difference increased, acting as a major barrier to community building. The Communist solution was loyalty to Communism, which was to override class, cultural, and ethnic differences. However, minorities were not assimilated, and a new social division, between loyalists and the disloyal, was created.

This tragic history—of a great civilization falling apart, then trying to restore its glory through radical change—is the subject of this chapter, which begins in the middle of the Ming dynasty.

A. A GREAT CIVILIZATION (MID-MING TO MID-CHING), 1400–1800

In this period China had a "brilliant" civilization. Seeing itself as the center of the universe—the *Middle Kingdom*—China had begun to withdraw from the rest of the world. After a century or so of authoritarian Mongol rule, which had brought considerable bureaucratic efficiency and Muslim administrators to China, political rule turned milder. Provincial administration, based on the Mongol model, gave the central government the ability to project its power throughout the country. Confucianism returned as the dominant ideology, pushing aside the multiculturalism of the Mongol age. Confucianism became increasingly rigid, focusing on required conformity rather than thoughtful pursuit of ethical behavior, the original ideal of Confucius. Economic changes occurred, too, as the Ming and Qing emphasized agriculture and agricultural development, rather than commerce, which had become extremely important under the Mongols. The class system changed little, with a gentry elite (eventually infused with the Manchu unable to maintain their apartness) at the top, the peasantry in the middle and the merchantry at the bottom. Confucian ideals demanded domination by the patriarchal family and the subordination of women. In general, conditions for women had worsened from about 1,000 C.E. on. Chineseness replaced the Mongols' stress on diversity. Definitions of Chineseness remained cultural. Increasing isolation characterized the Ming and the early Qing.

1. Place: China the Central Kingdom

In reaction to the Mongol conquest, the Chinese reaffirmed their superiority. China demonstrated this self-sufficiency in the early Ming period when it abandoned ocean-going trade/tribute expeditions. Led by the Muslim admiral, Zheng He, Chinese ships had sailed throughout Southeast Asia and reached the east coast of Africa. China then established *tributary states,* which recognized its superiority and sent tribute or gifts. However, in the 1430s the Chinese abandoned the sea voyages and turned insular. China especially focused on threats in the north.

The North. Symbolically, the emperor moved his capital from southern China to Beijing in the north. China was unable to destroy the Mongol threat, especially the early fifteenth century inroads of Timur the Lame (Tamerlane). A bit later, in 1474, the Chinese adopted a new strategy; they began to build the *Great Wall.* The Manchu invasion of the first half of the seventeenth century turned China's attention to the northeast, adding a valuable agricultural area. The Manchu were supporters of expansion into Central Asia but their energies were turned toward the consolidation of power in China.

Russian expansion in the Northwest was the first foreign policy challenge the Manchu faced. However, the Treaty of Nerchinsk of 1689 (see Chapter One) halted Russia's attempts to extend their political control into Chinese lands. Trade continued, though, as Russia's preoccupation with becoming part of Europe took precedence over the push to the East.

Expansion. Having halted the Russian advance, the Manchu began to expand in that area, taking Outer Mongolia in 1728, Xinjiang in 1759, and Tibet in 1792. The Qing acquired territory in the south, capturing *Miao* (*Hmong*) lands in a twenty-year period of conquest in the late eighteenth century, Taiwan in 1787, and Burma and Annam in Southeast Asia late in the eighteenth century. China doubled in size through these successful efforts at military expansion.

The Europeans. The mid-fifteenth century Ming decision to completely abandon interest in the sea could not be sustained as Europeans tried to establish control over ports as a vehicle for trade with China. The Portuguese, Spanish, and Dutch took the lead in the China trade in the sixteenth and seventeenth centuries. Portugal established the first port/colony on Chinese soil—Macao in 1557. By the early seventeenth century foreigners had gained control over a half dozen ports.

Influenced by these European efforts in the eighteenth century, the Qing began to engage in maritime trade. Chinese ships traded in Korea, Japan, Manchuria, the Ryukyus, and Taiwan. The Chinese also reestablished overland commercial ties with the West, primarily providing tea and silk as trade goods.

At the end of the eighteenth century, China demonstrated its splendid isolation, when it rejected overtures from the British King George III, whose diplomats, through the *Macartney Mission,* asked for recognition and trade opportunities. The Chinese rejected the British request but the persistent British would not take no for an answer.

Consequences of Isolation. China's self-isolation and lack of powerful neighbors with glorious cultures produced a country increasingly incapable of dealing with great challenges. Relative isolation separated China from Muslim science and mathematics as well as the Renaissance, Reformation, and Enlightenment of the West. Forced to abandon isolation in the early decades of the nineteenth century, the Chinese could not defend themselves against Western power, though they sheltered themselves from it as much as possible. In its isolation, China remained a well-administered empire.

2. Power: Imperial Bureaucracy and the Civil Service System

High-quality governance resulted from the longevity and dedication of emperors and from a civil service system that identified the most talented men in Chinese society. Confucian scholars developed the concept of a *dynastic cycle,* which described the rise and fall of dynasties. Initially a dynasty was filled with virtue and society prospered, morally, and materially. After this initial period of virtue, gradual decline set in. As rulers abandoned their virtuous ways, Heaven intervened, warning the ruler through natural disasters. However, emperors ignored such warnings. Rebellion then broke out and the victors, possessing the new *Mandate of Heaven,* assumed power with the support of the gods. We see this dynastic cycle at play during the Ming and Qing periods.

"Ming Absolutism." After a century of Mongol rule, the Ming sought to restore the power of the emperor and the central political institutions that had existed in the pre-Mongol period. They also built upon the much more effective administration the Mongols had introduced, especially at the provincial level. In addition, a number of Mongols remained in service to the Ming government.

At the center of the Ming system was the reintroduction of the civil service examination system. Individuals studied the Chinese classics of literature, philosophy, and history and then sat for examinations at the local, provincial, and court levels. The examinations were extremely difficult, testing detailed understanding of the classics and emphasizing style and calligraphy. Taking the exam for the first time in their late twenties or early thirties, some men (women were not eligible to participate) passed the exam at the local level, then could take the provincial exam, which only a small proportion passed. The few who passed the provincial examination then took an examination administered by the emperor himself. Those who passed the central exam became officials at the central government, those who passed the provincial exam were eligible for provincial offices, and those who passed the local exam were eligible for local government positions. The system was intended to identify for government service the most talented individuals. It also created a means of preserving a unified culture based on the Chinese classics.

Under the Ming, the emperor supervised the bureaucracy directly, having eliminated the office of chief minister. The Ming reestablished a centralized bureaucracy, with six central ministries—finance, personnel, ritual, law, military affairs, and public affairs. The system was hierarchical with provincial governors reporting to the central government. Prefects, the administrators of large cities, reported to provincial governors, and county magistrates reported to the prefects. Policemen, couriers, militiamen, and most importantly, tax collectors assisted each county magistrate. To ensure that officials carried out their duties in a responsible manner, *censors,* the personal spies of the emperor, checked up on officials at all levels of government. Punishment of those who challenged the emperor's power was in the hands of a special group known as the Embroidered Guard.

The Manchu Victory. Though Ming government was initially quite successful, rebellion and ineffective government later undermined the dynasty.

At one point, the *Jurchens* had ruled much of north China. Defeated by the Mongols, they were pushed into what is today Manchuria. Under Nurhachi, the Jurchens consolidated their power in Manchuria and put pressure on the Chinese frontier. However in 1626 the Ming defeated Nurhachi.

The Ming breathing space was quite brief. One of Nurhachi's sons, Hong Taiji, assumed power and incorporated a number of elements of Chinese culture into his regime. In 1636, Hong announced the creation of a new dynasty, the *Qing* (pure) and changed the name of his people to the *Manchu,* a word derived from Buddhism that meant "great good fortune."

In 1644, as rebellion and civil war broke out in China, battle between two Ming armies left the capital Beijing undefended. The regent for a Manchu boy emperor took advantage of the situation and led a Manchu army into the Chinese capital. By 1648, much of China had fallen to Manchu armies. Ming rebellions broke out intermittently, especially in 1652. Thereafter, consolidation of power became a central aim of the Manchu.

Early Qing Dynasty. The Qing followed two contradictory policies—continuation of many Chinese political institutions and preservation of Manchu separateness from the Chinese.

The Qing quickly reintroduced the civil service system and espoused *neo-Confucian* ideals of obedience to the ruler. They retained the basic structure of government, including the six-ministry system. Two co-presidents, one Manchu, and the other Chinese jointly presided over each ministry. Manchu held all of the top offices but Chinese controlled provincial and local government.

Three Qing emperors, *Kangxi* (1699–1722), *Yongzheng* (1722–1735), and *Qianlong* (1736–1799) dominated the eighteenth century. Continuity of rule was possible through these lengthy reigns. Kangxi devoted his energies to the consolidation of Manchu power. He made a distinction between the *inner court,* which supervised the *regiment* men and Manchu royalty and the *outer court,* the regular bureaucracy. Kangxi also developed the *palace memorial system,* a network of correspondence between the emperor and his provincial confidantes.

Yongzheng introduced a clear set of political objectives that included establishing the moral authority of the ruler, correcting the tax system, and improving the flow of intelligence from local areas and the provinces to the center. Yongzheng emulated Confucian ideals. He built upon a set of sixteen moral principles developed in the Kangxi period. Scholars were ordered to read these principles twice a month in each village.

To ensure that he had accurate information about what was happening in China, Yongzheng required that senior provincial officials report directly to him. He then relied upon a small group of advisers, the *inner grand secretaries.* Yongzheng also devoted much energy to revising the tax system. He operated under the Confucian idea that taxes should be low both to ensure the prosperity of the populace and to demonstrate the ruler's benevolence. The existing tax system had been unjust and graft-ridden.

Yongzheng introduced a system based on tax simplification and the elimination of fraud. A number of taxes were eliminated, leaving a *head tax* (tax on each person) and a land tax (15–20%) in place. Local tax collectors were to send all tax receipts to the provincial finance commissioner's office. Then provincial officials decided how the revenue was to be redistributed at the provincial and local levels. Thus during his brief reign, Yongzheng carried out political reform to enhance the power of the ruler, promote ethical behavior among the Chinese people, and create an equitable and honest system of tax collection.

Following two straight activist emperors, Qianlong adopted a much more hands off attitude. He, too, emphasized Confucian ethics and culture. Under his auspices the entire extant classics were republished as the *Four Treasuries* of Chinese wisdom. However, he gradually lost power. The Yongzheng tax system began to fall apart, corruption increased, political judgement became clouded, and Qianlong became dependent upon a favorite. The Chinese leadership failed to address emerging problems—especially the pressure on the land caused by rapid population increases. Confucian ideology could not preserve the glory and power of the Middle Kingdom.

3. Ideology: Confucianism and Religions

Confucianism survived the challenges of the alien religions of the Mongol period and, revitalized by the support of the Manchu, dominated the ideological scene. Christianity offered an alternative, as did Buddhism and Daoism. The latter two had, much earlier of course, been incorporated into the Chinese worldview.

Confucianism. Confucianism had a profound impact on two and a half millennia of Chinese history. It is hard to imagine any society more deeply influenced by a single set of ideas than China was by Confucianism.

Confucius and Early Confucianism. Confucius was a scholar and sometime bureaucrat active around 500 B.C.E., during the Zhou period. He responded to the increasing instability and turmoil associated with the collapse of strong central government and deepening social and political unrest. Students of his intellectual mentoring eventually wrote down his thoughts, collected as the *Analects.* Over time changes were introduced and even forged sections were added. Very broadly, a "final" version was created in the Han period (206 B.C.E.–220 C.E.)

Confucius developed a theory of *public ethics.* He sought to answer the question of how to maintain public as well as personal morality in an age of turmoil. He argued that ethical behavior was learned through relationships with others and would become automatic through the repetitive performance of ritual. Proper behavior was achieved through education and observation of the example of gentlemen's moral action.

He emphasized five basic human relationships: ruler-citizen, husband-wife, father-son, sibling-sibling and friend-friend. The first three (ruler-citizen, husband-wife, father-son) were vertical relationships in which the first had power over the second and the second was to obey the first. The last two (sibling-sibling and friend-friend) were relationships of relative equality and mutual respect.

It is important to understand that Confucianism was not a religion. Confucius focused on human relationships. Though he believed in deities and suggested that human beings should have a proper relationship with the gods, he emphasized that humans should not focus on trying to understand the heavens. Ethical behavior among human beings took precedence over *metaphysical* explanation.

Neo-Confucianism. Over time Confucianism changed, in response to historical developments of particular periods of history. *Neo-Confucianism* (New Confucianism) represented the most important modification of Confucianism. Confucianism changed in response to the appeal of Buddhism and Daoism, both of which had emotional and metaphysical levels. Both had become increasingly important in the Tang and Song periods (c. 700–1200 C.E.). Confucianism was broadened, especially in the work of the thirteenth century scholar Zhu Xi. He used two fundamental principles, *li* and *qi,* to explain the universe and humans' role in it. Li guided human behavior and explained the actions of heaven, or the gods. By following li, one would be assured of acting properly. Thus, for Neo-Confucianism an abstract concept facilitated ethical behavior, while from Confucius' perspective, human interaction enabled proper behavior. By the Qing period Neo-Confucianism had evolved into a doctrine that emphasized obedience to authority.

Early Qing Critiques of Neo-Confucianism. The Manchu conquest represented a disaster for many enthusiastic supporters of the Ming period. In the early decades of Qing rule a number of scholars criticized the intellectual developments of the Ming era. Ironically, their starting point was their rejection of foreign and non-Confucian rule and their desire for the restoration of a Chinese dynasty. This led them to try to identify internal developments that had so weakened China, from their perspective, that mere foreigners could conquer the country. They presented three main criticisms. Some scholars, such as Wang Fuzhi, condemned the idea that individual conscience determined ethical behavior. This led, they argued, to the destruction of national consensus on proper behavior, to lawlessness, and to moral decline. Others, such as Huang Zongxi, suggested the opposite, that over-centralization of the government had weakened the role of the scholar-bureaucrat. They proposed a reduction of the power of the central government, including the emperor, and a decentralization that would permit the moral power of the scholar-bureaucrat to act as an example of ethical behavior at the local level. Finally, others, such as Gu Yanwu, argued that Confucianism should abandon Neo-Confucian metaphysics and focus on morality.

Empiricism of the Eighteenth Century. In the eighteenth century scholars moved away from philosophical speculation and political theory, instead focusing on the discovery of facts, which they saw as the source of truth. The Chinese called this approach the *methodology of kaozheng*. Kaozheng began as a critique of the metaphysical speculation central to Neo-Confucianism. The methodologists argued that one should discover and analyze facts. The certainty, or truth, of facts would thus provide the basis for human action. They collected facts about geology, natural resources, history, and even Confucianism. Facts, not theory, thus became the basis for action. However, by the end of the century philosophical speculation had again returned to center stage, pushing aside methodology. Methodology was defeated at a time when Chinese leadership faced increasingly complicated and difficult practical problems. Many of these problems rose from the eighteenth century population explosion, which had implications for Chinese economic development.

4. Class: Economic Expansion, Class, and Protest

This period was one of relatively rapid economic growth, population increase, social differentiation, and social protests.

Economic Development. From the mid-Ming through the early Qing period China experienced substantial economic growth. Population explosion, improvements in agricultural productivity, and the flourishing of trade powered this growth.

The Ming Economy. At first the Ming economy shrank. The rebellions that drove the Mongols from power produced considerable property destruction. In addition, the country moved away from the Eurasian trade-oriented economy of the Mongol age. Maritime trade collapsed, too, as the Ming withdrew from ocean travel in the 1430s and a century later banned maritime trade.

Instead, the Ming devoted more attention to farming and especially the production of food, rather than commercial crops. This strategy produced modest economic growth. Important regional differences existed in farming. In north and northwest China hard grains, especially wheat and millet, were grown on small farms owned by individual peasant families. Some fruits, such as apples and pears, were grown as were soybeans and cotton. Life was harsh for North China peasants, who lived in a climate similar to the northern plains of the United States. Inadequate rainfall, soil erosion, and intermittent devastating flooding of the *Yellow River* heightened these difficulties.

In central China, the richest part of the country, wet rice cultivation and *double cropping* dominated. Climate permitted the growing of two crops per year on the same piece of land, thus increasing agricultural yields. Wet-rice farming required intensive labor. The silk industry was centered here, as was tea farming. Land was generally held by *lineage groups* (*clans*) and worked by tenant farmers rather than by individual families. In southeastern China the climate permitted triple cropping. In central and southeast China levels of income were higher and agricultural productivity per farmer much greater than in the north.

Increased productivity mainly came from more intensive cultivation of the land and secondarily from expanding the amount of land under cultivation, introduction of new crops, and improvements in agricultural technology.

Qing Economy. The economy changed dramatically under the Qing. In the early decades of Qing rule, the devastation caused by the Manchu invasion and rebellions against the Qing produced a devastating and lengthy economic depression. Banditry and an increase in civil disturbances, natural disasters, epidemics, and the breakdown of parts of the irrigation system added to the economic difficulties.

Economic recovery began in the late seventeenth century and lasted into the early nineteenth century. Once again, China became the wealthiest country in the world and along with England, India, and Japan had the highest economic growth rate. Several factors produced this long-lasting economic boom. Most important was a population explosion that continues almost unchecked even today. This population growth made possible the cultivation of lands that had gone out of use because of the seventeenth century population decline that may have been as high as 50 percent. Formerly marginal lands including the upland river valleys and southern Manchuria were planted, especially with new crops that did not require the rich soil needed for rice and tea. These strategies produced a 25 percent increase in land under cultivation. The population explosion also created many more consumers, thus stimulating craft production in a whole variety of areas, including cloth, glass, porcelain, brewing, and oil pressing. New crops were introduced and the area of cultivation of existing crops expanded. In the second half of the eighteenth century sweet potatoes, corn, and potatoes were introduced from the New World. Peanut plantings spread from southern to northern China. Early ripening forms of rice were introduced from Vietnam and gradually spread northward.

Interregional and maritime trade increased rapidly. Maritime trade with Southeast Asia revived, while Westerners began to carry Chinese products to Europe. More sophisticated banking and financial systems were introduced, facilitating the flow of goods. Finally, the Yongzheng tax reforms reduced the overall tax burden, leaving more money available for investment, as well as consumption.

Economic growth did not dramatically change the divisions between northern, southern, and southeastern farming. Changes in the social system were modest, too, while social unrest remained on a rather high level, at least intermittently.

Class and Protest. The Confucian model of society remained in place, giving China the illusion of stability. At the same time, periods of social or political protest erupted but were not sufficiently powerful to challenge the state or the elite.

Population. China's population grew very rapidly except for one sharp decline during the Ming and Qing periods. At the beginning of Ming rule, China's population was somewhere between 65 and 80 million. By the late Ming (1620) its population had more than doubled to approximately 150 million. The Manchu conquest, natural disasters, and epidemic disease produced a decline to approximately 100 million in 1681. Thereafter, population grew quickly, to 177 million in 1749, and to 301 million in 1790. Thus during the eighteenth century, China's population tripled. The population boom not only affected the economy, as suggested earlier, but also had an impact on class structure, social mobility, and protest.

Classes and Social Mobility. The Confucian model of class structure continued to dominate, especially in the Ming period. The gentry class emerged as the dominant social group. Since education played a central role in determining entrance into the gentry, some opportunities for mobility existed. The gentry class had a large measure of internal cohesiveness, in spite of regional differences. This cohesion, of course, was based on learning the Confucian classical tradition that included history, poetry, and philosophy. Confucius' *Analects* discussed the role of the "gentleman" (member of the gentry class) in providing moral leadership through ethical behavior for the rest of society. The gentry were held together by possession of government office or aspirations to hold such positions. Gentry status was determined by wealth, lineage (blood ties), education, and government post. Though much wealth was in land, a consequence of the expansion of the rural economy, silver, and luxury goods also formed an important part of a gentry family's "portfolio." The position of a gentry family was associated with the power of the lineage or clan to which it belonged. Ties of mutual support gave members of lineage groups increased power and influence. Of greatest importance was education that created opportunities to move into the government.

The nature and identity of the upper classes changed in the Qing period. The Ming gentry leaders lost most of their influence and political power when the Manchu came to power. The Manchu and the Chinese warlords who had formed part of the Manchu *banners* dominated government. The Manchu formed a new aristocracy, initially composed of foreigners who tried to retain their non-Chinese identity. If for the Chinese, the civil service examination system created opportunities for upward mobility, Manchu procedures established under Nurhachi provided for the gradual leveling of Manchu society. The Manchu aristocracy was divided into nine ranks. When the head of a family of a particular rank died, all members of the family moved down one rank. Thus, an aristocratic family might eventually become part of the commoners.

Peasants as the Middle Strata. Confucianism placed the peasants in the middle of society. Providing most of the labor for society, peasants produced the food and some other essential items for themselves and the rest of society. They thus played a worthwhile role in society. In reality, the peasants were at the bottom of society in economic terms and living conditions. In the Ming period, the reemphasis on agriculture led to some improvements in the status and living standards of the peasants. Economic factors and social situation were closely interrelated for peasants. Individual family smallholdings dominated in the north, while clan identity and tenant farming predominated in the south.

The Merchant Class and Urban Society. In spite of the de-emphasis on trade, merchants remained an important part of society, even if Confucianism placed them at the bottom. The boundary between merchants and artisans was blurred, for many artisans sold the goods they produced and thus were retail storekeepers.

Merchants became increasingly important in the Qing era, due to its economic growth. An urban intellectual culture flourished and more and more sons of merchants entered the bureaucracy—and thus the gentry class.

The Qing period also saw an increase in the size of the urban working class. Though mechanized factories would not appear for centuries, increasingly hand production was housed in large shops, rather than produced separately by individuals. These production facilities are generally called *manufactures.* From time to time those working in the same shops acted together to protest their treatment by shop owners. For example, in Suzhou, a major silk and cotton cloth production area in south China, workers struck in the 1720s, seeking higher wages, a hospital, an orphanage, and a meeting hall.

Beneath the workers, who were at the bottom of recognized urban society, were the "*mean people.*" This group included various kinds of social outcasts, including singers, "fallen people," beggars, hereditary servant groups, boatmen, oyster gatherers, pearl divers, and people who harvested hemp and indigo. In the years 1723–1731, Yongzheng issued a series of decrees that emancipated the mean people from their outcast status. However, in general, these decrees were ignored.

Protest. Protest was intermittent, geared either to specific events or a consequence of long existent injustices. Protest did not really threaten authority.

Two types of protest occurred in the Ming period, both a response to long-existing conditions. Unrest reached a peak toward the end of the Ming period. Urban protest was concentrated among workers in *manufacture* jobs, including porcelain and silk production. Rural protest broke out primarily among indentured servants, who sought their freedom, and tenant farmers, who refused to pay "unreasonable" rents. Protests were an indication of the inadequacies of living standards, unfair treatment of lower class people, and the weakening power of government. Rebellion weakened the Ming, making it easier for the Manchu to come to power in the mid-seventeenth century.

Protests against the Manchu victory occurred quite frequently through 1652 and then petered out. Opposition to the Manchu was strongest in the lower Yangzi River valley of central China, the wealthiest region of the country. Targets included landlords, who might be killed or their compounds destroyed; local officials, who were attacked by urban residents; and wealthy families who had mistreated their indentured servants or refused to grant them freedom at the appropriate time.

Millenarian movements and ethnic rebellion occurred in the eighteenth century. The most famous of the former were the *Wang Lun Uprising* of 1744 and the *White Lotus Rebellion* of 1799–1804. The Wang Lun rebels were linked to a Buddhist cult group, the White Lotus. They believed in the "Eternal

Venerable Mother"—a goddess that offered them invincibility. Peasants and persons from the large itinerant population formed the core support for the movement. The rebellion's goal was to destroy the Qing and replace it with a native Chinese dynasty. Imperial armies destroyed the Wang Lun rebels and their claims of invincibility. Claims of invincibility reemerged in the Boxer movement at the end of the nineteenth century (see section C.3). In 1799, the White Lotus Rebellion broke out, based on secret societies, the worship of the Eternal Mother and some of the same mystical elements as the Wang Lun Uprising.

In the 1780s two Muslim rebellions broke out in Gansu Province in Western China. Much of the population of this area espoused Islamic fundamentalism and most of the population was non-Chinese, both from a cultural and ethnic perspective. In the same era, *Miao (Hmong)* tribesmen in southwestern China rebelled.

5. Patriarchal Family

The patriarchal family dominated throughout society, lending some degree of stability to a changing country. The Chinese tended to idealize the family and reinforce its role through ancestor worship, whose goal was to keep ancestors from suffering in the afterworld and to secure their assistance in this world.

The Family. In southern China the family was embedded in the clan or lineage group. In northern China clan structures were much looser. Clans provided some degree of mutual security and mutual assistance for individual families in difficult times. Children frequently were hired out to work on clan holdings rather than for the individual family.

Marriages were arranged, with the wife moving in with her husband's family. Families were thus extended (several generations living together). Late marriage was common, especially in the peasantry. Women generally married in their late twenties, thus shortening the childbearing period.

The patriarch was extremely powerful, controlling the family in an authoritarian manner. The grandmother was the matriarch of the family. She possessed some economic power and generally sought to ameliorate the authoritarianism of her husband. Sons' wives were powerless unless they eventually became the matriarch, the wife of the senior male in the family.

Children were especially important to the family, in part because of the high death rate. Every family wanted to assure itself that there would be a surviving male son to conduct ancestor worship rituals after the grandfather died. One-third of all males died before their first birthday, while overall life expectancy was approximately thirty for peasants and no more than fifty for members of the gentry. Property was divided equally among all sons, producing smaller and smaller and less and less economically viable plots of land.

Education was an important function of the family, with fathers deeply involved in their sons' education. The Chinese increasingly emphasized the education of gentry daughters, especially focusing on the arts. In the eighteenth century some women became poets. However the shift to kaozheng scholarship (see section 3 above) required many years of dedicated endeavor, precluding almost all women from becoming scholars. Women were not permitted to sit for the civil service examination.

Sexual behavior was generally unregulated. Most wealthy men had one or more secondary wives, or *concubines.* Adultery and the rape of servants were quite common, while homosexual relationships were found both in the home and at the schools. Passion and jealousy, added to anger and abuse, especially child abuse, meant that Chinese families were quite far from the Confucian ideal of peaceful, rational behavior. Aware of the distance between reality and the ideal, the Chinese tried to develop ways of minimizing conflict within the family and of promoting solidarity.

Gender. Women had limited power. This was symbolized by the continuation of *footbinding,* especially among the Han (ethnic) Chinese. Minority and outcast groups did not do footbinding. The Chinese believed that small feet were a sign of feminine beauty. Therefore young girls would have their feet bound so tightly that bones could not grow. Mothers imposed this excruciatingly painful process upon their own daughters, even as they remembered their own suffering. At the same time, women from the elite secured educations and expanded their influence. Increasingly male attitudes toward women were criticized. For example, widow suicide was widely condemned.

6. Community and Diversity

China retained some difference in the Ming period and became increasingly diverse in the Qing dynasty, largely as a consequence of the Manchu triumph and the increased importance of ethnic identity.

Community. The Mongol conquest had reunited north and south China into a single political system, providing the basis for community, a major goal of the Ming. In spite of intellectual disputes among scholars, Confucian ideology and a common educational system provided a strong basis for unity among the educated classes. A common emphasis on the ideals of public ethics, family, effective government, and the prosperity of the people acted as a powerful basis for harmony. Finally, most of the population was Han Chinese, with a common nationality and common set of cultural values. Being Han Chinese was a powerful force for community among the Han.

Early Manchu rulers emphasized the unity of China, minimizing the differences between the Han and Manchu. Continuity thus confirmed the historical unity of China, now under foreign, Manchu rule.

Diversity. Diversity was based on ethnic and religious differences. Sometimes ethnic and religious identities were fused, sometimes not.

Ethnic-Identity. The Mongol conquest had brought in large numbers of Mongol and Turkic peoples, most of them Muslim. They remained fairly distinct from the Chinese (the Han Chinese). When the Ming came to power they focused on Han Chineseness, seeking to eliminate all vestiges of Mongol rule and culture. Ming authors used isolation from outsiders as well as propaganda that emphasized Chinese Han unity to develop a sense of Chinese community.

Ming efforts were overturned by the Manchu conquest. The Manchu tried to preserve their own cultural and ethnic identity through conscious separation from the Chinese. Chinese were not permitted to live in Manchuria. Manchu were banned from engaging in trade or manual labor. Intermarriage between

Manchu and the Chinese was prohibited. The Manchu retained their own religion—shamanism—while Chinese were not permitted to enter shamanistic temples. The Manchu kept their own language and social structure, organized around the banners and an aristocratic ranking system. The Manchu confiscated 1 million acres, transferring it to banner men. They looked down on the Chinese and treated them with brutality. In the eighteenth century Manchu leaders became *Sinified* but the Han Chinese never forgot that their rulers had foreign roots.

Intermediate between the Manchu and the Han Chinese were the Chinese bannermen. Having served the Manchu as military leaders and bureaucrats for many decades before the Manchu conquered China, the Chinese bannermen represented an amalgam of both cultures. They spoke Manchu and Chinese and combined Manchu militarism and Confucian public ethics.

Religious Difference. China lacked religious unity as well, though religious difference had less impact than ethnic difference.

Most Chinese combined several forms of religious worship in a *syncretic* mixture. They fulfilled the responsibilities of ancestor worship associated with Confucianism. Most were influenced by Buddhism, which had become a powerful force in China from the Tang period on. Buddhism included a variety of sects that had little in common. Yongzheng, for example, was a proponent of *Chan* Buddhism (better known in the West as *Zen*). Chan Buddhism emphasized meditation and self-reflection as the proper ways to seek perfection. Chinese were also *Daoists.* Dao, *the way,* meant an emotional relationship with nature and a rejection of rationalism.

Christianity was added to this mix, primarily through the efforts of the Jesuits (see Chapter Three for Japanese attitudes toward Christianity at this time). In 1692, Emperor Kangxi issued a toleration decree, permitting the practice of Christianity. He argued that since Confucianism was not a religion, Chinese Christians should be permitted to continue ancestor worship, which derived from Confucianism. However, in the early eighteenth century the Papacy prohibited Chinese Christians from engaging in ancestor worship. Kangxi ordered Jesuits and other Catholics to sign a statement indicating agreement with his perspective. He expelled Jesuits and others who refused to sign the statement. Though he did not ban Christianity, he halted its expansion—at least until the nineteenth century. Yongzheng did not ban Christianity either. However, he condemned it as a political faction that threatened Chinese harmony. Jesuit influence at court diminished, limited to a few areas of science. Christianity was thus seen as a potential political threat, just as Buddhism had been in the Tang period.

The Jesuits. As the counter-reformation raged in Europe, Jesuits began to appear in China in the first half of the seventeenth century. Though their goal was to convert the Chinese to Catholicism, most of their energies were diverted to providing technical skills to the Ming, including advice on the construction of cannon. The Jesuits were a conduit through which Western science and mathematics flowed to China. After Jesuit doctors successfully treated emperor Kangxi for malaria, he issued an Edict of Toleration.

However, the Papacy rejected Jesuit ideas for incorporating traditional Chinese religious beliefs, especially ancestor worship, into their Catholicism. By the mid-eighteenth century the popes banned "Chinese" Christianity. In response, the Chinese government banned Christian missionary work in China.

Conclusion. In the eighteenth century it became clear that efforts to create unity and harmony in China had not been entirely successful. China was neither as cohesive nor as homogeneous as Chinese leaders wished.

B. NINETEENTH CENTURY CHALLENGES

Few could have predicted that the glorious China of the Ming and early Qing periods would soon face tremendous challenges it had little ability to overcome. China faced both domestic unrest and foreign pressure and was unable to deal effectively with either. Confucianism faced its greatest challenge in two millennia—from Westernism and modernization. Social discontent, too, almost destroyed the Qing. The population explosion no longer acted as an economic stimulant; instead it dragged down the economy. The patriarchal family remained unchanged until near the end of the Qing dynasty, though challenges to it came from the alternative ideologies of rebellious groups and some Westernization of Chinese youth. Unity was further undermined by the rise of nationalism among the ethnic minorities and the Han Chinese. The Qing first tried to restore the Chinese past, then to reform the country. Neither strategy prevented the death of imperial China in the early twentieth century.

1. China and the Western World

China's ability to assimilate outsiders to the superior Chinese civilization collapsed in the nineteenth century and its efforts to preserve its dominant role in Asia and its independence weakened under the *Qing*. China was forced to submit to Western powers, especially the British. Ultimately China suffered military defeat at the hands of the Japanese, who had learned much more from the West than China had.

The British. Rebuffed by the Chinese at the end of the eighteenth century, within decades the British imposed their will upon the country. British actions had a powerful impact on the direction of Chinese history in the nineteenth century.

The Opium Trade. The British were unhappy with the *cohong* system. Through this method the Chinese government authorized certain merchants, organized in an international trade guild, or cohong, to engage in commerce with foreigners. Each member contributed 10 percent of his profits to a special fund, dispersed in case of emergency. This international trade was limited to the port of Canton.

The British East India Company (BEIC) traded woolens and metal products for Chinese tea. Dramatic changes in British-Chinese relations came after the British Parliament ended the British East India Company's monopoly of trade in Asia in 1834 (see Chapter Two). This led to greater competition, sharpened desire for access to additional Chinese ports, pressure to greatly increase opium exports, and the smuggling of opium into China. In 1835, the British sold 30,000 chests of opium to the cohong, in 1838 they sold 40,000.

Emperor *Daoguang* (ruled 1821–1850) recognized the consequences of the opium trade, both in terms of the drain on Chinese silver and moral issues facing the Chinese. Authorities considered two alternatives—legalization and prohibition. Daoguang chose the prohibition option and sent *Lin Zexu* to Canton to end the opium trade. Lin developed a comprehensive strategy that focused on the consumers, the small-scale dealers and the importers. He combined Confucian moral exhortation and force. Opium smokers, known as "opium eaters," were ordered to turn in their opium and their pipes. To ensure the success of this campaign, Lin organized peer pressure among numerous groups in southern China, whose responsibility was to identify opium users to the government. This plan worked. By the summer of 1839 the Chinese had surrendered over 70,000 pipes and 50,000 pounds of opium. In addition, drug dealers were arrested.

However, the international importers still had the ability to sell their goods in China. Lin ordered foreigners to turn over their opium supplies, without compensation. When the Western traders ignored his demands, Lin used the Chinese navy to blockade the foreigners' vessels. After six weeks, the Westerners surrendered 20,000 chests of opium. Lin Zexu destroyed the 3 million pounds of raw opium collected from users, dealers, and importers.

Next British opium traders lobbied Parliament, seeking compensation for their losses, punishment of the Chinese, and the reopening of the opium trade. Though Parliament did not declare war, it decided to send a naval fleet, as well as soldiers from India, to China. The British refused to halt the opium trade and withdrew to the island of *Hong Kong.*

The Opium War (1839–1842). This so-called war began with armed clashes in Canton harbor in 1839 and attacks by the Chinese population against the British commercial community. In the summer of 1840 the British blockaded Canton harbor then moved up the coast and set up a blockade on the lower Yangzi River delta. Next the British threatened Tianjin, a major port in north China. British representatives and local Chinese officials negotiated a treaty but both the British Prime Minister and the Chinese Emperor rejected it.

Conflict returned in 1841 as the gentry mobilized militia and peasants to attack the British in the Canton area. The British destroyed the Chinese forts in Canton Bay, invaded the city, and withdrew only after receiving a large "ransom." That autumn the British seized several major ports in central China and in the summer of 1842 they captured Shanghai. The British were now in a position to cut the country in half, blocking traffic on the Grand Canal and the lower Yangzi. When the British attacked the southern capital, Nanjing, the Chinese agreed to peace negotiations.

The British easily defeated the Chinese, largely because of naval superiority. The British wisely did not send forces inland, where logistical problems and numerical disadvantage would have hampered their efforts.

The Treaty of Nanjing and Other Chinese Diplomatic Defeats. The *Treaty of Nanjing* was the first of several treaties that opened up China to greater and greater Western presence and influence. China had little choice but to acquiesce to Western power, thus accepting the reduction of its sovereignty. Yet this treaty conflicted with the anti-foreign attitudes of most government officials and the gentry in southern China.

This treaty identified five Chinese ports that would be open to British trade, settlement, and diplomatic representation. Hong Kong was to belong to Great Britain forever. In addition, the cohong system was abolished. The British would have to pay tariffs only at the port of entry, not in interior China. China agreed to grant indemnities to the British equaling $21 million.

Ironically, the treaty that ended the Opium War did not mention the issue of opium.

The Americans soon forced China to come to terms, too. In 1844, the two countries signed the *Treaty of Wanghia.* Not only did the Americans receive the same rights of trade, settlement, and diplomatic representation as the British; the Americans also gained the right to establish churches in port cities. Finally, the Chinese accepted the principle of extraterritoriality. U.S. officials would use American law to try Americans accused of crimes in China, except for Americans trading in opium.

Though the unequal treaties were intended to open up China to Western commercial activity and to generate huge profits, Westerners earned only modest profits in China.

The treaties forced Chinese leaders to reappraise their foreign policy, which was based on the idea that China was the center of the world and all other states were inferior barbarians. Some officials concluded that the Westerners only wanted trade concessions and if the government continued to grant them, the Westerners would leave China alone. The loss of sovereignty, especially symbolized by extraterritoriality, seemed a minor issue. Other officials recognized that the treaties had raised the basic question of whether the Qing dynasty could survive the aggressive presence of the Westerners.

British-Chinese Tensions in the 1850s. Having secured major concessions from the Chinese in the 1840s, the British and other Western powers saw opportunities for even greater gains. The British used the illegal Chinese search of a British ship, the Arrow, to take the offensive. In December 1857, the British captured Canton and in the following year threatened the capital, Beijing. The Chinese gave in and signed the *Treaty of Tianjin.* This treaty identified ten additional ports, from Manchuria in the north to Hainan Island in the south, to be opened to British traders. The Chinese agreed on a tariff rate of 2.5 percent of the value of imports, with no transit fees. Opium importation was legalized, though only Chinese traders could sell it beyond the port cities. With a passport, the British were allowed to travel anywhere in the country, while missionary activity throughout China was legalized. Finally, the Chinese agreed to accept a British ambassador in the capital. This implied abandonment of traditional Chinese principles of diplomacy.

Conflict continued as Chinese mobs attacked British citizens. The British responded by assaulting Beijing, burning the summer palace, and forcing the Emperor to flee the capital. Additional concessions were made, including giving part of the Kowloon peninsula to Hong Kong for 99 years (until 1997).

Diplomatic Institutions. Forced to treat foreigners as equals and even superiors, the Chinese created institutions to formalize diplomatic relations. The government established a *Qing Imperial Maritime Customs Office,* with a British citizen, *Robert Hart,* in charge. The Customs Office worked with great efficiency and brought huge amounts of money into the Chinese treasury. The government also established the *Zongli Yamen,* or Foreign Affairs Office. Gradually the Chinese developed some degree of diplomatic skill in dealing with the Westerners.

Impact of Western Power. Western power undermined the Chinese treasury, at least temporarily, and weakened the economy, as silver was used to pay for opium. The Western presence challenged Chinese beliefs in their innate superiority over all other peoples. China was forced to deal with an external threat for the first time since the Manchu conquest. However, the Westerners did not wish to assume power in China. They saw China as a source of tremendous financial gain. Though it is difficult to see a direct correlation, many historians argue that the presence of Westerners, who were so different from the Chinese, created a measure of social dislocation and unrest in southern China. Certainly the gentry felt threatened by Western power and Christianity and urged the commoners to see the West as a force to be driven from China. Western power weakened the Chinese government, forcing it to ignore domestic problems, which exploded in a whole series of regime-threatening rebellions in the 1860s and 1870s. However, this regularization of relations with the West gave China a respite, until the appearance of the Japanese threat.

Japan and China. Japan began to build an Asian empire in the 1870s. In 1879, Japan annexed the Ryukyu Islands (see Chapter Three). China was not strong enough to defend its claims to the area. Increasingly the Chinese saw Japan as its main opponent. The Chinese government sought to ensure that Japan did not gain a dominant position in Korea, which China viewed as its tributary state.

However, conflict over Korea led to the *Sino-Japanese War* (1894–1895). Japan defeated the Chinese in both the southern and northern parts of Korea, and then crossed the Yalu River into Manchuria. The Japanese moved toward the Shanhaignan Pass, which led to Beijing. This threat, along with Japan's destruction of the Chinese navy in 1895, led the Chinese to sue for peace.

The *Treaty of Shimonoseiki* (1895) was a terrible defeat for China, which had always viewed Japan as inferior. Korea became a protectorate of Japan. China opened up four more treaty ports. Japan was guaranteed Taiwan, the Pescadores Islands, and the Liaodong area of southern Manchuria (Japan surrendered the latter under pressure from the Western powers), all claimed by China. Finally China paid an indemnity greater than the Japanese costs of prosecuting the war.

Scramble for China. Western powers renewed their interest in China at the end of the nineteenth century. The British acquired the rest of Kowloon, while France and Germany both occupied Chinese territory. American efforts to promote an *Open Door Policy* (equal economic rights for all Western power) may have slowed down the "slicing of the Chinese melon." However, China appeared vulnerable to partition by Western powers.

Boxer Rebellion, 1899–1901. Chinese defeat at the hands of the Japanese renewed Western interest in ensuring that the China trade prospered. It also promoted increased missionary activity. Finally, defeat combined with efforts at strengthening China through the Reforms of 1898. Reaction set in, manifested in "pure discussion"—vigilante attacks on the reformers, anti-missionary activity, and the Boxer Rebellion.

Boxers United in Righteousness formed in northern China in 1898. Influenced by the rituals of secret societies and the martial arts tradition, Boxers believed they were protected from Western power, including bullets. They attracted peasants and itinerant groups, who provided the muscle for their anti-Western acts. A number of women participated in the Boxers through separate women's organizations, such as Red Lanterns Shining and Cooking Pan Lanterns. The Boxers engaged in anti-Christian activity, including attacks on Chinese Christians and Western missionaries.

The Qing government, led by the *Dowager Empress Cixi,* hesitated at first. It could not decide whether to join the Westerners in opposition to the Boxers or to align with them. The Boxers, too, faced a dilemma. Originally they had sought to drive the Manchu from power but later they recognized that they needed military support from the government if they were to avoid defeat at the hands of Western military forces. Deciding to support the Boxers, Cixi declared war on the foreigners. However, the Qing armies ignored her and failed to provide military support for the Boxers.

By 1900, 20,000 foreign troops had arrived at Tianjin in northern China. Within ten days they captured the Chinese capital, forcing Cixi to flee to Xian, some 500 miles to the west. The Boxer movement was destroyed, while China was further weakened. Instead of greater independence from the West, China was now more completely subordinate to foreign powers.

In 1901, the Chinese signed the *Boxer Protocol.* The West humiliated China, requiring the Chinese to build a monument in honor of the 200 foreigners killed during the rebellion. China accepted a two-year ban on importing Western weapons. The Zongli Yamen became the Ministry of Foreign Affairs, completing the abandonment of traditional Chinese views of the world. The Chinese were to pay an indemnity equal to 333 million dollars, almost double the total Qing annual revenue. Finally, the government agreed to execute all Boxer leaders.

The Boxer Rebellion demonstrated growing nationalistic feeling among the Chinese. It followed the traditional pattern of rebellion but lacked the military power to stand up to the West. Western military power demonstrated how weak China was, provoking a final burst of reform that ended with the Revolution of 1911 that overthrew the Chinese Empire.

2. Imperial Weakness

During the nineteenth century China's political world became increasingly complex. In the first half of the century, authorities changed political institutions in response to pressure from the West. In the second half of the century, the dynasty tottered but survived. Political issues were framed by the question of what government should do to preserve and sustain the Qing dynasty and the Chinese Empire. In response to internal rebellion, the government embarked upon a *restoration program,* in many ways similar to that of the Meiji Restoration (see Chapter Three). During the last third of the nineteenth century, *self-strengthening* was the watchword, with much of it taking place through provincial-level initiatives. During the *One Hundred Days Reform,* the emperor championed change. Though he was pushed from power, within a few years the Qing dynasty, under the leadership of Cixi, introduced a number of reforms that led toward constitutionalism and electoral politics.

Tongzhi Restoration, 1861–1875. Primarily responding to domestic rebellions that almost drove the Qing from power, authorities embarked upon a program of restoration. These uprisings weakened the government, produced a shift of power toward the provinces, and caused tremendous destruction. The restoration was an effort to reestablish the kind of society China had been before rebellion and Western pressure. Some of the reforms were carried out by the central government, especially through the efforts of Prince Gong.

Provincial military leaders such as *Zeng* Guofan, *Li* Hongzhang, and *Zuyo* Zongtang sponsored others. Creation of the Zongli Yamen was one major reform. Tax systems were restructured. Efforts were also made to emphasize strict Confucian education.

Officials also devoted much energy to rural reconstruction. Irrigation systems and other waterways were rebuilt. As many as 20–30 million people died during the rebellions. Millions of refugees returned to their homes, while millions of émigrés were brought into eastern and central China, the main scenes of the rebellions. Chinese agriculture recovered very slowly for no efforts were made to promote agricultural modernization.

The Restoration also marked a shift of power to the local gentry. Civil service examination standards were loosened up, permitting many more persons to pass the exams and thus enter the gentry class. Even though many gentry did not secure government employment, they acquired a privileged position, including exemption from taxation and access to officials, ensuring that their concerns would be heard. The gentry created village defense organizations and also hired mercenaries to defend their lands and peasant villages from rebel forces.

Finally, the military was strengthened. Zeng Guofan created the Xiang army, well trained and loyal to him personally. Other regional military leaders did the same. Regional military leaders built arsenals, technical schools, and shipyards. Restoration enabled the Qing dynasty to last another half century but could not restore China to its previous brilliance.

Self-strengthening. A campaign of self-strengthening continued, based on the idea that one could preserve Chinese tradition through the selective adoption of Western technology and ideas. This required a modernization of the educational system. Self-strengthening had some support from Cixi, the aunt of the young emperor *Guangxu* (ruled 1875–1908). For Cixi, self-strengthening must not be at the expense of Manchu power.

Li Hongzhang was the most important advocate of self-strengthening. Li promoted industrial development. He championed study abroad for Chinese youth, especially through the *Hartford Plan.* During the 1870s over 100 Chinese students were sent to Hartford, Connecticut, where they received both Chinese and American educations. The program was cancelled when it became apparent that these Chinese graduates of an American high school would not be permitted to attend the U.S. military academies. After that, Li sent students to France, Germany, and Great Britain. Li also promoted military self-strengthening. Foreign military technology was important in the development of arsenals and ship building works. Such efforts had little broader impact on the economy as a whole. Built on the foundation of the restoration, self-strengthening preserved China but did little to strengthen it. More radical moves were needed.

Hundred Days' Reform (1898). By the late nineteenth century China had three options as it sought to develop enough strength to overcome domestic unrest, destroy Western power in China and achieve parity with Japan. It could continue the modest program of self-strengthening, gambling that quick action was unnecessary; implement dramatic reforms; or overthrow the reigning dynasty. Emperor *Guangxu* assumed power in 1898, determined to carry out dramatic reform that would quickly make his country independent of outside influences and capable of maintaining domestic order.

Guangxu was deeply influenced by three scholar-reformers, *Kang* Youwei, *Tan* Sitong, and *Li* Qichao. During the summer of 1898 Guangxu issued a number of decrees aimed at dramatic reform in five major areas. First, the emperor changed the examination system. He downgraded the significance of calligraphy and poetry, instead requiring questions on practical matters such as the current political situation in China. Second, since the exam was to be altered, education must change as well. Guangxu called for modern schools that included both Chinese and Western learning. He espoused vocational education in mining, industry, and railroads. He promoted the expansion of Chinese industry (import substitution) and encouraged increased production of tea and silk. Guangxu ordered the strengthening of the military, with a goal of building thirty-four modern warships and introducing Western military drill and training. Finally, he attempted to simplify the bureaucracy, eliminating superfluous offices.

The Emperor thought he had the support of Cixi, but she feared that his political restructuring would weaken the Manchu hold over the government and undermine her personal political power. She placed Guangxu under house arrest, announced that she would henceforth rule the country, and ordered the execution of leading reformers. Tan was executed but Kang and Liang fled China.

This effort to introduce major reforms quickly aroused a great deal of opposition, both from those who would lose power and from those who feared the Westernization of the country. However, after the defeat of the Boxer Rebellion and the Western capture of the capital city, Cixi turned to reform.

Constitutional Reform, 1905–1911. In 1901, after being forced to flee the capital during the Boxer Rebellion, Cixi issued a call for reform ideas. Reform followed two parallel tracks—provincial-led initiatives and central government-sponsored political change.

In the provinces *local self-government* was the key issue. Counties were quite large and the state found it difficult to ensure effective government at the county level and below. Provincial leaders proposed limited representative government at the local level, especially in the cities and towns. To some extent provincial leaders attempted to weaken the increasing power of the gentry. *Yuan Shikai,* general and governor, established an elected city council in Tianjin based on the recommendation of his "self-government bureau."

At the center Cixi moved toward revolutionary changes. She introduced educational reforms. She expanded the number of schools at all levels, emphasized practical and technical subjects and abolished the examination system. On the recommendation of a study group sent to Japan, the United States, and five European countries, in 1906 she promised to draw up a constitution, reform the bureaucracy, reduce the power of provincial governor-generals and hold a national assembly. In 1908, she announced that within nine years China would have a constitutional government based on electoral principles. Despite the deaths of Cixi and Guangxu in 1908, the momentum for reform continued. In 1909, elected provincial assemblies began to meet (as in Russia, the assemblies became a forum for criticism of the government—see Chapter One). Though they represented the elite, the delegates were elected. In 1910, Qing leaders agreed to call a provisional national assembly that year.

The move toward constitutional reform was diverted somewhat by the *railroad issue.* Until 1900 the Qing had been deeply opposed to railroad construction. Recognizing the need to move troops quickly from one place to another, the government changed its mind. By this time provincial authorities already had built a number of railroads. When the government tried to nationalize the rail lines, provincial leaders, especially the gentry, organized a strong campaign.

The military, too, strongly supported decentralization. Yuan Shikai dominated the *Beiyang Army,* the strongest army in China. This force was much stronger than the *New Army,* created by the central government.

As power *devolved* upon the provinces and that of the central government declined, more radical opposition began to appear. Just as in Russia, constitutional reform came too late to prevent the collapse of support for the monarchy (see Chapter One).

Revolution of 1911–1912. On the eve of the First World War the Qing dynasty fell from power, ending 4,000 years of imperial rule. Facing only weak opposition, the ruling elite could not maintain themselves in office. The collapse of the Qing was the final stage of the decentralization of power that had been occurring since the mid-nineteenth century. Revolutionary uprisings were localized, as well but spread across the country, driving the Manchu from power.

Opposition Groups. In the decade before the revolution, five main opposition groups or perspectives emerged. Kang Youwei represented the proponents of constitutional monarchy. His position gradually lost support, especially after the deaths of Cixi and Guangxu. Monarchy seemed increasingly superfluous.

Liang Qichao represented the nationalists. Opposed to revolution, he also felt that China was not ready for democracy. Instead, he argued, it needed a strong authoritarian leader who could weld together a unified Chinese nation.

Marxists lacked an organized movement in China but a number of intellectuals were influenced by the Russian Revolution of 1905 and had read some Marx. *The Communist Manifesto* was published in China in 1906.

Anarchists were more influential. They called for the elimination of all government and all economic authority. Influenced by Russian anarchism, they espoused revolutionary violence.

The *Revolutionary Alliance* of *Sun Yat-sen* was the most important opposition group. The Revolutionary Alliance combined a number of different factions of Chinese students in Japan. Sun called for the overthrow of the Qing and the creation of a republic. Only a republic, he believed, could successfully organize China's defense. He also argued that government must act to improve the living condition of the people. By the summer of 1911 it claimed 10,000 members, including students, soldiers, and representatives to the provincial assemblies.

Revolutions of 1911. The revolutions began in Wuhan in October 1911, a result of an accidental mix of factors. This prominence of accident, rather than conscious planning, paralleled the October Revolution in Russia (see Chapter One). The role of accident also demonstrated the weakness of the Qing dynasty. Radical youth had been infiltrating the army units stationed in Wuhan and claimed the support of 5,000–6,000 soldiers. Their goal was to turn the military against the Manchu and to use the troops to destroy the dynasty.

These youths accidentally detonated explosives while attempting to make bombs. When the police learned of the explosion they made plans to arrest the revolutionary leaders. To forestall this, the students organized a military mutiny against the authorities. When the governor fled, the revolutionaries appointed the commander of the local New Army as military governor. Within days the army mutinied in five other provinces. The military demanded a parliament, a constitution, an elected prime minister, and a Chinese (non-Manchu) cabinet.

In early November the newly elected national assembly chose Yuan Shikai as Prime Minister, a decision accepted by the emperor's camp. At the same time, province after province in southern and western China pledged loyalty to the Revolutionary Alliance. In December 1911, Manchu forces were driven from Nanjing in heavy fighting. In January 1912, Sun Yat-sen assumed the provisional presidency of a Chinese Republic. A month later the emperor abdicated, surrendering full power to Yuan Shikai.

The Qing dynasty fell quickly and easily, the victim of its own ineptitude, the unwillingness of the military to remain loyal, the rising tide of Chinese nationalism, and the fervor of China's youth. After almost 4,000 years, Chinese imperial power was destroyed, replaced by a fragile republican system. China soon disintegrated and a forty-year civil war ensued.

3. Confucianism and Its Challengers

During the nineteenth century, scholars sought to rework and revitalize Confucian ideals. They were challenged by Westernism, in the form of modernization and Christianity. This was a period without an ideological consensus.

Varieties of Confucianism. At the beginning of the nineteenth century Confucianism dominated Chinese thought. Especially in its Neo-Confucian guise, it stressed loyalty to the emperor who was expected to set a moral example for the people. Confucianism emphasized social harmony and order. Filial piety (respect for one's elders), the importance of agriculture, and a Spartan way of life were very important, too. However, Confucianism was not a monolithic system of thought. We can identify three main strains of Confucianism—practical learning or statecraft, moral philosophy, and empirical research based on the close study of texts (*kaosheng*). All traced their roots to the basic Confucian idea of virtue (*ren*). In the first half of the nineteenth century empirical research and statecraft became increasingly important, while moral philosophy played a secondary role. Along with this, a shift in "texts" occurred, which placed less emphasis on the classics and more on contemporary issues and non-Chinese ideas.

Confucian Critiques of Chinese Reality. For a number of thinkers the issue was how should Confucianism respond to a China facing increasingly serious problems? Confucian reformers identified China's problems and suggested that solutions could be found, in part, within the Confucian tradition. They frequently argued that Confucius was a reformer and that Confucianism was a reform doctrine, not one that reaffirmed and supported the status quo.

For example, early in the century Hong Liangji identified China's main problems as overpopulation, materialism, and corruption. He Changling and Wei Yuan collected a massive compendium of documents on Qing statecraft. The cumulative impact of these documents suggested that the Qing had been very successful rulers early on but now China faced a crisis. The Confucian formulation of the problem asked how to delay or halt the dynastic cycle of birth, growth, and collapse, since the Qing seemed to be in the latter stage. Some stressed that Confucian scholars should focus on practical issues of statecraft and economic leadership rather than engage in philosophical speculation of the Neo-Confucian type.

Gong Zizhen offered another answer in his analysis of the commentaries on the classic of Chinese history, *The Spring and Autumn Annals.* The approach of Gong, Wei Yuan, and others is known as the *New Text* method. Gong suggested that human history went through three ages—chaos, ascending peace, and universal peace. He criticized corruption, the examination system, inequality, foot binding, opium smoking, and trade with foreigners, seeing them as manifestations of the age of chaos. By resolving these and other problems, China could advance beyond the age of chaos to one of the stages of peace. Gong thus rejected the cyclical theory central to Chinese interpretations of their history for a linear model, similar to the idea of the inevitability of progress widely accepted in the West in the nineteenth century.

In the 1870s Wang Dao focused on the concepts of wealth and power, increasingly important in Confucian debate. In "On Reform," Wang, a journalist who had extensive contact with Westerners through living in Hong Kong for over two decades, predicted that within a century the Chinese would adopt all available Western technologies. Western ideas, though, would not replace Confucianism, which would remain at the heart of Chinese life. Within several centuries Confucianism would fuse with Western ideas in a broader harmony. He complained, "Alas! People all understand the past, but they are ignorant of the future" (parallel to the Japanese school of native learning). Wang recognized the dramatic and powerful impact of the West in forcing China to change. He also argued that Confucius was a proponent of change. Wang made specific suggestions, including eliminating the examination system, improving the military, modernizing education, and simplifying government. He also recognized that merely imitating Western technology, without implementing more profound changes, would leave China a weak country.

General and administrator *Zeng Guofan* sought to fuse the three main strands of Confucianism, moral philosophy, empirical analysis, and statecraft, though in practice he concentrated on statecraft. Zeng believed that one could combine practical self-strengthening with Confucian inner values to revitalize Chinese government and the economy. He called for renewed dedication to traditional Confucian learning, since its decline had produced spiritual collapse.

Feng Guifen expressed similar views, utilizing a comparative perspective. Feng argued that China must make selective use of Western ideas and technology. He called for changes in the educational system, including the introduction of the teaching of foreign languages, mathematics, and science. He wondered why Great Britain was small, yet strong and China large and weak. This comparative question—how could a country have an effective political system—led him to focus on Great Britain's efficient use of manpower, the agricultural revolution, close ties between the ruler and the subjects, and the nation's ability to propose and reach goals. Feng believed that China must first learn from the West and, by using Western knowledge, China could equal and surpass the West.

Late nineteenth century Western ideas attracted increasing support within China. Closely allied to Kang Youwei, Tan Sitong, and Liang Qichao, Tang Caichang introduced the ideas of Charles Darwin, Herbert Spencer, and Thomas Huxley to China. China must reform, he said, in order to survive in the struggle for existence. Yan Fu also promoted the ideas of *Social Darwinism.* Social Darwinism emphasized biological evolution, the struggle for survival, the constancy of progress, and White racial superiority. Western ideas were key weapons in China's struggle for existence, he argued. Yan took from Social Darwinism its emphasis on the existence of a universal pattern of evolution. He argued that China must change, if it was to survive Western pressure and internal turmoil. Only Western ideas could save China, he stressed, as he abandoned the idea that one could create a harmonious fusion of Confucianism and Western ideology.

Kang Youwei, the leading advocate of the Reforms of 1898 and one of the most radical of nineteenth century Chinese thinkers, argued in *A Study of Confucius as a Reformer* that Confucius was an advocate of political reform. Confucius had not recovered and transmitted ancient ways but had created a new ideology, Kang suggested. According to Kang, a proponent of New Text analysis, Confucius did not espouse the theory of dynastic cycles but proposed a system of linear development. Thus, Confucianism demanded reform.

In the nineteenth century a number of Confucian thinkers criticized Neo-Confucianism, argued that Confucius was a proponent of reform and change, and tried to synthesize Chinese and Western intellectual traditions. This latter effort represented one of the most far-reaching intellectual efforts of the modern world. However, it was extremely difficult to create a synthesis of two such different ideologies.

Christianity and the Missionaries. Western ideology also included Christianity. Christian missionary activity expanded substantially in the second half of the nineteenth century. This expansion was enabled by the unequal treaties between China and the Western powers. The treaties permitted missionaries to move freely around China. Missionaries represented Catholicism and a dozen Protestant sects. By 1900, approximately 500 Christian missionaries were operating in China. They came from a number of European countries plus the United States and Canada.

Christians attacked Confucian values and traditions and the gentry-dominated Confucian social structure. Missionaries created a different kind of educational system, one that was open to the poor and that emphasized Christianity and Western science and math. By 1900, missionaries had established some 2,000 schools. Missionaries translated a number of scientific and mathematical texts into Chinese. They also translated the Bible into Chinese and published a number of journals that provided the Chinese with a great deal of information about the Western world. Medical missionaries had great impact, as they healed the sick, reduced epidemic disease, and built 250 hospitals and clinics. Missionaries acted as agricultural extension agents, teaching Western agricultural practices to the Chinese. The missionaries, especially women, challenged traditional Chinese gender roles and offered an alternative model.

The missionaries sought to change China and thus challenged traditional ways of doing things and most importantly the idea that Confucianism was the highest form of ideological truth in the world. They thus raised the ire of many Chinese, including the gentry and peasants. As a result, anti-missionary protests, frequently incited by the gentry but carried out by peasants, increased dramatically by the end of the nineteenth century. The missionaries' challenge to traditionalism was at the heart of the turn of the century reaction that produced the Boxer rebellion.

Conclusion. The nineteenth century was an age of ideological debate and struggle. Intellectuals reached no new consensus, though the proponents of Western ideas and Confucianist reform clearly became more and more important. The debate continued through the next period of Chinese history. Intellectual conflict was matched by social change and conflict.

4. Poverty and Protest

In the first half of the century individuals and groups with ties to secret societies organized most protests. Population increases, poverty, gentry unemployment, ethnic conflict, Western pressure, the weakening of government because of factionalism, migration, and the decline in Manchu military power all contributed to a sharp rise in protest during the nineteenth century. Private and regional interests increasingly took precedence over public and central government concerns. Protests in the second half of the century threatened Qing power. Economic decline set in as silver flowed out of the country and government failed to maintain China's infrastructure, including the Grand Canal and the irrigation systems.

Secret Society Rebellion. Other insurrections followed the White Lotus Rebellion. One of the most important was the rebellion led by *Lin Qing* in 1813. Lin was influenced by a millenarian form of Buddhism and gradually built up support across impoverished rural parts of north China. He began to view himself as a charismatic leader, a future Buddha sent to lead the people of north China, who would soon face natural disasters. Lin argued that China could avoid or emerge successfully from such disasters by eliminating the Manchu emperor and replacing him with a Chinese Han ruler. When it came time for the group's planned attack on Emperor Jiaqing, Lin stayed at home and his followers were arrested. The executioner then sliced off Lin's head with a sharp sword.

In southern China *Triad* groups associated with the *Heaven and Earth Society* fomented rebellion. Initially sailors and criminals formed Triad groups, which later attracted peasants, both men and women. Triad groups had ties with gentry militia groups and martial arts organizations. They did not attack major cities but remained a constant irritant to authorities. The Triads, too, called for the overthrow of the Manchu and the restoration of the Ming to the Chinese throne. Anti-Qing feeling was stimulated by the inability of government officials to prevent foreigners from establishing a strong beachhead in the Canton area. Ethnic dimensions were present as well. The rebels retreated into mountainous areas inhabited by tribal groups, the *Yao* and *Zhuang.* In addition, farmers, known as the *Hakka* or *guest peoples,* who had moved from Jiangxi Province down into southeastern China, clashed with the local residents.

Taiping Rebellion. The greatest threat to the Manchu came from the *Taiping Rebellion* or Heavenly Kingdom of Great Peace Rebellion (1853–1864). The Taiping controlled large parts of southern China for over a decade and came close to overthrowing Qing rule.

Hong Xiuquan initiated the Taiping movement. Several times Hong failed to pass the civil service examination. The anxiety these occasions created and Christian missionary tracts eventually led Hong to believe that God had chosen him to drive the god-less Manchu from power and create heaven on earth in the form of a kingdom of equality and justice. Hong had a vision in which a golden-haired man called upon him to destroy the elder spirits, which he later identified as the Manchu. By the late 1840s Hong had joined a Society of God Worshipers. The movement quickly expanded in relatively remote areas beyond the government's reach.

The movement's appeal was based on a broad ideological platform. By outlining the Taiping's vision for China, we can understand what the rebels believed was wrong with the country. Hong called for the overthrow of the Manchu government and its replacement by a new "religious" leadership—a *theocracy.* Hong promoted gender equality. Civil service examinations were to be open to both men and women. Both men and women could hold office. The movement was puritanical, outlawing opium, alcohol, prostitution, foot binding, and dancing. Men and women were to live in separate barracks. This would abolish the hated patriarchal family. All economic goods, beyond what was needed for basic necessities were to be pooled and placed in a community warehouse, available to anyone who needed anything. The population was divided into groups of twenty-five families. The Taiping required military service of all men.

In spite of power conflicts among Hong and his chief lieutenants, the Taiping army captured a number of large cities in southern and central China and controlled the surrounding countryside. In 1853, the Taiping took Hankou, Wuhan, and Nanjing. They failed to capture Shanghai, in part because Western military forces supported the Qing. Finally in 1864 Qing troops recaptured Nanjing and the Taiping Rebellion collapsed.

More a militant military force than a government, the Taiping had only loose political control over the countryside. However, the rebellion had support from large numbers of peasants, the descendants of the "mean people," and minorities such as the Hakka.

The Taiping rebellion demonstrated the weaknesses of the central government's military forces and promoted the creation of gentry militias and regional military forces, thus contributing to decentralization. The rebellion pointed to causes of high levels of dissatisfaction with Manchu rule. Massive destruction and devastation accompanied the Taiping rebellion. It took China decades to recover from the economic losses produced by the rebellion. The Taiping was one of four major rebellions that challenged Qing power in the early years of the second half of the nineteenth century.

The Nian Rebellion. The *Nian Rebellion* occurred at about the same time as the Taiping. Unlike the Taiping, the Nian (*mobile rebels*) espoused no mystical religious ideology and had no clear goals. They had arisen as early as the 1790s northeast of the Huai River in central China and along the Chinese coast. The Nian had ties to the Triads and other secret societies and recruited to their ranks smugglers, thieves, and especially single peasant males. Female infanticide had left as many as 20 percent of the young males without an opportunity for marriage—and thus property ownership.

The Nian attacked salt merchants, seized peasant crops, and kidnapped wealthy landlords. Initially they were little more than criminal bands. After the Yellow River changed its course in 1855, causing widespread havoc, Zhang Luoxing emerged as Nian leader. The Nian then organized themselves into five armies and conducted guerilla activities near Beijing and Nanjing. Because the Nian operated close to the center of Qing power, the government sent large forces against them. The rebels held out in mountainous areas or retreated more quickly than the Qing armies could advance. Finally Li Hongzhang was assigned to defeat the Nian. After much fighting, in 1868 Li cornered the Nian in Shandong province and destroyed their armies and executed their leaders. Li's victory was made possible in part because of Western arms and the use of gunboats on the main waterways. The Nian rebellion illustrated the despair of the Chinese farmers, the devastating impact of rebellion, and the weakness of Qing military forces.

Muslim Rebellions. From 1855–1873, Muslim rebels fought the Qing in the province of Yunnan in the southwest and in Gansu and Shaanxi in the northwest. Muslims had first settled in China during the Tang period and came in larger numbers during Mongol rule. In the nineteenth century Muslim communities were scattered all over the western half of China, but especially in Yunnan and the Gansu-Shaanxi areas.

Insurrection broke out among Muslims in Shaanxi and Gansu in 1862. Chinese Muslims resented the discrimination they received at the hands of the Han. The government supported Han popular discrimination against the Muslims. These Muslims were influenced by the more emotional brand of Islam, Sufism, transported to China from Central Asia.

Ethnic tensions between the Muslims and the Chinese provoked conflict. A minor quarrel over the price of bamboo poles led to fighting and then to a Muslim insurrection. Qing soldiers in the area were Muslims and thus unreliable, while Qing authority was quite limited. The rebels took two large Shaanxi cities, Tongzhou and Xian. Later driven out of the two cities, the Muslim rebels retreated into Gansu province. Finally in 1868 Qing troops, led by Zuo Zongtang, defeated the Muslim rebels in the northwest. They refused to surrender, continuing to fight with desperation into 1871, holding the city of Suzhou until 1873.

In Yunnan Province the Qing government levied higher taxes on the Muslims than on the Chinese. The Muslims rebelled when the Chinese tried to forcibly take Muslim-owned gold mines. Rebels created a Kingdom of the Pacified South. Using divide and conquer tactics, the Qing captured the Muslim capital in 1873.

China was now quiet and could turn its attention once again to self-strengthening, reform and the Western threat.

5. Unchanging Family and Gender Roles

The nineteenth century saw few changes in the nature of the family and gender roles.

Family and Gender. Rebels, Confucian reformers, and missionaries all called for changes in the position of women. On a very modest scale a few gentry and middle class women began to receive western education, though they were not able to slip out of the grasp of the patriarchal family. Patriarchy; the extended family; mistreatment of women, especially daughters-in-law; and high levels of conflict within the family continued.

6. Community and Diversity

Community eluded China in the nineteenth century, as conflict based on difference increased substantially.

Weakening of Community; Rise of Diversity. Qing rule was weakened, preventing government from being the kind of unifying force it had been earlier. The examination system broke down when many individuals bought government offices, thus reducing the role of a common educational content and a sense of cultural unity. Disagreement among Confucian scholars also contributed to the disharmony.

Ethnic differences became increasingly important, while the definition of Chineseness based on acceptance of Chinese culture was disintegrating. The example of ethnic differences among the Westerners and Western racial hatred of the Chinese magnified the importance of ethnic conflict. Broadly, society was divided between the Manchu and the Han. Rebellion drove a wedge between the supporters of the Qing and their enemies, many of whom were Muslim and Turkic. Poverty and suffering among the masses had little impact on the gentry, which was increasingly isolated from this reality. Diversity and the violent expression of differences shattered the degree of community that had existed earlier.

C. REVOLUTION AND ANARCHY, 1911–1949

China disintegrated after the Revolutions of 1911. In place of centralized civilian government, warlords ruled bits and pieces of the country. Internal war devastated China and left the Chinese people worse off than they had been for many centuries. Civil war continued into the early 1930s, with the Nationalists emerging as nominal rulers of the country. Once in power, the Nationalists hesitantly sought to carry out reforms to modernize China and solve its staggering domestic problems. In general, reform efforts were unsuccessful. In this era of anarchy, dramatic social changes occurred. In the coastal cities, especially in educated families, women's position improved dramatically, while the patriarchal family began to weaken. Little remained of Confucian society to form a basis for community. Diversity and hatred flourished.

1. Occupied China

Western interest in China largely disappeared at the time of the First World War, only to revive later after the Japanese occupied much of the country. Especially from the 1920s on, China's main foreign policy challenge was how to preserve its independence from Japanese aggression.

China and the West. The West played a less activist role in China than at any time since the Opium War. The British were preoccupied with India and European affairs. The United States emerged from the First World War as the most powerful Western country with an interest in Asia. However, its main goal was to prevent Japan from becoming too influential. This objective led to the negotiations signed at the Washington Conference in 1921–1922 (see Chapter Three). In the 1920s, Russia supported the Nationalists and Communists, giving them organizational and military advice. In the late 1920s, the Western nations abandoned the unequal treaties signed with China in the 1850s. Germany provided military training and technology to the Nationalists in the 1930s. Insignificance, ironically, gave China more independence than it had had in many decades.

China and Japan. Japan replaced China as the most important Asian nation. For China, the Japan problem revived during the First World War (see Chapter Three). Throughout the 1920s the Japanese were much more conciliatory. Japan returned the Chinese territories and railways it had acquired during the First World War. It did not need to take a hard line since China was weakened by civil war.

Renewed Japanese activism came on the heels of the Nationalist victories that made them the nominal rulers of China. The Japanese intervened in Manchuria, killing the Manchurian warlord, *Zhang Zuolin* in 1928, when it appeared he would align with Chang Kai-shek, the Nationalist leader, rather than seek an independent Manchuria.

Again in 1931 the Japanese acted to maintain a presence in north China. The Mukden (Manchurian) Incident of September 1931 (see Chapter Three) led to the Japanese conquest of Manchuria, as the Chinese decided they were too weak to contest Japanese aggression. Japanese actions stimulated intense anti-Japanese feelings, especially in Shanghai where the population initiated boycotts of Japanese goods. Tension mounted, leading to a major battle between Chinese and Japanese troops in the Shanghai area in 1932. That same year the Japanese moved beyond Manchuria and took the north China province of Rehe. In 1933, the Japanese army pushed the Chinese back beyond the Great Wall, as far as Tianjin. The *Tanggu Truce* of 1933 required that the area north of Tianjin be a demilitarized zone, forcing Chinese troops even further south and leaving the Chinese capital virtually defenseless. Several quiet years then ensued as internal issues absorbed both China and Japan.

Second World War. The Second World War began with the Incident at Marco Polo Bridge (see Chapter Three) in July 1937. Within a month Japan had consolidated its hold over the Tianjin-Beijing area and was poised for the conquest of all of China.

The Conquest. Even though he recognized that China would have little success battling Japan in North China, Chiang Kai-shek concluded that he must resist Japanese advances. Thus, he decided to attack Japanese forces in central China, in the Shanghai area. In mid-August the Chinese airforce tried to bomb Japanese warships in the Shanghai port. Though the bombs missed their target, Japan immediately sent in substantial reinforcements. Fierce fighting lasted into mid-November, when the Chinese fell back to avoid encirclement. Japan now had a two front war, as it moved down from north China along the coast and pushed westward in central China. Nanjing, the traditional capital, which Chiang pledged to defend forever, fell in December. Nanjing first had been the scene of pillage and massacre by Chinese troops and then when the Japanese took the city, their soldiers raped at least 20,000 and murdered 40,000 soldiers and citizens. The *Rape of Nanjing* was the first of a series of inhumane acts of violence carried out by the Japanese military.

The Nationalists fled up the Yangzi River, with the Japanese in pursuit. In late summer the Chinese halted their retreat at the industrial tri-city of Wuhan. At the end of October, a ruined Wuhan surrendered to the Japanese. Canton was taken about the same time. Japan now controlled most of eastern China, especially the coastal areas and the major river valleys. Chiang Kai-shek retreated to the Sichuan Basin in southwest China, with his wartime capital at Chongqing (Chunking).

The Japanese Occupation. With the front line stabilized until another Japanese offensive in 1944 extended the area under their control, the Occupation lasted almost seven years. The Japanese controlled the eastern half of China, where much of the population, almost all of the industry and most of the best agricultural land was located. The Chinese controlled the western half, which except for the Sichuan Basin was barren and impoverished. The Japanese created puppet governments to administer Japanese China, while the Nationalists held the Southwest and the Communists the Northwest.

Rather than occupy China with a very large military force, the Japanese created several regional puppet governments, led by Chinese and controlled by Japanese military advisers. The Japanese had several goals, including pacification and exploitation of a region's natural resources. Japan established *development corporations* to coordinate economic activity and mobilize China's industrial and agricultural capacity to meet Japanese war needs. They made little effort to convince the Chinese to be cooperative.

Manchukuo (Manchuria) was the model. There, the last emperor, Pu-yi, was placed in power, though he was a mere figurehead, controlled by the Japanese army. Other regional "Chinese" governments were established in Mongolia, north China (with Beijing as its capital), central China, and the Japanese colony of Taiwan. Though there was some exodus from the coastal areas to "free China," most people remained in their homes, subject to Japanese brutality.

The Chongqing government of the Nationalists faced difficult problems. Most important was the military question of how to defend southwestern China from the Japanese. The romanticism associated with supplying the Chinese with assistance did much to promote sympathy for China among the peoples of the West. These efforts included the *Flying Tigers,* American pilots who volunteered to fly American-purchased planes for the Chinese; the supply of goods over the *Burma Road;* and, after it was interdicted by the Japanese, the supply flights from India over the *hump,* the Himalayan Mountains.

The Nationalists also tried to establish a civilian government in the southwest and destroy the power of local warlords who still remained fairly independent. The Nationalists carried out tax reform, built infrastructure, and campaigned against opium. Chiang gained the support of Yunnan by permitting its warlord, Long Yun, to remain fairly independent. Yunnan was important because it was located at the end of the Burma Road and was the site of airport facilities for supply flights from India. As one would expect, in wartime, the military played a dominant role in decision-making.

The Communists faced similar problems, with the added burden of occupying the most impoverished area of China. The Communists controlled two parts of northern China, with headquarters in the more remote area, Shaanxi Province. Thus the Communists had to focus more attention on ensuring an adequate food supply. They were somewhat more accessible to Japanese offensive moves and thus had a less secure location. Finally the Communists tried to enforce centralized leadership and complete loyalty to Communism, while the Nationalists remained a coalition of leaders and military forces.

Japanese forces had less solid control over parts of north China, thus permitting Communist guerilla actions. Guerilla campaigns, such as those of 1940 and 1941, backfired because the Japanese responded with the mass murder of civilians and the destruction of large numbers of Communist soldiers in battles. For example, in 1941, the Japanese conducted the inhumane "three alls" campaign—"kill all, burn all, destroy all." Japanese revenge weakened popular support for the Communists.

In the Communist capital *Yan'an,* Mao Zedong consolidated his power and the party built up support among the peasants in north China. To ensure loyalty to the Communist Party, Mao conducted a *Rectification Campaign* that purged those, especially intellectuals, who disagreed with his positions. The Communists also created a number of special interest groups, each of which focused on a specific part of the population, such as youth or women. The Communists introduced a program of modest land reform that cemented the loyalty of poorer peasants and maintained food production.

The Communists and Nationalists also positioned themselves for the future power struggle that would determine who would rule China after the war. The two camps sometimes spent more energy fighting each other than they did opposing the Japanese. In 1941, the two sides went to war with each other. When the Communists tried to move down into central China, the Nationalists rebuffed their efforts. The Nationalists also imposed an economic boycott that prevented supplies from reaching Communist-controlled territory in the northwest.

Chinese morale plummeted in 1942 and 1943. In 1944, the Japanese launched a final offensive that extended their power in north China, as they seized much of Hunan Province, and pushed within several hundred miles of the Nationalist capital in the south. Also, in 1944, the Americans began to bomb Japan itself. When the Nationalists and Communists concluded that the Americans would drive the Japanese from China, they both mobilized for the important fight—for control of post-war China. In August 1945, the Japanese surrendered, leaving China embroiled in another civil war.

2. The Politics of Anarchy

The struggle to succeed the Qing as rulers of China was first fought on the floor of Parliament, then among rival armies. *Warlords*—generals with private armies who controlled territory and aspired to rule all of China—sliced up China during the First World War. Gradually ideological parties, the Nationalists and Communists, emerged. By the late 1920s the Nationalists had beaten the Communists and coopted or defeated most warlords. Establishing their capital in Nanjing, the Nationalists responded to China's huge problems. However, the reform efforts of this *Nanjing Decade* met with little success. The Nationalists' main goal was to achieve the final destruction of Communism; reform was secondary.

China in 1912. The Revolution that destroyed Qing rule did not solve China's problems. Instead, the destruction of the remnants of centralized power made it more difficult for the nation to deal with issues it had not effectively addressed earlier. Obviously the most important immediate problem was to reestablish effective government. Serious economic problems remained, made worse by natural disasters. Refugees fled from areas of natural disasters, producing a decline in agricultural output. Chinese governments had always faced these kinds of problems and had handled them with varying degrees of success. However, in a period in which there was no recognized national authority, it was much harder to respond to natural disaster. At the same time, China was changing, though its pace of modernization was considerably slower than that of its neighbor, Japan (see Chapter Three for the Meiji modernization). Modern infrastructure and industrial methods were being introduced. Confucianism was being challenged in more profound ways than it had been for many centuries. Instead of proposing modification of Confucianism, the dominant approach in the second half of the nineteenth century, proponents of Westernism now challenged it directly. Efforts to respond to the political vacuum began as soon as the dynasty fell.

Republicanism or Dictatorship? Two major forces emerged out of the rubble of the Qing dynasty—the military might of *Yuan Shikai* and the political power of Sun Yat-sen's *Revolutionary Alliance.* The conflict between the two groups revolved around the issue of constitutional government. The dying Qing dynasty had called into session a National Assembly, which quickly drafted a constitution and selected Yuan Shikai as Prime Minister.

In January 1912, Sun Yat-sen held a meeting of a *National Council,* representing Revolutionary Alliance groups. The Council confirmed Yuan as provisional president and prepared a draft provisional constitution. This document proposed guarantees of civil rights and the calling of a bi-cameral parliament within a year. Once the Parliament convened the National Council was to dissolve itself and Yuan would resign, so that new presidential elections could take place. The Revolutionary Alliance then organized itself into a nation-wide political party, the *Guomindang* or *National People's Party* (generally known as the Nationalist Party) so that it could seek a commanding majority in the parliament.

Elections in 1912 gave victory to the Nationalists. In spring 1913, the political leader of the Nationalists, Song Jiaoren, was assassinated, reportedly on orders of Yuan Shikai. Yuan went on the offensive in 1913, dismissing pro-Nationalist military governors and local officials. In the summer his armies captured Nanjing, the center of Nationalist power. In the autumn he forced the Parliament to elect him to a five-year term, dissolved the Nationalist Party, and ejected its members from the Parliament. Dictatorship had triumphed over republican, representative government.

Dictatorship of Yuan Shikai. Yuan's rule was tragic, sad, and brief. Though he gained recognition from foreign powers, his efforts to maintain power in China collapsed. Maintaining the illusion of constitutionalism, Yuan called together a group of government officials, who prepared a *constitutional compact* that gave him almost total power. He could not finance his government, especially its military, and was forced to depend on foreign loans. Though an authoritarian and brutal ruler, Yuan tried to continue the late Qing reform agenda. He promoted public education that would include both the Confucian classics and modern subjects. He campaigned against opium smoking and worked to restore the damaged infrastructure, such as the irrigation system.

Yuan declare himself emperor in 1915. This act backfired, as key allies and supporters abandoned him. It was clear that few people in China supported monarchy. His power play had turned into a farce that ended with his sudden death in 1916. The death of Yuan was the death knell of centralized government. Military leaders seized power in various parts of the country, each acting independently, each seeking to acquire enough power to capture the former capital of Beijing and establish a new dynasty.

The Warlord Era. Thus the warlord era began. After the fall of the Qing, warlords dominated China for almost two decades. Warlords were military men who controlled specific territories and used military might to add to their holdings and dreamed of reuniting China under their leadership.

Brutal Warlords. Very broadly, we can identify two main types of warlords. Some warlords were brutal, only interested in acquiring power, using any means possible. They oppressed the civilian population with heavy taxes, requisitions of food and other goods, and the drafting of males into their armies. Such warlords frequently espoused Confucianism but actually represented the behavior that Confucius had condemned 2,500 years before. Among them was the "dog meat general," called that because he fed enemy soldiers to the packs of dogs that followed his army. Most of the conservative, brutal warlords were found in northern China.

Reformist Warlords. In the south and the west, some reformist warlords could be found. They, too, carried out Confucianist puritanical campaigns against opium smoking, cock fighting, swearing, spitting, drunkenness, and prostitution. But they also promoted education and economic modernization. Because the south was better off economically, these warlords could levy more reasonable tax rates. Since the population was greater, their induction of young men into the military had less impact on the villages. The "republican" warlords generally believed that it would be possible to institute republican government after order was restored but that the transitional period of authoritarian government might be quite lengthy.

Warlords controlled all of China for most of the 1920s, fighting among themselves, frequently shifting loyalties to maximize their relative power or preserve a measure of independence. Gradually the Nationalist Party, itself largely a warlord force, moved against other warlords, offering alliance or military conflict.

The Nationalists. During the 1920s the Nationalists possessed the single-most powerful military force in China. Its principal goal was to defeat its rivals and establish a nation-wide government. Its relationship with warlords was straightforward. It either secured alliances with particular generals or it sought to defeat them on the battlefield. Its other main foes were the Communists and the Japanese. The Nationalists moved from alliance with the Communists to determined efforts to destroy them. The Nationalists generally avoided battle with the Japanese or were defeated by them.

Surviving Warlords. In the early 1920s Sun Yat-sen emerged as military governor in Canton, his earlier flirtation with republicanism smashed by Yuan Shikai and his warlord successors. Sun turned abroad for support. In early 1923, Sun and a Soviet Communist emissary, Adolf *Joffe,* negotiated an alliance. Sun needed expertise in military and organizational matters if he was to compete with other warlords. Lenin had proposed that the Soviet Union support national liberation movements in countries that were not yet ready for a socialist revolution. In addition, the Soviets worried about Japan's power on the Asian mainland, especially because of its reluctance to leave the Soviet Far East after the Russian Civil War. The Soviets tried to develop ties with a number of factions in China, including the Nationalists. The Soviets also sought to dominate the small Chinese Communist Party.

In October 1923, Sun Yat-sen signed an agreement with another Soviet agent, Alexander *Borodin.* Borodin forced the Communists to accept an alliance with the Nationalists. The Soviets promised to provide military training for Nationalist officers and suggested the Soviet Communist Party structure as an organizational model. Chinese Communists were to join the Nationalist Party individually. While the Nationalists focused on military affairs, the Communists concentrated on mass action, especially working with youth, women, and labor organizations. This unholy alliance did not last long.

The Struggle With the Communists. Sun Yat-sen's death in 1925 led to a power struggle within the Nationalist Party and to a break between the Nationalists and the Communists. Sun's probable successor was murdered later that year and the right wing of the party, the Western Hills group, was blamed. At the same time, the left wing of the party, without Sun's moderating pressure, moved closer to the Communists. *Chiang Kai-shek* occupied the middle ground in the party. The Nationalists' military victories over warlords in the Canton area, made possible by Soviet military training, gave Chiang Kai-shek confidence that his military was strong enough to challenge and defeat the Communists.

Chiang's first clash with the Communists came in March 1926. Perhaps misjudging the intent of a Communist gunboat that appeared at the island of Whampoa, the location of the Nationalist military academy, Chiang placed Canton under martial law and briefly arrested several Communist leaders. Both Chiang and the Soviets wished to continue the alliance and sought to minimize the growing Nationalist-Communist estrangement. Borodin and Chiang agreed that no Chinese Communist would be permitted a leadership role in the Nationalist Party and that the Communists would not criticize Nationalist policies. Nationalists were not to join the Communist Party.

The political cease-fire lasted a year, broken by the *Shanghai Spring* of 1927. The Nationalists had begun what would become a victorious *Northern Expedition,* already gathering support from a number of powerful warlords. The alliance between the Communists and the left wing of the Nationalist Party was now threatened. Communist power seemed endangered. At the same time, Stalin was in the midst of a power struggle in the Soviet Union and needed to prove that his China policy was successful and not a basis for criticism (see Chapter One). Thus, Stalin ordered the Communists to continue to cooperate with the Nationalists.

In March 1927, Communist-led trade unions in Shanghai called a general strike, which attracted the support of 600,000 workers. By the end of the month, Nationalist armies had pushed into central China and entered Shanghai. Chiang decisively supported the Chinese and foreign business communities. He also met with the leaders of the Shanghai underworld, especially the powerful *Green Gang.* The gangsters formed a Society for Common Progress.

In mid-April, the Society for Common Progress, often aided by Nationalist troops, attacked the headquarters of the major unions. Hundreds of unionists were killed or wounded. Chiang thus had destroyed the most powerful Communist force—the Shanghai trade unions—leaving the Communists desperate and deeply wounded. However, even this attack on the Communists did not lead to Soviet abandonment of its alliance strategy.

Criticized by Trotskii, Stalin insisted on strengthening the ties between the Nationalists and the Communists, while trying to manipulate the Nationalists to move to the left. Nationalist generals attacked the Wuhan stronghold of the Communists and left wing Nationalists. The position of the Communists and left wing nationalists was further undermined when the powerful warlord *Feng Yuxiang* aligned with Chiang Kai-shek and pressured the Nationalist left wing to break with the Communists.

Stalin finally changed his strategy and ordered the demoralized Communists to organize peasant rebellions. Mao and others led a series of *Autumn Harvest Uprisings* that failed utterly. Communist soldiers briefly captured the major city of Nanchang but were soon driven out. Unwilling to admit his mistakes, Stalin (December 1927) called for a Communist insurrection in Canton. The Communists established "communes" in some neighborhoods of Canton but the insurrection collapsed within two days.

The experiences of the Communists in the late 1920s had a profound impact on the future direction of the Communist Party, a future further advanced by the Nationalist encirclement campaigns and the Long March. Driven out of Shanghai in 1927, a number of Communists drifted into rural areas of Jiangxi Province in the Jinggang Mountains of southern China. By the end of 1928 Nationalist armies had driven the Communists eastward into another mountainous area along the border between Jiangxi and Fujian provinces. By this time the Nationalists were preoccupied with north China politics, especially concern over the power of the independent warlord Zhang Xueliang. Their own isolation and Nationalist preoccupation with north China gave the Communists a brief breathing space. Mao Zedong spent his time organizing the peasants and promoting modest land reforms. At the same time, he realized that his understanding of the peasants was quite limited, so he also spent much time in the formal study of peasant life.

By the early 1930s, a dozen small Communist organizations operated in remote areas of south China, sometimes forming small governments called *soviets,* after the Russian example. Internal squabbles, especially between Communists who moved to the countryside in 1927 and those who abandoned the underground urban sites in the early 1930s, marred Communist efforts.

The Nationalists made intermittent forays against the Communists, using a strategy of economic blockade and military *encirclement campaigns.* By the summer of 1934, the Communist leaders of the largest soviet, the *Jiangxi Soviet,* decided to abandon the area, fearing an imminent Nationalist attack. In mid-October 1934, 80,000 Communists left Jiangxi, eventually arriving in a remote part of Shaanxi Province in northern China in October 1935. By the time the Communists reached Yan'an in Shaanxi Province, only 10 percent of the original force of 80,000 remained. This *Long March* had covered over 6,000 miles of difficult terrain, ranging from mountains to swamps, from tropical weather to frigid climates. They crossed nine of China's eighteen provinces with Nationalist armies in pursuit. In mid-December 1934, the Nationalists trapped and almost destroyed the Communist army.

At first glance, it appeared that the Long March was a terrible defeat for the Communists. They had lost their urban power base. They had become isolated from the proletariat—whom they saw as the essential revolutionary force. They had abandoned the populous and relatively wealthy south for the impoverished northwest. The Communists had lost the power struggle with the Nationalists, and thus an opportunity to share power in a Nationalist government.

However, the Communists ultimately benefited from the Long March. In many ways, it made possible Communist victory in 1949. The Communists were forced to abandon the Western Communist ideology for one that fit China—a backward, poor, peasant country. The working class was quite small. In contrast to Russia, power was geographically more widely dispersed in China. It would have required a much larger Communist Party and a much larger military force to come to power in urban China. In addition, the Japanese occupied almost all major Chinese cities during the Second World War. Undoubtedly, the Communists would have been destroyed if they had remained in the cities. Finally, the Long March affected the psychology of the survivors. They felt they owed a debt to fallen comrades, which could only be repaid through a Communist triumph over the Nationalists. The survivors saw themselves as unique, with a special mission. The remnants of the Communists represented courage, endurance, and willingness to overcome almost insurmountable obstacles.

Nanjing Decade, 1928–1937. By the late 1920s, much of populated China was in the hands of the Nationalists. With their capital in Nanjing in the south where their strongest power base was located, the Nationalists were in a position to respond to the challenges of governance and the serious problems facing China.

The Nationalist Power Structure. Chiang Kai-shek was the most powerful leader of the Nationalist Party, serving as military commander in chief, head of the Nationalist Party Central Executive Committee that made key decisions, and chairman of the State Council. Government was divided into five major bureaus—Executive, Legislative, Control, Judicial, and Examination. The Executive Bureau supervised the central ministries, economic planning, the military, province-center relationships, and appointment of local officials. The Legislative Bureau was primarily a rubber stamp outfit that gave some legitimacy to the leaders' actions. The Control Bureau investigated abuses in the government. The Examination Bureau supervised civil service examinations.

Chiang Kai-shek created a cadre of personally loyal supporters through a number of training groups, including the Nationalist Party Central Political Institute and the Whampoa Academy. The Chen brothers controlled ideology, while secret police functions were in the hands of two other loyal allies. The secret police concentrated on opposing Communist activity.

The Problems. Chiang and his allies faced a complex set of very serious challenges. First, they needed to extend the power of the central Nationalist government throughout the country. Second, poverty and the lack of economic development placed severe limitations on the Nationalists. Third, they had to deal with foreign pressure. Fourth, the Party attempted to increase its security and preserve its power. Fifth, it needed to create an ideology that could supplement or replace Confucianism. Sixth, it faced the challenge of Japanese aggression. The Nationalists offered responses to all of these problems.

The Solutions? The Nationalists made some efforts to respond to China's problems. The decline in central control over the provinces had begun in the mid-nineteenth century. The warlord era left Chiang's government with little influence beyond the large cities and the reach of its armies. The Nationalists needed control over the countryside in order to maintain themselves in power, fund governmental activities, and respond to China's problems. They issued a County Organization Law that kept the old system of counties but divided each county into wards of 10–50 townships. A number of villages formed a ward. Villages were divided into neighborhoods and neighborhoods into the *baojia system,* in which groups of ten families had joint responsibilities for ensuring proper behavior, paying taxes, etc. Merely creating a hierarchical structure did not ensure good government. Officials were corrupt; they oppressed the peasants and encouraged the continuation of traditional social behaviors such as footbinding.

Poverty stalked the countryside, while the cities were much more advanced. Rural poverty had worsened because of the devastation of warlord activities, increased taxes, higher rents charged by exploitative landlords, and the worldwide agricultural depression of the 1920s. Peasants who mainly grew cash crops, such as silk, cotton, soybeans, and tobacco, were especially hard hit.

Several strategies existed for dealing with rural poverty. Earlier, expansion of the amount of land under cultivation had been a very successful means of increasing agricultural output. Now, only limited amounts of arable land remained untilled. However, restoration of irrigation systems increased the amount of land under cultivation, while land that had gone out of use because of the devastation of the warlord armies was again farmed. Second, one could change ownership patterns. A shift from tenant farming to ownership created an incentive for more productive farming. Since much of the Nationalist support came from the gentry, this alternative was politically dangerous. Agricultural modernization was a third option. This included new higher-yield grains and mechanization, which would be viable only on large-scale farms. Such a gigantic project was beyond the ability of the Nationalist government and flew in the face of the Chinese tradition of small farms worked with intensive labor. Other aspects of agricultural modernization were much more promising, with much of the effort carried out with minimal government support. James *Yen* and *Liang* Shuming were the leading agricultural reformers.

Yen worked in Hebei Province in north China. He promoted literacy and tried to create *model villages.* In the model villages, peasants were taught basic literacy, hygiene, and more productive agricultural methods. His efforts were based on the agricultural extension agent model popular in the United States. Yen also promoted rural light industry and local self-government.

Liang Shuming emphasized agricultural research and its dissemination. Based at the Shandong Rural Research Institute, Liang also tried to create model communities, emphasizing economic development and education. Rather than impose programs from above, Liang proposed mutual assistance efforts from below. Agricultural reform did not end the impoverishment of the peasantry, though some improvements in agricultural productivity resulted.

The Nationalists successfully secured independence from Western powers, especially the elimination of unequal treaties and the acquisition of control over tariff policies and revenue.

The Nationalists attempted to entrench themselves in power in three ways. They tried to co-opt warlords who had remained independent. By 1933, most warlords had aligned with the Nationalists. Second, the Nationalists tried to destroy the Communists. Finally, the Nationalists employed a very active police and secret police operation, supported by pro-government vigilantes, the *Blue Shirts.* The Blue Shirts directed their attacks against Communists, as well as supporters of democracy.

The Nationalists also tried to create an ideology that retained Confucian ethics and combined it with Nationalism. No ideological consensus was successfully constructed in the Nationalist period.

Finally, the Nationalists tried to avoid dealing with the Japanese problem. Not until the Japanese had taken most of north China did the Nationalists stand up to the invaders.

Conclusions. The Nationalists had little success extending their power into the countryside. They promoted greater industrialization but achieved little agricultural growth. Westerners withdrew from China, in part due to Nationalist pressure but also because of the turmoil in the country. Ideological conformity was suggested but not achieved. The Nationalists utterly failed to resist Japanese aggression.

Why were the Nationalists' achievements so limited? First, they held power for less than a decade and the problems they faced were almost insurmountable. Long-term programs were needed, not quick fixes. The Nationalists also lacked the governmental structure to implement major reform. In addition, most of the Party leaders were primarily interested in their own power and not in reform. For the Nationalists, national integration had to come before social and economic reform. Preoccupation with the Communist "menace" diverted the Nationalists from reform as well. Finally, most social and economic reforms would have attacked the gentry and business classes that were the backbone of the Nationalist Parity. The Party could not afford to alienate its strongest supporters.

3. The Politics of Ideology

With the collapse of the Chinese Empire, its defining ideology, Confucianism, was more and more called into question. Alternative ideologies emerged, including republicanism, nationalism, communism, and liberal democracy. Very broadly, the basis issue was one of timing. Should China focus on achieving national independence or domestic renewal first? This issue had faced Russia and India at about the same time (see Chapters One and Two). None of the competing ideologies achieved the kind of dominant position that

Confucianism held for the previous 2,500 years. The intellectual disarray was provoked by the *May Fourth Movement* attacks on Confucianism.

May Fourth Movement. In the Chinese context, the term *cultural revolution* is usually applied to radical efforts to transform China and Chinese Communism through violence in the 1960s. However, the term is equally valid when applied to the intellectual upheaval that emerged from student and labor protests in 1919. The term May Fourth is applied both to the protests and to the intellectual ferment that had already begun but which the protests intensified.

Student protests broke out on May 4, 1919, when news of the Versailles Treaty settlement that ended the First World War reached China. China had been virtually ignored at Versailles, in part because no legitimate Chinese government had been recognized. In addition, the Shandong Peninsula, earlier dominated by the Germans, was assigned to Japan. University students in Beijing organized small demonstrations, which led to clashes with the police. Students from middle schools, high schools, and universities joined a Beijing student union. Students then established similar groups in other large cities. The business community supported the student demonstrations, as did workers in large factories. In Shanghai, for instance, 60,000 workers in 43 factories struck in support of the student protests.

The protests stimulated a rethinking of Confucian ideas and promoted a quest for alternative visions for the country in response to China's humiliation. The May Fourth Movement was an attempt to reassert the value of Chinese culture. The intellectual movement criticized Confucianism and proposed alternatives.

Critique of Confucianism. Confucianism took much of the blame for China's failure to remain powerful and independent. Many thinkers attacked the patriarchal family, arranged marriages and Confucian education. They condemned classical Chinese language as remote, elitist, and impractical.

Translated into Chinese, Henrik Ibsen's *A Doll House* presented a dramatic critique of the patriarchal family. In the play, the heroine, Nora, left her husband, thus escaping from male domination. Many Chinese women sought to become Noras, unbinding their feet, going to universities, and pursuing public careers.

The opponents of Confucianism presented their ideas in new journals and newspapers; the most important of which took the French name, *La Jeunesse Noveau* (*New Youth*). Fiction writers also actively engaged in the debate over China's future. The most important literary participant was *Lu Xun.* With great caution and less optimism than other representatives of the May Fourth generation, Lu Xun warned women that they might not achieve their goals of freedom. In the short story, "The True Story of Ah Q," Lu satirized the Revolution of 1911, suggesting that little had changed and little could be expected in the way of reform. Lu's realism was, unfortunately, an accurate portrait of China in the 1920s and 1930s. Writers offered ideas for solving China's problems, especially the absence of true independence, poverty, and backwardness. Less attention was given to political instability and the lack of political unity.

Peking University was the center of the intellectual ferment. Yan Fu and Cai Yuanpei, presidents at Peking University, gave protection and legitimacy to the new thinkers. *Chen Duxiu,* dean of the university, founded *New Youth,* led the attack on Confucianism, called for the use of everyday Chinese rather than the classical language, and emphasized the importance of science and democracy.

Some thinkers, such as *Hu Shi,* took a pragmatic approach. China's problems could be solved through the application of Western science, technology, and social thought. Others held a more ideological perspective, arguing that one needed a broad framework of understanding in order to solve China's problems.

The "cultural revolution" was influenced by a number of foreign visitors, including philosophers John Dewey and Bertrand Russell, Albert Einstein, Margaret Sanger (the leading advocate of birth control), and the Nobel-prize winning Indian novelist, Rabindranath Tagore. All of these outsiders provided ideas for reviving China.

Republicanism. Sun Yat-sen was the leading representative of "republican" thought. His ideas were developed before the Qing dynasty fell and changed little thereafter.

Sun called for actions that would ensure Chinese independence. Thus he promoted Chinese nationalism. His views can be termed republicanism because he opposed the establishment of a new monarchy yet did not feel that the Chinese people were ready for democracy. He introduced the concept of *tutelage.* China would pass through three stages of political development. After coming to power, the Nationalists would first rule China through the military and the tutelage or dictatorship of the Nationalist Party. Only members of the Nationalist Party would have rights of citizenship in this stage. Once the Chinese people were adequately prepared, democracy could be introduced. Government would consist of five branches—executive, legislative, judicial, military, and censorate (to supervise the population and ensure moral behavior). Finally, Sun made vague statements in favor of improving the conditions of the people. His ideas remained at the center of Nationalist Party ideology.

Nationalism. Nationalism was the most powerful ideology in this period. For many, achieving the goals of nationalism must precede the solution of China's domestic ills. *Liang Qichao* was one of the leading advocates of nationalism. He was deeply influenced by his understanding of Japan's path to modernization. Japanese thinkers clearly had understood that survival depended on the ability of a country to quickly strengthen itself so that outsiders would not try to determine its fate. This survival of the fittest concept also applied to China, Liang argued. He insisted that the Chinese people develop a sense of loyalty to China and identify themselves as members of the Chinese nation before they addressed other problems. According to Liang, China must regain the sense of superiority it had possessed before the arrival of the Westerners. Though he claimed to support democracy, he emphasized that even dictatorship was a good political system if it contributed to national independence.

Chinese nationalism changed after the Nationalists came to power. Increasingly, nationalism became less a clarion call for opposition to "Western imperialism" and more a justification for Nationalist Party rule. Chiang Kai-shek sought to mobilize the Chinese people through a mass activity known as the *New Life Movement.* In many ways this was an attempt to return to the superficial elements of Confucianism. Chiang claimed that the New Life Movement would create the basis for true national unity and patriotism. He sought to unify the Chinese under the tight control of the Nationalists, who would ensure that the people behaved properly. Chiang campaigned against spitting, smoking, illicit sex, cock fighting, gambling, and even short skirts. The New Life Movement, however, did not breathe life into Chinese nationalism, which defined itself in part through its opposition to Communism.

Marxism. In this era Marxism had limited appeal, in part because its analyses and objectives seemed so unreal to most Chinese intellectuals. It is easy to see significant differences between early Marxism and the later Yan'an Maoism.

Early Marxism (1920s). Small Marxist circles began to form in China about the time of the May Fourth Movement, with Li Dazhao and Chen Duxiu playing a key role. Marxism had some influence because the Russian Soviets condemned imperialism and abandoned claims to Chinese territory. Soviet Marxism appealed to the Chinese Communists because it seemed to parallel their emphasis on opposing imperialism and strengthening the country through modernization. Yet much of Marxism seemed barely relevant to the Chinese.

Chinese Marxism accepted the general outline of western Marxism but modified it. Li Dazhao suggested that Marxism lacked an ethical component and that the emphasis on class struggle was inappropriate in a society of good people who acted on the basis of mutual assistance. Chen Duxiu also rejected the idea of armed proletarian uprisings. Instead, he suggested that the Communists would win power as a regular political party in a republican state. Chinese Marxists also rejected Marx's economic determinism. Instead the Chinese Marxists emphasized the importance of *voluntarism,* from the Latin word for *conscious will.* Individuals acting on the basis of will (determination) could change the material world, thus accelerating development, and move directly to socialism. Revolutionary consciousness, according to Li Dazhao, depended on a person's intellectual perspective, not social origins. By collapsing the stages of historical development through the leadership of the intelligentsia, a process of *permanent or interrupted revolution* would take place. Actually, since the Communists had little hope of coming to power, their early revisions of Marxism, and its application to China, were mainly intellectual musings. Changed conditions forced them to abandon their initial ideas.

Yan'an Maoism. In the Yan'an period, the Communists moved to create a kind of Chinese Marxism, which we will call *Maoism.* They were forced to retreat from their urban power base in the most modern and westernized part of China into one of the most remote and impoverished areas of northwest China. The Communists, clearly under Mao's leadership by 1934, adapted to their new conditions, which Mao chose to portray as opportunities. Mao emphasized the revolutionary role of the Communist elite, primarily the survivors of the Long March.

Since the Communists now were located in a rural area, peasants were their only hope for potential allies. To secure support from the peasants, the Maoists emphasized education, democratic centralism, and nationalism. They downplayed social reform or social revolution. Mao emphasized the role of propaganda in teaching the peasants about Maoism. For revolution to be successful it was necessary to transform people's consciousness, he argued. Thus he developed the concept of the *mass line.* The Communists proposed ideas to the peasants, listened to their responses, and then finalized policy. Leadership would follow consultation, with the Communists making and implementing policy. (In Soviet Communism the term *democratic centralism* is used to denote this strategy.)

By the 1930s, most Chinese had come to see the Japanese as the main threat to Chinese security. Most Chinese yearned for a leadership that would drive the Japanese from Chinese soil. Pledging to do so was one means by which the Communists gained considerable support. They applied these ideas on a small-scale in northwest China from the mid-1930s through the end of the Second World War.

Liberalism. Liberalism had little impact, perhaps because it was the most Westernized of Chinese ideologies, perhaps because it seemed so alien to the political anarchy of post-imperial China. *Hu Shi* was the most important Chinese liberal. Hu saw individualism, self-enlightenment, critical reasoning, and civil rights as the central themes of liberalism. He rejected classical liberalism's minimization of the role of government. Drawing from Confucianism, Hu suggested that government should create opportunities for all citizens to be well-educated individuals capable of applying critical reasoning to politics. Hu's democracy was a community, not a group of isolated individuals. Yet he also championed individual rights and individual initiative. Democracy, thus, permitted individuals to reach their full potential.

Education would prepare the Chinese to participate in a democracy. Hu championed the *vernacular* so that education would be available to everyone. Cultural Revolution should precede democracy, for democracy could only work if society consisted of well-educated, critical thinking individuals. Educated at Columbia University in the United States under the leading philosopher of American pragmatism, John Dewey, Hu Shi emphasized the need for experimentation and practical efforts to improve China. He criticized the theorists, especially the Marxists. By the 1930s, Liberalism had largely died out in China.

Conclusion. In this period in which no national political authority existed that was capable of imposing its will, the educated classes were relatively free to pursue a variety of ideological orientations. Confucianism crashed, after almost 2,500 years of being the dominant set of ideas. However, it was difficult to build a post-Confucian consensus. Instead, Nationalism, Republicanism, Marxism, and Liberalism shouted out their intellectual wares. Nationalism had the weakest ideological structure but the greatest impact. The well-reasoned liberalism of Hu Shi had little influence. The ideological conflict was paralleled by the Chinese people's struggle for existence.

4. Poverty and Modernization

China was a land of contrasts, with rural poverty and Westernized urban pop culture at the extremes of the continuum. The tragic destructiveness of the warlord era added to nineteenth century economic decline. For most Chinese people, this was an age of poverty and great suffering.

The Economy. The Chinese economy grew very slowly in this period, with most of the growth associated with industrialization. Industry, however, was only a minor sector of the economy. Warlord devastations prevented increased agricultural output. Population grew more rapidly than the economy, producing a lowering of overall living standards.

Gentry. The gentry class remained the most important class in society. It quickly adjusted to the fall of the Qing dynasty and to the reduced importance of Confucian learning. The gentry attached themselves to warlords and to the Nationalist Party. Thus the class preserved much of its political power. Its influence in the countryside, where most people lived, went unchallenged. Its economic position was weakened by the devastations of civil war; the modest increase in the importance of the urban economic sector, dominated by the business class; and the decline in gentry income from local government duties. The class experienced some decline in its cultural leadership, for the anti-Confucian intellectuals came partially from the urban classes and the wealthy peasantry.

Peasants, Poverty, and Protest. The broad dimensions of rural China remained unchanged, including differences between north and south and the poverty of a majority of peasants. The plight of rural China can be blamed on its entrance into the global economy, environmental devastation, technological backwardness, and overpopulation. Overpopulation created a labor surplus that urban China could not absorb.

Four main categories of peasants existed, including managerial farmers (who owned more land than they could work and hired laborers), rich peasants, middle peasants, and poor peasants (landless laborers employed as farm workers or tenant farmers). The economic position of the peasants declined due to warlord activity, natural disasters, and the impact of the world agricultural depressions of the 1920s and 1930s.

The peasants responded to their poverty with individual and group strategies. Most families merely suffered. Sometimes they reduced the number of mouths that had to be fed by selling a son or daughter. At other times peasants acted collectively, especially under Communist influence in 1926 and 1927. In 1927, the Communists proposed land distribution schemes that would set maximum size farms at 10 acres. Generally, and especially in the early 1930s, peasants directed their anger against local authorities. Ironically, peasants usually directed their anger toward bailiffs and farm managers, and not the landlords. The government easily crushed peasant unrest.

Industry and the Urban Classes. Chinese industry grew rapidly from 1911 to 1937. Existing industries expanded production and new ones were built, generally with foreign capital. The industrial sector expanded first in heavy industry—coal, steel, and iron—centered in the Wuhan area. The British dominated coal mining, which employed some 50,000 workers. Textiles, located primarily in the Shanghai area, were another major industry. The Chinese owned a majority of mills but the British and Japanese between them owned approximately 40 percent of them. Shipbuilding for coastal and river traffic developed into a major industry, as did cigarette manufacturing.

In spite of political instability, foreign investors continued to send money into China, with the Japanese investing primarily in Manchuria and the British in the south. Perhaps 10 percent of China's investment capital came from foreign sources.

Industry represented the most dynamic component of the economy and drew large numbers of workers into the cities. Still, industry represented only about 10 percent of the GDP.

The working class was quite diversified. A gray elite of skilled workers in more modernized facilities earned relatively high wages. Those in small consumer goods plants were badly treated and poorly paid. Work hours were similar to those in most countries in the early stages of industrialization and might have been a bit shorter than the norm. High rates of industrial accidents and inadequate housing made conditions worse.

Working class protest occurred on a far broader scale than did peasant unrest. From May 4, 1919, through 1922, strikes increased in number and volatility. The January 1922 Hong Kong and Canton seamen and long shore men's strike gained the support of some 120,000 and produced major gains. Though the strikes might have represented the launching point for a major strike movement, warlords began to crack down on labor unrest. Beatings and arrests punctured the dynamism of the strike movement. A small wave of strikes broke out in 1934–1935 but the police crushed them with great brutality.

The business class grew wealthier from industrial activity, railroad investment, and commerce. The class increased in political power, especially with the collapse of Confucian education. Less conservative than the gentry, the business class supported the Nationalists and the small democracy movement.

Conclusions. Modest social change, increasingly rapid social mobility, and very limited amounts of protest characterized the nation in the period of anarchy. Poverty increased for a majority of peasant families, while economic conditions improved for wealthier peasants and most urban residents, especially the business-commercial class. Within the middle class a professional-intelligentsia strata increased in size and significance. China's class structure began to resemble those of Japan and Western societies.

5. Family and Women Undergoing Change

This period saw dramatic changes in the family and in the position and roles of women. The changes were most profound among the middle classes in the cities and less substantial in the gentry. Peasants remained tied to the status quo.

Gender and Family. A very small suffrage movement emerged soon after the collapse of the Qing. *Tang* Yunying led a modest women's protest in 1912. Women demanded that the new constitution provide for male-female equality and women's right. Police broke up the rally and the government ignored the women's proposals.

More substantial changes occurred in the position of women within the family. Changes had begun in the late Qing but accelerated after the May Fourth Movement. In *New Youth,* Chen Duxiu criticized Confucian tenets of filial piety (obedience to the eldest males); he condemned the subservience of women and called for widows to have the right to remarry. The intelligentsia attacked the patriarchal family, the lack of education for women, arranged marriages, concubinage, and foot binding.

Changes came quickest in the large cities. Beginning in 1920, women gained admittance into Beijing University. Coeducation at the secondary level became common. In the countryside, however, little changed.

Women entered the workforce in increasing numbers. Since the emergence of the textiles industry women had formed a majority of industrial workers (approximately two-thirds of the workforce). Women also comprised a majority of workers in the new cigarette industry. Many of them came from rural areas, while some were the spouses of urban workers. Female factory workers were paid less than men and treated harshly by bosses and male workers. In rural areas, women in poor families tended to work in the fields and in the households. Wealthier peasant women worked only in the home.

Greater literacy among women, economic opportunities, and male acceptance of some emancipation of women weakened but did not destroy the patriarchal family.

6. Diversity and Community

Community in the form of national unity was a dream, diversity a reality. The Imperial Office and Confucianism had given China a large measure of community. But the collapse of the Qing dynasty and the attacks on Confucianism left China adrift, searching for political unification and national unity.

Difference Dominates. Political conflict among warlords, Nationalists, and Communists undermined the quest for unity, even though all political factions had a common goal of reunification of China under a single political system. China was divided into a number of separate states, even after the Nationalists had conquered the country. Not even the presence of grave danger—the Japanese threat—could unify the Chinese. Social harmony, never fully realized, was replaced by increasing social conflict. Ideological conflict resulted from efforts to find a common ideological basis for Chinese behavior. Nationalism came closest to providing a basis for unity.

D. CHINESE STALINISM, 1949–1957

Thirty years after its formation, the Communist Party assumed power in China in October 1949. Deeply influenced by their experiences in isolated, rural areas, the Communists gained advantage over the Nationalists during the Second World War and, utilizing superior military tactics, won a civil war that lasted from 1945–1949. Once in power, the Communists embarked upon the transformation of China. They moved gradually because their power was limited. Relatively isolated, China had some potential for ties with either the United States or the Soviet Union but not with both. Creation of a stable, effective government was a priority. Maoism became the only acceptable ideology, though Communists could not always agree on what Maoism should be like. Cautiously but relentlessly the Party introduced social and economic changes. The gentry class was destroyed or disappeared, while great mobility was available to those who were Communists. The Chinese followed the Soviet model of economic development, thus the name Stalinism for the period, but focused on gradual collectivization of agriculture and nationalization of industry and central planning. The Party ordered the destruction of the patriarchal family and espoused equality for women. Finally, the Communists emphasized unity but introduced a new basis for determining difference—loyalty. They also tried to manage the national minority problem.

1. Civil War Victory and International Dilemma

The Communists rather easily defeated the Nationalists in the Civil War and then turned to the Soviet Union for economic models and assistance.

Civil War. Historians identify the period of fierce fighting after the Second World War as the Civil War but conflict between the Nationalists and the Communists had begun as early as 1926. When the Second World War ended, both sides scrambled to gain military advantage in strategic areas, strengthen their position with foreign allies, mobilize support from the people, and provide government for the areas they controlled. Military action was interrupted several times as the United States sought to mediate a compromise sharing of power.

The Course of the Civil War. Both sides realized that Manchuria held the key to victory. The Americans airlifted large numbers of Nationalist soldiers from southwest China to north and east China. However, Communists troops were closer to Manchuria and the Soviets accepted the Japanese surrender there and delivered large stocks of weapons to the Communists.

As the two sides prepared for the ultimate struggle, the United States tried to force the Communists and Nationalists to negotiate a settlement that would avoid civil war. It is not clear that either Chinese side was serious about negotiations. Instead both saw negotiations as providing a lull in which they could build up their military advantage. Finally, in January 1946, both agreed to a cease-fire and the calling of a national assembly. However, the leaders of the Nationalist Party decided on a strong presidency, with Chiang Kai-shek to hold that office. When the first attempt at negotiations collapsed, war returned to Manchuria in July 1946. Though American President Harry S. Truman threatened to withdraw American assistance if the Nationalists did not return to the negotiating table, domestic political pressure in the United States made it impossible for Truman to carry out the threat. In January 1947, the chief U.S. negotiator left China, admitting that U.S. efforts to prevent civil war had failed.

Occupying a strategic location and possessing the most advanced industrial complex in China, Manchuria was extremely important to both sides. With a stronger military, the Nationalists gained control of southern Manchuria. They then forced the Communists to retreat into central Manchuria. The Communists took advantage of a harsh winter to march across frozen rivers and carry out surprise attacks against Nationalist strongholds. The Nationalist forces began to crack. Concentrated in large cities, they gradually lost the surrounding territories and were liable to encirclement and siege by the Communists. Nationalist soldiers' morale collapsed and the Communists forced large Nationalist forces to surrender in the major cities of Manchuria. The balance of power had shifted, as up to one million Nationalist soldiers surrendered and gave up large stores of weapons. The Communists now had a larger military force than the Nationalists did. In addition, victory in Manchuria boosted Communist morale and destroyed that of the Nationalists.

At this point—in the late spring of 1948—Chiang Kai-shek faced a momentous decision. Should he retreat into the south, where his strength and popular support was still substantial? This would mean the loss of north China and an end to dreams of Chinese unity. Or should the Nationalists continue to fight in north China, in hopes of somehow defeating the Communists? Chiang Kai-shek could not abandon his desire to be ruler of all China, for national unity had always been a central goal of the Nationalists. Yet this strategy was quite a gamble, for if the Nationalists were again defeated in north China, the south would be open to relatively easy Communist conquest. Chiang Kai-shek decided to make a stand in north China.

During the spring of 1948 the two sides fought fierce battles for control of strategic cities in north China. The Nationalist front lines held but their losses were quite heavy. The Nationalists made a stand at Xuzhou on the Huai River, the traditional dividing point between north and south China. They held on for over two months but at the end of 1948 the city fell. In early 1949, the Communists took both Tianjin and Beijing. It seemed clear that the Nationalists could no longer defend themselves against the Communists. Chiang Kai-shek decided that the Nationalists would retreat to the island of Taiwan, rather than try to establish a Nationalist "warlord kingdom" in southwest China that would be impregnable against the Communists and might later provide a base for offensives against the Communists. In April 1949, the Communists captured the Nationalist capital of Nanjing. Shanghai fell in August and Canton in October. On October 1, 1949, Mao Zedong announced the establishment of the People's Republic of China.

Reasons for the Communist Victory. Communist victory resulted from Communist advantages and Nationalist disadvantages. The Communist military leadership made effective strategic decisions. When they were outnumbered in north China and Manchuria they concentrated on guerilla warfare and gaining the support of the rural population. When the Nationalists retreated into the cities, the Communists turned to siege tactics. With the defeat of Nationalist armies in Manchuria, the balance of power shifted and the Communists turned to conventional warfare, using their advantage in manpower and weaponry against the demoralized Nationalists. The Communists clearly had a sense of destiny and a clear set of goals. They operated in their main areas of support while they were relatively weak and gradually extended that base. The Communists portrayed themselves as the only group that could bring unity to China and liberate it from outside influence, ideas that especially appealed to youth and the business community.

The Nationalists had the disadvantage of being in power when the Japanese invaded and were thus blamed for China's defeat and humiliation. They could not overcome this perception. After the war the Nationalists failed to effectively deal with serious problems, including inflation, unemployment, and corruption within the Party's leadership. They thus fought the civil war without much support from the people. The Nationalists had lost elite divisions and key military leaders during the lengthy period of Japanese occupation. So when the Nationalists faced the Communists they did so with soldiers, who were poorly trained, with low morale. They were led by inexperienced, brutal, and frequently incompetent officers. Chiang Kai-shek intervened in battlefield decision-making, often changing his mind on strategies to be pursued. Only massive U.S. assistance and the use of huge numbers of American troops could have saved the Nationalists from defeat once they had lost key cities in

Manchuria. U.S. leaders had little desire to prop up a corrupt, unpopular, ineffective, and undemocratic regime.

International Initiatives. Its diplomatic experience limited to wartime and civil war negotiations, the Communists hesitantly began to develop a foreign policy. Their foreign policy was based on four key tenets: affirmation of China's independence, recovery of Taiwan, alliance with the Soviet Union, and support for Third World non-alignment. The broader context was that China no longer counted globally. This motivated the Chinese Communists to aggressive rhetoric, if not action.

Taiwan. Chiang Kai-shek and the Nationalists quickly consolidated their power over the Taiwanese, thus making dissent almost impossible. The Communists moved large numbers of troops to the coastal area adjacent to Taiwan but did not attempt to invade immediately. Their invasion plans were interrupted by the Korean War.

The Soviets. In desperate need of assistance for industrialization, the Chinese turned to the Soviet Union. In 1950, the two signed a trade agreement. The Soviets sent in large numbers of technical advisers and even shipped entire factories to China. In a difficult economic situation itself, the Soviet Union sold military material to China and provided it with economic development loans. In addition, the Chinese adopted the Stalinist model for rapid economic growth. Neither the Japanese model nor the Western one was available for political reasons. Also, both models focused on consumer goods rather than heavy industry and emphasized a more gradual approach than the Communists wanted. Acceptance of Soviet aid brought with it the expectation that the Chinese Communists would follow the Soviets in terms of foreign policy.

The United States and the Korean War. Initially, the United States neither recognized the People's Republic of China as the legitimate rulers of China nor took any actions against it. Policies changed with the outbreak of the Korean War (1950–1953). The decision to go to war was made by the North Koreans with the strong support of the Soviets. The Chinese Communists were aware of the plan to attack South Korea. When the war broke out the Americans decided to provide naval protection for Taiwan. Chinese authorities intensified anti-American propaganda. An atmosphere of witch hunts existed in China, with the Americans viewed as the "evil empire." In part the Communists used the Americans as an excuse for domestic repression.

By October 1950, the United Nations Forces had begun a major offensive that was driving the North Koreans toward the Chinese border. The Chinese then sent in troops to aid the North Koreans. Eventually 2 million Chinese soldiers fought in the war and Chinese forces pushed the Americans back near the original dividing line between North and South Korea. Negotiations dragged on, eventually producing an armistice in July 1953. Chinese casualties reached over a quarter of a million. The costs of the war were huge, postponing economic development. The Communists used the war to stimulate patriotism and conduct campaigns against potential and real domestic enemies as loyalty became all-important. China also turned inward, isolating itself from much of the world, as it had done in the Ming period.

Non-alignment. Later, *Zhou Enlai* developed a foreign policy strategy that sought to end Chinese isolation, mainly through ties with Third World, non-aligned countries (most of whom were not non-aligned but pro-Soviet). The

Chinese formed close ties with India and participated in the Bandung Conference in Indonesia in 1955 (see Chapter Two for India's role in this). The Chinese played a leadership role in condemning "American imperialism." Though recognized by the Communist countries and much of the non-aligned group, China remained an outsider to international politics, especially since it was denied membership in the United Nations.

2. A New Government

The Chinese Communists made restoration of order a key objective. This meant establishing local urban and rural governments as well as a national political system. For most of the early years of Communist power, government essentially remained a military dictatorship. The new political system was one in which the Communist Party controlled the government and a small number of Communist leaders determined policy.

Advantages. The Chinese Communists came to power in a much more advantageous situation than the Soviet Communists had. The Chinese Communists had over a decade of experience in governing a territory that numbered 40 million people. They understood that the population must be treated well, the Communists disciplined, and crime and corruption eliminated. They recognized the value of moderate reform plans, which would not alienate powerful local figures and productive farmers. Instead of making enemies, their goal was to seek allies; even among those they considered representatives of the Nationalist camp. The Communists used the mass line idea to communicate with the people. They also recognized that the military, with its built-in structure of decision-making, could play an important role in civilian governance.

Goals. Finally, the Communists had a clear sense of what they wished to accomplish once they were in power. They outlined their major policy goals in September 1949. This *Common Program* called for civil rights, equal rights for women and men, rural reform that included rent reduction and land redistribution, the expansion of heavy industry, and universal education.

Having spent the previous decade in rural China, the Communists entered the cities with mixed feelings. On the one hand they saw cities as the evil centers of immorality and exploitation. At the same time, they recognized that urban areas would be the location of heavy industry. The Communists established local governments, initially retaining officials from the Nationalist era. They gradually added Communists to city governments, with the ultimate aim of having a well-trained cadre of Communist urban officials. They also extended government down through the wards and eventually to street-level committees. The Communists moved quickly to eliminate corruption, crime, and immorality. They built up support through massive propaganda campaigns, using radio, the theater, and film. They established interest groups willing to support Communists, including trade unions, women's organizations, and youth groups. The Communists' achievement in establishing order and effective, clean government in the cities was a huge one.

Central Government. Communists dominated the central government. The Central People's Government Council, chaired by Mao Zedong, occupied the top of the government. This organization worked closely with the other major administrative body, the State Council, or Cabinet, headed by Zhou Enlai. The State Council supervised the twenty-four ministries or departments.

Though this structure suggests a high level of centralization, in reality authority was dispersed more broadly, mainly as a consequence of the tremendous power of the military. China was divided into six regional military commands. Within each command were four major officials—the government chairman, a first party secretary, a military commander, and an army political commissar. Chinese military-political leaders, including Gao Gang, Peng Dehuai, Rao Shushi, Lin Biao, and Deng Xiaoping, dominated these regional commands. Actually, these powerful regional leaders modified or ignored decisions of the center.

Chinese Communist Party. The Chinese Communist Party was structured parallel to the government. Authority was in the hands of the *Standing Committee of the Politburo;* under it were the *Politburo* and the *Central Committee.* In the original Standing Committee were Mao, Zhou, Liu Shaoqi, Zhu De, and Chen Yun. The Standing Committee was the true center of Party power.

Very quickly the Communists created local and central governments able to maintain order and achieve significant reforms. The Communist Party also sought to ensure an ideological monopoly for Maoist thought.

3. Maoism, Ideological Conformity, and Maoism Questioned

When the Communists came to power, they sought to ensure that Communist thought gained an ideological monopoly. Through propaganda, they promoted Maoism, frequently called *Yan'an Communism.* The Party conducted campaigns to coerce doubters into at least superficial acceptance of Communism. However, toward the end of this period, reform seemed to hit a dead end, and Mao asked China's intelligentsia to propose a new path to higher levels of Chinese Communism.

Yan'an Communism. Maoist ideas derived from the experiences of the Communists in Yan'an after they were driven out of southern China. Yan'an Communism was modified by the need to create a nation-wide socialist society, which meant the addition of Soviet Communist ideas.

Yan'an Communism built upon earlier criticisms of Marxism as well as the experiences of the Long March and the Yan'an period. Chinese Marxists viewed human will as the primary force for revolutionary change. Socialist revolution could come about in any type socioeconomic formation. Revolution need not wait until a society reached an advanced capitalist stage. Thus revolutionary heroism replaced economic development as the most important motor for human progress.

Instead of the proletariat, the peasantry provided the mass support needed for revolution. The Communists used socioeconomic categories, including poor peasants, middle peasants, and rich peasants. Poor peasants naturally supported revolution, while middle peasants could be brought over to the side of revolution. This focus on peasants as revolutionaries also led the Communists to idealize the countryside as pure and the cities as cesspools of iniquity.

The idea of permanent revolution was reinforced as well. Permanent revolution meant that Communists would constantly struggle to achieve higher and higher levels of socialism, without a pause for rest and consolidation.

Additions from Soviet Communism. As the Communists came to power they began to realize that Yan'an Communism provided only a partial set of guidelines and that ideas that explained how to make a successful revolution were not very helpful in ruling a country and carrying out a socialist transformation. The Chinese turned to the apparently successful Soviet model (see Chapter One). Stalinism meant centralized decision-making in the hands of a very small group. It emphasized the use of force to achieve goals. It also promoted rapid economic growth through mobilization of labor, capital, and materials to stimulate heavy industry. The needs and rights of individuals must be ignored, in the name of the cause—building socialism.

Repression. Soon after coming to power, the Communists carried out four repression campaigns intended to ensure loyalty, identify potential opponents, and change behaviors. The targets were the Communist Party, the government bureaucracy, the educated classes, and supporters of the Nationalist cause.

The "Resist America and Aid Korea" campaign identified foreigners as potential enemies. Persons were accused of being Western spies, property was confiscated and foreign business assets frozen or confiscated. A number of foreigners were imprisoned and tortured. Christian church properties were confiscated and Chinese Christianity declared illegal.

Another campaign was directed against "counterrevolutionaries." The campaign targeted former Nationalist supporters, including soldiers. This "Suppression of Counterrevolutionaries Campaign" identified millions of "enemies of Communism." Millions were identified as counter-revolutionaries, who lost their civil rights and access to careers and jobs.

In addition to these campaigns against opponents of Communism, other campaigns had more specific targets. The *Three Antis* campaign was directed against corruption, waste, and inefficiency among Party and government bureaucrats, as well as business leaders. In addition, workers were mobilized to attack foremen and company executives.

The *Five Antis* campaign was directed against the "bourgeoisie," the urban middle class, and the rural landlord class. Bribery, tax evasion, theft of state property, cheating on government contracts, and stealing state economic data were targeted.

By the end of 1952, the campaigns had ended. Millions of people were identified as outsiders, unfit for inclusion in Chinese Communist society. Loyalty, whose dimensions and definition were determined by the Party, became a major criterion for determining difference in this period and thereafter.

"One Hundred Flowers." Although many intellectuals had been purged in the repressive campaigns of the early 1950s or forced to go through lengthy training sessions at "revolutionary colleges," Mao called for their assistance in 1956. By this time Chinese Stalinism had produced effective government, national independence and unity, rapid industrialization through state planning, and collectivization of agriculture. The Chinese had moved more quickly and with greater success than had the Soviets in the 1920s and 1930s. Mao believed that these early achievements had reached a plateau and that permanent revolution required China to move relentlessly to higher stages of socialism. The problem was that Mao and other Party leaders had no idea what a higher stage of socialism should look like. Mao invited the intellectuals to critique the early achievements of Chinese Stalinism and to propose ideas for future advancement. In the sloganeering style of his speech, Mao called for "letting a hundred flowers blossom and a hundred schools of thought contend."

Reluctantly, the intelligentsia participated in the Hundred Flowers campaign during May and early June of 1957. Unexpectedly, they were quite critical of the Stalinist heritage. They condemned the Party for authoritarianism and the bureaucracy for inefficiency and corruption. They attacked the radical economic reforms for increasing inequality and leaving the peasants as impoverished as they had been under the Nationalist regime.

The intelligentsia offered alternatives, implicit in their criticism of Chinese Stalinism. They called for democracy, civil rights, and a multi-party system. The educated classes wanted policies that would improve the standard of living of the peasants. They argued that China had traded subordination to the West for subordination to the Soviet Union, thus belying the statement that China was now truly independent.

The protests went beyond statements of the intelligentsia to include student protests and the creation of a "Democratic Wall" at Beijing University. At this point in early June, Mao turned off the tap of freedom of expression. By the end of 1957, 300,000 members of the intelligentsia had been labeled "rightists." They lost their jobs and many were sent to labor camps or to collective farms. Pressured by the Party, some committed suicide. The blossom of freedom was destroyed by the herbicidal mixture of fear, torment, and torture.

4. Economic Stalinism

The Communists followed the broad outlines of Stalinist economics that included collectivization and rapid industrialization through centralized planning. They tried to secure popular support for radical reforms before implementing them and used a gradualist approach. Collectivization emerged out of a program of land redistribution and rural equalization.

Collectivization. During the Yan'an decade the Communists discovered that radical rural experimentation produced opposition and reduced farm output. At the same time they experimented with various types of gradual, modest land redistribution. This was followed by a gradual, three-stage introduction of collectivization. Collectivization, as you recall, is state ownership and management of farmland, with peasants transformed into slave-like workers.

Land Reform. Land reform preceded collectivization. Redistribution of land began during the war and accelerated as the Communists expanded out of their northwest China base. This took place gradually, based on Communist experience during the war and on the gradual consolidation of Communist power in the country. Land reform was a strategy to destroy the power of the wealthy, and sometimes absentee, landlords, gain the support of the peasant masses, and create an economically egalitarian (and thus socialist) countryside. The Communists recognized that land reform should not take the property of the most productive individual landowners, since the country could not afford any loss of farm output. The process was not peaceful, for the Communists organized *struggle meetings* to arouse peasants to attack the landlords and wealthiest peasants, beat or kill them, and seize their property. Landlord counterattacks produced internal war within villages. Land redistribution went nation-wide in 1950 and concluded by the end of 1951.

As much as 40 percent of the farmland changed hands. Land reform did little to increase productivity, while the turmoil in the villages probably hindered farming. Yet the Party needed more capital for industrial investment. In spite of their rural orientation, the Communists decided to "squeeze the peasants," as the Soviets had done in the 1920s (see Chapter One). Peasants were forced to sell over one-quarter of their harvest to the state at very low prices. Yet, industry needed still more capital. The Communists then turned to *collectivization.*

Collectivization. Collectivization had as its ultimate aim the creation of a Soviet-style agricultural system. However, the Chinese used somewhat different methods, in part because they had so recently come to power and in part because they understood the need to introduce rural change gradually.

In a first stage, peasants were asked to join *mutual aid teams,* in which labor, tools, and draft animals were shared. These teams were quite small, encompassing half a dozen or so families, mostly smallholders. At first mutual aid teams were disbanded after each harvest but eventually they operated year-round. Generally by 1952 or 1953, mutual aid teams were combined into larger units of 30–50 families to form *lower-stage agricultural cooperatives.* At this point land was pooled, along with labor, tools, and draft animals. Land remained privately owned but was worked jointly. After the government took its "share" of the harvest, the remainder was allocated to peasants based on the acreage each family contributed and the amount of work each family provided.

By 1955, officials were grouping lower-stage agricultural cooperatives into *higher-stage agricultural cooperatives,* essentially collective farms. Each collective farm contained several hundred households. In theory, peasants still owned the land. They also retained private plots, used primarily for growing vegetables that could be consumed or sold at market. By 1957, almost all peasants were organized into collective farms.

Collectivization was not a spontaneous action by peasants. The Communist Party directed it. Just as land reform produced high levels of violence, so did collectivization. Somewhere between several hundred thousand and 2 million people died in the collectivization process, primarily in southern China. Collectivization led to increased agricultural output, though a substantial portion of the increase came from the private plots and the elimination of boundary strips, which marginally increased the amount of land under cultivation. Collectivization created rural equality and gave the state control over the peasants, solidifying the Communists' rural base. Gradualism also played an important role in transforming the urban economy.

Nationalization and Rapid Industrialization. Since the Communists had little experience with the industrial sector of the economy and needed to rebuild and expand industry, initially they did not intrude in the industrial economy, except to coordinate the supply of raw materials and to support trade unions.

The Communists decided to follow the Soviet model, which involved state ownership of industry; mobilization of labor through propaganda and coercion; long-range central planning; extensive (rather than intensive) exploitation of labor, capital, and raw materials; and an emphasis on heavy industry rather than consumer goods. The Soviet method appeared to have been a successful strategy for rapid modernization and this made it appealing to the Chinese. In addition, Soviet aid to China was incorporated into and geared to Soviet five-year plans, forcing the Chinese to follow the Soviet approach.

Once again, the Chinese moved more slowly than their Soviet counterparts had. Initially the Communists encouraged factory owners to follow Western market principles. Private ownership and entrepreneurship were confirmed. This period is sometimes known as *national capitalism.* The repression campaigns of the late 1940s and early 1950s "softened up" the business community, making it open to Communist proposals for changing principles of ownership. First, factory owners agreed to transfer half of their assets to the state. By 1955, the state had demanded and owners had acquiesced in the transfer of the remaining assets. Thus private enterprise was nationalized. Another basis for nationalization came from the confiscation of Japanese-built industry in Manchuria and in major coastal cities, especially Shanghai, and the factories of Nationalist supporters who fled to Taiwan.

Nationalization, completed in the middle of the First Five-Year Plan of 1953–1957, was essential to the success of centralized long-range planning. Though planners had received some training in the Soviet Union, they had little experience and little accurate data to inform their decisions. The First Five-Year Plan called for high expenditures in heavy industry, especially, coal, iron, and steel. It produced a sharp growth rate in the industrial economy, though it was hard to see how the growth could be sustained. The transformation of the Chinese economy had an impact on Chinese social structure, too.

Social Change. The Second World War and the initial period of Chinese Stalinism produced revolutionary changes in social structure. The gentry class was destroyed through deaths in the war, flight to Taiwan or Southeast Asia, and Communist repression. A new upper class emerged—the Chinese Communist *cadre* (party activists). The intelligentsia that had developed in the late nineteenth century was browbeaten and crushed by the Communists and most of its members were declared disloyal, and thus beyond society. A new Communist intelligentsia slowly emerged. The business class, which had been an important social group in the Nationalist era, was also destroyed by the mid-1950s. The working class became increasingly important. For skilled workers and other permanent employees guaranteed wages gave them some security (the *iron rice bowl*). Differentiations within the largest class, the peasantry, generally disappeared. The peasants remained near the bottom of the social ladder. At the bottom were unskilled workers, day laborers, and large numbers of immigrants from the countryside who were unemployed and frequently homeless. This class numbered in the millions.

The era was characterized by tremendous social mobility. Upward mobility was available to those who could demonstrate their loyalty to the Communists Party and who found roles and jobs in the new society. Downward mobility characterized former supporters of the Nationalists, the intelligentsia, and the business community. Social stability arrived very slowly. Radical change also can be seen in family and gender roles.

5. Family and Gender Revolutions

Having begun to change in the first half of the Twentieth Century, the Confucian family system that determined gender roles was largely destroyed in the early years of Communism. The Communists saw the Confucian family as a relic of the past and as a bulwark of conservative opposition to the radical changes the Communists wished to introduce.

Changes in the Family. The Communists sought to destroy the traditional family through law and peer pressure (struggle meetings). In 1950, the government issued a *Marriage Law.* The law granted women equality with men, eliminated the bases for legal male domination of the family, and gave unmarried, divorced, and widowed women the right to own land in their own names. Women were given divorce rights equal to those of men. Concubinage was outlawed, replaced by monogamy. However, it was not enough to issue decrees; it was necessary to ensure that the new law was enforced.

The Communists decided to implement the law at the grass roots level, using struggle meetings. Communist work teams went from village to village organizing women to attack the most authoritarian patriarchs. Patriarchs were dragged into the village center, accompanied by drums and catcalls. There they were threatened and sometimes beaten. They were to be an example to other males who retained the old ways and treated women cruelly.

Women's Rights. In the cities, where most of the population was young and many were single, it was easier to implement the changes. In addition, a start toward greater rights for women had already been made in the Nationalist period.

Women moved into the workforce in great numbers, many migrating from the rural areas to the cities in search of work. In general women worked menial jobs rather than skilled ones.

A number of prominent female intellectuals were purged in the repression campaigns of the late 1940s and early 1950s. Among them was *Ding Ling,* one of the great Chinese writers of the Twentieth Century. Women played a peripheral political role. The wives of some party leaders had some influence but only one woman held a post as minister in the government. The rhetoric of equality was applied in the home but not in the public arena.

6. Loyalty and Minority Policy

The Chinese Communists changed the rules of diversity and community. In Imperial China, culture—classical learning and the acceptance of Confucian ideals—determined whether one was Chinese. Ethnicity and race were not very important, though in the second half of the nineteenth century the Chinese began to exclude those whose ethnicity was non-Chinese and especially those whose religion was Islam. Under Communism, political loyalty replaced cultural identity as the main basis for community.

Loyalty. Loyalty to Communism replaced tolerance of differences, becoming the primary determinant of membership in Chinese society. Class origins as well as behavior were used to identify disloyal groups, groups that lost citizenship rights, employment, and access to education for themselves and their relatives. The repression campaigns of 1949–1952 were used to identify and punish those whose loyalty was questioned or questionable. Thus enormous pressure was applied to ensure ideological conformity. Parallels exist between the ideological uniformity expected in the imperial period and the ideological conformity in the form of belief in Communism in the Maoist era. Ideological conformity was a constant, except for the Republican era of 1912–1949, which was one of ideological disarray. The nature of the dominant ideology changed, of course.

National Minorities. The Communists also recognized the existence of national minorities and minority issues. When the Communists came to power the country possessed over fifty minority groups with a population of about 30 million (6–7% of the population). Most of the minorities were Muslims and lived on the periphery of China. Those in the north were mainly the remnants of Mongol and other Central Asian invaders, who had not assimilated to Chinese culture. Those in the south had been pushed to the edges of China by the southward movement of the Han Chinese 1,000 years earlier. Some were driven into mountainous areas along the border with India and Southeast Asia. Others were pushed into mountainous or upland areas within south China.

A number of members of minority groups had joined the Communists after the Long March. Thus it was easy for the Communists to develop an initial strategy of permitting the minorities to remain outside the radical changes that affected the Han Chinese during the first half of the 1950s. However, when the Communists sent work teams into minority areas to identify potential Communists and encourage modernization, they were met with suspicion and resistance.

That resistance was greatest in Tibet, which was loosely incorporated into Communist China in 1950. At first the Chinese policy emphasized gradual assimilation. The *Seventeen Point Agreement* of 1950 reflected this strategy. Tibet would be permitted to retain its traditional culture, while recognizing that Tibet was part of China. When the Communists tried to introduce Stalinist reforms among the East Tibetans in Western China, many East Tibetans fled to Tibet. The Tibetans were poised to offer resistance to Chinese actions.

Pressure to adopt a different policy came with the push for rapid economic growth and modernization. By the end of the First Five-Year plan minorities were no longer exempt from the radical social and economic changes recently introduced in the rest of China.

Conclusions. The emphasis on loyalty remained a constant in the Communist era, while the Party vacillated between policies of acculturation of the minorities and cultural autonomy for them.

E. AGE OF MAOIST RADICALISM, 1956–1976

After less than a decade of profound change, China seemed ready to relax and take the time to fully absorb changes already introduced. Mao Zedong and other members of the "leftist" faction of the Communist Party used the intelligentsia's critique as motivation for continuing permanent revolution. However, new radical reforms turned out to be flawed and brought great misery to the people. China moved from relative isolation from the rest of the world to being the object of attention of the two superpowers, the United States and the Soviet Union. Intense political conflict within the party first gave victory to the radicals, then briefly to the *modernizers.* The radicals returned to power through the Cultural Revolution, tearing the party and Chinese society apart in the process. Political conflict took place on the ideological level as well. Mao Zedong and the radicals championed permanent revolution, social equality, decentralization, peasant revolutionism, and voluntarism. Proposals for permanent revolution, the *Great Leap Forward* and *People's Communes,* were intended to solve economic problems through radical decentralization of economic decision-making and by giving priority to rural development. Leftist radicalism also challenged the very institution of the family, weakened it and sought to replace loyalty to the family with loyalty to Mao Zedong. Thus community was to be created by shifting the primary focus of loyalty away from the Communist Party and to Mao himself. However, the radical initiatives made unity more difficult, though they did contribute to a reduction of urban-rural differences. Overall, the two decades of permanent revolution caused enormous hardship and pain to the Chinese people, parallel to the sufferings under Soviet Stalinism (see Chapter One).

1. From Isolation to World Power Status

Relatively isolated in the mid-1950s, China became recognized as a major power by the end of the radical age. Both the Great Leap Forward and the Cultural Revolution forced China to focus on domestic affairs. When China participated in world affairs it directed more and more energy to relationships with the two super powers—the Soviet Union and the United States.

Third World Revolution. In a marginal way, the Chinese fomented Third World revolution. They encouraged revolutionary movements in southern Africa, especially in Mozambique, and in the Middle East, primarily giving support to the anti-Israel Palestinian Liberation Organization.

The Sino-Soviet Split. One of the most important global events of this era was the Sino-Soviet split. The Chinese had resented having to subordinate their interests to those of the Soviet Union. When Stalin died and Khrushchev began a modest program of liberalization, the Chinese Communists attacked him. The Hundred Flowers Campaign and the Great Leap Forward represented Mao's subtle criticism of the Hungarian Uprising of 1956 and the dangers of liberalization, China's belief that war with capitalism was inevitable and a rejection of Stalinist economics. These campaigns drove the two sides further apart.

In 1957, tensions lessened as the two nations signed a "technology for national defense" agreement that may have promised Soviet assistance in the development of a Chinese atomic bomb. In the late 1950s the Soviets helped the Chinese develop uranium mines, a nuclear weapons test site and ballistic missile capability. As Khrushchev pushed for peaceful co-existence with the West, Mao "went ballistic," leading the Soviets in 1960 to withdraw technical assistance used in the construction of Chinese atomic weapons. By 1961, the Chinese had begun to publicly attack Khrushchev and the Soviet Union. His condemnation of Chinese Communism at the Twenty Second Party Congress led to a Chinese walk out and further deterioration of the relationship.

Tension peaked in 1969, with border clashes along the Ussuri River boundary between the two countries. Altogether almost 1,000 soldiers, mainly Chinese, died in the skirmishes. Obviously the Soviets attempted to take advantage of a China weakened by the Cultural Revolution. The border conflict had several consequences. The Chinese military became determined to end the Cultural Revolution, seeing it as a grave threat to national security. The prestige and status of the military was enhanced, in spite of obvious inferiority to Soviet troops. Finally, the Chinese recognized the need for better relations with the United States as a counter to the Soviet threat.

The Chinese–U.S. Alliance. The Chinese Communists and the United States had flirted with an alliance during the Second World War and the ensuing civil war. From 1948 until the beginning of the 1970s, the two were bitter enemies, though throughout the period they regularly held discussions in Poland. The first step toward rapprochement came in 1971 when the United States withdrew its objections to transferring the permanent seat on the U.N. Security Council from Taiwan to the People's Republic of China. In April, *ping-pong diplomacy* began. A U.S. table tennis team visiting Japan was invited to play exhibition matches in China. Secretary of State Henry Kissinger soon arrived in China and made arrangements for President Richard Nixon to visit China, a trip that took place in February 1972. The two sides drew up a vague communiqué that called for U.S. technical support for China and scientific, academic, and sports exchanges. Both agreed to work toward diplomatic recognition of each other. This normalization of relations between the two countries was based on a mutual threat, the Soviet Union. The U.S.–Chinese ties isolated the Soviet Union, forcing it into a military buildup it could neither sustain nor afford. The U.S.–Chinese arrangement thus played a role in the collapse of Communism in the Soviet Union.

2. The Chinese Communist Party—Divided and Destroyed

Radical social and economic change damaged the Chinese Communist Party. The Party split into two fairly distinct factions. On one side were the "Leftists," supporters of Mao and permanent revolution. On the other were the "Modernizers," (sometimes called moderates or "Rightists"), pragmatic conservatives who initially favored one of two approaches—either continuation of Stalinist economics or a shift to a Leninist-style New Economic Policy (see Chapter One). The Great Leap Forward led to internal conflict within the Party. The Cultural Revolution produced warfare among Party factions and the disintegration of the Party.

Politics of the Great Leap Forward. By the mid-1950s, Mao Zedong consolidated his power. Leadership of the "revolution" and the successful transformation of China into a Stalinist society gave Mao unimaginable authority. With this authority he had little difficulty introducing radical changes.

In political terms, the Great Leap Forward produced significant decentralization of political decision-making. The reduction of the power of the central government and central Party cadres contributed to the dissatisfaction with Mao that emerged as early as the end of December 1958. Attacks on Mao and criticism of the Great Leap Forward at the Wuhan meeting of the Central Committee led him to resign as head of state. Further criticism took place at the Lushan party conference in July 1959. Peng Dehuai condemned the Great Leap Forward, leading Mao to accuse him of "rightist opportunism." Mao took the criticism personally and mobilized enough support, in spite of the failures of the Great Leap Forward, to force Peng to resign as Minister of Defense. Clearly, Mao still had sufficient power to weather any criticism and to transform the criticism into charges that his opponents had betrayed Communism.

Still, by the early 1960s Mao had been moved aside, permitting the moderates, led by *Liu* Shaoqi, to dismantle the Great Leap Forward institutions and to propose the kind of mixed economy that existed in the Soviet Union in the 1920s. The political conflict over the Great Leap Forward and Mao's responsibility for it split the Party deeply.

The Politics of the Cultural Revolution. The apparent victory of the modernizers was a *pyrrhic* one. Mao soon began to rebuild his political power, especially with the assistance of the military, and turned a 1963–1964 campaign against him into a program of mass mobilization—the Great Proletarian Cultural Revolution. This led to civil war, known as the *Cultural Revolution,* which destroyed the government and the Party. The military briefly assumed power at the end of the Cultural Revolution. Gradually the moderates regained control of the government and rebuilt the Communist Party, holding off attacks from the defeated radicals. Mao's death signaled the end to radicalism but did not halt power struggles at the top of the Party.

Military Support. *Lin* Biao, new Minister of Defense, orchestrated a massive propaganda campaign within the military. He championed the mythology of the omnipotent and all-powerful Mao and the desperate need to return to the concept of permanent revolution. The radical camp gained a number of other allies, including Mao Zedong's third wife, *Jiang* Qing. Security forces and ideological functionaries were brought on board, too.

The Allegorical Campaign. Initially the increasingly powerful radicals and the pragmatic conservatives fought each other through literature and allegory. *Wu Han,* a historian and writer, was the central figure in this struggle. His essay on a prominent political figure of the Ming period used *allegory* to attack permanent revolution, the Great Leap Forward, and Mao's radical clique. The radicals established a power base in Shanghai and from there attacked Wu Han's ideas. Party leaders were being forced to take a stance on the Great Leap Forward and other radical initiatives.

Beginnings of the Cultural Revolution. By 1966, two groups had formed within the party, one promoting moderation and the other radicalism. The Group of Five espoused the moderate position of Liu Shaoqi and *Deng Xiaoping.* The radical group met in Shanghai under the general leadership of

Jiang Qing. Initially a majority of party leaders accepted the moderate approach, which wished to treat Wu Han's writings as merely academic debate and to support gradual economic reforms. The radicals argued that the opponents of Mao were actually an "anti-Party group" and reconfirmed the need for a radical vision for China. Wu Han was described as the gardener of a field of "anti-socialist poisonous weeds."

Compromise and conciliation no longer seemed possible. Mao became even more convinced that Stalinist bureaucratization and the Party's inability to produce innovative ideas endangered the Chinese revolution. Conflict within the Party fused with the frustrations of disgruntled urban youth to initiate the Cultural Revolution.

Youth and the Cultural Revolution. The 1960s were a period of global student unrest—from Berkeley to Kent State, from Paris to Tokyo. China was not immune. The moderates could not prevent a purge of the cultural bureaucracy in the late spring of 1966. This led students to direct verbal attacks against the cultural elite in Beijing and against university professors. Obviously the professors were a convenient target for student protests. In May, unrest spread to secondary schools and students began to be called *Red Guards.* Under the influence of the radicals, students came to see themselves as the next and true revolutionary generation, whose opportunities were being squandered by the moderates. Examinations were cancelled as the school year came to a close, giving students free time to pursue radical vigilante actions. Professors were taunted and subjected to public humiliation. Their property (especially books) was destroyed. Masses of students were drawn to Beijing where Mao greeted them and encouraged them in their activities. Students went on a rampage in the fall. Since all schools were now closed, students had the leisure to engage in Red Guard activity full time. Red Guards beat or tortured to death thousands of intellectuals. Many more were sent to impoverished collective farms, to "learn from the people." The levels of hatred expressed by the youth indicate how dissatisfied they were. They had been taught to give total loyalty to the Communist Party. Now they attacked it and transferred that total allegiance to Mao and the radicals. The radicals used the cover of student violence to purge the Communist Party, eventually dismissing the moderate leaders Liu Shaoqi and Deng Xiaoping.

January 1967 Uprising. By 1967, the Cultural Revolution had spread beyond the intelligentsia and now engaged the energies of factory workers, too. Red Guard groups, acting independently, expressed their rage toward the system and their faith in Mao by attacking state property and government offices. Later radicals sacked the Ministry of Foreign Affairs building and torched secret correspondence.

In January, the radicals stormed the ramparts of power in Shanghai and established the Shanghai People's Commune. However, Mao finally became concerned about the extent of violence and the destruction of formal power. He, too, felt threatened by the anarchic behavior of the rebels. Mao urged the formation of revolutionary communes in each province, with power to be shared among the Red Guards, the military, and Maoist Communist Party officials. The army assumed greater importance. While continuing to publicly support the Cultural Revolution, it also began to restore order. Generally the army destroyed working class Red Guard units and left the students alone.

Red Guards clashed with the army more and more frequently. In Wuhan in July 1967 the army destroyed the power of the large group of local Red Guards. Two key leaders of the Cultural Revolution were sent to Wuhan to condemn the military's actions. Army units opposed to the Cultural Revolution kidnapped one of them. Then Zhou Enlai and crack paratroop units flew in to halt the military mutiny. Still, the military and radicals fought more and more frequently all across China. The struggle was uneven since the military had superior firepower and organizational skills.

By the autumn of 1967, most of the radical leaders also came to the conclusion that the country was in the midst of anarchy and order needed to be restored. Gradually the army gained the upper hand. However it was only in the summer of 1968 that relative order was restored. The radical leaders then initiated a massive purge that crushed the grass roots radicals as well as supporters of the moderates. Those who were neither executed nor imprisoned were forced to go through indoctrination training, known as *May Seventh schools,* to ensure that they would accept the correct socialist line. These schools combined indoctrination with hard labor on collective farms. Internal exile became the fate of millions of Chinese youth who had believed deeply in Mao. Yet, he had now turned against them.

Lin Biao and the Collapse of Military Dictatorship. By 1969, the military, led by Lin Biao, had consolidated its power throughout China. The regular governmental and party structures had been destroyed by the Cultural Revolution. Only the revolutionary communes, now dominated by the military, could quickly provide administration for the country.

Two years later the military's efforts to dominate China were blunted. Mao developed a plan to weaken the power of the military. A number of senior officials were forced to undergo indoctrination. Lin Biao's key supporters in the high command were dismissed. Mao also shifted military commanders to different localities in order to undermine their regional power bases. The military command in Beijing was changed as Mao brought in officers personally loyal to him. Finally, in May 1971, Lin Biao was killed in a plane crash. The official account was that Lin had planned to murder Mao Zedong and that when the plot was discovered Lin and his family tried to flee to the Soviet Union. Unfortunately, their jet ran out of fuel and crashed in Mongolia. It is not known whether this story is true. It is clear that Lin died in May 1971, thus marking the collapse of a very brief military dictatorship.

Under the leadership of Zhou Enlai, previous government institutions were recreated and the Communist Party organizations resurrected. By 1973, the moderates had reestablished the political system that had existed before the Cultural Revolution.

Last Ditch Radical Campaigns. Though the Red Guards had been destroyed and order reestablished, the radical leaders still retained much power. In fact, at the 1973 Party Congress radicals gained greater influence in the Politburo while the military lost half of the seats it had previously held on the Central Committee. The radicals attacked Confucius and Western music in order to rekindle the flame of radicalism. The flame, however, had been extinguished forever.

Symbolic of this was a devastating earthquake and the deaths of Zhou Enlai and Mao Zedong, all in 1976. Their deaths brought an end to an era of barbaric *internecine* warfare. Mao had sought to demonstrate the validity of permanent revolution, mobilize a new revolutionary generation, and consolidate his political position by destroying his enemies. He achieved none of these goals.

3. Ideological Battles—Permanent Revolution vs. Moderation

The Great Leap Forward and the Cultural Revolution demonstrated how difficult it was for the Chinese Communists to define the nature of Chinese Marxism. Most agreed that Stalinism was no longer an appropriate vehicle for moving China to a higher stage of socialism. However, there was bitter conflict over what should replace Stalinism. Many of the radical perspectives were drawn from the Yan'an experience, an ideology largely abandoned in the Stalinist phase. Both the radicals and the moderates sought to articulate their vision, the radicals more clearly in the Great Leap Forward and the moderates after the Cultural Revolution. The debate between the two sides hearkened back to the debate over isms during the May Fourth Movement.

Radical Vision of the Great Leap Forward. The Great Leap Forward attempted to actualize the theory of permanent revolution. Mao seemed convinced that Stalinism had brought about a fossilization of Chinese life that would prevent any further progress toward higher stages of socialism. He believed that permanent revolution required that constant struggle be employed to destroy conservative institutions, ways of thinking, and other barriers to achieving higher and higher levels of socialism.

Radicalism suggested that economic development should result from dispersing economic resources and upgrading the technological skills of those least familiar with technology—the peasants. This *populism,* or idealization of the revolutionary potential of the peasants, permeated radical thought. Mao's emphasis on human will played a role in two ways. First, he believed that peasant will could transform the countryside into a modern sector of Chinese life. Second, the emphasis on human will was translated into the idea that economic growth resulted from labor intensity rather than extensive use of capital, labor, and materials. Mao's emphasis on peasant effort was still a strategy for exploiting the peasants, no matter how much he suggested that Stalinism had exploited the peasants and the Great Leap Forward would emancipate them. Finally, Mao's campaign had echoes of the earlier puritanical condemnation of urban life.

Modernization. The moderates argued that the party should avoid ideologically based decisions and radical changes. Powerless to prevent the Great Leap Forward, they could only point out its faults later. The moderates rejected the idea of permanent revolution, though they too accepted populism and voluntarism. Economic modernization, from their perspective, must be achieved through industrialization.

Radical Thought and the Cultural Revolution. Mao articulated his ideas of permanent revolution much more clearly in the run up to the Great Leap Forward. Though the Cultural Revolution had strong ideological overtones, Mao's radicalism was less clearly defined.

The ideology of the Cultural Revolution emphasized the great patriarch—thus espousing the great man in history perspective. Once again the radicals stressed permanent revolution and condemned the stagnation of Chinese socialism after the Great Leap Forward. The radicals attacked the "four olds"—old customs, old habits, old culture, and old thinking.

By this time Mao had lost faith in populism; he no longer considered the peasants capable of the self-sacrifice he needed. The collapse of the Great Leap Forward had proved that he could not count on the peasants. Instead he looked to a new revolutionary generation—China's youth. For him students had become the new masses.

The radicals emphasized the importance of indoctrination. Human will remained supreme as young people could be motivated to carry out Cultural Revolution through propaganda campaigns. Finally, the Cultural Revolution was anti-Western and anti-Soviet. China must be self-reliant. It must carry out permanent revolution without the help or interference of outsiders (see Stalin's "Socialism in One Country" in Chapter One).

Moderating the Cultural Revolution. Initially, the moderates were concerned with saving their lives and later with rebuilding the nation's political structure. They spent little time presenting a clear ideological alternative to radicalism. Radicalism had such a destructive impact on China that little ideological justification was needed to oppose it. The moderates emphasized stability and order. They condemned spontaneity and undisciplined behavior. They stressed the importance of state leadership and the bureaucracy. Modernization was clearly a goal. Though there was a price to pay, including greater inequality, bureacratism, and corruption, the ultimate benefits outweighed the harm, they argued. Most of all, change must be gradual.

4. Economics of Radicalism

Both the Great Leap Forward and the Cultural Revolution had a tremendous impact on the Chinese economy. The Great Leap Forward was based on fairly clear economic goals and included a strategy for achieving those goals. The Cultural Revolution did not offer an economic strategy but had serious economic consequences. Both the Great Leap Forward and the Cultural Revolution greatly damaged the country.

Great Leap Forward. Initiated in 1957, by the end of the 1950s the Great Leap Forward (GLF) had been abandoned, clearly a terrible and destructive economic failure. We have looked at the political and ideological background to the Great Leap Forward. Economic policy was at its core.

The Great Leap Forward responded to Mao's need for permanent revolution and his support for a rural technological revolution. It also attempted to solve specific problems. The agricultural growth rate was slowing, hardly able to keep up with the population growth, especially since large amounts of grain were shipped to the Soviet Union to repay loans. The economy could not provide the capital necessary for industrial development and thus the GLF was an effort to reduce the need for capital. Finally, the GLF was viewed as a means of drawing much of the excess labor out of the cities and moving it to the countryside.

The Great Leap Forward had six major components. First, the Great Leap Forward introduced much more ambitious industrial production goals, including more than doubling steel production. Much of the increase was to be achieved by a doubling of the industrial workforce. Second, it was a plan to decentralize economic decision-making. This reduced the power of the central bureaucracy and placed decision-making closer to the point of production. In theory this would reduce the amount of bad decision-making. Of course this plan required either that central bureaucrats be reassigned to local level management or that new people (peasants) be trained for management positions.

Third, the GLF emphasized rural technology. Its goal was to extend technology to the countryside, in part to ensure that the entire population would be modernized through the use of technology. In addition, rural technology was seen as simpler and less costly, thus reducing capital investment needs. Collective farms were encouraged to establish low-tech factories that would produce consumer goods. Thus, rural factories produced light bulbs and other relatively simple objects. Sometimes small steel mills, generally known as *backyard furnaces,* were built. The volume of steel produced was substantial but the quality was quite low. No nationwide coordination of production existed, so some goods were produced in great quantities and others failed to meet demand.

Fourth, a massive propaganda campaign accompanied the Great Leap Forward. Peasants were told they were building an ideal future of equality, productivity and wealth. Few believed the propaganda for very long. Fifth, the educational system was expanded and reorganized. In addition to increasing the number of students at all levels, 30,000 agricultural middle schools and 400 "red and expert" universities were built. All schools were to engage in productive labor as part of the educational curriculum.

Finally, beginning in the fall of 1957, rural society was restructured into 26,000 *People's Communes.* Some economists call this the introduction of *state-feudalism.* Communes, with an average population of 25,000–30,000, were to be responsible for all aspects of rural life. A commune determined economic development and investment strategies. It mobilized the local population for infrastructure projects, such as new irrigation systems or reforestation. It coordinated propaganda campaigns. It also organized "people's militias" that trained daily in order to be able to defend China against possible invasion. At least 30 million and perhaps as many as 220 million served in the militias. The communes also sought to eliminate the private family, replacing it with communal duties.

The communes were a failure, bringing with them disillusionment and political conflict. They could not coordinate economic activity; they failed to maintain peasant enthusiasm for the experiment, and they diverted peasant labor from agriculture, producing a sharp decline in agricultural output. In addition, to feed the larger urban population, the state took 40 percent of the harvest. The Great Leap Forward produced a famine during which at least 20 million people died.

Moderate Plan for Economic Restoration. The dislocation, devastation, and loss of life forced China to abandon the Great Leap Forward and to quickly introduce policies to ameliorate its damage. The Party accepted a five-point program proposed by Chen Yun, head of central planning. These policies remained in effect until the collapse of government during the Cultural Revolution. The 30 million people who had moved to the cities during the 1950s were permanently moved back to the countryside. Rural factories were dismantled. Private plots were reestablished, totaling 6 percent of the farmland. Private markets were reopened. Finally, individual households were made responsible for setting their own production goals, rather than have them imposed from above. In reality, the collective farms once again became the basic rural organization. The shift toward a mixed rural economy led to increased agricultural production. Centralized planning once again concentrated on determining and coordinating production goals. Though the moderate plan produced economic recovery, it also brought back into favor bureaucracies, the cities, and corruption—all of which Mao found unacceptable. By 1965, agricultural production had reached 1957 levels. However population had increased even faster, reducing the per capita food supply.

Economics of Cultural Revolution. Mao did not propose radical economic experiments during the Cultural Revolution. Its economic impact was indirect, though devastating. Educational and scientific research institutions were closed. This meant that scientific and technological innovation stopped. Peasants' living standards were reduced because they had to provide food for the millions of Red Guards who roamed all over China, many of them trying to duplicate the Long March or go to the "holy shrines" of Maoism. Especially in 1967 and 1968, factory production was seriously interrupted by worker participation in the Cultural Revolution and by breakdowns in the supply of goods to factories because the rail system was being used primarily to transport the millions of Red Guards. Military costs went up, both to supply the peasant militia with weapons and to produce a military buildup because of the Soviet threat. Much money had to be expended to rebuild and restore property destroyed by the Red Guards. The Cultural Revolution produced a significant economic decline but did not create major structural changes.

Return to Stalinism. Though the radicals continued to call for mobilization of the population to work harder, the Stalinist economic system was reestablished. Zhou Enlai, Chen Yun, and Deng Xiaoping led those who called for a return to the traditional Stalinist system. They were influenced by the *Petroleum Group,* which recognized the need for foreign investment and *technology transfer.* Because the United States was the world's leader in oil industry technology, the Chinese drew up a long-range plan for the purchase of U.S. oil technology equipment. However, the Stalinist system no longer met the needs of a China so far behind the industrial nations of the world, for whom technological innovation was a key to economic growth.

Conclusions on the Economy. Radical economic changes had damaged the Chinese economy, while Stalinist strategies reached the limit of their usefulness. New approaches were needed and in the late 1970s a number of experiments took place, leading toward what would become the Four Modernizations.

Social Structure. In this period, Chinese social structure came to resemble that of other Communist countries. Communist party leadership and its families sat at the top of society. Just beneath them was a technical/bureaucratic elite that filled government positions and leadership positions in the economy. In the middle was the intelligentsia, including teachers and writers. Further down were three lower classes: white collar workers, industrial workers, and peasants. At the bottom of society was the unskilled work force, composed primarily of peasant immigrants from the countryside.

5. Redefinition of the Family and Gender Roles

Radical experiments were not limited to the economy. During the Great Leap Forward attempts were made to destroy the private family. These attempts at family reform were the most hated parts of the Great Leap Forward. Actually the Cultural Revolution did even greater damage to the family, especially that of the intelligentsia.

People's Communes and the Family. Efforts were made through the People's Communes to destroy the private family. Party workgroups organized anti-family meetings. In a number of cases, families were physically broken up. Men and women were placed in separate barracks, as were the children and elderly. The commune, not the family, assumed responsibility for raising children. The commune assigned domestic duties in rotation. Communal dining rooms replaced meals at home. Some radicals saw this as a strategy for destroying the family. They had not been content to attack the patriarchal family or perhaps they recognized that earlier efforts to destroy patriarchy had failed. Most importantly, however, elimination of the private family meant that its former members could spend much more time working for the commune.

The Great Leap Forward also brought changes in the position of women. A substantial number of women moved into positions of importance, especially at the commune-level. The Party also argued that the Great Leap Forward continued the Communists' efforts to promote equality of men and women, in this case focusing on the equality of work. The communes also reduced women's domestic role, especially in child rearing. During the GLF the birth rate went down dramatically, further reducing women's traditional role.

Cultural Revolution and the Family. The Cultural Revolution further undermined the family and totally destroyed some individual families. It also promoted emancipation of Chinese young women.

The radicals attacked the family as a relic of the past. The Cultural Revolution broke up families in several ways. Most obviously, the party promoted efforts to turn children against their parents. Red Guards verbally and physically abused their parents and betrayed them as "enemies of the Cultural Revolution." Parents, in turn, could not understand why their children were acting so "strangely." In addition, "enemies" were imprisoned or sent to do hard labor at collective farms. At the end of the Cultural Revolution millions of Red Guards were sent to remote parts of China and forbidden to return to their urban homes. Many came home only a decade later and many never reunited with their families. Finally, the freedoms youths gained by participating in the marches and trips all over China gave them an independence they would not have obtained until a later age under normal conditions. Middle school students became adults by participating in the Cultural Revolution.

The Cultural Revolution brought no substantial changes in gender roles, though Jiang Qing became a role model for many female Red Guards. There was a kind of asexual comradeship among the Red Guards of both sexes who traveled together all over China.

The weakening of the most basic institution in Chinese society—the family—and the familial conflict that became very common during the Cultural Revolution was paralleled by the failure of efforts to build community based on loyalty to Maoist radicalism.

6. Loyalty and Ethnic Unity

Radicalism placed intense pressure on the Chinese people to be loyal to Mao. Lack of loyalty meant automatic dismissal from the ranks of respected citizens. The propaganda campaigns of the Great Leap Forward also emphasized conformity. For the first time, the Communists made major efforts to incorporate minorities into the main stream of Chinese Communist life.

Loyalty. Though the Communists had permitted some political diversity in the Stalinist period, the repression campaigns had severely limited people's ability to be different. The Hundred Flowers provided a final opportunity for divergence from the Communist Party, even though difference and conflict continued within the party leadership. In the era of permanent revolution, the Party placed even greater emphasis on loyalty. A simple formula for loyalty was applied during both the Great Leap Forward and the Cultural Revolution—class origin. Someone from a peasant or working class background was automatically termed loyal and thus had rights of citizenship, including access to education and exemption from suspicion. Someone from a middle class, intelligentsia, or gentry background was automatically suspect, considered disloyal, and thus barred from citizenship.

During the Great Leap Forward peasants quickly understood that it was better to do what the Party wanted you to, even if you didn't perform tasks conscientiously or well. The alternative was exclusion from the category of the loyal.

During the Cultural Revolution, the radicals placed even greater emphasis on loyalty, with class background, and attitude toward the Cultural Revolution (i.e., radicalism) the key determinants of loyalty and citizenship. Disloyalty produced loss of jobs; exclusion from the party; verbal and physical abuse; and imprisonment, exile, or execution.

Ethnic Minorities. The Party also made major efforts to force national minorities to conform to state policy. No longer were minorities given some degree of freedom from participation in the Maoist society. The Party abandoned the attitude that minorities were not yet ready to undergo the kind of modernization expected of Han Chinese. Just as collectivization had been extended into minority areas, the People's Communes and the Cultural Revolution reached them as well.

No longer left alone, minorities increasingly resorted to rebellion. The most important rebellion in this period occurred in Tibet in 1959. Unrest among Tibetans in southwest China spread into Tibet itself. The Chinese military was sent in to crush the uprising. Brutal destruction of religious property and human life were followed by martial law and Chinese military occupation. The

Dalai Lama, head of the Tibetan religion, *Lamaism,* fled to India where he continued to call for resistance to Chinese rule. Though community and national unity were goals of the Chinese Communists, their actions reinforced diversity and fostered disunity.

F. FOUR MODERNIZATIONS, 1980–1989

During the early 1980s the basic direction of Chinese policy took a dramatic 180-degree turn, except in the area of politics. Chinese participation in the global economy replaced isolation. Both Stalinism and radicalism were abandoned, replaced by the Four Modernizations' view that China's principal goal was modernization and economic growth. The Four Modernizations established a mixed economy. The program included the privatization of agriculture, a return to rural capitalist markets, private manufacturing in the countryside, some private entrepreneurship in urban industry, decentralized management, global exports and the importation of Western technology, as well as a major emphasis on economic growth. The patriarchal family returned as a consequence of economic change. Diversity became more prominent, with economic change and greater freedom of action for minority groups, central forces in the increasing diversity. People paid lip service in terms of loyalty to the party. Much of what took place in China fell more and more beyond the zone of Party control. Efforts to promote democracy were crushed at Tiananmen Square in 1989. The Communist Party sought to remain firmly in power politically, while permitting a great deal of economic freedom, as well as modest private liberties.

1. China and the World

The Chinese played a much more active role in the world economy than previously and successfully eliminated the last vestiges of colonialism in China by recovering Macao from the Portuguese and Hong Kong from China. The Chinese military buildup seemed increasingly dangerous. Relations with the only superpower, the United States, produced low-level conflict but growing anxiety, with the two countries differing over trade policies and human rights. However, China had much more global power than it had had since the early Qing and the kind of independence from foreigners it had not enjoyed during the previous 200 years.

Hong Kong and Macao. The return of Hong Kong was of great value to the Communist Chinese. First, it was of great symbolic importance, since Hong Kong represented the last vestiges of Western imperialism in China. Second, it was a city-state with great wealth, high-tech skills, and port facilities for international trade. Finally, insistence on the return of Hong Kong made it easier for the Chinese to make a believable claim to Taiwan.

The British had controlled Hong Kong since 1840. In 1898, they had acquired a 99-year lease on a small part of the mainland next to Hong Kong, the so-called "New Territories." That lease expired in 1977. In 1984 the British and Chinese reached an agreement by which the former would return Hong Kong to China in 1997. China would control foreign policy and defense, while Hong Kong would retain a large measure of economic independence, making it similar to other special economic zones that were introduced as part of the economic reforms known as the Four Modernizations. Hong Kong was to have a representative form of government, though in reality the Chinese Communists ensured that pro-Beijing persons led the Hong Kong government.

U.S.–Chinese Relations. The Nixon initiative of 1972 was followed by an U.S. decision to normalize diplomatic relations with China. Full diplomatic relations were established at the beginning of 1979. This led to an influx of Chinese professors and students, wishing to attend American universities. The Chinese also began to purchase large amounts of American goods, including Boeing jets. Coca-Cola soon opened a bottling plant in Shanghai. Most importantly, the Americans began to send China high tech military goods used for defensive purposes, such as advanced radar systems.

The Chinese and the Russians. Tensions with the Soviet Union remained high during the 1980s, especially as it pulled Vietnam more and more fully into the Soviet orbit and began to use Vietnamese naval bases as warm water ports. As part of his new diplomacy (see Chapter One), Gorbachev sought to improve relations with China. The Chinese were hardly willing to compromise. They insisted that the Soviet Union withdraw its troops from the Soviet side of the Soviet-Chinese border; remove its troops from Afghanistan; and end Soviet support for the Vietnamese occupation of Cambodia. Trade and cultural exchanges expanded, but the key issues remained unresolved. The Soviets eventually abandoned their military efforts in Afghanistan, providing a rationale for the Chinese to accept a visit from Gorbachev in 1989. Gorbachev's visit coincided with the run up to the Tiananmen Square massacre, so the visit came to naught. The Gorbachev trip thus confirmed the Chinese in their decision to permit capitalist economic development but reject political reform.

The Chinese-Vietnamese War. Now little remembered, the brief Chinese-Vietnamese War of 1979 seemed at the time to be the start of a Chinese Communist aggressive campaign to assert primacy in Southeast Asia.

Vietnam, fully under Communist control by 1975, invaded Cambodia in January 1979. In mid-February a large Chinese army attacked Vietnam. Chinese motives are not entirely clear but leaders attempted to placate the military, which feared the modernizers would neglect the military's needs and prevent Vietnam from dominating all of mainland Southeast Asia. However, within three weeks the Chinese began to withdraw from Vietnam, having suffered heavy casualties. After that, the Chinese limited themselves to bluster and threats but generally pursued a peaceful foreign policy.

China and Africa. In the 1970s, China became deeply involved in Africa. Their motivations were two-fold. First, the Chinese sought to relive their romantic period of national liberation by helping the last colonies in Africa achieve independence. Thus Chinese support for revolutionary movements in the Portuguese colonies. After independence, these countries received financial support from China, primarily in the area of infrastructure construction. Secondly, Chinese activism in Africa was a means of undermining the Soviet Union's revolutionary credentials, thus strengthening the Chinese in their conflict with the Russians.

2. Survival of the Communist Party

In comparison with the Cultural Revolution, the period after Mao's death appeared relatively peaceful in the political sphere. However, intense political conflict continued within the Communist Party. In the second half of the 1970s, the modernizing faction destroyed the remnants of radicalism and then in the late 1980s defeated the resurgent Stalinists.

However the greatest political conflict took place not within the Party but between the Party and Chinese youth. This struggle was over what is generally called the *Fifth Modernization,* demands for democratization, and political reform. Initially the young people had considerable support from the public but the use of overwhelming military force destroyed the youth movement and silenced support from the rest of society. The Party sought to promote economic freedom while maintaining a Communist monopoly over political power.

Trial of the "*Gang of Four*." A public show trial of the radical leadership, including Mao's wife, Jiang Qing, fascinated and entertained the Chinese during the two years following Mao's death. The Trial of the Gang of Four sought to publicly humiliate the radicals and demonstrate the consequences of being a radical. Imprisoned in 1976, the radical leaders were brought to trial in 1980 and sentenced in early 1981. The trial failed to elicit the public confessions the Modernizers wanted. People wanted to forget the time of troubles that was the Cultural Revolution and get on with their lives in "modernizing" China.

Defeat of the Stalinists. Upon Mao's death, the head of security *Hua* Guofeng seized power. An opponent of the Cultural Revolution, he proposed a return to Stalinist structures. Hua had been the personal protégé of Mao and had little support beyond the security apparatus. Aided by the military, Deng Xiaoping returned to prominence in 1977. He then began to build a coalition of modernizers.

At the *Third Plenum* (special conference) of the Communist Party in 1978, victims of the Cultural Revolution were rehabilitated and began to return to party leadership positions. In addition, the plenum approved the key ideas of the Four Modernizations. Deng next launched a campaign against Hua and in 1980 replaced him as premier (head of government). Deng dominated Chinese politics through the mid-1990s.

Political Decentralization. The Four Modernizations affected the political system in two major ways. First, they contributed to a measure of decentralization of political power. A small group, with Deng Xiaoping at the head, controlled central policymaking. However, power increasingly devolved to the provincial and local levels. Second, central economic institutions lost many of their functions and more and more economic decision-making took place at lower levels. China was moving toward becoming a coalition of relatively independent provinces. The central Party was determined to maintain control but saw dissidence as a greater threat than decentralization.

Tiananmen. Just as the May Fourth demonstrations against the Versailles Treaty assumed a broader identity as the intellectual and cultural rejection of Confucianism, *Tiananmen* assumed a broader identity as the cumulative intellectual and cultural rejection of Communism. The massacre of students at Tiananmen Square in early June 1989 climaxed a decade of increasing support for democracy. *Wei* Jinsheng, a leading dissident, applied the term *The Fifth Modernization* to the pro-democracy movement. The Hundred Flowers Campaign and then the Democracy Wall movement of 1978 included calls for democratization but did not lead to major protests against the Communist Party. Tiananmen got mixed up in internal Party conflicts and led to massive student protests in the large cities of China in the spring and early summer of 1989.

The emergence of a *Neo-Stalinist* faction in the mid-1980s led to renewed conflict within the Party. The Neo-Stalinists feared that modernization, with its emphasis on economic growth and prosperity, would have negative consequences. Modernization reduced the need for a large Party bureaucracy and transferred power both to the regions and beyond the government. The Neo-Stalinists also condemned the corruption and materialism that accompanied modernization. Finally, the Neo-Stalinists longed for days of campaigns and causes, of sacrifice and glory. Now Western pop culture and making money were all-important. What had happened to Communism, they wailed?

Though the Party had promised greater freedom of expression to the literary community and the intelligentsia as a whole in the mid-1980s, the Neo-Stalinists had sufficient influence to convince the Party to crack down on student protests that began at the end of 1986. Thirty thousand students and an equal number of townspeople demonstrated for freedom and democracy in Shanghai. Next the protest movement spread to other large cities in southern China and then to Beijing. In January 1987 students held a massive demonstration for democracy and freedom at Tiananmen Square in Beijing. *Hu Yaobang,* one of the most important modernizers and head of the Party, was dismissed as head of the Communist Party, a scapegoat. Another reformer, *Zhao* Ziyang, replaced him as head of the party. Clearly the modernizers were under attack.

The death of Hu Yaobang in April 1989 acted as a catalyst for student protest. Students organized a series of demonstrations to honor Hu and call for democracy. Beijing students organized sits-ins at Party headquarters and in front of the residences of the Party leaders and held a massive demonstration on Tiananmen Square. Students also began to boycott classes. Rallies and marches grew larger and larger. In Beijing over 100,000 demonstrated on the anniversary of the May 4, 1919, march. Similar demonstrations took place throughout urban China. By mid-May the sit-in at Tiananmen became more serious, as students initiated hunger strikes. Zhao Ziyang met with the students, apparently expressing some support for their position.

Yang Shangkun, a leading military officer and close ally of Deng Xiaoping, then declared martial law. Troops thought to be loyal to Yang were brought to Beijing but for two weeks city residents blocked them from removing students from Tiananmen. The army seemed reluctant to use force against ordinary citizens. Finally, at the end of May Deng rallied enough support from the military to permit the use of all force necessary to destroy the protest movement. Zhao Ziyang appeared isolated, as Deng moved to support the Neo-Stalinists. Zhao was then dismissed as head of the Party.

In Tiananmen, some student leaders began to urge that the sit-in be called off. Enthusiasm was dissipating and crime and disease entered the square. Ironically then, art students created a thirty-foot Lady of Liberty, whose appearance revived the protesters' morale.

On the night of June 3-4, elite military forces surrounded Tiananmen Square. The students then decided to disband, but they were gunned down by the military as they tried to leave the square. Thousands died and many more were arrested. Some leaders fled the country or went into hiding. The military also crushed student movements in some seventy major cities.

Tiananmen destroyed the democracy movement and appeared to threaten the survival of the Four Modernizations.

3. The Death of Chinese Communism and the Birth of the "Fifth Modernization"

After the death of Mao, Communist ideology lost its grip on society. The Communist Party did not. In essence, market ideology and concepts of individual freedom replaced Chinese Communist ideology, while democracy challenged the Party. In the early 1980s the Party's critique of Maoism provided a justification for the Four Modernizations and paralleled the reappearance of Marxist humanism and its emphasis on the importance of the individual. This emphasis on individualism was at the heart of the pro-democracy movement, the "Fifth Modernization."

Critique of Maoist Radicalism. In 1981, the Party leadership embarked upon a critique of the two decades of permanent revolution. This was not an easy task. Mao's prestige had been damaged but not completely undermined. The Chinese did not want to repeat the Soviet experience of the "thaw" (see Chapter One), when criticism of Stalin led some to reject Communism and the right of the Communist Party to rule the Soviet Union. Nor did the Chinese leaders wish to give hope to the pro-democracy movement, which had been crushed at the end of the 1970s. Party leaders praised Mao's role in leading the Communists to power and introducing the Stalinist reforms but criticized his devotion to permanent revolution, his emphasis on class enemies within the Party, and his leadership of the Cultural Revolution. The critique of the Cultural Revolution provided justification for the ideas of the Four Modernizations.

The Four Modernizations. Certain ideas provided support for the market economics of the Four Modernizations. Most important were the rejection of centralized planning and support for market factors such as demand, price, and profit. The modernizers argued that market mechanisms were a means of achieving the socialist goals of economic development and modernization. Clearly neither Stalinism nor the Great Leap Forward had achieved those goals. Modernizers thus called for a reduction in the sphere of Party control and the expansion of *economic civil society*. Individual responsibility was to replace state control. Concerned that individualism would be contrary to Party goals, the modernizations gave not only individuals but also collectives, such as villages and local governments, the right to engage in market activity. Along the same lines, the proponents of the Four Modernizations carefully argued that economic freedom supported the "leading role of the Communist Party," a given that could not be questioned. Political freedom, on the other hand, would destroy the leading role of the Communist Party, the Neo-Stalinists feared.

Marxist Humanism. In the 1950s, Communists in Europe, especially in Eastern Europe, became influenced by the ideas of *Marxist humanism.* They reinterpreted ideas Marx developed early in his career in the light of the experiences of the Stalinization of Eastern Europe. In some of his early works Marx had used the concept of alienation to criticize capitalism. Capitalism, he argued, had alienated individuals from their essential humanity. Under socialism, alienation would disappear, producing individual freedom. Thus human history was moved forward not by the struggle among classes but by the gradual reduction of individual alienation, and by implication, increases in individual freedom.

In China, *humanists* also used the concept of alienation to criticize Communism. Stalinism, they believed, had led to the alienation of the people from their leaders and to the alienation of the peasants from the Party. Humanists condemned the system by which loyalty was determined on the basis of class origin.

Marxist humanists flourished after the death of Mao. They argued that the goal of socialism was to ensure that individuals had an opportunity to realize their needs and become fully human. Individualism took priority over collectivism.

Wang Ruoshi was the leading advocate of humanism in the 1980s. He argued that there were universal human needs, especially the need for self-realization. Good policies fostered the satisfaction of individual needs; bad policies alienated or separated individuals from their natures. He attacked the political dictatorship of the Communist Party, which caused the alienation.

A leading Party intellectual, Hu Qiaomu, led the Party's counter-attack. He emphasized that ordinary ethics, such as concern for the elderly or the sick, provided the only acceptable form of humanism. He rejected the idea that alienation could be used to explain historical development. Hu also condemned the idea that the Party had caused alienation. Alienation could not exist under socialism, he said. He also criticized the Maoist notion of the inevitability of conflict within the Party under socialism. Hu reiterated the validity of historical materialism as the only theory accurately explaining human development. However, humanism became increasingly important as a theoretical justification for the Four Modernizations and for democracy.

Democracy—The Fifth Modernization. Building on the legacy of the Hundred Flowers campaign, a number of individuals began to espouse pro-democratic ideals. This led to the *Democracy Movement* of 1978. Criticism of the Cultural Revolution through the so-called *literature of the wounded* (candid, semi-autobiographical accounts of individual suffering), led to demands for democracy, presented mainly in *wall posters.*

Wei Jingsheng, the central figure in this movement, posted an essay, "The Fifth Modernization," in Beijing in December 1978. Democracy, he asserted, was the fifth modernization. The Four Modernizations would be meaningless unless accompanied by democracy and individual freedom. He argued for popular sovereignty, the idea that political power resided in the masses, not in the Communist Party. The people had given the Communists permission to rule China. However the Party had created a political dictatorship that had destroyed the independent power of the people.

Wei had been a socialist, who argued that democracy was necessary if China was to go beyond the Stalinist system to a higher level of socialism. Economic development required democracy. Thus the base, social and economic development, would be determined by the superstructure, the ideas and institutions of democracy. Increasingly, Wei's criticism hinted at opposition to the very existence of Communism. He argued that the Party had not solved China's problems, in spite of thirty years in power. Its failure was a result of its emphasis on the collective to the neglect of the individual.

Beginning with a mid-December, 1978 demonstration in Tiananmen Square, protests expanded in size and spread to other major cities, such as Shanghai and Hangzhou. In early 1979, the Party cracked down on the pro-democracy movement. Wei and other leaders were arrested. Wei was sentenced to fifteen years in prison.

A new thaw surfaced in late 1984 when Communist leaders assured the Chinese Writers Association that the Party would permit freedom of expression. In January 1985, it issued a charter to the writers that promised them democracy and freedom of expression as long as they remained faithful to the Communist Party. Hu Yaobang appeared to be the most prominent Party spokesperson for this stance.

In 1986 and 1987, there was another surge of dissident ideas. Once again writers used allegory to condemn Communism and the Chinese Communist Party. Some authors portrayed a China soon to be destroyed. The mandate of Heaven was about to be taken from the Communists and chaos would follow, some suggested. Others focused on the joys of materialism made possible by the market economy, thus balancing the pessimism of some authors.

Fang Lizhi, an astrophysicist and university vice-president, moved the debate back to the basics of democratization. Fang argued that power must be shared, decisions made openly, and freedom of debate protected. Influenced by Fang, students began to demonstrate for democracy, first in Hefei, where he worked, then in places like Wuhan, and finally in Beijing and Shanghai. In the latter city 30,000 students demonstrated for democracy in late December 1986. In early January 1987, Beijing students defied a ban on demonstrations and held a large rally in Tiananmen Square. The Party cracked down once again. Fang was dismissed from the Party and from his university post. Authorities also dismissed Liu Binyan, a journalist well known for his exposes of Party corruption and materialism. Hu Yaobang was blamed for the pro-democracy movement and dismissed as head of the Party. The development of a pro-democracy ideology led almost inexorably to the Tiananmen massacre in 1989. Chinese democratic thought spilled over the boundaries of support for the Communist Party. Many came to the conclusion that democracy and Communism were incompatible. Certainly this was the view of the Party. Democracy meant civil rights, popular sovereignty, representative governments, and an end to the political power monopoly of the Communist Party. After Tiananmen, democratic thought went underground, waiting for the next opportunity to oppose the political monopoly of Chinese Communism. Ideological conflict and diversity were matched by the controversial economic proposals of the Four Modernizations.

4. Four Modernizations and Their Economic and Social Consequences

Much of this part of the chapter has focused on certain aspects of the Four Modernizations, such as the political battle over it and the emergence of pro-democratic ideals. In this section, we will look at the economic program of modernization. The Four Modernizations comprised the modernization of agriculture, industry, education and technology, and the military. The modernization of agriculture meant a shift to private ownership of the land and rural capitalist markets. The modernization of industry involved private enterprise and foreign technology and investment. The modernization of education enabled large numbers of Chinese professors and students to study abroad, primarily in the United States. The modernization of the military remained on the back burner until the mid-1990s.

Modernization of Agriculture—the *Responsibility System*. The Four Modernizations were based on experiments conducted in Sichuan province in the 1970s, under the leadership of Hu Yaobang and Zhao Ziyang. The modernization of agriculture was introduced first and retained strong support throughout.

The responsibility system was at the heart of the modernization of agriculture. Neither of the previous agricultural systems—collectivization and people's communes—had produced the levels of agricultural productivity China needed as its population passed one billion. China had much less agricultural land per capita (little more than 10% as much as the United States) than most other countries and the amount of land available for agriculture was shrinking. Several traditional solutions were available. Population growth, in spite of massive migration to the cities, meant that more labor was available to continue intensive agriculture. Some progress was made in the introduction of more productive strains of grain through the Green Revolution (see Chapter Two). Large-scale mechanization was not really feasible.

The Communists decided on a new incentive plan—the *responsibility system,* private markets where peasants could sell much of their harvests, and engage in side-line manufacturing. The responsibility system entailed a systems of contracts by which the peasants were responsible (hence the term responsibility system) for sending a certain amount of grain to the state at set prices (initially set at about 20% of the harvest). In return, the government was responsible for guaranteeing that peasants could use a particular piece of land forever. In 1987, the government transferred ownership to the individual peasant households that worked the land. Land could be bought and sold, inherited, and subdivided without government permission.

Peasants also gained the freedom to farm. After they provided a set amount of grain to the government, peasants were free to grow whatever crops they wished. Most households diversified, planting garden crops and commercial ones, since profit margins were much higher than for grain.

Private markets emerged all over rural China and then in the cities. Peasants sold grain and other farm goods at these markets, with prices set by supply and demand. They thus had an incentive to be as productive as possible.

Third, peasants and rural governments (and later individuals in the cities and urban governments) were permitted to organize private industrial production. These small-scale factories were reminiscent of the Great Leap Forward idea of rural industry, except that now peasants provided the management and received the profits. Small rural industry produced for the domestic and global markets. Action-figures, Barney tablecloths, Christmas ornaments, etc., all came from Chinese rural industry. Manufacturing was the single-most important component of rural economic growth.

Modernization of Industry. This modernization was introduced more slowly and almost always had ideological and political opposition. Opposition was strongest in the period 1989–1992, in reaction to Tiananmen. Elements of the modernization of industry included privately owned industry, the shift of state industry into private hands (on a very modest scale), the end to centralized planning (including prices and wages), decentralization of decision-making among state firms, application of the concept of bankruptcy to state-owned industry, an end to the iron rice bowl guarantee and the possibility of unemployment for factory workers, special economic zones, capitalistic financial institutions including the stock market, international trade, and foreign technology and investment.

Most private manufacturing concentrated on consumer goods, while the state retained ownership of the "rust-belt" heavy industries such as iron and steel. Private firms did not have production quotas, nor were they required to produce specific products. Factories were free to produce whatever they wanted to. This led to a shift away from heavy industry, with negative consequences for military needs. With the exception of a small list of basic goods, firms were free to charge whatever prices they wished. Central planning remained in effect for state-owned firms, though they, too, gained some degree of independent decision-making power. In theory firms that were unprofitable could be closed down by the state or forced into bankruptcy. In reality bankruptcy was seldom declared and the state propped up inefficient, unprofitable firms, for fear of working class unemployment and unrest. The same concern affected employment practices. Though enterprises were free to lay off workers and lower wages to reduce costs and maintain profits, most firms did not do so. In the private commercial sector, employment was dependent upon high-quality work and wages were generally low.

A global-oriented economy replaced the *autarkic* Chinese economy of the decades of permanent revolution. This globalization was based on three components. Initially, the Chinese planned to use foreign investment and foreign technology. They saw the need to catch up after a decade or more in which almost no real scientific and technological research took place (due to the Cultural Revolution). China had neither the knowledge nor the money to modernize quickly, so it turned to the outside world, just as Japan had done a century before (see Chapter Three). The Chinese emphasized the importation of foreign technology and encouraged foreign companies to invest in joint ventures. The Japanese, especially, invested in China, with annual foreign investment levels of 5 to 10 billion dollars. However, foreign firms found it difficult to make money in the Chinese market, in spite of local partners.

Special economic zones were one venue for foreign investment. Eventually fourteen special economic zones were established along the Chinese coast. The most important was *Shenzen,* near Hong Kong. Chinese business law did not apply in the zones. Goods produced in the zones could be exported abroad and later imported into China. The special economic zones were reminiscent of the Western treaty ports system of the nineteenth century. Finally China adopted a pro-export model for economic growth, patterned after the Japanese.

The modernization of industry played a central role in the rapid growth rates China produced in the 1980s. In the 1980s, China had the highest growth rate in the world, 10–12 percent per year. However, the modernization of industry created or made more obvious certain problems.

Modernization of Education and Technology. If China was to sustain high rates of economic growth and become a global economic power it needed a well-educated workforce and highly educated scientific-technological elite. To achieve the former, schools were given some degree of independence in curriculum and encouraged to stress science and math. In addition, enterprises, local governments, and the state sent tens of thousands of Chinese professors and students abroad to study. Thousands of other students went independently, their way paid by parents.

The government recognized that it could not afford the labs and research facilities world class scientists needed. Nor could its educational system produce such scientists. The state believed that sending students and professors abroad could be a shortcut to the rapid creation of new scientific elite. It assumed that the returning scientists and students would bring back the knowledge and experience they had acquired in the most advanced scientific communities in the world. The scientists could then apply that knowledge for the benefit of China and its economic development.

However, the policy failed. A majority of those who studied abroad decided not to return to China. This was true in spite of American government efforts to limit the stays of Chinese scholars and students. The Tiananmen massacre led both the Chinese and the Americans to change their policy. The Chinese government concluded that those who had studied abroad had become contaminated with democratic ideas and would only be troublemakers if they returned to China. The American government began to view the students and professors as political exiles.

Modernization of the Military. Stung by its defeat at the hands of "little Vietnam," the Chinese military gradually abandoned Maoist and Yan'anist military concepts. Into the 1980s, Chinese military doctrine was based on two ideas, the superiority of guerilla warfare over conventional warfare and the huge advantage of manpower over weaponry. Now, China understood the importance of employing the most modern weapons, the best delivery systems, and the latest air and missile defenses. This meant importing military technology from the West, as well as from India.

The Rosy Picture Fades—Consequences of the Four Modernizations. Though at first almost universally praised, the Four Modernizations later came under attack. To some extent the problems facing the Four Modernizations were part of a conservative Neo-Stalinist political campaign against Party reformers. But there was certainly a valid basis for much of the criticism.

The Four Modernizations led to higher levels of inequality, materialism, and corruption and to a reduction in the role and extent of Communist Party power. Not every rural family gained from the Four Modernizations, especially if the family had little good land and lived some distance from major urban centers. The concentration of productive farming and industrial growth along the coast and the river valleys divided the country into the wealthier coastal region and the relatively poor interior west. In the cities some individuals acquired huge wealth, while others barely survived as day laborers. The Four Modernizations broadened the gap between the rich, increasingly westernized east and the poor, isolated west and heightened overall inequality. Now the elite consisted of the wealthy, as well as the party cadre. Clear class distinctions emerged, as China's social structure came to resemble that of the industrialized nations, an upper business class, a middle class of professionals, and two lower classes, workers, and peasants. Materialism and corruption accompanied the Four Modernizations. Corruption centered on privileged access to economic decision-making was most common among local Party officials. They took bribes and diverted state production onto the private market (pocketing the profits themselves). People began to desire modern consumer goods. In the 1960s and 1970s people had wanted bicycles, radios, watches, and sewing machines. During the era of Four Modernizations ordinary Chinese sought the "Eight Bigs"—a color TV, refrigerator, stereo/CD player, camera, motorcycle, fancy furniture, washing machine, and electric fan. The wealthy wanted a foreign luxury car, furs, the latest Paris and Tokyo fashions and a detached home. Children begged for "Transformers" and other Western toys.

The Four Modernizations affected the family and gender roles and produced a decline in social services and educational opportunity. Since local governments had been primarily responsible for providing social services, when they turned to investment in industry they had less money available for health care, pensions, and assistance to the elderly. Children's labor was more valuable in the family factory or farm than in the schools, so many families took their children out of school so they could work.

Conclusion. In spite of technical economic issues, political partisanship and social problems, the Four Modernizations benefited China greatly. They provided goals and methods that were transforming China from a country alien to the rest of the world into one whose pattern of development followed that of Japan and the West. The Communist Party still felt threatened by the potential consequences of the coexistence of a capitalist economy and an authoritarian political system. It appeared to be capable of walking on this tightrope well into the twenty-first century.

5. Gender and Family Under "Capitalism"

For the first thirty years of Communist rule, the Party had taken the initiative, executing a series of policies to change gender roles and the family. In the era of the Four Modernizations, change was generally unintended, an accidental consequence of the reforms.

Gender Roles. The position of women changed only modestly. The *Marriage Law of 1980* reiterated the main provisions of the Marriage Law of 1950 but with much greater specificity. The new law prohibited the physical abuse of wives and reinforced women's right to divorce. Divorced women were guaranteed the right to sue if they were not given a fair share of jointly owned property. The state increased the minimum age for marriage to twenty-two for men and twenty for women. The promulgation of this new marriage law demonstrated that "old practices" and unequal treatment of women continued. Girls were still sold into marriage, widows were forced to remarry, bride prices were extremely high, and child brides were still frequently purchased. Physical abuse remained common. *Female infanticide* increased, largely in response to China's efforts to limit the population explosion.

With the return of private property, boys were again much more important than girls were. A son was needed to inherit the family's property, most Chinese believed. Daughters were less valuable. If a family did not have a son, the birth of a daughter might lead to female infanticide.

Women remained active in the economic affairs of the family, more frequently working in the fields than earlier because many men took jobs in industry. Urban women participated in the new Westernized pop culture of disco, Coke, and Kentucky Fried. Women did not acquire greater importance in political affairs. Only about 20 percent of government and party officials were female, and then primarily at the local level.

The Family. The Four Modernizations produced changes in the family. The family survived earlier Party efforts to weaken and destroy it. In fact, the family became stronger under the Four Modernizations. Fathers became increasingly important, especially as economic decision-makers. The family became more of a cohesive work unit than earlier. Economic activity again became the center of family life. In the countryside, patriarchy continued to prevail.

Population and the One-Child Policy. For the first 25 years of the People's Republic of China, little attention was paid to China's rapidly growing population. Mao generally believed that population growth was good. The larger China's population, the greater its security and the more productive it would be economically, he argued. Radical initiatives, including the Great Leap Forward and the Cultural Revolution, acted as a break on population growth.

However, in the 1970s, state policy changed, as the population explosion came to be viewed as a threat not an advantage. Population had increased from approximately 700 million in 1964 to slightly over one billion in 1982. Leaders concluded that the country could no longer permit unlimited procreation. Through propaganda campaigns and sanctions against families with more than three children the party had pushed the fertility rate down from 4.2 percent in 1974 to 2.2 percent in 1980. But China could not afford a population growth rate of 300 million a decade. In 1979, the Party turned to the *one-child policy,* a variation of the responsibility system. The state declared that urban families could have only one child, while rural families were limited to two. Couples were encouraged to sign a contract agreeing to have only one child. If they fulfilled their part of the bargain, that child would be guaranteed access to housing, education, and a "good job." Couples that went over the limit would be fined and might even lose their jobs or private farm plots. Women were forced to have abortions against their will, though forced sterilization was dropped. China is a society in which sons are seen as an essential asset for preservation of the ancestral, family line. Abortions and sterilization of females increased. Female infanticide levels probably reached 200,000 per year in the 1980s. Incentives, threats, and coercion dramatically reduced the rate of population growth. Today China has come close to its goal of only 1.2 billion people.

6. Less Community and More Diversity

What held Chinese people together in the last two decades of the twentieth century? Obviously the Han Chinese had a strong sense of pride in Chinese accomplishments because of the Four Modernizations. The government promoted the interests of the Han Chinese at the expense of minorities, in part out of a concern for security on its western flanks. Yet differences were mounting.

Ethnic Unrest. Minorities comprise 8 percent of China's population and are mainly located in the strategic borderlands. Efforts at forced assimilation of ethnic minorities were abandoned after the Cultural Revolution. The application of the Four Modernizations actually increased the relative freedom of the minorities. Greater freedom led to increased demands for even greater independence and resentment when the Chinese tried to impose their will on the minorities. Ethnic protest returned for the first time since the Tibetan Uprising of 1959. Active protest movements were strongest in Tibet and *Xinjiang.*

Tibet. Chinese policy toward Tibet paralleled the Four Modernizations, including introduction of the responsibility system and modernization to maximize Tibet's economic potential. Tibet received some informal autonomy, as the Communists reduced the number of Party bureaucrats and permitted some freedom of religion.

Ironically, this policy of moderation only encouraged dissent. Anti-Chinese demonstrations broke out in 1987. Instead of using force, the Communists permitted some public religious worship. The public gathering for the Great Prayer Festival in 1988 produced major anti-Chinese riots and a Chinese crackdown. Unrest simmered throughout the 1990s. The goals of the two sides were incompatible. The Chinese favored assimilation of the Tibetans to "modernized" China, while the Tibetans sought autonomy and religious independence. The government promoted immigration of Han Chinese into Tibet, though their numbers remained small.

Xinjiang. Located in northwest China, Xinjiang was inhabited mainly by Turkic Muslims of varied ethnic origin, including Uyghur, Mongol, Uzbek, and Tajik. Chinese migration to Xinjiang reduced the Turkic population proportion to about 60 percent.

Initially the Communists treated Xinjiang like Tibet—permitted autonomy and did not try to force Communist policies upon them. In 1957, Mao tried to introduce Stalinization, including collective farming, a system alien to the nomadic Turkic peoples. Many fled to the Soviet Union.

In the early 1960s, increasing unrest in Xinjiang culminated in riots protesting the ban on emigration to the Soviet Union. Occupying a strategic area along the Soviet-Chinese border, Xinjiang had become a pawn in the Sino-Soviet conflict. To counter the pro-Soviet tilt of the Xinjiang people, Chinese authorities encouraged massive Chinese migration to northwest China. The two peoples lived side by side, with separate existences.

The collapse of the Soviet Union, along with the emergence of Islamic fundamentalism among the Muslims of the Soviet Union changed the dynamics in

Xinjiang. Chinese authorities responded with brutal force to halt the emergence of Islamic consciousness and demonstrations. In 1990, the Chinese government crushed a Uyghur national liberation protest movement.

Conclusion. The decline in support for Chinese Communism, weakening of the idea of loyalty as a key determinant of unity, and increasing economic differentiation contributed to a decline of community in Communist China.

G. CONTEMPORARY CHINA, 1990–PRESENT

Since Tiananmen (1989), China has become a major world power, another Asian success story. China has come to see the United States as a rival and the old enemy, now Russia, as a potential friend. The Communist Party has remained all-powerful and has been characterized by stable transitions from one leader to the next. Democratic ideals have not become a threat to the power of the Chinese Communist Party. Ideological statements are primarily a justification of why an authoritarian political monopoly by the Communist Party is compatible with capitalism. China has become a much more capitalistic country; as privatization continues, the government reduces the public sector and consumer demand heightens. Exports still drive the economy. Women have borne the brunt of the continued transition to capitalism, while some women have succeeded as entrepreneurs and business leaders. The government concerns itself primarily with slowing the population increase. Unrest still marks the minority areas, especially Tibet and Xinjiang.

1. Against "Hegemony"

Since the 1989 Tiananmen Massacre, China has played an active role in global affairs, focusing its attention on relations with major world powers but also aggressively expanding its economic and political influence in Africa and Southeast Asia. Its relationship with its former rival, Russia, has improved substantially, while its bond with the United States has weakened. It maintains a tension-filled relationship with India.

China and Russia. Gorbachev's 1989 visit to China and the Tiananmen Massacre of Chinese university students marked a dramatic change in China's relationship with its former Communist ally turned enemy. Resolution of major differences followed the collapse of the Soviet Union. Russia and China moved closer together in an effort to counter the "hegemony" of the world's sole remaining power—the United States.

The warming of Chinese-Russian relations was gradual but became quite evident by the mid-1990s. In 1996, China and Russia agreed to a "strategic partnership," directed against the United States. Each agreed not to target nuclear weapons against the other and not to carry out a nuclear first strike. Arms sales agreements were reached, with the Russians selling surplus, and rather out of date, weapons to China. Both declined to defend the other in case of an attack by a third party. At the same time the two countries took the lead in the formation of the Shanghai Cooperation Organization, whose other members were Central Asian states. Common concerns included stability, energy and delivery systems, Islamic fundamentalism, nuclear proliferation in South Asia, the drug trade, and immigration. The strategic relationship was reconfirmed by a 2001 Treaty of Good Neighborliness, Friendship, and Cooperation and by a 2005 joint communiqué of agreement to work together for peace and stability. In recent years the Russians have taken modest actions that have angered the Chinese, including abandoning a pipeline deal and issuing an invitation to meet with the Dalai Lama, the spiritual leader of the Tibetan people.

China and the United States. Chinese-U.S. relations have continued to cool from the 1990s to the present.

The 1990s. Though mutual diplomatic recognition had come at the end of the 1970s, improvements in relations were halted by Tiananmen and the subsequent U.S. ban on trade with China. In the Clinton years (coinciding with the continued domination of Chinese policy by Deng Xiaoping) the key issues facing U.S.-Chinese relations were a trade imbalance, human rights, the Taiwan question, and Chinese fears of American hegemony in a uni-polar world.

China exported much more to the United States than the United States shipped to China, creating a huge trade imbalance. The imbalance was due to much cheaper Chinese labor costs, Chinese laws that made it difficult for foreign companies to operate in China, and Chinese undervaluation of its currency, which made Chinese goods cheaper and thus more competitive in the United States and the rest of the industrialized world.

The United States sought to minimize conflict with China by very cautiously raising the issue of human rights, including forced labor camps, the imprisonment of Chinese dissidents, and repressive measures against religious groups and ethnic minorities. China, however, openly rejected American concerns about human rights, leading the United States in the twenty-first century to generally downplay the issue.

Twenty-First Century. Taiwan is an abrasive issue. Though the United States agreed to sell only defensive military equipment to Taiwan, first President George W. Bush in 2001, 2004, and 2008 and then President Barack Obama signed high-priced arms deals with Taiwan that included some offensive weapons. At the same time, China had promised in the late 1970s not to try to take Taiwan by force. Yet in 1995–1996 China mobilized a huge invasion force in Fujian Province, across from Taiwan, and conducted missile exercises in the Straits of Taiwan. In 1998 Clinton promised not to use military force to prevent the peaceful reunification of Taiwan to China. Chinese saber-rattling in the South China Seas have sustained tension over Taiwan.

As China's economy has grown (almost as large as Japan's but only one-third the size of the United States') in the twenty-first century, China has begun to address its future geo-political role in a world in which China may become the second most powerful country in the world, after the United States. China has had some difficulty defining its future goals. On the one hand China is determined to have a geographical periphery, almost a no-man's land in which no other major power has much influence. This is parallel to the Soviet post-World War II goal of a buffer zone surrounding its borders. It appears that China's strategy toward the United States is one of moderation, officially a "peaceful rise." At the same time, responding to China's increased capability and increasing nationalism, there is much support for *China's Dream* (the title of a recent Chinese book, which could not have been published without official government approval), which features a future, inevitable war with the United States. Concern about domestic instability has also produced caution in China's foreign policy.

More recently, tension has continued over Chinese trade policies, as well as concerns over safety and environmental issues. Toxic ingredients in medicines, cosmetics, and pet food as well as lead in toys have created friction between the two countries. President Obama's meeting with the Dalai Lama and conflict over cyber freedom and human rights continue to promote a tense relationship.

China and India. In the 1980s, border tensions between China and India continued with no apparent resolution in sight. In the 1990s relations improved. The border issue was set aside, replaced by *confidence-building measures*, including agreements on scientific-technical and cultural exchanges. However, after India tested a nuclear weapon in 1998, China turned cool toward India.

Relations have improved in the twenty-first century, as the two largest countries in the world sought to take the measure of the other and to define the other's intentions and capabilities. The two have very different political systems—India has a decentralized democracy and China a centralized authoritarian government. India's economy is based on the service industries and domestic trade, with modest amounts of involvement in the international economy. China has an export-based industrial economy with a limited domestic market. Both have huge pockets of poverty that they seem incapable of erasing.

The two are national security rivals. China has successfully blocked Indian efforts for international recognition through a permanent seat on the United Nations Security council. Both are nuclear powers with fairly large militaries. Both seek to increase their influence in Southeast Asia. Both contest for increasingly scarce natural resources. Both are concerned about religious fundamentalism and separatist movements weakening national security. Both will continue to be Asian rivals as the twenty-first century continues.

China and Southeast Asia. China's relationship with Southeast Asia has several dimensions. First there is a large Chinese diaspora of 30-40 million. China has security goals that involve a Southeast Asian security buffer zone and preventing a Southeast Asian tilt toward Japan, India, or the United States. In addition, China seeks economic advantage in Southeast Asia. The Southeast Asian nations seek to avoid a commitment to China.

National Security. Into the mid-1980s China still promoted insurgencies and national liberation movements in Southeast Asia. More recently China has adopted a much more sophisticated set of national security goals. China sees Southeast Asia as a potential part of a national security buffer zone. Security, the Chinese believe, rests in part on building up a buffer zone around China's periphery, consisting of countries that are pro-China or at least not pro-United States. China has sought to participate in regional security organizations, such as ASEAN (Association of Southeast Asian Nations). In response, however, Southeast Asian nations are increasingly concerned about the expansion of China's military capability. Chinese claims to South China Seas island chains, the Spratly and Paracel Islands, worry the countries of Southeast Asia. Finally, China has tried to enlist the countries of Southeast Asia in China's efforts to isolate Taiwan, an unsuccessful move so far.

Economic Drive. China has several motives for deeper economic involvement in Southeast Asia, though ties with the area are weaker than those with South Korea and Japan. China sees Southeast Asia as a market for Chinese goods. China has sought to create an indebtedness dependency through infrastructure loans, especially to Indonesia and the Philippines. China has also proposed a Free Trade Area to include China and the countries of Southeast Asia. Nations of Southeast Asia recognize that such a structure would primarily benefit Chinese exports and not Southeast Asian exports to China. China also sees Southeast Asia as a source for energy supplies. Thus Chinese economic moves in Southeast Asia have had limited success.

Conclusions. China has decided that Southeast Asia is an area ripe for increasing Chinese influence and for achieving Chinese national security and economic goals. Southeast Asia has not aligned with these Chinese strategies.

2. Chinese Communist Party Monopoly

China's Communist Party monopoly of political power has continued. The Party leadership has been characterized by the ability to sustain continuity of policy and orderly transitions from one administration to another. Government policies, focused on continued economic growth, have secured the support of the Chinese people. At the same time, citizens have greater freedom, though civil rights are still hardly present.

From Power Conflicts to Stability. Initially, a power struggle raged within the Party. Clearly Deng Xiaoping had lost a great deal of credibility and authority. For a while it appeared that Li Peng, who had risen to a top leadership position, would take power. However, gradually *Jiang* Zemin consolidated his position, assuming predominant authority upon the death of Deng. After his death, a quiet power struggle took place, from which Jiang Zemin emerged victorious. Jiang spent the latter part of the 1990s consolidating his power. In general Jiang continued the Deng position—to promote a market economy and permit no threats to the Chinese Communist Party's monopoly of power. Jiang remained in power until 2001. He was succeeded by *Hu Jintao* (2001–2007), who led an administration of technocrats and experts, including Premier Wen Jiabao. Throughout, the military remained a powerful force, which had to be placated by high budgets. The current continuity of leadership contrasted sharply with the intense rivalries of the early 1990s. No major changes are expected at the 2012 Communist Party Congress.

Policy Directions. State policy has emphasized two main directions: socialist market economics and global respect. The Party also launches periodic campaigns against corruption, but with little success. The *four cardinal principles,* announced in 1992, call for economic growth through capitalism. Within this general directive, emphasis has changed over time. Primarily, building capitalist components in the economy has been replaced by efforts to eliminate the unproductive segments of the public sector. At the same time, the Communist Party has announced that its goal is to ensure that most people are "moderately well off." Little attention has been given to applying this to the impoverished rural population of the interior and the west.

Modest Freedoms without Civil Rights. The Chinese have greater private and personal freedoms than in earlier periods. In addition, some NGOs (non-governmental organizations) have been permitted to function, especially domestic charitable organizations that carry out tasks the Party has neglected. Some historians talk about the modest emergence of a "civil society." A civil society is one in which the citizens organize to assume a number of responsibilities that would seem to belong to the government. For example, "Project Hope" is a charitable organization, whose main function is to build and run primary schools in the poorest areas of China.

Civil rights are still largely non-existent. There is some evidence that the judicial system is becoming fairer and that a person is no longer considered guilty unless proven innocent. Still 90 percent of the executions in the world occur in China. When a Chinese Democracy Party formed in 1998, it was quickly declared illegal. Censorship and government control over the media make freedom of public expression very difficult. To ensure that the Internet does not become a forum for the criticism of the Chinese system, the government has introduced an Internet police force. Government officials act as Internet commentators, giving direction to discussion on the blogs.

Religious freedom is virtually non-existent. Chinese religious groups, such as Buddhists, Muslims, and Daoists are regularly discriminated against. Intermittently Christianity is subject to repression. The government has reserved its fiercest action against unorthodox religious groups that demonstrate publicly. The strongest government action has been against the group, Falun Gong, which focuses on public exercise as a form of religious expression.

Corruption remains a serious problem. Though it is rampant within the economy, it has spread throughout society, too. For instance in soccer there are "black whistles," referees who take bribes to affect the outcome of matches.

3. Communist Thought and Nationalism

Chinese leaders still espouse "Communist" ideas, especially in terms of political power. Some expression of support for democratic ideals surfaces from time to time but has little resonance. Only a renewed sense of Chinese nationalism seems capable of offering an alternative to dead Chinese Communist ideology.

One attempt at Communist Party thought was the *Three Represents,* announced in 2000. Seeking to justify Communist Party behavior, these phrases suggested that the Communist Party represented the most advanced forces in China, China represented the most advanced culture in the world, and Party actions reflected the fundamental interests of the masses.

Chinese nationalism is not new to the Communist era. Mao has also mobilized the Chinese people on the basis of this attempt to restore Chinese dignity and world standing. Chinese nationalism still represents a quest for influence commensurate with China's recent rapid economic growth and increased global influence. (See Chapter Three for a parallel Japanese revival of nationalism based on economic success.)

4. Capitalism and Inequality

Rapid economic growth has been accompanied by increasing economic difficulties and by increasing economic inequality. It was not clear in the two years after Tiananmen whether market socialist economics would survive or be replaced by a return to the economic Stalinism of the past. From the early 1990s, the Party has supported market socialist economics, first emphasizing building capitalism and then in the late 1990s placing increased emphasis on reducing the economic role of state-owned enterprises. Still China remains a poor country.

Building Capitalism. By 1992, the conversion to capitalism was again on track. Deng Xiaoping ended price controls, encouraged private enterprise, and tried, unsuccessfully, to eliminate excess labor from state-owned firms. Exports continued to be promoted. Forty percent of Chinas' exports are to the United States, a trade that has reached about half a trillion dollars annually. To 2005, most exports and the main focus of light industry were cheap goods, produced by hand or with low-tech methods. Socks and children's toys were the two most important export items. Thereafter, factories shifted to goods requiring medium levels of technology, such as cameras and washing machines. The automotive industry has also become a major engine for exports, as has steel. Half of the world's cameras are produced in China. Domestic consumption, especially of luxury goods that are frequently imported, has also stimulated the economy. China's growth rate has reached levels similar to those of Japan in the 1950s and 1960s. In the 1980s and 1990s, the growth rate has been about 9 percent per year. In the twenty first century, the growth rate has risen to 11–12 percent per year, but declined to 7–8% after the 2008–2009 global economic crisis. China now has the third largest economy in the world with a GDP of a bit less than $5 trillion.

Restructuring State Enterprise. State firms have been badly managed and rampant with corruption. The government's response to the inefficiency of state-owned companies, which weaken overall economic growth, has been to close some companies and to reduce work forces in most. By 2001, one-third of the industrial workforce in state enterprises had been laid off. This produced much personal suffering and an unemployment rate of approximately 20 percent.

Economic Problems. Rapid economic growth has not come without consequences. The Chinese economy remains wasteful, using up huge amounts of energy and raw materials. The economy is deeply dependent on imports of petroleum and other raw materials, whose prices rise and fall and threaten to slow Chinese economic growth. Corruption is everywhere. Financial institutions are inefficient and badly run, making raising money for capital investment rather difficult.

Environmental Problems. China faces very serious environmental problems, largely due to its strategy of rapid economic development. Belatedly it has become concerned with global warming, reduction of pollution, and production of clean energy alternatives.

Today, China is the globe's largest producer of carbon dioxide, with levels continuing to increase. Air pollution, symbolized by the absence of blue sky in the coastal areas and river basins, results from automobiles and diesel trucks, extensive use of coal to create power, and desert dust. Deforestation and desertification are found all over the plateaus of Western China. Drought and overuse of the waters of the Yellow River in northern China mean that the river no longer flows to the sea. Global warming has led to the melting of glaciers that form the headwaters of Chinese (and Indian) rivers and thus to markedly reduced water flow.

Inequality. Inequality is one result of the nature of Chinese capitalism. Though Mao Zedong sought to minimize inequality through radical programs, such as the unsuccessful Great Leap Forward, his successors have recognized the problem. Discussion and rhetoric have been their main responses. Dealing with inequality would force difficult decisions and reduce the rate of economic growth, which is so important to sustaining public support for the party and for maintaining respect for China abroad. There is great inequality between standards of living in the cities and in the countryside. Coastal areas are much richer than the interior. A majority of China's population has an income of less than $1 per day, similar to Pakistan and Bangladesh (see Chapter Two). The primary response of the impoverished is to migrate to the cities, where they start out as day laborers and perhaps gain a better life than the one they abandoned.

5. Gender, Family, and Capitalism

While the state has focused on population control it has largely ignored the brutal impact of capitalism on the lives of older women.

As China entered the twenty-first century its population growth rate declined. Today, China's population is about 1.3 billion. The government continues a modified one-child policy. In the countryside families can have two children, in the cities only one. Ultrasound is widely used to determine the sex of a child. If the child is a female, the mother is much more likely to have an abortion. This has produced a ratio of 1.2 male births to 1.0 female birth. Under capitalism living standards have improved and life expectancy has lengthened to 72 for women and 68 for men. This represents much greater life expectancy than in Russia or lesser-developed countries.

As in Russia, the transition to capitalism has been especially hard on older women. In China, older urban women are most likely to lose their jobs.

Though the nuclear family now dominates in the cities and women have some economic power and rights within the family, in the rural areas little has changed. Patriarchy still dominates there.

6. Double Minorities

Officially China portrays itself as a *unitary multi-ethnic nation.* Minorities living in the western borderlands have challenged China's emphasis on loyalty and conformity.

Tibet. Tibetans, living in the Tibetan administrative unit and in other parts of western China, again protested Chinese policies of cultural and religious restrictions (including expulsion of monks and nuns), modernization of the economy, and encouragement of Han Chinese in-migration. Protests lasted from 1987 into 1990, at which time China introduced martial law and cracked down on dissidents.

In 1996, the Dalai Lama, émigré head of the Tibetan religion, Lamaism, called for "genuine autonomy" for Tibet, within China, noting that Tibet had become a "hell on earth" due to Chinese policies. The Chinese government rejected the demand for autonomy. China's response has been to intensify efforts to promote Han immigration to Tibet. This strategy has not been very successful, as only 6 percent of Tibet's population is Han Chinese. Also, China built a railway line into Tibet to facilitate movement of military forces into Tibet to quell unrest.

Thereafter, Tibet remained quiet until 2008, when Tibetans again protested Chinese rule and policies. Unrest continued into 2009, when numerous Tibetans refused to celebrate Tibetan New Year. In March 2009, monks attacked a police station.

The Tibetan situation is at a stalemate. Tibetans want autonomy for Tibet and areas of western China where the population is mainly Tibetan—thus autonomy for a "Greater Tibet." The Tibetans also seek recognition of their religion and the safe return of their religious leader, the Dalai Lama. The Chinese goal is order, exploitation of recently discovered mineral resources, and border security. Border security is part of the broader strategy of creating a border zone on the periphery of China that will ensure safety from external forces (in this case India).

Xinjiang ("New Frontier"). Xinjiang in northwest China is a greater threat to Chinese national security and unity than Tibet. Xinjiang borders Russia as well as several Central Asian nations. China's worries about Uyghur (the largest ethnic group in Xinjiang), and its national liberation movements, intensified after the breakup of the Soviet Union, which left Russia and three independent Muslim states on its western borders. Systematic persecution of Uyghurs increased after large-scale Uyghur pro-independence demonstrations in 1997. September 11th is used as an excuse, as the Chinese government has falsely claimed that the Uyghurs have ties to al Qaeda. Some twenty Uyghurs ended up in the American prison at Guantanamo but have recently been released. China has argued that the threat of Islamic fundamentalism requires tighter control over Xinjiang and more repressive measures.

Chinese in-migration has dramatically transformed the ethnic dimensions of Xinjiang. Today about 45 percent are Uyghurs (Turkic Muslims), 40 percent are Han Chinese and 7 percent are Kazakh. The rest of the population is of Persian or Turkic origins. Ironically, because of oil and gas extraction, Xinjiang is one of the wealthiest areas of China, second to the southeast China coastal areas.

Chinese policy can be summed up in the slogan, "Go West," a broad strategy of economic development, infrastructure projects, and Han immigration. In Xinjiang the program of urban construction, infrastructure, and industrial development is led by the Xinjiang Products and Construction Corps, a semimilitary organization. Beyond this "modernization" strategy, China emphasizes the need for order and stability. However, this strategy backfires because its main methods are religious repression and the condemnation of Muslim separatists as al Qaeda terrorists.

The Uyghurs have reacted by organizing demonstrations and riots and even attempts at uprisings. Student protests in the 1980s were followed by a failed uprising in 1990 and then the Chinese massacre of demonstrating separatists in 1997 during the holy month of Ramadan.

The situation thereafter remained quiet until 2007. Since then there has been continued unrest, which culminated in bloody rioting in the capital, Urumqi, in 2009. Estimates are that 150 demonstrators were killed, 1000 wounded, and 1400 imprisoned. Here, too, no resolution of the conflict is in sight, given Chinese authoritarianism, inflexibility, and intolerance of religious expression.

CONCLUSION

In the modern period China moved from being the most powerful and probably most advanced country in the world to being a troubled country that had difficult dealing with its problems.

China saw itself as the center of the universe, the "middle kingdom." China had been open to invasion and foreign conquest throughout its history but had successfully incorporated the outsiders into Chinese culture. However, the Ming tried to change China's orientation and transform it from an open society into a closed one. This strategy failed and new invaders swept the Ming from power. In the nineteenth century, Western powers forced China to accept a dangerous Western presence. China simply could not stand up to the West. During the Second World War the Japanese occupied much of China, even setting up Chinese puppet governments. During the Communist period China rejected the West, turned to the Soviet Union and remained relatively isolated. From the 1970s on, China gradually entered the world scene, aligning with the U.S. against the Soviet Union, supporting revolutionary movements and engaging in international trade.

Chinese government had an authoritarian political system throughout. China—both in the imperial period and under the Communists—sought to maintain centralized control through ideological conformity and a gigantic bureaucracy. The government had great power over people's lives and, especially under the Communists, used that power first to carry out radical change and then to introduce capitalism. Supporters of pluralism issued faint calls for democracy but their voices were ignored or repressed.

Two ideologies played a vital role in Chinese history—Confucianism and Communism. Both had much in common. Both emphasized obedience to authority, proper behavior, and the central role of government. Both made little distinction between public and private spheres. Confucianism dominated Chinese life until the twentieth century. Western ideas weakened Confucianism's hold on Chinese life. Confucianism crumbled through warlordism, war, and revolution. Communism became the new all-powerful ideology, though there was fierce debate between champions of permanent revolution and modernization. Western ideas, especially capitalism, and less importantly, liberalism, began to influence the Chinese toward the end of the twentieth century.

At the beginning of the modern era the Chinese economy was one of the most productive and the Chinese people among the wealthiest in the world.

However, by the nineteenth century, the Chinese economy was disintegrating. Significant recovery has taken place only in the last few decades. Thus China suffered through almost two centuries of real economic weakness. Poverty, overpopulation, and economic backwardness produced the economic difficulties. Chinese society contained a fairly distinct social structure, with mobility made possible through education (the civil service examination system) and commerce. The class system collapsed during the first half of the twentieth century. When the Communists came to power they pledged to create a society without social distinctions. However, membership in the Communist Party provided the basis for the emergence of a "new class." The Four Modernizations introduced new types of inequality based on access to powerful Party leaders and entrepreneurial success. The Four Modernizations also produced greater geographical inequality, with a wealthier coastal area and an impoverished central and western China.

Patriarchy dominated Chinese history, with the senior male of the extended family generally exercising brutal authoritarian power. Patriarchy has been challenged twice, first by the May Fourth Movement attacks on Confucianism in the 1920s and 1930s and by marriage reform strategies under the Communists. Women gained some degree of independence in the twentieth century, especially under the Communists. Patriarchy has made a comeback through the introduction of a market economy.

Loyalty has been a core value in Chinese history. For most of its history, China has emphasized the unifying power of Confucianism. The examination system ensured that all educated people understood and accepted the key Chinese values. Those values spread beyond the educated classes and throughout society. The Chinese assimilated outsiders effectively, minimizing the significance of original ethnic difference. Chineseness was a cultural concept not an ethnic identity. In the nineteenth century, ethnic and religious identity became increasingly important, reducing the unifying power of Confucianism. Western ideas further weakened the power of Confucianism as a community-building force. When the Communists came to power they reestablished the centrality of loyalty, this time loyalty to Communist ideals. People were divided into two categories, those loyal to Communism and those considered as potential opponents of Communism. The Communists, too, faced the rise of national and ethnic identity, especially in the non-Chinese and Muslim populations of western China. With the decline in support for Communist economic ideas, the Communists faced the possibility that loyalty could no longer act as a force for unity.

Name: ______________________________ **Date:** ____________________

Chapter Four: China

IDENTIFICATION: IMPORTANT TERMS AND VOCABULARY

Autumn Harvest Uprisings (316)

banners (290)

Blue Shirts (319)

Boxers United in Righteousness (298)

cadre (335)

Chiang Kai-shek (315)

cohong (295)

concubines (293)

Daoism (the way) (294)

Deng Xiaoping (340)

devolved (302)

Dowager Empress Cixi (299)

dynastic cycle (284)

encirclement campaigns (316)

female infanticide (360)

Fifth Modernization (351)

footbinding (293)

gentry (282)

Great Leap Forward (338)

Guomindang (National Peoples Party) (313)

Name: ________________________________ Date: ____________________

Chapter Four: China

KEY QUESTIONS

A Great Civilization, 1400–1800: What enabled China to be one of the most powerful and important countries in the world, 1400–1800?

Nineteenth Century China: What were the main challenges facing nineteenth century China and why wasn't China able to respond effectively to them?

Revolution and Anarchy, 1911–1949: Why was China so filled with conflict and chaos in the four decades after the collapse of the Chinese Empire?

Chinese Stalinism, 1949–1957: Why was the Chinese Communist Party able to transform China into a "Stalinist" society so easily?

Maoist Radicalism, 1956–1976: What were the consequences of two decades of radicalism?

Four Modernizations, 1980–1989: Why did China abandon socialism and turn to capitalism?

Contemporary China, 1990–Present: What has enabled China to become a world power?

Chapter Five

South Africa

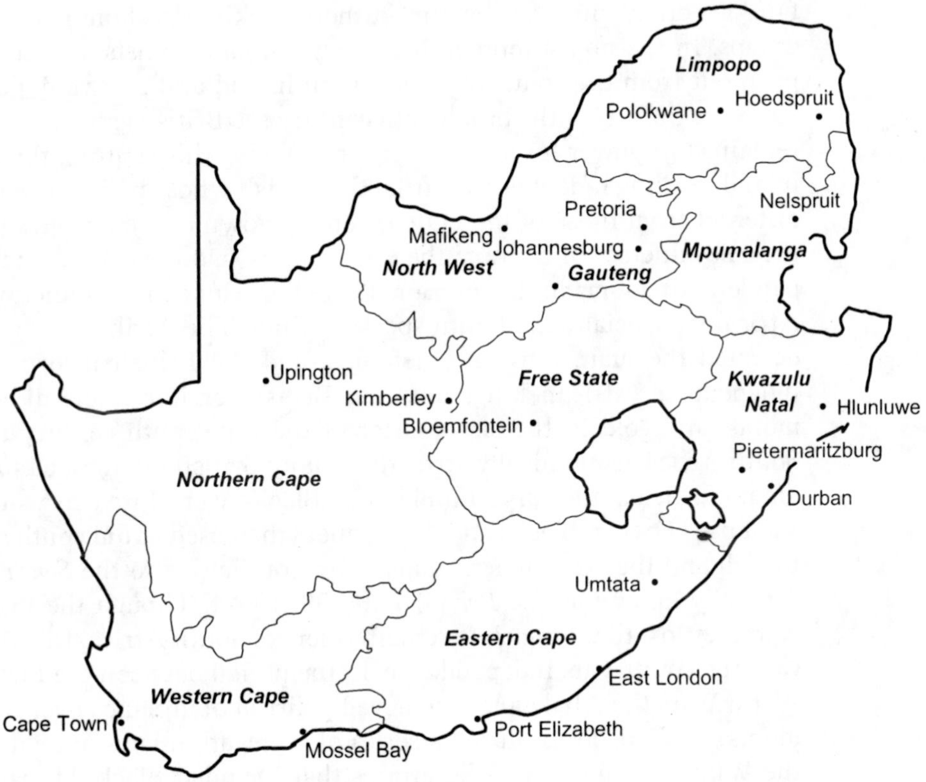

Introduction

Competing Communities: Before the Europeans, 1500–1652

Dutch Colonial Period, 1650–1800

British Century, 1800–1910

Triumph of the Afrikaaners and Segregation, 1910–1948

Era of Apartheid, 1948–1991

Rainbow Society, 1991–Present

Conclusion

INTRODUCTION

Racial conflict dominated the history of South Africa. Before the arrival of Europeans, Africans with different ethnic identities and different socioeconomic structures fought each other. The initial inhabitants were *hunter-gatherers,* followed by *pastoralists.* Gradually Bantu-speaking immigrants who were farmers and livestock owners spread into South Africa, especially into the eastern half. The relationship between farmers and pastoralists and hunter-gatherers was sometimes one of peaceful trade relations and at other times warfare, generally initiated by the farmers seeking to dominate the other two groups. In the mid-seventeenth century Dutch colonists arrived and began to push out from the southwest coast both inland and eastward along the coast. At the beginning of the nineteenth century the British gained South Africa and remained in power for about a century. During this century, the Dutch moved inland, seeking independence from the British whose political beliefs were very different from those of the Dutch, better known as *Afrikaaners* (or *Boers*). By the mid-nineteenth century the Afrikaaners had created two relatively independent kingdoms in the interior. There they came into conflict with the Black Africans, especially the Bantu-speaking Zulu. The Afrikaaners and the British defeated the main African chiefdoms, and the British incorporated the last independent African kingdoms into British territory. The discovery of diamonds and gold in the last quarter of the nineteenth century made interior South Africa economically attractive. Many British immigrated to the gold and diamond fields and large numbers of Blacks were hired to work the mines. Violence between Blacks and Afrikaaners increased as did conflict between the British and the Afrikaaners. This latter conflict led to the *South African War,* generally known as the *Boer War* (1899–1902). Though the British won the war, they lost the stomach to remain rulers of South Africa. In 1910, the British gave the country its independence. In the period between the First and Second World Wars the Afrikaaners achieved political dominance over the British residents. They also introduced a series of segregation laws, intended to separate the Whites from other racial groups that included Black Africans, Coloureds (mixed racial groups and descendants of the hunter-gatherers), and Asians. After the Second World War the *National Party* introduced *apartheid,* racial separation based on White racial superiority, brutally enforced by the state. Apartheid lasted half a century. Finally at the beginning of the 1990s apartheid was abandoned and a Black majority government came to power. Facing immense social and economic problems, the new government announced that it would create a *rainbow society* in which people of all races would prosper and live together peacefully without prejudice and without discrimination.

A. COMPETING COMMUNITIES: BEFORE THE EUROPEANS, 1500–1652

Before the Dutch put down shallow roots in South Africa in 1652, geography largely determined political, social, and economic patterns. Three broad groups competed for resources: the hunter-gatherers, the pastoralists, and the mixed farmers. The latter group gradually gained domination over the other two. The hunter-gatherers lived in small groups, the pastoralists had loose systems of federations, while the mixed farmers had more elaborate political systems based on chiefdoms. Religion was most well developed among the mixed farmers who believed in *animism,* the idea that physical objects had supernatural powers. They also called on the assistance of *shamans,* or priests. Hunter-gatherers hunted game and gathered wild plants. Pastoralists grazed cattle and other livestock. The mixed farmers grew grain and other crops and possessed livestock as well. The family was most important among hunter-gatherers and the clan among the other two categories. Difference was based on ethnicity, language, and primary economic activity.

1. The Geographical Landscape

Geography played a very important role in determining settlement patterns and economic activity. Rainfall was the key determinant, dividing South Africa into three major zones.

Geography. Located in the southern hemisphere, South Africa was about 1,000 miles from north to south and 1,000 miles from east to west. Its oceanic coastline was also about 1,000 miles. The Atlantic and Indian Oceans met off the coast of southwestern South Africa. The Atlantic currents coming from Antarctica were very cold, while the Indian Ocean currents were quite warm. Most of the population lived along the coast.

Western South Africa was desert-like, averaging about five inches of rain per year. In the east, forty inches of rain per year was common and along the coast, the climate was subtropical. A transitional semi-arid zone in the middle averaged about twenty inches of rain, though severe drought sometimes hit the region.

Most of South Africa was plateau with a steep cliff or *escarpment* running parallel to the coast about 100 miles inland. Rivers were navigable only by boats with a very shallow draft. Rivers thus did not become major paths of commerce. The Vaal, Orange, and Limpopo were the most important rivers. Soil was generally of rather poor quality, thus limiting agricultural productivity. Iron, gold, and copper were found in abundance. Iron was used for weapons and tools and gold and copper for ornamentation.

Population Patterns. The hunter-gatherers, known as the *San* or *Khoisan* (the Bushmen or Hottentots, as they were known in the West), were the earliest known inhabitants of South Africa and were located on the edges of the deserts in the west. The San, a Stone Age people, reached South Africa about 10,000 years ago. The Iron Age pastoralists, or *Khoekhoen,* settled in the Cape of Good Hope area some two to four thousand years ago, having migrated from what is today northern Botswana. They spread along the southern coast. The mixed farming groups migrated from West Africa as well as from the area around Lake Victoria in East Africa. Their migration, about 1200–1700 C.E., was a response to population explosion. They were Bantu-speakers, using the *Nguni* (from which the *Xhosa* and *Zulu* languages originally came) and *Sotho* languages. They moved in gradually, yet dramatically increased the population of South Africa. Migration was generally peaceful but sometimes took the form of military invasion, followed by colonization. Initially the Bantu speakers settled east of the transitional rainfall zone but population pressure drove some of them into the transitional area. The Nguni located along the coast and the Sotho, Pedi, and Tswana settled on the plateau.

2. Political Systems

Each of the three socioeconomic types possessed a different political structure, all of them quite simple.

Hunter-gatherers. The hunter-gatherers had little in the way of a political system. They were organized into small nomadic bands, ranging in size from 15 to 100 people each. Political power was in the hands of the males most skilled in hunting and determining hunting areas.

Pastoralists. Pastoralists were organized into clans loosely tied together in coalitions of chiefdoms or tribes. Hereditary chiefs made decisions after consulting clan leaders. Pastoralists' political structures were rather fragile and clans shifted from one chiefdom to another.

Mixed Farmers. The basic political unit for mixed farmers depended on ethnic heritage and economic conditions. These ranged from small hamlets along the East Coast to towns in the northwest, where in-migration was heaviest. Adult males participated in local government. The mixed farming areas were divided into a number of separate chiefdoms. A hereditary chief, known as a *paramount,* ruled the chiefdom. The chief made decisions after consulting his counselors. He was the richest person in the kingdom and controlled the labor of a large number of people. The chief's primary role was to resolve conflict, especially issues of cattle ownership. Thus, he promoted harmony and healed wounds. From time to time the chief called a *pitso,* a gathering of all of the adult males of the kingdom. At these meetings, chiefs were sometimes openly criticized and factions threatened to leave the community unless the chief accepted their position. In this period, government was simple and its responsibilities quite limited.

3. Religion

We have little detailed knowledge of the ideology or beliefs of hunter-gatherers and pastoralists. Rock paintings indicate the existence of religion. Yet, we can identify the main characteristics of the farmers' religious beliefs.

Religion was family based, as farmers showed great respect for elders and ancestors. The farmers believed that ancestral spirits had a great deal of control over people's lives. Therefore, they sacrificed livestock to placate these spirits. Sometimes, especially during a crisis such as a drought, they turned to shamanistic religious specialists or priests, known as *dingaka,* believed to have the power to intercede with the ancestors. Witchcraft was also important. Certain evil individuals were believed to have the power to turn themselves into animals and birds and injure or kill people.

4. Economies

Each of the three groups engaged in a different form of economic activity.

Hunter-gatherers. Hunter-gatherers lived very simple lives and lacked a sense of private property beyond items such as clothing and weapons. They hunted wild animals and gathered wild grains and berries. They moved in a limited area and were self-sufficient.

Pastoral Economy. The pastoralists were nomads who raised livestock, especially cattle. They ranged over broad areas and were most vulnerable to drought. Over time, social inequality emerged, with some families owning larger herds than others.

Mixed Farming Economy and Society. The mixed farming economy was based on agriculture, livestock, metallurgy, and trade. The farmers used *swidden agriculture;* that is they worked a piece of land for several years and when productivity declined, they left it fallow and farmed new land. Obviously this method required relatively large amounts of land and resulted in overall low productivity. The farmers raised sorghum, millet, melons, yams, beans, and tobacco. They herded sheep and cattle and did some hunting as well. Some farmers specialized in metalworking. Long distance trade was common, though there was no professional merchant class. Farmers traded with the next village and that village with one further on.

The mixed farming communities were hierarchical, with clear gradations in wealth. The wealthy developed *patron-client relationships* with the poor. The poor herded the cattle of the rich and in return received milk and some of the calves.

5. Families and Gender Roles

Family and gender roles varied, depending upon socioeconomic type. Among hunter-gatherers and pastoralists, a pronounced division of labor existed between the sexes. In mixed-farming communities, male domination prevailed.

Hunter-gatherers. The nuclear family dominated among hunter-gatherers. A clear division of labor existed. Men hunted and engaged in craft production and in artistic activity. Women were responsible for the household, childcare, and collecting edible plants, small snakes, lizards, and insects.

Pastoralists. The clan was the primary socioeconomic institution among pastoralists. Men herded the livestock, while women were responsible for the household and childcare.

Mixed Farmers. The *extended family* was common among mixed farmers. An extended family was one in which three or more generations lived in the same household. The senior male controlled the extended family, thus establishing patriarchy. Parents arranged the marriages of their children. Marriage was an economic relationship, reinforced by the exchange of property between the two families. The *bride price* or *lobola* was quite common. The bridegroom's parents gave cattle to the bride's family to seal the marriage agreement.

Men dominated women in a number of ways. The division of labor was advantageous to men. Men cleared fields, while boys tended cattle. Men made leather clothing and had much leisure time for conversation and drinking.

Women raised the children, ran the household, and did farm work. Women worked the fields communally, though the harvest from a piece of land went to a particular family. A strong sense of private property emerged in mixed farming communities.

Wealthy men were *polygamous* (they had more than one wife). The *great wife* was the mother of the male heir to the family's property.

Families were authoritarian. Young men went through initiation procedures that instructed them in the community's beliefs, which included absolute obedience to the patriarch. Community unity was all-important and individualism a threat to the well being of the community.

6. Community and Diversity

Ethnic and linguistic diversity created differences among chiefdoms and social groups. Community unity produced a sense of unity at a lower level.

The hunter-gatherers were *Khoisan* (San). They spoke dialects of a single, common language. The pastoralists were mainly *Khoekhoen.* The mixed farmers were Bantu-speakers, using a number of related languages from the Bantu language group.

The boundaries of political units were somewhat fluid and people moved from one unit to another. Identity was based on geography. For example, everyone who lived in Xhosaland was viewed as a Xhosa, even though they might come from different ethnic groupings.

B. DUTCH COLONIAL PERIOD, 1650–1800

The construction of port facilities followed Dutch exploration. The term Dutch refers to the people of Holland, that is, the Netherlands. Though the Dutch initially had no intention of inviting White settlement into South Africa, Dutch immigrants arrived in increasing numbers. They gradually spread from the Dutch Cape Colony along the coast and inland. The Dutch easily gained domination over the Khoekhoen, who lived near the coast, and then in the 1770s fought bitter wars with the Bantu-speakers further inland and along the east coast. The Dutch settlers established a government relatively independent of the motherland. Gradually a kind of racial Christianity emerged to guide the behavior and beliefs of the Dutch settlers. The native population continued to be motivated by their own religious beliefs. Trade and agriculture formed the base of the South African economy. White and Black South Africans had different social structures. Relative equality characterized the Whites, who enslaved some Blacks, as well as Asians. Few Dutch women came to South Africa initially and White families formed only gradually. Black family structures changed little from earlier periods. The arrival of the Whites made diversity more complex and community more difficult. South Africa remained a country with a very small and relatively isolated White population and a large number of various African Black tribes frequently at war with each other. The arrival of the Dutch had a long-term profound impact on South Africa but its immediate effect was limited.

1. The Dutch Arrival and Settlement

The borders of South Africa had been porous, permitting the immigration of large numbers of Blacks from both West and East Africa. Before the arrival of the Dutch the coastal area had existed without much outside contact.

European "Discovery." Portuguese explorers gradually moved down the west coast of Africa. In 1487, Bartholomeu Dias rounded the Cape of Good Hope and sailed as far as Algoa Bay on the east coast of southern Africa. During the next century the Portuguese sent annual naval expeditions to the Indian Ocean and the east coast of Africa. South Africa was an area to be sailed past; it had little economic value to the Portuguese. The decline in Portuguese naval power and competition from other Europeans changed the situation. Though the English traded with the Khoekhoen, they showed no interest in acquiring territory in South Africa. However, in 1652, Jan Van Riebeek of the *Dutch East India Company (DEIC)* built a fort at the Cape of Good Hope.

The Dutch Cape Colony. By the seventeenth century Holland had superseded Portugal as the world's leading maritime trading power. Founded in 1602, the Dutch East India Company, the world's largest trading enterprise, dominated Dutch global trade. The initial Dutch post in South Africa was intended as a stopping point for ships headed back to Holland or going to the Dutch East Indies (Southeast Asia). Ships took on fresh water and supplies that the company's traders purchased from the local Khoekhoen population.

The post became a colony when the company gave land to its employees (1657), who became free burghers (citizens), and permitted gradual expansion inland beyond the immediate port area. This expansion, begun by 1660, pushed the Khoekhoen off their grazing lands. The Khoekhoen strategy was to steal plow animals so that the Dutch couldn't farm. However, the Dutch extended forts out into the land taken from the Khoekhoen and planted thick hedge to separate themselves from the Khoekhoen. The Dutch also began to import slaves, primarily from the Dutch East Indies. The colony expanded as more and more DEIC employees received land in exchange for promises to provide the company with grain and vegetables. The DEIC also began to encourage immigration. In 1679, it began to authorize settlement eastward beyond the Cape peninsula. By 1700, the colony's population had grown to about 2,500, including 1,200 Whites, primarily Dutch and French Protestants. About half of the inhabitants were slaves, mainly from the Dutch East Indies. Efforts to transplant Dutch-style labor intensive farming to South Africa were not very successful. Gradually farmers built up larger holdings, producing livestock, wine, and grain. Many small holders sold or gave up their lands and moved to Cape Town, where they became artisans and unskilled dockworkers.

Khoekhoen-Dutch Relations. The creation of larger holdings also came at the expense of Khoekhoen pasturelands. Some 4,000–8,000 Khoekhoen lived in the Cape peninsula. They traded with the Dutch, selling sheep and cattle for iron, copper, and brass objects. Peaceful trade relations were replaced by conflict in the 1660s, when the Khoekhoen attacked Dutch settlements. A more aggressive Dutch program of expansion led to warfare that lasted from

1673–1677. The Dutch fought three wars with four different Khoekhoen chiefdoms. Superior firepower and organizational skills gave victory to the Dutch. Vigorous expansion became official Dutch policy. Dutch efforts led to the disintegration of Khoekhoen society in the early eighteenth century. Khoekhoen were pressed into service to the Dutch as servants or livestock herders. Khoekhoen chieftains surrendered to the Dutch in 1713. Smallpox (1713–1767) delivered the final blow to Khoekhoen independence.

Further Dutch Settlement. During the rest of the century more and more immigrants arrived from Holland, but also from Germany, Switzerland, and France. They and the coastal settlers spread inland as far north as the Orange River and as far east as the interior deserts, some 400 miles from Cape Town, and east into the mixed-farming area 450 miles away. By the 1790s, some 16,000 settlers inhabited the Cape Colony. These interior settlers were known as *trekboers* (migrating farmers).

Inland the trekboers came into contact with hunter-gatherers, the San. In the 1770s, warfare broke out between the hunter-gatherers and the trekboers, with the well-armed trekboers victorious. By the end of the eighteenth century the pastoralists and hunter-gatherers could offer no further resistance to Dutch expansion. Beyond the trekboer frontier to the north of the Orange River were people of mixed background, including runaway slaves and criminals. These people, known as *griquas,* had organized themselves into chiefdoms similar to those of the African Blacks.

The Whites also expanded along the southern coast into the frontier area of Khoekhoen and Xhosa mixed-farming communities. The Dutch fought major wars with the Xhosa in 1779 and 1793.

The British and the End of Dutch Rule. Dutch rule collapsed because of two factors. First, in 1794, the DEIC went bankrupt, reducing Dutch interest in South Africa. In addition, the British captured Cape Colony during the Napoleonic Wars, the century-long conflict between the French and a coalition of the other Europeans, led by the British. The Treaty transferred the Cape Colony into British hands. The arrival of the British coincided with the westward expansion of the Xhosa.

2. Colonial Government

Three types of political systems emerged in the Dutch period. The Dutch created a colonial government. Frontier governments appeared in spite of Dutch efforts to maintain control over the growing colony. Black political structures remained largely unchanged.

Dutch Government. The Dutch established a government to rule White-controlled areas and determine relations between Whites and Blacks. It is important to understand that a private corporation, the Dutch East Indies Company, ran the colony. At the top of the political system were the Governor-General, headquartered in the Dutch East Indies, and the Council of Seventeen, in the Dutch capital of Amsterdam. Direct administration of the Cape Colony was in the hands of the local governor and the Council of Policy, composed of employees of the DEIC. Company employees also formed a majority on the Court of Justice. Frequently, conflict took place between the company officials and increasingly wealthy and independent settlers.

Governors and other leading officials sought to make decisions that were economically beneficial to themselves, losing sight of the overall purpose of the colony—to facilitate DEIC trade and profits. In 1700, the directors of the Council of Seventeen prohibited officials from owning land or engaging in trade. This helped shift the balance of political power away from local company officials and toward the settlers.

Conflict between settlers and company officials continued. The free burghers complained to DEIC administration, accusing local DEIC officials of corruption. The governor tried to arrest over sixty free burgher petitioners but then the DEIC removed the governor and other key officials. The Dutch government tried to limit the problem by prohibiting further land ownership and trade. Increasingly this local conflict got caught up in Dutch political issues, including the conflict between conservatives and republicans and the collapse of Dutch maritime trade supremacy. Colonial authorities also came into conflict with governments created by the trekboers.

Frontier Governments. While the colonial government in Cape Town exercised nominal control over all settlements, the trekboers acquired increasing independence. The colonial government attempted to establish local governments headed by company officers, the *landrosts.* In reality, trekboers dominated local government through their own officials known as *heemraden* and *veldkornets.* Existing officials submitted lists of candidates to the governor, who appointed six heemraden for each district. Veldkornets were appointed to maintain law and order in subdivisions of the district. Tension between trekboer interests and those of the DEIC were played out in local government institutions.

African Governments. Trekboer expansionism and military victories undermined pastoralist and hunter-gatherer political institutions. However, the chiefdoms of the mixed-farmers were as yet untouched by White expansion. Within the chiefdoms conflict frequently broke out over who should be paramount chief.

3. Dutch Christianity

Thousands of miles away from the Netherlands, the colonists began to introduce modifications to Dutch Reformed Christianity.

The idea of a *state church* was transferred to the Cape Colony. The DEIC appointed and funded the local *Dutch Reformed Church.* The Dutch Reformed Church was a branch of Protestant Calvinism. Calvinism emphasized God's sovereignty over the world. It emphasized human sin and a "fallen" world. Christ would thus create a "New Jerusalem" in South Africa. Gradually Christianity began to take hold in the colony, primarily along the coast. Though missionary activity began in 1734, the DEIC opposed such endeavors (see similar attitudes of the British East India Company in Chapter Three). At this time, the idea that Christian meant White began to have some influence.

Religion remained increasingly important to the Black populations in the seventeenth and eighteenth centuries. However, the initial contact between missionaries and the African Black population did not immediately produce changes in native religious patterns.

4. Trade, Agriculture, and Social Structure

Trade and agriculture dominated South Africa. Black society remained unchanged, though influenced by slavery. Social differences emerged in White society, based on political power, wealth, and geography.

Trade and Agriculture. Agricultural goods, imports, and locally produced craft products provided the basis for trade. Initially trade and agriculture were associated with providing DEIC trading ships with fresh goods. As Cape Town grew and other cities emerged, local trade became increasingly important. A shift to large-scale farming came in the early eighteenth century, when the government began to offer farmers 6,000-acre plots of lands. Though the government retained ownership of the land, the farmer could sell rights to the land, purchase rights to more land and pass the right to use a piece of land to heirs. In effect, this created a dual system of private ownership and rented lands. The trekboers used large amounts of land to graze livestock, including sheep, and to grow grains, vegetables, and sugar cane. Some farmers, especially French colonists, produced wine. Farming in the interior was largely for subsistence, while farmers near Cape Town generally engaged in commercial agriculture.

Black Society. For mixed farmers, little changed, as chiefs dominated local communities. White power largely destroyed the independence of the traditional elite in hunter-gatherer and pastoral communities. Commoners frequently became servants or laborers for Whites.

Slavery. Slavery began with the importation of people from Angola and West Africa, taken from captured Portuguese slave ships. However, throughout the Dutch period a majority of slaves came from Madagascar, India, Sri Lanka, and Indonesia and not from Africa. Most of these slaves were Muslims. By the early eighteenth century slaves outnumbered the Whites. In 1717, there were 2,700 slaves, 2,000 free burghers, and 744 DEIC officials. In 1793, there were almost 15,000 slaves and 14,000 Whites. The slave population grew slowly, with continued importation of new slaves offsetting high *mortality rates*.

In the early eighteenth century most Whites owned only a few slaves, while senior officials owned larger numbers. Later, the proportion of Whites who owned slaves declined, largely due to the immigration of individuals who could not afford slaves. In 1750, there were fewer than 700 slaveholders (10% of White families).

Slaves had few rights and their legal position was determined by the *Cape Slave Code* of 1754. They could neither marry, nor control their children's lives, nor acquire property, nor make legal contracts. They were required to obey their masters completely. Slaves could be bought, sold, and inherited by Whites. Female slaves were frequently used as prostitutes for sailors on liberty. However, enslavement generally did not include physical abuse since slaves were valuable property.

Most slaves accepted their fate. Slave rebellion was almost unknown. A minority fled to the frontiers, where they became *griquas*. Runaways would be beaten, even executed if caught. Others formed bands and turned to crime, robbing White settlements. Slaves who lived in White households became acculturated to White life, converted to Christianity, and learned Dutch. Slaves could be emancipated, if they bought their freedom; men at the age of twenty-five, women at twenty-two.

Masters freed few slaves, so the freed population was quite small (somewhat more than 12,000 near the end of the eighteenth century). Most former slaves lived in Cape Town, where they became servants, artisans, and small retail storekeepers. Initially freed slaves had the same rights as Whites but by the late eighteenth century they were subject to "*pass laws.*" They needed the government's permission to leave one city and move to another. Overall, racial lines were somewhat fluid, certainly much less rigid than in the twentieth century.

White Society. Initially, White social structure was based on one's position within the DEIC. Then gradually White society split into two groups, company employees and free citizens (artisans or farmers). Over time social structure became increasingly complex, especially within the citizens' group, where wealthy farmers and merchants intermingled with the company leadership. In the middle were small traders, innkeepers, farm overseers, and ordinary farmers. At the bottom were poorer Whites, including both low-level Company officials and the landless without steady incomes.

The expansion of settlement inland created a variant in trekboer society. Local officials were at the top of society, but a large middle group of independent farmers existed, too. At the bottom were frontiersmen, who lived from hunting and trading with the Black communities, and tenant farmers. They also hired increasing numbers of pastoralists, primarily to herd livestock.

5. Family and Gender

Black families changed little unless they were affected by White expansion. White society was male-dominated, in terms of both numbers and power.

The Black Family and Gender Roles. Black families remained male-dominated, with clear gender-based divisions of labor. Men tended the livestock and did light field work. Women did the heavy field work, as well as performing household duties.

White Male Domination. Throughout the Dutch period White men outnumbered White women by three or four to one. The family was patriarchal but the small size of the female population and Dutch law gave women some privileges. Women could be more selective in marriage, ignoring the poorest males, who perforce remained single, and marry into the middle or upper ranks of White society. Women could accumulate property, since legally they owned half of the family's wealth.

Slave women were an even smaller proportion of the population. Since slaves could not marry, slave families did not form. Slave women worked hard jobs and were frequently treated as prostitutes for sailors and as mistresses for their owners. The offspring of relationships between White men and slave women were considered slaves. Sometimes White men freed their slave mistresses and married them. Racial mixing was more common in the Dutch period than later.

6. Diversity and Community

Great diversity and some toleration of difference characterized the Cape Colony in its first half-century. However, the Cape Colony came to be divided along racial lines by the second half of the eighteenth century.

The Racial Divide. Whites overpowered the non-Whites with whom they came into contact. In this period the Whites came to dominate the Khoekhoen, some Xhosa communities, and of course the slaves. Over time White demands for land outweighed the mutual benefits of trade between Whites and Khoekhoen. Whites gradually took over Khoekhoen lands, driving the Khoekhoen into less hospitable areas or subordinating them to White economic activity. Khoekhoen became servants, herders, and manual laborers for the Whites. The Whites used military power to destroy the political structures that bound Khoekhoen communities together. As a result, individual Khoekhoen faced White power, an uneven match.

The Language Divide. Language also divided the peoples of South Africa. Dutch was initially the principal language of the Whites, though French was also common. Indigenous people generally spoke their own native languages. Some slaves spoke Dutch; a few retained their original language. Asian slaves commonly used Portuguese Creole. Rather gradually a simplified dialect of Dutch became the language of the White settlers and those who came into contact with them. This dialect became a distinct language, known as *Afrikaans* ("the African language"). All aspects of South African life, including language, became more complex after the British assumed power.

C. BRITISH CENTURY, 1800–1910

The British dominated South Africa during the nineteenth century. By the end of the century they had conquered all of the African chiefdoms and tribes and incorporated them into the British South African political structure. This increase in British power angered the settlers of Dutch descent, the *Afrikaaners,* or *Boers,* culminating in the South African War of 1899–1902. At war's end the Afrikaaners gained a large measure of autonomy from the British colonial government. The century also saw the emergence of a strong sense of racial superiority among the Afrikaaners. The discovery of gold and diamonds transformed the economy from a commercial-agricultural one into an industrial-global one (the so-called "*mineral revolution*"). These economic changes produced two new social groups, the capitalist-industrialist and working classes. The migration of Black labor to the minefields and cities and the arrival of unmarried British immigrants disrupted families and in the case of Black families gave women much more power than previously. Racial conflict intensified, as race became the single-most important force in South African history.

1. The British Conquest of South Africa

Whites secured control over all of South Africa in this period. The British expanded from the Cape Colony eastward, eventually fighting fierce wars with the Zulu who had moved from the north down along the east coast. Before mid-century many Boers had migrated inland from the Cape Colony, escaping British governance. In the second half of the century the British acquired Natal along the east coast and the Afrikaaners gained control over the central plateau areas. After the discovery of mineral wealth, the British made a determined effort to force remaining independent chiefdoms to accept British rule. By the end of the century, Whites ruled all of South Africa. However, the Whites were not united and the British and Afrikaaners fought each other in the Boer War, the world's first bloody, brutal war of the twentieth century. Though the British won, they soon abandoned South Africa, which then became an independent country.

Reasons for White Victory. Whites gained political control over all of South Africa in the nineteenth century for several reasons. Most importantly, they decided to defeat and conquer the non-White chiefdoms and tribes. Among the advantages that Europeans had globally in the eighteenth and nineteenth centuries was the ability to articulate political goals, develop strategies to achieve those goals, and organize society to support their aims. The Europeans also had a huge military advantage, both in weaponry and fortifications, that Blacks could not overcome. The Whites also had considerable mobility and the *logistical* capability to move supplies, food, and equipment with them. The absence of Black unity weakened their ability to defend themselves against the Whites. The Whites faced separate chiefdoms, which frequently fought against each other. In a sense, the Whites brought order to an area of southern Africa where warfare and conflict were endemic. Of course, White actions fostered conflict, as well.

Conquest of the Xhosa. Having already devastated the Khoekhoen, the Europeans then moved along the east coast into Xhosaland. The Xhosa formed the strongest chiefdom along the southeast coast of South Africa. They resisted European expansion in the War of the Axe in 1846 and in the Mlajeni War of the early 1850s. By 1847, the British had reached the Great Kei River and in 1855 they incorporated Xhosaland into British South Africa. Soon after that a cattle disease destroyed much of the Xhosa wealth and brought psychological despair to the nation. They were in no position to offer further resistance to the British.

Conflict with the Zulu. The struggle with the Zulu was more challenging for the Europeans. The Bantu-speaking Zulu possessed a warrior kingdom, having expanded their power by conquering local chiefdoms. Around 1810, the Zulu defeated two northern Nguni peoples, the Ndwandwe and the Mthethwa. The famous *Shaka* provided Zulu leadership. Zulu victories resulted from the weakening of local chiefdoms as well as their own military superiority. Zulu expansionism produced a massive movement of peoples, especially of defeated military forces. Military bands engaged in *mfecane* (the term means "grinding" but describes territorial conquest through military force), abandoning the east coast and moving into the central parts of South Africa. Their expansion led to the destruction of the political kingdoms they defeated and to further massive migration to the northern edges of South Africa, to areas that are now the states of Malawi, Zambia, and Tanzania. Many Blacks fled into the Cape Colony, too. The series of Zulu-inspired wars weakened the Blacks and made it easier for Whites to conquer the eastern parts of South Africa. Warfare and migration led to the formation of four larger kingdoms, the Zulu, Ndbele, Swazi, and Sotho, as well as a number of smaller chiefdoms. The Zulu also fought a series of wars with the Afrikaaners, who were expanding into the eastern parts of the country.

The Great Trek, 1836–1842. Parallel to the mfecane, the Afrikaaners migrated in large numbers out of Cape Colony and into central and eastern South Africa. This *Great Trek* resulted from Afrikaaner disgust with the British and the unwillingness and inability of the Afrikaaners to accept British rule and values.

Two chief sources of conflict existed. First, the Afrikaaners felt betrayed by the British government's decisions to ban the slave trade (1807) and then slavery in the British Empire (1833). By escaping inland, they hoped to perpetuate their slave-holding society. Second, the Afrikaaners resented the loss of independence that came with the transfer of South Africa from the Dutch to the British. Armed flight was the Afrikaaner solution.

Large numbers of Afrikaaners moved from south of the Fish River to the area between the *Vaal* and Caledon Rivers in central South Africa. Eventually they moved north to the Limpopo River, essentially the northern border of South Africa. In 1836, the Trekkers defeated the Ndebele, who then fled northward into what is today Zimbabwe. The Boers next moved eastward to Zululand where they defeated the Zulu in the epic *Battle of Blood River* (1838). Many Afrikaaners settled in this area, Natal. Ironically, the Zulu defeat led many Blacks, earlier driven out by the Zulu, to return to Natal.

When the British annexed Natal in 1842, most of the Afrikaaners moved back into the *highveld* (high plateau) area between the Vaal and Caledon Rivers. The Afrikaaners then drove the Sotho and Tswana peoples out of the highveld, which they had entered after the flight of the Ndbele. A *Griquas* state competed for power in the highveld. In 1848, the British annexed the area between the Orange and Vaal Rivers, calling it the Orange River Sovereignty. It seemed the Afrikaaners could not escape British rule. After the Afrikaaners defeated local chiefdoms, the British then annexed the defenseless areas. The Afrikaaners seemed to be doing the British government's dirty work.

However, the British soon decided to limit their direct rule to the Cape Colony and the Natal. In 1854, the British signed two agreements with the Afrikaaners, the *Sand River* and *Bloemfontein Conventions,* that gave the Afrikaaners relative autonomy in the *Trans-Vaal* and Orange River regions. After decades, the Afrikaaners now appeared free to live their lives without much British interference.

The Highveld. The situation in the highveld was quite complicated. Black communities tried to rebuild political structures after the mfecane. British missionaries arrived, intent upon converting the Africans to Christianity. From 1850–1865, intermittent warfare took place between the Afrikaaners and the main Black kingdoms, the Sotho, Pedi, Tswana, and Venda. The battles with the Sotho were especially fierce, leading the British to annex the Sotho lands, or Basutoland. By 1870, South Africa consisted of the British areas of the Cape Colony, Natal and Lesotho; the Afrikaaner states of the Transvaal and the Orange Free State; the Black kingdoms on the northern frontier, the Tswana and Venda; and the Swazi, Zulu, and Mpondo in the east.

British Takeover of Natal. Large numbers of Blacks fled into the Natal, desperately trying to escape a Zulu civil war of the 1860s and 1870s. The British decided to annex Natal in order to establish order and institute direct rule there. They set aside land for the Blacks, the *reserves.* The situation in Natal became increasingly complex with the immigration of large numbers of people from India, beginning in the 1860s. The Indians fled the poverty of their homeland, yet remained within the British Empire.

Final Conquest of the African Chiefdoms, 1870–1900. After 1870, the British used military force to destroy the independence of the remaining Black chiefdoms and then incorporated them into British or Afrikaaner territories. Resistance to the British was hampered by internal discord among the Blacks. Individual chiefdoms seldom cooperated together against the Europeans and there was much internal conflict within many chiefdoms, especially over who would be chief. By 1900, the British had incorporated all of the indigenous chiefdoms into White-dominated South Africa.

Zulu Resistance. The Zulu put up strong resistance to the British. The victory of *Chief Cetshwayo* in a Zulu civil war led to the expansion of the Zulu in Natal. Initially the Zulu aligned with the British governor, Shepstone. However, in 1877, he annexed the Transvaal and dropped his ties to the Zulu. Two years later the British invaded Zululand. At first the Zulus inflicted major defeats on the British, at *Isandhlwana,* for example. Eventually the British used divide and conquer tactics and, aided by the renewal of civil war among the Zulu, destroyed the Zulu capital, Ulundi. In 1887, the British attached part of Zululand to the Transvaal and the rest to Natal.

Collapse of the Other Chiefdoms. The other kingdoms fell easily to superior British military power. A rebellion by the Xhosa and Thembi was crushed in 1881, after lasting four years. The British peacefully incorporated the Mpondo into the Cape Colony in 1894. The Pedi, under pressure from the Swazi and the Afrikaaner and influenced by German Lutheran missionaries, easily submitted to the British in 1879. After a rebellion in 1880, the Sotho cooperated with the British.

Conquest of the Tswana took more than twenty years. The Tswana lived in the Kimberley mining area. In 1871, the British annexed the Tswana lands and in 1880 incorporated them into Cape Colony, following the Tswana insurrection of 1879. Later more Tswana territory was annexed and added to Cape Colony in 1895. This provoked another rebellion in 1896–1897.

The Swazi had created a chiefdom out of the remnants of previous mfecane. Hated enemy of the Zulu, the Swazi chiefdom was first added to the Transvaal and, in 1902, annexed by the British and treated as a separate colony, Basutoland.

The Venda on the northwest frontier defended themselves against the British and Afrikaaner into the 1890s. In 1898, however, the Whites, aided by the Swazi and Tsonga, captured the Venda stronghold. With the demise of the independent Venda kingdom, all of South Africa came under the political control of the Whites. The Blacks were concentrated in specific areas, including Basutoland, Botswana (Bechuanaland), Transkei, Zululand, Swaziland, and the reserves in Ciskei and Natal.

Conclusion. It took the Whites much of the nineteenth century to gain control over all of South Africa. The indigenous chiefdoms resisted militarily but their efforts were unsuccessful. The gap in military technology and organizational ability was even greater than it had been earlier. In addition the chiefdoms were weakened by decades of warfare—with the Whites and with each other. At the end of the century, war between the two White groups—the Afrikaaners (Boers) and the British replaced warfare between Whites and Blacks.

The South African War (1899–1902). A century of violence for South Africa ended with the South African, or Boer, War. The war broke out as the British tried to incorporate the two Afrikaaner states into a united South Africa.

The Run-up to the War. Efforts to achieve unity through diplomatic negotiations failed. British Colonial Secretary Lord Carnarvon tried to convince the separate states to meet together to form a single British colony. When this failed, he authorized Shepstone, governor of Natal, to annex the Transvaal. In 1880, a small rebellion in the Transvaal led to an Afrikaaner invasion of Natal, where British troops were easily defeated. The British government in London agreed to give the Transvaal "complete self-government." However, the issue of the relationship of the two Afrikaaner states to the British Empire remained unresolved.

The emergence of an emotional Afrikaaner nationalism and the influx of large numbers of non-Afrikaaners made the situation more volatile in the Transvaal mining areas. The *Uitlanders,* non-Afrikaaner Whites, outnumbered the Afrikaaners. The Uitlanders identified with the British, though their ethnic backgrounds were much more varied.

Under a new president, Paul Kruger, Transvaal moved to establish its independence from the British. At the same time, a new British Colonial Secretary, Joseph Chamberlain, decided that the British must assert their control over the wayward Afrikaaner republics. He gave support to the ill-fated *Jameson Raid.* Cecil Rhodes, the dominant figure in the diamond trade and a person whose company controlled Southern Rhodesia (today Zimbabwe), organized a plot to seize power in the Transvaal. At the end of 1895, Leander Jameson led a group of 500 armed police into Transvaal. The uprising expected from the Uitlanders never materialized and Jameson and his men were arrested.

The Afrikaaners and British found no basis for cooperation. Instead, animosity grew. Chamberlain concluded that the British would have to use military force to prevent the Afrikaaners from gaining control of all of South Africa. The new British High Commissioner in South Africa plotted for the annexation of the Transvaal. Both sides issued ultimatums in 1899 and the war was on, initiated by the Afrikaaners.

The War. The war was marked by brutality on both sides. Though the British eventually triumphed, the victory was hard-won. The British had a 5:1 advantage in manpower and superiority in weaponry. However, the Boers had the advantage of terrain, mobility, and guerilla tactics. The Boers were determined to win; the British were less enthusiastic fighters.

The war went through three phases. Initially the Afrikaaners advanced into Natal and the Cape Colony, using three lines of attack. They held off British counterattacks at the end of 1899 but bogged down in sieges of British troops in Natal, Kimberley, and the northwestern part of the Cape Colony.

During the second phase, the British won a series of important victories in 1900. They captured major Afrikaaner cities including Bloemfontein, Johannesburg, and Pretoria, the capital. The British annexed the two republics, the Transvaal and the Orange River Colony. The war appeared over.

However, in the third stage the Afrikaaners resorted to guerilla warfare and lightening quick raids into Cape Colony. The British then turned to the systematic destruction of Afrikaaner territory. Farms and crops were destroyed and civilians (mainly women and children) were placed in camps. The British built blockhouses and stretched barbwire fences around areas, then systematically destroyed Afrikaaner guerilla groups within these enclosed area. In 1902, the Afrikaaner army surrendered.

The Peace of Vereeniging. The *Peace of Vereeniging* (1902) provided a temporary solution for South Africa. The treaty called for a system of temporary military rule, which would be gradually transformed into a civilian administration. Dutch would be taught in the schools and no decision about political rights for the non-Whites would be made until self-government was introduced. Thus the British surrendered the right to determine the future of race relations in South Africa.

The End of British Rule. When a new government came to power in England in 1906, it decided not to pursue British domination of the Afrikaaner provinces. The British accepted an Afrikaaner proposal for Transvaal self-government. Pro-independence groups also came to power in the Orange River Colony and the Cape Colony. Only Natal wished to remain a British colony. In 1908, representatives of the four colonies drafted a constitution for an independent South Africa. In the following year parliaments of the four colonies approved the new constitution. The British accepted the independence of the new Union of South Africa in 1910.

2. Colonial Governance

Three forms of governance existed in South Africa during the nineteenth century. First, there was British colonial government. Second, each White province had its own governing structure. Finally, the African chiefdoms retained their traditional structure, with a chief, assisted by a council of elders.

British Colonial Government. As in India (see Chapter Two), the British government provided South Africa with a bare bones administration and little oversight from London. The British, however, offered a more activist government than the Dutch East Indies Company had. The British began to impose their political culture and principles upon the colony. By 1834, British magistrates without local ties had replaced the system of *heemraden* and *veldkornets.* British policy goals differed from those of the Dutch East Indies authorities and

Afrikaaner local officials. The British sought to limit White migration into the interior and opposed slavery. Both of these policies were in direct opposition to the views of the Dutch.

As the British annexed territories and added them to either Cape Colony or Natal, British administration was gradually extended throughout much of South Africa. In mid-century a more formal governmental structure was established with a governor-general for all of South Africa and governors for individual colonies. Natal and Cape Colony had legislatures in which officials in the executive branch were represented but not dominant. The White populations elected the majority of legislators. The British government in South Africa reported to the Colonial Secretary in London, who was a member of the Cabinet.

Afrikaaner Government. Afrikaaners sought to preserve their traditional forms of local government and to strengthen them through demands for autonomy for the Transvaal and the Orange Free State. In general, the Afrikaaners had an ambiguous attitude toward the British government. In 1834, British administration superceded the Dutch system of rather autonomous local governments run by district *heemraden* and local *veldkornets.* However, the Great Trek permitted the reestablishment of autonomous Afrikaaner governance in the interior.

In 1854, the Orange Free State adopted a constitution that created a unitary republic. Male citizens elected a legislature, or *Volksraad.* Citizenship was open to White males who had lived in the territory for six years and had registered for military service. Citizens directly elected a president for a five-year term. The president was aided by an executive council of officials and Volksraad representatives. Civil rights were guaranteed for citizens, while the Constitution was almost impossible to amend.

In 1860, the Transvaal drew up a constitution similar to that of the Orange Free State, except that it gave supreme authority to the elected *Volksraad,* not the elected president, and prohibited equal rights for non-Whites. Initially, political conflict was intense in the Transvaal and constitutional government very fragile. Over time greater stability emerged, especially through the efforts of strong presidents. Since the Transvaal was the site of substantial immigration, the *Volksraad* tried to prevent *Uitlanders* (immigrants) from gaining control of the government. The *Volksraad* passed a law limiting citizenship to naturalized citizens who had lived in the Transvaal for at least fourteen years. Few *Uitlanders* sought political rights; their main objective was to earn money in the mining industry.

Native Governments. Battered by warfare within tribes, between tribes, and with the Whites, the Blacks found it difficult to maintain effective government. In general, tribes were still ruled by chiefs, whose power was based on wealth, prestige, and military support. Councils of elders aided the chiefs.

In the reserves of Natal and increasingly in other parts of South Africa, Blacks came under the direct control of White colonial government. Shepstone applied the system of indirect rule used in India. He manipulated and controlled African chiefs, making them colonial officials responsible to the colonial government and not to their own people.

3. Native, Racist, and Civilizing Ideologies

Some African tribes developed fairly elaborate ideological justifications for their actions, while the Afrikaaners increasingly turned to a racist ideology. The British provided an alternative set of ideals, too.

Native Ideologies. Both the Zulu and Xhosa developed fairly sophisticated sets of ideas. A Xhosa ideology developed in reaction to conquest by the British and to epidemic cattle disease. The Xhosa combined traditional religious beliefs and Christian missionary ideas. Prophets, including teenage girls, announced that they had received visions that explained how the Xhosa were to survive. The Xhosa were to destroy all of their remaining cattle and abandon farming. In this way, thus, the Xhosa would purify themselves and destroy the witches that had caused pollution, death, and defeat. Then ancestors would return and establish a golden age. Xhosaland was in a state of war between those who believed the visions (and thus sought to create a new religion) and those who rejected such ideas. The believers won out and in 1857 some 400,000 head of cattle were slaughtered and at least 40,000 Xhosa subsequently died of starvation. Thereafter, the Xhosa turned more and more to Christianity and to the leadership of Tiyo Soga, who returned from Scotland to preach Presbyterianism, practical education, and submission to the British.

The ideology of the Zulu was not that of a people in despair but of a nation confident in its own power. Zulu supremacy was an ideological strategy for incorporating various Nguni people into a single nation. Their beliefs justified militarism, brutal punishment of dissenters, and the primacy of the royal family. Coercion, ceremony, and magic were used to secure support for Zulu suprematism.

Afrikaaner Racism. Despising the native peoples and hating the British, Afrikaaners developed an ideology that justified their sense of superiority. The Afrikaaners argued for "states' rights," parallel to the position of American Southerners. They suggested that their freedom depended upon the right to dominate and/or enslave non-Whites. They emphasized that the natural relationship between the Afrikaaners and Blacks was a master-servant one. The Afrikaaner definition of civilization was based on Dutch Reformed Christianity. Christianity confirmed and justified the superiority of the Afrikaaner.

By the 1880s, Afrikaaner ideology had separated into two main strands, generally called *idealistic* and *pragmatic.* A Dutch Reformed minister, S. J. *duToit,* articulated most clearly the idealistic program. He pointed out the uniqueness (thus superiority) of the Afrikaaners. The Afrikaaners, he said, had been chosen by God to dominate South Africa and civilize the "heathen" Blacks and other non-Whites. Other Dutch Reformed ministers espoused similar ideas of Afrikaaner unity and exclusivity. It was thought that to mix with others, both geographically and genetically, would weaken the Afrikaaners and undermine their ability to dominate South Africa.

The duToit position had less appeal than that of the pragmatists, represented by Jan *Hofmeyer,* from Cape Town. He called for harmony among all whites, cooperation with the British and unification of South Africa. His goals were largely political, with the ultimate objective an Afrikaaner-dominated, unified South Africa. Hofmeyer was influenced by the Social Darwinist idea of the survival of the fittest, the fittest being the Afrikaaners. However, he saw this as an evolutionary process.

British Civilizing Mission. In the first half of the nineteenth century the British in South Africa were deeply influenced by the humanitarian reform movement taking place back in Great Britain. In the mother country British reformers sought to civilize the lower classes, through example, laws, and Christianity. Their goal was to make England a more civilized society. This idea of a humanitarian mission to civilize "others" was applied in India (see Chapter Two) and in South Africa. Education, based on the British model, was seen as the primary means of civilizing the Africans. In addition, White example, modernization of infrastructure, and Westernized employment were viewed as ways to civilize the primitive Blacks. To become Christian was to become civilized, too.

Evangelical Missionaries. Missionaries played a practical role, articulating an ideology of civilization and attempting to transform the lives of the indigenous people. By the end of the nineteenth century two-thirds of all native people had become Christians. The missionaries frequently acted as advocates for the native peoples and tried to protect them and cushion them against rapid change. They created mission schools and hospitals and provided role models for the Westernization of a small Black elite, primarily in the Cape Colony. The missionaries acquired large amounts of land for their mission stations, which served as refuges for the indigenous people.

Missionary activity began among the Khoekhoen in the first half of the eighteenth century. German Moravians were the first to arrive. At the end of the century the *London Missionary Society* assumed a leadership role in missionary activity. This group espoused a radical form of evangelism that emphasized racial and economic equality. A strong sense of justice led it to argue for the indigenous peoples and to condemn their unjust treatment by the Whites.

At the British Parliament, John Philip agitated on behalf of the Khoekhoen. In 1828, he convinced Parliament to pass a resolution asking the colonial government to treat all peoples of South Africa equally. The resolution stated that the indigenous people of South Africa should have the same rights and freedom as the Dutch and English. This led the governor of Cape Colony to issue *Ordinance 50* (1828), which gave Khoekhoen and other indigenous people equality with Whites before the law. In effect, the Ordinance freed all Khoekhoen who had been enslaved.

Conclusion. Thus a variety of ideologies existed in South Africa in the nineteenth century. They were quite varied but had several common elements. First, all addressed the issue of race relations. All espoused the superiority of one racial group over all others, whether British, Zulu, or Afrikaaner. Finally all responded to the instability resulting from warfare, military aggression, and the expansion of White power.

4. "Mineral Revolution": From An Agrarian Age to An Industrial One

During the nineteenth century South Africa was transformed from a rural society, based on agriculture and local trade, into a participant in the global economy, based on the mineral extraction industries. These changes affected all social groups within the country.

Rural Economy, to 1870. Initially, South Africa played a minimal role in the British global economy of the nineteenth century. Most agricultural production, especially corn, was either for subsistence or for feeding the urban populations. Cattle and sheep ranching produced for local markets. Craft production met the needs of urban consumers. In general rural farmers produced most of the craft items they consumed. Gradually, White merchants gained control over local and inter-regional trade, displacing Black traders.

Wine and wool represented the main exports to Great Britain. During the 1860s, for instance, wool represented three-fourths of all exports. Though the British government promoted a modest program of modernizing infrastructure (including roads and railways), South Africa remained an economic backwater. Whites dominated the economy, while Black farming communities were devastated by the destructiveness of warfare and disease.

Pre-industrial Society. We can see clear differences between White and non-White social structures. In general, all Whites were seen as members of a race superior to all non-Whites. We can also see differences within White and Black societies.

White Society. Top government officials and wealthy farmers, especially those who produced wine and wool for the export market, dominated White society. A small middle class composed of the intelligentsia, minor government officials, shopkeepers, and artisans resided in the cities. Rural White society consisted of the wool and wine estate owners, a middle group engaged in sugar cane production and using hired labor from India, and lower class White farmers, mainly Afrikaaners. The Afrikaaners were poor farmers, especially in the Transvaal and the Orange River Province. Frequently they raised cattle and sheep but had to buy grain from Black farmers.

Indians. Beginning in the 1860s, White farmers in Natal began to import laborers from India since they could not get enough Black workers after the end of slavery. The Indians came as *indentured servants,* who signed a contract to work for a five-year period. After they had fulfilled their five-year obligation they could remain in South Africa on their own, renew their work contract for another five years, receive a small plot of land as their own property, or receive a free return passage to India. Natal law required that 25 Indian women be imported for every 100 men. This created some opportunities for marriages and settlement. Very few returned to India, instead taking one of the above options. By 1911, Indians outnumbered Whites in Natal.

Black Societies. Substantial differences existed among Black peoples. Tribes that retained some degree of cohesion were generally divided into the political/economic elite (the chiefs and the key families) and ordinary farmers. Zulu society was more clearly structured into two groups—a military elite and a mass of ordinary farmers. Where tribal structures had broken down, such as among the Khoekhoen and Xhosa, individuals generally worked as hired laborers for White farmers. No upper class existed.

Emancipation of Slaves. The British Parliament banned the slave trade in the Empire in 1807. This meant that additional slaves could only come from procreation among the existing ones. White farmers responded to the labor shortage by working existing slaves harder. The British government soon intervened, ordering the governor to issue a law setting maximum work hours, types of punishments, and minimum standards for food and clothing. Local compliance was at first minimal but the British government persisted. The government appointed Protectors of Slaves who were to ensure compliance with the legislation. Slavery was abolished in 1828 through the Ordinance of 50. However, in the interior Afrikaaners frequently ignored the law. As noted previously, the evangelical Christian missionaries acted as a powerful lobby for the abolition of slavery in South Africa. In 1833, the British Parliament banned slavery throughout the British Empire. The law also emancipated all slaves in the Empire and provided for modest compensation for former owners, with a five-year period of transition.

Mineral Revolution, 1870–1910. The discovery of gold and diamonds transformed the South African economy and society, which became wealthier and more industrialized. South Africa became a capitalist country. As the economy grew rapidly, an industrial labor force emerged, composed of Afrikaaners, White immigrants or Uitlanders, and Black laborers. The economic core of the country shifted from the coastal areas to the interior.

Diamond Mining. Gold and copper mining had begun in the Transvaal and Cape Colony in the 1860s but the discovery of diamonds in the Transvaal in 1867 led to a huge gold and diamond rush. Kimberley became the center of the world's richest diamond mining region and Johannesburg became a major gold mining area.

At first, Whites mined diamond claims individually with the assistance of a few Black laborers. Consolidation came quickly, however. Mechanized mining, which required substantial amounts of capital, replaced hand mining. By 1872, four companies controlled most of the diamond fields. Cecil Rhodes, mentioned earlier in conjunction with the Jameson Raid, gradually gained control of the Kimberley mining area, through *DeBeers Consolidated Mines.* Rhodes and his partners acquired a diamond mining monopoly. However, the mines were so rich that they flooded the global diamond market with South African stones, reducing profits for DeBeers and other diamond companies. The firms turned to a marketing strategy that limited the number of diamonds on the world market, thus sustaining high prices and huge profits. A London diamond group agreed to purchase DeBeers diamonds and prevent an increase in the quantity of diamonds it sold.

Gold Mining. In 1886, gold was discovered along the Witwatersrand, the watershed between the Limpopo and Orange Rivers. Large amounts of gold were easily accessible, though the ore was of rather low grade. Rhodes and other diamond magnates quickly captured the gold mining industry. South African gold mining benefited from the development of the *MacArthur-Forrest Process,* which simplified extraction of the gold from the mined rock. By the turn of the century South Africa was producing over a quarter of the world's gold. In contrast to diamond mining, gold mining was not dominated by a single firm. Instead over 100 companies owned gold mines.

Demand for Industrial Goods. Commercial activity flourished and domestic trade expanded greatly. The mining industries created a demand for other products as well, from food and consumer goods to textiles and leather products. Thus mining stimulated the development of light industry, and later of heavy industry. However, the importation of cheap foreign goods hindered the development of local industry. In other words, *import substitution* did not become a viable economic strategy. The influx of large numbers of White immigrants and of Black laborers encouraged agricultural production, too.

Social Change. The discovery of diamonds and gold had a profound impact on South African society. A wealthy class of millionaires emerged for the first time. This wealthy industrial capitalist class, composed primarily of British, attempted to dominate South Africa. However, the Afrikaaners, who had much less wealth, resisted.

A large working class emerged, though its cohesion was broken by racial and ethnic differences. Most of the skilled mining and supervisory responsibilities fell to White miners, especially Uitlanders. Afrikaaners made up only a small portion of the skilled mining workforce in the nineteenth century. Black migrant workers provided unskilled labor. The Whites were relatively well paid and had a sense of class-consciousness. They organized unions and struck for higher wages and better treatment. The Blacks were poorly paid and badly treated and performed most of the purely physical labor. Owners sought to mechanize operations but also preferred to hire as many Black workers at cheap wages as possible and to minimize the number of well-paid jobs set aside for White workers. Thus race determined internal divisions within the working class.

Industrialization affected rural society in two ways. First, the demand for food products increased dramatically, making farming more profitable than it had ever been. In addition, both the Afrikaaners and the Black communities opposed the use of Black labor in the mines. They preferred that Black labor continue to farm. However, the allure of mining jobs and the possibility of wealth, along with a desire to escape from the authoritarian controls of Black family and tribal constraints and Afrikaaner brutality, drove many Black men to the cities and the mining communities.

5. Gender and Family In An Era of Change

Neither the family nor gender roles changed much until the diamond and gold rushes of the last third of the nineteenth century. Mining had a significant affect on the family and gender roles among both Whites and Blacks.

White Family. White families had a different structure and internal dynamic than Black families. Both urban and rural White families tended to be nuclear ones. Both Afrikaaner and British families were patriarchal but fathers were more authoritarian in Afrikaaner families. Most Afrikaaner families were rural and their family size was much larger than that of the mainly urban British families.

Industrialization reduced the importance of the family through migration of male labor to the mines. More and more persons were single and not a part of any family. Many males remained single throughout their lives. In contrast to other societies undergoing industrialization, women did not enter the job market in great numbers. Women did not hold any political power, either formally or informally. Women did not have the right to vote in the nineteenth century.

Black Family. Few changes occurred in Black families until the opening up of the minefields. Patriarchy and clear division of labor between the sexes prevailed. The bride price was used to cement marriage, which continued to be an economic arrangement.

With the development of mining in the interior, large numbers of single males, as well as married men, emigrated to work in the mines. The absence of single men, along with the devastation of the male population through warfare, meant that more and more women did not marry. When a married man left home to work in the mines, the wife assumed much greater responsibility. In addition, chiefs acquired much more power over the women who remained behind. At times the burden on women was so great that it produced high levels of anxiety and child abuse. The disruption of family life was severe.

6. Race, Diversity, and Community

South Africa became increasingly diverse. The actions of various groups generally widened difference and increased diversity-based conflict. Efforts to build community were modest and largely unsuccessful. No racial group maintained a unified identity.

Racial Mosaic. By the end of the century, four major racial groups existed in South Africa—the Whites, the Blacks, the Coloureds, and the Asians. Serious differences and frequent conflict marked both White and Black communities. The Coloured category included a number of different groups. The Asians, who were recruited into South Africa in the second half of the century, were diverse in terms of caste identity, religion, and ethnicity.

Afrikaaners. The Afrikaaners espoused a sense of racial superiority over all other residents of South Africa, including the British and other White Europeans. Increasingly the Afrikaaners showed hatred for the British, who were unwilling to accept, at least during the first half of the nineteenth century, the racial ideologies of the Afrikaaners. From the time of the Great Trek in the 1830s on the Afrikaaners lived on the frontier and emphasized their pioneer spirit. They consciously sought to create an isolated community, totally separate from the Blacks and with minimal contact with the British.

Their frontier way of life and relative freedom within South Africa was shattered by the discovery of diamonds and gold, which produced a massive influx of outsiders, whose way of life was alien to the Afrikaaners. Uitlanders gained controlled of most of the wealth of the mining region and occupied key administrative and skilled labor positions. The Afrikaaners either remained as farmers or sent their sons to hold low-level administrative positions, primarily supervising unskilled Black labor. Neither able to prevent outsiders from disrupting their way of life, nor to remain in isolation from the rest of South

Africa, the Afrikaaners resorted to political solutions—to deny outsiders political rights in the Afrikaaner interior states.

Afrikaaner relations with Blacks were based on military supremacy and control over Black labor on Afrikaaner farms.

The British. At the beginning of the century the British acquired the colony of South Africa from the Dutch. Initially, only a few British administrators came to South Africa. In the 1820s, the government recruited some 20,000 British immigrants through an organized program and gave them large tracts of land for settlement and farming. The *1820 Settlers* arrived first. In the last third of the century the British and other Uitlanders rushed into the mining areas, quickly gaining a dominant role in that environment and outnumbering the Afrikaaners in the newly burgeoning cities. They were a threat to Afrikaaner domination of the interior.

Coloureds and Griquas. The Coloureds were descendants of the hunter-gatherers and pastoralists, the non-Bantu speakers (including the Khoekhoen), and emancipated slaves, many of whom were originally from Southeast Asia. The abolition of slavery and the emancipation of the Khoekhoen led to the formation of a distinct racial category, the *Cape Coloureds.* The Coloureds were primarily urban residents engaged in crafts production and retail trade. In the Cape Colony initially they had the same political rights as Whites. Many of the Coloureds converted to the Dutch Reformed type of Christianity. However, in 1857, the Dutch Reformed Church Synod (church council) created separate White and Coloured church organizations. In a sense the Coloureds were driven out of the Whites' Dutch Reformed Church. Then in 1861, Coloureds were banned from attending church schools.

The Griquas were people of mixed race, the descendants of White-Black and White-Khoekhoen sexual relations. The Griquas were pushed out of the Cape Colony and into the interior some time before the Afrikaaners began the Great Trek and created their own separate states there.

Blacks. The term African is usually used to describe the Bantu-speaking Black population. However, we will use the term Black to avoid defining African to include only some residents of South Africa. The Bantu speakers had migrated into South Africa, gradually gaining control of the high rainfall areas and much of the transitional zone. Moving into the transitional zone they pushed out the pastoralists. The Blacks were not united; they formed a number of distinct tribes, though the boundaries between tribes were quite fluid. The tribes frequently fought with each other. In general military victory led not to the subordination of the losers to the winners but to the forced migration or flight of the losers to another area. The Zulu played a dynamic role in conquering territory and driving out indigenous inhabitants. Tribes also broke apart. For example, tension within the Xhosa led to its division into three separate tribes. In the 1860s and 1870s, internal conflict weakened the Zulu, which eventually broke into two factions. Thus no racial group maintained a single identity.

Asians. Asians first came to South Africa in the seventeenth and eighteenth centuries as slaves. These Southeast Asians eventually became part of the Coloured population after emancipation in the nineteenth century. Beginning in the 1860s, persons from India were recruited to work on farms in the southeast part of the country. After completing their term of indenture they moved to cities and became artisans and retail traders. At the turn of the century a number of Chinese were recruited for manual labor on infrastructure projects. Almost all of them were sent back to China at the end of their terms of work.

Community. Modest efforts were made to overcome difference, reduce animosity, and build community. Certainly the abolition of slavery was the most important effort to reduce difference. However, the slave population was fairly small and former slaves were soon identified as Coloureds. In Cape Colony all males were considered citizens and had the right to vote and hold office if they had sufficient property. In reality, Whites dominated the political process and Coloureds and Blacks never formed more than 15 percent of the electorate, even though they were a majority of the population. The idea that race was irrelevant to citizenship gradually was abandoned.

Religion provided another basis for community. The London Missionary Board and the American Board of Commissioners for Foreign Missions both sponsored missionaries, who sought to protect the Blacks and Coloureds from discrimination and brutal treatment. The missionaries argued that conversion to Christianity could civilize the non-Whites. Thus Christianity formed a bond among the various racial groups, at least in theory. The Dutch Reformed Church decision to force the Coloured congregations out of the White Dutch Reformed Church undermined this position. Broadly, in the first half of the nineteenth century, the British emphasized that they could civilize the various people of South Africa. The British thought that Western Civilization would provide a basis for community that would overcome racial differences. In the second half of the nineteenth century the British abandoned this position, moving toward the Afrikaaner stance of White racial superiority. Among the Black Africans community was based on ethnicity and was not national in scope.

Diversity. Diversity was a more powerful force than community. Racial differences were too great to bridge, especially when the Afrikaaner saw themselves as superior to all others. Afrikaaner strategies included total separation of the races or military and forceful domination of non-Whites. The nineteenth century saw the gradual extension of White power over all of South Africa, whose population was overwhelmingly Black. Difference was reinforced by White economic domination. This is evident in White control over the best farmland, with Blacks owning less desirable and more remote farmland or working as agricultural laborers for Whites. Industrial jobs and wages also demonstrated White domination and Black subordination. Blacks and Coloureds lost the right to dig for diamonds soon after the discovery of the diamond fields. Whites owned and managed mines and monopolized the better paying skilled jobs. In the minefields White wages were eight times those of Blacks. In Natal the British government set aside *reserves,* lands only available for Black settlement. In a number of parts of South Africa especially in the interior mining areas, Blacks were required to have *passes* to enter towns or mining sites or to work in the mines.

Conclusion. During the nineteenth century, opportunities for building community fell to racism and visions of White supremacy. By the time South Africa became independent the groundwork was laid for the separation of races that culminated in apartheid.

D. TRIUMPH OF THE AFRIKAANERS AND SEGREGATION, 1910–1948

South Africa became the first African colony to gain its independence. In contrast to other African states that gained their freedom later, South Africa's independence did not result from a war of national liberation and did not give political power to the majority population, the non-Whites. Instead Whites comprised most of those with rights of citizenship. Independence and the structure of the country's Constitution undermined the ability of the British to continue to rule South Africa. Afrikaaners were euphoric over independence. Afrikaaner parties increased their power, eventually defeating the British. Afrikaaner domination was accompanied by the articulation of an ideology of Afrikaaner supremacy. The government introduced a series of segregation measures, including geographical separation, economic discrimination, educational discrimination, and denial of political rights to non-Whites. Continued industrialization, some modernization of agriculture, and segregationist legislation affected gender roles and the family. South Africa became one of the most unequal and unjust societies in the world during this period.

1. Independence and Loose Ties with Great Britain

Independence gave South Africa freedom to determine its own foreign policy, though it remained loosely tied to Great Britain, especially in economic terms.

Independent Foreign Policy. South Africa sought to eliminate any legal basis for continued British influence. In 1934, the South African legislature passed the *Status of the Union Act.* According to this law, no act of the British Parliament would apply to South Africa unless the law also passed the South African legislature. The Afrikaaners wanted to ensure that membership in the British Empire would not lead to British interference in South African affairs. However, the South Africans could not sever all ties with the British, especially because of intermittent crises that renewed South African emotional attachment to the British. The South Africans provided strong support for the British war effort during both world wars. However, during the Second World War many Afrikaaners expressed sympathy with the Nazis, especially because of the similarity of their ideologies of racial superiority.

In addition, South Africa sought regional domination—to be the most powerful country in southern Africa. Because the rest of southern Africa remained colonies of the European powers, South Africa had limited political influence. However, it benefitted from its economic relations with its neighbors.

2. Political Triumph of the Afrikaaners

South African politics was dominated by the struggle between the Afrikaaners and the British and by the creation of a body of segregationist legislation. The two were interrelated.

The Constitution of the Republic of South Africa. The Constitution of 1909 provided for an independent South Africa. South Africa was to be a unitary state rather than a loose federation. Each of the four colonies became a province within the Union. The country would have a parliamentary form of government rather than a strong presidency. The executive branch of government was to be responsible to the *House of Assembly,* the lower house of the legislature. The Senate had very little power and was elected indirectly. The Constitution contained no bill of rights, as the Afrikaaner colonial constitutions had. Laws could be amended by a simple majority vote. Thus the legislature was all-powerful and the other two branches of government quite weak.

Membership in Parliament was limited to White men, while each province retained the franchise laws it had possessed under the British. Those franchise laws could only be amended by a vote of two-thirds of the members of each house of Parliament. In Natal, property qualifications meant that only a few Blacks, Indians, and Coloreds could vote. In the Cape Province, any literate male who owned a home and land worth seventy-five pounds could vote, unless he lived in the reserves. In 1909, 85 percent of the registered voters were White, 10 percent Coloured (mixed blood or Asian), and 5 percent Black.

The Constitution also gave *delimitation commissions* the right to periodically redistrict, with considerable variance from the one man–one vote principle. The delimitation commissions ensured that the rural voters, primarily Afrikaaners, had proportionately greater representation than the urban residents did. Both Dutch and English were designated as official languages. The Constitution represented a political victory for the Afrikaaners who gradually gained a dominant political position within independent South Africa.

Decline of British Power. The *South Africa Party* won the first elections in 1910. It tried to build a coalition between the Afrikaaners and the British and to ensure that the wealthy mining executives supported the Party. However, when the government ordered the military to crush a powerful mine workers' strike, the South Africa Party lost considerable support in the Afrikaaner working class. The National Party, a militant Afrikaaner organization, aligned with the Labor Party to win the election of 1924. This coalition (the Pact Government) remained in power until 1933. It carried out policies that favored the Afrikaaners and discriminated against non-Whites. It granted economic benefits to the Afrikaaners and provided protection for White workers against the possibility of Blacks competing successfully for the better jobs. The coalition promoted Afrikaaner cultural identify, especially through 1925 legislation that made *Afrikaans* an official state language.

Radicalization. The Great Depression produced changes in the political structure. Many blamed the National Party-led coalition for the country's failure to quickly recover from the Depression. In 1933, the South Africa Party and the National Party formed a coalition government, with National Party chief Hertzog continuing as prime minister and Smuts, leader of the South Africa Party, as deputy prime minister. The coalition was confirmed in power by 1933 elections in which 144 of 158 seats went to the coalition partners. In the following year the two parties merged as the United Party. Opposition was fragmented. The Labor Party collapsed, a British ethnic party (the Dominion Party) emerged, and an extremist Afrikaaner faction, the Purified National party, broke away from the National Party.

The Purified National Party became increasingly influential, pushing the United Party to support segregation. In 1938, the Purified National Party and the secret *Afrikaaner Broederbond* (*Afrikaaner Brotherhood*) organized a celebration of the anniversary of the Great Trek which strengthened an emotional pro-Afrikaaner ideology. In the 1938 elections the Purified National Party gained 20 percent of the seats.

The outbreak of the Second World War in Europe in 1939 led to intense political conflict in South Africa. When Parliament decided to support the British, Hertzog resigned as Prime Minister, and Smuts became head of the United Party. A number of United Party activists turned to the Purified National Party.

Thus the Afrikaaners came to dominate the political system and gradually became more and more racist in their perspective.

3. Ideology of Afrikaaner Supremacy

The clear ideology of Afrikaaner superiority over others emerged in this period. Once freed from the "liberal" tendencies of the British, the Afrikaaners could espouse and implement an ideology of racial domination.

Afrikaaner Supremacy. This ideology had an increasingly powerful impact on the Afrikaaners. A number of organizations promoted Afrikaaner ideology and used the Great Trek as a symbol around which Afrikaaners rallied. The Broederbond played the most important role, but the Federation of Afrikaaner Cultural Associations, the Rescue Association, the Purified National Party, and the Dutch Reformed Church all campaigned for the Afrikaaner ideology.

This ideology had a number of key components. First, Afrikaaner ethnic identity was more important than any other element of identity. Second, Afrikaaners argued for the purity of the White (i.e., Afrikaaner) race. Since other racial groups were inferior, Afrikaaners must not permit or participate in any racial mixing. In *A Home for Posterity,* G.S. Cronje argued that the Afrikaaners could not survive unless they totally separated themselves from the Blacks. This meant complete geographic separation and the removal of all Black labor, including industrial workers and household help, from the White economic world. Third, the ideology was anti-British, broadly rejecting Western civilization. Deep resentment of nineteenth century British efforts to impose their values on the Afrikaaners produced an Afrikaaner sense of cultural superiority. Fourth, rigid, conservative forms of Christianity, represented by the Dutch Reformed Church, inspired this superiority. The Church emphasized an Old Testament authoritarianism and righteousness. Finally, ideologists argued that the superiority of the Afrikaaners must be maintained through special economic privileges, including subsidies to farmers and protection of industrial workers against job competition.

Black Alternative. Founded in 1913, the *African National Congress (ANC)* also sought to outline its views and to influence the Black population to accept its perspective. In 1943, the ANC adopted a platform, *Africans' Claims in South Africa,* a vision of a society with neither discriminatory legislation nor informal discrimination. Blacks would have equal rights with Whites, including political rights. The ANC also called for "economic justice," including the redistribution of land and the legalization of collective bargaining rights for unions.

4. Industrialization and the Great Depression

Independence produced major changes in the economy of South Africa. Industrialization became more and more important, while greater emphasis was placed on the agricultural modernization of large farms. The government took a more active role in leading the economy, introducing policies of state ownership, import substitution, and regional economic domination. Racial discrimination still played a central role in economic development. The economy tripled in size, a growth rate of about 7 percent per year. At the same time, the economic boom of the 1920s dissolved in the Great Depression of the 1930s, as South Africa became part of the global economy.

Industry. Mining remained the most important source of economic growth, with gold mining relatively more important than in the nineteenth century. Some increase in mechanization produced only modest changes in production. Unions became increasingly powerful. Blacks were prohibited from organizing unions but the all-White Mine Workers Union was extremely powerful. In 1923, White mine workers struck to prevent owners from opening up jobs to Blacks who would be paid lower wages. Though the army crushed the strikes, the mine owners backed away from their quest for cheaper, non-White labor sources. In addition, the mineworkers had sufficient political clout to drive the South African Party, which had sided with mine owners, from power. In 1920, Black industrial and mine workers also struck; their strikes were quickly crushed.

Agriculture. Two major trends occurred in agriculture. First White farm owners, especially the Afrikaaners, received substantial assistance from the government, which promoted modernization of agriculture, including mechanization and the introduction of more productive strains of grains. Second, during the Depression many Blacks lost their farms, which were taken over by Whites. Former Black farm owners became tenant farmers, while those who had been sharecroppers or tenant farmers frequently became hired laborers. The period saw a substantial decline in the living standards of rural Blacks, even when male family members worked in industry. The reserves were characterized by overcrowding and severe pressure on the limited amounts of agricultural land.

Class. Race determined class. Whites automatically occupied higher status than non-Whites. Among Whites, the status of Afrikaaners rose. By the end of the period Afrikaaners had almost reached the social level of the British population. In large part this rise in Afrikaaner status resulted from their greater political power and their larger population. Still, there was a large Afrikaaner lower class. The National Party especially sought to implement policies that would aid the poor whites. Blacks remained lower class, with industrial and mining workers faring better than rural Blacks.

5. Gender Roles and the Family

Stability characterized the White family, as well as gender relations among Whites. Black families were increasingly disrupted by the flow of male labor to the cities.

White Families. Few changes occurred in the White family. The Afrikaaner family, especially, retained its patriarchal nature. White women generally confined their roles to the domestic sphere. They ran the households, especially supervising the work of Black female servants. Embittered by the Boer War, many middle-class Afrikaaner women became active in the movement to defend Afrikaaner rights and developed assistance programs for poor working-class Afrikaaners. They thus promoted Afrikaaner solidarity across classes. White women gained the right to vote in 1931, thus expanding their public role.

Black Families. Black families continued to be disrupted by economic change, not only by industrialization but also by the decline in the economic viability of Black farming. Increasing numbers of males left the rural areas to work in the cities, leaving women with greater responsibility and power. In addition, large numbers of Black women moved to the cities, as well, taking jobs as domestic servants or in the retail trade in Black communities. In the rural areas many households became female-centered. The fluidity of class in the Black community contrasted with the increasing rigidity of class in general.

6. Community, Diversity, and Segregation

Segregation made community building across racial lines impossible. Community building took place primarily within the Afrikaaner population. Segregation and discrimination created greater difference and deepened the divide between people of different races.

Creation of a Segregated Nation. The South African Whites, especially the Afrikaaners, established a segregated society. Segregation took many forms, economic, geographic, educational, and political. Segregation represented a strategy to preserve Afrikaaner "superiority" and to create structures that would preserve public stability and order.

Geographic Segregation. Whites acquired most of the Black farmland and authorities placed some Blacks on reserves. These policies were initiated as early as the first years of independence. In 1913, the government passed the *Natives Land Act.* The law prevented Blacks from buying or leasing land outside the reserves and banned Black sharecropping in the Orange Free State. Essentially Blacks and Coloureds lost the farmland they had once possessed in Afrikaaner areas. The law was not applied in the Cape Province so Blacks continued to have the right to own property there until changes in law in 1936. The 1936 *African Native Trust Act* provided government funding to purchase additional land to be set aside for reserves. This action reduced Afrikaaner holdings in eastern South Africa by 7 percent. By the Second World War approximately 12 percent of the land of South Africa was in the reserves. Whites possessed most of the best land, while reserves were scattered throughout the country.

The government sought to limit Black access to the cities through a series of pass laws. A system of passes tied many Blacks to the soil, as laborers for White farmers. Whites also issued passes permitting their farm workers to work in the cities. In the Transvaal, Blacks who entered White urban areas had to report for a work permit within twenty-four hours. The *Natives (Urban*

Areas) Act gave local city governments the right to establish urban districts for Black residency only. Blacks could then be required to live in the areas specifically set aside for them. This produced urban geographical segregation. A number of urban Black or Coloured communities were thus created, such as the "District Six" Coloured community in Cape Town. The law was not universally applied and in a number of major cities, there was little or no residential segregation.

Economic Segregation. Whites had exclusive rights to skilled better-paying jobs. Whites were covered by the *Apprenticeship Act* of 1922, which established a certain minimum level of education in order to become an apprentice and thus enter a number of careers. Blacks were thus excluded. Whites could organize in trade unions and seek improved conditions through collective bargaining and strikes. They gained paid vacations and pensions upon retirement. Blacks were prohibited from organizing unions and lacked these fringe benefits. White miners lived in decent housing, while Blacks huddled in crowded barracks, hardly fit for living.

Political Segregation. Primarily in the former British areas, Coloureds and some Blacks had had the right to vote. In other areas they did not have the right to vote. However, in 1936 all non-Whites were disenfranchised, losing the right to vote and hold office.

Discrimination in Education. Blacks and Coloureds received an inferior education. Those who went to school attended mission schools. Only a few hundred Blacks per year received the equivalent of a high school diploma. The quality of non-White education was low, schools were badly funded, and teachers ill-prepared for their jobs. Only the South African Native College at Fort Hare, a missionary-founded university, provided Blacks, Coloureds, and Indians with post-secondary education.

Resistance to Segregation. Opposition to segregation came largely from three organizations: the *African Political Organization,* representing Coloureds; the *South African Indian Congress;* and the African National Congress (ANC), representing Blacks. Abdullah Abdurahman led the Coloured organization. R.R. Pather and Abdulla Ismail Kajee headed the South African Indian Congress. Pixley ka Isaka Seme, Alfred Mangena, Richard Msimang, and George Montsioa directed the ANC. These organizations were either established at the end of British rule or in the early years of independent South African. White liberals, such as Edgar Brookes, worked with these groups to promote a multi-racial alternative to segregation. They used moderate tactics and had modest goals. As in the Indian and Algerian independence movements (see Chapters Two and Six), the leaders were middle-class men (lawyers, journalists, and clergy), with Western educations and intelligentsia careers. Their goals were modest and political, initially limited to seeking the franchise for middle-class non-Whites. They believed that after middle-class non-Whites gained the right to vote, the same rights could be extended to lower-class non-Whites. Their efforts had no significant impact.

More radical strategies included strikes by Black workers and Mohandas Gandhi's emphasis on peaceful civil disobedience. Coming to South Africa to defend the economic rights of Asians, Gandhi gradually developed the methods for non-violent protest that he would later make famous in India. He organized demonstrations and encouraged participants not to resist police efforts to break up the rallies.

Toward Modest Reforms. Proposals for modifying the segregation laws came from White professors at Witwatersrand University and the Institute of Race Relations. In addition, some members of the business community began to conclude that economic segregation damaged the business community and company profits.

The government became concerned with racial questions during the Second World War. The *Fagan Commission,* appointed to study segregation, suggested in 1948 that the pass laws be eased and that Black labor be permitted to compete with White workers on an equal footing. The Fagan report was the last straw for the Afrikaaner extremists, who used the report to promote the National Party platform and to propel it to victory in the 1948 elections. The victory of the Nationalists led to the creation of apartheid.

E. ERA OF APARTHEID, 1948–1991

The completion of the racist system of apartheid finalized trends already evident in the introduction of slavery and the subordination of the Khoekhoen in the seventeenth century. Still, one should not see this as an inevitable process. The abolition of slavery and missionary efforts to ameliorate the condition of Blacks, as well as a move to weaken segregation during and immediately after the Second World War, suggest that South Africa could have taken a different path. It did not, however. South Africa became increasingly isolated from the rest of the continent and from the rest of the world. The National Party came to power in the 1948 elections and remained in power through the end of apartheid. A champion of apartheid, the National Party used its Afrikaaner base to create an authoritarian and frequently brutal administration. Apartheid represented the most powerful and dominant ideology in the period but we can also identify two strains of opposition thought—White liberalism (primarily British) and Black consciousness. The economy grew rapidly until the mid-1980s, fueled by the global demand for diamonds, gold, uranium, and semi-precious stones. Initially apartheid contributed to economic growth but by the 1980s it played a significant role in the economic slowdown. Apartheid and economic development continued to foster the breakup of the Black family as males moved to the industrial sector in large numbers and women increasingly sought work as household servants for the White middle class. Apartheid contributed to a strengthening of urban families. Apartheid produced among Afrikaaners, especially those in the rural areas, a deep sense of insecurity that promoted family cohesion and patriarchy. Despised by all except a slight majority of Afrikaaners, apartheid was abolished at the end of the 1980s, contributing to the global transformation symbolized by the destruction of the Berlin Wall.

1. Isolated South Africa

Geographically isolated, South Africa retained economic ties with the Western industrial countries before the 1980s. Thereafter its isolation deepened with the world's condemnation of apartheid and the introduction of economic boycotts and *divestment*.

A Different Path. During the 1950s and 1960s almost all African peoples gained their independence from European colonial powers (see Chapter Six for Algeria). Since South Africa had gained its independence from Great Britain early in the twentieth century, it followed a different path. Avoiding the wave of decolonization that brought native peoples to power in the rest of the continent, Whites continued to rule South Africa, primarily through apartheid.

Apartheid led to the country's diplomatic isolation. South Africa's response was two-fold. It attempted to maintain ties with the Western industrial powers by portraying itself as a *bastion* of anti-Communism. Second, it sought to create a buffer zone between itself and the stronger African states by controlling its neighbors and using military force to expand the zone of South African political influence.

As early as 1960 the United Nations condemned apartheid and in 1977 the Security Council urged all members of the UN to participate in an economic embargo of South Africa. In response, the South African government argued that apartheid had prevented Communists from coming to power in strategically important southern Africa.

Great Britain was South Africa's main economic partner. It provided 40 percent of foreign investment, controlled most of the banking industry, and acted as South Africa's major trading partner. In general the British were quite slow to oppose apartheid. In the 1960s, the United States ended arms shipments to South Africa, supporting the United Nations' position, but did not halt economic relations. In the early 1970s, the United States tilted toward South Africa, at least pretending that there was a Communist threat. Under Jimmy Carter (1977–1981) the United States once again condemned apartheid. By the mid-1980s, the United States clearly expressed its opposition to apartheid. It adopted a policy of *constructive engagement,* encouraging the South African government to reform apartheid. From the mid-1980s American firms began to withdraw their investments and presence from the country. In general South Africa was able to maintain some relationship with the Americans and British, thus avoiding total economic and political isolation. By the end of the 1980s, South Africa was essentially isolated diplomatically, besieged by efforts to force it to abandon apartheid.

Domination of Neighbors. South Africa also sought security through domination of its neighbors, employing both economic and military means. It used the South African Customs Union to incorporate the economies of Lesotho, Botswana, and Swaziland into the South African economy. Through the Anglo-American Corporation of South Africa, the South African Whites had substantial economic interests in the above countries, as well as in Zimbabwe, Zambia, and Namibia. The military intimidated its neighbors and tried to prevent them from becoming a haven for exiled African National Congress activists. South Africa occupied Namibia and supported conservative revolutionary groups in Angola and Mozambique. In 1988, it invaded Angola, where it lost several major battles with Cuban military units and their Angolan allies. Next Cuban troops withdrew from Angola and South African soldiers from Namibia. The African National Congress closed its bases in Angola but South Africa kept the only Namibian port, Walvis Bay, which had been part of South Africa since 1884.

2. National Party Dictatorship

The National Party dominated South Africa from 1948 to 1991. It used its power to introduce and sustain apartheid.

Initial Strategies. The National Party won an overwhelming victory in the 1948 elections, running on a platform of fear. It argued that only it could prevent Blacks from coming to power. Its main opponent, the United Party collapsed. In its place several small parties emerged, none a threat to National Party domination.

Afrikaaners replaced British in the bureaucracy, while the lower level clerical staff, comprised mainly of Blacks, was docile and loyal. Afrikaaner control over the bureaucracy ensured that the laws of apartheid were carried out enthusiastically. The size of the bureaucracy increased dramatically, since it took large numbers of government officials to implement apartheid.

Early on, the security forces began to play a powerful role in the government. In 1950, Parliament passed the *Suppression of Communism Act.* The law gave the Ministry of Justice the right to take any action it wished against anyone identified as a Communist. Any one could be *banned* (not permitted to appear in public in a group of three or more). Authorities could prevent a so-called Communist from publishing or confine him/her to the home without visitors. In the early 1970s, the State Security Council became more powerful than the Cabinet. Chaired by Pieter Willem Botha, the State Security Council included the Minister of Defense, other military leaders, and the heads of the security and regular police.

Reform without Change. Some cracks in the National Party leadership appeared in the late 1970s. Prime Minister B.J. *Voerster* was forced to resign because of scandal and was replaced by *Botha.* Leadership in the Party shifted from persons with rural ties to those from the urban professional and business elite. Thus a better-educated and more cosmopolitan group gained control over the Party. This change did not immediately lead to any modifications of apartheid. Botha tried to convince the English-speakers to support apartheid and the government's campaign to suppress its opponents.

In 1984, the Nationalists issued a new Constitution, a strategy for maintaining apartheid. The Constitution preserved racial distinctions. According to this Constitution, a new Parliament was to be formed, consisting of three chambers: a House of Assembly of Whites, elected by White voters; a House of Representatives of Coloureds, elected by Coloureds; and a House of Delegates of Indians, elected by Indians. Blacks were given no representation. The White House of Assembly had more seats than the other two houses combined, so Whites could pass any laws they wished and prevent the passage of bills they opposed. A multi-racial Cabinet representing Whites, Coloureds, and Indians dealt with national affairs such as taxes, foreign policy, defense, state security, justice, economic affairs, and Black issues. Each "race" was to have its own cabinet responsible for local matters, such as education, health and welfare, and local government. An electoral college in which Whites had 70 percent of the seats elected the State President. The President had a great deal of power, including control over Black affairs. The new Constitution was an attempt to co-opt the Coloured and Indian populations into supporting the Whites and apartheid. The promise of greater power for Coloureds and Asians was not realized. President Botha appointed only one Coloured and one Indian to the multi-racial cabinet.

In a parallel move, the government established four metropolitan urban regions, as well as four rural regions, each with its multi-racial Regional Services Council, with representation of Whites, Coloureds and Asians. The responsibilities of each regional government were divided into general affairs, the responsibility of the multi-racial Councils, and local matters, for which uni-racial councils were created. A central authority, that is the National Party, appointed members of the metropolitan and regional governments.

State of Emergency. When these reforms failed to bring greater support to apartheid, the government introduced a state of emergency, lasting from 1985–1986. The police acquired the right to arrest, detain, and interrogate anyone without a warrant and without proof of cause. Authorities deployed the army to maintain order in the Black and Coloured townships. They arrested large numbers of opponents of apartheid and prohibited the media from covering unrest. Emergency rule halted the unrest but did not solve the government's problem. Apartheid had less and less support, while even Afrikaaners began to call for reform. Very modest reforms did not bring renewed acceptance of the general outlines of apartheid, but led instead to demands for further reform.

Weakening of Control. The National Party's hold on the country began to weaken. The Party had no answers to the question of what to do about apartheid. Efforts to co-opt the non-Blacks and ease "social apartheid" satisfied no one. The 1987 elections showed a serious decline in National Party support. Nationalists received only 52 percent of the vote for the House of Assembly of Whites. Extremist supporters of apartheid, forming the Conservative Party, came in second with 26 percent of the vote. In 1988 local elections, the Conservatives took power in most of the towns in the Transvaal. The Coloured and Indian Assemblies used their voice to condemn apartheid and refused to cooperate with the apartheid government. A Party in crisis upon the death of Botha in 1989, it turned to F.W. *DeKlerk*. This decision paved the way for a radical shift in National Party policy.

3. The Visions of Apartheid and of Its Opposition

Apartheid ideology reigned in this period, though increasingly a White liberal critique of apartheid and a Black consciousness movement threatened the monopoly of the apartheid ideology.

The Vision of Apartheid. Afrikaaner ideology changed little in this era. This vision, however, became a reality. It was taught in the home, schools, and in the Dutch Reformed Church. The Great Trek, the victory over the Zulus at Blood River, and the "triumph" over the British in the South African War all demonstrated the validity of the apartheid vision of Afrikaaner supremacy, according to the supporters of apartheid.

Apartheid became a strategy for White domination and survival. The Afrikaaners used a *separate but equal* argument. All races had the right to separate development toward an ideal future. But only the Whites were ready to enter the "Promised Land." The Coloureds and Indians were in an intermediate category, needing some supervision by the Whites. The Blacks, on the other hand, were not ready for independent, separate development. Thus, paternalistically, the Whites would have to provide the Blacks with guidance for many generations (see parallels with the Nationalists in China in Chapter Four).

White Liberalism. White criticism of apartheid was immediate. White opposition to apartheid came from many churches and from the English-speaking intelligentsia. In 1948, all of the religious organizations in South Africa, except for the Dutch Reformed Church, condemned apartheid. In 1962, a splinter group, led by C.V. Beyers Naude, broke from the Dutch Reformed Church, forming a *Christian Institute* that called for the abolition of apartheid. In 1968, the South African Council of Churches condemned apartheid as anti-Christian. However, Afrikaaner clergy continued to support apartheid. Finally, beginning in 1978 some Afrikaaner clergy began to criticize apartheid.

White writers were especially critical of apartheid. *Alan Paton's Cry, the Beloved Country* issued the most famous literary condemnation of apartheid. In the 1970s, other writers such as Andre Brink, Nadine Gordimer, J.M. Coetzee, and the playwright Athol Fugard attacked apartheid. Black and Coloured critics were prohibited from publishing and were forced to write in exile. For example, the famous novelist Bessie Head wrote her most powerful novels in rural Botswana. Other members of the primarily British intelligentsia also condemned apartheid, mainly from a liberal perspective. They saw apartheid as a form of slavery that denied non-Whites civil liberties and an opportunity to achieve justice and equality.

Black Consciousness. South African *Black consciousness* was part of a global movement that began in West Africa and Paris and spread gradually throughout Africa and to the United States, the Caribbean and Brazil. In South Africa Black consciousness was reflected especially in poetry readings and street theater. Black consciousness recognized that efforts to stop violence could not destroy apartheid but actually worsened the lives of the South African Blacks. First, Blacks needed to develop a sense of pride in themselves and in the Black community. Black pride and unity were prerequisites for the overthrow of apartheid. The apartheid government preferred the emphasis on Black consciousness to overt acts of terror. Black consciousness gradually influenced the Black community, eventually leading to a number of peaceful economic protests in the 1980s.

4. Apartheid, Diversity, and Community

Apartheid divided South Africans into racial groups and provided some basis for community *within* separate groups. Government-determined racial identity promoted divisiveness for the country as a whole but acted as a unifying force for individual groups. Apartheid affected every aspect of life in South Africa. It was reflected in geography, economics, class, education, and criminal justice.

Racial Definitions. The first step toward *apartheid*—total separation of the races, enforced by the government with violence and brutality—was to establish a legal definition of races. Law divided the population into four categories—Whites, Coloureds, Asians, and Bantu (the Blacks). Differences within racial groups thus disappeared and boundaries between races became rigid. Gradually the proportions among the races changed. By 1980, South Africa had a population of 7 million Blacks, 4 million Whites, 2 million Coloureds, and almost 1 million Indians.

Political Discrimination. Only Whites retained the right to vote and hold office. Coloureds and Blacks, who had had limited political rights in the Cape Province, lost those rights in the 1930s. Only those who lived in the Black *homelands* had political rights and then only to vote and hold office in the homeland.

Geographical Apartheid. Geographical separation of the races was made more complete. The *Group Areas Act* (1950) identified geographical areas in which only one particular race could reside. Blacks lived in race-based *townships* (suburbs) or in homelands. In a number of cases Blacks, Coloureds, and Asians were moved out of areas they had lived in for decades. Space was needed for White expansion and for geographical barriers between the races. For example the Coloured community in Cape Town was moved out of its traditional residence, District Six, to an area further from the city. Many Indians were moved out of Asian neighborhoods in Durban.

Creation of the homelands was another form of geographical apartheid. The homelands built upon the idea of reserves developed earlier. In 1951, the government abolished the Natives Representative Council and divided the reserves into ten homelands. Blacks, under the supervision of Whites, administered the homelands. By the 1970s, several of the homelands had acquired nominal "independence." Homelands were expected to be economically self-sufficient, a goal unrealizable given the lack of natural resources and the poor quality of the agricultural land. Opposition to the homeland structure was limited. The only major rebellion occurred in Pondaland (in eastern South Africa) in 1959.

Strict limitations were placed on the mobility of the rural Black population. Non-White rural residents could visit an urban area for only seventy-two hours. A non-White without a pass (permission to be in a White area) could be arrested.

Economic Difference. Economic separation was more difficult to achieve since the White population was not large enough to fill all of the jobs required by the economy. Thus segregation was based on type of employment. Whites retained the skilled, high-paying, and managerial jobs in industries, while Blacks held the unskilled jobs. Early in the 1970s, White factory wages were six times those of Blacks, while the average White miner earned twenty-one times as much as a Black mineworker. Real wages for Blacks were lower than in 1911.

During the 1970s and 1980s, the wages of Black workers rose proportionately, especially in mining. More and more Blacks moved up into semi-skilled and even skilled jobs. In 1982, White wages were four times that of Blacks and six times as high in mines. In addition, Black workers were the first let go during economic slowdowns. In the late 1970s, the Black unemployment rate was 26 percent, the White unemployment rate very small.

In 1979, the legislature repealed the law that reserved certain jobs for Whites. Blacks were also permitted to establish trade unions, giving them access to industrial mediation courts and the right to strike. A number of Black trade unions formed. They became increasingly militant, with strikes more and more common. In 1987, for instance, the National Union of Mineworkers organized a three-week strike that involved half a million Black miners.

Separate and Unequal Education. Apartheid reached its greatest depth in education. Separate schools were established for White Afrikaans-speakers and for White English-speakers. In addition, the central government assumed control over Black education, previously in the hands of mission schools. The Nationalist government feared that mission education would produce insufficiently submissive Blacks. In addition, the mission schools could not educate enough Blacks to meet the country's economic needs. In 1953, the *Bantu Education Act* transferred control over Black schools to the central government. In the 1960s, the government began to supervise the education of Coloureds and Asians. Segregation was strengthened in higher education too. The 1959 *Extension of University Education Act* halted a trend toward non-White enrollment at universities. The law required the Cabinet to approve the enrollment of a Black in a White university. New universities were set up for specific groups, for Coloureds, Indians, Zulu, and Transvaal Blacks. Fort Hare College was reserved for Xhosa students.

Education was also unequal. Black education was on a much lower level. Compulsory education applied to Whites but not to Blacks. The government spent ten times as much per White pupil as it did for a Black child.

"Social" Apartheid. Separation of the races applied in informal public settings as well. The government tried to prevent casual social contacts between people of different races. Transportation, elevators, beaches, parks, public toilets, churches, cinemas, theaters, restaurants, hotels, and hospitals were race-specific. Sports teams were not integrated, nor could teams of different races play each other.

Social apartheid not only kept the races apart, it created superior public services for Whites and inferior ones for non-Whites. Obviously, even with inferior quality services for the non-Whites, apartheid was costly.

Interracial sexual activity, including interraccial marriage, were prohibited, punishable by imprisonment.

Enforcement of Apartheid. The government enforced apartheid with great brutality. Central to this was a legal system that permitted the government to do anything it wanted to persons who either failed to obey the apartheid laws or tried to oppose apartheid. The *Suppression of Communism Act* (1950) gave the Minister of Justice the power to ban those who supported Communism (i.e., opponents of apartheid). The *Public Safety Act* (1953) gave the government the legal right to act illegally, that is, it gave authorities the right to declare a state of emergency allowing it to issue decrees that had the force of law but need not be confirmed by parliament. In the 1950s and 1960s, a whole series of laws strengthened the power of the police. Police could arrest people and hold them indefinitely without trial. The government could ban any organization. Police determined whether or not public meetings were permitted. The *Bantu Laws Amendment Act* (1964) gave the government the power to expel a Black from a White farm or White city without cause. In general the courts had no authority to declare the actions of the government, the police, or security officials illegal. In addition, *BOSS (the Bureau of State Security)* became increasingly powerful in maintaining apartheid and attacking its opponents.

Resistance to Apartheid. In spite of the overpowering force authorities could and did use against anti-apartheid activity, resistance was almost immediate. Obviously the vast majority of non-Whites, and Whites, too, simply obeyed the law and passively accepted their treatment at the hands of authorities. Very broadly, resistance went through three phases: Gandhi-style passive resistance (see Chapter Two), terrorism, and broad-based economic boycotts. The three phases overlapped.

Moral Resistance. Christian church organizations criticized apartheid from the beginning. Faculty at the Universities of Cape Town and Witwatersrand also opposed apartheid. The National Union of South African Students organized major protests in 1959 when Blacks were denied entrance into White universities. Black Sash, representing middle class English-speaking women, organized passive resistance campaigns. The Liberal Party, primarily composed of British, opposed apartheid.

Opponents of apartheid organized a "*defiance campaign.*" The African National Congress led the opposition to apartheid. When several radical youth, including Walter Sisulu, Oliver Tambo, and Nelson *Mandela,* entered the leadership in 1949, ANC began to focus its energies on opposition to apartheid. At first it promoted non-violent protest, influenced by Gandhi's satyagraha campaign (see Chapter Three). In 1952, ANC and the South African Indian Congress organized a campaign of passive resistance. Thousands were arrested for refusing to obey the apartheid laws. When passive resistance turned to massive disturbances, ANC called off the campaign. In 1955, ANC organized the Congress Alliance, a coalition of opposition groups that adopted a *Freedom Charter.* The Charter claimed that political power emanated from the will of the people (the concept of *popular sovereignty*). It called for civil rights; equality before the law; the right to vote and hold office regardless of race; equal pay for equal work; a minimum wage and forty-hour work week, as well as fringe benefits; free medical care; and free, compulsory, and equal education.

The Federation of South African Women organized demonstrations against application of the pass laws to Black women. Almost 300,000 protested at government headquarters in 1956. In 1957, Blacks in Johannesburg and Pretoria boycotted the bus systems. Teachers that opposed unequal education were dismissed, leading to a decline of the teachers association by the late 1950s.

Peaceful protest led to government repression and did not produce any modification of apartheid. Dissatisfied with the results of peaceful protest, a number of ANC leaders turned to more radical measures in the early 1960s.

An Eye for an Eye—Violent Resistance. The 1960 *Sharpesville Massacre* acted as a catalyst for radicalization of resistance to apartheid. Even before this, however, Robert Sobukwe and others condemned the moderate position of ANC and formed a *Pan-Africanist Congress* (PAC) in 1959. In 1960, the PAC began to campaign against the pass laws. In Sharpesville the police fired on a crowd, killing 67 and wounding almost 200. Rallies, strikes, and riots followed, lasting for several weeks. The government responded by outlawing ANC and PAC and arresting almost 20,000 people, over half of them Blacks.

ANC leaders went underground, determined to use force against force. Mandela and other ANC leaders formed *The Spear of the Nation;* the PAC organized a terrorist group, "Pure." Young White professionals and students established the African Resistance Movement. All three groups launched terrorist campaigns, bombing police stations, post offices, and transportation facilities. PAC was the most militant of the resistance organizations. In 1963, most of the Spear leaders, including Mandela and Sisulu, and PAC leader Sobukwe, were arrested and sentenced to life imprisonment on Robben Island, off the coast of Cape Town. Government action destroyed the terrorist campaign and open resistance to apartheid. Authorities continued to apply violence, including murdering youth activist Steve Biko in 1971 and carrying out the massacre of school children at *Soweto* in 1976. Student demonstrations spread to other towns, too. Students were protesting the use of Afrikaans as the language of instruction. Militancy revived, but in exile, as a number of Black youth fled to nearby countries where they participated in paramilitary training.

Modification of Apartheid. Opposition to apartheid intensified in the 1980s, leading the Nationalists to offer very modest reforms, in hopes of staving off the need to abolish apartheid. The government tried to maintain the levels of force but violence no longer silenced its opponents.

Revival of Protests; Economic Boycotts. In 1983, representatives of over 500 organizations established the *United Democratic Front,* whose goal was to end apartheid. Protests intensified. In 1983–1984 residents of the homelands boycotted the bus system. Riots and protests against the Black governments of the homelands increased. In 1985, bus and school boycotts, strikes, and clashes in the townships expanded, becoming more violent. A general breakdown of authority occurred, leading to a sharp increase in Black against Black violence. *Inkatha,* representing the Zulu, clashed with the United Democratic Front. The business community lost its faith in apartheid, especially when economic decline set in. Black boycotts of retail trade demonstrated the importance of non-White customers. The country seemed on the verge of anarchy and collapse. Increased government brutality could no longer stem the tide of protest.

Retreat from Apartheid. In a sense, the retreat from apartheid paralleled Gorbachev's reform activities in the Soviet Union in the 1980s (see Chapter One). From the mid-1970s the state stopped enforcing social apartheid. The Nationalist government decided on a strategy of modest reform as a means of preserving apartheid, White domination, and National Party rule. In 1977, it halted segregated transportation in Cape Town and opened White-only beaches to everyone. In 1986, the government repealed the pass laws for those non-Whites who did not reside in the homelands. It permitted employers to hire homeland workers with government permission. In the same year the government ended the ban on interracial sexual activity and interracial marriage. It legalized multi-racial political organizations. Once again it confirmed an end to the policy of reserving certain jobs for Whites. Hotels, restaurants, theaters, transportation, and other public facilities were desegregated. Sports teams from different races were permitted to compete against each other.

Repealing "social apartheid" did nothing to reduce the political monopoly of the National Party, the political and economic domination of the Whites and inequality in employment, political rights, and education. Few were satisfied with modest reforms. The implementation of these small reforms demonstrated, many thought, the weakness of apartheid, and its inevitable future demise. Afrikaaner extremists argued for a return to total apartheid and a repeal of the modest concessions of 1986. Violence increased. Clearly the modest retreat from apartheid failed. Would the White government continue to use violence to preserve apartheid? Or would it abandon apartheid? Betting people put their money on the first option. They were wrong, for in 1989 the new leader of the National Party, F.W. DeKlerk, initiated actions that led to the abolition of apartheid and to the creation of Black rule in a "Rainbow Society."

5. Class, Economics, and Apartheid

The South African economy grew substantially until the 1980s. Thereafter the country faced economic stagnation and recession. Increasingly South Africa found itself both a beneficiary and a victim of global economic trends. Economic development accelerated the growth of a well-educated middle class of professionals and business people.

Economy. As a semi-industrialized country, South Africa had one of the highest growth rates in the world in the first years after the Second World War. The economy grew by approximately 10 percent per year in the late 1940s and continued to grow into the mid-1980s. After that GDP declined, accompanied by a sharp increase in inflation (almost 20% in 1986).

Rapid growth resulted from participation in the global economy, especially because of the demand for minerals. South Africa produced 65 percent of the world's gold, 42 percent of its platinum, 42 percent of its vanadium, and 33 percent of its chromium. South Africa was also a leading producer of diamonds, coal, asbestos, copper, nickel, phosphates, silver, uranium, and zinc. Since so much of the economy depended on global demand for minerals, changes in that demand affected South Africa's growth rate.

Manufacturing was less important, though there was a noticeable shift to heavy industry and away from consumer goods. Mineral extraction reached the global market but the South Africans could not compete on the world market of manufactured products. Since most of the population of South Africa was Black and impoverished, domestic demand was quite limited and this hindered the growth of the domestic economy. The lack of skilled workers and the poor quality of work by illiterate Blacks also hampered manufacturing.

Large-scale farming, primarily by Afrikaaners, received huge government subsidies. These farms produced for the urban market, while Black farms were primarily subsistence operations.

Class. Apartheid had a tremendous impact on the social system. Very broadly, the Whites were at the top of society, followed by Indians and Coloureds, with Blacks at the bottom. There were also significant differences within racial categories.

The White upper class consisted of the Afrikaaner political elite and the Afrikaaner and British business leaders. The business community was clearly divided into two ethnic groups, with Afrikaaner business represented by the Afrikaanse Handelsinstitut and the British by the Federated Chamber of Industries.

The middle class was composed primarily of the intelligentsia, most of whom were British. The British dominated the cultural realm and the universities. The intelligentsia gradually moved into opposition to apartheid. Rich Afrikaaner farmers can also be considered part of the middle class.

As a whole, the working class increased in size, importance, and income. Both White and Black workers benefited from economic growth, though the wages of Whites remained much higher than those of Blacks. However, Blacks increasingly moved up into semi-skilled jobs and in a few cases into skilled ones. The strict division into White and Black jobs slowly eroded, especially after a 1979 law abolished the requirement that certain employment categories be White-only. Strikes grew increasingly common, among Black, as well as White workers, especially miners.

In the countryside, no major changes occurred in class structures. However, urban class distinctions eroded slightly through economic change. The economy served the goals of apartheid less and less well, while apartheid increasingly undermined economic development.

6. Family and Gender Roles Under Apartheid

Apartheid continued to be a key determinant of family and gender relations. It both corroded and reinforced the family and strengthened and undermined gender roles. Male domination continued, based on law and tradition, such as the Bantu Law Code of 1891 that turned tribal custom into law.

Afrikaaner Family. Apartheid reinforced patriarchy and family cohesiveness, especially among rural Afrikaaner families. By law women were inferior to men. Women had the right to vote but generally followed the will of their husbands or fathers. They demonstrated hostility toward the opponents of apartheid, especially Black women. Afrikaaner women isolated themselves in the home and played neither a significant economic nor political role. A few Afrikaaner women received a university education and became teachers or even university professors. British women were much more active in the political arena, including opposition to apartheid. British women dominated the main women's organization, the Federation of South African Women. They also played an important role in the *Black Sash,* a group that provided legal advice, education, and job-training skills for Coloured and Black household servants. In 1983, white women were granted equal property rights.

Black Family. Apartheid and industrialization continued to have a destructive effect on the Black family. Males still streamed into the cities, leaving women in charge of the family and responsible for running the farm and holding Black society together. Increasingly Black and Coloured women also migrated to the cities in search of employment as servants. In the rural areas and the townships women frequently left their children behind, to be raised by grandmothers or grandfathers. Unemployment was much higher among Black and Coloured women than among Black and Coloured men.

Most women were peasants, affected by high infant mortality rates and the psychological consequences of losing babies to death. In addition the government applied stricter restrictions on abortion for non-White women.

Family abuse continued, accompanied by much male alcoholism. Women lacked equal property rights. Polygamy continued, unrestrained by the state. Half of all Black children were born to unmarried women and were thus members of single-parent families.

Black women played an important role in the non-violent campaigns against apartheid. In 1954, 8,000 protesting women were arrested. In 1956, 20,000 Black women protested the introduction of the pass laws. Women also opposed the pass laws, which were first applied to them in 1961. Urban Black and Coloured women were also active in the economic boycotts of White retailers in the mid-1980s. Especially active were organizations such as Manyano, the largest Black women's organization, the YWCA, and the ANC Women's League.

Apartheid weakened the power of non-White men, and strengthened the position, power, and influence of non-White women.

Coloured Family. Many of the Coloured families were Muslim (see Chapter Six for details on the impact of Islamic law on the family). This meant that males could divorce and women generally couldn't. Also, women had property rights, especially useful for Coloured women from the merchant class.

Asian Family. Economic goals continued to characterize the Asian family. The purpose of the family was to promote upward social and economic mobility. It was recognized that women—through education and employment—could facilitate this aim.

F. RAINBOW SOCIETY, 1991–PRESENT

The abolition of apartheid was the most significant event in the history of contemporary South Africa. Changes occurred in the White population, among the non-Whites, in the country as a whole and globally. Whites declined as a proportion of the country's population, from 21 percent in 1936 to 19 percent in 1960, 15 percent in 1985, and 13 percent in 1993. The relative decline of the White population made it more difficult to sustain White rule. English-speakers expressed their opposition to the injustices of apartheid more and more vocally. In addition, Afrikaaners began to move toward the English-speakers' position of reform or repeal of apartheid. Insecurity and fatalism infected the White population. They began to conclude that increasing police brutality would not strengthen apartheid. Since partial reforms had not worked, or at least appeared not to work, repeal of apartheid seemed the only possible solution.

Changes occurred in the non-White populations, too. Economic conditions improved for non-Whites relative to the Whites. The non-White populations became better educated, as well, in spite of educational apartheid. Blacks were also concluding that violence would not destroy apartheid, therefore alternative strategies were needed.

The South African economy began a long, steady decline. GDP declined by 1 percent from 1980–1987. Many blamed apartheid for the long-term economic decline. Apartheid administrative costs were quite high. Social apartheid meant the costly duplication of public services. Apartheid also hindered economic growth by preventing improvements in the quality of the non-White workforce. South African manufacturers were not competitive in the global market. Economic boycotts and the withdrawal of foreign investment prevented modernization of industrial plant. Demand for the raw materials produced by South Africa declined, reducing income from mineral extraction.

Global political isolation and the collapse of Communism had a major psychological impact on apartheid. If one of the most authoritarian and seemingly invincible political systems in the world—the Soviet Union—could disintegrate so easily and if the Soviet Union could do nothing to retain control over the Eastern European satellites, what could the Whites of South Africa do to preserve apartheid? Nothing, many concluded. The elimination of apartheid unleashed a whole series of changes as momentous as the arrival of the Whites had been in the mid-seventeenth century.

South Africa's isolation from the world disappeared, especially in the economic arena. New constitutional provisions balanced unitary and decentralization interests. The African National Congress, led by Nelson Mandela, achieved a dominant electoral victory in the first four elections. Mandela outlined ideas for a "rainbow society," in which people would still identify with a particular race but share political power, rebuild South African society, and reform the economy. Initially the revolutionary political transformation did not produce major changes in gender and family relationships. South Africa consciously tried to create a Rainbow Society—a community based on diversity.

1. Reasons for the End to Apartheid

Apartheid was abolished because of five major factors. Apartheid became too costly to maintain. Efforts to reform it actually weakened support for the apartheid system. Opposition increased and became more moderate at the same time. Some of the increase in opposition resulted from White supporters of apartheid deciding that apartheid no longer made sense. Finally, the collapse of the Cold War removed the remnants of support for an anti-Communist apartheid state.

Economic decline and the increasingly devastating impact of both domestic and international economic boycotts weakened support for apartheid. The high costs of policing apartheid and heavy military expenditures strained the government's budget. The government found it more difficult to provide subsidies to lower-class Afrikaaners. The economic costs of maintaining apartheid had increased beyond its personal benefits to Whites. The White business community became disenchanted with apartheid and began to call for its elimination.

Reform momentum made the elimination of apartheid seem almost inevitable. Modest reforms, such as the elimination of "social" apartheid, satisfied neither the Afrikaaner hardliners nor the opponents of apartheid. Half-measures suggested the government's lack of commitment to the continuance of apartheid and encouraged its opponents to believe that the end to apartheid was near.

Changes occurred in the opposition camps, too. On the one hand, more and more people began to oppose apartheid and to become more vocal in their rejection of apartheid. At the same time, the radicals, especially the African National Congress, began to moderate their position and to signal willingness to compromise with the government.

Some Afrikaaners abandoned apartheid and for the reasons mentioned. They, along with the liberals, who were primarily of British descent, now formed a majority among the White population. Thus, only a small minority (perhaps 10%, of the country's population) continued to support apartheid in the late 1980s. When most of the nation, including its elite, came to the conclusion that apartheid was doomed, it certainly was. That led the National Party to cut its losses as much as possible and to make a deal that would preserve some White privilege—political and economic.

Finally, the ending to the Cold War also played a role. Symbolically, if one entrenched and seemingly invincible, as well as unjust, system could topple, how could any other entrenched, invincible, and unjust system hope to survive? (See Chapter Four, China, for an alternative view.) Further, the end to the Cold War meant that neither super power had any national security reason to support either side in the conflict over apartheid. The United States no longer had any need of anti-Communist partners and Russia could not afford to provide financial support for the opponents of apartheid, including the Communist Party in South Africa.

2. Isolation Ends

The peaceful overthrow of the apartheid regime ended South Africa's political quarantine and opened up the country to renewed participation in the international economy. At the same time, South Africa's interest in playing a global role was weakened by a preoccupation with very powerful domestic issues.

Globalism. Though the African National Congress had socialist leanings before it came to power, the collapse of Communism in Eastern Europe and the Soviet Union made it easier for South Africa to tilt toward the West. The United States became a major trading partner and source of investment for South Africa, as deep-seated anti-Americanism gradually dissipated. South Africa became a respected member of the international community, reflected in its abandonment of nuclear weapons development and in its support for nuclear non-proliferation. South Africa also championed the anti-land mine campaign.

Africa. In addition, exploiting its sense of superiority, South Africa began an aggressive strategy of influencing its neighbors and supporting human rights in Africa. Domination of southern Africa became its major goal. South Africa played an important role in the African organization *African Renaissance,* whose goal was to promote political harmony, good government, and economic development in Africa. At the same time, however, South Africa supported fraudulent elections and the preservation of power of a dictator, who controlled neighboring Zimbabwe. South Africa sought to control the economies of its neighbors to the benefit of South African economic growth.

3. Constitution-Building and Political Conflict

The introduction of a new political system accompanied the diplomatic changes. Discussion between representatives of the National Party and the ANC preceded the decision to eliminate apartheid. Its repeal required the development of new constitutional structures based on universal adult participation in the political system. The struggle over a new Constitution revealed new fault lines in South African politics, with the main issue whether South Africa would remain a centralized unitary state or become a federal system with some measure of decentralization.

Violence, such an important part of the apartheid political structure, carried over into the new era. The ANC easily won the national elections from 1994 to the present. South African people faced the issue of whether to take revenge against those who had created and administered apartheid and acted in an inhumane, brutal fashion or to try to develop a system of reconciliation. This led to the actions of the *Truth and Reconciliation Commission,* which sought to carry out justice and to create mechanisms for reconciliation.

Repeal of Apartheid. Though the repeal of apartheid seemed to take place very quickly, the announcement of its end was preceded by half a decade of informal discussions. In the mid-1980s, the head of the Afrikaaner extremist group Broederbund met with Thabo *Mbeki,* an ANC leader and President of South Africa, 1999–2008. In 1985, Prime Minister Botha offered to free Nelson Mandela if the ANC would renounce the use of violence. Mandela rejected the proposal but he and representatives of the Nationalist Party and South African security forces began a series of secret discussions. In January 1989, Mandela and Botha met personally to discuss how to implement a peaceful transition from apartheid to majority rule. This time, Botha rejected the Mandela offer. Soon after that Botha resigned because of illness.

His successor, Frederick Willem DeKlerk, decided that the Whites could no longer be assured of ruling South Africa and that it was necessary to negotiate an agreement with ANC. In February 1990, DeKlerk legalized ANC, the Pan-Africanist Congress, and the South African Communist Party. He announced the introduction of civil rights, including freedom of assembly and freedom of the press. He also released all political prisoners, most importantly Mandela.

In 1990, the government cancelled the state of emergency and repealed all apartheid laws. It is clear that apartheid's control over South Africa was as fragile as Nicholas II's power in Russia in 1917, and thus easily toppled. Mandela and DeKlerk agreed to lead South Africa toward a non-racial, democratic society. Negotiations to determine the structure of a future South Africa began at the end of 1991. These negotiations were difficult, since the Afrikaaner extremists and the ANC extremists and other radical Black groups, as well as the Zulu Party *(Inkatha Freedom Party)*, either boycotted the proceedings or frequently threatened to bolt the discussions. Violence continued, as all sides sought to use force to affect the direction of negotiations.

Democratic Political Institutions. Negotiations took place at *CODESA* (The Convention for a Democratic South Africa), composed of some 200 delegates from the major political groups. Eventually the two major players, the ANC and the National Party, agreed on basic principles to be applied to the future political system. The political system would guarantee civil rights, universal adult suffrage, an independent judiciary with the powers of *judicial review,* and the elimination of the homelands. Whites would be guaranteed political power disproportionate to their numbers. The chief issue of contention was whether the political system would be centralized or decentralized. The ANC favored a winner-take-all centralized political system. Some Whites argued for an autonomous White province, while Inkatha, led by Mangosuthu Buthelezi, wanted autonomy for the Natal, where it was strongest. The Whites and the Zulu feared that they would be excluded from power in the future since it was obvious that ANC would be the majority party. This situation paralleled that of the Congress Party in India after independence and that of the Liberal Democratic Party in Japan from the mid-1950s (See Chapters Two and Three).

Increased violence halted negotiations for almost a year. Finally ANC agreed to the sharing of power. The Nationalists and ANC agreed to prepare an interim constitution and hold elections in April 1994. The Parliament elected in 1994 would write a permanent constitution, to be ratified by referendum.

The interim constitution divided South Africa into nine provinces, generally cutting across previous boundaries and across racial lines. A National Assembly (or lower house) of 400 would be elected by *proportional representation.* Proportional representation is an electoral system that gives each party the number of seats in Parliament that is proportional to its share of total votes. That is, if a party won 40 percent of the votes, it would get approximately 40 percent of the seats in the legislature. This differs from the winner-take-all system of the United States, where each seat is won by the party with the most votes in that district. And though a party might win 40 percent of the overall vote, it might win few seats if it lost many contests by a small margin. The Senate of 90 would consist of 10 delegates from each province, elected proportionally. The National Assembly would elect the President. Any party that won 80 or more seats in the National Assembly would have the right to select an executive deputy president. Any party that won twenty or more Assembly seats would receive cabinet positions in proportion to the number of seats it won. Civil rights were guaranteed. Eleven languages were declared official languages. This interim constitution could not be amended, only replaced by a permanent constitution.

ANC Government. The ANC easily won the elections of 1994. Several major political forces refused to register for the elections, including the Conservative (Afrikaaner extremists) Party and the Inkatha Freedom Party. Both joined together in a *Freedom Alliance,* demanding that South Africa be a loose federation of semi-autonomous states, rather than the centralized state pushed by ANC and incorporated into the interim constitution. Rebellion in Kwa-Zulu Natal led to its takeover by the South African government. The Freedom Alliance fell apart, as the Inkatha finally agreed to participate in the elections.

In spite of a great deal of pre-election violence, the elections themselves were relatively peaceful and honest, with participation rates of 90 percent in 1994 and 75–80 percent since then. The ANC won 63 percent of the vote, the

National Party 20 percent, and Inkatha 10 percent, with no other party winning more than 3 percent. Failure to win two-thirds of the vote prevented ANC from being able to amend the constitution at will. The ANC won control of seven provinces; the National Party won in the Western Cape Province, with support from the Coloured as well as White populations; and the Inkatha Freedom Party won in KwaZulu-Natal. Now ANC controls the governments of all nine provinces. In May 1994, Mandela was elected president of South Africa, replaced by Mbeki in 1999.

The executive branch (the presidency) dominates the legislative branch. Almost 1,000 pieces of ANC-sponsored legislation have passed. Not a single ANC-sponsored bill has been defeated. At the same time the courts have acted to limit the power of the executive, declaring executive actions and new laws unconstitutional in about half of the cases brought before it. Initially an auditing commission set up to investigate government financial activity uncovered numerous cases of fraud and bribery. However, by about 2001, ANC had been able to halt the commission's actions.

Problems. The ANC-dominated government faced tremendous problems. It introduced a series of reform programs (some to be discussed in detail in section 5), wrote a permanent constitution, and gradually strengthened the central government and reduced the rights of the provinces.

The new government reorganized the bureaucracy, the military, the police, and local and provincial government. The ANC had agreed that no bureaucrats would lose their jobs in the reorganization of government. Many agencies were closed, however, including the homeland governments, and their employees were transferred. It was easier to shift personnel than to change the attitudes of the apartheid bureaucrats, most of whom opposed the new government. The new authorities announced that their goal was to use affirmative action to make government reflect the racial composition of the population as a whole. This was a long-term process since so few qualified non-Whites were available to serve in the new government.

The government also restructured the military. This required fusing the South African army of apartheid, the homeland military forces, and the guerilla and para-military groups of the ANC and PAC. The various military units were combined and the guerilla forces given military training. The apartheid-era army resented these changes and the guerillas resisted regular military discipline.

It was even harder to create a post-apartheid police force. With much difficulty the new White leaders of the police and security forces worked to create a single, unified central police force. The police only gradually accepted the idea that their main responsibility was no longer to enforce apartheid.

The transition to a non-apartheid structure brought with it a large measure of lawlessness, as the resort to force had been part of the arsenal of strategies for most groups under apartheid. Eventually the crime rate began to decline, as political violence diminished. However, the murder rate remained extremely high, ten times as high as in the United States, where the murder rate was one of the highest among Western nations. In South Africa the murder rate was 61 for every 100,000 residents; in the United States it was 10 per 100,000.

Provincial government was also restructured. New provincial leaders had difficulty in establishing authority and many were not well qualified. New urban governments, known as *transitional councils,* were established to integrate White areas and non-White townships. Later, elected city councils replaced the transitional councils. The new city governments were responsible for public utilities and local services and labored under inadequate budgets and tax bases. Most non-Whites had refused to pay local taxes, rents, and mortgages, so tax revenues had only been sufficient to provide for services to the Whites. The new city governments had to convince the non-Whites both to pay their previous obligations and higher taxes as well.

Preparing a permanent constitution was a major task. Many had accepted the interim constitution, even though it did not satisfy them, because they believed there would be a chance to introduce different ideas for the permanent constitution. Therefore, debate over the permanent constitution produced less willingness to compromise. Though the ANC wished to have a political monopoly, it did not have the two-thirds majority needed to eliminate power sharing.

Democracy was further confirmed in South Africa by the 1999 elections. When Mandela decided not to seek reelection, Mbeki from ANC was elected President, with the same sort of margin as the ANC victory in the first elections in 1994. In 2004 elections Mbeki was easily reelected and ANC continued to dominate the political system.

4. An Ideology for a "Rainbow Society"

Nelson Mandela articulated most clearly the values of the rainbow society. He argued that it was possible to create a non-racial democracy.

Political tolerance was to be championed. Freedom of expression permitted debate about the truth. From this debate, actual truth would emerge. Nelson Mandela espoused ideas similar to those of nineteenth-century liberalism as advocated by Englishman John Stuart Mill. Mandela argued that all legitimate government derived from the consent of the governed and that South Africa must be a society of laws and not of men. He called for guarantees of civil rights, using the broader term human rights. For Mandela, political rights were not enough. People needed economic opportunity; Thomas Jefferson's "pursuit of happiness." Economic change, therefore, was central to Mandela's quest for a successful non-racial democracy. The new constitution was to represent the ideals of the rainbow society: humanity, equality, civil liberties, and human rights. This new society was to be non-radical and non-sexist. Politically the constitution and the rule of law were to be separate.

5. Economic Reforms and Class Changes

Apartheid was repealed during a period of economic crisis. The introduction of a post-apartheid state did not quickly resolve the economic problems (The situation in Russia was quite similar; see Chapter One).

Economic Situation. Economic depression ended only in 1993. South Africa suffered from a high inflation rate and massive unemployment (43% among Blacks). Divestment had sucked capital investment out of the country and capital returned only gradually. South Africa's emphasis on using labor intensiveness to produce wealth left it non-competitive in world manufacturing markets, where technology was increasingly important. This was similar to the situation at the end of Communist rule in Russia. The emphasis on exporting raw materials, especially minerals, could not sustain economic growth. High levels of non-White poverty depressed the local market for retail goods. Parallel to Algeria after independence (see Chapter Six), South Africa faced a serious problem of human capital flight after apartheid. One to one and one half million emigrated. This included 45 percent of doctors and 25 percent of all university graduates, who moved to the U.S.

New Economic Policies. The new government soon abandoned interest in state planning and socialism. Instead it sought to promote economic justice, with economic growth to be a by-product. Central to achieving this goal was the *Reconstruction and Development Program (RDP)*. The RDP focused on public works projects that would both create jobs and modernize the infrastructure of the townships and rural areas. The goal was to build 300,000 new homes a year, all with access to water, electricity, and sewers. Expansion of the electrical grid moved more quickly than housing construction did. Obviously the project would cost a great deal of money and tax rates were already relatively high. Economic recovery, which began in 1994, provided some increase in government revenue. Heavy foreign investment did not take place. In 1996, the government introduced the *GEAR* program (Growth, Employment, and Redevelopment) to promote economic development. Since then, the government has reduced its role in the economy.

Results of these policies were mixed. By 2004, economic growth had reached 4 percent and has hovered around that figure until the global economic crisis of 2008–2009. However, unemployment rates still rested at 25 percent. Improvements in living standards came very gradually. Most of the South African poor recognized that the process of raising living standards would be slow.

Land reform was another major objective of the government. In 1995, it promulgated a five-year plan for the redistribution of farm land. The government's goal was redistribution of about one-third of the land. Land redistribution was to be based on purchase, not forced confiscation, so initially only a few pilot projects were initiated.

The government also emphasized better education—both to promote equality and to foster economic growth. The educational problems were immense. A century of funding White schools well and non-White schools quite inadequately meant that the costs of making non-White education equal to White education were very high. School facilities were inadequate, too few school buildings were available, and too few qualified teachers could be found. Subjects had been taught from a pro-apartheid perspective. New textbooks were needed, especially in the humanities and social sciences. Efforts to integrate students of different races needed to take place. Educational goals were not met.

Inequality Continued. Centuries of inequality and decades of apartheid had left South Africa a deeply unequal society. Abolition of apartheid did not quickly overcome inequality. Whites remained at the top of society, Blacks at the bottom. Only gradually did a small Black elite and a larger Black middle class emerge. In general, the desperately poor remained desperately poor. Half of the national wealth was in the hands of the top 10 percent, while the lowest

44 percent of the population held 1 percent of the nation's wealth. Most of the wealth was in the hands of the Whites. Wages for White workers were still six times that of wages for Black workers. Based on the key statistical measure of inequality, the GINI coefficient, in the 1990s South Africa had the second highest level of inequality in the world (0.58, with the higher the number, the greater the inequality).

6. Transition in Gender and Family Issues

The end to apartheid did not immediately bring significant changes in the family. Changes in the position of women and male-female relations were unclear.

Opposition to Apartheid. Women had been prominent in opposition to apartheid. Black and Coloured women had marched in protest against the pass laws and participated in economic boycotts. Liberal White women had greater freedom to organize in opposition to apartheid than men did, for they were not viewed as capable of significant political action.

Politics. Women, however, played a limited role in the new society, in spite of efforts to participate in the constitution-building process. All adult women gained the right to vote and hold office. Women have become an increasingly large proportion of representatives in Parliament, 28 percent in 1994 and 36 percent a decade later. However, few had prominent positions in the transition team, the Cabinet, and the state bureaucracy. The most prominent woman was Winnie Mandela, Nelson Mandela's estranged wife. One woman became Speaker of the House.

New laws have increased women's rights. In 1996, women were granted the right to have abortions. In 1998, domestic violence was made illegal. This law was a response to South Africa's extremely high level of sexual violence. Under the Maintenance Act of 1998, former partners were required to provide financial support for mothers and their children.

Customary Law. Though the Constitution called for male-female equality, it also reconfirmed customary or tribal law, which applied in the Black communities and discriminated against women. Under customary law, women were treated as minors. Males had control over inheritance, property rights, and marriage and divorce.

7. Community and Diversity

After several centuries, during which race was used to divide people and create separate groups, informally and legally, the post-apartheid period was one in which races were encouraged to work together. Derived from U.S. activist, Jesse Jackson, the slogan "rainbow society" was used to describe and promote racial tolerance and racial equality. Initially, however, the African National Congress sought to "play the race card"—in favor of the Blacks.

Mosaic. Post-apartheid South Africa continued to resemble a mosaic. Seventy-seven percent of the population of 47 million was Black, 11 percent White, 9 percent Coloured, and 3 percent Asian. Significant differences existed within each racial category and within tribal identities, as well. Though socioeconomic differences existed between Afrikaaners and English-speakers, those differences were narrowing. The difference in political attitudes toward apartheid also narrowed, as a majority of the Afrikaaners also came to support its repeal.

Conflict between Zulu and Xhosa and Zulu and Sotho was intense in the Witwatersrand area. In the Natal the Zulu supporters of Inkatha fought with pro-ANC Zulu. At least a million political refugees had fled to South Africa from nearby countries, especially Mozambique. Their assimilation into the South African life was difficult.

The interim and permanent constitutions created provincial boundaries based on ethnic identity, thus preserving and reinforcing those identities. Eight of the nine provinces had a single dominant ethnic identity. Tendencies toward autonomy and intensified tribal identities were evident especially among the Zulu but also among other large tribes, including the Xhosa, Tswani, Pedi, Tsonga, and Venda.

Language differences were dealt with by authorizing eleven official languages, with English, in practice, the main language of communication among groups (see Chapter Two, India, for parallels). The educational system, too, was to be language-based.

Responding to the demands of the Whites and Zulu, the constitutions emphasized cultural autonomy for each racial grouping, but especially for the Zulu and Whites.

Finally, a new multi-racial upper class of administrators, businessmen, and intelligentsia began to emerge.

The image of the rainbow celebrated diversity but also suggested that there would be little interracial mixing.

Rainbow Policies. The ANC-dominated government employed a number of strategies to reduce racial differences and identity. A *Truth and Reconciliation Commission* investigated the brutal actions of the apartheid period. If individuals admitted their inhumane behavior, they were forgiven and exempted from punishment. If an individual refused to admit guilt, he or she could later be brought to trial. The goal was to overcome the legacy of apartheid by an airing of apartheid era behavior. After this, forgiveness would reign, at least theoretically (see similar strategies in Chapter Six, Algeria).

Affirmative Action was introduced, with racial quotas for openings in the government. The government promoted geographical mixing of races, and this began to occur as Blacks and Coloureds moved into White areas. Improving education for non-Whites was a long-range plan for moving toward racial equality. Through these rainbow society policies, South Africa reduced the levels of inequality and difference, though the country remained far from being a cohesive community.

CONCLUSION

South African history revolves around the issue of race and identity.

South Africa remained isolated from the rest of the world throughout most of its history. It had porous borders, however. Immigrants as well as invading military forces moved into South Africa from the north. Westerners arrived by sea and gradually expanded inland. Gradually over two and one half centuries, the Whites, Dutch, and British, conquered the various tribes, finalizing the process in the late nineteenth century. The discovery of diamonds and gold brought South Africa into the global economy. However, the introduction of apartheid led to a new era of isolation that lasted until late in the twentieth century.

Governments were varied and minimal until the establishment of an independent South Africa in the early twentieth century. From that point on government became more powerful. Race determined citizenship. Whites had political rights, including the right to vote and hold office. Over time the Afrikaaners gained control of the government, at the expense of the British. White-only democracy lasted until the end of apartheid, after which universal suffrage was introduced. The government used its power to encourage and legalize discrimination and racism.

Ideologies generally offered religious perspectives. Native religion and Dutch Reformed Protestantism played a powerful role. Eventually the supporters of apartheid offered an ideology based on racial separation and White superiority. After apartheid was abolished, ideas of interracial democracy offered a direction for the future.

Race affected economics and social structure. South Africa had an agrarian-pastoral economy through the first half of the nineteenth century. Economic contacts with the rest of the world were limited to providing supplies for ships sailing between Europe and Asia. With the discovery of diamonds and gold, the South African economy came to rely on exports from mining. In the twentieth century, South Africa began to build an industrial economy, primarily to meet domestic (White) consumer demand. South Africa was divided into two social groups—Whites and non-Whites. Though some Whites were upper class, others middle class, and still others lower class, all of White society had much higher status and power than did non-Whites. There were fewer social distinctions among non-White groups than among Whites. Interracial mobility was impossible.

Most families were patriarchal with senior males more powerful in Afrikaaner families than they were in other social groups. Other racial groups had a large single male population separated from the family due to urban employment. This meant that women had greater power and independence.

Race divided South Africans and made community-building impossible before the end of apartheid. Apartheid sought to establish and legalize racial difference and separation. With the fall of apartheid, the idea of a rainbow society espoused the goal of interracial equality and an eventual end to racial identity.

Name: ______________________________ **Date:** ________________

Chapter Five: South Africa

IDENTIFICATION: IMPORTANT VOCABULARY AND TERMS

1820 Settlers (403)

African National Congress (ANC) (407)

African Political Organization (410)

African Renaissance (424)

Afrikaaner Broederbond (Afrikaaner Brotherhood) (406)

Afrikaaners (Boers) (380)

apartheid (380)

Bantu Laws Amendment Act (418)

black consciousness (415)

BOSS (Bureau of State Security) (418)

bride price (lobola) (383)

Cape Coloureds (403)

Cape Slave Code (388)

constructive engagement (412)

DeKlerk (414)

dingaka (382)

divestment (412)

Dutch Reformed Church (387)

Evangelical missionaries (398)

extended family (383)

Fagan Commission (411)

GEAR (Growth, Employment, and Redevelopment) (429)

Great Trek (392)

Griquas (386)

homelands (416)

Inkatha Freedom Party (425)

Mandela (418)

Mbeki (425)

mfecane (391)

mineral revolution (390)

mortality rates (388)

National Party (380)

Ordinance 50 (398)

pass laws (389)

Peace of Vereeniging (395)

polygamous (384)

rainbow society (380)

Reconstruction and Development Program (RDP) (429)

separate but equal (415)

Shaka (391)

shamans (381)

Sharpesville Massacre (419)

South African Indian Congress (410)

Soweto (419)

Suppression of Communism Act (413)

swidden agriculture (383)

Name: ______________________________ **Date:** __________________

Trans-Vaal (392)

Truth and Reconciliation Commission (425)

United Democratic Front (419)

Zulu (381)

Name: ______________________________ Date: ________________

Chapter Five: South Africa

KEY QUESTIONS

Competing Communities—before the Europeans, 1500–1652: What enabled the "mixed-farmers" to conquer the hunter-gatherers and the pastoralists?

Dutch Colonial Period, 1650–1800: Define the most important characteristics of Dutch Christianity.

British Century, 1800–1910. What enabled Whites to dominate the non-White populations during the "British Century"?

Triumph of the Afrikaaners and Segregation, 1910–1948: Why did the Afrikaaners establish segregation?

Era of Apartheid, 1948–1991: What role did violence play during the apartheid period?

Rainbow Society, 1991–Present: What produced the collapse of apartheid?

Chapter Six

ALGERIA

Introduction

Muslim Algeria, 1500–1830

French Colonial Rule, 1830–1954

Civil War and National Liberation, 1954–1962

An Independent, Radical Algeria, 1962–1988

Second Civil War, 1988–1999

Contemporary Algeria, 1999–Present

Conclusion

INTRODUCTION

Algeria has a fascinating history, illustrating the impact of Islam in North Africa. Its past included national liberation, socialism, religious fundamentalism, and democracy, as well as issues of multi-ethnicity in an Islamic state.

Geography has played an important role in the history of Algeria. Algeria stretches from blue Mediterranean waters through inland highlands to the hot sands of the *Sahara* desert. The northern part of Algeria consists of coastal hills and plains, the Atlas Mountains, the High Plateaus, and the Sahara Atlas mountain range. This fertile area is the location of much of the country's population and all of its large cities. Here farming for the market is common. Further south, the eastern areas of the High Plateaus have bountiful rainfall, while the western half is rather arid. *Pastoralism* dominates the western half, while the eastern half is an area of subsistence farming and pastoralism that includes *Kabylia.* Eighty percent of the country is Saharan desert. An area to be crossed for commercial purposes, Saharan Algeria contains vast oil and gas reserves.

The coastal regions dominated most of its history, though tensions between the peoples of the highlands and those of the coastal areas continue down to today. Centralizing authorities, from the *Ottoman sultanate* through the French colonial government to the army-dominated governments of independent Algeria have always faced *centrifugal* forces and demands for regional and ethnic autonomy.

Islam has been the dominant ideology for over 1,000 years. From time to time *secular* challenges, French civilization, and later socialism, emerged. Algerian nationalism assumed importance in the twentieth century.

Until the mid-twentieth century Algeria was predominately an agricultural-commercial society. Only with the discovery of oil toward the end of the French period has industry become important. Patriarchy had been enforced and reinforced by Islam, though there was some weakening of male domination in the French period and during the war of national liberation (1954–1962).

Diversity has been present since the arrival of Arab warriors who converted the native peoples, commonly known as *Berbers,* to Islam. Tension between the Arab invaders and colonists and the native population continued throughout the Muslim period. Diversity was made more complex with the arrival of the French. Large numbers of colonists, French as well as northern Mediterraneans, flowed into Algeria. French became the culture of the educated classes. Tension between Islam and French, or Western, civilization was ironically most intense along the coast, while the Berbers of the interior found it easier to balance their native culture with that of the French. After independence, some groups resisted efforts to transform Algeria into an Arab-Islamic state. The conflict over these efforts at transformation, along with the rise of Islamic fundamentalism, led to civil war that lasted throughout the 1990s. In the early Twenty-First Century, Algeria continues to deal with the fallout from the latest civil war.

A. MUSLIM ALGERIA, 1500–1830

Islam had swept into North Africa a century after its founding in the Arabian Peninsula, meeting fierce resistance from the native population, the Berbers.

After several waves of Arabic invasion and immigration, native dynasties ruled for several centuries. Upon the collapse of Mongol power, Ottomans, Turkic peoples from Central Asia, came to power in Anatolia (today's Turkey). Ottoman power spread across North Africa in the sixteenth century. The Ottomans ruled Algeria through local representatives, or *deys,* whose power derived from Turkic soldiers. In reality Algeria was relatively independent. Islam provided a set of beliefs accepted by almost all Algerians, though divisions existed within Islam. Algeria was an agrarian-commercial society, whose wealth was generated in part through pirate activity in the Mediterranean Sea. Patriarchy determined the nature of the family and gender roles. Islam and Ottoman rule provided some degree of community. However, the primary division was between a multi-ethnic coastal area, inhabited by Turks, Arabs, mixed Turkic-Berber peoples (*Koloughlis*), Moors (descendants of Muslim refugees from Spain), Jews, and nomadic Berbers, who controlled the interior.

1. Ottoman Turkic Expansion

The Turks replaced Berber dynasties in eastern Algeria and a loose federation of Berber tribes in the western half. The immigration of large numbers of Muslims, who fled Spain after the Christian reconquest at the end of the fifteenth century, supplemented the Berber population.

Turkic pirates, led by the brothers Aruj al-Din and Khair al-Din, captured coastal Algeria in the early sixteenth century. By 1545, the Ottoman Sultan assumed ultimate authority, with Khair as governor-general. Eastern and central Algeria became a province of the Ottoman Empire, while the western coastal section was divided into small, semi-independent states. The interior Berber tribes, led by chiefs (*tariqa*), remained independent until the French conquest.

Ottoman power declined in the second half of the eighteenth century, weakened by domestic rebellion, and increased British and Dutch naval action against the pirates.

2. Decentralized Political System

The *dey,* or governor-general, ruled Algeria with the city of Algiers as his capital.

The dey's power was based in part on his military, the *Janissaries*-Ottoman soldiers from Anatolia and the Balkans. The troops were personally loyal to him, and lacking local ties, did not support dissidence and rebellion. The power of the dey weakened beginning in the mid-eighteenth century, when the deys began to use Algerian troops. The pirates or *corsairs* had great power since their activities provided most of the government's income. Though the dey paid tribute to the Sultan, Algeria was basically independent.

3. Islam

Islam, one of the great religions of the world, played an overwhelming role in Algerian life.

Islam means the total acceptance of God (Allah) and requires total submission to his will. Islam is a monotheistic religion (belief in a single supreme deity). In the mid-seventh century Allah presented his commandments to

Muhammad. These were recorded in the Muslim Holy Book, the *Qu'ran.* Muslims followed five basic religious practices, the *five pillars.* Muslims declared their total submission to God. They performed prayers five times a day, with Friday noon communal prayers the most important ones. Muslims were to give alms to the needy and fast during the holy month of *Ramadan.* Finally, if at all possible, they were to take a pilgrimage to Mecca, the original site of the religion. Islam provided believers with detailed rules of behavior. These rules were laid out in the *Qu'ran,* the direct word of Allah. In addition, Islamic law (*shar'ia*) included traditions (the *hadith*), collections of the thoughts of Muhammad, analogy, scholarly interpretations, societal consensus, and established custom. *Shar'ia* thus determined how a person should act in almost every possible situation.

4. Traditional Economy

Farming, pastoralism, and commerce were the main components of the economy. Piracy provided income to the government and wealth to the pirates but had a minimal impact on the economic lives of most Algerians.

Along the coast, grain and fruits were grown and some were exported to Europe. Inland, some grain was grown in the highlands. Nomads used the desert areas for livestock herding. Agriculture productivity declined during this period and French markets disappeared. Piracy replaced agriculture as the main source of wealth.

Social structure was quite simple. Most Algerians were peasant farmers; a small minority was full-time traders, and a few formed a small political elite.

5. Patriarchy and Islam

Islam provided guidelines for male domination, though there was some ambiguity in its perspective. The *Qu'ran,* interpreted narrowly by *hadith,* defined the nature of the family and the relative roles of males and females.

The *Qu'ran* stated that men and women were equal before God, meaning that they had the same religious obligations. However the *Qu'ran* also assigned men and women different rights and responsibilities based on physical differences. Males were responsible for providing economically for all members of the family. They were to treat women with justice, kindness, and benevolence. Women had the right to own personal property, including the *dowry* provided at the time of marriage. They could freely dispose of their property. A woman could inherit property, though a male received twice as much as did a woman.

Marriage was viewed as a civil, almost economic, contract. Men were permitted four wives; though only the wealthiest of men had more than one. The *Qu'ran* encouraged monogamy. Divorce was permitted, though frowned upon. It was easier for husbands than wives to obtain divorce.

According to *hadith,* women were to be veiled and isolated. The veiling and isolation of women in the house was most common in middle and upper class urban families. Ottoman influence reinforced this isolation of women.

6. Community and Diversity

Islam provided some sense of community. However difference was more potent. Difference was based primarily on lifestyle, language, and ethnicity.

In the interior Berbers sought to maintain a separate way of life. Relative isolation, language, and sect differentiated the Berbers from the coastal population. At the same time, each Berber tribe was distinct from other Berber communities.

The urban coastal areas held a mixture of great diversity. Berbers were found in the cities but so were people descended from various groups of invaders and immigrants. Arabs came first, some from Egypt and others from the eastern Mediterranean. Turks, Moors (an Arab-Spanish mixture), Koloughlis (people of mixed Turkic and Berber descent), and Jews followed them. The coastal cities contained cosmopolitan populations. Trade across the Mediterranean had promoted diversity and a degree of tolerance.

B. FRENCH COLONIAL RULE, 1830–1954

The arrival of French domination brought about basic changes in political structure, ideology, class structure, and community and diversity. Fewer changes occurred in the economy and in family and gender relations.

1. French Conquest

The French used military force to gain control over Algeria. In response to unrest and rebellion, France imposed a two-tier system of control and citizenship. French and other colonists were considered French, while Muslims were automatically considered inferiors.

The French conquest of Algeria came about almost by accident. When the dey hit a French diplomat with a fly swatter, the French took advantage of this "incident" to invade Algeria in 1827. The French King, Charles XII, was quite unpopular and saw an opportunity to rebuild his support by demonstrating French global power. Though Algeria was conquered, revolution overthrew Charles XII three years later.

Resistance to the French was quite strong, with Emir *Abd al-Kadir* leading the opposition. Initially basing himself on the west coast at Oran, al-Kadir later created an independent Berber state of Kabylia that survived until 1839. From 1839 to 1847, al-Kadir waged a holy war (*jihad*). Using great brutality, the French general Bugeaud defeated al-Kadir and extended French power beyond the coast and through the high plateaus to the edge of the Sahara desert. Berber tribes held out in Kabylia until 1857. In 1871, a tribal leader in the Constantine area of eastern Algeria rebelled but French forces brutally crushed them. Periodic uprisings continued into the 1890s.

2. French Colonial Government

The French government in Algeria sought to ensure quiescence among the local population, establish the French as the dominant political and social group in the country, and use Algeria as a source of agricultural products for France and a market for French goods. In spite of the absence of official encouragement, by 1847 over 100,000 Europeans had immigrated to Algeria. Eventually the Europeans formed over 10 percent of the country's population (see parallels with South Africa in Chapter Five).

In 1851, France divided Algeria into three coastal units—Oran, Algiers, and Constantine. These territories were considered part of France and were ruled by French civilian administrators. Berbers and Arabs outside these areas were under French military rule. With encouragement from the French Emperor, Napoleon III, large numbers of French settlers pushed beyond the coastal areas and into the interior. He also granted large amounts of land to favorites and political allies. Once colonists had moved into the interior, the political structure based on distinct French and Arab-Berber areas disintegrated.

This required changes in French rule. Napoleon III first announced the creation of an Arab Kingdom in the interior, which he would rule directly as emperor. Muslims would be granted French nationality. Neither the French colonists nor the Muslims supported the plan.

Then in 1871, especially in response to rebellion in the Constantine area, the French tightened their control over Algeria. Europeans in the three coastal territories were given representation in the French Parliament. French authorities confiscated large quantities of tribal lands and made them available for colonization. The French placed Kabylia under martial law and punished Muslims without reference to the judicial process. European settlers thus became French citizens and Muslims remained second-class persons. The colonial government levied extra taxes on the Muslims, restricted their travel and limited their education. The only way to avoid French political domination was to assimilate to French culture and convert to Roman Catholicism. The French thus ruled Algeria through military power and discrimination.

3. French Nationalism vs. Islam

The French emphasis on the superiority of their culture met little open resistance until after the First World War. While most of the people remained deeply committed to Islam, they avoided direct confrontation with Western power. Eventually, the challenge to French cultural superiority led to Algerian nationalism.

French Nationalism. Perhaps more insistently than the British, the French claimed cultural superiority. This was not a contest between French Catholicism and the Islamic religion but between French culture and an inferior Muslim civilization. Throughout, though, the French believed that education would transform the non-French into French citizens. Thus the barriers between the French and the Muslims were less than those between the British and Afrikaaners on the one hand and the Whites and Blacks on the other in South Africa and between the British and the Indians in South Asia (see Chapters Five and Two).

Algerian Nationalism. Among the educated Muslim Algerians, opposition to French rule and French cultural superiority slowly began to develop. Before the Second World War, most Algerian nationalists continued to propose that Algerians receive greater political rights within the French orbit.

Ironically, the Algerian independence movement began among Algerian émigrés in France. In 1925, *Messali al-Hadj* founded the *North African Star* (*Etoile Nord-Africaine*) movement. Sheik Abdelhamid Ben Badis, Ferhat

Abbas, and Muhamed Bendjelloul espoused a moderate position. Abbas favored the integration of the Muslim community into France. Messali called for independence from France but he was in a minority. In 1937, Messali and a few others formed the pro-independence Algerian People's Party. Ben Badis founded the Association of Reformist Ulema, which emphasized Islamic values.

Dramatic changes in Algerian views came during the Second World War. Most French in Algeria supported the pro-Nazi French government, while most Algerians supported the Allies, especially after the 1942 Allied liberation of Algeria. In February 1943, Abbas proposed a *Manifesto of the Algerian People.* The Manifesto called for Arabic as the official language of Algeria, a constitutional assembly empowered to draw up a new constitution and a union of the *Maghreb* nations of Morocco, Algeria, and Tunisia. The proposal did not address the role of Islam, thus reflecting the dominant secular thinking of Algerian nationalists. The "Free French" government issued a decree that extended French citizenship to less than 10 percent of the Muslim population. Abbas then joined with Messali al-Hadj to form the Friends of the Manifesto of Freedom, which called for an independent Algeria.

The end of the war brought forth massive riots, especially those in *Setif,* as demonstrators called for Algerian independence. Up to 15,000 Muslims died, while French authorities arrested similar numbers. The brutal repression that followed the riots pushed more Algerians into the pro-independence camp. Abbas founded the Democratic Union of the Manifesto, which urged an autonomous, secular state associated with France. This seemed to represent the majority opinion of educated Muslim Algerians. Messali, however, called for a completely independent Algeria and organized a Movement for the Triumph of Democratic Liberty. With the formation of an Algerian terrorist group, the Special Organization, the civil war and war for national liberation began.

4. Modernization and Exploitation

Under the French, Algeria remained an agricultural-commercial society, though some industrialization took place from the late nineteenth century on. However, land and wealth shifted to the French settlers. The economy grew quite gradually. The class structure became much more complicated as a result of the French conquest.

Agriculture. A dual agricultural economy developed in the French period. Most Muslim farmers continued to carry out subsistence farming, growing barley, wheat, figs and olives, on marginal lands. European colonists acquired the most fertile land, pushing out the Algerians. Some Muslims became agricultural laborers on colonial lands. The farms of the Europeans were large and in the twentieth century generally mechanized. Their farms were commercial operations, primarily exporting to France. They grew wheat, grapes, olives, tobacco, citrus fruit, and vegetables. Subsidized by the government, the European farms produced two-thirds of Algeria's agricultural goods.

Industry. Some industrialization took place in the period between the world wars, but the first major industrialization drive began in the 1950s, just before the civil war. Instead, French investment flowed into banking, finance, and infrastructure. The French built an extensive road, railroad, and postal communications system, as well as port facilities and airports.

Class. The social structure became increasingly complex. The Europeans transformed the traditional system in which most people were farmers. A small elite of the French and Muslim intelligentsia, businessmen, and French officials occupied the top of the social structure. Below this group were the European farmers. At the bottom of society were the native farmers and workers. Upward mobility was available to most Europeans and to Muslims with French educations.

5. Issues in Family and Gender

Colonial conquest had a modest impact on family and gender issues.

In general, the Muslim family, especially among the peasants, did not change. However, French colonial families and Muslims with French education saw a loosening of patriarchy. Fathers no longer had total control over the family. After the First World War, some Muslim women entered the urban workforce. Except for employment, though, women had no roles outside the household.

6. Colonial Conceptions of Citizenship and Diversity

During the colonial period, Muslims ceased to be the only residents of Algeria. Over 10 percent were Europeans, primarily from France but also from Spain and Italy.

In 1900, Algeria had a population of 4 million Muslims, 300,000 French and 200,000 other Europeans. Within the Muslim population, the Berbers remained a distinctive group, looked down upon by the coastal Arab population. Thus both the Europeans and the native Algerians lacked internal unity.

Islam provided a sense of community, while ethnicity preserved diversity. The French offered an alternative basis of community—French culture—which actually made community-building more difficult. For the Muslim community, ethnicity had been the major divisive force. For the French, culture determined difference. The French made a clear distinction between European civilization/French culture and Muslim culture. Initially the French made a distinction between French, Jewish, and Muslim cultures but by the end of the nineteenth century European Jews in Algeria were viewed as French. Thus French culture was secularized.

The French divided Algeria into two segments, French and Muslim. The French had special privileges, the Muslims special disadvantages. Muslims could breach the boundary between the two groups with French educations, especially if they renounced their religion.

C. CIVIL WAR AND NATIONAL LIBERATION, 1954–1962

Civil war (the French perspective) or national liberation (as termed by the Algerians) destroyed French rule over Algeria. Dissatisfaction with French power intensified during the Second World War. A modest and generally moderate Muslim political reform movement became radicalized and transformed into a broad nationwide movement. French proposals for reform came reluctantly, generally opposed by the French settlers in Algeria, the *pied noirs.* French offers fell short of independence. By the end of 1945, the Algerian Muslims would accept nothing less. The Civil War/War of National Liberation was fought with great brutality, destroying the lives of millions and leaving the country economically and demographically devastated. Born in war, independent Algeria stumbled toward freedom.

1. Geography of Independence

At the beginning of the Civil War, Algeria had a population of 9 million Muslims and 1.5 million Europeans. The Civil War led to the withdrawal of almost all Europeans, dramatically changing the ethnic and social composition of the country.

2. Political-Military Struggle

The Civil War began formally in 1954 but its opening can be traced to the formation of pro-liberation terrorist groups. Though the war produced an independent Algerian state, it brought untold misery to the Algerian people.

The Run-up to the Civil War. Beginning with the Setif riots, the French and the Algerians sparred, trying to decide whether Algeria should be independent or remain a part of France. Terrorist attacks that began in 1949 pushed both sides toward a decision. The French drew up a new constitution that declared all Algerians citizens and French and Arabic as official languages of Algeria. The country was to have an elected bicameral legislature. However, the French sought to manipulate the elections to prevent Abbas' Democratic Union and Messali's Democratic Liberty from participating.

In 1954, Democratic Liberty established a Revolutionary Committee of Unity and Action, led by nine *historic chiefs.* The organization changed its name to the *National Liberation Front* (*FLN*) with a military force, the *Army of National Liberation* (*ALN*).

The War for Independence. Both sides fought with great brutality. Neither the French nor the Muslims were united. The Algerians of French descent fought for an Algeria that would remain within the French sphere. Eventually the government of General *deGaulle* overruled the French Algerians and negotiated independence with the Algerians. Within the Muslim camp bitter political struggles also took place.

Rebellion began in eastern Algeria at the end of 1954, and then spread into Kabylia and to the Oran area near the border with Morocco. By early 1956, all of northern Algeria was in flames. The ALN and Algerian terrorist organizations attacked the French army and security forces. Muslim weapons included assassinations, economic sabotage, and urban terrorism. The French used intimidation, executions, and massive military force. By 1956, the various independent Algerian political groups had joined the FLN, which announced that socialism would be introduced after independence.

From 1956 to 1958, the French military took the offensive, generally winning the Civil War. The French kidnapped five of the nine FLN "chiefs" and imprisoned them in France. The French controlled the coastal area and the Sahara, while the ALN built up strength in the highlands and mountains of the interior. In 1956 the French turned to a much more sophisticated set of strategies. The French shifted from defense to offense, emphasing mobile warfare and the use of helicopters to transport troops. France tripled the size of its military in Algeria (a "surge"), special operations using commandos and special forces located and destroyed guerilla bands in the interior. The French sought to deny the FLN support by resettling rural communities from the interior to the coastal areas. The ALN responded with a campaign of urban terrorism.

From 1958–1960, the *pied noirs* (French settlers) tried to force the French government to support continued French power in Algeria. In May 1958, the French Algerians organized a coup d'etat in Algiers in support of deGaulle. DeGaulle came to power in France and initially supported the French Algerians. He promulgated a new constitution leaving Algeria part of France. The Constitution was supported not only by the French Algerians but also by a majority of the Muslims in Algeria. However, deGaulle abandoned the Constitution and in September 1959 concluded inaccurately that the FLN was winning the Civil War. He thus proposed self-determination, that Algeria would determine its future through the ballot box.

This turnaround and the increasing likelihood that the rebels would assume power led the French Algerians to rebel against deGaulle in April 1960. Four French generals in Algeria organized an uprising against deGaulle. They created a secret armed terrorist organization, the *Secret Army Organization (OAS)*. The insurrection disintegrated when most military units remained loyal to deGaulle.

Negotiations began at Evian in France in May 1960. The negotiations dragged out for almost two years, while FLN terrorism did not let up. However, the end was in sight. In March 1962, the *Evian Accords* were signed. The agreement called for a cease fire, recognized the FLN as the sole legal government of Algeria, promised independence after a brief transition, guaranteed freedom and property rights for the Europeans, and permitted France to retain strategic naval bases and other military installations in Algeria. The OAS conducted a terrorist campaign whose purpose was to sabotage the accords. The FLN intensified terrorist acts as well. Finally on July 1, 1962, an Algerian referendum confirmed Algerian independence. The Civil War brought independence to Algeria, along with economic devastation and the transformation of the Algerian community.

3. Ideology of Violence/Mythology of National Liberation

The Civil War left a deep imprint on the psyche and values of the Algerians. Civil War ideology had three components.

First, violence was viewed as a legitimate and necessary function of the state. Violence had defeated the French Algerians and forced deGaulle to accept Algerian independence, so it was claimed. Violence required secrecy and total obedience to authority, thus promoting political authoritarianism.

Second, victory over the French after almost 125 years of French rule legitimized single-party rule and the infallibility of the FLN. Similarly to the Chinese

Communists (see Chapter Four), the FLN activists just knew they were invincible and infallible. Historians describe this as a mythology of revolution.

Finally, the war produced the idea of national unity based on *Algerianity/ Algerianess,* Islam, and the Arabic language. Thus uniformity of belief and the creation of a homogeneous society became goals of the new government.

4. Economic Costs of the War

The Civil War also produced huge demographic and economic losses. It had a devastating impact, especially on the more modern sector of the Algerian economy.

Demographic losses were huge. Approximately 10 percent of the entire population died, while half a million Muslims fled to nearby countries. By the time the war had ended, almost all of the 1.5 million Europeans had migrated to Europe. Many Muslims left the countryside and crowded into the cities, which were unprepared for them in terms of housing, infrastructure, and employment. Most of the educated population and most of those with administrative, technical skills left the country, making economic development difficult.

Property damage was tremendous. Oran, the second largest city and the major center of French culture, was almost totally destroyed. The costs of reconstruction provided jobs and produced economic growth. However the capital, materials, and labor used for reconstruction were just not available for economic development. Algeria, thus, entered the era of independence in economic shambles. Only the discovery of large oil and gas reserves during the war provided some economic potential.

5. Revolutionary Women

The Civil War provided women with an opportunity for activity outside the home and loosened the bonds of patriarchy.

Women played a very important role in the ALN during the civil war, acting as runners and intelligence operatives. They were able to act with greater freedom than men were, since all Muslim males were automatically suspected of being members of the ALN. In this way, women acquired much greater independence. They also played an important economic role, especially in agriculture, with many men away in the ALN. The large number of deaths affected mothers and wives, giving women greater freedom because the patriarchal male of the family was interned or killed. The war shifted the demographic balance, leaving a much larger female than male population. This affected family creation in a society in which everyone was expected to marry. After the war, women quickly were "returned to their apartments," again subordinate to males.

6. Creation of a New, All-Muslim Community

The Civil War reduced Algeria's diversity, though the new degree of community was much less than the new government wished.

Obviously the departure of most Europeans left Algeria a Muslim community. However, wartime unity based on the need to achieve a common objective of national independence through warfare was a fragile one. Within the Muslim community three splits were patched over and set aside during the war. The conflict between Arabs and Berbers, differences between those who had strong French cultural ties and those who did not, and differences among the Muslims became quite apparent after independence.

D. AN INDEPENDENT, RADICAL ALGERIA, 1962–1988

Independence brought to power the leaders of the wartime FLN and ALN. Intense political conflict was a constant, as various factions within the FLN vied for control. Authoritarian rule, more dictatorial than that of the French, characterized the FLN. The military played a central role throughout. Their support was essential for every government. The new leaders sought to achieve contradictory goals, most clearly evident in the area of ideology, where socialism, Arabism, and Islamicization vied for domination, while French culture remained a powerful motive force. The government introduced socialism, including state planning, nationalization of industry, and collectivization. Tremendous wealth generated by oil and gas masked the failings of Algerian socialism. Patriarchy was reconfirmed, especially due to the greater power of Islam and the weakening of French culture. The effort to create a united Algeria with a single non-French culture floundered because of resistance to Arabic replacing French as the predominant language, Berber opposition to Arabization, and the lack of a national consensus on politics and economics.

1. Algeria and the World

For the first time in a century, Algeria had the ability to define its relationship with the rest of the world. Algeria played a relatively important role in global politics from independence into the 1980s, in spite of its relatively small population. The revolutionary aura surrounding the victory over the colonial power, France, as well as the increased importance of Muslim states in general, gave Algeria a basis for exerting broad influence beyond its borders.

Non-alignment and National Liberation. During the first three decades of independence, Algeria supported rebellion against colonialism and imperialism. Algeria implemented this policy primarily through support for the Palestine Liberation Organization, which was headquartered in Algiers for much of the period. Ahmed Ben Bella (president, 1962–1965) supported terrorist revolutionary groups. His successor, Houari Boumedienne (1965–1978), talked about a New World Economic Order no longer dominated by the West. Algeria also gave military support to Egypt during the Arab-Israeli War of 1967. Boumedienne and his successor, Benjedid Chadli, believed that Palestinian independence could be achieved only through the use of terrorism, which would finally break Israel's hold over Palestinian lands. Algeria also played a leading role in the non-aligned movement (see Chapter Two for India's role in this). In the 1976 National Charter, Algeria pledged its support to third-world nations. Algeria severed diplomatic relations with Egypt in 1978 after Egypt and Israel signed the Camp David Agreement, which provided for peace between the two countries and transferred small amounts of Israeli-held land to the Palestinians. Algeria also offered support to a number of other national liberation movements in Africa. It aided Khomeini in his campaign to drive the Shah of Iran from power.

The Maghreb. After Ben Bella, Algeria focused its attention on the Maghreb (Northwest Africa) and the Arab world. In the 1960s Algeria supported the idea of a Greater Arab Maghreb, which would have a common religion—Islam—and a common language—Arabic. However, Morocco, Tunisia, and Algeria found it difficult to surrender autonomy to a broader political structure.

Algeria, Morocco, and the Western Sahara. Algeria shifted back and forth between friendship with its neighbors and conflict with them. This is especially true of Algeria's relationship with Morocco. In 1963, Algeria and Morocco clashed over definitions of their common border, especially after the area claimed by Morocco turned out to be rich in iron deposits.

Both Algeria and Morocco sought to control the Western Sahara. In 1975, Morocco occupied the Western Sahara, formerly a Spanish colony. Algeria feared this would enable Morocco to become the dominant Maghrebian state. In addition, Algeria did not want a strong neighbor on its southwestern border. At first Boumedienne supported the Polisario Front, the Sahrawi (Saharan) separationist movement. In 1976, Moroccan and Algerian troops clashed at the border. Algeria recognized the anti-Moroccan Saharan Arab Democratic Republic government in exile and hosted it in Algeria. Algeria broke diplomatic relations with Morocco and threatened war, then backed down.

Relations worsened again in the mid-1980s after Algeria and Tunisia signed a treaty of alliance. Morocco then aligned with Libya. In response Algeria stepped up its support for Polisario. By the late 1980s, Algeria was preoccupied with domestic economic problems, while Morocco was much stronger than earlier. Algeria backed away from a policy of confrontation with its western neighbor.

Algeria and France. Even though Algeria had fought a bloody Civil War to gain independence from France, the latter remained very important to Algeria. France and Algeria forged a special economic relationship. DeGaulle gave preferential treatment to Algeria, including loans and technical assistance, as a way of offsetting the economic losses resulting from French re-emigration to France. Over one and a half million Algerians also settled in France. Ben Bella signed a fifteen-year oil production agreement. Algeria remained culturally dependent upon France and refrained from attacking French imperialism.

Algerian-French relations deteriorated when Algeria turned to socialism and nationalized the oil industry, much of which had been French-owned. Though the French retained minority ownership, they withdrew technical support for the Algerian oil industry, the central engine for the economy. At the same time, the French changed their strategy toward the Maghreb, concluding that France would benefit from treating Algeria, Tunisia, and Morocco equally, rather than showing favoritism toward Algeria. When socialist Francois Mitterand became French president, he returned to the earlier approach of a special relationship with Algeria.

The Super Powers. The super powers, the Soviet Union and the United States, were less important to Algeria. During this period Algeria was officially non-aligned but actually pro-Communist. Ben Bella promoted close economic ties with the Soviets. Boumedienne combined sharp public rhetoric in favor of the Soviet bloc with little actual support. In the 1970s, the Soviets provided military and technical aid, thus bringing the two nations closer together. Chadli moved away from a pro-Soviet position, in part because of concerns about the poor quality of Soviet military assistance.

The United States was seen as the main symbol of imperialism, but the two countries had little contact. During the Arab-Israeli War of 1967, Algeria broke diplomatic relations with the United States. Anti-American propaganda in the 1970s and 1980s was accompanied by increasingly important economic ties. Diplomatic ties were renewed in 1974 and the Algerians played an important role in the release of the American hostages in Iran in the early 1980s.

2. One-Party, Military Rule

Algeria was dominated politically by the FLN, with the army playing an important role behind the scenes. Political factionalism and conflict were endemic in the Algerian political system. Conflicts were based on power as well as policy.

Ben Bella, 1962–1965. Ahmed Ben Bella became the first president of independent Algeria. Facing huge challenges, he sought to consolidate his power in a one-man dictatorship. Ben Bella cleverly outmaneuvered two rivals, including Houari Boumedienne. Unrest in the military almost led to a civil war among rival factions. Algerian society was deeply divided, with a minority of Algerians remaining pro-French and the Berbers, especially the Kabyle, opposed to a centralized government.

A constitution provided Ben Bella with some legal legitimacy. According to the Constitution, Algeria was to be a one-party (the National Liberation Front), socialist state with Arabic as the state language and Islam as the state religion. Ben Bella personally appointed most members of the legislative body, the National Assembly. It then selected Ferhat Abbas as President and Ben Bella as Prime Minister. Ben Bella soon forced the resignation of Abbas. Real power was located in the FLN and its leading body, the Politburo, not in the formal institutions of government.

Ben Bella's power was threatened by a series of rebellions in 1964 centered in the Kabyle area. The Front of Socialist Forces, led by Hocine Ait Ahmed, led the opposition to Ben Bella. In 1965, Boumedienne and his supporters arrested and imprisoned Ben Bella when he tried to bring the Front of Socialist Forces into his government.

Ben Bella outlined his objectives in the 1964 Charter of Algiers. Algeria was to be a socialist state, with the economy organized around principles of workers' self-management. Modern Standard Arabic, rather than the Algerian Arabic dialect, would be the official language. Those who were not completely loyal to the goals of the Charter, and thus the dictatorship of Ben Bella, were to be purged from the FLN. Ben Bella, thus, spent most of his time and energy attempting to eliminate opposition and increase his power. He paid little attention to the problems facing his country.

Boumedienne, 1965–1978. Boumedienne, too, devoted much energy to consolidating his power. He assumed the positions of President, Prime Minister and Minister of Defense. However, he also recognized the need to work with the various factions rather than try to ride roughshod over them. Still he had to deal with unrest in Kabylia and the attempt by a socialist group within the military to overthrow him. Boumedienne was also wounded in an assassination attempt.

Boumedienne emphasized the need to develop a new post-French system of local government. Discussions and rather broad input led, with much delay, to the National Charter of 1976. The Charter guaranteed civil rights and ownership of private property that would not be used to exploit others. The National Assembly was to be chosen by universal suffrage, with candidates selected by the FLN. Since the number of nominees was to be three times the size of the Assembly, voters would have some choice. The National Assembly would nominate the president, who would be approved by a national referendum.

Boumedienne implemented policy in two major areas—cultural change and economic transformation. Arabization was a major goal. This meant transforming the elite into Arab-speakers rather than French-speakers and using Arabic in education, government, and the media. French was to be downgraded and Berber was not to rise to the position of a national language. Algerian nationalism was to be emphasized by idealizing the war of liberation and by promoting a sense of Algerian identity.

He launched an agricultural revolution, introducing collectivization. Using oil and gas revenues, Boumedienne promoted industrialization. Nationalization of industry, especially oil and gas, showed his commitment to socialism. He also built up his own position by demonstrating his ability to defend Algerian interest against imperialists.

During the Boumedienne regime, the military, with its leaders drawn from those officers trained in France, gained strength. Bureaucrats and technocrats, most of them French-speakers, became increasingly important in the FLN and in the government.

By the time Boumedienne died of a rare blood disease in 1978, Algeria appeared to have achieved his goals—Arabization and modernization. However, the radical changes he introduced produced cracks in Algerian unity and unrest surfaced soon after his death.

Chadli Bendjedid, 1979–1988. Chadli Bendjedid sought to achieve two contradictory goals—economic and political liberalization and preservation of his and the FLN's dominant role in Algeria. (Mikhail Gorbachev faced similar problems in Russia. See Chapter One.) Political liberalization provided an opportunity for Islamic fundamentalist political power to emerge, while economic liberalization clashed with Islamic fundamentalist tenets. Chadli, the highest-ranking officer in the army, was a compromise candidate. He recognized the need to work with the factions, while consolidating his own personal power and strengthening his support within the military and the FLN. Chadli slowly moved toward political liberalization. He understood that the FLN could no longer act independently of society, since its role as the group that brought independence to Algeria was now like a thread-bare coat. Some two-thirds of the population had been born after the War of Liberation. Many people would not support the FLN just because it had "made the revolution." (The same thing happened to the Soviet Communist Party only much more slowly.)

Chadli pursued Islamic and Arabic fundamentalism, at a time when minorities were becoming more and more active politically. He also sought to transform state socialism and move toward a market economy. Unfortunately, the state socialist economy began to falter and oil and gas income declined in the 1980s.

Thus Chadli's efforts to introduce significant changes in a society that was losing faith in his political leadership produced minority unrest and the rise of Islamic fundamentalist militancy. The crisis began in 1988 and continued to the end of the century. Ideological conflict became more and more apparent in this period, as Chadli pushed the Arabization-Islamicization agenda of Boumedienne.

3. Clash of Ideologies

The leaders of the FLN had tried to establish an Algerian identity that would replace the divided identities of the French colonial period. They created a mythology of national liberation. At the same time they espoused contradictory ideals. Arabization and Islamicization can be seen as traditionalist and native ideologies. Socialism and nationalism represented modernist, outside sets of ideas. Traditionalism and modernism were like particles suspended in a potion of revolutionary victory. The mixture was ultimately explosive.

Mythology of National Liberation. Algerian nationalism acquired its final form through the idealization of the war of liberation. The mythology portrayed the war of liberation as the central event in Algerian history. Independence resulted from the efforts of the Army of National Liberation, the FLN claimed. The army thus embodied the ideals of Algeria and created a single identity—Algerian nationalism. National goals thus could be achieved through violence and by supporting the FLN. FLN heroism was seen as capable of achieving every goal possible (see Chapter Four for the Chinese Communist emphasis on the role of will that emerged from the Long March experience).

Modernizing State Socialism. If nationalism looked to the recent past, state socialism was seen as the means of achieving the future—a modern Algeria. The Stalinist model deeply influenced Algerian socialism but the Algerians also recognized the significance of the modifications introduced in Indian state planning. Algerian leaders also had to take into consideration the spontaneous actions of the lower classes. Algerian socialism included nationalization of industry, collectivization of agriculture, and long-range state planning. In addition, it also included the idea of worker self-management. Workers were initially seen as capable of providing enterprise-level managerial and decision-making skills. Yugoslavia provided Algeria with a model for worker self-management.

From Authoritarianism toward Pluralism. Algerian leaders saw authoritarianism as the appropriate form of governance for Algeria. Both the French colonial experience and Islam provided support for authoritarian rule. Strong political leadership was seen as essential to the modernization of Algeria and the creation of a single national identity. A kind of paternalism was at work as well. The Algerian people, so it was believed, were not ready for any political system except authoritarianism.

Yet there was also a minor key in the political tune—support for pluralism or democracy. Democratic ideals were espoused primarily by the left wing of FLN, still strongly influenced by French values, and by the Berbers, especially the Kabyle. Chadli initiated the shift away from authoritarianism and tentatively toward pluralism. He sought to build a broader base in order to strengthen his position. Most supporters of pluralism saw democracy as a way of defending minority rights.

Arabization. *Arabization* was based on the assumption, not terribly accurate, that Algeria had been an integral part of the Arab world, from the Arab conquest on. However, the French occupation and the French colonial period had severed Algeria's close ties with the rest of the Arabic world, it was believed. Now that Algeria was independent, it again must become part of the Arab world. To achieve this, Algeria needed to support the Arab cause in the Middle East and transform Algerian culture into an Arabic one. The main means of doing this was Arabization—making Arabic the language of business, government, education, and culture. The government decided that Modern Standard Arabic, not Algerian Arabic, should be the state language. Thus identity with the Arab world superceded the creation of an Algerian national identity. Support for Arabization emerged slowly but accelerated in the 1970s and 1980s.

Islamism. *Islamism,* too, was based on questionable assumptions about the Algerian past. True, most Algerians had converted to Islam before the year 1000 but Algerian Muslims were not especially traditionalist in perspective. Algerian Islam contained a number of competing sects with different interpretations of Muslim truths. Islamism sought to reestablish a culture of traditionalist Islam, initially in reaction to the increasing influence of secular French thought.

Though some Islamic theologians emphasized a traditionalist approach, into the 1980s secular and leftist bureaucrats dominated government action. In the 1960s, Islamism revived, centered in the journal *al-Qiyam (Values)*. The Islamists argued that colonialism had brought forth decadence. Now it was time to return to Islamic law. In the 1970s, an Islamist alternative emerged to challenge Boumedienne who tried to please both the modernizers and Islamic traditionalists.

The traditionalists built upon predecessors from the colonial period. In 1974, Abdellatif Soltani condemned the Boumedienne government for using Western systems of thought including socialism, liberalism, and toleration. Instead, Algeria should function through a literal interpretation of the *Qu'ran* and *hadith.* The National Charter of 1976 reiterated that Islam was the state religion of Algeria. The question, of course, was what should be the nature of Algerian Islam.

A partial answer came from the *battle of the mosques.* From the beginning of the Chadli period the mosques (Muslim places of worship) became a center for the discussion of political issues. Going beyond political discussion, that is condemnation of Westernism and modernization, Ben Bella established the Movement for a Democratic Algeria, which supported Islamism. Ben Bella thus suggested that if traditionalist Islam was to achieve its goals, it needed to become a political movement and not just a religious one. Islamists began to coalesce around three key figures, Soltani, Ahmed Sahnoun, and Abassi Madani. They condemned Western influence and attacked socialism as sinful. They espoused Islamic economics and attacked the consumption of alcohol and the liberation of women. Islamism became the most powerful idea during the Second Civil War, 1988–1999.

Berberism. The Kabyle intelligentsia sought to combine support for Westernism and French culture with idealization of traditional Berber life. Political pluralism and political decentralization, they argued, were necessary to preserve Berber culture. Berberism appealed to a majority of the Berbers but had little broader impact.

4. Economic Revolution, Oil, and Poverty

The government of Algeria sought to transform the Algerian economy from a capitalist one integrated into the French economy into an autonomous, socialist economy. Algeria began independence facing serious economic problems, including an unemployment rate of 45 percent, the departure of most of its technical personnel and the loss of French markets. The annual growth rate peaked at almost 10 percent in the years 1979–1984. At the same time the unemployment rate ranged from 17–22 percent and the foreign debt increased. When not even huge oil revenues could reduce poverty, Chadli explored the alternative of moving toward a market economy. This change promoted unrest and rebellion, though during the Second Civil War Algeria's leaders continued to move toward capitalism.

State Socialism. After some debate about what the economy should be like, Algerian leaders decided on *state socialism.* State socialism had four major components. First, the government transformed workers' self-management into centralized planning. Second, authorities nationalized finance, transportation, industry, and especially hydrocarbons (oil and gas). Third, the government introduced a plan for rapid industrialization. Finally, it initiated a form of collectivized agriculture.

State Planning. Initially independent Algeria seemed to be moving toward a system of decentralized decision-making. Many enterprises were taken over by workers during the Civil War, especially when management and technical personnel fled to France. The *March Decree* (1963) legalized self-management—that is worker seizure of factories and enterprises that had belonged to the French government or colonials. However, very quickly the government reduced the independence of these workers' self-management groups.

State planners developed a series of long-range plans, beginning with the First Four-Year Plan (see Chapters One and Two for other descriptions of long-range planning models). The first plan (1970–1973) emphasized the oil and gas industry and put little investment into agriculture and infrastructure. In addition the plan sought to shift industry inland, since it had previously been concentrated along the coast. The First Four-Year Plan led to an increase in oil and gas production. However, the neglect of agriculture forced the government to import food, thus diverting capital. In addition, authorities failed to achieve their goal of creating industrial sectors in the interior. Other plans, including the Second Four-Year Plan, maintained the emphasis on the oil and gas industry and other industrial developments to the neglect of agriculture and social services.

Nationalization. Enterprises abandoned by their French owners and those owned by the French government in Algeria were easily nationalized. Nationalization was most common in the late 1960s, when mining, manufacturing, insurance, the oil and gas industry, and agriculture were nationalized. The large French petrochemicals firm, Sonantrach, was taken over by the government in 1971. Nationalization gave the government access to the revenues from hydrocarbons but also meant that the government absorbed losses produced by inefficient manufacturing firms. Nationalization was an essential component of state planning but required a large and costly bureaucracy. Nationalization made possible the rapid industrialization drive.

Rapid Industrialization. Once Boumedienne came to power, Algeria embarked upon a program of rapid, large-scale industrialization. Its goal was to be self-sufficient by 1990. Thus rapid industrialization was a strategy of *import substitution.* Rapid industrialization produced much larger industrial capacity, which only gradually began to pay off. The quality of production was rather low, since Algeria lacked the managerial and technical expertise to successfully carry out rapid industrialization.

Priority was given to heavy industry, using the slogan *industrializing industries.* Metallurgy, chemicals, and heavy machinery were emphasized. Algerian leaders assumed that the development of heavy industry would create the basis for light industry. Since light industry was more labor intensive and heavy industry more capital intensive, it was assumed that the future expansion of light industry would absorb the excess rural population flooding into the cities. The government assumed that revenues from oil and gas would provide sufficient capital to pay for rapid industrialization. In spite of increases in refinery capacity, Algeria was forced to borrow large amounts of money abroad.

Collectivization. When the FLN came to power in 1962, agriculture consisted of two components. Relatively large and productive farms, once owned by Europeans, were taken over by the state. These new state farms had large personnel staffs that had little familiarity with agriculture. The farm workers were not very productive. They had little incentive to work hard or well, since they had traded the old French master for the new Algerian bureaucratic boss. At the same time about 75 percent of the land was worked by small farmers. Their soil was of poor quality, their farm techniques out of date, and their income too small to permit investment in agriculture. By the end of the Ben Bella regime, Algeria imported almost one-third of its food. Something had to be done.

After several years of planning, Boumedienne introduced an *agrarian revolution.* He nationalized public lands, lands formerly owned by Europeans, communal land, and tribal lands. They were redistributed to poor peasants in seven- to ten-acre plots. The land remained state property. These peasants were required to "rent" equipment from Agricultural Productive Cooperatives of the

Agrarian Revolution. (This system followed the Chinese Communist model for the introduction of collectivization. See Chapter Four.)

During the second stage, 1973–1975, the state partially nationalized and redistributed Algerian-owned large holdings. The government established 6,000 model agricultural cooperatives (collective farms). Some land was collectivized and turned over to FLN activist-managers, who had little rapport with the peasants. Wealthy farmers avoided nationalization by dividing up their land and giving it to family members in plots below the minimum acreage for nationalization. Parallel to the actions of Soviet peasants during collectivization, farmers protested by slaughtering livestock and destroying citrus groves.

Collectivization did not create a more productive agriculture, primarily because of the lack of trained managers and agronomists, low levels of state investment and resistance from the peasants. Nor did collectivization produce greater rural equality.

Efforts to transform the Algerian economy into a socialist one did not create a viable economy. By the end of the Boumedienne period the economy was stagnating. If socialism didn't seem to be able to achieve the government's goals, so Chadli concluded, perhaps a move toward a market economy would be more successful.

Economic Liberalization. Algeria's economic problems were so great that the 1980s are called the *Black Decade.* A special task force analyzed the problem and produced *Les Cahiers de la Reforme* (*Reform Registers*). The group concluded that the command economy was not working. It proposed that Algeria turn to private enterprise and replace state planning with decentralized decision-making. Economic reform, the movement away from socialism, met much resistance on ideological grounds. There appeared to be, however, no alternative to economic reform.

In 1980, Chadli introduced a new First Five-Year Plan, emphasizing investment in agriculture, consumer goods industries, and social infrastructure. He implemented the plan at a time when oil and gas revenues were declining sharply. Chadli divided the state oil monopoly, Sonantrach, into thirteen companies and dissolved 70,000 state farms, transferring the land to private farmers. In 1987, the government abolished the collective farms, turning the land over to groups of two to three families each. These changes in the structure of agriculture led to an increase in food production. In 1987, Chadli gave public sector enterprises control over decision making. At the same time, new huge structures, which were really trusts, assumed responsibility for up to 200 firms each. Reflecting its powerful role in the economy, the government ordered each trust to be profitable, locate sources of raw materials, and find markets for finished productions. Two-thirds of state firms thus acquired autonomy. In 1988, the National Planning Council replaced the Ministry of Planning, thus downgrading the significance of centralized planning. The state retained ownership of industry, so de-nationalization did not occur. The Chadli reforms paralleled the perestroika reforms of Gorbachev (see Chapter One).

Chadli's efforts to restructure the economy, especially in moving toward enterprise decision-making and private ownership and management of farmland came too late to halt economic decline. The reforms also alienated a large number of FLN bureaucrats and state officials and led to serious protests in the late 1980s.

Persistence of Poverty and the Emergence of Protest. Poverty remained a serious problem. The population continued to grow much faster than job creation. State control over the economy had produced low levels of productivity. It was thus impossible to raise the living standards of ordinary Algerians.

A violent society since the end of the Second World War, Algeria was never free of social and political unrest. The number of industrial strikes increased from 22 in 1969 to 500 in 1977. Unrest accelerated in the mid-1980s, in part because of rising expectations. In 1985, massive demonstrations protested terrible housing conditions. In the following year strikes and protests broke out in most major cities and continued into 1988. This all culminated in the October Days of 1988, which eventually led to the destruction of much of the structure of rule created at the beginning of independence.

From Equality to Class Differences. With the exit of most Europeans during or right after the war of independence, Algeria was left essentially with a single social class—a lower class. The differences between urban and rural were minimal. Only a tiny French-educated Algerian elite and the leaders of the FLN can be seen as an upper class.

Over time, clear social differences emerged, based on privilege and access to scarce resources. A "*new class*" emerged, parallel to the Soviet Union's bureaucratic/party elite. The intelligentsia grew in size as well and formed a middle class that also included the new technocratic-managerial personnel. Increasing differences in wealth enabled a small minority of Algerians to live a European-style way of life, with European cars, villas, and French fashions. The sons and daughters of this wealthy group came to be known as "chichis." With rapid industrialization, an industrial working class emerged that was urban and increasingly differentiated from the farm workers, who became state employees rather than farm owners, at least until late in this period. At the bottom of society were the day workers and the large number of unemployed.

State socialism produced significant economic growth. However, low productivity, low quality, and high cost hampered the economy. Increasingly, economic problems and social inequality combined to produce high levels of protest. If the leaders sought to move forward in terms of economic development, they tried to turn backward in family policy and the definition of gender roles.

5. Return to Patriarchy

Though women had played a very important role in the War of Liberation, after the war the government and Islamic activists pushed for male domination and the renewed seclusion of women in the home. Ironically, independence brought a return to traditional beliefs.

Gender. Gender attitudes and the nature of the family derived from Islamic religious beliefs, especially the *Qu'ran* and were interpreted by *hadith* in a restrictive fashion. They were further narrowed by Islamic fundamentalism. Though men and women were equal before God, they had different rights and responsibilities due to biological differences.

Women were expected to remain in the home, with work outside the house acceptable only on a temporary basis. However, industrialization and the expansion of bureaucracy meant that women had opportunities to go into the workforce and they took advantage of those opportunities. Women were pressured to wear the veil when they went out in public. In the early 1960s, Islamists began to campaign against "immodestly dressed women." According to the *Qu'ran,* only women in Muhammad's family were to be isolated and required to wear the veil in public. *Hadith* extended this to all women, arguing that the covering of women with cloth was an act of love and obedience to *Allah.* Women were to confine themselves to the private space of the home, where their primary function was to bear children and raise them properly.

Boumedienne introduced modest improvements in the position of women, including greater political rights and social freedom. Islamists had hoped that Boumedienne would place greater limitations on women and reinforce patriarchy.

The family was the basic social institution in Algeria and marriage the norm for almost all Algerians. The *Family Code of 1984* regulated marriage and the family and was closely patterned after the *Qu'ran* and *hadith.* Families were patriarchal and patrilocal. The patriarch made all important decisions. Women were dominated by men—first by their fathers and then by their husbands. In public men and women led separate lives; in private, their lives intersected. The ideal was for women to remain secluded in the household, focusing their energies on domestic family responsibilities.

The extended family continued in the rural areas and remote interior. In the cities the nuclear family (husband, wife, and unmarried children) became quite common. This change resulted from urbanization, education, and greater opportunities for women in wage labor. Marriages were less frequently arranged than in the past and in the cities delayed marriage became common. In 1966, women married at eighteen (the minimum age for marriage) and men at twenty-four (the legal minimum was twenty-one); in 1986, the average age of marriage for women was twenty-four and for men twenty-seven. Late marriage resulted primarily from greater opportunities to stay in school and from urban poverty, which meant that few people could afford to marry early. Except in some Berber areas of southern Algeria, monogamy was almost universal.

The birth rate, and thus family size, remained high until the 1990s. As late as 1986, on average Algerian women gave birth to six children. Until the 1980s the government believed the country was underpopulated, a consequence of the loss of life during the war of independence, the emigration of Europeans, and later the wage emigration of more than a million Algerians. Thus, they argued, government should encourage a high birth rate. In the 1980s, however, the government introduced a program of *birth spacing* (increasing the time between pregnancies) and made contraceptives available. In addition, the birth rate was reduced by 25 percent by delaying marriage and by women not having children as late in life as previously.

Economic opportunities for women were limited by the emphasis on privacy and isolation. Islamist pressure to maintain women in traditional roles limited the employment of women. Approximately 7 percent of the urban workforce was female. However, in the countryside women worked in the fields as well as in the household. Economic needs as well as the assumption that the woman was still isolated led to this.

Since independence, women have been increasingly silenced politically. The *Tripoli Charter* of 1962 guaranteed political and civil rights to women. The residue of revolutionary valor combined with socialist ideas to briefly sustain political rights for women. A few women were elected to the relatively powerless National Assembly, while the FLN front organization, the *Women's National Union,* sought to ensure the loyalty of women to the FLN. Though women had the right to vote, until the late 1980s the male family head cast the vote for all members of the household. Generally excluded from the political process (as were most males until the late 1980s), women attempted to apply pressure on the government through demonstrations. During the years 1980–1984 women protested against proposed restrictions that were eventually put into the Family Code of 1984. Their demonstrations slowed down the process but did not prevent the eventual promulgation of the Family Code.

Women played a very prominent role in Algerian culture. Their efforts aroused considerable opposition since they invaded the traditional male bastion of culture-creation. Women found it difficult to publish and women writers were publicly harassed. Leading female intellectuals and writers, including Assia *Djebar,* Leila Sebbar, and Nina Bouraoui, generally went into exile in France and published in French.

6. Conformity and Resistance

At independence Algeria was essentially a new country. The Europeans had fled and massive population movement had occurred. The new leaders of Algeria, influenced by the kind of psychological unity they had experienced in the Civil War, sought to create a singe, unified, cohesive Algeria. However, Algeria was a multicultural society, which made unity quite difficult. The FLN sought to create harmony on the basis of a common ideology, language, religion, and cultural/ethnic identity. Socialism was expected to provide a single socioeconomic structure. The FLN was to be the only political force, thus eliminating divisive political conflict. *Modern Standard Arabic* was to replace French as the national language. Islam was to be the state religion. Algerians were to identify with the Arabic world.

Eliminating French Culture. Algerian leaders agreed that it was essential to reject French culture and language, since it was the language and culture of "imperialist oppressors." The French had departed but they had left behind a culture hard to erase. French was the language of government and of culture. The officer class was French-trained, while managers, engineers, and technicians functioned in French. Education was conducted in French and the curriculum was designed to create French citizens. Thus one of the tasks of the new leaders was to eliminate French cultural and linguistic influence. This was slow work.

Creating a New Culture. The leaders of independent Algeria sought to create a new culture that would have nothing in common with colonial culture. This involved an emphasis on the use of Arabic, confirmation of the primacy of Islam, and identification with the "Arabs."

Modern Standard Arabic. Ben Bella decided that Modern Standard Arabic should be the official language of Algeria (see Chapter Five for the issue of language and identity in South Africa). Boumedienne tried to minimize the use of French and also encouraged the use of Modern Standard Arabic. The decision to use modern Standard Arabic as the national language, rather than the Algerian Arabic dialect, posed significant problems. Most Algerians spoke Algerian Arabic and not Modern Standard Arabic, which was based on classical Arabic. Arabic-speaking teachers had to be brought in from Egypt and other countries to teach Modern Standard Arabic. Not enough teachers were available and their efforts were not very successful. French continued to be the language of the educated Algerians and the language for social mobility.

Chadli increased pressure for the compulsory use of Modern Standard Arabic. Proponents of Arabization replaced moderates in the Ministries of Information and Education. The government prohibited courts from operating in French. They ordered radio stations and newspapers to use only Arabic. Efforts were made to ban the use of French in the government. Algerian Arabic and the Berber languages were to be confined to the home. Student protests at the University of Algiers in 1979 and the rise of Islamic conservatism pushed Chadli to Arabization.

Islam. With the retreat of the Europeans, almost all Algerians were Muslims. Thus it was natural and quite easy for the government to declare Algeria an Islamic State. At the same time, the government did not wish to be hampered by the ideas of Muslim leaders. Algerian Muslims were Sunni, the variant without a highly structured priesthood. Ben Bella tried to use the main Muslim journal, *Values,* in religious education activities in the schools. By the mid-1960s, Boumedienne had concluded that *Values* and other Muslim religious publications and organizations were a threat to his desire to transform Algeria into a secular state, motivated by nationalism and patriotism, not by religious faith. In the 1970s, he faced increased pressure from Muslim leaders. In response, the National Charter of 1976 designated Islam as the state religion. Religious influence increased under Chadli, eventually leading to Islamist fundamentalism and the idea that Algeria should be a theocracy (religious state).

In the 1980s, the Islamists, those who wished Algeria to be a religion-dominated state, were disorganized and lacked leaders with a national stature. Responding to the emergence of Islamic fundamentalism at the University of Algiers, Chadli accepted part of the Islamist program, as reflected in the 1984 Family Code. Eventually the *Front for Islamic Salvation (FIS)* offered an alternative vision of how to create community in a fragmented society—through religious conformity.

Arabization. Most problematically, the government carried out an Arabization campaign, arguing that Algeria was an integral part of the Arabic world and that Algerians were Arabs. Boumedienne believed that Islamization and Arabization could not be separated and that each reinforced the other. In reality the non-Berber Algerians were of mixed ethnicity and generally did not view themselves as Arabs. The emphasis on Arabization created a conflict between Algerian identity and a kind of Pan-Arabism. Thus Arabization made it more difficult to achieve community. The Berbers especially resented the idea of Arab-based nationalism.

Kabylia and Berberism. The Berbers were found in the interior of Algeria but consisted of distinct peoples, including the Kabyle, the Chaouia, and the M-zabite. The Berbers in general, and especially the Kabyle, opposed Arabization in terms of language and Arab nationalism. The Kabyle had played an important role far greater than their numbers would suggest. As a minority they concluded that by associating themselves with French culture, they would, ironically, secure the best chance for social advancement and preservation of Kabyle culture. The Kabyle were, thus, the most westernized Algerians, and Kabyle intelligentsia were quite familiar with Western political ideals. The Kabyle formed much of the Algerian intelligentsia and played an important role in administration and business. Many of the most important Algerian authors were Kabyle. Most Berbers sought cultural autonomy; only a small minority wanted an independent Berber kingdom.

1960s. Cultural Programs. In the 1960s, the Kabyle pushed for recognition of *Tamazigh* (the Berber written language) as a state language. Their requests were denied. Tamazigh was written in the Latin script. Amazigh was the name for the oral dialect. In the 1960s, the Kabyle established a number of cultural organizations that promoted Kabyle ideals in France, since a large number of Algerian immigrants came from Berber communities. Ben Bella and Boumedienne rejected Berber demands for some measure of cultural autonomy, fearing that this would lead to an independence movement. The FLN also worried that it would be impossible to create a single national identity if it granted the Berbers some degree of cultural autonomy. The FLN group also argued that the Berbers were descendants of the Arabs, rather than the indigenous people of Algeria, whom the Arabs pushed into the interior.

The Kabyle sought to play an independent political role, too. Led by Hocine Ait Ahmed, the Kabyle formed the Front of Socialist Forces (FFS). In 1964, Ait Ahmed was arrested and sentenced to death for treason, defined as opposition to the FLN government. His arrest was a bitter blow to the Kabyle political and cultural movement.

The Kabyle turned to efforts at cultural survival. In 1968, a *Berber Cultural Movement* was formed for that purpose. The Berbers demanded political pluralism, opposed Arabization, and focused on language and cultural issues. Gradually the anti-government Kabyle coalesced around the Berber Cultural Movement. In the 1970s, the government's emphasis on Arabization had led to efforts to destroy Berber culture. In the mid-1970s Kabyle protested the plan to reduce the hours of Kabyle Radio. The government sentenced a number of Berbers to death or long prison terms for bombing the FLN's newspaper offices.

Tizi Ouzo Spring (March 1980). The *Tizi Ouzo Spring* was the first major Berber protest, for twenty years of repression had forced the Berbers into quiescence. The death of Boumedienne, a rabid anti-Berber, seemed to create an opportunity for the Berbers to push for cultural autonomy. Economic liberalization seemed to presage political pluralism. At the same time the Berber Cultural Movement grew in strength.

Tizi Ouzo, located in Kabylia, had the only French-language university in Algeria. The government banned a lecture by Mouloud *Mammeri,* a prominent Kabyle activist and a leading Algerian writer, even though the topic was seemingly apolitical, ancient Berber pottery. Students immediately rioted and held sit-in strikes. The unrest spread to the capital city Algiers, where security forces crushed street demonstrations. In mid-April Berber activists called a general strike in Tizi Ouzo. A sit-in strike spread from the university to hospitals and factories. At first security forces could not break up demonstrations, as students attacked government buildings. Eventually the military crushed the insurrection, killing over thirty, wounding 200, and arresting hundreds, including some activists in the Front for Socialist Forces.

The Chadli government's response was rather complex. In addition to repression, the government proposed concessions. It offered to create a chair of Kabyle Studies at the university in Tizi Ouzo and reestablish a chair in Berber Studies at the University of Algiers. Chadli also promised to set up a committee to review cultural policies but later withdrew the offer.

Protests continued into 1981, then dissipated. Kabyle leaders did not want to provoke another round of government repression. In 1981, the FLN prepared a Cultural Charter. The charter issued vague promises to recognize the popular cultural heritage of Algeria but made no specific mention of the Berbers. In response the Berber Cultural Movement called for a general strike to protest the Cultural Charter. Systematic repression followed, including arrests, denial of the right to travel abroad, and dismissal from jobs. Chadli, needing to consolidate his authority, gave strong support to Arabo-Islamicization. Yet, during the rest of the 1980s, a quiet emphasis on Berber culture and Tamazigh continued to ferment in Kabylia.

The Tizi Ouzo Spring did not yield immediate results. However it prepared the Kabyle to use insurrection against the government and to support Kabyle cultural autonomy and political pluralism.

Conclusion. Government resistance to recognizing the rights of minorities and its insistence on conformity led to Kabyle-initiated violence and made community more difficult to achieve. Cultural resistance was turning into political opposition.

E. SECOND CIVIL WAR, 1988–1999

The War of Liberation, or the First Civil War, was a bloody affair in which the key issue was whether Algeria should be independent. Riots in 1988 led to a constitutional crisis and to state and Islamist terrorism that resembled a Second Civil War. Algeria's relationship with the world revolved around foreign investments and how to halt the Civil War. Political liberalization under Chadli led toward what appeared to be a victory for the Islamists (conservative Muslims), whose influence had gradually increased during the 1980s. Support for the Islamists came more from those angry with the FLN government than from the ideas of Islamic fundamentalism. At this point the military seized power and cancelled upcoming elections. The Islamists responded with a campaign of terrorism. Military attacks against the Islamists increased the death toll, which overall totaled some 120,000. By the time of the 1997 elections the Civil War had begun to wind down. Open and relatively honest elections in 1999 moved Algeria toward a pluralist political system. During this decade Islamic fundamentalism established itself as the most powerful ideology, while the modernizing nationalism of the FLN lost all credibility. The minority Berbers espoused democracy most clearly. Economic liberalization continued, while the Civil War brought further damage to the economy. Islamic fundamentalism sought to use violence and intimidation to reinforce traditional patriarchy. The Islamists sought to create community through conformity to conservative Islam. Their efforts produced wounds that were difficult to heal. Algeria began to recover in the early years of the twenty-first century.

1. The Second Algerian Civil War and the World

Foreign policy, especially relations with France, the European Community, and the United States, revolved around the issue of Islamic fundamentalism and the Civil War. At the same time Morocco remained a thorny issue. As the power of the FLN disintegrated, it sought to reestablish its identity as a champion of the Third World against Western imperialists by supporting Iraq in the Gulf Crisis of 1990–1991. However, Algeria had less influence in world politics than at any time since independence.

Diplomacy of Civil War. More than any other country, France displayed concern about the Second Civil War. French interests were three-fold. France wanted to make sure that its economic interests in Algeria were safe. It also worried that the Civil War would spill over into France (as it did), where a million and a half Algerians lived. Finally, France saw an opportunity to reestablish its traditional influence over Algerian affairs.

Opposed to Algeria becoming an Islamic state, France feared that Islamic fundamentalism would sweep across the Middle East, destabilizing that area. The French provided large amounts of money to prop up the Chadli regime. After the Chadli government collapsed in 1992, the French generally supported military rule, even while publicly calling for an end to terrorism and a peaceful resolution of the crisis.

Just as the Civil War broke out, dramatic changes produced the collapse of Communism in Eastern Europe and a substantial decline in the power of Russia. A bi-polar world had been transformed into a new world system in which the United States was the only super-power. Therefore, American attitudes toward the Algerian crisis assumed great importance. The United States announced its support of pluralism and assumed a greater role as a customer for Algerian gas and oil. At the same time, the U.S. issued only a mild protest against the military takeover in 1992. Further, the United States was reluctant to criticize Algeria for violation of human rights. U.S. policy changed in 1994. From that point on, the United States put increasing pressure on the military government to negotiate with its political foes. The U.S. supported the *Sant' Egidio agreement,* which called for a negotiated settlement and Islamist participation in elections. The U.S. encouraged the elections of 1997 and 1999. However, Algeria was not very important to U.S. diplomatic strategy.

Morocco. Contacts with Morocco were generally strained. Improved relations led to a renewal of diplomatic ties in 1991. The Maghrebian states moved closer together in response, concerned about their economic futures because of the 1992 establishment of the European Community. However, the military coup again led to a worsening of relations, especially as the Civil War spilled over into Morocco. For example, in 1994, Algerians Islamists murdered Spanish tourists in Morocco. Morocco was deeply concerned about the spread of

Islamic fundamentalism into its country. Relations improved as the Civil War came to a close.

Third World Revolutionism. Independent Algeria had always been a strong supporter of anti-imperialist actions and especially as applied to the Middle East. Both major opponents in the Civil War, the FLN and the Islamists (Front for Islamic Salvation), supported Iraq, especially after the Gulf War opened. This decision isolated Algeria from all of the other Islamic countries in the Middle East with the exception of Libya.

Marginalization. The Second Civil War era left Algeria marginalized in world politics. Several factors help explain the weakening of Algerian global influence. Economic decline meant that the country could ill-afford to provide material support for anti-Western forces. Preoccupation with domestic events, primarily the Civil War, meant that Algeria had little opportunity to exercise broader influence.

External events were important, too. Rapprochement between the Palestinian Liberation Organization and Israel undercut Algeria's radical credentials. The revolutionary surge of the 1970s dissipated and the revolutionary overthrow of established governments seemed hardly likely to happen. Finally, the demise of Communism and the Soviet Union marked a dramatic shift in power. The Soviet Union could no longer promote anti-Western behavior. It certainly could not support such activity with military and financial assistance. Algeria thus could only play a significant role in the world if it carried out dramatic changes in the direction of its foreign policy, little changed since independence was achieved in 1962.

2. From One-Party Rule to Military Dictatorship, and Then Toward Democracy

The Civil War broke out in response to riots in October 1988. These riots represented and reinforced disillusionment with the FLN and its program. Political liberalization led to the mobilization of opposition, largely coordinated by Islamists or Berbers. The electoral conflict turned into military rule and then into a bloody civil war. Eventually the military decided to restore political liberalization. This meant reduced political influence for the military, open elections, and universal electoral participation. Ironically, late in the Civil War universal suffrage produced governments that had close ties to the military.

Black October, October 1988. Riots in October 1988 produced a political crisis that led to the overthrow of the FLN, the threat of an Islamic Republic, terrorism, civil war, and ultimately a return to pluralism.

In early October 1988, riots broke out among youth in lower-class suburbs of Algiers, and then spread to main shopping streets and to government buildings. When authorities could not put down the disturbances quickly, they declared a state of siege, enabling the military to take any actions necessary, without concerns about legality. For instance, security forces fired on an Islamist demonstration in Algiers, killing 200–500 and arresting 3,000–4,000. Order was restored after Chadli made a public announcement promising political reforms, an end to the state of siege, and a halt to FLN abuse of power. The riots gave the Islamists an opportunity to openly oppose the government.

Unrest had been building throughout the 1980s, primarily in response to economic problems. Oil and gas revenues declined sharply when OPEC refused to limit production. Foreign debt piled up. Authorities introduced an austerity program that included lower subsidies for food, reduced imports, and a wage freeze. The lower classes were hit hardest, as their costs of living rose significantly. In addition, the rapid increase in population put severe pressure on resources and contributed to a high unemployment rate. Algeria's population doubled in the 1980s to 23 million. Though there were real bases for discontent, the riots had been spontaneous. Black October represented the most significant domestic unrest since independence. It destroyed the myth of the army as the defender of the people, undermined the power of FLN, and forced the government to move toward pluralism.

Movement toward Pluralism, 1989–1991. Chadli combined continued economic liberalization with political liberalization. He fired the heads of the FLN and military security forces and separated the army and FLN. Then he proposed a referendum to approve changes in the Constitution. The President would be responsible to the National Assembly and not the FLN. In addition the President would be a symbol of the unity of government and the nation but not the symbol of party-state union. The late 1988 referendum passed almost unanimously. Chadli then ran for president and won 81 percent of the vote.

In 1989, a new Constitution was promulgated and approved by a national referendum, opposed only by the Islamists and Boumedienne socialists. Socialism was abandoned and Algeria ceased to be a one-party state. Thus FLN lost its monopoly of political power. The president was to have a five-year term, with increased authority over defense and foreign policy. A number of political parties were legalized but those based on religion, regionalism, gender, race, or support for violence were excluded. The Islamic Salvation Front (FIS) was legalized. The most important political parties were the FIS, the Front of Socialist Forces (FFS), Ben Bella's Movement for a Democratic Algeria (MDA), and Said Saadi's Rally for Cultural Democracy (RCD).

Electoral laws were promulgated in July 1989, introducing a modified form of proportional representation. If a party received a majority of votes in a district, it won all seats from the district. If no party won a majority of votes, seats would be determined by proportional representation.

Chadli appointed Mouloud Hamrouche as a reformist Prime Minister and General Khaled Nezzar as Minister of Defense. The army remained the ultimate authority. Chadli was not a democrat; he saw democracy as a strategy for co-opting the political goals of his opponents, especially the Islamists.

A formal Islamist organization emerged only in early 1989, though Islamist preaching had become increasingly influential during the 1970s and 1980s. Twenty-eight Islamist preachers founded the Islamic Salvation Front. Its ruling body was a council, the *Madjlis ech-Chava.* The group's main objective was to establish an Islamic republic dominated by the religious ideals of Islam.

FIS was not a united organization. In fact, it was divided into a number of factions, the most important of which were the *Algerianists* or *Djeza'ara* and the *Salafis.* Led by Abassi, the Algerianists espoused a moderate Arab-Islamic-Nationalist transformation of Algeria. They favored pluralism. Fundamentalist religious leaders with close ties to terrorist organizations such as the "*Afghans*" and the Algerian Islamic Army (GIA) dominated the *Salafis,* who were led by Ali Belhadj. The Afghans were Algerians who had fought against the Soviets in Afghanistan and now played an important role in the terrorist campaign. Initially the moderate Islamists dominated FIS and sought to come to power through the vote.

Municipal and provincial elections took place in June 1990. Algeria was divided into 1,541 municipalities and 277 provinces (*wilaya*). The elections were primarily a contest between the FLN and FIS and resulted in a huge victory for FIS. Fifty-five percent of the vote went to FIS and 31 percent to FLN. In the municipalities FIS won 853 seats, the FLN 487, and the Rally for Cultural Democracy 87. FIS won control in 32 wilayas, the FLN in 14, and the Rally in 1. FFS and the Movement for Democratic Algeria (MDA) both boycotted the election, thus strengthening the showing of the FIS. Only 65 percent voted, indicating the strength of FFS and MDA and generally disillusionment with politics. The vote for FIS was primarily directed against FLN rather than an expression of positive support for the Islamists. Some of the FIS vote was also a protest against Westernism and modernization. FIS was also the best-organized and fastest growing political party.

After the elections, FIS conducted a puritanical campaign, announcing that it would conduct vigilante activities to ensure that Islamic law was enforced. FIS opposed the wearing of shorts and swimwear on the streets at beach resorts, criticized Algerian pop music, condemned the sale of alcohol, and called for an end to co-education. The vigilante campaign, directed especially at women, intensified over the next few years.

Alarmed, the FLN changed the election law in April 1991, shifting from proportional representation to single-member districts. In addition, election campaigning was banned at churches and schools. Husbands were prohibited from proxy voting for their wives. In response, the FIS called a protest strike for late May. The strike had little impact outside the capital, Algiers. The strike revealed the serious split within FIS and its ruling council.

Strikes and demonstrations continued, forcing Chadli to reintroduce a state of siege and postpone the elections indefinitely in June 1991. Abassi threatened a holy war unless the army withdrew from the districts where the FIS had come to power. FIS leaders, including Abassi and Ali Belhadj, were arrested. After some indecision the *Afghans* initiated out a campaign of terrorism.

The military thus returned to power in Algerian politics. It opposed political liberalization and sought to prevent the Islamists from coming to power and creating an Islamic Republic.

Weakened, Chadli resigned as head of the FLN but remained as president. In October, the electoral laws were further reformed. The number of electoral districts was increased, the minimum voting age was lowered to twenty-five, and proxy votes of all types were banned. December 26, 1991, was set as the date for the first round of national elections. If no party won a majority of votes in a district, a run-off election would be held in mid-January 1992.

Running a well-organized campaign, the FIS easily won in the December first round elections. FIS received 47 percent of the vote. Large numbers of pro-democracy parties split the democratic vote. One million voters failed to receive their registration cards by election time, perhaps distorting the outcome. FIS appeared poised to come to power upon completion of the second round elections.

Civil War: Military Rule and Civilian Terrorism, 1992–1995. Within the government and military leadership, serious debate took place in early January 1992 over whether to permit the second round of elections. Chadli led those who favored holding the elections, while Nezzar represented the opposite view. Nezzar, supported by the military, then forced Chadli to resign. The military leaders organized what would soon be called the *Higher State Council,* abolished the Constitution and cancelled the elections. This military coup d'etat, carried out to prevent an expected Islamist government, led Algeria into a bloody civil war. The military could neither maintain order nor protect the population.

Higher State Council. The Higher State Council ruled Algeria for about two years. Focusing its attention on destroying the Islamic terrorists, the Council failed to address Algeria's other main problems: social and religious unrest, economic crisis, misgovernment, constitutionalism, and the role of religion. Within the Council, the modernists, supporters of economic development, prevailed, led by *Mohamed Boudiaf,* who had been a foe of Ben Bella in the 1960s.

Boudiaf created a new political organization, the National Patriotic Rally. He struggled to combat government corruption. He sought to improve the economy and preserve the secular-nationalist nature of Algeria against the threats of the religious parties, especially FIS. Boudiaf supported democratization and promised elections by the end of 1994, if security had been reestablished.

Instead, violence accelerated. Boudiaf arrested FIS leaders, prohibited political activities in the mosques and banned FIS. Abassi and Belhadj were sentenced to twelve-year prison terms. A State of Emergency lasted throughout 1993.

The actions of the military helped radicalize the FIS, including the Afghans. At least sixty distinct Islamic terrorist organizations existed, with a total membership of 10,000–15,000. The extremists generally believed that armed struggle and the holy war were the only legitimate means of fighting military rule. Initially the *Islamic Salvation Army (AIS)* was the leading Islamist terrorist group. The AIS tended to direct terrorist acts against security forces and junior level civil servants. At the same time, AIS hoped that FIS would come to power through constitutional means. AIS support was strongest in the rural parts of Algeria. Later the *Islamic Army Group (GIA)* led the more extreme terrorist wing of the Islamist movement. The GIA's greatest strength was among the unemployed youth of the large cities. From February 1992 to November 1993, 6,000 persons were killed. Some attacks were bold ones, such as a bombing at Algiers airport, in which 120 were killed and over 100 injured.

In June 1992, Boudiaf was assassinated, probably by military extremists. Personnel and policy changes occurred in rapid succession, reflecting the military's search for effective yet submissive leadership for the government.

The government responded to increased terrorism by expanding its antiterrorism campaign. Special security forces, called "ninjas," were especially active. Algerians were forbidden to join "foreign" terrorist organizations, possess weapons, and distribute subversive literature. Officials set a curfew for Greater Algiers and neighboring provinces. Torture was used against prisoners.

Secret *death squads,* undoubtedly sponsored by the military, carried out executions of the Islamists.

By the summer of 1993, violence had so escalated that the Higher State Council began to consider negotiating with opposition forces. However, talks broke down because the government would neither negotiate with nor legalize FIS.

Within the military, two groups emerged, the *eradicators* and the *conciliators.* The eradicators favored harsh repression of Islamists and promoted a modernizing, secular vision for the Algerian future. Few Algerians agreed with their vision. The conciliators believed that the military could remain in power if it compromised with the opposition, including the FLN and the FFS, and recognized Algeria as an Islamic state. Eradicators dominated the Higher State Council and the military leadership.

Violence and military action intensified during the winter of 1993–1994. Military and secret police offensives drove the Islamist terrorist groups out of the cities and into remote areas. From the interior the terrorists could only intermittently raid security, military, and government installations in the cities. FIS gave its support to the more moderate AIS as a counter to the more radical GIA. The GIA was weakened by secret police infiltration of its organization. In desperation the GIA turned to attacks on women (especially the wives and daughters of government officials), merchants, and shopkeepers and Kabyle and to random bombings intended to create an image of overpowering GIA strength.

Zeroual Administration. The appointment of Minister of Defense Lamine *Zeroual* as president in January 1994 marked a turning point. Zeroual was known for his honesty, lack of interest in politics, and sympathy for the Arabist-Islamic definition of Algeria. Zeroual braved military opposition to open direct talks with the FIS and made a symbolic gesture by releasing two FIS leaders. He worked out a deal with military leaders, briefly abandoning attempts at dialogue with the FIS in exchange for the consolidation of his power. Once Zeroual believed his power position was secure, he opened negotiations with Abassi and Belhadj, who remained in prison. Abassi accepted the ideas of political pluralism and the need for the party that lost an election to leave office. Abassi and Belhadj were then moved from prison to house arrest. Violence increased, however, leading both the military and FIS to abandon negotiations in the fall of 1994. It thus appeared that the Civil War would continue indefinitely, with no sign of a let up in violence and no one willing to return to the bargaining table. Ironically, changes began to occur after the government rejected a proposal from the opposition parties in January 1995.

Return to Pluralism, 1995–Present. Terrorism continued almost unabated but became less of an impediment to political changes and perhaps a major stimulant to the return of pluralism. Change began with the *Sant' Egidio* agreement.

Sant' Egidio was a religious order in Rome devoted to peaceful resolution of conflict. Its sponsorship enabled the main opposition parties, including the FLN, FFS, FIS, and MDA to sign a *National Contract.* FIS agreed to accept political pluralism and *alternance* (abandonment of power if a party lost an election). The agreement condemned violence against foreigners and civilians and condemned the more radical extremists group, the Islamic Army Group (GIA), while approving continued attacks on the government by the Army of Islamic Salvation (AIS). Berber rights were recognized, while a future Algeria was to be Islamic, with Arabic and Tamazight as state languages.

In the spring, Zeroual and Abassi entered negotiations, but FIS was too badly split to accept a negotiated settlement. Zeroual pushed ahead anyway. National elections held in November 1995 helped Zeroual consolidate his power and move toward more substantial political reforms. In Algeria's first free national elections, Zeroual won 61 percent of the vote for president. The voters rejected both military dictatorship and Islamist extremism.

In 1996, Zeroual announced constitutional changes that left the military in power but introduced some political pluralism. The presidency was to be an elective office. The national assembly could be composed of members from many different parties. After national assembly elections were held, local elections would follow. Zeroual called for a referendum to approve the constitutional changes.

On the basis of these changes Algeria held National Assembly elections in 1997. The pro-government National Democratic Rally was the leading vote getter with 33 percent. A moderate Islamist party, the Movement for a Peaceful Society, came in second with 14 percent. The FLN, which had recovered somewhat, won 14 percent of the vote. The two Berberist parties won 9 percent of the seats. FIS boycotted the election. Zeroual established a coalition government of representatives of the top three vote-getting parties.

Pluralism was confirmed by 1999 elections, which marked the end of the Civil War. Abdelaziz *Bouteflika* was elected President, while a more moderate National Assembly began to struggle with the restoration of peace, reconciliation of Islamists and non-Islamists, and poverty and economic underdevelopment.

3. Conflicting Ideologies

As you would expect during a period of fierce political warfare, ideological conflict was equally intense. The decade of civil war produced dramatic changes in the relative significance of various ideologies. The ideology of national liberation lost most of its influence. Islamic Fundamentalism remained very powerful. Berberism and pluralism became more important than previously.

National Liberationism. Hardly challenged until the late 1980s, the reigning ideology of national liberation had gradually ceased to have a deep impact on people's lives. The heroism of bloody victory over the French and the creation of a new society no longer held the attention or loyalties of the majority of Algerians, who were born after independence. The ideology of national liberation had been transformed into a set of modernizing goals based on Marxism and a set of international power goals that meant support for national liberation movements abroad. These ideas no longer appeared workable since Communism had collapsed in the Soviet Union and almost every nation was now independent of western imperialism. The failure of the modernizing goals to provide Algerians with an adequate standard of living led many to turn to an alternative, which both criticized national liberationism and offered a very different vision of what Algeria should be like.

Islamist Visions. Supporters of Islamism were not united. *Islamic Revivalism* referred to efforts to increase Islamic influences in public life. Very broadly, most Algerians supported the increased importance of Islam in their public lives.

Islamic Fundamentalism (Islamism) sought to revive "pure Islam" and impose upon twentieth century believers the *Qu'ran* and *hadith.* Islamic fundamentalism was extremely pessimistic, anti-Western, and anti-modern. Fundamentalists believed that Islam had been deeply weakened by contact with the decadent West. From their perspective, only the destruction of Western influence, and its replacement with Islamic ideas of the pre-Western era could restore purity. The fundamentalists proposed the creation of a *theocracy,* an *Islamic Republic.* Though Islamists agreed on what should be done, they differed in terms of strategies. *Pragmatists,* the Djeza'ara, supported democracy as a means by which the Islamists could come to power, not as an end. The pragmatists rejected the idea of using violence against civilians and foreigners. The *Puritans* believed that people should be forced to follow the traditional Islamic ways and used vigilante action to achieve these goals. Everyone was a target for them. Justice, morality, and retribution were their slogans. They saw themselves as conducting a *jihad,* or holy war, against those who were not true believers.

Berberism. One-fifth of the Algerian population, the Berbers, articulated a somewhat different vision for Algeria, generally without much success. Much of the Algerian intelligentsia initially came from the Berber population, which saw French culture as a means of bolstering Berberism against the dominant Arabic-speaking Algerians. The Berbers rejected Arabization, both in terms of the primacy of the Arabic language and the mythology that the Arabs were true Algerians and the Berbers were not. The Berbers accepted the modernizing goals of the national liberationists and saw themselves as playing a major role in the achievement of those goals. However, the Berbers favored decentralization of power, which was directly at odds with national liberationist methods of modernization—centralized economic and political decision-making. Instead, the Berbers were the primary proponents of civil rights, pluralism, and democracy.

As the Civil War wound down, national liberationists came back into power but did not try to reestablish their discredited socialist modernizing strategies, supporting capitalism instead. Islamism remained a powerful force but began to abandon vigilante tactics. Berberism had no appeal beyond the Berber lands, especially Kabyle. Pluralism, too, seemed a goal for a minority. Thus Algeria exited the Civil War unable to agree on a set of values and beliefs beyond independence, economic development, and Islam.

4. Economic Crisis and Social Unrest

The economic crisis of the 1980s produced massive unrest and gave many an excuse to violently oppose the government. During the Civil War the government tried to continue to develop policies designed to pull Algeria out of its economic difficulties by turning to capitalism.

Economic Liberalization. Economic liberalization continued, despite opposition from the bureaucracy, FLN, and the trade unions. The government called for the completion of the transformation of Algeria into a market economy. It emphasized continuation of reforms that granted enterprises autonomy of decision-making. The state increased investment in private agriculture in order to promote increased productivity. Ironically, the government promoted foreign investment at a time when to do so was increasingly risky. The Money and Credit Law of 1990 permitted foreign companies to invest in Algeria. Soon foreign firms were permitted to buy up to 49 percent of the shares of Algerian companies, including the gas and oil monopoly, Sonantrach. In part, the effort to encourage foreign investment in the oil industry was meant to compensate for the failure of Sonantrach to conduct much exploration and develop new oil fields. Finally, the Bank of Algeria, rather than the government planners, was given responsibility for managing investment strategies. Economic liberalization produced modest economic growth.

5. Punishing Opposition to Patriarchy

Among the major goals of the Islamists was the restoration of patriarchy, which they feared (incorrectly) was disintegrating. Women had gained the right to vote and were carrying out this right, without permitting their husbands to cast votes for them. Women were prominent in the intellectual opposition to fundamentalism, which threatened the meager rights women had.

At first the FIS sought to use persuasion, even providing veils for women who were found in public without them. Islamists offered marriage counseling for "uppity women." They called on women to leave the workforce and remain in the home. The Islamists supported gender segregation in the schools and universities. However, more and more often the Puritans used violence, conducting a terrorist campaign against women. At the height of the Civil War the wives and daughters of government officials were targets and females in the intelligentsia had to flee the country or go into hiding. Islamists found women an easy target. The Second Civil War struck a blow at women's rights, as women were primary victims of terrorist attacks.

6. Islamic Conformity vs. Diversity and Tolerance

The Islamist vision of community was one in which everyone would accept the tenets of Islamic fundamentalism, with no opportunity for dissent. Acceptance of Islamic ideals was not voluntary but would be enforced through violence.

Islamism rejected the idea of diversity. The modernizers offered a secular vision, while the Berbers called for recognition of the rights of non-Arabic speakers. As a consequence of the Civil War it appeared that there would be some recognition of Berber language and culture.

The end to the Civil War and steps toward political pluralism suggested that Algeria might be moving toward a sense of community based on the Islamic religion, with some degree of diversity based on language and ethnicity.

F. CONTEMPORARY ALGERIA, 1999–PRESENT

By the end of the twentieth century, relative peace had returned to Algeria, permitting the achievement of goals intermittently and ineffectively pursued during the Second Civil War. Algeria pursued an activist foreign policy that included efforts to promote peace in the eastern Mediterranean and in sub-Saharan Africa. Algeria also promoted increased participation in the global economy. Having experienced the violence associated with the conflict with Islamic fundamentalism during the Second Civil War, Algeria supported the United States after September 11th (2001). Conflict with Morocco demonstrated continuity in terms of place. The Algerian government sought to encourage domestic peace through a broad strategy of amnesty for participants in the recent civil war. Algerian democracy operated through a strong presidency and a national legislature dominated by a pro-government party. Islamism and national liberationism had little appeal, while democracy and moderate Islamism were more influential. Economic privatization continued, in tandem with globalization, leaving Algeria a rapidly growing free market economy. A large underclass sustained itself in spite of gradual declines in unemployment and poverty. Surprisingly, women's position underwent substantial improvement, reflected especially in 2005 amendments to the Family Code of 1984. Berber riots challenged the emphasis on conformity. Algeria seemed on the way to a more peaceful society, characterized by successful problem-solving.

1. Activist Foreign Policy

After the Second Civil War, Algeria returned to an activist foreign policy, though with somewhat different aims than those of the 1950s and 1960s. Initially that foreign policy focused on support for the Palestinians and the promotion of peace-keeping activities in sub-Saharan Africa. Algeria also sought to strengthen its role in the global economy. Algeria was an early supporter of the United States after September 11th and continued to actively participate in the "war against terror." Conflict with Morocco continued, as peace still eluded the Maghreb.

Activist Foreign Policy. Having harbored the key components of the Palestinian organization for a number of years, Algeria continued to offer strong support for the Palestinian cause. In practice that meant criticism of Israel and Israeli settlement on lands that were Palestinian before the Six Days War of 1967. In addition, Algeria encouraged peace initiatives led by other Arab nations. Algeria also supported efforts to reduce conflict in sub-Saharan Africa, especially in West Africa. Algeria's location on the northern edge of the sub-Saharan region meant that peace to the south was important to Algerian national security.

Participation in the Global Economy. During the Second Civil War Algeria had reduced its trade ties with its traditional partner France. Once peace was restored, the Algerian government and the increasingly powerful private sector corporations sought to reaffirm an interest in participating in the global economy. Algeria sought increased economic relations with American companies, parallel to its pro-American foreign policy. In addition, the Algerians recognized the value of not limiting its trade relationship to France. Instead, Algeria sought improved economic ties to the European Community, a market much larger than that of just France. Algeria also pursued membership in the World Trade Organization, which would give it access to foreign markets at reduced tariff costs.

Algeria and September 11th. Al-Qaeda's attack on the United States on September 11, 2001, resonated with the Algerian government and people. Algerian sympathy for the United States resulted from a common experience of struggle against Islamists and a foreign policy strategy of seeking common cause with the West. Algeria quickly offered its support to the United States. More specifically, Algeria joined joint anti-terrorist operations in the Sahel, the dry lands south of the Sahara Desert. Islamist terrorists were hiding out in these remote areas along the borderlands of several countries. Algeria participated in the *rendition* program by which captured al-Qaeda operatives and other terrorist suspects were quietly placed in detention centers, where the Geneva Convention rules against torture could be ignored. Algerian airports were a transit point for the movement of captured suspects and Algeria may have run one or two detention camps. Ironically, this high level of support for the American war against terrorism seems to have produced few tangible benefits for Algeria, other than its removal from the State Department list of countries unsafe for Americans.

Continued Conflict with Morocco. Algeria and Morocco remained at odds. Levels of tension have decreased but the two countries still see each other as rivals for domination of the Maghreb. Though divided over what to do about the Western Sahara, a common problem of Islamic fundamentalist terrorism has produced some cooperation.

2. Domestic Peace and Democracy

With the end of the Second Civil War both the government and most rebels concluded that domestic peace and reconciliation were necessary. (See Chapter Five for South Africa's program of reconciliation, which became a model for Algeria, as well as the remnants of the former Yugoslavia.) Essentially all sides were asked to forget the violence that had racked the country for a decade and to pledge to live together peacefully. Domestic peace was only possible with a sharing of power through democratic elections. Though Algeria retains a strong presidency, the nation has now gone through about a decade of elections, whose results have been accepted by almost all parties.

Domestic Peace. The Algerian government developed a broad strategy for achieving domestic peace through a general amnesty for participants in the Second Civil War. In this way both government authorities and rebels would be exempted from punishment for their brutal behavior during the War. Islamists who surrendered to the government would be reintegrated back into Algerian society and not remain outcasts. Not everyone accepted the effort to establish domestic peace. Small scale violence continued, led by the largest armed Islamic fundamentalist group, the *Salafists.* Many Algerians were also uneasy about the fate of the 4,800 "*disappeared people,*" presumably kidnapped, killed, and unaccounted for. Many of the disappeared people were the innocent victims of government and Islamic fundamentalist executions. The political agreement to end all violence and grant amnesties was confirmed by the *Civil Concord Law* of 2000. Further, in 2005, the government held a referendum on the amnesty program—98 percent voted in favor of continuing this program for domestic peace.

Democracy and Party Politics. Algeria became a democracy based on several broad political principles. Universal suffrage was realized. In addition freedom of expression was clearly defined in connection to democracy, with an emphasis on an independent media and open political debate. The political system functioned through a bicameral legislature. The Lower House operated on the basis of popular sovereignty, while the Upper House combined elections and presidential appointment of one-third of its membership. A strong presidency remained the key political institution.

Six major political parties emerged. The Assembly of National Democracy (RND) represented the government. The long-existing Front for National Liberation (FLN) split into factions and failed to recover its lost dominant role. The Rally for Cultural Democracy (RCD), espousing socialist views, worked closely with the FLN. The Party for a Society of Peace (MSP) reflected the views of moderate Islamists. The Berbers' Front of Socialist Forces (FFS) continued to be the most fervent supporter of democracy and the main champion of minority rights, while no longer expressing loyalty to socialist ideas. The main Islamic fundamentalist organization, the Front for Islamic Salvation (FIS), disbanded and its supporters joined the MSP and the RND or opted out of active participation in politics.

Shifts in electoral support were reflected in successive elections. In the 2002 legislative elections, political support was widely distributed. FLN won 34 percent of the seats, while the pro-presidential party, RND won 18 percent, the moderate Islamists, the MSP, won only 7 percent. The 2004 presidential election showed much more consensus, with the government party, the Assembly of National Democrats' candidate, winning 85 percent of the vote and the FLN candidate garnering only 6 percent. This reelection of Bouteflika demonstrated support for pluralism within the context of a strong presidency, which used the powers of office to generate support.

In the 2007 parliamentary elections, the vote was widely dispersed, with FLN winning 23 percent, the pro-government RND 10 percent, and MSP almost 10 percent. Other parties received smaller vote totals. In the 2009 presidential election, Bouteflika easily won a third term after inducing the national assembly to amend the constitutional limit of two terms. Some people believe Bouteflika used government resources to give people economic incentives to vote for him. He doubled the salaries of legislators, erased farmers' debts, and doubled the size of college scholarships. At the same time, the opposition was diffused and unable to mount a credible campaign for an alternate candidate. Thus, the strong presidency was reaffirmed and reinforced.

3. Decline of Inflexible Ideology

The intense conflict and expressions of hatred that reflected various political forces during the Civil War produced a backlash after the Civil War ended. Those sets of ideas expressed with so much vehemence and so little flexibility lost most of their appeal. Instead more moderate positions—democracy and moderate Islamism have had the greatest influence.

4. Economic Growth and Continued Inequality

With the close of the Second Civil War, the Algerian economy grew rapidly, largely through profits from oil and natural gas exports and a modest program of *import substitution.* Globalization and privatization also were central to economic growth. Algeria remained a society of substantial inequality, with a large underclass largely resulting from high unemployment. Social problems became more evident while social unrest mainly resulted from perceived and actual local government incompetence.

Economic Growth. Algeria's economy has grown rapidly since the late 1990s. It doubled between 1995 and 2000, with most of the expansion in the last years of that half-decade and has almost doubled again between 2000 and 2005. Currently the growth rate is almost 7 percent a year.

Economic growth has been possible for a number of reasons. In part, economic expansion has resulted from the abandonment of ineffective economic strategies, based on state ownership and direction. The effort to shift toward privatization also interrupted economic activity. In addition, the end to intense internal turmoil, which continued throughout the 1980s and culminated in the Second Civil War, no longer hampers economic development.

Beyond the elimination of these forces that dragged down the economy, positive changes also have had an effect. The government broadened the privatization program of Chadli Benjedid until 2001, focusing on piece-meal privatization, then accelerating privatization more broadly. Not only were industries, including oil, natural gas, and metals extraction privatized, but the government gave up its monopoly over import and export trade, producing new efficiencies and flexibilities. Today Algeria has a liberal, free market economy. Sharp increases in global oil and natural gas prices reached 30 percent of GDP and produced both substantial growth and a positive trade balance.

The industrial and agricultural growth rates are much lower than overall economic performance. Algeria's exports are largely oil, natural gas, minerals (especially iron and zinc), wine, and olive products. Most of Algeria's foreign trade is with the European Community countries, but substantial trade with Russia is a legacy of rule by the Front for National Liberation. For example, in 2006, Russia and Algeria signed an agreement by which the Russians cancelled an old 5 billion dollar debt in exchange for the purchase of 8 billion dollars worth of Russian armaments.

Agriculture remains important, employing about 15 percent of the workforce. Rich soil and proximity to European markets is offset by frequent droughts in recent years and by technological backwardness on the farms of small holders.

Continued Inequality. Algeria remains a country with substantial inequality. Some of that inequality is geographical. Much of the country's non-petroleum wealth is generated in the coastal areas. Cities possess considerable social and economic inequality, with a small wealthy business class and professionals and a very large group of industrial workers and the unemployed. In the Berber interior, small subsistence farms predominate, characterized by a low standard of living.

Poverty is a serious problem for Algeria, with over 20 percent of the population falling below the official poverty line. Poverty is closely aligned with the unemployment rate, which has been about 25–30 percent. High unemployment results from a number of factors. Rapid population growth exceeds job creation. Population growth has declined to about 1.5 percent per year. However, the labor force has grown at an even more rapid rate, as increasing numbers of young people have reached working age. High unemployment results in large part from the transition from public corporations to private enterprise. In the process half a million workers have lost their jobs.

Poverty has been a central factor in the saliency of social issues and in the expansion of public unrest. A decline in the potency of Islamic fundamentalism has loosened informal restrictions on crime, suicide, drug trafficking, and prostitution, whose rates have soared. Dissatisfaction has produced public protests at the local level. Local government has been been blamed and has been the object of protests directed against local incompetence.

5. Surprising Changes in Family and Gender

Unexpectedly, changes have occurred in the position of women. The sharp reduction in Islamic fundamentalist influence has certainly influenced changes in thinking about women's rights in Algeria. Public discussion of issues such as domestic violence has become common, leading to a 2004 prohibition against sexual harassment. The literacy rate for women has increased substantially, while women now form a majority of university students. More and more women have made their way into the workforce but still face relatively low wages and few opportunities for advancement. A major change has come with the 2005 amendments to the 1984 Family Code, which defines relationships between men and women. Actual advances, however, have not always kept pace with legal changes. Still urban women, at least, are quite optimistic about possibilities of further improvements in their lives.

Open Discussion of Issues Facing Women. In recent years Algerians have engaged in much public discussion of issues facing women. The conversation about sexual violence generally condemns the abuse of women. Much of this discussion has been about domestic sexual violence against women, including marital rape, rape, and incest. Frequently the practice has been for a raped woman to be forced into marriage with her rapist.

There is also much talk about the plight of unmarried mothers. That single mothers exist is now recognized. However, unmarried mothers are generally viewed negatively, with little appreciation of the challenges they face.

Literacy and Employment. After a decade of attacks that forced women back into the home, women have returned to educational institutions in great numbers. This has resulted in a high rate of literacy for women. Women, especially, have enrolled in universities and higher technical schools. Increasingly women have sought degrees in the hard sciences and engineering, and not just in education or medicine.

Female employment has increased as well, now at 14% of the labor force, women dominate many professions. Most doctors are female, as are 70% of lawyers and 60% of judges. Women have penetrated traditionally male occupations, such as bus and taxi drivers. However, equal pay for equal work does not exist and women find few opportunities for job advancement.

Legal Changes. According to the Algerian Constitution all citizens are equal and discrimination on the basis of sex is illegal. Major changes have occurred in the legal position of women. The new 2004 penal code prohibited sexual harassment, though mechanisms for redress are weak.

2005 amendments to the 1984 Family Code brought substantial improvements to the legal position of women. Yet, one can still see subordination of women embedded in the Code. It is a wife's duty to obey her husband. Women still need a male guardian. However, women now can decide who the guardian will be. Marriage is defined as an equal partnership, with equal relations between husband and wife. Both men and women may define in writing their rights within the marriage. Inheritance rules have not changed. Sons inherit two-thirds of the family's property and daughters inherit the remaining one-third. The rights of divorced women have been modified. They can now become the guardians of their children. No longer does the husband automatically receive the children in a divorce. Polygamy remains legal but now a man needs government approval to have more than one wife. Women who marry non-citizens cannot pass on to their children the rights of Algerian citizenship. In contrast, if an Algerian male marries a foreign woman, she becomes a citizen, as do their children.

Changes in the legal position of women and a more liberal attitude toward women's rights have hardly touched the countryside. Apparently, the exodus of young women from the countryside results both from the power of rural patriarchy and the depth of rural poverty.

Conclusion. In general, in the years since the close of the Second Civil War, the position of Algerian women has improved measurably. However, patriarchy is still especially strong in the rural areas and laws only partially reduce it for the cities.

6. Community and Diversity

Algeria remains a society that praises and seeks unity. However, recent years have brought some recognition of rights for the Berber minority and acceptance of the independence of local governments.

The Berber Question. The Algerian government tends to address the Berber question only when the Berbers threaten social peace by engaging in riots, demonstrations, and strikes. Riots in Berber lands in 2001 and 2003 led to modest improvements in political and language rights for the Berbers. Since then Berbers have actively participated in the political process and have continued, unsuccessfully, to champion Berber cultural autonomy.

Traditional Village Autonomy. Traditional village communities (the *arsh*) retain their independence from the hierarchical structure of the central government. They form independent local governments, with the power to make local decisions related to the agricultural cycle, infrastructure, and conflict resolution.

CONCLUSION

The history of Algeria is that of a diverse, complex, and fascinating country. Islam provides a framework for that history.

Given its geographical location, Algeria was open to immigration and invasion, first from the heavily populated areas of eastern North Africa, and then in the nineteenth century from France. For most of the period, Algeria was under the thumb of outside powers, first the Ottoman Turks and then the French. Some degree of independence existed in the century before the French conquest and fully after the Algerian War of Liberation in the 1950s. After independence, Algeria sought to play a broader role in the Middle East and Africa.

Authoritarian government existed for almost the entire modern period, though governments had little control over people's lives. The French promoted economic development and French domination. After independence, strong authoritarian rule produced major changes in Algeria. Efforts to create a pluralistic alternative to authoritarian rule produced a Second Civil War that ended as the twentieth century closed.

Islam provided a dominant ideology for Algeria. As a religion, Islam outlined detailed rules of private and public behavior. Western culture challenged Islam in the French period and continued to have some influence thereafter. Islamic fundamentalism sought to eliminate all modern and non-Islamic ways of thinking and behaving.

Algeria was a pastoral-agricultural society for most of its history. After the First World War the French began to promote industrialization in a limited way. After independence the ruling party tried to introduce a Stalinist-style system of state economic planning and control. Though some industrialization took place and the gas and oil industries became the center of the Algerian economy, poverty and economic suffering increased. Economic problems and overpopulation combined to produce massive discontent. Relative equality characterized Algeria before the French period. In the French period society was divided into the French or Europeans and the Muslims. The French formed an upper class and the Algerians a lower class. Among the Algerians the basic distinction was between the French-educated intelligentsia and the peasants and craftsmen. After independence and the flight of most Europeans, Algeria had a relative equal society. The political leaders and their military allies soon formed a "new class," with special privileges and a near-monopoly on power.

Islam outlined a system of patriarchy. Though it defined certain rights for women, common practice, called traditions, reduced women to insignificance. French civilization produced very modest changes, while the War of Liberation gave urban women a great deal of freedom. After independence was confirmed, patriarchy returned, supported by the authoritarianism of the government and by Islamic tradition. During the Second Civil War Islamic militants attacked women in public, trying to force them to conform to very traditional ideas of female subservience.

Islam provided an overarching basis for community-building. However ethnic diversity, language difference, and cultural conflict weaken such efforts. The Berbers rejected Arabization and sought cultural autonomy. In the modern period clashes occurred between French culture and Islamic culture. After independence the government tried to strengthen community-building efforts by espousing ideals of revolutionary fervor. Algeria remains a society in which difference remains very important.

Name: ______________________________ Date: ____________________

Chapter Six: Algeria

IDENTIFICATION: IMPORTANT TERMS AND VOCABULARY

2005 amendments (479)

Abd al-Kadir (443)

Afghans (468)

Algerianists (467)

Algerianity (449)

al-Qiyam (455)

alternance (470)

Arabization (455)

battle of the mosques (455)

Berbers (440)

birth spacing (460)

Black Decade (458)

Bouteflika (471)

centrifugal (440)

Civil Concord Law (476)

corsairs (441)

de Gaulle (447)

dey (441)

disappeared people (475)

Djebar (461)

dowry (442)

Evian Accords (448)

Name: ______________________________ **Date:** ____________________

theocracy (Islamic Republic) (472)

Tizi Ouzo Spring (463)

Tripoli Charter (461)

Women's National Union (461)

Name: ______________________________ **Date:** ____________________

Chapter Six: Algeria

KEY OBJECTIVES

Muslim Algeria, 1500–1830: Name the five pillars of Islam.

French Colonial Rule, 1830–1954: Why were Muslims not considered capable of being French citizens?

Civil War and National Liberation, 1954–1962: Why were the non-European Algerians able to defeat the French and gain independence from French control?

An Independent, Radical Algeria, 1962–1988: What were the main goals of independent Algeria's foreign policy?

Second Civil War, 1988–1999: What produced the rise of militant, fundamentalist Islam in Algeria?

Contemporary Algeria, 1999–Present: How was Algeria able to end domestic conflict and create a relatively peaceful society?